SOCIOLOGY & EMPIRE

SOCIOLOGY & EMPIRE

The Imperial Entanglements of a Discipline

EDITED BY GEORGE STEINMETZ

Duke University Press · Durham and London · 2013

#809028608

Library of Congress Cataloging-in-Publication Data
Sociology and empire : the imperial entanglements of a discipline / George
Steinmetz, ed.
pages cm — (Politics, history, and culture)
Includes bibliographical references and index.
ISBN 978-0-8223-5258-7 (cloth : alk. paper) —
ISBN 978-0-8223-5279-2 (pbk. : alk. paper)
1. Imperialism.   2. Sociology.   I. Steinmetz, George, 1957–   II. Series: Politics,
history, and culture.
JC359.S693 2013
306.2—dc23
2013005287

Contents

Conclusion
Understanding Empire
RAEWYN CONNELL
489

Preface

The idea for this collection began to emerge during the 1990s, when I started working on the connections between ethnographic discourse and German colonial policy. At that time, colonialism and empires were central topics of discussion in the weekly workshop I ran with David Laitin at the University of Chicago and in the book series David and I edited together.[1] One notable feature of that workshop and book series, however, was that almost none of the scholars working on imperial topics came from sociology. I started to supervise sociology PhD dissertations on imperial topics during the early 1990s, but most of the theoretical and empirical references in these theses came from anthropology and history, and to a lesser extent from political science, geography, literary criticism, and cultural studies. It seemed that there was almost no disciplinary memory of earlier sociological work on imperial themes. Scholars of colonialism who had described themselves as sociologists—including Richard Thurnwald, René Maunier, Jacques Berque, Georges Balandier, Albert Memmi, Roger Bastide, St. Clair Drake, Peter Worsley, and Clyde Mitchell—had been written out of the field or recategorized as anthropologists or area specialists.[2] There was little awareness in sociology, outside a few specialized departments, of colonial research by people who had always been identified with sociology, such as E. A. Ross, Albert G. Keller, Robert Michels, E. Franklin Frazier, Pierre Bourdieu, or Anouar Abdel-Malek (who edited *Sociology of Imperialism*; Abdel-Malek 1971). Immanuel Wallerstein was known for world-system theory but not for his earlier work on colonial Africa.[3]

As the essays in this volume suggest, however, the period from the mid-1970s to the mid-1990s was an anomalous one in the history of academic sociology in terms of the relative lack of interest in colonialism and empires. There were several reasons for the disappearance of imperial studies within sociology in the 1970s. The first was the collapse of European colonialism and its replacement by less overt techniques of American imperial influence. Second, postwar sociology had rejected its own disciplinary legacies of historical sociology and marginalized the émigré German sociologists who tried to instill into U.S. sociology elements of the rich historicism that had flourished in Weimar Germany (Steinmetz 2010c). If sociology was a science of the present, and if empires belonged to the dustbin of history, there was no longer any reason to study empires or colonies. A third reason for this turning away from empire was postwar sociology's entrenched methodological nationalism (criticized by Martins 1974). The U.S. nation-state became a naturalized unit of analysis, understood as a container of social processes. Sociologists fell back on studies of domestic phenomena occurring inside that national container.[4] Since the 1990s, an explicit critique of methodological nationalism has become more prevalent in the social sciences (Taylor 1994, 1996), including sociology (Beck 2006). A fourth factor was the emergence of historical sociology out of its defensive crouch vis-à-vis the rest of the sociological discipline. Once historical sociologists no longer felt compelled to legitimate themselves in pseudo-scientific ways, they were free to stop proving they were sociologists by ignoring work on imperial history being done by historians. Imperial political formations reentered the general social scientific field of vision in this same period. Two milestones were the translation of Carl Schmitt's *Nomos of the Earth* (Schmitt 2003) and the discussion of *Empire* (Hardt and Negri 2000).

I discovered more fruitful conditions for colonial and imperial studies in sociology once I moved to the University of Michigan at the end of the 1990s. Michigan has long been a hotbed of research on colonialism, postcolonialism, and empire across the social sciences and the humanities. More unusual at Michigan is the emphasis on colonial and imperial history inside the Sociology Department itself.[5] The long-serving chair of the Michigan Sociology Department, Robert Cooley Angell, had argued in 1962 that sociology had reached its highest stage of development due to the "throwing off of colonialism in the 1950s" and the resulting "great interest in the underdeveloped world."[6] As a result of Angell's hiring efforts[7] and those of some of his successors, Michigan has long been one of the few U.S. sociology departments filled with "area" specialists in Africa, Asia, Latin America, and Europe, some of them trained in anthropology or history.[8] Michigan was also the center of the new historical sociology that took off in the 1970s, starting with the recruitment of Charles Tilly in 1968. Tilly discussed empires and their decline and the specific dilemmas of postcolonial states, and endorsed an explicitly "historicist" epistemology (Steinmetz 2010a; Tilly 1975, 1990, 1997a). Nonetheless, even at Michigan there seemed to be little awareness of earlier sociological contributions to the study of empire and colonized cultures, some of them historically associated with the Michigan department itself.

In light of the sociology's disciplinary amnesia about its own engagement with colonialism and empire, one of my aims in putting together the present volume has been to recover earlier sociological work in this area. Sociology can never aspire to be a cumulative science in which earlier work can be safely discarded.[9] Ongoing social research always remains connected to its own past in ways that distinguish the human sciences from the natural sciences. The much vaunted reflexivity of social science requires historical self-analysis. Intellectual history or the historical sociology of social science is an integral part of all social science.[10]

The task of reconstructing earlier sociological discussions is urgent in light of mounting critiques of the latent and manifest colonial assumptions and imperial ideologies informing current sociological theory and research (Bhambra 2007; Connell 2007; Steinmetz 2006a). There is an urgent need not only for research and theoretical work on empires but also for critical reflection on the ways sociology has been shaped by empire. Pierre Bourdieu once argued that a "social science of 'colonial' 'science' [was] one of the preconditions for a genuine decolonization of . . . social science" (1993b: 50), but he was never able to carry out this project himself. André Adam explored "the condition of sociology in the colonial situation" but limited his attention to sociologists studying colonial Morocco (Adam 1968: 18). The current discussion was inaugurated in the English-speaking world by a 1997 *American Journal of Sociology* article by Raewyn Connell (see also the conclusion of the present volume).

A related intervention began more than a half decade ago with a flurry of books and articles by C. Wright Mills. Mills discerned the emergence of a new and distinctive form of American imperialism in the 1940s and 1950s, and he connected this new imperial formation to an intensified threat to the autonomy of social scientists and intellectuals in general. For Mills, scientific autonomy was the precondition for any public engagement by the sociologist (Mills 1959b: 106). Bourdieu's subsequent arguments for scientific autonomy as the basis for responsible public interventions by social scientists are phrased in almost identical terms.[11] Mills's *Sociological Imagination* contained a scathing critique of the forms of narrow-gauge policy research he called "abstracted empiricism." The problem with this style of sociology, according to Mills, was not just its specialization but its dependence on the goals, interests, and directives of the "power elite"—governments, corporations, and the military. Mills insisted that "if social science is not autonomous, it cannot be a publicly responsible enterprise" (106). In 1948 Mills had already called in the pages of the *American Sociological Review* for the creation of "a third camp of science" (1948: 272), and he pointed to the growing entwinement of policy-oriented social science with U.S. imperialism. In *The Sociological Imagination*, Mills associated the positivist demand for prediction and control with the aims of military powers. Mills argued that "different theories" of imperialism were needed "for different periods" (1958: 72). Mills had already suggested in *Character and Social Structure*, which he and Hans Gerth had drafted during World War II, that the United States had become a new kind of empire, one that "expand[s] its military area of control by establishing naval and air bases abroad without assuming overt political responsibility" for the direct governance of foreign political bodies, in contrast to European colonialism (Gerth and Mills 1953: 205). This new form of American empire was connected, for Mills, to baleful effects on American intellectuals. On the one hand, the emergence of what he called the American "supersociety" entailed an enormous increase in decisionistic power within international policymaking and capitalist production—an "enlargement and centralization of the means of history-making" (Mills 1958: 30, 115–116). Correspondingly, the potential power of the intellectual had also increased markedly. Intellectuals therefore had a central role to play in resisting "war thinking" (137). At the same time, many social scientists were now "experts" and were only as free as their masters allowed them to be, as Mills suggested in an article that attacked what he called "crackpot realism." This article was accompanied by an illustration (next page) showing an expert (at left) advising the political and military sectors of the power elite on matters geopolitical.

Mills's initial response to the power elite's tightening grip on science was to argue that the intellectuals' "first job today is to be consistently and altogether unconstructive" (1958: 157). At a more "constructive" level, however, autonomous intellectuals could attempt to reclaim the "expropriated" means of cultural production and constitute themselves as an independent and oppositional group (Mills 1944; 1958: 160–161). An important basis for this collective project would be the university, which Mills hoped could become a "world intelligence center for the people," a "permanent third camp

CRACKPOT REALISM

BY C. WRIGHT MILLS

Image from C. Wright Mills, "Crackpot Realism" (1959a).

in world affairs rather than . . . a cradle from which retinues of experts are drawn at will by statesmen" (1948: 272).

Today we are confronting two crises that are often experienced as separate but that are actually interwoven: "the crisis of the universities" and "the crisis of empire." In the United States, military sources made up the largest share of social science funding from World War II until well into the 1960s, and this important source of research support never disappeared. Since 2001, funding for social scientific counterinsurgency and military research expanded along with jobs in these areas, while university jobs disappeared. These trends pose a severe threat to sociologists' hard-won scientific autonomy.[12] In the United States, as in Britain and elsewhere, there is increasing pressure "to make academic research serve political ends" (Guttenplan 2011). The most extreme example of this has been the involvement of anthropologists and sociologists in the Human Terrain Project and as "embedded" advisers with American troops in Afghanistan (Cohen 2007; Der Derian 2010; Kelly 2010; Mulrine 2007; Price 2011). The goals of the Defense Department's Minerva Project, which is remarkably similar to the 1960s Project Camelot (Wax 1979), include finding techniques to "support more effective, more culturally sensitive interactions between the US military and Islamic populations."[13] The problems that motivated C. Wright Mills a half century ago are still, or once again, our own.

NOTES

1. See the essays in Steinmetz (1999) for a summing up of the work of this series. My turn to colonialism in the early 1990s was inspired by the work of David Laitin and other University of Chicago colleagues, especially Jean and John Comaroff, Prasenjit Duara, Andrew Apter, Ralph Austen, Barney Cohn, and my first PhD student, Suk-Jun Han, now vice president of Dong-A University in Korea (see Han

1995). I discussed German colonial welfare policy briefly in Steinmetz (1993) and gave my first presentation on German colonial culture that year at the Smart Museum of Art, in the series "Kultur/Kommerz/Kommunikation: Interdisciplinary Perspectives on Germany and Austria, 1890–1945."

2. Thurnwald was a professor of sociology, ethnology, and ethnic psychology (*Völkerpsychologie*) at Berlin University and founded the journal *Sociologus* (called *Zeitschrift für Völkerpsychologie und Soziologie* until 1932). Maunier was a student of Mauss and author of *Sociology of Colonies* (Maunier 1932, 1949). Balandier insisted on his identity as a sociologist during the first two decades of his career, when he carried out his important work in French West Africa (Steinmetz 2010a). Bastide held the sociology chair at the University of São Paulo for sixteen years, starting in 1938, and edited the *Année Sociologique* from 1962 to 1974 (De Quieroz 1975). Berque defined himself as a sociologist throughout his entire academic career, as did Memmi. St. Clair Drake's doctorate was in anthropology (Drake 1954), but he had coauthored the famous study of Chicago, *Black Metropolis*, with a fellow graduate student in sociology (Drake and Cayton 1945) and was a sociology professor at Roosevelt University in Chicago from 1946 until 1973 and head of the sociology department at the University College of Ghana between 1958 and 1961. Drake's PhD dissertation was on race relations in the British Isles, and some of his later work focused on colonial and postcolonial West Africa (e.g., Drake 1956, 1960). Mitchell (born 1918), was trained in sociology and social anthropology in South Africa, was an assistant anthropologist, senior sociologist, and director of the Rhodes-Livingston Institute in Northern Rhodesia, taught African studies and sociology at the University College of Rhodesia and Nyasaland (1957–1965), was professor of urban sociology at the University of Manchester (1966–1973), and finally became sociology professor and official fellow of Nuffield College, Oxford, in 1973 (Oxford University, Rhodes House, MSS. Afr. s. 1825 [80^A], "Personal Data"). Peter Worsley (born 1924) earned his doctorate in social anthropology from Australian National University in 1954 but went on to become the first lecturer in sociology chair at Hull University (1956) and the first professor of sociology at the University of Manchester (1964–1982) (Peter Maurice Worsley curriculum vitae, in author's possession). Anouar Abdel-Malek has a *doctorat de sociologie* from the Sorbonne; see Gale Research, *Contemporary Authors* (Detroit: Gale Research Co.), online. Accessed 1/13/2013.

3. Although the early work by Bourdieu and Wallerstein on colonialism has gained more recognition in recent years, Frazier's interest in colonialism, which emerged while he served as chief of the Division of Applied Social Sciences of UNESCO (1951–1953), is still less familiar; see Frazier (1955).

4. It would be a simplification to attribute the widespread acceptance of methodological nationalism entirely to processes occurring outside the ivory tower during the Cold War. The geopolitics of informal empire after 1945 could also have encouraged an international or transnational sociological epistemology. Historical changes are rarely expressed directly in social scientific doxa, as can be seen in the continuing interest of German and Italian sociologists in colonialism long after their respec-

tive colonial empires had disappeared—that is, after 1918 and 1945, respectively (Steinmetz 2009a, 2009b; see also chapter 4).

5. See especially Adams (1994), Chae (2006), Clarno (2008, 2009), Decoteau (2008), Göcek (1987, 2011), Goh (2005), Gowda (2007), Hall and Rose (2006), Paige (1975), and Pula (2008).

6. Angell, notes on seminar "What Does History Offer Sociology" (ca. 1962), in Robert Cooley Angell papers, Bentley Library, University of Michigan, folder "Outlines of Talks."

7. Especially important was the hiring in sociology of Horace Miner, an anthropologist who had retrained himself during World War II as a specialist in North Africa (Miner 1953, 1960, 1965). Angell also hired David F. Aberle, an anthropologist who studied Hopi, Navaho, and Ute culture. By (re)introducing the study of the internally colonized American Indians into U.S. sociology, Aberle's hire broke with the notorious academic division of labor according to which anthropology is assigned to the "savage slot" (Trouillot 1991).

8. As the essays in this book demonstrate, Trouillot's (1991) analysis does not fully capture the division of ontological labor between sociology and anthropology, which was variable across period and geographic setting. Sociologists studied colonized cultures from the beginning of the academic discipline, and this included the internally colonized Native American. During its early decades the *American Journal of Sociology* carried articles on American Indians by Ohio State sociologist Fayette Avery McKenzie, founder of the Society of American Indians (McKenzie 1911) and by Kansas sociologist Frank Wilson Blackmar (1929). Native Americans are discussed in Durkheim ([1912] 1995) and Durkheim and Mauss (1969a). Important sociological studies of American Indians since the 1960s include Champagne (2006), Cornell (1988), Garroutte (2001, 2003, 2008), Nagel (2006), Pollock (1984), Snipp (1985, 1986, 1992), Wax (1971), and Wax and Buchanan (1975).

9. One of the most fruitful recent examples of redeploying earlier sociological theory was Michael Mann's (1986) return to Gumplowicz and Oppenheimer (discussed in chapter 1), who theorized the military sources of state expansion and empire formation.

10. All cultural producers need to familiarize themselves with the historical genesis and development of the fields in which they are active in order to understand the *illusio* to which they themselves are subject. They need to have a sense of the existing forms of autonomous and heteronomous practice within the field. Even in a natural science field like mathematics or geology, participants need to be aware of the external powers and institutions to which heteronomous scientists are linked, the ways in which autonomous scientists have tried to insulate themselves from forms of external dependency, the typical strategies of dominated newcomers and consecrated elites in the field, and so forth. The need for self-reflexivity is especially pronounced in the social and human sciences, however, because of certain peculiarities of these *Geisteswissenschaften*. First, human beings are capable of consciously or unconsciously changing their own practice in response to social science; this is one of the "looping effects" between social science and its objects of analysis discussed

by Hacking (1995). Second, the inherently meaning-laden character of human practice necessitates an interpretive, hermeneutic approach to understanding practice. Explanatory social science therefore usually appears in textualized forms, which are better suited for representing interpretive, meaningful action than numerical data or statistical models. Social science writing, like all writing, has to rely on rhetorical forms, tropes, narrative plot structures, and other stylistic devices. In social scientific writing it is likely that some of these literary forms are inherited from earlier social science writing. Third, reflexivity about one's own position is crucial for minimizing or at least perceiving processes of transference and countertransference that arise in the interpretation of social practice. Fourth, the intrinsically political character of social life makes value-free social science a chimerical goal; the best that can be hoped for is a reflexive understanding of the array of political stances toward social objects and one's own position in this space of possibilities. What some see as sociological navel-gazing is thus an integral part of all genuine social science.

11. Bourdieu (1999/2000, 2001); Bourdieu and Wacquant (1992: 187–188). For a more recent intervention connected to Mills and Bourdieu, see Burawoy (2004, 2006).

12. Scientific autonomy is related to academic freedom and freedom of speech but is not an identical concept. On the former, see Bourdieu (1991b, 1993a, 2000, 2001, 2004); on the U.S. concepts of academic freedom and freedom of speech, see Finkin and Post (2009); on the history of the German approach to freedom of science, teaching, and the universities, on which the American concept was originally based, see Laaser (1981) and Müller and Schwinges (2008).

13. See Department of Defense, BAA (Broad Agency Announcement) No. W911NF-08-R-0007, at http://www.arl.army.mil/www/default.cfm?page=362. The Defense Department agreed to allow peer review of proposals, but the Minerva program's definition of fundable projects was determined by American military and geopolitical interests. See David Glenn, "Pentagon Announces First Grants in Disputed Social-Science Program," *Chronicle of Higher Education*, December 23, 2008; and http://www.ssrc.org/programs/minerva-controversy/.

ONE

Major Contributions to Sociological Theory and Research on Empire, 1830s–Present

GEORGE STEINMETZ

INTRODUCTION: A HIDDEN GENEALOGY

Sociologists have analyzed empires throughout the entire history of their discipline.[1] This chapter offers an overview of the major theoretical and conceptual developments in sociological research on empires, imperial states, and colonial societies during the past two centuries. I will focus on sociologists' theoretical and empirical contributions to understanding the forms and developmental trajectories of these political entities.

The genealogy of sociological research on empires is largely a hidden one. The most general reason for this invisibility is disciplinary amnesia (Agger 2000: 168), that is, sociology's general lack of interest in its own past. Another reason is the ritualized practices of training sociologists, undergirded by references to a handful of founders (Connell 1997). Sociology often seems committed to a vestigial view of science as progressing in a linear fashion, and this approach discourages investigations of earlier thinkers. Even among sociological specialists in empire there is little knowledge of the contents and the contours of sociological work on empires.[2] Colonial researchers who were seen as full-fledged participants in the sociological field during their lifetimes, such as Roger Bastide or Richard Thurnwald, are retroactively reassigned to anthropology. Thus sociologists attribute theories of colonial syncretism and transculturation to cultural anthropology and literary criticism, for example, even though these theories were partly pioneered by sociologists. A more detailed investigation, as inaugurated in the first part of this volume, finds that sociologists have conducted imperial research since the beginning of the intellectual field of sociology in the nineteenth century. There have been huge changes in emphasis and argumentation over time, of course. Sociological interest in ancient empires declined after the 1920s and resurfaced briefly during and after World War II (Eisenstadt 1963; Freyer 1948; Rüstow [1950–1957] 1980; Weber 1935) and again with the resurgence of historical sociology in the 1980s (Goldstone and Haldon 2010; Mann 1986). There have also been geographical shifts in the center of sociological interest in empire, with a concentration in France, Germany, and Italy during the interwar and immediate post-1945 periods and in the United States since the 1990s. This chapter will not map out these geographical shifts in much detail, much less try to explain them, but the chapters in the first section will fill some of these lacunae.

What follows is an overview of sociological resources for research on empires and the intellectual history of sociological research on empires. I am especially interested in the ways sociologists have analyzed the *forms*, *developmental trajectories*, *determinants*, and *effects* of empires. Let me briefly clarify these terms. "Forms of empire" concerns definitions of empires, colonies, and related imperial formations. Here the major sociological contributions include theories of colonialism and models of twentieth-century empires in which the sovereignty of dominated states is left largely intact even as they are brought under the sway of an imperial power. The word *trajectory* refers to the ways sociologists have described the developmental paths of geopolitical history. Theories of "alternative," "multiple," and "entangled" modernities have largely replaced earlier views of societies as moving along a common path from tribe to state to empire, or from tradition to modernity.

With regard to the *determinants* and *effects* of empires, I identify four main theoretical developments. First, earlier theories of empire typically sought to identity a single, primary, determining source of imperial politics. Contemporary sociological work, by contrast, emphasizes conjunctural, contingent, multicausal patterns of causality. Second, earlier theories tended to foreground political, military, or economic causal mechanisms, whereas current work integrates all these factors with attention to ideological, linguistic, psychic, and cultural processes. Third, earlier theories tended to be "metrocentric," locating the driving source of imperial expansion and techniques of colonial governance in the global core. A more recent set of theorists twisted the stick in the opposite, "ex-centric," direction, emphasizing the power of events, processes, and structures in the peripheries to shape the forms and even the very existence of colonialism (Robinson 1986). Most recently, analysts have integrated the metrocentric and ex-centric optics, analyzing imperial systems as complex, overdetermined totalities in which powerful impulses may come from both directions, with cores shaping peripheries and vice versa. Theorists of imperial "fields" of social action, including colonial science (Petitjean et al. 1992; Steinmetz 2009a), development policy (Garth and Dezalay 2002), and the colonial state (Steinmetz 2008a), see those fields as sometimes being located entirely within the core or the periphery and at other times spanning these imperial spaces (Go 2008b; Steinmetz 2012c). The fourth, overarching development is the movement within political and historical sociology away from a focus on states as the highest-level order of political organization. Empires are increasingly understood as encompassing states and as having emergent properties that cannot be reduced to the properties of states (see chapter 9).

Since I am interested in charting theoretical contributions to the study of empires here and not in conducting a sociology of sociology, I will follow a diachronic organizational scheme. A diachronic approach is especially appropriate since it allows us to see how theorists and researchers are drawing on, rejecting, reconstructing, suppressing, or simply overlooking earlier members of their discipline. These patterns of disciplinary memory and amnesia, continuity and disavowal, can yield valuable insights for the sociology of science. Even if transdisciplinarity (Steinmetz 2007c) is a necessary goal in the human sciences, sociologists are best advised to enter into transdisciplinary encounters with a good understanding of their own discipline and its history. A diachronic analysis is useful for restoring to sociology some sense of its own accomplishments. This is especially important in the field of empire and colonial studies, which have been completely dominated in recent years by other disciplines. As we will see, several insights that have been claimed in recent years by postcolonial theory, anthropology, or history were actually pioneered by sociologists.

Of course, a transnational approach to the history of modern sociology (e.g., Heilbron 1995; Platt 2010; Schrecker 2010) needs to be combined with nation-based comparisons (e.g., Abend 2006; Levine 1995; Wagner et al. 1999) if we are interested in understanding the field's evolution. National intellectual fields are often distinct enough to produce radical misunderstandings when exiles or texts circulate without their original contexts (Bourdieu 1991b). The symbolic capital of sociological ideas or individual sociologists undergoes radical devaluation or inflation due to migration (Cusset 2003; Steinmetz 2010c). Each imperial state had a nationally specific system of higher education and unique intellectual traditions. Sociologists were recruited from a differing array of disciplines in each country during each period of disciplinary foundation and refoundation. Sociology has therefore often had strong national peculiarities (Heilbron 2008) in spite of streams of international and transnational circulation. At the same time, because of the central role of emigration, exile, and scholarly exchange in many scholars' lives, it can be highly misleading to assign sociologists or their schools and ideas to one or the other national tradition. The dangers of error due to a nation-state-based approach are exacerbated in the case of imperial sociologists, many of whom spend a great deal of time overseas in research sites or historical archives, interacting with scholars and laypeople from the colonized population and from other metropolitan nations. The socio-spatial contours of imperial social-scientific fields are shaped by the analytic object itself—by the empires being studied.

The discussion that follows is broken into four periods: 1830–1890, 1890–1918, 1918–1945, and 1945 to the present. Each period corresponds to important global developments and events in imperial practice and to developments in sociological theories of empire. It is important to caution against two possible readings of this periodizing scheme. Most of the imperial sociologists I discuss lived through more than one of these four periods, and some, including Alfred Weber and Richard Thurnwald, were active scientifically in at least three of them. In the discussion that follows, I usually introduce individual scholars in the context of the historical period when they first entered the intellectual or academic field. If I were engaged in an explanation rather than a presentation of their work, I would also discuss their social and psychic background *before* they entered the sociological field, since, *pace* Pierre Bourdieu, the professional field is not the only field "with which and against which one has been formed" (2007: 4).[3] Second, this periodization is not meant to suggest any necessary or direct connection between science and imperial politics, each of which is usually able to remain relatively independent of the other. Indeed, patterns of sociological attentiveness to questions of colonialism and empire have often been extremely independent of ongoing geopolitics. For example, German sociologists became more, not less, interested in colonialism after World War I, even though Germany had lost its colonies and stood little chance of regaining them (Steinmetz 2009b).[4] Nonetheless, ongoing imperial events do often shape intellectual thinking about empire.

Some of the most original sociological contributors to the study of empires and colonialisms include Ludwig Gumplowicz, Friedrich Ratzel, Gabriel Tarde, J. A. Hobson, Max and Alfred Weber, Maurice Leenhardt, René Maunier, Carl Schmitt, Paul Mus, Roger Bastide, Jacques Berque, Albert

Memmi, Georges Balandier, Paul Mercier, Immanuel Wallerstein, and Michael Mann. It is their contributions that I emphasize here, rather than the work of the many sociologists involved in practical imperial policy-making or anti-colonial activism.[5]

WHO IS A "SOCIOLOGIST"?

Who counts as a sociologist? Any disciplinary history must offer a working definition of the discipline in question. The extant research presents a spectrum of minimalist and maximalist definitional strategies. At one extreme, a discipline like sociology is defined as including anyone who defines himself or herself as a sociologist or who conducts research or teaches on topics he or she designates as "sociological." This approach has the drawback of willfully ignoring the social processes of boundary creation that are emphasized in all social theories and that are especially prominent in intellectual and scientific life (Bourdieu 1993a; Luhmann 1995: 28–31). Equally problematic, I think, are studies that count as a sociologist anyone who publishes in a predefined list of sociological journals or uses the word or the language of *sociology* in their publication titles (Fleck 2007: 189; Hardin 1977). This approach begs the methodological question of determining which journals count as sociological and how these journals are hierarchically arranged—questions that are stakes in the sociology field itself. This approach ignores the complexities of interactions across disciplines rather than directly thematizing and theorizing these interactions (Bourdieu 1991b; Steinmetz 2011b).

A third approach counts as a sociologist only those with a doctorate or advanced degree in sociology or holding a professorship or research position in the field.[6] This approach might seem more realistic, since, as Bourdieu (1996a: 226) notes, "one of the most characteristic properties of a field is the degree to which its dynamic limits ... are converted into a juridical frontier, protected by a right of entry, which is explicitly codified, such as the possession of scholarly titles, success in competition, etc., or by measures of exclusion and discrimination, such as laws intended to assure a *numerus clauses*." But scientific and academic fields vary historically and geographically in their divisions and degree of specialization and codification. A strict definition based on "juridical frontiers" would imply that before the 1960s sociology existed only in the United States, where it "became a university and college supported discipline much earlier and to a much greater extent ... than it did elsewhere" (Morgan 1970: 170) and where there were already about a thousand sociology professors in the interwar period (Walther 1927: 1).

The only sociology post in a British university before 1945 was at the London School of Economics, however, and before 1961 "there were chairs of sociology in only five universities" (Platt 2002: 181). In France and Germany, two of the three countries—along with the United States—in which sociology is usually seen as having first emerged as an intellectual and academic discipline, there were no advanced sociology degrees until the last third of the twentieth century. In France there were only four sociology professorships in 1952 (Clark 1973: 33). In Germany there were fewer than fifty full-time or part-time sociology professors before 1933, even if we include teachers in the technical, commercial, labor union, women's, and "people's" colleges (*Frauenhochschulen* and *Volkshochschulen*; Fleck 2007; Lepsius 1983). Many of the founders of sociological associations and journals never held university positions in sociology. Max Weber obtained a professorship with "Soziologie" in its title only at the very end of his life, but he was widely acknowledged as a sociologist during his own lifetime and was seen as the discipline's most important figure by German sociologists during the Weimar Republic.[7] Pierre Bourdieu, who was recognized in a survey of British sociologists in 2001 as one of the ten most important sociologists of the twentieth century (Halsey 2004: 171), earned an *agrégation* in philosophy at the École normale supérieure but never wrote a doctoral thesis (Lane 2000: 9; Lescourret 2009) and never studied sociology while a student. Indeed, most of the great French sociologists of the mid-twentieth century earned an agrégation in philosophy but not a sociology degree.[8] Treatments of the history of sociology by American sociologists before 1945 focused on European, especially French and German, thinkers, as evidenced by Eubank's project on the "makers" of sociology and by overviews by Albion Small (1923–1924) and Harry Barnes and Howard Becker (1938). It would be a definitional absurdity if none of the founders or masters of sociology counted as sociologists.

What these examples illustrate is that there is no formal or deductive methodological rule that can adequately define membership in an academic field. Pierre Bourdieu's theory of semiautonomous fields offers a preferable solution to the problem (Bourdieu 1993b). As with any other kind of field, a scientific or academic discipline can best be understood through a historical reconstruction of its genesis, starting with its founders or *nomothets*—the founders of the scientific *nomos* (Bourdieu 1996a)—and tracing it forward. There is a constant process of genealogical reconstruction through which new figures are recognized and included by subsequent generations as disciplinary members or founders while others are expunged from the field's history or forgotten. Scientific genealogies and canons are therefore constantly being revised. Decisions on inclusion in and exclusion from the field can be discerned only by reconstructing the judgments of acknowledged members of a field at any given moment. These "acknowledged members" will usually be direct "descendents" of the field's nomothets. Reconstructing the horizon of recognition and nonrecognition according to contemporary actors' own understandings of the situation is the only realistic criterion for determining who actually belongs to a specific sociological field, in order to avoid anachronistic oversights or inclusions. These considerations suggest that a discipline cannot be defined according to a priori definitions, strict academic credentials, precise institutional affiliations, or some arbitrary chronological cutoff point.

A field historical approach reveals that scholars' membership in sociology can change drastically from one period to the next. In *The Structure of Social Action*, Talcott Parsons included as one of his four disciplinary founders Alfred Marshall, who is rarely read by sociologists today. The reverse process, by which previously ignored figures are inducted into a field, is illustrated by the reception of Siegfried Kracauer in German sociology. Kracauer "went largely unnoticed in sociological circles . . . in the scholarly world" of Weimar Germany (Frisby 1986: 161), even though he had studied with Georg Simmel and published on "sociology as a science" and on the white-collar masses (Kracauer 1922, 1928). This began to change after 1945, when a German sociology lexicon noted that his works "had not been sufficiently explored by German sociology until now" (Mierendorff 1959: 280). Nowadays Kracauer is included in German collections of the key works of sociology (e.g., Käsler and Vogt 2000: 230–233) and in some sociological encyclopedias (Gilloch 2006), and he figures both as a topic and as a theorist in current sociological research (Schroer 2007; Staubmann 1999). An extreme example of a fluctuating membership in the field is presented by Alfred Weber, Max Weber's brother. Alfred Weber taught and supervised many of the rising stars of German sociology and social science at Heidelberg between 1918 and 1933 (Demm 1997). He also made a number of lasting contributions, including the very concepts of historical and cultural sociology (*Geschichts-Soziologie* and *Kultursoziologie*). Alfred Weber is credited with the concept, popularized by Karl Mannheim, of a "socially free-floating intelligentsia" (*sozial freischwebende Intelligenz*; Demm 2000b: 264). After 1945, however, Talcott Parsons joined forces with the new rising star in German sociology, René König, to marginalize Alfred Weber, declaring him a nonsociologist (Demm 2000a: 220). Alfred Weber's ostracism from the field was enhanced by the combined forces of postwar Americanization, political conservatism, and suspicion of any and all German intellectual traditions, including those of someone like Weber, who had renounced his professorship when the Nazis came to power and moved from liberalism to Social Democracy after the war. Most recently a small countermovement has succeeded in publishing Alfred Weber's collected works and pushed to reestablish him as a founding sociologist (Bräu et al. 1997–2003; Demm 2000b; Kruse 1990, 1999).

Field autonomy is, of course, always *relative* autonomy—relative to external forces, institutions, and movements. Because of the vulnerability of field dynamics to external determination, it is sometimes possible to determine the membership of a field using information other than the judgments of direct field participants. One familiar form of external determination is when a university administration overturns a department's department to hire or grant tenure to a scholar who has also been endorsed by referees from the disciplinary field. An even more extreme instance of external determination of scientific fields is the Nazi purge of German universities starting in 1933. This led to a dramatic narrowing not just of the personnel in sociology through the firing of Jewish and Leftist academics but also of the styles and topics of acceptable research and teaching (Klingemann 1989, 2009; Paulsen 1988). The German sociology field effectively lost almost all of its autonomy. After 1945, membership in the (west) German sociological field was influenced not just by patterns of emigration and return but also by American foundations and universities and policy decisions of the American occupiers. For example, Siegfried Landshut earned his doctorate under Alfred Weber and wrote an ill-fated habilitation thesis on the "critique of sociology" (Landshut 1929; see Nicolaysen 1997: 103–115). In 1933 Landshut emigrated to Egypt and then to Palestine and then taught at Hebrew University. He returned to Hamburg in 1951 as a professor of political science, a new discipline that was being heavily promoted by Americans at the time (Bleek 2001: ch. 8).

Goudsblom and Heilbron (2001) distinguish between two periods of sociology's formation: as an *intellectual* discipline (1830–1890) and as an *academic* discipline (1890–1930). The latter is defined in terms of shared ideas and the existence of "units of teaching, research, and professional organization" (Heilbron 1995: 3). This suggests that sociology existed as a field before it had dedicated professorships, departments, or courses of university study, and that we need to extend our analysis back to at least 1830. The word *sociologie* was used as early as the 1780s, by the Abbé Sièyes (Guilhaumou 2006) and was popularized by Auguste Comte in the early nineteenth century.[9]

Academic sociology emerged in the late nineteenth century in the United States, Japan (Akimoto 2004), Russia (see chapter 2), and in most other European countries and somewhat later in the colonized countries and the global peripheries: after the 1911 Republican Revolution in China (Gransow 1992), during the 1920s in India (Mukherjee 1979), and after 1945 in Australia (Germov 2005; Macintyre 2010), for example.[10]

In sum, the boundaries of "sociology" in each geographic or historical instance can best be established by considering the dual processes of recognition and institutionalization. The first of these criteria refers to practices of inclusion and exclusion of potential members by the founders of the disciplinary field and by each subsequent group of insiders. The second criterion refers to institutional mechanisms such as the attainment of an advanced degree that can strengthen claims to membership in a given field and, equally important, strengthen an individual's investment in that field.[11]

EMPIRE, IMPERIALISM, COLONIALISM, AND THE STATE: WORKING DEFINITIONS

The overarching concept in any discussion of imperialism and colonialism is *empire*. An empire can be defined minimally as a relationship "of political control imposed by some political societies over the effective sovereignty of other political societies" (Doyle 1986: 19; see also Eisenstadt 2010: xxii–xxiii). Empires are also defined by a restless expansionism, which, *pace* Gumplowicz (see below), is not characteristic of all nation-states. The word *empire* initially referred to large agrarian political organizations formed by conquest (Goldstone and Haldon 2010: 18; Koebner 1955, 1961; Pagden 2003). Rome was the prototype and original referent of this "watchword" (Koebner 1954: 122),[12] but it became conventional for historians to extend the word to such diverse polities as Achaemenid Persia, Akkad, and China from the Qin Dynasty to the Qing. Ancient empires typically combined militaristic expansion with mechanisms aimed at stabilizing conquered populations by offering peace and prosperity in exchange for subjection and tribute (Mann 1986: 145; Pagden 2003: xvi–xxiii, 13, 26). One result of the endless waves of territorial conquest and political incorporation in the ancient world was that empires were multicultural or cosmopolitan, although some integrated the conquered populations into the core culture to a greater extent than others.

The second keyword in the present discussion is *imperialism*. This polemical neologism was coined in the nineteenth century to decry Napoleon's despotic militarism. It was subsequently applied to the regimes of

Napoleon III and other oppressive rulers (Koebner and Schmidt 1964: 1–26; Spann 1923: 838). As Arthur Salz noted, the addition of *-ism* to *Imperium* added connotations of illegitimacy and anachronism and suggested "a sort of hubris and extravagance" (1931: 4). Historians quickly extended the word backward in time to Rome itself (Jones and Phillips 2005), which was now cast in seemingly redundant terms as an "imperialist Imperium." Eventually imperialism was used to describe the behavior of empires at all times and places (e.g., Mann 1986: 176). The contributors to the often authoritative *Geschichtliche Grundbegriffe* (Fisch, Groh, and Walther 1982) contend that the word *imperialism* remained semantically frozen as a "counterconcept" serving only "to vehemently attack the political strategies of others" (Jordheim 2007: 125). This is largely accurate for the nineteenth century, but the idea was transformed into a more objective concept around the turn of the century. Arthur Salz defined as imperialist all efforts by a state to increase its power through territorial conquest.

A different definition of imperialism, associated with J. A. Hobson, Achille Loria, Rudolf Hilferding, Rosa Luxemburg, Nikolai Bukharin, Vladimir Lenin, and a host of Marxists (Brewer 1990), recast the political word *imperialism* in economic terms. Imperialism came to mean, for many people, capitalism's quest for investment opportunities, raw materials, or sources of lower-cost labor power outside its national boundaries. Several German writers including Otto Hintze ([1907] 1970), Joseph Schumpeter ([1919] 1951), Walter Sulzbach (1926), and Arthur Salz (1931) immediately pushed back against this economic narrowing of imperialism by reasserting the concept's political character and attacking the idea that capitalists were inherently warmongering (Sulzbach 1942).

In order to retain the original meaning of imperialism as geopolitics while also differentiating it from colonialism, it should be understood as a form of political control of foreign lands that does not necessarily entail conquest, occupation, and permanent foreign rule. Imperialism is thus "a more comprehensive concept" than colonialism, since it "presupposes the will and the ability of an imperial center to *define* as imperial its own national interests and enforce them worldwide in the anarchy of the international system." This means that empires often treat colonies "not just as ends in themselves, but also [as] pawns in global power games" (Osterhammel 2005: 21–22).

The third keyword in this discussion, *colonialism*, is based on the Latin verb *colere* (meaning to inhabit, till, cultivate, care for) and on the related word *colonus* (meaning tiller of the soil), which points in the present context to the Roman *coloni* (Weber 1891, 1998a). The words *colony* and *colonization* are also linked to the expansion of the Roman Republic. Colonia*lism* as a word and a modern practice emerged in the eighteenth and nineteenth centuries. Colonialism is distinguished from both imperialism and settler "colonization" (Belich 2009; Elkins and Pedersen 2005) in three main ways. First, in colonialism, territorial takeover through conquest or purchase is followed by the seizure of sovereignty and durable foreign rule over the annexed space.[13] Imperialism, by contrast, leaves sovereignty largely in the hands of the dominated polities and may not involve any movement by the imperial power into foreign territory. Second, modern colonialism does not necessarily involve the installation of settlers in conquered territories. This stands in contrast to "colonization," which always involves settlement in and as a "colony." Third, modern colonial rule is organized around assumptions of racial or civilizational hierarchy that are enforced through law and administrative policy. These official inequalities prevent almost all colonized subjects from attaining citizenship status and rights equal to the colonizers.[14] By contrast, ancient empires often integrated the conquered completely into their culture. Since modern imperialism does not claim sovereignty over the dominated peripheries, it is in no position to implement policies there, except in short-term emergency situations.[15] Of course there is a spectrum of variations of sovereignty and legal-political differentiations between conquerors and conquered, dominant and dominated. Many political situations are located in an intermediate zone between colonialism and imperialism. Indeed, powerful modern states almost always combine different imperialist and colonialist strategies rather than choosing between them (Steinmetz 2005a). Colonial strategies sometimes morphed into imperialist ones, and vice versa.

A final key term in the present discussion is *the state*. During the second half of the twentieth century most sociologists used the word *state* when referring to political organizations that had historically been called empires. An entire subfield of "the sociology of the state" emerged on the heels of the earlier German *Staatswissenschaft*, or state science, in which concepts of empire were almost entirely absent. Whereas early sociological textbooks like Giddings's *Elements of Sociology* (1915: 284–287) and Park and Burgess's *Introduction to the Science of Sociology* (1924: 725–726) had included discussions of empires, comparable textbooks and encyclopedias after 1945 avoided the topic. This started to change only very recently (e.g., Ritzer 2007).

Any discussion of empire needs to specify the place of *the state*, just as the sociology of the state often cannot grasp its object fully without also attending to empires.[16] States figure at three main points in the analysis of empires. First, there is always a state at the core of every empire (Schmitt [1941] 1991: 67).[17] An empire, as Friedrich Naumann ([1915] 1964) suggested, can be imagined as a solar system, with the core state representing the sun and the colonial or imperial peripheries in the role of planets. The planets in the imperial solar system may themselves possess two different kinds of states. On the one hand, colonizers usually smash existing native polities or refunction them to create colonial states. Colonial states are controlled by the foreign invaders but are also relatively autonomous from the core metropolitan state and the conquered population (Steinmetz 2008a). On the other hand, colonial powers typically rely on some version of indirect rule. Residual native polities (homelands, Bantustans, tribal reservations, etc.) therefore coexist with colonial states (Lugard 1928; Mamdani 1996); the colonized retain some influence over their own internal affairs, even if they cannot participate in the affairs of the central colonial state.[18] The third way in which states figure into discussions of empire concerns imperial developmental trajectories. States may eventually obtain empires, as was the case for the United States. Conversely, empire-possessing states may devolve into states *simpliciter*, as with the dismantling of the Austro-Hungarian and Ottoman empires after World War I. The relationship between empire and state needs to be clarified before one can begin the discussion of empires. But sociologists have often ignored this distinction, referring to empires as states. In fact, one of the greatest sociological analysts of empire formation, Ludwig Gumplowicz, framed his entire analysis as a study of "states."[19]

My main topic is colonialism, imperialism, and empires, but states will also be considered here as the coordinating centers of empires, as the origins and endpoints of empires' historical trajectories, and as offshoots of metropolitan power in the colonies. As mentioned above, my specific topics are the *origins, forms,* developmental *trajectories,* and *effects* of empires. Sociological analyses of these objects fall roughly into four broad classes, variably emphasizing political, economic, cultural, or social processes and causal mechanisms. Historical sociologists since Max Weber have recognized that social events and objects are almost always conjuncturally overdetermined and cannot be explained by a single causal mechanism or law (Steinmetz 2010a; Tilly 1995). An adequate explanation of any aspect of an empire will therefore need to combine political, economic, cultural, and social mechanisms. The theories presented here should be understood not as mutually exclusive but as potential building blocks for a more adequate, multicausal account of imperial history.

FOUR PERIODS OF SOCIOLOGICAL RESEARCH ON EMPIRE
1830–1890

The first period was bookmarked at one end by the French invasion of Algeria, which signaled the onset of the second wave of European colonialism, and at the other by the parceling out of Africa among the European powers.[20] This period also saw the founding of sociology as an intellectual disciplinary field (if not yet an academic one). Several of the key founders of the intellectual field of sociology, including Auguste Comte, analyzed colonialism, while others directly advised imperial governments or participated in colonial policymaking (e.g., John Stuart Mill and Alexis de Tocqueville).

Proto-Sociologists as Colonial Analysts, Critics, and Policymakers:
Comte, Tocqueville, and Marx

Auguste Comte and Alexis de Tocqueville, who are today generally considered to be two of the founders of modern sociology, also represent two poles in the discipline's permanent struggle between critics and supporters of empire and over sociologists' proper relationship to politics. Comte tutored a student who participated in the French expeditionary force to Algeria in 1830 (Burke 2002: 41) and anticipated Durkheim ([1912] 1995) and Hobhouse, Wheeler, and Ginsberg (1915) in using evidence from contemporaneous non-Western cultures as proxies for earlier stages of European development. But Comte was no supporter of colonialism. In the *Cours de philosophie positive* he argued that early-modern colonialism "opened new opportunities for the warrior spirit by land and sea," thereby prolonging "the military and theological *régime*" and delaying "the time of the final reorganization" (Comte [1830–1842] 1975: 128–129). Comte believed that "Catholicism, in its decay, not only sanctioned but even instigated the primitive extermination of entire races" and created a system of colonial slavery, which he called "a political monstrosity." Countries in which investors became "personally interested" in overseas colonies saw an increase in "retrograde thought and social immobility" (720). Comte concluded his discussion with an optimistic diagnosis of the cunning of history, however, reasoning that while colonialism "systematically destroyed the races of men," it simultaneously undermined the belief in racial inequality by demonstrating to Europeans that positive science and industry were "destined to include the whole human race" (129–130). Comte's argument about the negative effects of colonialism on metropolitan political culture was repeated by British liberal social thinkers like Herbert Spencer, Leonard Hobhouse, and J. A. Hobson and was taken up by more recent critics of "empire as a way of life" (Maskovsky and Susser 2009; Steinmetz 2003a; Williams 1980) and in postcolonial discussions of the centrality of the imperial margin in metropolitan culture (Said 1993).

Like Comte and later Hobson, Tocqueville warned against the creation of a large class of French military heroes returning home from colonial wars and assuming "distorted proportions in the public imagination" (2001: 78). But while some readers of Tocqueville's *Democracy in America* have mistakenly believed that its author rejected "every system of rule by outsiders no matter how benevolent" (Berlin 1965: 204), this was far from the case. After visiting the Algerian colony, Tocqueville wrote several reports on it for the French Parliament. In a long essay in 1842 he insisted that France could not abandon the Algerian colony without signaling its own "decline" and "falling to the second rank." The Algerians, he wrote, must be fought "with the utmost violence and in the Turkish manner, that is to say, by killing everything we meet" and employing "all means of desolating these tribes" (Tocqueville 2001: 59, 70–71). Securing French control of the colony would require the creation of a sizable settler community. Tocqueville's study of British rule in India ([1843] 1962) confirmed his strong support for European colonialism. He rejected the social evolutionary view of the colonized as an earlier version of the colonizer in favor of a theory of unbridgeable difference and asymmetry, arguing that the fusion of Arabs and French into "a single people from the two races" was a chimerical goal (Tocqueville 2001: 25, 111). This antievolutionary stance pointed toward European native policies of "indirect rule" or "associationism" in which the colonizer tries to preserve cultural difference within a hierarchical, dualistic legal framework.

Karl Marx offered an influential account of the sources of European global expansion and the effects of colonial rule on the colonies.[21] Capital accumulation for Marx is an inherently expansive process, leading to the "entanglement of all peoples in the net of the world market, and with this, the growth of the international character of the capitalist regime" (Marx 1976: 929). In the final chapters of volume 1 of *Capital*, Marx connected the processes of primitive accumulation occurring at the "dawn of the era of capitalist production" to "the discovery of gold and silver in America, the extirpation, enslavement and entombment in mines of the indigenous population of that continent, and the conversion of Africa into a preserve for the commercial hunting of blackskins." These "idyllic proceedings" overseas, according to Marx, were "the chief moments of primitive accumulation." The colonial system spurred the concentration of capital, as the "treasures captured outside Europe by undisguised looting, enslavement, and murder flowed back to the mother-country and were turned into capital there." Marx suggested that colonialism played a "preponderant role" in the period of manufacture but that its importance receded in the era of machinofacture (Marx 1976: 915, 918). Marx died in 1883, however, just when the second scramble for overseas colonies was beginning and too late to comment on the new forms of colonial expansion. His comments on imperialism as the centerpiece of primitive accumulation and colonies as sites for high rates of exploitation and profit (Marx 1967: 150–151) were picked up by later Marxists (e.g., Harvey 2003).

Marx also wrote a series of articles for the *New York Post* in which he described colonialism as clearing away the cobwebs of Oriental despotism and feudalism and allowing capitalism to take root in the peripheries (Marx 1969). Although this more "optimistic" reading of colonialism has been rejected by most twentieth-century Marxists (but see Warren 1980), Marx's comments on the Chinese Taiping Rebellion in 1853 seem less in thrall to nineteenth-century civilizational prejudices. In an article entitled "Revolution in China and Europe," Marx prophesied that "the next uprising of the people of Europe . . . may depend more probably on what is now passing in the Celestial Empire . . . than on any other political cause that now exists" ([1853b] 1969: 67). This was a precocious statement of the thesis of the "colonial boomerang," described by Jean-Paul Sartre (1963: 20) as a form of violence that "comes back" at the colonizers "who have launched it." Herbert Marcuse restated this thesis, arguing that "by virtue of the evolution of imperialism, the developments in the Third World pertain to the dynamic of the First World," and that "the external revolution has become an essential part of the opposition within the capitalist metropoles" (1969: 80, 82). More recent versions of the boomerang thesis include Michael Mann on the ways in which imperial Rome provided the "semicivilized" Germanic tribes with the military and economic techniques that sustained Rome's "assassination" (1986: 294) and Chalmers Johnson (2000) on "blowback" against the American Empire.

Gumplowicz and the Origins of the Nonbiological Militarist Theory of the Formation of States (and Empires)

A signal contribution to the analysis of empire was made by the Polish-Austrian sociologist Ludwig Gumplowicz (1838–1909). To my knowledge, Gumplowicz was the first writer to use the adjective "sociological" (*soziologische*) in a German language book title (Gumplowicz 1883). Gumplowicz's understanding of geopolitics was shaped by his personal experience as a subject of the Russian and Austro-Hungarian empires (Barnes 1919a: 401–402). Some commentators have misleadingly characterized Gumplowicz as a proponent of "nineteenth century racist theory" (Mann 1986: 54), a Social Darwinist (Johnston 1972: 323–326), or even a forerunner of fascism (Lukács 1981: 691). In fact, after his very early book *Raçe und Staat* (1875), Gumplowicz "distanced himself... from the anthropological-biological concept of race" (Mozetič 1985: 199) and criticized thinkers like Spencer and Schäffle who compared society to a biological organism. He insisted that the "laws of social life were not reducible to biological ... factors, but constituted a field of investigation *sui generis*" (Weiler 2007: 2039). Although Gumplowicz did describe human history as an eternal "race struggle" (*Rassenkampf*), he defined "race" [*Rasse*] not in biological terms but as as a "social product, the result of social development." Although race was a sociological phenomenon, Gumplowicz argued that the social classes in Western countries "nonetheless behave toward one another as races, carrying out a social race struggle" (1909: 196–197, note 1). Warfare was not determined by racial differences; instead, warfare imposed a racial format on struggles between groups and nations (Gumplowicz 1883: 194).

Like many other nineteenth-century thinkers influenced by Darwinism Gumplowicz argued that society was "an aggregate of groups continuously struggling against each other since time immemorial." Each group feels superior to and tries to exploit every other group—a process Gumplowicz called "ethnocentrism" (*Ethnocentrismus*; Gumplowicz 1879: 254). Warfare was the "compelling" (*zwingende*) force in human history, domination (*Herrschaft*) "the pivot of all events in the historical process" (Gumplowicz 1883: 194, 218). The "wars of civilized nations are essentially nothing but the 'higher forms' of ... primitive wars of plunder and pillage" (166). The culmination of a history of "almost uninterrupted warfare" was the creation of states, which tend to grow ever larger (176). Following Gumplowicz, sociologists like Tilly (1975: 73–76; 1990: ch. 3), Collins (1978: 26), and Mann (1984) have argued warfare drives state expansion, in a process limited only by resource constraints and the countervailing force of other states pursing the same goals.

Gumplowicz did not, however, refer to the largest or highest-order political organizations as *empires*. He typically used the word *Reich*, or empire, only when referring to the polities that historians had always called empires, such as Rome. Intriguingly, Gumplowicz broke with this pattern only once, when discussing the United States, which he saw as "seeking today to unify itself with the South American states into a large American *Reich*" (1910: 157). Gumplowicz's failure to develop a systematic conceptual language to talk about empires probably stemmed from his association with the discipline of *Staatswissenschaft* (Gumplowicz 1875: iv), an academic field that avoided the topics of colonialism and imperialism, according to Lindenfeld (1997: 292). Central European "state theory" from Hegel to Max Weber largely aligned the idea of empire with ancient history and the idea of the state with modernity.

Reading Gumplowicz *symptomatically*, however, we can extract some useful ideas for distinguishing between modern states, empires, and overseas colonies. Territorial political organizations that originate in conquest are almost always confronted with problems of ethnic or cultural heterogeneity. Gumplowicz distinguished between the subset of "national states" in which "a more or less general culture has covered up the originally heterogeneous component parts" and another subset of "states with a 'nationally more mixed' population," like the Austro-Hungarian Empire (Gumplowicz 1883: 206). This second group of states was characterized by the fact "that the heterogeneous ethnic components relate to one another in a condition of super- and subordination, that is, in a relationship of domination" (*Herrschaftsverhältnis*; Gumplowicz 1883: 206). The ongoing subjection of conquered territorial populations or minorities, along with restless political expansiveness, is the defining characteristic of empires as opposed to nation-states.

Friedrich Ratzel: World History as a Tendency Toward the Formation of Giant Empires

Friedrich Ratzel, who described his work as being located at the "border region between geography and sociology" (1897: 3), saw giant empires as the starting point and culmination of all political development. Ratzel grounded his analysis in a supposed general "natural" law reminiscent of Gumplowicz according to which all peoples are animated by the impetus to expand and conquer. "Nature," he wrote, "does not allow a people to stand still in the long run" (Ratzel 1882, vol. 1: 116). Ratzel added a cultural dimension to this argument, suggesting that "the more nations become conscious of global spatial relations, the more they engage in the struggle for space" (Hell forthcoming; Ratzel 1923: 264–267). For Ratzel, world history was a succession of "politically expansive powers" or empires, all of them modeled on Rome, although many of these were "larger than Rome." He rejected the idea, popular in Europe since Polybius (1979), of a "deeply rooted law of dissolution of large empires" and did not believe in "some inexorable law of rise and decline, but in the alternation of expansion and contraction of spaces across time" (Hell forthcoming).

1890–1918

The second period began with the completion of Africa's partition and ended with the collapse of the Ottoman, Russian, and Austrian empires and the transfer of the German colonies and Ottoman provinces to new northern overseers under the League of Nations Mandate system. This period also saw the creation of the first university chairs in sociology and the founding of sociological associations and departments. Key figures in each national sociological field contributed to the study of empire during this period, including Franklin Giddings (1900) and William Graham Sumner (1911) in the United States; Max Weber (1998a, 1998b, 2010), Alfred Weber (1904), and Leopold von Wiese (1914a, 1914b, 1915) in Germany; René Worms (1908) and Gabriel Tarde (1899) in France; and Hobson (1902) and Patrick Geddes (1917) in Britain. An international "congress of colonial sociology" was held in Paris in 1900 (*Congrès international de sociologie coloniale* 1901). René Worms, founder of the Institut international de sociologie, presided over the Sociology and Ethnography section of the annual French Colonial Congress starting in 1907 (Anonymous 1907).

Sociologists and Practical Imperial Policy, 1890–1918

In the British, French, German, and American overseas colonies, policies for governing the colonized—so-called native policy—was largely elaborated in situ by colonial officials at the level of the colony's headquarters or even at the district and local levels (Delavignette 1939; Goh 2007b; Steinmetz 2007b). Professional social scientific research played only a minor role in colonial policymaking before 1918, however, even if native policies drew on ideas from a broader archive of ethnographic representations that included but was not limited to anthropological texts (Steinmetz 2007b). Nonetheless, metropolitan social scientists began to reflect seriously on the practical aspects of colonial policy and to propose ideas to government officials. Between the 1870s and the 1890s the geographer Ferdinand von Richthofen corresponded with German statesmen and published detailed guidelines for seizing and governing a future German colony in China (Steinmetz 2007b). Friedrich Ratzel elaborated on his preference for "colonies of settlement" over "colonies of exploitation" (1923: 102–105), a preference linked to Ratzel's notorious concept of *Lebensraum*, or living space (Neumann 2009: 136). Ratzel's main statement on the idea of Lebensraum appeared in a Festschrift for the founding German sociologist Albert Schäffle (Ratzel 1901). In his book-length essay on colonialism, Schäffle distinguished between what he called "passive colonization" and

FIG 1.1 · Sociologist Richard Thurnwald during a research trip in the German colony of New Guinea before World War I.

the forms of "active political colonization" (*politische Aktivkolonisation*) that Germany was involved in at the time of his writing (Schäffle 1886– 1888, part 2: 126). Passive colonization designated the kinds of activities undertaken by German missionaries, traders, and explorers in the decades and centuries leading up to the Scramble of the 1880s. Alfred Vierkandt, who held the first sociology chair at Berlin University, published a book on two of the categories that played a central role in the formation of German colonial policies: the ideas of *Kulturvölker* and *Naturvölker*, or "cultural and natural peoples" (1896). Richard Thurnwald, who would go on to teach sociology and ethnology at Berlin University after World War I, carried out field research before the war in the German colony of New Guinea (Figure 1.1).

Max Weber's hyperimperialist political views were directed mainly toward support of Germany's projection of its power on a world stage (*Weltpolitik*); he was largely indifferent to overseas colonialism (Mommsen 1984). Alfred Weber argued that German capitalists could profit handily by doing business in other countries' empires and did not need German colonies (Weber 1904). During World War I, Max and Alfred Weber lent active support to plans hatched by Liberal politician Friedrich Naumann ([1915] 1964) for indirect German hegemony over the countries to the east. Germany would lead this "transnational federation of states" while "respecting the freedom of the smaller nations and renouncing annexation" (Alfred Weber, in Demm 1990: 207, 209). Dutch sociologist S. R. Steinmetz (1903) extensively analyzed indigenous "customary law" in European colonies. Patrick Geddes, the most frequently cited sociologist before 1950 in the pages of the British *Sociological Review* (Halsey 2004: 174) and the first sociology professor in India at the University of Bombay, devised a theory of imperial urbanism (Geddes 1917: ch. 11) and a program of ameliorative colonial urban planning (Geddes 1918). Geddes's work was promoted by British officials in India who believed that blight was a source of growing anticolonial sentiment (Meller 1990: 299).

The Comparative Method, Evolutionary Social Theory, and Imperialism

The comparative method, as it used to be called (Steinmetz forthcoming-a), was rooted in the assumption that sociology should seek general laws, following the example of the natural sciences—or at least, emulating the natural sciences as they were incorrectly understood. Pareto (1893: 677) wrote that "it is by comparing civilized with savage society that modern sociologists . . . have been able to lay the basis for a new science." Many of the members of Émile Durkheim's inner circle were connected to colonialism as an analytic object, research setting, or source of information. Durkheim relied on information gathered by European colonial officials, travelers, and missionaries on non-Western and colonized peoples to build an evolutionary theory of society. Maksim Kovalevsky, a sociologist and legal historian at St. Petersburg University, followed Sir Henry Maine (Mantena 2010) in framing his comparative research at the scale of the Russian Empire, understood as a "diverse space that could accommodate the comparative exploration of social forms" and the different temporalities of a universal process of social evolution (chapter 2; Timasheff 1948).

Although sociologists now disparage evolutionary and modernization theories as empirically feeble and politically conservative, these ideas were politically progressive in certain contexts. In Third Republic France after the Dreyfus affair, Durkheim's evolutionary analysis in *Elementary Forms of Religious Life* suggested a commonality among all cultures, from Australian Aborigines to contemporary French. According to early Russian sociologist Evgenii de Roberti, an evolutionary sociology offered a powerful critique of "superstitions and errors" by suggesting that even backward Russia would one day converge with liberal Western societies (Resis 1970: 226).

Evolutionary social theories were revived after 1945 under the guise of modernization theory. The modernization framework was also partially progressive in its rejection of European colonialism and colonialism's "rule of difference" (Chatterjee 1986), although it simultaneously laid the intellectual groundwork for the global American Empire (Gilman 2003). The idea of modernity as a singular "point of convergence" (Taylor 2001: 181) has long accompanied empire. The opposite perspective, which sees civilizations as developing along differing paths, already emerged in the eighteenth century (Herder [1784] 1985) and the Romantic era. I will defer discussion of these ideas until later, since they have again emerged in full force.

Empire as a "World State": Gabriel Tarde

Gabriel Tarde was perhaps the first sociologist to envision the culmination of political history as a unitary world state, which he called an "empire."[22] In *Les transformations du pouvoir* (1899) and *Psychologie économique* (1902), Tarde claimed to discern a general tendency toward the centralization of political powers and the "agglomeration of states into larger units" (Lazzarato 2002: 382–385; Toscano 2007: 601). While criticizing French colonial conquest as a "veritable national cannibalism" and a "collective form of slavery," Tarde praised the Roman Empire for encouraging "competition open to all creative and generous small nations, whose inventions would remain sterile and unperceived without [the empire]" (1899: 161). Like Rome, a future centralized empire would transform *"an illogical diversity into a logical diversity,"* systemizing and intensifying the many "unruly differences and oppositions" (177; Toscano 2007: 600). Although the idea of a world state had been advocated by many earlier theorists of international relations, from Francisco Suárez to Christian Wolf and Immanuel Kant, they all had rejected the idea of universal empire "in the Roman sense" (Hill 1911: 116). Tarde, however, suggested that the preservation of "diversity" within a global political organization had a specifically imperial dimension. Tarde distinguished this form of empire from *imperialism*, which, although it "may have been the only method for pacifying populations by crushing them two millennia ago" was now "nothing more than a . . . monstrous despotism combined with a gigantic and collective rapaciousness" (1902, vol. 2: 441).[23] More recent theories of global political unification have been divided as to whether political history will end in a megastate (Naroll 1966) or giant empire (C. Schmitt [1955] 1995), and whether such unification will preserve cultural difference or eliminate it.

J. A. Hobson: Imperialism as a Function of Capitalism and as the Ruin of Democracy

The most famous contribution to the study of empire from this period is Hobson's *Imperialism*, published in 1902 and still in print. Although Hobson never held a university position, he was a member of the editorial committee of the British *Sociological Papers*, attended the meetings of the British Sociological Society, and published in journals like *Jahrbuch für Soziologie* and the *American Journal of Sociology*. Hobson wrote in his autobiography that he "might wish to claim the title of sociologist" (1938: 64, 71–81). He had a far-reaching influence on subsequent discussions by redefining imperialism as a mainly economic phenomenon rather than a primarily political one.[24] According to Hobson, imperialism was driven by overaccumulation, underconsumption, and finance capital's search for new markets and investment outlets. Imperialism signaled a repudiation of free trade. It did not benefit capitalism as a whole but only sectional interests (Hobson [1902] 1965: 49, 59, 67). Imperialism could be eliminated, he suggested, by redistributing wealth domestically and thereby raising consumption levels (75, 81, 83).

The second half of *Imperialism* focused on the wider effects of empire, especially in Britain itself. Contrary to Marx, Hobson argued that imperialism's impact on the global periphery was catastrophic. The sources of the "incomes expended in the Home Counties and other large districts of Southern Britain," he wrote, "were in large measure wrung from the enforced toil of vast multitudes of black, brown, or yellow natives, by arts not differing essentially from those which supported in idleness and luxury imperial Rome" (Hobson [1902] 1965: 151). Politically, the trend in the colonies was toward "unfreedom" and "British despotism," except with regard to white settlers (151). Turning to the imperial homeland, Hobson echoed Spencer (1902a, 1902b) and many other British Radicals and New Liberals (Porter 1968) in arguing that imperialism struck "at the very root of popular liberty and ordinary civic virtues" in Britain and checked "the very course of civilization" (Hobson [1902] 1965: 133, 162). Governments use "foreign wars and the glamour of empire-making, in order to bemuse the popular mind and divert rising resentment against domestic abuses" and to distract attention from "the vested interests, which, on our analysis, are shown to be chief prompters of an imperialist policy" (142). Imperialism overawes the citizenry "by continual suggestions of unknown and incalculable gains and perils the . . . sober processes of domestic policy," demanding a "blind vote of confidence" (147–148). Jingoistic ideology cements a hegemonic bloc that unites various social classes in support of imperial adventures (Hobson

1901). Empire degrades daily life in the metropole by cultivating a military habitus that "unfits a man for civil life," training him to become "a perfect killer" (Hobson [1902] 1965: 133–134). British children are taught a " 'geocentric' view of the moral universe" and their playtime is turned "into the routine of military drill" (217).

Hobson's argument that "autocratic government in imperial politics naturally reacts upon domestic government" ([1902] 1965: 146–147) was echoed by his sociologist colleague Leonard Hobhouse (1899, 1902, 1904). It anticipated Arendt's (1958) argument about imperialism's corrosive effect on democracy and more recent discussions of the reflux of empire into metropolitan culture by postcolonial theorists (Said 1993). Hobson continued to revise his analysis of imperialism between the wars in response to criticisms of his economic narrowing of the concept. By 1926 he argued that "power-politics furnish the largest volume of imperialist energy, though narrow economic considerations mainly determine its concrete application" (Hobson 1926: 192–193).

Otto Hintze, Max Weber, Robert Michels, and the Noneconomistic Explanation of Ancient Empires and Modern Imperialism

Resistance to the economically straitened definition of imperialism set in swiftly among German-speaking social scientists. German sociologist Robert Michels explained Italy's turn toward colonial aggression with reference to population pressure, national pride, and the "natural instinct for political expansion" (1912: 470, 495). In his 1907 essay "Imperialismus und Weltpolitik," historian Otto Hintze insisted on imperialism's inherently political character. Hintze also distinguished between Roman "ancient imperialism" and "modern imperialism." Ancient imperialism had been oriented toward political expansion and conquest and was based on a "relatively closed civilization," one "that refuses the right to exist of everything foreign that cannot be assimilated" (Hintze 1970). Modern imperialism overcomes the ancient orientation toward world domination, seeking instead a balance among the great powers. Napoleon promoted a "great federative system" of empires that would "give the world its laws," rather than accept a British global domination of politics and trade. After 1815 a liberal era of free trade and industrialism "seemed to replace the era of mercantilism and militarism." Toward the end of the century, however, Britain began to reorganize its colonial empire in the face of mounting challenges to its global domination. Other colonial empires were created in response to the British one and in competition with one another. The goal of present-day imperialism was not a single world empire but a system of smaller world empires coexisting side by side—a sort of Westphalian system of larger units, on a grander scale. Hintze's analysis here resonated with Hobson's discussion of "Imperial Federation" in the penultimate chapter of *Imperialism* (Hobson [1902] 1965: 328–355).

The nonlinear path of social scientific history is sharply illustrated by the case of Max Weber, whose work staked out many of the arguments currently being rediscovered by sociologists of empire. Weber came to be known as a theorist of the state and bureaucracy in U.S. sociology, but he was just as much a historical sociologist of empires. Weber's work on empires and imperialism is spread across many different texts, starting with his 1891 habilitation thesis on Rome (Weber 2010) and continuing through *Economy and Society* (Weber 1978). Weber defended a nonteleological and nonlinear approach to civilizational history, exploring the reasons for Rome's decline, arguing that the great world civilizations each followed distinct developmental paths, and describing the West's modernity as a mix of progress and dystopia. In his writing on the Roman Empire he paid equal attention to core and periphery, centralizing and decentralizing impulses. Perhaps most important, Weber distinguished carefully among different types of higher-order political organization, including states and empires. Although his careful definition of the state is widely accepted, Weber's work is also a corrective to a historical sociology that is organized exclusively around states rather than empires.

At the center of Weber's analysis of Rome was the movement away from a compact, contained central state and outward toward the far-flung empire of conquests and the decentralized structure of manorial power. Another key theme for Weber was the political determination of economic facts, and this informed his analysis of Rome.[25] "Ancient capitalism was based on politics," he wrote (Weber 1998b: 364). The network of Roman roads "served the army, not commerce." Rome's decline resulted from the shift in the political center of gravity from the cities to the countryside, which was at the same time a move from a predominantly commercial economy to a static, subsistence-oriented "natural economy" concentrated in the latifundia. Weber signaled his argument about the primacy of politics by altering the normal Marxist usage of the words "superstructure" and "infrastructure," describing the expansion of the Roman exchange economy and international trade as "a sort of superstructure [*Ueberbau*]," "a thin net," resting on the "infrastructure [*Unterbau*] of natural economy" ([1896] 1924: 294). Over time the Roman slavery-based rural estate became an autarkic "*oikos*," "independent of markets" and satisfying its own consumption needs (Weber 1998b: 359;

2010: 151). Landowners and *coloni* began to flee the cities for the rural manors (Weber 2010: 163–164). Whereas the earlier "basis of Roman public administration" had been located in the cities, over time the rural estates were "removed from urban jurisdiction" and "great numbers of rural properties ... started to appear alongside the cities as administrative units." The large landowners and their interests gained a "new prominence in the policies of the Later Roman Empire" (Weber 1998a: 401; 1998b: 360). The central state was increasingly organized along "a natural economy basis," with the fiscus "producing as much as possible what it needed" and relying on in-kind payments and tribute (Weber 1998a: 405). As the army was dispersed to the peripheries to protect the great landowners, it was increasingly professionalized and de-Romanized, its members recruited locally (Weber 1998b: 361). The Roman cities "crumbled" and "came to rest on [the rural manors]" like "leeches" (Weber 2010: 164, 166). Weber thus attributed the empire's collapse to the "shift of society's centre from the coasts to the hinterland" and the "throttling" of capitalism (Weber 1998b: 358), rather than to the barbarian invasions, the rise of Christianity, or any of the other proximate causes emphasized in the literature of his own era.

Weber also analyzed Rome's expansion as a process of conquests and colonial settlement. Most of Rome's growth occurred under the Republic, which actually became an empire, analytically speaking. At least a third of the land in the conquered polities was "divided among Rome and its allies" (Weber 1998b: 306). The impetus for Roman expansion was both political and economic: "Rome provided for her landless citizens (*cives proletarii*), the peasantry's offspring," through "distributions of land and colonial foundations." Indeed, distribution of conquered land was "what the hoplite army fought for" (307). The inhabitants were treated differently in each of the "citizen colonies," sometimes being "simply incorporated into the ranks of the colonists," elsewhere being "reduced to the status of commoners" or some other unequal status (Weber 2010: 46–47).

Weber's discussion of imperialism in *Economy and Society* adopted some of the arguments of writers like Hobson. He allowed that "one might be inclined to believe that the formation as well as the expansion of Great Power structures is always and primarily determined economically" (Weber 1978: 913). Capitalism in the present had shifted from a generally pacifist orientation to an aggressively imperialist stance, Weber asserted. At the same time, Weber continued, that while "the economic importance of trade was not altogether absent; yet other motives have played their part in every overland political expansion of the past." "Empire formation" in general "does not always follow the routes of export trade" (914–915). Territorial political organizations were motivated toward expansion by concerns deriving from the "realm of 'honor'" or the quest for the "prestige of power," even if they "vary in the extent to which they are turned outward" (910). The specifically "political drives for expansion" might be reinforced by capitalist interests, but at the same time "the evolution of capitalism may be strangled by the manner in which a unified political structure is administrated," as in the late Roman Empire (915). Echoing Ibn Khaldun's theory of imperial overstretch,[26] and Alfred Weber's refutation of the economic benefits to German capitalists of a colonial empire (Weber 1904), Max Weber suggested that "countries little burdened by military expenses ... often experience a stronger economic expansion than do some of the Great Powers" (901). The relations between economic and political impulses varied over time; sometimes they were mutually reinforcing, but other times politics trumped or violated economic imperatives.

1918–1945

The third period saw the consolidation of European colonialism and the rise of anticolonial movements, especially in India. At the beginning of this period, discourses of cultural pessimism and degeneration combined with the collapse of the Ottoman, Austro-Hungarian, Russian, and German empires to reinvigorate ancient theories of imperial cycles. Sociologists continued to propose theories of imperialism that avoided economic reductionism. A sizable group of ethnologists, sociologists, and ethno-sociologists theorized colonial cultural syncretism and anticolonial resistance. At the end of the period social scientists began analyzing Nazism as a form of empire. Some discussed geospatial spheres of influence without territorial annexation as the dominant emerging form of empire.

Discourses of Degeneration and the Cyclical Rise and Fall of Empires

The early twentieth century saw a revival of ancient theories about cycles of empires. Since Polybius (1979), empires have been shadowed by discourses about their inevitable demise (Hell 2008, 2009, forthcoming). These arguments gained a new urgency at the end of the nineteenth century with the rising tide of theories of cultural degeneration. One of the most influential statements of cultural pessimism was Oswald Spengler's (1920–1922) *Decline of the West*, a wide-ranging narrative of the rise and fall of civilizations and their crystallization as empires in their final, degenerate phases. The idea of the cyclical rise and fall of nations and empires was elaborated by the fascist demographer and sociologist Corrado Gini (Gillette 2002: 40–41; see chapter 4). Indeed, there has been a periodic—dare I say cyclical?—return of the idea of cycles of empire (see Eisenstadt 1963; Ferrari 1896; Gini 1938, 1941a, 1941b; Mann 1986: 168; Naroll 1966) and of the inexorable demise of empires (Eisenstadt 1967; Kennedy 1987; Motyl 2001; Tilly 1997a; Wallerstein 2003), as well as continuing sociological fascination with the reasons for the decline of empires (Sassen 2006: 92, note 35).

Sociological Accounts of Imperialism: Oppenheimer versus Schumpeter, Salz, Sulzbach, and Davy

At least one leading sociologist from the interwar period, Franz Oppenheimer, accepted the Marxist argument about the capitalist roots of imperialism. Where Oppenheimer's thought diverged from Marxism was in combining the militaristic theory of the state with an approach that privileged economics causally and politically. Oppenheimer also followed Gumplowicz, whom he called a "pathfinder," in arguing that the state is a "social institution that is forced by a victorious group of men on a defeated group, with the sole purpose of regulating the dominion of the former over the latter and securing itself against revolt from within and attacks from abroad" (Oppenheimer 1919: 10). This was a universal theory: "all States of world-history have to run the same course or gauntlet, torn by the same class-struggles . . . through the same stages of development following the same inexorable laws" (Oppenheimer 1944: 551). The second volume of Oppenheimer's *System der Soziologie* was entitled *Der Staat*. Like his short 1919 book with the same title, this was organized according to a historical sequence running from the primitive "conquest state" through maritime, feudal, *Ständesstaat*, and absolutist forms of the state. Rather than culminating in constitutionalism, however, as in the 1919 book, Oppenheimer now concluded with a utopian vision of a "classless society," a "true 'democracy'" (1926: 795), one in which capitalist landlord ownership would be abolished and large industrial firms would be owned by the workers (740, 744). By reforming land tenure patterns and encouraging communal colonization,[27] the living standards of the poorest classes would be raised and class differences abolished (Oppenheimer 1926: 764, 772; 1958: 87, 90). His utopia's political form would be a consensually governed federative republic at the national level and a "federation of free federations" or *Eidgenossenschaft der Staaten* at the global level (Oppenheimer 1926: 731, 795, 794, 797). Centralized states, with their emphasis on sovereignty and monopolization of violence, would cease to exist (773–774). The "sovereign" in this world federation would be the law (804).

Although Oppenheimer referred to Rome as a Reich and a *Kaiserreich* (Oppenheimer 1929: 401, 382) and to the formation of a number of medieval *Reiche* (Oppenheimer 1933), he used the word *Reich* mainly as a name, not as a concept. The only generalization Oppenheimer offered was in his definition of "primitive giant empires" as collections of even more primitive conquest states, and his argument that these empires typically collapse back into a "pile of individual states" (1926: 584). But Oppenheimer did discuss "imperialism" at some length. The medieval Arab empires engaged in "aristocratic exclusive imperialism" (Oppenheimer 1933: 692). The final volume of *System der Soziologie* described colonialism as a continuation of a "politics of plunder" (Oppenheimer 1935: 1292). "Capitalism" in its highest stage, which was the penultimate stage before the classless society, was essentially imperialist (Oppenheimer 1926: 788). Wages in capitalist countries were too low to ensure that workers could "buy back their products," so capitalists were driven to seek foreign markets and to seek surplus profits from the "proletarians of foreign countries" (789–790). The "struggle over the world market" was therefore a "vital need of the capitalist bourgeoisie" (790), leading to war and protectionism. The Roman Empire, Oppenheimer now claimed, had also been driven toward expansion by the limited capacity of the "domestic market" (1929: 332).

Most members of the second generation of German sociologists—those who earned their doctorates or obtained their first university posts during the Weimar Republic—amplified the critique of economistic accounts of colonialism and empire. Austrian economist Joseph Schumpeter, who moved to Bonn University in 1925 (and from there to Harvard in 1932), published an influential essay on imperialism in 1919 in *Archiv fur Sozialwissenschaft und Sozialpolitik*, the leading journal in the nascent German field of academic sociology. Schumpeter defined imperialism here as the "objectless disposition on the part of a state to unlimited forcible expansion" (1951: 6). He traced the "birth and life of imperialism" not to capitalist economic motives but to the atavistic drives of the declining aristocratic ruling class and to appeals to "instincts that carry over from the life habits of the dim past," especially the "instinctive urge to domination" (7, 12). Schumpeter claimed that imperialism was "best illustrated by examples from antiquity" (23). Against Hobson and the Marxists, Schumpeter insisted that "the bourgeois is unwarlike" and that imperialism could "never been have evolved by the 'inner logic' of capitalism itself" (97). For Schumpeter, Marxist accounts were part of a broader rationalizing disavowal of the irrational sources of the primitive urge to dominate.

Schumpeter's arguments were adopted by the Frankfurt University sociologist Walter Sulzbach, who argued that "the imperialism of modern capitalist countries can be regarded as an out-flow of the policies of military and political leaders who, pretending to represent the vital national interests of their peoples, are using entrepreneurs and foreign investors as pawns in order to justify their policy of aggression." Sulzbach distinguished "sharply between the political elite and the business leaders and stipulate[d] antagonistic interests of the two" (Hoselitz 1951: 363; Sulzbach 1926). Nationalist fervor rather than capitalism was responsible for imperialism (Sulzbach 1929). From the 1920s through the 1960s Sulzbach continued to argue that the bourgeoisie "everywhere defended disarmament and agreement between nations" and that "really big capitalists" had very little interest in territorial expansion (Sulzbach 1959: 168, 210). Along similar lines, the Heidelberg social scientist Arthur Salz published a synthetic study of imperialism that defined it in political terms as encompassing efforts by a state to expand its power through the conquest of territory.[28] The economic definition of imperialism was misleading, Salz insisted: imperialism existed before capitalism; capitalist accumulation is often peaceful (Salz 1931).

French sociologist Georges Davy, a member of the original grouping around Durkheim, rejected the economic approach to empire in *From Tribe to Empire: Social Organization among Primitives and in the Ancient East*, a study coauthored with Egyptologist Alexandre Moret. Their central argument, as summarized by historian Henri Berr, was that "the enlargement of societies is accomplished by violence" and that "imperialism" was itself "inspired by the 'will to growth'—a brutal will" (1926: xix, xxiv). They also relied on Durkheim's theory of totemism to make sense of the centralization and monopolization of power in ancient Egypt, adding a symbolic dimension to discussions that had hitherto foregrounded politics and economics (Moret and Davy 1926).

Theories of Colonial Transculturation, Mimicry, and Anticolonial Resistance
Theories of colonial hybridity, syncretism, and transculturation might seem peripheral to the history of sociology if one limited one's vision to recent decades, when these discussions have been dominated by literary theorists and cultural anthropologists. The pioneers of these theories, however, were mainly students of Marcel Mauss who defined themselves as sociologists or ethno-sociologists, or British social anthropologists, many of them students of Max Gluckman, who were equally at home in the two disciplines.[29]

In the middle decades of the twentieth century, colonial sociologists and social scientists stopped looking for pristine, untouched native cultures and became interested in processes of colonial transculturation. The background for this shift is complex. Colonial governments had been less concerned with "primitivism" among their subjects than with the danger of large numbers of partially assimilated "natives." Concern about the "illegibility" of culturally mixed subjects was a key motivation behind the colonial state's focus on "native policy," whose aim was to urge the colonized to adhere to a stable, uniform definition of their own culture (Steinmetz 2003b). Most native policy sought to restrict the colonized to a codified version of their "traditional" culture. Social scientists oriented their research toward discovering the coherent "traditional" culture that native policy would try to reinforce. Colonial social scientists therefore typically sought out informants familiar with tradition or untouched by Western culture, around whom they could construct their narratives. In British-ruled Tanganyika in the 1920s, for example, colonial governor Donald Cameron instructed his district officials to become amateur anthropologists and to gather information on ancient tribal traditions, which colonial policy would then seek to resurrect (Austen 1967). More autonomous social scientists, like Durkheim, were also most interested in unassimilated natives, albeit for different reasons—as evidence for theories of evolutionary development.

By the time Claude Lévi-Strauss published *Tristes tropiques* in 1955, the idealized figure of the "noble savage" had been dismantled. Lévi-Strauss could only allude wistfully to his "great disappointment" in the Brazilian Indians, who were "less unspoiled than [he] had hoped." Their culture was now "a compromise," entirely lacking in "poetry" (Lévi-Strauss 1997: 154, 172). For most of the colonial social researchers who started calling themselves sociologists during the middle decades of the twentieth century, however, it was these less "poetic," syncretic cultures that proved most interesting.

One of the first sociological analysts of colonial transculturation and resistance was Maurice Leenhardt, who interpreted the messianic "Ethiopian" church movement in southern Africa as a form of subaltern resistance via appropriation of the colonizer's culture (Leenhardt [1902] 1976). In his subsequent work Leenhardt interpreted indigenous New Caledonian culture along similar lines. Following an initial period of brutal expropriation and cultural decimation, the French Oceanic colony had become a syncretic society. Transculturation ran in both directions between Europeans and Melanesians, in a process Leenhardt called a *jeu des transferts* (play of cultural transfers; Leenhardt 1953: 213). Along similar lines, sociologist

Gilberto Freyre, a student of Franz Boas, analyzed colonial Brazil as a "hybrid society" ([1933] 1946). Anthropologist Melville Herskovits developed a theory of "acculturation" under conditions of colonial slavery and argued that the mixing of European and African traditions was a "fundamental . . . mechanism in the acculturative process undergone by New World Negroes" (1941: 184–185; 1937, 1938).[30] Herskovits eventually replaced the concept of syncretism with *reinterpretation*, defined as forms of "cultural borrowing" that "permit a people to retain the inner meanings of traditionally sanctioned modes of behavior while adopting new outer institutional forms" (Herskovits and Herskovits [1947] 1964: vi).

Many ethno-sociologists contributed to theories of the culturally transformative effects of colonialism in the interwar period. Richard Thurnwald addressed the "crisis" in native life that had been precipitated by sustained contact with the colonizer's culture and technology (Thurnwald 1931–1935, vol. 1: 21–22). Thurnwald analyzed cultural mixing by distinguishing between "culture" and "civilization," echoing Alfred Weber (1920–1921). Societies could be arranged along a scale in terms of their "civilizational" level, defined in terms of technology and technical knowledge, but such linear comparisons were impossible at the "cultural" level (Thurnwald 1935: 4; 1939b: 422–423). In 1936 Thurnwald discussed the "crisis of imperialism" and the emergence of anticolonialism in an "awakening Africa" (1936: 80), and argued that "inherent in imperialism is the 'hybris,' the overbearing insolence of the dominant stratum," which "inescapably leads to its nemesis," in the guise of "a new generation of natives . . . which has been educated in schools by Europeans, in ways of thought that are European, and in using devices introduced by Europeans" (84).[31]

Many of Marcel Mauss's students began focusing on colonial hybridity between the wars. As mentioned above, Durkheim had been uninterested in the partly Westernized Other or cultural *métissage* resulting from imperial contact. The publications that resulted from expeditions sponsored by the Paris Ethnological Institute tended to ignore "everything that did not correspond to the image of a preserved Africa" (De l'Estoile 2007: 148). But in *L'Afrique fantôme* (Leiris 1934) and "The Ethnographer Faced with Colonialism," Michel Leiris attacked "the tendency to attach oneself by preference to peoples one can qualify as relatively intact, either out of a love of a certain 'primitivism' or . . . exoticism." The most "authentic" Africans, Leiris insisted, "the most interesting, humanly," were the ones that ethnographers usually saw as "mere imitators" of Western culture (Leiris 1989: 124–127). René Maunier, promoter of a field he called *colonistics* (*la colonistique*) and author of *Sociology of Colonies*, was another forerunner of theories of anti-colonial resistance and cultural melding. Maunier conceptualized colonization as a "social fact" involving "contact" between two "hitherto separated" societies (Maunier 1949: 5–6). Although Maunier's definition of colonialism did not emphasize the centrality of racism or the colonial "rule of difference," he specified that colonialism was always based on a "doctrine of domination" (29, 19). Analyzing the rise of independence movements in the colonies, Maunier argued that "colonization itself organized the space of Algerian nationalism and gave it its main idea" (Henry 1989: 143). Maunier also discussed the reciprocal imitation between colonizer and colonized, adumbrating a theory of colonial mimicry (*mixité*). For Maunier, colonial cultural mixing included not just the "fusion" or "racial and . . . social blending of the two groups" but also the "conversion of the conqueror by the conquered" (1949: 124, 535). Roger Bastide, a specialist in Afro-Brazilian religion, developed a "sociology of the interpenetration of cultures" (1948, 1960) based on the concepts of *bricolage* from Lévi-Strauss. According to Bastide, the "gaps" in collective memory resulting from the collective trauma of the uprooting of African slaves from their homeland were selectively filled in by homologous or structurally similar materials found in the new culture (Bastide 1970–1971). The Afro-Brazilian *candomblé*, which resembled a mystical trance, was for Bastide a coherent religious system (Bastide 1958, 1970–1971). Mexicanist Jacques Soustelle studied the Otomi Indians,[32] whose culture he described as a veritable "clash of civilizations" and "an original synthesis" (1937: 253; 1971: 132, 137). Indian converts "were not so much renouncing their old beliefs as incorporating them into a new body of faith and ritual," forging a "Hispano-Indian and Christiano-pagan syncretism" (Soustelle 1971: 137, 121). If many of these ideas sound familiar today it is because they were articulated so powerfully during the middle decades of the twentieth century by a number of anthropologists and ethno-sociologists (Steinmetz 2009a).

A final twist was the integration of psychoanalytic concepts to the analysis of colonized consciousness and anticolonial movements. Although this approach is usually associated nowadays with authors like Wulf Sachs, Octave Mannoni, and Frantz Fanon, it was also developed by sociologists working in French colonial North Africa. Jacques Berque, a sociologist specialized in Northern African societies, argued that the Algerian war was "not just 'sociological' . . . but also . . . psychoanalytical: reaffirmation of a mutilated unconscious" (Berque 1958: 102). Sociologist Albert Memmi framed his analysis of the "sociology of relations between the colonizer and the colonized" (1957) explicitly around the question of the importance of adding a psychoanalytic to a Marxist economic lens (Memmi 1967: xiii). Sociologist André Adam explored the "contribution of psychoanalysis to the knowledge of North African societies" (1965).

Nazi Germany and the Postwar United States as Empires: Arendt, Neumann, Schmitt, and Aron

In the middle decades of the twentieth century some social scientists began arguing that empires were increasingly based on indirect and informal control of peripheries rather than permanent occupation and foreign overrule. This theory of informal empire developed largely as a reflection on the geopolitics of the United States and pre–World War II Nazi Germany. In the early 1920s Arthur Salz discussed the new, highly "elastic" form of U.S. imperialism in Latin America that "leaves its victims with the appearance of political autonomy and is satisfied with a minimal amount of political violence" (1923: 569). After World War II Hans Gerth and C. Wright Mills (1953: 205) described the American strategy as one in which "one power may seek to expand its military area of control by establishing naval and air bases abroad without assuming overt political responsibility" over "foreign political bodies." Franz Neumann (2009: 136) noted that empires often eschew conquest altogether in favor of something "midway between influence and outright domination." Starting in 1942 Carl Schmitt discussed the new American nomos that would install itself "upon the ruins of the old" ([1942] 1997: 59). In a postwar discussion of "the new *nomoi* of the earth," Schmitt held out the possibility of a "combination of several independent *Großräume* or blocs" that could counterbalance the American and Soviet nomoi (Schmitt [1950] 2003: 355). Schmitt developed his concepts of the *Großräum* (great space) and the *nomoi of the earth* as a modern form of empire in which the controlling state renounces "open territorial annexation of the controlled state" but absorbs a "space far exceeding the boundaries of the state proper" into its own "spatial sphere" (252, 281). René Maunier echoed Schmitt in comparing U.S. hegemony over the Western hemisphere to German plans to dominate Central Europe (Maunier 1943: 141). Similar ideas underlay discussions after the war of a future European federation as a counterweight to the United States (Anter 2008; Joerges 2003; Kaiser 1968; Masala 2004). Alexandre Kojève proposed a Mediterranean, French-led nomos that would encompass northern Africa and provide a counterweight to American dominance (Howse 2006; Kojève 2002). Raymond Aron suggested that France should unify the European nation-states against the three great "empires"—the United States, Soviet Union, and United Kingdom—by "coordinating them, tightening their relations to one another, and to instill in them little by little the idea of a larger order" (1945: 358–360, 368). Although Aron insisted that France itself would not "rise to the level of the empires," his vision of a French-led hegemonic federation closely resembled Schmitt's model of empire as Großräum or nomos.[33] More recent discussions of unified Europe as a nomos or counterempire have their origins in these wartime and immediate postwar discussions.[34]

Many of the same ideas were used to analyze Nazi Germany as a kind of empire. Hannah Arendt (1945–1946, 1950) analyzed overseas imperialism as a "prefiguration" of Nazi totalitarianism. Franz Neumann's *Behemoth* compared Hitler's foreign policy to the U.S. Monroe Doctrine and sketched out a theory of "great spaces" as empires (Neumann 2009: 130–218). Nazi geopolitical theory traced its lineage back to Ratzel, who shattered "traditional conceptions of the state" and emphasized the need "to develop a popular consciousness of large spaces" (Neumann 2009: 139). Geographer Karl Haushofer argued that "the category of great power must be replaced by world power" (Neumann 2009: 144). German world power, for Haushofer, would be anticolonial, supporting the self-determination of colonized and racial minorities (Neumann 2009: 144). "Geo-jurisprudence" would "reformulate international law in terms of vassals, dependencies, protectorates, and federations worked out on geopolitical principles" (151). The culmination of this analytic move from states to empires was represented by Schmitt, with whom Neumann had studied in Germany. Schmitt had already analyzed imperialism as a practice of ordering transnational space prior to the Nazi seizure of power (Schmitt [1932] 1940). In 1941 Schmitt proposed a model of the Monroe Doctrine for Germany, shortly before Hitler himself proclaimed a "German Monroe Doctrine" (Schmitt [1941] 1991). Schmitt labeled this supranational political order Großräum, or greater space; subsequently he introduced the concept of the geopolitical nomos ([1942] 1997: 371; [1950] 2003). Schmitt contrasted "the regional, anti-universalist space principle" of the Germans with the universalistic, abstract space principle of the British empire (Neumann 2009: 158). This meant that "there is no longer one international law but as many as there are empires, that is, large spaces" (158). Schmitt argued that "the decline of the state . . . represents a major practical trend," and he refused "to call the legal relations between the rival empires international law," a term that had "been misused for imperialistic aims" (159–160). Within a given empire or Großräum, Schmitt argued, "the conqueror imposes a hierarchy of races," and within "countries dominated by

Germany," the "German minority receives the status of a dominant minority" (163, 165).

Sociologist Wilhelm Mühlmann, a student of Richard Thurnwald, developed a program for distinguishing the ethnic groups in the Nazi-occupied eastern territories that were amenable to re-Germanization and absorption—a process he called "trans-folking" (*Umvolkung*).[35] According to Mühlmann, "Subjective ethnic conversion under the superior weight of the foreign ethnic gradient corresponds to surrendering to the enemy in war. . . . The suffering ethnos constitutes small . . . ethnic islands that become ever more tightly surrounded and finally give way before the flood of the stronger ethnic group" (1942: 296). This was a theory for German domination of the east that stopped just short of advocating racial extermination of those not suited for assimilation.[36] It resembled the European colonial practice of evaluating individuals on a case-by-case basis to determine whether they could receive "white" or European legal status (and be employed as collaborators).[37]

1945–PRESENT

After 1945 the United States and Soviet Union struggled for influence over the newly independent postcolonies. Since 1990 there has been a shift to a unipolar global system. Most recently, China has started to challenge American hegemony (chapter 10). Sociological thinking about empire and related topics was dominated initially in this period by modernization theory, which was then challenged by theories of dependency, underdevelopment, and the world system. Social scientists from the former colonies became increasingly prominent in these discussions (e.g., Alavi 1981; Appaduri 1991; Chatterjee 1993; Gaonkar 2001; Goh 2005; Hermassi 1972; Mamdani 1996; Mazrui 1968). The most recent period has seen a proliferation of multicausal, historical analyses of empires, exemplified by the work of Michael Mann (1986, 2003; chapter 7), and of colonies.

Modernization Theory and Neo-Marxist Responses

After 1945 modernization theory was closely associated with American foreign policy, which eventually came to reject European colonialism (Louis and Robinson 1993; Sulzbach 1963; Williams 1959) in favor of a view of all cultures as equally suited for democracy, capitalism, and the American way of life. Modernization theory itself subsequently came under attack as imperialist and neocolonialist (Hermassi 1972: 3; Mazrui 1968; Tipps 1973). Marxists began analyzing the exploitation of the global peripheries through mechanisms that bypassed colonial rule, such as unequal conditions of exchange (Frank 1969).

A powerful alternative approach was developed by Immanuel Wallerstein. After working for more than a decade as an Africanist, Wallerstein began to examine the structural constraints preventing postcolonial Africa from succeeding economically and politically (Wallerstein 1971). His answer was presented in *The Modern World System* (1974–2011), whose historical arc swept from the conquest of the New World to the nineteenth-century "settler decolonization of the Americas." Wallerstein argued that there are two kinds of world systems or intersocietal divisions of labor: *world-empires,* with a single political authority, and *world-economies,* organized politically as a plurality of competing sovereign nation-states (Wallerstein 1979: 5; 2004: 57). The capitalist world economy initially treated Africa as an "external area"; after about 1750 Africa became a "periphery" providing slaves; after 1800 "the slave trade was gradually abolished," facilitating "the reconversion of [African] production to cash cropping" and preparing the continent for the "imposition of colonial administration," which "made it possible to establish [European] primacy" in African "economic transactions" (Wallerstein [1970] 1986: 14–16). World system theory explains the historical ebb and flow of waves of colonial annexation and decolonization in terms of shifts in the degree of hegemonic centralization within the global core. If a single state (or group of states) dominates the core economically and politically, it enforces free trade and eschews colonialism; when there is no hegemon, each core state throws up protectionist barriers and tries to secure exclusive access to markets and raw materials in the periphery, which often involves setting up colonies (Bergesen and Schoenberg 1980; Boswell 1989).

The Historical Sociology of Colonialism after 1945

A new historical sociology of colonialism started to emerge during the 1950s and 1960s among French sociologists. Georges Balandier (1951) analyzed colonialism as a unique, overdetermined social formation, a Sartrian "situation." In *Sociologie actuelle de l'Afrique noire,* Balandier compared the differing responses to colonialism by the Gabonese Fang and the Bakongo of the French Congo (Balandier 1955a: 14–15). The differences were due to a mix of internal and European-induced factors. The Fang had become "unemployed conquerors" lacking any central leadership; the Bakongo had been involved in the slave trade and were more rooted in their territory, more hierarchical, and better acquainted with other tribes. The French government attempted to curtail the prominence of Bakongo in the colonial administration during the 1930s but ended up strengthening the modernist elite's anticolonialism, which filled "the 'political void' that resulted from the diminished authority of the traditional chiefs" (Balandier 1955a: 354–355). Balandier's *Sociologie des Brazzavilles noires* focused on Bakongo urbanites who had resettled in Brazzaville. He found that urban Bakongo did not abandon their traditional culture or their connections to rural countrymen and that they developed a "precocious awareness of the inferiority created by the colonial situation" (Balandier 1955b: 388). Balandier's coauthor Paul Mercier rejected linear developmental models, emphasizing the "considerable discontinuities in the development of colonial societies" and "multiple determinants, sometimes in contradiction with one another" (Mercier 1954: 65, 57). Cultural practices "that seem to be 'traditional' in these societies actually represented 'responses' to relatively recent 'challenges'" (Mercier 1966, p. 168, note 1). Mercier criticized the application to African societies of Western and Marxist concepts like social class and nationalism (Mercier 1954, 1965a, 1965b).

In his earliest publications, Pierre Bourdieu blamed Algerian underdevelopment not on the Algerians' own shortcomings but on the "shock effect of a clash between an archaic economy and a modern one" (1959: 55). In *Sociologie de l'Algérie* he asked how different groups of Algerians reacted to this "clash of civilizations" (Bourdieu 1958: 119). Bourdieu described the Kabyle as a historical society that had been continuously reshaped by episodes of conquest by Arabs and Europeans (16). Discussing Algeria's Arab speakers, he argued that few societies "pose the problem of the relations between sociology and history more sharply," since they had "suffered the most directly and the most profoundly from the shock of colonization" (60). The second edition of *Sociologie de l'Algérie* included a discussion of French land annexations and settlements, which produced a "tabula rasa of a civilization that could no longer be discussed except in the past tense" (Bourdieu 1961b: 125, 107–118). Bourdieu insisted on the "special form this war acquired because of its being waged in this unique situation," namely, a colonial one (1961a: 28–29). The radical transformation effected by uprooting, resettlement, and war was the subject of a book Bourdieu coauthored with his Algerian student and colleague, sociologist Abdelmalek Sayad (Bourdieu and Sayad 1964).

According to the Althusserian theory of the *articulation of modes of production* (Coquery-Vidrovitch 1969; Rey 1973; Wolpe 1980), colonialism typically combined capitalist and noncapitalist modes of production in ways that were functional for capitalism, lowering the costs of reproducing labor power and yielding higher profits (Coquery-Vidrovitch 1988). Hamza Alavi (1981) called the combined social formation a *colonial mode of production*.

Despite this theory's residual economic reductionism and functionalism, it was more open to the complexity and uniqueness of historical processes and events than were earlier Marxist approaches (Berman and Lonsdale 1992; Dedering 1988).

The "peripheralist" or "excentric" approach argued that resistance and collaboration by the colonized is at least as important as impulses coming from the core in determining whether European states engage in colonialism at all and in shaping colonial rule (Robinson 1972, 1986). Collaboration by the colonized provides an explanation for the colonial state's frequent decisions to preserve traditional social structures (Robinson 1986: 272, 280). The peripheralist approach drew on the earlier studies of creative reinterpretation of Western culture by Herskovits, Leenhardt, and other students of Mauss.

Since the 1960s, historical sociologists of empire have drawn on various elements of this diverse theoretical legacy. In an excellent study of nationalist movements in French North Africa, Elbaki Hermassi (1972) emphasized the effects of the differing length of colonial occupation, the class identities of colonial rulers, the character of native policies, and the strength of the precolonial autochthonous state. Mahmood Mamdani's analysis (1996) of South African apartheid built on the articulation of modes of production framework, arguing that the traditional mode of production in South Africa—"decentralized despotism"—was produced by the colonizers' reliance on collaborators and "indirect rule" and was accompanied by "customary law" and "tribalization." The capitalist structure of South African urban zones, by contrast, was a result of direct colonial rule. Here Africans were excluded from civil freedoms and subjected to racialization rather than tribalization (Mamdani 1996: 18–19).

Other recent historical studies of empire by sociologists have drawn on neoinstitutionalist theory. In *Bandits and Bureaucrats* (1994), Karen Barkey showed how endemic banditry challenged the Ottoman state and how that state managed its relations with these former mercenary soldiers through deals and patronage. In *Empire of Difference* (2008), Barkey developed a "hub and spoke" model of the Ottoman Empire's approach to ruling. In an empire shaped like a rimless wheel (Motyl 2001), the cultures located at the end of each "spoke" are connected only to the core but not to one another, explaining the empire's ability to persist for such a long time.

Another set of approaches are broadly culturalist. David Strang (1990) analyzed decolonization by using a cultural world systems approach. Julia Adams (1994, 2005a) drew on principal-agent theory and combined it with a cultural analysis of the meanings of family and gender in the early modern

Netherlands in order to understand the form of colonial merchant capitalism and state formation. In *Orientalism*, Edward Said posited an "absolute unanimity" between Orientalism and empire, in which "from travelers' tales, and not only from great institutions like the various India companies, colonies were created" (1978: 104, 117). An outpouring of work inspired by Said and Michel Foucault emphasized the effects of European representations of the non-West on subsequent colonial and imperial activities. Some applications of this theory greatly exaggerate the homogeneity of Western discourse about the non-West and underestimate the role of nondiscursive mechanisms in shaping colonial rule. Nonetheless, this approach provided an essential corrective to earlier theories of empire that ignored or failed to specify the independent effect of discursive and cultural processes. In *Colonizing Egypt*, Timothy Mitchell (1988) argues that a generic European modern consciousness was replicated in the self-modernization of nineteenth-century Egypt and other parts of the colonized world. Steinmetz (2003b, 2007) demonstrated that precolonial archives of ethnographic images and texts codetermined subsequent colonial native policies (see also Goh 2005, 2007b, 2008). Go (2008a), in a study of American colonialism in the Philippines and Puerto Rico, reframed Herskovits's reinterpretation theory, looking at the ways the uniform American colonial project of "democratic tutelage," that is, efforts to restructure domestic politics in these two colonies, was differentially interpreted by two groups of colonized elites and at the ways in which these reinterpretations shaped the formation of divergent colonial states. One type of response by these native elites involved accepting the language of the imported concepts while reinterpreting them in terms of familiar concepts and practices; another response by the colonized accepted both the language and the meaning of the imposed concepts. Theories of cultural "incommensurability" (Steinmetz 2004) and "multiple" or "alternative" modernities (Appadurai 1991: 192–194; Eisenstadt 2002; Gaonkar 2001a) returned to earlier arguments against uniform models of social development, first presented by Herder and elaborated during the initial decades of the twentieth century by the *Kulturkreislehre*, or theory of cultural regions, an anthropological school based in central Europe.

Historical sociologists now recognize that powerful states usually pursue a mix of imperialist and colonialist strategies (Steinmetz 2005a). During the eighteenth century the Austro-Hungarian Empire treated Belgium (the Austrian Netherlands) in an imperialist manner as a pawn in a future game of "territorial barter," while treating Hungary as a colony whose best lands were redistributed "to foreigners, mostly German nobles" (Kann 1974: 89, 74).[38]

American foreign policy at the end of the nineteenth century similarly reveals a combination of imperial technologies. After subjecting most Native Americans to formal colonial rule under the system of Indian reservations, the United States embarked on a career of overseas colonialism in the Philippines, Puerto Rico, and the Pacific (Go 2008a) while pursuing a noncolonial imperial approach in China (the "Open Door" policy) and Latin America (the Monroe Doctrine).

Historians and sociologists have called attention to the ways in which generic European state formation resembled colonial conquest (Bartlett 1993; Given 1990; Lustick 1993; see also chapter 9). Unlike colonial state formation, however, state formation inside Europe usually involved territorial annexation followed by the effacement of hierarchical legal distinctions between conqueror and conquered. The distinction between European state-making and overseas colonial state-making is to some extent a question of the duration of foreign domination. European colonizers deferred their colonies' independence far into the nebulous future in their imaginations and did everything possible to squelch the growth of Asian or African nationalism (Steinmetz 2007b). Conquerors in modern Europe, by contrast, usually set out immediately after territorial annexations to convert, assimilate, and nationalize the conquered populations. Within Europe the conquering state tried to turn "peasants into Frenchmen" (E. Weber 1976), or into Britons or Germans, as the case may be. In modern colonies, however, the goal was most often to turn "peasants into tribesmen." State formation in this respect was fundamentally different in the core and in the colonized periphery.

Most recently, colonial historians have drawn on Pierre Bourdieu's theory of social fields. If the metropolitan state is analyzed as a field, as Bourdieu (1996b; 2012) suggested, overseas colonial states may represent a distinct type of field characterized by competition for specific forms of symbolic capital and by particular forms of relative autonomy from the metropolitan state and other fields in the colony (Steinmetz 2008a). Colony and metropole are also linked via additional transnational fields, such as scientific ones (Steinmetz 2012c). Bourdieusian field theory can also be reconstructed to make sense of imperial global relations (Steinmetz 2012c).

Michael Mann's Theory of the Sources of Social Power and the Question of Ancient and Modern Empires

One of the most comprehensive approaches to empire has been developed by sociologist Michael Mann. The first volume of Mann's *Sources of Social Power* provides a subtle and multifaceted account of ancient empires that avoids the temptation of forcing imperial history into a single, linear evolutionary box. If Mann's key causal mechanisms and certain "higher-order crystallizations of power" are repeated over time, the specific events and power formations are the result of contingent accidents and nonuniversal patterns (Mann 1986: 503). Mann draws on Marx and Hobson for his theory of the profitability of empire, on Weber for his historicist methodology of contingent multicausality, on historical sociologist Wolfram Eberhard (1965) for his notion of world time (Mann 1986: 30), and on Polybius for his analysis of imperial cycles. Mann defines the state in Weberian terms (Mann 1993: 55) and notes that states' territorial boundaries "give rise to an area of regulated interstate relations," which take two forms—"hegemonic empire" and "multistate civilization" (1986: 27). Empires' expansion, like that of states, is driven by warfare and conquest. Imperial power increases via the "caging" of populations. Mann distinguishes between "empires of domination," which lack a true core and "extensive" control over the entire imperial territory, and "territorial empires," which spread their power over an entire imperial space. Rome was the first and last true territorial empire in Europe (338). The existence of empires led to greater prosperity via a sort of "welfare state imperialism," at least in the ancient world (257, 265). Ancient empires employed four strategies of domination: rule through clients (indirect rule); direct rule through the army; "compulsory cooperation"; and the development of a common ruling-class culture. Mann rejects any notion of general evolutionary paths but treats the historical development of empires "dialectically," tracing the production of countertendencies to imperial strategy. At the most general level, he identifies a dialectic of centralization and decentralization—also described as a cycling between empires and "multi-power-actor civilization" (the latter defined as a decentralized international society governed by diplomacy, shared rules, and cosmopolitan difference). This multi-power-actor civilization may in turn "generate its own antithetical, interstitial force," leading to a new round of empire formation (161, 167, 537). In addition to centralization versus decentralization, empires generate four specific contradictions: (1) between particularism and a countervailing universalism; (2) between the project of cultural uniformity—the "development of a common ruling-class culture"—and the cultural diversity or "cosmopolitanism" of the various conquered peoples; (3) between hierarchical organization and egalitarianism; and (4) between drawing a sharp line against external "barbarians" and a civilizing orientation toward the barbarians. Empires encourage these countervailing practices "unconsciously" or "unintentionally" (363, 537). World religions like Christianity and Islam are the interstitially emergent products of imperial rule. Such religions are *transcendent* powers that cut across empire's concentrated military, political, and economic power networks. They are contrasted to the *immanent* imperial ideologies that cement ruling-class culture within empires.

In *The Sources of Social Power*, Mann implies that the category of empire belongs mainly to the ancient world, and that the modern world is a world of states rather than of empires. This seemingly arbitrary sorting conforms to the linear evolutionary thinking common to most postwar Anglo-American "historical sociology," and it seems to violate Mann's own antievolutionary strictures, which are closer to pre-1933 German sociological historicism (Steinmetz 2008c). For example, Mann states that "a territorial empire was never resurrected in Europe" after Rome (Mann 1986: 338). If central Europe had some "would-be empires of domination" there were no genuine ones (Mann 1993: 274). Mann qualifies as "states" (300) several polities that historians typically refer to as Reiche or empires (e.g., the Burgundian, Habsburg, and Austrian empires). He mentions that Prussia/Germany created itself by "mopping" up smaller states (288), but he does not compare this process to the violent expansion of the Roman Empire.[39] European overseas colonialism, which was ignored in volume 1 of *Sources*, is dealt with only peripherally in volume 2.

This changed in *Incoherent Empire* and other recent work, in which Mann analyzes the American Empire by using the earlier model of the four sources of social power—ideological, economic, military, and political—as well as a "dialectical" method similar to the one he employed so effectively in his analysis of ancient empires. In terms of military power, Mann argues, the United States vastly outguns its rivals, but its interventions lead to the proliferation of guerrillas, terrorists, and weapons of mass destruction among rogue states (Mann 2003: 29–45). With respect to economic power, Mann notes that U.S. protectionism, neoliberalism, and unwillingness to finance postinvasion "nation building" all combine to "produce political turmoil and anti-Americanism" (70). "American political powers," Mann continues, "are *schizophrenic*: in international politics they are large, but oscillating unsteadily between multilateralism and unilateralism; and when trying to interfere inside individual nation states they are small" (97). American ideological power, finally, is weakened by a contradiction between "democratic values" and "an imperialism which is strong on military offense, but weak on the ability to bring order, peace and democracy afterwards" (120). By distinguishing between the four sources of social power Mann is able to mount a critique of world system theory and other approaches that see economic and military imperialism as being closely connected. He argues that the American neoliberal, floating dollar offensive that began during the 1970s and the military imperialism that has intensified since the late 1990s were pushed by different interest groups with different motivations and had very different consequences: "Whereas the economic intensification was carefully calibrated to American interests and succeeded in preserving American global dominance, military intensification was more ideologically and emotionally driven and has failed," partially undermining American dominance (Mann 2008: 149).

OVERVIEW OF SOCIOLOGICAL CONTRIBUTIONS TO DATE

Throughout the discipline's history sociologists have been writing about the (1) forms, (2) trajectories, (3) effects, and (4) determinants of empires. With respect to the first dimension, Hintze and Weber distinguished between ancient empires and modern imperialism. Mann (1986) developed a useful distinction between empires of domination and territorial empires. Tarde and Schmitt discussed the possibility of a singular world empire qua "world state" or "global nomos." Hintze and Schmitt also considered the alternative possibility, a system of multiple coexisting empires. Various theorists identified the emergence of a new form of empire in the twentieth century, that of "informal imperialism," one that "leaves its victims with the appearance of political autonomy" and constrains them only with "a minimal amount of political violence" and "intimidation" (Mann 2008; Salz 1923: 569).[40] This informal model first appeared as a project for a German *Mitteleuropa* around World War I and was transformed into a theory of and for the Nazi Empire. The supposedly anticolonial United States (Gerth and Mills 1953) and mid-nineteenth-century Britain (Gallagher and Robinson 1953) were both described as informal empires. The concept of "colonialism" was distinguished from ancient and informal empires in terms of the permanent seizure of foreign sovereignty by the conqueror and the implementation of a "rule of colonial difference" (Chatterjee 1993; Steinmetz 2007b, 2008a). Ratzel (1923) codified nineteenth-century debates among colonial advocates by distinguishing between settler and exploitation colonies. A number of historians inspired by Althusser and Poulantzas theorized colonial societies by using the concept of articulation of modes of production. Mamdani (1996) described South African apartheid as an articulation of both political and economic models: nationalizing, capitalist direct urban rule combined with tribalizing, noncapitalist, indirect rural rule. Perhaps the most general lesson is that the state is not necessarily, or even typically, the dominant form of political organization. The "historical sociology of the state" needs to be closely articulated with the "historical sociology of empires."

The theorists discussed in this chapter also offered differing accounts of the *developmental trajectories of empires.* Gumplowicz and Ratzel claimed that warfare led to the centralization of political power and the "agglomeration of states into larger units." Arendt identified a passage from overseas imperialism to continental totalitarianism. Other writers focused on cycles of empire (Gini), patterns of the rise and fall of empire (Spengler), or waves of hegemony and nonhegemony correlating with different articulations of the global core and periphery (Wallerstein). According to Mann (1986: 168), the ancient world was characterized by both a cycling of empires and an upward historical trend in the overall accumulation of collective social power. Steinmetz (2005a) argued that Great Powers typically engaged in a mixture of different imperial strategies vis-à-vis different parts of the world, rather than alternating between colonialism and informal imperialism as world system theory suggested.

Some discussions of imperial trajectories focus on empire's *impact* on the metropoles. Comte, Hobson, and others noted that imperialism strengthened militarization and despotism in the core countries. Writers from Ibn Khaldun (1967: 128–129) to René Maunier (1949: 201) and Paul Kennedy (1987) analyzed imperial overreach. Theories of imperial blowback (Johnson 2000; Sartre 1963) see imperial interventions returning to haunt the core, in ways ranging from the contagion of revolution from south to north (Marx [1853b] 1969) to more diffuse cultural effects. Other discussions of the effects of empire focus on the peripheries. Karl Marx ([1853a] 1969) argued that colonial exploitation paradoxically paves the way for the development of capitalism and modernity in the colony (Warren 1980). This prediction, if not the details of Marx's analytic model, echoed arguments by mainstream colonial propagandists and missionaries throughout the modern colonial era and recalled historians' descriptions of the Romans' civilizing impact on the conquered barbarians. Rejecting these theories of empire as the road to improvement, other social scientists thematized the "development of underdevelopment" and "dependency." Berque saw colonialism as "destructuring a structure without [being] able to restructure it" (Bouhdiba 1964: 179), creating *"une nuit structurale de la planète"* ("a planetary structural night"; Berque 1964: 106). A distinct group of writers from Herder to Appadurai have described civilizations as moving along separate paths, rather than being arranged along a uniform path. Colonialism is condemned here for imposing hierarchy and uniformity. Compatible arguments were made by theorists of colonial transculturation (Leenhardt, Freyre, Herskovits, Leiris, Thurnwald, Bastide, Maunier, and Bhabha).

Finally, this chapter has reviewed a number of *explanatory theories* of the forms and trajectories of empire, explanations focused on political, economic, cultural, and/or social mechanisms. Broadly economic theories trace imperialism back to capitalist interests, including the need for new markets, investment opportunities, sources of cheaper labor power, or sites for new rounds of primitive accumulation. Broadly political theories emphasize a general tendency toward warfare and expansion (Gumplowicz, Ratzel, Oppenheimer) and the impetus to create "great spaces" or nomoi (Schmitt). Theorists of "social imperialism" trace the ways in which empire is used to integrate masses and classes within the imperial core (Mann 1993; Weber 1998a; Wehler 1972). Broadly sociological theories of empire emphasize four main causal processes: (1) an atavistic urge to domination rooted in the class habitus of older social strata (Schumpeter); (2) patterns of collaboration and resistance and other social structural features of the peripheries as determinants of imperialism (Balandier, Robinson, Go); (3) principal-agent relations (Adams) or network structures (Barkey); and (4) the colonial state as a Bourdieusian field of competition over field-specific symbolic capital (Steinmetz). Theories of cultural forces driving empire emphasize the impact of dreams of conquest (Hobhouse, Thurnwald), racism and Orientalism (Said), or precolonial ethnographic representations of the colonized (Steinmetz, Goh).

These political, economic, cultural, and social determinants should not be understood as mutually exclusive. Michael Mann, like Max Weber, rejects the idea of transhistorical general laws and pseudoexperimentalist comparison in favor of a more historicist (Steinmetz 2011a) strategy that identifies contextual patterns and contingent concatenations of mechanisms as the sources of imperial strategies and forms (Bhaskar 1986). Future research on empires should remain open to comparison but should not emulate a poorly understood form of natural science (Goldstone 1991: 40; Steinmetz 2005b). Comparisons can be carried out across empirical features of empires (Osterhammel 2009) or causal mechanisms (Steinmetz 2004). Causal *mechanism tracing* can explore the differing ways in which a single mechanism works in diverse contexts. Comparison may also be used to "focus on what is of central importance in a society, despite all analogies, and use the similarities of two societies to highlight the specific individuality of each" (Weber 1998b: 341). With these more historicist forms of comparison in hand, social scientists should be well equipped to push imperial analysis in new directions.

NOTES

1. Sociologists have also admired, advised, criticized, and openly opposed empires. This chapter is not intended as a complete historical sociology of imperial sociology, so I bracket sociologists' political postures and projects vis-à-vis empires here. My forthcoming book will provide a more complete intellectual, political, and institutional history of sociology from this standpoint (Steinmetz forthcoming-b).

2. For an important exception see André Adam's critical bibliography of sociology, ethnology, and human geography of Morocco, which examines "the condition of sociology in the colonial situation" (1968: 18).

3. Of course, Bourdieu explicitly cautions that his *Sketch for a Self-Analysis* is "not an autobiography" but rather a "sociological analysis, excluding psychology, except for some moods" (2007: epigram and "preparatory notes" included in "Publisher's Note to the French Edition"). For a more detailed discussion of Bourdieu's sketch and its strained relation to psychoanalysis, see Steinmetz (2013).

4. In this chapter I do not have room to explore the conditions of production of sociological knowledge of empire and the patterns of heteronomy and autonomy (see Steinmetz 2007a, 2009a) or the effects of scientific knowledge on empire (Steinmetz 2003a, 2007a).

5. The largest group of heteronomous policy-making colonial sociologists were those working for the French Organization for Colonial Scientific Research (ORSC, later renamed ORSTOM) and French Institute of Black Africa (IFAN); see Steinmetz (2012a).

6. In a study of American sociology during and after World War II, Abbott and Sparrow (2007: 287) define as sociologists only those with PhDs in sociology. This approach would exclude as sociologists many people who were in fact recognized members of it, including those who were imported from government and wartime agencies after 1945 (Turner and Turner 1990: 88). At the University of Michigan alone, it would exclude anthropologists Horace Miner and David Aberle and historian William Sewell, all of them hired in sociology under the initiative of the Sociology department at the time (Steinmetz 2007b: 344–345). It would exclude all of the refugee sociologists from Nazi Germany, none of whom had sociology doctorates (Steinmetz 2010a).

7. Max Weber was the most frequently mentioned name at all of the meetings of the German Sociological Association between 1910 and 1933 (Käsler 1984) and was called the most important "maker of sociology" by the German sociologists interviewed by Earle Edward Eubank in 1934 (Käsler 1984: 41; 1991). His fame continued through the Nazi period but lapsed after 1945 in West Germany and reemerged in the 1960s. A survey of British sociologists in 2001 found that Weber was named far more often than anyone else as the sociologist in the twentieth century who had contributed most to the subject (Halsey 2004: 171).

8. Conversely, those who hold sociology doctorates may fail to find employment in the discipline or move into other disciplines and professions. From a field-theoretic standpoint they will usually not be counted as members unless they continue publishing and participating in the disciplinary field. It is important to recall that field theory does not argue that individuals can participate in only a single specialized field, although it is impossible to participate in a large number of different fields given the costs of admission, the psychic burden of investment, and the corporeal tasks of adjusting one's habitus to each new domain. As Lacan (1991: 141) writes, "libidinal investment is what makes an object become desirable." On "investment" in fields, see Bourdieu (2000: 166) and Steinmetz (2013).

9. As for the "predisciplinary history" of (Western) sociology, it covers the period "from about 1600 to the middle of the nineteenth century" (Heilbron 1995: 3). Covering this period would have stretched the current volume beyond acceptable limits. Wickham and Freemantle (2008) distinguish between sociological thinking in the period 1550–1700 and the emergence of sociology as a discipline in the late nineteenth century.

10. On university sociology in France see Karady (1976, 1979) and Mucchielli (1998); for Germany see Käsler (1984); for Austria see Fleck (1990); for Britain see Abrams (1968), Halliday (1968), Soffer (1982), and Halsey (2004); for Italy see Nese (1993) and Santoro (chapter 4 of this volume); on sociology in Arab counties see Sabagh and Ghazalla (1986); for Tunisia see Zeghidi (1976) and Ben Salem (2009); for Algeria see Madoui (2007); for Egypt and Morocco see Roussillon (2003); for brief case studies of sociology in a number of countries during the 1990s, see Mohan and Wilke (1994).

11. Charles Tilly's relations to the academic history field provide a good example of disciplinary membership strengthening a scholar's *investment* in a field and members' *recognition* of the newcomer. Before coming to the University of Michigan in 1968, Tilly's main connections to historians had been in the French archives and through isolated publications in *French Historical Studies* and *History and Theory* (Tilly and Stave 1998). Starting in 1968, however, Tilly was a full, paid member of a leading history department, at the University of Michigan, where he supervised history PhD candidates. His recognition as a historian reached the point that he was described in 1997 by Eric Hobsbawm as "almost certainly the [sociologist] most respected by historians and political scientists" (Hobsbawm blurb on the back cover of Tilly 1997b). Tilly's own identification with history reached the point where he described himself as having "become much more historicist over time" (Tilly and Stave 1998: 189).

12. The noun *imperium* originally signified the power to command and punish, specifically the power of princes, magistrates, and officials (M. Weber 1978: 650, 839).

13. The intentions of imperial planners and dominant groups in the local colonial state are more central to this definitional issue than the actual duration of foreign rule. Nazi-occupied Poland was clearly colonial, for example, even though the general government in Poland lasted just five years and even though the general government "witnessed a conflict between the two ideal types of colonialism, the settlement-oriented ss and the exploitation-oriented civil administration" (Furber and Lower 2008: 377). By contrast the American invasion of Iraq in 2003 was never intended to

become a permanent colonial occupation, even though the United States deployed certain techniques and terminology reminiscent of colonialism (Steinmetz 2005a).

14. As with all rules, there were of course many exceptions to the so-called rule of colonial difference (Chatterjee 1993) involving individuals or entire groups among the colonized (Steinmetz 2007: 218–239).

15. The U.S., of course, maintains *status of forces agreements* with all countries in which its troops are stationed in its "empire of bases."

16. Skocpol (1979: 47), for example, describes Czarist Russia and Qing China as "old-regime *states*" rather than empires, thereby eliding some of the specifically imperial determinants of these empires' revolutions, which is her object of investigation. An imperial optic would emphasize sources of the weakening of the French ancien régime that remain invisible in Skocpol's metrocentric analysis, including the uprisings in France's overseas colonies. The Chinese state is better understood as an empire than as a state even in the nineteenth century. Here an imperial optic would read the Taiping and Xinhai revolutions as doubly anti-imperial, directed against both Manchu rule (Gasster 1998) and European pressure. Skocpol's third case, Russia, was of the three the most obviously an empire even in the Roman sense, ruled by a czar (Caesar) and encompassing "most of the space over which the Empire of Genghis Khan formerly extended" (Aron 1945: 358); it was also a colonial power vis-à-vis many of its indigenous populations, as Sorokin, founder of Skocpol's own Harvard Sociology department, had argued in his earliest work (see Sorokin 1990, discussed in chapter 2 of the present volume).

17. The possible exception to this rule is the ancient "empire of domination," a formation that was "in almost perpetual campaigning motion" (Mann 1986: 145) and had no statelike center.

18. This is true in the cases analyzed by Dirks (1987) and Gowda (2007).

19. Centeno and Enriquez (2010) incorrectly suggest that "such distinctions as 'empires' and 'states' are artificial, imposed upon what is clear only in hindsight, and that the distinction may have not made much sense to anyone even as late as the nineteenth century." In fact, the opposite is the case: it is social scientists themselves who have elided the distinction, starting with Central European *Staatswissenschaft* and continuing to the historical sociology of the state in the last third of the twentieth century. Political leaders and jurists clearly recognized the difference, as demonstrated by the nomenclature used to distinguish the levels of the *Reich* (empire) and the constitutive states in post-1870 Germany, for example. As Chae (see chapter 14) notes, the "Great Japanese Empire" was explicitly named after Western empires, such as the British, and this nomenclature was even adopted in (precolonial) Korea, as the "Great Korean Empire" (1897–1910). Specialized Colonial Offices existed in the British, French, German, and other European states to govern empires, and they were quite distinct from these state's noncolonial departments. The American Bureau of Indian Affairs was an office long specialized in the regulation of the internal colonial empire over Native Americans.

20. See this book's cover, a reconstruction by artist Yinka Shonibare of the Berlin West Africa Conference of 1884–1885.

21. Marx was obviously not a sociologist during his lifetime, and he died before the language of sociology had entered the German language. But Marx has been adopted as a founder of the disciplinary field.

22. Constantin-François Volney (1796) had also discussed this possibility.

23. In terms of the definitions I set out at the beginning, Tarde's "empire" was actually a "state," since it involved not a hierarchy between centers and peripheries but pluralistic cultural coexistence.

24. Although Hobson did not refer to Marx in *Imperialism*, elsewhere he discussed *Capital* and referred to "the constructive economic theory of Marx and his followers" (1898: 195).

25. As Christ (1982: 112) notes, Weber's discussions of ancient history paid little attention to the cultural processes like charisma and religion that later preoccupied him so intensely.

26. According to Ibn Khaldun, the earliest exponent of this theory (Maunier 1949: 201), "if the dynasty then undertakes to expand beyond its holdings, its widening territory remains without military protection and is laid open to any chance attack by enemy or neighbour. . . . A dynasty is stronger at its centre than it is at its border regions. When it has reached its farthest expansion, it becomes too weak and incapable to go any farther" (Ibn Khaldun 1967: 128–129).

27. Oppenheimer's emphasis on communal colonization was also central to his contributions to early Zionist discussions (Oppenheimer 1958).

28. Salz's disciplinary affiliation once he came to the United States was with economics (Kettler 2005), but while still in Heidelberg he was categorized more broadly as a social scientist (Mussgnug 1988).

29. On the interactions between sociology and social anthropology in British colonial research from the 1940s through the 1960s see Steinmetz (2012a, forthcoming b).

30. Anthropologist Herskovits published extensively in the three leading American sociology journals (e.g., Herskovits and Willey 1923).

31. Thurnwald returned from a leave of absence in the United States and East Africa to Berlin University in 1936 and immediately began accommodating himself to Nazism; see Thurnwald (1938); Timm (1977); Steinmetz (2009a). In 1942 Thurnwald asked the university's *Dekan* for a reduction in his teaching load because he was working on "a series of reports on the labor deployment of foreign workers" for the Ministry for Armaments and Munition (Reichsministerium für Bewaffnung und Munition). Thurnwald to *Dekan*, Oct. 31, 1942, Thurnwald personnel file, Humboldt University Archive, Berlin, vol. 6, p. 200. Thurnwald became a member of the Nazi Party's Colonial-Political Office in 1939 and a Nazi Party member in 1940. Thurnwald to Westermann, Feb.–May 1946, in Thurnwald personnel file, Humboldt University Archive, Berlin, vol. 6, p. 238.

32. On Soustelle's later political roles in Algeria, see Le Sueur (2001).

33. In an unmistakable reference to Schmitt without naming him, Aron referred to "theorists of great spaces" ("*théoriciens des grands espaces*"). See Aron (1945: 368).

34. An exhibition at the European Commission headquarters in Brussels in 2004 described the European Union (EU) as the return of the Roman Empire, and in July 2007, the president of the European Commission suggested that the EU could be likened to a "nonimperial empire." See Evans-Pritchard (2004) and "Barroso: European Union Is 'Non-imperial' Empire (long version)," uploaded by EUXTV on July 10, 2007, http://www.youtube.com/watch?v=-I8M1T-GgRU&mode=user&search=/.

35. The project of assimilating ethnic Germans in Nazi-occupied Eastern Europe ultimately failed but not for want of trying (E. R. Harvey 2005). Within the Auslandswissenschaftliche Fakultät at Berlin University, Mühlmann's strategies were ultimately marginalized by the even more radical "racial faction," which was strengthened by the impending loss of the war and mounting Polish resistance (Klingemann 1989: 21).

36. Mühlmann went on to head one of the most prestigious departments of sociology and anthropology at Heidelberg starting in 1960 (Michel 2005), and was highly regarded as an analyst of the Mau-Mau and other late colonial uprisings. His 1961 edited volume on "revolutionary third world messianisms" was translated from German into French by Jean Baudrillard (Mühlmann 1968). He struck an apologetic tone when discussing colonialism, however (Mühlmann 1962: 187), and his racist ideas soon became public and led to a mounting wave of criticism against him (Sigrist and Kössler 1985).

37. French colonizers in Algeria had treated Algerian Jews as requiring "regeneration" to qualify for assimilation (Birnbaum 2003).

38. Another example of mixed strategies can be seen in the German Kaiserreich. The Kaiserreich's sovereign was called the Kaiser, his title a Germanization of "Caesar"; the literal translation of the name Kaiserreich is "Emperor's Empire." The Kaiserreich constituted an "empire" vis-à-vis its constituent kingdoms, duchies, principalities, and free cities, which were subject to the emperor but independent in certain respects. The Kaiserreich engaged in a variety of imperialist but noncolonial practices, such as the efforts to influence Turkey and China through military advisers and scientific and cultural missions (Kaske 2002; Kloosterhuis 1994; Kreissler 1989). The Kaiserreich also became a full-fledged Kolonialreich (colonial empire) after 1884 through the annexation of overseas colonies in Africa, Oceania, and China.

39. More recently Michael Mann (2004: 83) suggested that "only Austria possessed a European empire," apparently unwilling to acknowledge the imperial status of Germany.

40. Michael Mann's (1993) sketch of ancient Athenian imperialism resembled this model.

PART I

NATIONAL SOCIOLOGICAL FIELDS
& THE STUDY OF EMPIRE

TWO

Russian Sociology in Imperial Context

ALEXANDER SEMYONOV, MARINA MOGILNER,
AND ILYA GERASIMOV

THE RUSSIAN DILEMMA

From a modern functionalist point of view, despite its obvious specificity
and peculiarities, the Russian Empire "was made" of the same basic elements as other composite polities of its day and faced similar challenges. It
is the arrangement of those "elements" and their specific historical and cultural contexts that made the Russian case so special. This explains why Russian intellectuals conceptualizing the structure and dynamics of society so
easily operated with theories and models produced by their West European
peers and had so much difficulty applying them to the Russian imperial
context. To understand the challenges faced by Russian sociologists (both
academics and those theorizing society for practical purposes), we suggest
the interpretation of Russian historical experience by means of focusing not
on political institutions and social structures but on practices and social
relations that characterized Russian society.

To make sense of this "Russian dilemma" by way of counterfactual comparison and without delving into nuances of Russian history, imagine that
sometime in the late nineteenth century the British islands sunk to the sea
bottom, overnight, leaving the British Raj in India without its overseas
metropole. All other key elements of administration, social infrastructure,
and cultural relations remained intact: the viceroy, the British colonial personnel, and the native Indian staff of colonial institutions; the division between "dominion" and "suzerainty" states; the religious strife among Hindus, Muslims, Buddhists, and Christians; the cultural distance between the
colonizers and colonized, overlapping with the social distance within the

"white" milieu. Everything was the same, except the retired colonial officers had not sailed "home" but had settled amid their former colleagues and subjects. Native Europeanized intellectuals, such as Jawaharlal Nehru, still experienced frustration with the attitude of the British elite, but there was no metropole society left into which they might aspire in vain to integrate or which insisted on their subaltern status. In short, all the conflicts and social and cultural differences of the "imperial formation" remained in place; the only thing that had disappeared is the structurally imposed clear-cut demarcation between "them" and the subaltern Other. This minor change would have dramatically transformed the lived experience of such an imperial society and complicated the metanarratives of its description. The cultural, social, or racial distance would have become effectively conditioned by circumstances, social context, or locality, as both dominant social groups and subaltern Others would be integral parts of the same society. Colonization, along with attendant Westernization and modernization, would have become a factor of internal politics, losing any external subject or agency. The disappearance of the externally imposed normative social hierarchy would have prompted the proliferation of hybrid (or rather composite) social identities that poorly fit into any single system of social status. Nobility, ethnicity, confession, economic standing, service record, and education would have formed combinations competing with each other, rather than with the universal standards of good old Britain. Still an imperial society, this imagined India would be poorly described in the categories of "economic exploitation," "colonial domination," some homogeneous "metropole," and equally homogeneous "subalterns." Such an India never existed, but a society in many aspects resembling this picture of an empire without a distinctive metropole and unambiguously alienated colonial subjects can be found in Russian history. The historical Russian Empire can be analyzed within the analytical framework developed by modern social sciences as a phenomenon *sui generis* exactly because it featured all the key elements of "Western" imperial formations; only they were set in a specific historical context that defied any monological schemes of imposing and sustaining difference and distance. Given that Russian social sciences were thoroughly integrated into the European and, later, transatlantic intellectual context largely insensitive to the specificity of Russian internal imperialism, it becomes a challenging task to identify those trends in Russian social thought that reflected on the specificity of the local imperial situation. Yet a scrutiny of the development of Russian social theories and sociological discipline in the Russian Empire is capable of locating different modes of relationship between sociology and empire. Moreover, this scrutiny can contribute to the historical understanding of empire by taking into account the process of making sense of Russian imperial experience of diversity in the field production of modern knowledge.

Besides the "spatial" specificity of the Russian Empire that did not have a clearly localized "core" and "periphery," the empire was characterized by a "chronological" displacement. Russia was invariably presented as a remnant of a bygone epoch in the family of modern nations. The dominant model of modern social (and sociological) discourse that was formed under the impact of the Enlightenment paradigm in Western Europe had a built-in definition of social norm based on the contrast with "Asiatic," "barbarous," and "underrationalized" societies that included Russia along with the Ottoman Empire and other East European and "oriental" polities (Wolff 1994). Otherwise mutually controversial views of legal theorists and moral philosophers (from Hobbes to Rousseau and from Pufendorf to Montesquieu) shared a common convention that a regular polity was formed by people of the same culture (that is, language, religion, and customs). The imagined political union was a result of a natural historical process: be it a public contract based on general consensus or an integrating experience of subjecthood in the same kingdom for a long time. Russia was almost universally seen as a violation of those norms: its territory was an arbitrary conglomerate of lands acquired through (illegitimate) conquests, and its population was not only excessively socially stratified but, what is worse, included many different peoples alien to each other. This diverse population was not rationally organized or justly governed. Long before France or Germany themselves reached any degree of internal cohesion and cultural integration, Russia was seen as an example of a hopelessly backward polity. This stereotype could not be deconstructed simply by curing the alleged European "Russophobia": at stake was the very normative definition of Europeanness as the true West and the embodiment of modernity.

Russian intellectuals inherited this authoritative understanding of the normative Europe as part and parcel of their education and socialization into modern European culture, and there were no alternative cultural traditions and norms in educated Russian society, at least since the eighteenth century. It is not surprising, then, that even representatives of the social elite expressed quite critical views of their native country (that occasionally brought them to political or religious dissent): the man of (European) culture should be an opponent of anything primordially "Russian."

Although Russian educated society had been engaging European social theories at least since the time of Peter I, it may be argued that a truly

theoretical social discourse emerged in Russia only after the 1840s. The enthusiastic reception of Hegelianism by Russian intellectuals (most notably,
by the so-called Moscow circle of university students and younger lecturers) played a seminal role in the development of all major intellectual currents of the epoch: the proto-nationalist Slavophilism, the proto-socialist
anarchism, and early versions of liberalism. In the philosophy of Hegel,
Russian intellectuals found a rare combination of "social structure" and
"social dynamics" enveloped in the model of self-propelled historical development of the Absolute Spirit that went through several stages marked by
distinctive social regimes. The figure of Mikhail Bakunin is paradigmatic
for this early period of Russian Hegelianism: he explored both the ultra-
conservative interpretation of Hegelian idealism, and its revolutionary connotations of adjusting the existing social order to the ideal and desirable
model (Pirumova 1970; Randolph 2007). By switching between the politically polar interpretations of the same theory, Bakunin demonstrated his
primary interest in the sociological model as such, rather than in any of its
specific applications. Eventually Bakunin became known as the founding
father of Russian anarchism, who envisioned the ideal society as a federation of independent local communities. Although among the first Russian
Hegelians there were people with more articulated sociological views and
different political ideals than those of Bakunin, his example is telling because of the series of conscious choices he made (Berlin 1978; Walicki 1979).
He found it necessary to take an anti-imperial stance in order to fully accommodate the theoretical system of his choice. By applying the principles
of a just society (based on the free public contract) and historical progress
to Russia, he arrived at the conclusion that this imperial conglomerate
should be ruined by a popular uprising. All categories of the oppressed (peasants, ethnic and religion minorities, and criminals) should revolt to get a
chance for a free expression of their subjectivity. In this logic, the "true"
Russia should be reassembled from ground zero as a free political union of
self-determined subjects. Thus this proverbial "typical Russian" and anti-
system activist resolved the imperial dilemma quite in line with the dominant episteme of modern European sociological imagination.

The fundamental trope of the Russian Empire's backwardness grafted
onto the discourse of European modernity made the next generation of Russian intellectuals particularly attentive to Marxism. Even those not sharing
extreme political views took very seriously the famous motto from Marx's
early *Theses on Feuerbach* (little known to their European peers): "The philosophers have only interpreted the world, in various ways; the point is to

change it" (thesis 11). The Russian imperial dilemma made this idea central for Russian social thinkers: a proper interpretation of Russian "irregular" society amounted to (or made imperative) its radical transformation.

These imperatives of political philosophy also explain why evolutionism became a key formative factor for Russian social sciences. In the Russian context of dual underdevelopment (Russia versus Europe, backward regions of empire versus territorial and nonterritorial loci of modernity), the idea of a universal evolutionary path promised the eventual catching up with historical leaders in some distant future. A regular taxonomic classification, so typical of early stages of social sciences, almost automatically acquired a developmental vector in the imperial heterogeneous social landscape. This is why the initial optimistic evolutionism successfully survived criticism that caused its subsequent rejection or serious revisions in Europe and the United States. Beginning in the 1870s, Russian populist-inspired ethnography increasingly embraced evolutionism as a way out of particularism and a means of scientific rehabilitation as a science of modernity. Russian physical anthropology embraced evolutionism from the moment of its academic institutionalization in the mid-nineteenth century (Mogilner 2013). The key to evolutionism's persistence in imperial Russia was its ability to function as a modern and scientifically legitimate imperial ideology: it placed Russia as the unfortunate alter ego of European modernity on the universal civilization ladder, granting a hope of its eventual normalization in the future. What was open to debate was the price to be paid for this normalization.

• • •

THERE ARE NO CONVENTIONAL canons for telling the history of Russian sociology in the nineteenth and early twentieth century, not least because this multifaceted discipline did not produce a comprehensive self-descriptive narrative (beyond superficial outlines for college survey courses and encyclopedia entries) prior to the dramatic overhaul of the structure of social sciences after 1917. Sociology was all but outlawed throughout much of the Soviet period as a field of competing explanatory models of society's functioning and organization. This happened because one specific (Marxist) sociological doctrine became the major source of political legitimacy of the regime, and as such it did not allow any room for criticism and rival interpretations. Even the eventual reemergence of sociology in the Soviet Union and its legacy for post-Soviet sociology remains the most contentious issue in the self-reflection of the contemporary sociological profession (Firsov 2001), and there are differing interpretations as to what extent the legacy of the pre-1917 sociology has been actually reclaimed by modern-day Russian sociologists (Golosenko and Kozlovskii 2005; Medushesvkii 1993). Today we witness attempts to invent a distinctive and coherent national sociological tradition (Yadov 2008). As was mentioned above, most Russian sociologists and a good part of social thinkers saw themselves as belonging to the general European intellectual tradition, speaking the analytical language and discussing problems that originated in European and transatlantic contexts, and this fact alone makes futile any attempts to "nationalize" Russian sociology.

As was long ago pointed out, both Russian "nativists" and "Westernizers" belonged to the same modern European cultural tradition, their ideological preferences and prejudices notwithstanding (Walicki 1975). Therefore, there was nothing specifically "Russian" about their social theories and models, except for their political biases and possible better acquaintance with local realities. One fundamental divide between the camps of Russian intellectuals was sustained by the opposition between the universalist legacy of the Enlightenment and particularism of the Romantic tradition. Another important difference was between theorists who became interested in social theory for practical (political) purposes and those who came to sociology out of general (academic) epistemological interest. Typically for the imperial situation, one opposition relativized the difference between the parts of another opposition, and vice versa. Thus, the proverbial strife between the Russian populists and Marxists in the late nineteenth century looks like a petty disagreement on issues of secondary importance when epistemological foundations of social analysis are taken seriously. Indeed, although they had serious political differences, both populists and Marxists operated basically within the same conceptual framework: they debated the prospects of the class society, capitalism, and premodern social forms in Russia but not the validity of those concepts. Similarly, to politicized social thinkers (be it Lenin or Mikhailovsky), the argument between neo-Kantians and phenomenologists was little more than scholastic rhetoric, concealing their fundamental agreement on the legitimacy of the existing social order. Still, the suggested elemental classification of Russian sociologists is helpful for the purposes of their classification and interpretation of their intellectual genealogies and agendas.

THE CASE OF RUSSIAN POPULIST SOCIOLOGY

The specific Russian context with its "imperial dilemma" in one way or another affected those scholars who dealt with abstract and general theoretical problems of sociology and those politicized intellectuals mostly interested in practical application of their ideas. They could choose from several options in finding a place for Russia on the map of mainstream social development: to redefine "Russianness" by criticizing its *Sonderweg* interpretations or revealing some "true Russianness" that would not hamper its progress; to deconstruct (or practically dismantle) the empire; to remap the very normative Europeanness, in order to eliminate the structural stigmatization of Russian society; or any combination of the above.

These distinctive discursive strategies became possible not before the fundamental conceptual agreement was reached between different streams of Russian social theory that the terrain of the social was the sui generis foundational base that determined the shape of the state, law, culture, and human agency.[1] It may be seen as yet another Russian peculiarity that this complex "social sphere" was initially envisioned as a social body (society = the people), and only later, by the early twentieth century, did it become conceptualized as a social structure. This explains the preponderance of "populism" in Russian sociology of the nineteenth century—a very diverse conglomerate of concepts and approaches that had just one common trait: the centrality of "the people," rather than social institutions and practices. Both revolutionary and conservative "populists" were preoccupied with the problem of relations between the individual and the group and the foundations of groupness and collective social action. A series of consecutive individual choices and group actions were conceptualized teleologically as "history."

On the theoretical level, populist writers and ideologues, such as Petr Lavrov and Nikolai Mikhailovsky, directed their criticism at Social Darwinism, Herbert Spencer's organicist social theory, and Durkheim's theory of social facts and disciplinary autonomy of sociology (Vucinich 1976: 15–66). This criticism of both organicist theories and arguments in favor of autonomy of sociological knowledge by Russian authors reflected the overwhelming concern of Russian social thinkers with locating the agency of modernity (and, more broadly, of the historical process) in the peculiar context of underdevelopment. This criticism provided the affirmation of the ideological and moral mission of the Russian intelligentsia as the subject of society's self-cognition and hence transformation (Wortman 1967). Russian society could become modern by following the vanguard stratum of "the people," and conversely, the intelligentsia as the advanced social group had to demonstrate its superiority not only intellectually but also morally, by providing a clear ideal of the better social compound. As a result, the "subjective school" of Russian populist sociology blended into a single whole the study of society, moral judgment, and utopian socialism.

Yet apart from the theory of critically thinking intellectuals, populist sociology in its substratum followed the Western vision of holistic and determining nature of social order and construed the Russian peasant commune as the bounded social structure that lay at the foundation of Russian society. This holistic humanist tradition of the Russian intelligentsia was obsessed with the fear of any type of human "fragmentation" and "alienation," whether a "differentiation" within the capitalist society or a "narrow specialization" of the individual. Regardless of party affiliation, social activism based on this worldview acquired a form of body politics, be it individual terror or an educational "going to the people" campaign: the conscious personality was seen as both the means and the end of social interaction, and no formalized routine (institutional or technological) was tolerated in the process. The idealization of the peasant social order in populist rendition was based not so much on faulty and superficial social analysis but rather on the double premises of the nature of Russian society (i.e., "people") and Western modernity. If the eventual goal of modernization was socialism, Russia was best fitting into this ideal as a country of elemental peasant communitarianism, rather than, for example, the society of many nationalities, or rich resources, or diverse climatic zones, and so forth.[2]

Incidentally, whenever Russian sociologists spoke about "the people," they implied first of all the broad stratum of a legally and economically unprivileged population. The same rhetoric coming from an intellectual with a double identity (the Russian cultural and ethnic Ukrainian or Jewish) almost immediately altered the communicated meaning from social emancipation into national liberation. This was the case of Mikhailo Dragomanov and his polemics with Russian revolutionaries over the question of distinctiveness of populism in the Ukrainian lands where "Only an illogical populist cannot become a Ukrainophile and the other way round. And from which end one is going to start this combination is a matter of personal choice" (Dragomanov 1881: 125; Miller 2000: 220–223; von Hagen 2007). For quite a while, Russian intellectuals did not notice this subversive characteristic of the populist discourse in the situation of imperial diversity. In fact, many of them even did not pay attention to Russia's imperial diversity, treating Russia as an analog to an idealized France or other European "nation." The populist focus on the social body of the "people" made them ignore political institutions of the Russian state, which spanned the regionally, confessionally, and ethnically heterogeneous space of the Russian Empire and enveloped variegated groups of population into structures of imperial citizenship (Burbank 2006). This changed in the second half of the nineteenth century, as the Russian Empire ceased to resemble the ideal type of traditional, land-based, and composite polity (Hosking 1997) in which social and cultural differences were made invisible to the sociological eye by the differentiating regime of imperial policy, if this ideal type can be said to have ever adequately captured the history of the Russian Empire. The policies of the modernizing empire and colonialism and the processes of social mobility and cultural hybridity (Gerasimov 2009; Suny 2006) made even the populist sociologists ponder the question of how to account for the fabric of imperial society and address the question of diversity.

Among the populist sociologists of the late nineteenth century, Gleb Uspenskii and Sergei Iuzhakov registered the presence of imperial diversity more than their populist peers. Both Uspenskii and Iuzhakov followed the developing process of resettlement/colonization, which involved empire's agricultural population (Breyfogle 2005; Breyfogle, Schrader, and Sunderland 2007; Sunderland 2004). Both authors were noted populist writers and correspondents of central populist periodicals. Uspenskii traveled as a free-lance journalist, and Iuzhakov was employed as secretary to the construction company of the Ussuri railroad in the Far East. Uspenskii and Iuzhakov followed the movement of agricultural communities to the steppe regions, South Caucasus, Siberia, and Far East and witnessed the encounter between the resettled peasant communities and the local population (Iuzhakov 1894; Uspenskii 1908). Uspenskii wrote about the impact of capitalism in the form of land speculation and peasant land acquisition in the Urals region (Ufa and Orenburg provinces) that together led to the "vanishing of the Bashkirs," which had been the titular service estate holder of the lands (Steinwedel 2002). Iuzhakov drew a picture of the heterogeneous social and cultural composition of the city of Vladivostok and the Far Eastern region, which included the Russian military and navy personnel, Russian peasant communities, Chinese borderland bandits (*hunghutzu*), Chinese and Korean laborers, and Japanese prostitutes, as well as merchants and convicts of different faiths and origins. However, the analysis of both authors remained persistently focused on the state of affairs of the peasant communities. Those communities might have been made of different groups of Eastern Slavic ("Great Russian" and "Little or Southern Russian") or non-Slavic populations, yet in the eyes of the populist authors they comprised the common social structure and the privileged object of social analysis.

Following the concerns of populist sociology writ large, Uspenskii and Iuzhakov refocused their travelogues from the heterogeneous context of resettlement/colonization toward the discussion of the prospects for development of a social order based on the spread of education, technology, and communal solidarity. The substratum of holistic and bounded definition of society made the populist sociologists ignore the processes of interaction and hybridization in the imperial social fabric and, in the case of Iuzhakov, deny Vladivostok's heterogeneous social milieu the very "name of society." It is indicative that in his descriptions of individualism, unchecked pursuit of profit, and corruption of Vladivostok, Iuzhakov used the term "Eastern America" (1894: 101). The "vanishing Bashkirs" did indeed vanish from Uspenskii's account of the injustices of the governmental resettlement policies and the plight of uneducated Russian peasants. Noting the threat to communal solidarity in the form of the waged labor of "alien origin" in the peasant economy of the Far East, Iuzhakov called for the elimination of the "alien" population[3] from the territory together with the extermination of the menace of the Far Eastern tigers (stopping slightly short of the call for ethnic cleansing [Iuzhakov 1894: 94–97]).

The case of late nineteenth-century Russian populist sociology reveals a type of relations between sociology and empire that cannot be accommodated in the political dimension of sociological endorsement or critique of empire. This case demonstrates the epistemological aspect of the relationship between paradigms of modern knowledge and empire, in which the nonrecognition of diversity and interconnectedness of the social space of empire was the effect of "learned ignorance" (Stoler 2009: 247) of sociological discourse, in that it was underpinned by the perception of society as a holistic social order. The case of Russian populist sociologists of later generations also calls into doubt the interpretation of Russian non-Marxist socialism as fundamentally different from populist ideologies and movements of Central Europe, which showed predisposition toward nationalizing politics and ethnic nationalism. One can argue that Iuzhakov's sociological analysis of the Far East as "Eastern America" encapsulated the potential development of the vision of society as a holistic and bounded structure into a program of ordering the space of empire through exclusion and homogenization of territory and population.

EVOLUTIONARY SOCIOLOGY AND COMPARATIVE METHODOLOGY OF SOCIAL SCIENCES

Apart from the populist tradition that was politicized and centered on the "social body," there was a different type of sociology in Russia, motivated primarily by the academic interest in social sciences and epistemology. It was constituted by Russian imperial universities and, later on, private educational institutions together with the rich networks of professional associations and nonformalized intellectual circuits. This context gave rise to a cluster of social sciences, including the late-coming discipline of academic sociology. Before the 1905 revolution, sociology was generally understood in the Comtean key as a science of generalization of different fields of knowledge about society. Therefore, the boundaries of specialization were not rigid, and there were multiple junctures that connected jurisprudence, ethnography, political economy, physiology, psychology, and history to the science of society. These crossing points were underpinned by commonly held paradigms of positive science and evolutionism. Although it is difficult to separate the nascent field of academic sociology from the politically engaged social theory of the period before the 1905 revolution, it is still possible to see that academic sociology was increasingly defined in reference to the analytic methodology of academic sociology in the United States and Europe.

It is instructive to take a closer look at the world map of sociological knowledge as it was pictured by representatives of Russian academic sociology. As a self-appointed advocate of Russian "subjective sociology" and the defender of Comtean understanding of social sciences, Nikolai Kareev of St. Petersburg University viewed the world map of the science of sociology as inhabited by national schools and intellectual traditions and claimed the parity of the Russian populist sociology, which advanced the critique of monism, integrated social psychology into sociological theorizing, and anticipated the neo-Kantian turn in philosophy of social sciences (Kareev 1907: 67–69, 223–225, 253–255; 1996: 43–88, 355). The appearance of sociological literature in a national language was interpreted by Kareev as a sign of belonging to the "civilized nations" (including the newcomers, such as Japan) and the reflection of the advanced position of that nation in terms of social and political development (Kareev 1907: 336, 394). The schools of academic sociology were also reflections of respective "national" political and historical contexts. Thus the late reception of Auguste Comte in Germany was, according to Kareev, due to the historical hegemony of idealist philosophy. The central role of the competition between "races" in the sociology of Ludwig Gumplowicz (see chapter 1) could be explained by the presence of struggle between nationalities in the Habsburg monarchy (Kareev 1907: 394–395). The Russian national tradition of sociology was, according to Kareev, based on the following foundations: the emergence of theoretical sociological thinking in the milieu of progressive political thought and the synthetic character of the Russian sociological tradition, which had the benefit of familiarity with all European sociological traditions and thus was able to relate them to one another and solve paradoxes and contradictions of sociological theorizing in an overarching synthesis (Kareev 1907: 396). The presence of diversity and empire was patently not part of the Russian context or research agenda of Russian sociological tradition.

Contrary to Kareev, Maksim Kovalevsky saw the world map of sociological knowledge as related not only to national traditions and contexts but also to the structures of empire. Maksim Kovalevsky was a versatile scholar of comparative and public law, economic history, political institutions, and ethnography (Aresen'ev et al. 1917; Boronoev et al. 1996; Kaloev 1979; Medushesvkii 1993: 119–162; Pogodin 2005; Safronov 1960; Vucinich 1976: 153–172). He perceived his main vocation and achievement to be in the field of sociology or in what he defined as "genetic sociology." His contribution to the development of European sociology and promotion and institutionalization of academic sociology in Russia was acknowledged in the honorary title of the "dean of Russian sociology" and the fact that the first Russian sociological society was named after him. Kovalevsky was a showcase of cosmopolitan scholar-globetrotter, who connected academic circles in St. Petersburg, Moscow, and Khar'kov (his native city in modern-day Ukraine) with Vienna, Berlin, London, Paris, Stockholm, and Chicago. His early academic career as a student of public law and the federalist regime of the Habsburg Empire was changed in the direction of sociology and comparative study of law by his visit to England. In his memoirs, Kovalevsky acknowledged that his main research projects on ancient and comparative law, comparative study of communal land tenure, ethnography of traditional societies in the Caucasus, and history of economic development of Europe prior to capitalism were all conceived of during his stay in England, when he was able to familiarize himself with English and American literature on ethnology and sociology (Kovalevsky 2005: 90–97, 161). Kovalevsky's conversion to the comparative methodology of social sciences happened under the influence of Henry Sumner Maine and his comparative studies of "traditional societies" (Kovalevsky 1891: 3–5; Mantena 2010). Kovalevsky did not fail to note that Maine combined his scholarship with the administrative position of legal expert in the Indian Office. The universalism of empire in the sense of outreach of imperial rule beyond the home society and comparative evolutionary sociology were interconnected, and the meeting point was the imperial archive as the site of production of knowledge and power (Kovalevsky 1890a: 8; Mantena 2010: 57). With the help of Maine, Kovalevsky gained access to the archives of the Indian administration and was able to launch his first comparative research project on communal land tenure. This project and other explorations by Kovalevsky of evolution of forms of society in relationship with ancient custom and historic law were routed by ethnographic and administrative documentation of different imperial archives and mapped the synchronous terrain of traditional societies in British India, the Spanish American colonies, French Algeria, and the Russian Caucasus (Kovalevsky 1879; 2005: 160–161).

Comparative methodology as espoused by Kovalevsky was an integral component of evolutionary theory. It could ascertain the universality of historical stages of development of law, forms of social organization, and culture and therefore could provide the foundation for the "unity of history," that is, the formulation of scientific laws of general evolutionary development from the primitive human aggregates to the modern individualistic society (Kovalevsky 1880; 1890b: 1–7; 1902a). In Kovalevsky's conception, a scientific law had to be necessarily universal in order to be scientific, and evolution had to be self-generating in order to be evolution. From this vantage point Kovalevsky criticized Gabriel Tarde's theory of invention and imitation (Tarde 1895), noting that imitation of the superior society by the inferior could exist only as modification and adaptation of cultural influences to the local historical and cultural context (Kovalevsky 1997: 17–18, 37). Kovalevsky clearly saw the political implications of evolutionary sociology. It could scientifically reject the claim of uniqueness of Slavic peoples encapsulated in the communal social order and land tenure, their separation from the European "historical peoples," and the latter's "naturally given" social order of nuclear family and private property (Kovalevsky 2005: 157–59). Therefore, evolutionary sociology contained a scientifically grounded projection of Russia's self-generated and inevitable overcoming of social and political backwardness and convergence with European forms of social and political organization (Kovalevsky 1902b).

At the same time, Kovalevsky's evolutionary sociology and comparative method were the tools of conceptual organization of the space of the Russian Empire. Following the example of Maine, whose comparative research was framed by the expanse of the British Empire, Kovalevsky conceived of the Russian Empire as the diverse space that could accommodate the comparative exploration of social forms belonging to different phases of universal evolution. Kovalevsky studied the mountainous peoples of the Caucasus, "Little Russian" and Great Russian peasant social organization, and encouraged his students to pursue research in the Cossack customary law. This research produced the panoramic view of different temporalities of social evolution from Caucasian kinship societies to modern "individualistic" society of

Europeanized higher and middle classes of the empire. The grid of the social evolutionary map of empire was located not only in the spatial dimension of the Eurasian space but also in the social axis between the cities and the countryside (Kovalevsky 1891: 33). While the comparative method allowed Kovalevsky to conceptually unite the diverse space of the Russian Empire, evolutionary sociology provided tools for ordering the space of empire into the hierarchy of social and cultural forms. Kovalevsky understood the conceptual ordering of the space of empire not only as a scientific exercise but also as instrumental knowledge that could help the work of imperial administrative and judicial systems and justify the exceptional treatment of certain groups of population.[4] At the same time, his writing on traditional societies in the Caucasus is permeated by disappointment with the difference of the Russian situation from the situation in the British Empire. The Russian imperial authorities were not showing a predisposition toward the employment of instrumental knowledge for the benefit of more rational government of empire (Kovalevsky 1890a: vi–vii). Reflecting on the instrumental value of his research, Kovalevsky displayed an ambiguity: on the one hand, he encouraged interventions based on the idea of progressive reform of legal and social customs of underdeveloped classes of population and "primitive" peoples. On the other hand, he opined in favor of the retention of customary law and structures of traditional society on the basis of the idea of interdependency of law and social organization in a given society and as a way to uphold the stability of the empire through the practices of indirect rule (Kovalevsky 1902b: 280–281).[5]

The evolutionary sociology of Kovalevsky in its second aspect—mapping hierarchies of social advancement toward the norm of the modern society in a given political space—informed his conservative attitude toward the liberal reforms of the early twentieth century. His evolutionary credo that "history does not know leaps" placed him in the position of a critic of radical liberal reformism propagated by the Constitutional-Democratic Party in the context of the 1905 revolution and liberal reforms. The concept of traditional society underpinned his advocacy of exclusion of certain groups of Russian imperial society from modern citizenship based on political participation and equality of civil rights: "Let us imagine a Caucasian mountaineer who discusses some articles of the Criminal Code while being convinced that blood should be wiped away only by blood or compensated with cows and sheep. . . . When a circuit court sentences the murderer-Circassian to hard labor in Siberia, the closest relative of his victim follows him there to exercise the duty of revenge. Such facts are often mentioned in the courts' minutes and administrative correspondence" (Kovalevsky 1905: 2).

Throughout his career, Kovalevsky remained a scholar committed to the pursuit of comparative sociological research. He viewed favorably the development of American sociology and its platform of empirical study of social structures and behavior. Kovalevsky became part of the research project headed by the Chicago sociologist William Thomas, a specialist in race psychology, criminality, and immigration (Ross 1991: 304, 348, 251).[6] The project was devoted to the study of social structures of East European peasantry in connection to the social behavior of peasant immigrants from Eastern Europe in the United States, which also included the comparison of immigrants of peasant extraction with the "Negro question" in the United States (Thomas and Znaniecki 1918–1920). Kovalevsky endorsed the project and helped to recruit Russian participants. He consulted William Thomas on general theory of social evolution and comparative method (Thomas 1912a). As a representative of the empirical dimension of sociological research, Thomas was unimpressed by the promises of "genetic sociology." In response to Kovalevsky, Thomas stated:

> There is a principle called parallelism of development, meaning that different groups living quite apart develop nevertheless similar institutions. It is apparent that this law holds in general, and especially for what may be called the primary social expressions—approval of bravery, censure of treachery, property rights, tribal organization, feud, simple mechanical inventions, magic, the representative arts, and some "shalt nots" answering to the Hebrew commandments. But certain secondary and specialized attitudes, like representative government, free schools, scientific experimentation, and the equal recognition of women, originate slowly or not at all, but are imitated with extreme facility when conditions are favorable. (1912b: 741–742)

There was a conceptual gap between the evolutionist sociology of the nineteenth century that Kovalevsky continued to represent down to the early twentieth century and the new functional and structural sociology grounded in presentism and empirical research. Although Kovalevsky did not resolutely part with his version of sociology steeped in a historical vision of the progressive development of social forms, the case of the international collaborative project on peasant societies and global migration demonstrates his openness toward the new paradigm of functional and structuralist sociology. Kovalevsky was one of the few Russian intellectuals and scholars who parted from the traditional Eurocentric orientation of the Russian intelligentsia and traveled to the United States in 1881 and 1901 to familiarize himself with the social realities of American society (Kovalevsky 2005: 304–337). He invariably included reviews of American sociology in his surveys of current sociological scholarship and referenced with approval the American model of assimilation in his political pronouncements on the strategies of social transformation of the Russian Empire in the early twentieth century.[7] Kovalevsky's student Pitirim Sorokin inherited this predisposition toward American functional and structural sociological research and continued his mentor's work on the comparison of social realities of Russia with those of the United States.

INSTITUTIONALIZATION OF ACADEMIC SOCIOLOGY

The institutionalization of Russian sociology occurred first in the framework of the university in exile. It was the Russian Higher School for Social Sciences founded in Paris in 1901 by Ilya Mechnikov, Maksim Kovalevsky, Evgenii de Roberti, and Iurii Gambarov. The school was an outgrowth of the activity of the International Association for Promotion of Science, Art, and Education, which launched its activities in the framework of the Paris World Fair in 1900. The Russian World Fair lectures provided the basis for organizing the permanent university in exile, staffed by dissident professors and an émigré student body. Institutionally, the establishment of the school was made possible by association with the École pratique des hautes études (Gutnov 2004).

Following the Comtean classification of sociology as a generic science, the founders of the émigré university installed the broadly conceived sociological paradigm at the foundation of the entire curriculum, with evolutionary theory and comparative method as its cornerstones. Apart from courses on sociological theory, the curriculum included courses in Russian and European social history, philosophy, psychology, experimental biology, comparative history of law, public and civil law, political economy, criminology, ethnography, and physical anthropology. These courses were structured in such a way as to give a general introduction to social sciences and provide different disciplinary perspectives on the key questions of the sociological theory of the day. This effort was made possible by the collegial spirit of Russian academics and help from European academics, including Alfred Espinas, Marcel Mauss, Gabriel Tarde, Émile Vandervelde, and René Worms, who also taught at the school.

The Russian Higher School for Social Sciences was part of the broader phenomenon of pre-1917 Russian political emigration. The core members of the Russian faculty were academics living in Europe by choice or having been ousted from university positions by the imperial authorities for political views or defense of university autonomy. The typical student of the school was someone who was barred from the Russian Empire for revolutionary or oppositional political activities. There were also a number of female and Jewish students enrolled in the school who could not enroll in the universities in the Russian Empire due to discriminatory admission policies. This political context helps explain the prime role of sociology at the Paris School. While the Russian imperial government saw sociology as a politically suspect field of scholarship, the faculty and especially the students conceived of sociology as a modern form of knowledge that could be instrumentalized for the purposes of liberal or socialist politics.[8] From the viewpoint of the liberal faculty of the school, sociology was the form of modern objective and applied knowledge and also the form of consciousness of modern society in Russia that was coming of age according to the laws of evolution. Sociology as a form of knowledge was stripped of the metaphysical elements of previous political and philosophical doctrines, or so the Russian sociologists in exile thought. While having many elements in common with Marxism, sociology was free of the reductionism of historical materialism and was particularly suited for scientific exploration of the manifold factors that shaped the economic, social, and political condition of society and the political ideologies that operated in that society. As such, it was a form of critical theory that could "purify the social consciousness of superstitions and errors" and provide correctives for one-sided political visions, according to de Roberti (1905a: 44).

The specific character of the school as the university of Russian political emigration brought burning political questions of liberal and revolutionary politics to the heart of education. The school's organizers encouraged visits by politicians and public figures as guest lecturers. Thus, Vladimir Lenin gave a lecture on Marxist approaches to the agrarian question in Western Europe and Russia; Viktor Chernov, the leader of the Socialist Revolutionary Party, lectured on the critique of organicist theories; and various representatives of Russian liberal opposition gave their perspectives on the future of liberal political reforms in Russia.

Apart from the Russian party debates that raged through the life of the school, there was another dimension of the politicization of social knowledge: the heterogeneous space of the Russian Empire came to be represented in the framework of non-Russian national movements and their political claims. The school invited lectures from those scholars who at the same time were representatives of national movements in the Russian Empire, like

Mykhailo Hrushevsky, a historian of the Ukraine, leader of the Ukrainian national movement in Habsburg Galicia and Russian Ukraine, and future head of the independent Ukrainian state. Representatives of the Polish intelligentsia spoke about the historical conflict between the Russian and Polish nationalities and the prospects for reconciliation. The school's organizers emphasized the importance of the question of imperial diversity and sought to represent it in the curriculum. Several scholars introduced the question of the empire's diverse socioeconomic and cultural order. Ivan Luchitskii, a member of the Ukrainian national movement in the middle of the nineteenth century and a historian with a strong preference for evolutionary sociology, lectured on Ukrainian communal land tenure. Fyodor Volkov, a Ukrainian intellectual and European-trained scholar of physical anthropology, covered the ethnography and physical anthropology of the Slavic population of the Russian Empire. Mikhail Tamamshev offered courses on Islam and the Caucasus.[9]

Already at the foundation of the school, Evgenii de Roberti and Maksim Kovalevsky planned to use it as a model to create a new type of social science curriculum inside Russia (de Roberti, Gambarov, and Kovalevsky 1905: vi). Favorable conditions for the continuation of educational experimentation emerged after the 1905 revolution. The model of the Russian Higher School for Social Sciences served as a template for the sociological curriculum at the St. Petersburg Psycho-Neurological Institute (Akimenko 2007; Ivanov 1998). This institute was even more peculiar than its Paris predecessor. It was the realization of a utopian dream of a group of avant-garde Russian natural and social scientists who sought to create the science for the future: an experimental synthetic science focused on humans as psychosociological phenomena. The author of the idea and mastermind behind the actual project was the academician Vladimir Bekhterev, a famous Russian neurologist and psychiatrist. He argued that a modernizing Russia badly needed, yet did not have, an institute that would synthesize new social knowledge with the natural sciences and the "sciences of the Psyche." He observed that "Our universities do not have anthropology departments. Our ethnographers have no place to study their discipline. We need to rearrange these sciences on a very broad basis" (Russian Society for Normal and Pathological Psychology 1904). The institute, which had private status and operated on a budget of private donations and tuition, encompassed a number of experimental clinics and a Psycho-Pedological institute (Psycho-Neurological Institute 1907). Sociology was institutionalized in the form of a dedicated chair and inscribed in a very unusual curriculum that offered courses in anatomy, physical anthropology, criminal anthropology, theories of degeneration, pedology, and social sanitation, among others. As a private institution, the Psycho-Neurological Institute accepted students indiscriminately, attracting especially those who were banned from imperial universities for political offenses, whose admission was restricted on the basis of their nationality (Jews), or who could not compete with better prepared *gimnazia* graduates for university admission. The register of students at the Psycho-Neurological Institute in 1909–1917 has survived only partially. It contains 5,120 names in total, including as many as 40 percent non-Russian students—Armenians, Jews, Tatars, Germans, and others.[10] These students were actively absorbing knowledge that had instrumental meaning for the future scientific reordering of the archaic imperial society and imperial political order based on the perception of difference as a norm rather than as a deviation. Application of a systemic sociological approach to the Russian imperial context revealed that any attempts at society's rationalization would require a rearrangement of differences rather than their leveling. The ideal future (modernity) of Russian imperial society could have been more rational, institutionalized, and efficient, but it would be no more one-dimensional and monological than the old imperial "backwardness." Russian experts in the human sciences were gradually becoming aware of this epistemological difficulty.

The emergence of institutionalized sociology during this period was not dominated by one particular paradigm. The populist school coexisted with the neo-positivist school of social psychology and structural and functionalist sociology, and they developed alongside neo-Kantian sociological reflections on the objectivity of social knowledge and value judgments, which were brought into the Russian context by the student of Max Weber, Bogdan Kistiakovsky (Heuman 1998; Vucinich 1976: 125–152). At the same time, the political context of the Russian Empire of the Duma monarchy placed the emerging field of disciplinary sociology at the intersection of ideological movements that sought to redefine the epistemological positioning and political value of social order, social agency, and modernity (Semyonov 2009). On the one hand, Russian political Marxism tried to replace the pluralist theoretical foundation of sociological analysis with economic determinism and the utopian program of a radical remaking of the social order and even human nature. The presence in Russian Marxism of both the modernizing and utopian aspects explains why later in the early Soviet period sociology replaced history as a mandatory subject in the school and university curriculum and why the multiple schools of institutionalized sociology of the early twentieth century, whether the neopositivist sociology of Sorokin or neo-Kantian scholarship, came to be targeted by Bolshevik ideological censorship and political persecution. On the other hand, the experience of the 1905 revolution gave further impetus to the system of "moral foundationalism" and idealist critique of social reductionism of any sort, including sociological inquiry that interpreted cultural values and legal norms as socially determined (Kolerov 1996; Walicki 1987). In the continuum between Marxist reductionist views of social science and moral and metaphysical transcendence of the logic of social sciences, there existed other variants of politicized social theory, such as the version offered by Petr Struve, who enthusiastically embraced the notion of the survival of the fittest in the competition between the states for the status of great power and control of territory (Struve 1908).

SOROKIN'S "UNITY IN DIVERSITY"

An attempt at a dynamic model of sociological analysis of imperial diversity was produced by the new generation of scholars that began their studies after 1905, most notably by Pitirim Sorokin, who was trained from the start of his academic career as a sociologist. Sorokin's early biography is a reflection of the dynamically changing fabric of Russian imperial society. Born to a mixed Great Russian and Komi (Zyrian) family, Sorokin was a beneficiary of the Orthodox missionary activities in the Russian North. The Orthodox seminary allowed Sorokin to exit the world of rural crafts and embark on a journey across the social and political space of late imperial society. He moved from the countryside to the city, engaging in the groundwork of revolutionary propaganda on behalf of the Social-Revolutionary Party in the 1905 revolution; experiencing prison life as a political convict; climbing the ladder of the academic profession; being appointed in 1917 as a personal secretary to the head of the provisional government, Alexander Kerensky; fleeing the Bolshevik forces in the underground of the civil war; and founding the sociological department at Petrograd University (Golosenko 1991; Johnston 1995; Sorokin 1950, 1963). Citing the method of what may be called participant observation (Sorokin 1944: 7–8),[11] Sorokin repeatedly mentioned that his life experience informed his interest in sociology and the directions of his sociological research, from the study of mechanisms of social regulation in his first major work, *Crime and Punishment, Achievement and Reward*, to his major sociological works on social stratification and the impact of the war and famine on social behavior, which were completed prior to his expulsion from Soviet Russia in 1922. Drawing on his research experience and increasingly seeing sociology as an applied science after the 1917 revolution, Sorokin advocated before the Soviet government a system of sociological education that would encourage empirical research in the loci of rapidly changing society and that would immerse sociologists in the practices of cultural production and building a new system of education in Soviet Russia (Sorokin 1920, 1923, 1991).

Nikolai Kareev rightly pointed out that Sorokin was a representative of a new paradigm of sociology that signaled a departure from the traditions of Russian sociology in the nineteenth century. This was so not only because Sorokin's theoretical interlocutors were coming from American sociology or because he was one of the few scholars in early twentieth-century Russia whose professional specialization in sociology benefited from the institutionalization of sociological discipline in the Psycho-Neurological Institute and in the Russian sociological society.[12] Sorokin's sociology marked the watershed in the development of Russian sociology because "unlike the previous sociological research that had been concerned with the problem of development of society, [he] prioritized the problem of the formation of society" (Kareev 1996: 263).

Indeed, for Sorokin the very existence of society in late imperial Russia was far from obvious. He conducted his first research project on the ethnography of the Komi people in his native provinces of the Russian North, in 1908 and 1909 (Nesanelis and Semyonov 1991; Sorokin 1918, 1990). This research was made possible by his appointment to the expedition that was supposed to produce expertise for the colonization of this region and the resettlement of peasants into the provinces. He was fully aware of the political implications of the work of this commission, as colonization was the motto of the governmental policy of solving the agrarian question without expropriating the lands of the landowning nobility and of nationalization of empire. While making his ethnographic research on the Komi people, Sorokin exposed the work of the commission as fraudulent in misunderstanding the culture and customary law of the local population, underestimating this population's land hunger, and overestimating the availability of free land for colonization, thus revealing the colonialist aspiration of governmental policy and the conflict-ridden space of empire.

Defining sociology as an autonomous science of the general forms of social interaction, Sorokin's main question was not how knowledge of society is possible but how society as a space of social relations is possible: "why do people live together on a given territory? Why do they enter into intercourse?

Why do they gravitate toward one another and do not run away? ... The very fact of coexistence and interaction between people is usually taken for granted as something that does not require explanation" ([1920a] 1993: 358–359). Influenced by Leon Petrazycki and his interpretation of law as a psychological and social mechanism of self-regulation in society, Sorokin's first major sociological work was dedicated to exploration of the impact of mechanisms of social regulation on the emergence of social cohesion (Sorokin 1914). Formally subscribing to the evolutionary sociology of his mentor Kovalevsky, Sorokin displayed no interest in ascertaining the vector of social progress in the sequence of historically formed social orders. Instead, he presented an abstract picture of the work of coercion and reward in the spread and internalization of the social norm in social behavior.

Sorokin produced his major sociological synthesis in the *System of Sociology* in the early Soviet period, which ran against the ideological current of the day[13] and was dedicated to the problem of social structure. It is important to note that the red thread in this work is the theory of social cohesion and interconnectedness based on the premise of inherent heterogeneity of social space. The two volumes of the *System of Sociology* conceptualized the structure of society from the level of the individual and the formation of elementary social groups through the level of cumulative social groups (class and nationality) and aggregate social collectivities (the population of a country or the world). Defining the notion of the social through the concept of interaction, Sorokin paid special attention to conflict and antagonism, presenting them as forms of social connectedness. On all levels of analysis, Sorokin stressed the plurality of social groupness and interaction, picking intellectual and political fights with monistic descriptions of society seen through the prism of class or nationality. The element of social dynamics was presented by Sorokin in the form of the emergence, persistence, or collapse of social groupness. The second meaning of social dynamics was encapsulated in the changing configuration of the social structure. Using material from the civil war in Ukraine, Sorokin described the multiple fronts of the war and the plural social configurations that supported these fronts. Those included the struggle between "Reds" and "Whites," the clash between Russian nationalism and Ukrainian nationalism, the conflict between the urban political forces and rural movements, and the anomie that pitched one village against another. Sorokin attempted to conceptualize his open-ended view of the plurality of social groups and interactions with the concepts of "network" and "multiple souls": "Networks of interaction ... resemble the network of telephone connections in each given moment. The number of telephones is the same, but not all of them are in conference at the same time.... The individual is the outcome of projections of the system of social groups that compete or coexist with each other" (Sorokin [1920b] 1993: 30, 571). The attempt in *System of Sociology* to construct a dynamic model of "diversity in unity" displayed many tensions. In particular, Sorokin was never able to reconcile his theoretical stance of objective sociology and the study of forms of "real social collectivity" with the promise of the dynamic model of network analysis and multiple identities.

Sorokin's academic career after his forced emigration in 1922 is beyond the scope of this text, but it must be noted that in his writing on sociology of revolution and comparative analysis of the Soviet Union and the United States one can see a departure from his work of the Russian period. His sociology of revolution focused on the critique of revolution and its purported claim to bring about a significant transformation of social structure. Thus Sorokin's sociology of revolution stressed the moment of reproduction of the major structural division of society into rulers and ruled and introduced a novelty in the form of value judgment of "normal" and "abnormal" social groups in the revolution (Finkel 2005: 160; Sorokin 1922, 1925). His writing on the Russian nation emphasized the structural, transhistorical unity of the Great Russians, Ukrainians, and Byelorussians and downplayed the presence of conflicts and tensions in the space of the Russian Empire (Sorokin 1944: 29–31, 33–47; 1967).

POSTSCRIPT: THE UTOPIAN SOCIOLOGIST OF PROGRESSIVIST EMPIRE

The Russian Empire disappeared virtually overnight, leaving its former inhabitants not without a metropole, which had never been a spatially homogeneous locus anyway, but without a conceptual framework for embracing the variety of local customs and cultures within a single imagined political community. The new rhetoric of revolutionary social engineering marginalized the language of empire and the discourse of fundamental social heterogeneity within the borders of new Russia. Imperial domination of colonies and oppression of minorities could now be located only in the world of imperialism or in Russia's past, as was claimed in the writings of the historical school of Mikhail Pokrovsky (Barber 1981; Pokrovsky 1966). Within the Soviet Union, the dominant trope of social evolutionism and even revolutionism presented all the existing social and cultural differences as remnants of the old regime, to be effectively erased or reintegrated in the ultimately homogeneous society of the future. Ironically, much of this social engineering

and discursive manipulation had clear imperial and even imperialist implications, but it would be misleading to read unequivocally a hidden imperial
agenda into the social analysis of Soviet scholars. The episteme of Soviet
social sciences had a complex genealogy of its own and requires a special
deconstruction and examination.

Incidentally, the last outstanding sociologist of the Russian Empire remained unknown in this capacity, while his ideas summarized several decades of Russian scholars contemplating the analytical model of complex
open-ended societies. This unlikely imperial sociologist is Alexander Chaianov
(1888–1937), who became briefly prominent in the Western social sciences in
the 1970s as an anointed forerunner of peasant studies, the economics of
developing societies, and the emerging field of gender economics (Durrenberger 1980; Harrison 1977; Tannenbaum 1984; Thorner, Kerblay, and Smith
1968). In Russian studies, he is known as an original theorist of peasant economic rationality and peasant farm theory and as an activist in the rural
cooperative movement (Harrison 1975; Jasny 1972; Shanin 1972; Solomon
1977, 1978). He was severely criticized by Bolshevik authors in the 1920s and
by British and Indian Marxist critics in the 1970s for his nonclassical economic theories (Harrison 1979), but this is the only formal link between
Chaianov and the sociology of imperial "irregularity." Apparently, he
viewed the significance of his work differently, as we may judge by the bits of
personal information that survived the confiscation of his personal papers
after his first arrest in 1930. In 1906, Alexander Chaianov entered the elite
Moscow Agricultural Institute, which provided exceptional training in biology (the renowned geneticist Nikolai Vavilov was his classmate) and economics. Although his graduation thesis was dedicated to establishing the
southern boundary of the spread of the three-field system of crop rotation
in Russia and he spent much time analyzing peasant farm surveys, already
in spring 1909 he had admitted to his classmate and girlfriend, Ekaterina
Sakharova, that his true calling was sociology.[14] Before that, in October
1908, in a letter sent to his academic adviser, Aleksei Fortunatov, he mentioned his two notebooks of "sociological researches," of which he most valued his attempt to relate data from experimental psychology to certain social facts. He mentioned in particular the founder of modern psychology
in France, Theodule Ribot, as his source of inspiration in his theory of
personal motivation (Chaianov 1998: 110). In another letter to his professor,
Chaianov explicitly expressed his disagreement with the dominant understanding of sociology as dealing exclusively with abstract models and ideal
types: "I see sociology not as some abstract science of universal society but,

on the contrary, the science of . . . that actual society bustling and busy around us, the science that not only deconstructs the processes of social life into constituent factors, not only explains and differentiates phenomena, but the science capable of showing further directions for social life" (113). In this letter, Chaianov tried to explain to his positivist mentor that he was interested in the mechanisms regulating the processes of societal self-organization, rather than the general taxonomy of social forms and structures that are insensitive to specific historical and economic circumstances. The next documented statement of Chaianov's sociological views survived because he published it under the disguise of a literary work on utopia. Written in the second half of 1919 (and published in 1920), the small book *Journey of My Brother Alexey to the Land of Peasant Utopia* was published under a pen name and was set in 1984, almost two decades before the publication of George Orwell's *1984* (Chaianov 1976, 1977). Awkwardly written, lacking a formal finale, the novella is remarkable for its complex ideological message (Gerasimov 1997). Of special interest is an extensive fictional obituary of one Arsenii Bragin, "a great sociologist" and "patriarch of the science which he founded," incorporated into the text of the novella. His name may be read as a pun on Chaianov's name,[15] while his life circumstances stress important episodes of Chaianov's own biography.[16] Bragin is a fictional alter ego of Chaianov who embodied his ideal of social scientist and his understanding of sociology: "Bragin, who went from social technology to social theory, was fond of saying that the way to create a science of sociology was, first, to accumulate experience in the scientific study of individual practical social problems and, second, to find methods to express social phenomena quantitatively" (Chaianov 1977: 113). Bragin became famous for his field-defining studies, such as "The Rate of Social Change and Method of Measuring It" (which addressed the problem of quantitative description of social processes), "The Theory of Creation, Maintenance and Destruction of Reputation," and the multivolume "Theory of Political and Social Forces." These were stages of the realization of his "entire life's program which he had sketched out for himself in a youthful note" (113), probably the very same note by Chaianov from 1908 that was quoted above. Obviously, Chaianov did not believe in the self-sufficient heuristic value of statistical or taxonomic aggregation of empirical data (Bourgholtzer 1999: 77–78), and he was interested in the sociology of dynamic, open-ended systems, which only partially depended on social structures (such as public opinion or "reputation"). True to his early conviction that the ultimate task of sociology was "showing further directions for social life," Chaianov demonstrates the sociopolitical consequences of social analysis conducted by Bragin and his colleagues and followers. In the utopian Russia of 1984, state institutions are customized to suit local needs and peculiarities: "there is parliamentarism in Yakutsk *oblast'*, while the monarchists of Uglich have set up a local prince . . . , on the other hand, in the Mongolo-Altai territory, a 'governor-general' appointed by the central authority rules alone" (Chaianov 1977: 98). All urban centers had been rebuilt into "garden cities," and the economy is dominated by small production units integrated into cooperative networks. This is a hodgepodge of localities and regional peculiarities, bound together by the social system oriented toward rationalizing the application of available natural and human resources. The ruling political class consists of a loosely organized but distinctive community of experts. To sum up, the utopian society demonstrates the realization of Progressivist ideals (be it the urban-reform, antimonopolist rhetoric; the cult of rational managers; or fundamental disregard for institutionalized politics). But these general ideals of transatlantic Progressivism (Rodgers 1998: 5) are customized to serve the specificity of Russia as empire: certainly a great power but also a social space of the utmost internal heterogeneity. The sociology of this Progressivist empire faces the central challenge of balancing the need for achieving overall coherence with the accommodation of individual and local differences (in theory and practice). In the novella, Chaianov struggles to find a formula to embrace the domination of society by the political class of experts through what can be best described as governmentality, while at the same time avoiding the simplified language of colonialism and exploitation. He attempted to model and analyze the modern, or rather postmodern, Russia as an empire of multiculturalism and diversity, democratic and efficient, and yet still trapped in the dilemmas of the internal hegemony of knowledge and power over the otherness of local knowledge and concerns.

. . .

CHAIANOV'S PROJECT OF A "postimperial" sociology of imperial society brings us to the moment of rupture of Russian history in 1917. This rupture was brought about by the revolutions of 1917, the collapse of the imperial space, and the remaking of empire in the form of the Soviet Union. It would be a caricature view of 1917 to conceive of it as an unbridgeable boundary in Russian history between the late imperial period and the early Soviet period. For the questions concerned in the present essay it is important to note two processes that constitute the watershed in terms of the development of social sciences and the sociological reflection on empire.

Many historians have pointed out that the Soviet Union continued the pathways of the Russian Empire, including the retention of nondemocratic forms of rule focused on "management of vast territory and multiethnicity" (Lieven 2000). Others contend that the Soviet approach to diversity marked a departure from the Russian Empire. The Soviet politics was geared toward the reification of the category of class. Soviet nationality policy aimed at producing a bounded sense of nationhood for the multiple nationalities of the Soviet Union together with the territorial arrangement of multiethnicity in ethnically ascribed administrative territories. The result was the combination of an ideological regime, state-sponsored evolutionism, the dominance of the categories of class and ethnicity in state policy and the episteme of the social sciences, and ethno-territorial federation (Hirsch 2005; Khalid 2006; Martin 2001; Suny and Martin 2001). This was a radical unmaking of the irregular imperial society of differences as the context that had informed the development of Russian sociological reflection. As we argued, it was this context that was refracted in early Russian social theory and sociological inquiry in various ways, including the revolutionary tradition of unmaking the empire, the populist traditions of "learned ignorance" about empire, the evolutionary approach of normalization of the Russian Empire in the European continuum of imperial formations, and the quest for the dynamic model of sociology of imperial society of difference.

The relationship between the system of social sciences and the ideological regime in the early Soviet history was characterized as much by repression and censorship as it was by ambiguity. Arguably, the Soviet regime did not immediately have a ready, comprehensive social theory-cum-ideology beyond the revolutionary rhetoric and praxis. The announced "socialist" revolution, however, implied a radical transformation of the entire society on the basis of properly understood laws of its historical development, and sociology and social thinking therefore acquired supreme political importance. In search of a new social orthodoxy, the new regime encouraged the development of a "true" Marxist social science by establishing a number of institutions of higher learning and think tanks (such as the Sverdlov Communist University, the Communist Academy, and the Institute of Red Professorship). At the same time, the regime embarked on a large-scale process of negative selection, vigorously filtering out all of those ideas and their proponents who sounded alien to communist ideologues. This filtering included forced political emigration (this was the fate of Sorokin), arrests (Chaianov), and censorship.[17] Gradually, the negative selection turned to former ideologues of the socialist revolution themselves, such as the charismatic historian Pokrovsky. The two processes, filtering alien elements and creating the true Marxist sociology, eventually converged in the late 1930s, when the Stalinist canon of social sciences was enshrined in a series of discussions and the classic text *History of the Communist Party of the Soviet Union (Bolsheviks): Short Course* (Commission of the Central Committee of the C.P.S.U. [B.] 1939). By this time, the social scientists who had survived were forced to accept the new orthodoxy. This period marks the end of the most creative and critical social theorizing that spanned the early twentieth century and the 1920s. But this happened not before a series of theoretical contributions to the initial Marxist sociology was provided by Soviet social scientists, most notably, the theory of historical sequence of socioeconomic formations.

NOTES

The authors wish to thank Sergei Glebov, George Steinmetz, and Charles Steinwedel, whose criticism helped to improve this essay. Alexander Semyonov acknowledges the support of the Center for Fundamental Research of the National Research University–Higher School of Economics.

1. See the analysis of those aspects of European sociology that defined the voluntarism of the French Revolution and redefined politics from the viewpoint of the foundational nature of the social in Wolin (1973: 349; 2004).

2. Cf.: "They acted as utopian socialists, rather than empirical sociologists, when they thought of escaping capitalism by blending the complexity of industrial technology with the simplicity of *obshchina* cooperation" (Vucinich 1976: 63).

3. The term used by Iuzhakov is *inorodtsy* (literally: of different origin, often translated into English as "aliens"). It was initially a legal category for description of nomadic and seminomadic groups of the population in the Russian Empire. At the close of the nineteenth century, it acquired a new meaning: to designate all non-Russian groups of population in contradistinction to the "Russian people." See the complex semantic evolution of this key category of imperial politics analyzed in Slocum (1998).

4. Kovalevsky's students reflected their mentor's preoccupation with instrumental social knowledge. Mikhail Nikolaevich Kharuzin (1860–1888) was directed by Kovalevsky to the study of customary law in the Russian Empire. He wrote the definitive study of the Don Cossack customary law (Kharuzin 1885). Mikhail Kharuzin bridged the worlds of scholarship and imperial bureaucracy, serving as a secretary of the ethnographic division of the Society of the Lovers of Natural Sciences, Anthropology, and Ethnography and as the senior officer in the governorship of Estland.

5. Concluding his ethnographic observations on the role of customary law in the life of North Caucasus mountaineer societies, Kovalevsky writes that "I do not reject the value of the mountaineer courts that had been established previ-

ously [by the imperial authorities in the Caucasus].... such an idea, i.e. to have in the court of justice the elected from the people representatives and to give them a possibility to adjudicate cases in accordance to the 'adat' (custom), should be regarded as fruitful and should be taken into account in the nearest reform of our legal statutes and their application to the needs of the Caucasus" (2005: 612–613).

6. Kovalevsky got involved in the project with the help of Samuel Harper, who was an American scholar of Russian political institutions and the son of the first president of the University of Chicago. Harper was tutored by Kovalevsky. Harper was also involved in Thomas's sociological project. Beyond that project, Harper was involved in the mission of the United States Department of Labor headed by W. W. Husband, which sought to empower the authorities of Ellis Island with adequate knowledge about the flows of immigration and hold in check the German shipping companies that were largely responsible for transportation of immigrants from Eastern Europe (Harper 1945: 78–80).

7. Kovalevsky referred to the United States when he advocated the abolition of civil inequalities among the peoples of the Russian Empire: "History has proven to us that the language and culture of the most numerous group of population enters into everyday circulation without any coercion: the language of this group becomes the language of commercial deals, of the stock exchange and banking. In other words this language becomes not just the language of the state but the language of citizenship. Having resettled to America, Germans keep their schools, yet their children without exception speak English because this is the language of everyday civility. Defined by Turgenev as rich, melodic and 'great,' the Russian language gave emergence to the most remarkable literature in the past century, so it does not need the aide of bureaucrats of the Ministry of the Interior or the Ministry of Popular Enlightenment. The use of this language in everyday civility makes this language not just the language of the state or of its cultured groups, but also the language of commerce and everyday life" (Kovalevsky 2002: 257–258).

8. The school's students were eager to participate in political debates and turn the classes into a struggle between political platforms, chiefly socialist-revolutionary and social-democratic ones. They also demanded a more visible public profile for the school vis-à-vis current Russian politics. (See note 9.)

9. Hoover Institution of War, Peace, and Revolution, 1901–1904, Boris Nikolaevsky Collection, Box 78, Folder 11; Course catalogs, Box 78, Folder 9; "Kocharovskii Affair," Letters and pamphlets of student organizations reporting on the political clash that happened in the course by Professor Kocharovsky, Box 78, Folder 10; Letter from students calling for a public expression of the attitude of the school to the Kishinev pogrom.

10. Central State Archive of St. Petersburg 1909–1917, F. 115, Op. 2, Vol. 1, 5120d. The institute shared the fate of the Paris school in that the Russian government perceived its curriculum as dangerous and leading to the formation of subversive views on the side of the youth. The government several times contemplated the banning of educational activities of the institute, leaving it with research-only functions.

11. Sorokin was indebted to his mentor Leon Petrazycki in his thinking about introspective observation and observation of human behavior as methodologies of sociological research (Sorokin 1956: 1154).

12. Sorokin first enrolled in the Psycho-Neurological Institute and then continued his studies in the Law School of Petrograd University under the guidance of Maksim Kovalevsky, Evgenii de Roberti, and Leon Petrazycki. In his official autobiography, Sorokin notes that he was trained as a professional sociologist from the start of his career.

13. The publication of Sorokin's *System of Sociology* was carried out against the system of Bolshevik ideological censorship. The print run of the first edition (ten thousand copies for each of the two volumes) sold out within two weeks before the confiscation order came (Golosenko 1991: 84).

14. Russian State Archive of Economy, Moscow, F. 328, Op. 1, Ed. khr. 8, L. 158.

15. The original Greek meaning of "Arsenii" and "Alexander" are close, while "Bragin" refers to a traditional peasant fermented alcoholic drink, just as "Chayanov" refers to an equally popular (but nonalcoholic) beverage, tea.

16. Thus, Bragin is credited with creating "the political power of the scattered peasantry" and becoming a political leader of the peasant party. Chaianov was accused in 1930 of creating a fictional anti-Soviet Peasant Labor Party, but in 1917 he had indeed contemplated the creation of a "Broad Peasant Party" (Gerasimov 2009: 212).

17. To get the sense of the zeal with which the censors went after politically benign but sociologically "alien" texts, suffice it to mention that in 1919, the Petrograd Commissariat of Press, Agitation, and Propaganda prohibited the Cooperative Publishing House from publishing *The Prince and the Pauper* by Mark Twain, the historical novel *Prince Serebriannyi* by Aleksei Tolstoi, the economic treatise *The Paper Money* by M. Bogolepov, and *The State Bankruptcy* by A. N. Zak. The only permitted book was *The Moon* by G. Klein (Sandomirskii 1919: 24).

THREE

Sociology's Imperial Unconscious

The Emergence of American Sociology in the Context of Empire

JULIAN GO

The inhabitants of southern, central, and western Europe, call them Aryan, Indo-Germanic, or anything you please ... have led the civilization of the world ever since there were any records. ... The several nations into which this race is now divided are the products of compound assimilation of a higher order than that of other nations. As a consequence ... this race has become the dominant race of the globe. As such it has undertaken the work of extending its dominion over other parts of the earth. It has already spread over the whole of South and North America, over Australia, and over Southern Africa. It has gained a firm foothold on Northern Africa, Southern and Eastern Asia, and most of the larger islands and archipelagos of the sea. It is only necessary to understand the modern history of the world and the changes in the map of the world to see this.

—LESTER WARD, first president of the American Sociological Society,
in *Pure Sociology* (1903: 238–239)

INTRODUCTION

The St. Louis World's Fair of 1904 was in many ways an imperial affair. While it had exhibits on airships and automobiles, among many other modern novelties, it also put the new modern empires of the world on display. The nineteen million visitors to the fair could witness a reenactment of the recently ended Boer War: British and Boer troops played out the battles of the war against a backdrop of "a village of Zulus, Swazies, and other South African tribes" (Rydell 1984: 179). Visitors could also witness a parade on the Pike that included two thousand peoples from around the globe, mostly from Europe's recently established colonies in Africa and Asia. Between sipping sodas and eating hot dogs, visitors could even view living ethnological exhibits of pygmies from Africa, Kwakiutl Indians from Vancouver Island, or re-creations of "Cairo Street" and the "Empire of India." The mostly American attendees could also see their own empire. The fair was to serve as a commemoration of the purchase of the Louisiana Territory—which is why the fair was also known as the Louisiana Purchase Exposition—and accordingly ethnological exhibits included various Native American tribes as well as Geronimo himself (Francis 1913: 254–299). There were also exhibits on America's more recent colonial acquisitions, including Puerto Rico and the Philippines. One part of the Philippine exhibit involved some twelve hundred Filipinos. They stayed in model huts and villages, replicas of their exotic originals, and visitors were invited to watch as these "savage" tribes conducted their daily activities. Visitors stood with curious amazement (and sometimes horror) as the scantily clad Igorots, from the highlands of central Luzon, sacrificed and ate dog (531).

The St. Louis Fair condensed the imperial tenor of the turn of the twentieth century, but it also condensed another aspect of the times: the emergence of American professional social science. A committee of American academics had organized a Congress of Arts and Sciences to be held concurrently with the fair. As the director of the Congress explained, the Congress would enable scholars of various disciplines to "discuss their several sciences or professions with reference to some theme of universal human interest"—in this case the theme was "The Progress of Man since the Louisiana Purchase." Speakers were organized into distinct sections, including the Natural Sciences, Philosophy, and Religion; Medicine and Surgery; Law, Politics, and Government; and Applied Science. Sociology was one of the many other disciplines represented. Albion Small (editor of the *American Journal of Sociology* [AJS] and later president of the American Sociological Society) was a member of the organizing committee, and he had invited prominent sociologists to provide their own insights on the "Progress of Man." The European speakers were Ferdinand Tönnies and Gustav Ratzenhofer. The roster of American speakers included Lester Frank Ward, Franklin Giddings, George Edgard Vincent, William I. Thomas, and Edward A. Ross—all of whom would later take their turn as presidents of the American Sociological Society formed the subsequent year.[1] They gave their lectures at the Congress at the very same time that fairgoers outside were watching reenactments of the Boer War and living exhibits of Filipinos eating dog.

These two dimensions of the St. Louis World's Fair, the imperial and disciplinary-sociological, raises a larger question. Was not American sociology influenced in one way or another by the wider imperial context and culture in which it emerged? After all, American sociology became institutionalized in the United States just as imperialism was proliferating around the world and profoundly transforming the geopolitical order. Just as the Department of Sociology was established at the University of Chicago in 1893 and the first doctorate in sociology in the United States was awarded at Cornell, the French were colonizing the Ivory Coast, Laos, and Guinea; the British South Africa Company was invading Matabeleland in current-day Zimbabwe; and Queen Liliuokalani was surrendering her Hawaiian kingdom to the United States. A year later, the same year that Franklin Giddings was appointed chair and professor of sociology at Columbia (marking the first full professorship in sociology in the United States), England took Uganda as a protectorate, France seized Madagascar, and the Sino-Japanese War erupted. In 1895, as the AJS published its very first issue, Japan seized Taiwan, Britain turned Bechuanaland into a protectorate and raided the Transvaal Republic against the Boers, and the Cuban rebellion against Spain was unleashed. In 1901, the year that the Sociology Department at the University of Minnesota was established, England was adding Tonga and Nigeria to its empire, and the U.S. government was violently suppressing an anticolonial insurgency in the Philippines, occupying Cuba, and solidifying its colonial regimes in Samoa and Puerto Rico. American sociology was institutionalized as the new imperialism of Britain, Germany, France, Japan, the United States, and other powers was under way.[2] Was not this new world of empire a part of American sociology's imaginary?

Most studies of sociology's emergence bracket this question. Instead, traditional approaches probe and compare the content of the early sociologists' theories, treating them as autonomous systems abstracted from the social context of their production and reception (e.g., Hinkle 1980). Studies that do examine social context focus on the influence of social processes and dynamics within the United States. They trace how early sociology grappled with issues of immigration or domestic class conflict (Ross 1991), the ways in which it articulated with dominant corporate interests (Schwendinger and Schwendinger 1974), how it was shaped by turf wars with other disciplines (Camic 1995), or its need to establish its scientific legitimacy and assert its authoritative voice in American society (Breslau 2007; Haskell 1977). All of these accounts are valuable, but they forsake the geopolitical and global context for the domestic and local. Even the few studies that do expand their lens to the global arena warrant extension. Connell (1997) makes the novel move of tracing how European sociology in the early twentieth century had imperialist origins, but as critics point out, his analysis does not fully address American sociology. It stays focused on the imperialist origins of British and French sociology.[3] Studies of W. E. B. DuBois rightly recapture how DuBois's sociology was injected with geopolitical and imperial concerns, but we are then left with the impression that he was the exception that proves the rule (Morris 2007).[4]

This chapter attempts to rectify the elision. The goal is not to embark on a "guilt trip" and accuse early American sociology of being imperialist (cf. Collins 1997). Nor is it to anachronistically hurl charges of "racism." The goal is more humble. Focusing on the sociologists who are considered to be American sociology's founders (i.e., the first presidents of the American Sociological Society: Lester F. Ward, William G. Sumner, Franklin H. Giddings, Albion Small, and Edward A. Ross) and examining articles published in the discipline's main journal, the AJS, I consider the ways in which the global context of empires and colonialism might have influenced, guided, or articulated with the research and theory of American sociology in its formative years. In this sense, my approach should be uncontroversial. As have many other studies, I situate early American sociology in its sociohistorical context. But the approach differs from existing studies because it urges us to reconsider exactly which context should be foregrounded. While most existing studies demarcate the context to the boundaries of the United States, my goal is to push further and think about how the world of modern empires might have resounded in sociological thought.

GLOBAL DIFFERENCE: FROM EUROPE TO THE UNITED STATES

It will prove useful, for a start, to look across the Atlantic and consider one of American sociology's key influences: European sociology. Admittedly, sociology in Europe in the decades surrounding the twentieth century was itself complex; its manifestation in Britain, France, and Germany took varied forms. But if there was one shared interest at all, it was "progress" (though not among the German sociologists; Steinmetz 2009a). Working from social evolutionary assumptions, many European sociologists (though not necessarily all) were ultimately interested in the development or advancement of modern European societies, which is also to say that they were concerned with original or "primitive" societies in order to better understand development (Hawkins 1997). Such concerns had long been a part of European thought, but what is critical is the way in which European sociology pursued them. Specifically, European sociologists mapped evolution not by examining historical progress per se but historical progress as could be discerned across contemporaneous societies. They sought to understand chronological difference by reference to sociospatial difference. To explain "segmentary societies," Durkheim referred not only to ancient Hebrew society but also to the Kabyle in contemporary Algeria. Benjamin Kidd's work contrasted "civilized peoples" not with their earlier history but with the "less developed" races in non-European societies (Kidd 1894, 1898). Understanding historical difference meant synchronic comparison; it meant an interest in "global difference" (Connell 1997).

According to Connell (1997), this comparative framework, with its emphasis on global difference, is telling. Specifically, it suggests an intimacy between sociologists' mode of thought and European imperialism. "The idea of global difference was ... given to [sociologists] by the process of economic and colonial expansion, inscribed in the social structure of the empires that the North Atlantic powers constructed" (1519).

To be sure, the late nineteenth century was an important period of new imperial expansion and consolidation. Difference was the very structure of the new order. The rising empires created hierarchical social, political, legal, and administrative divisions between metropole and colony, citizen and subject. Along with these practical divisions came an explosion of difference talk at home and abroad; an unprecedented discursive proliferation about the "civilized" versus the "uncivilized," the "superior" versus the "inferior"; and a new emphasis on racialized difference and biology, blood, and stock. As new colonial states proliferated, the task of cataloging and comprehending such differences became more and more critical. Colonial governance demanded knowledge. Furthermore, a popular culture of imperialism at home was unleashed. Victorian middle-class readerships of new periodicals and literature expanded. World expositions and fairs displaying primitiveness become common. Popular cognizance of imperial endeavors and foreign peoples rose to new heights. Throughout all of this discourse, the assumption remained: colonized or would-be colonized peoples in the non-European world were not only inferior but inferior because they represented the earlier stages of historical development that modern Europeans had already undergone (MacKenzie 1986; Porter 2004; Said 1993).

European sociology and its scheme of global difference was part and parcel of this culture of imperialism. In contrasting advanced societies with contemporary primitive societies, and assuming that the latter represented historically prior incarnations of the former, European sociology rearticulated the practical and theoretical differences posited between the metropole and colony, the self and Other, while reinscribing the popular assumption of the white man's superiority. In Europe, sociology reproduced the imperial gaze. It was informed by and referred to a wider culture of imperialism while often sharing its social evolutionary assumptions. Even critics of imperialism, like Herbert Spencer, worked from the same assumptions (Sylvest 2007; Weinstein 2005: 97–102). In this sense, Connell's point that European sociology "was formed within the culture of imperialism and embodied a cultural response to the colonized world" is perfectly plausible (Connell 1997: 1519).

But what about sociology across the Atlantic? It is well known that American sociologists worked within social evolutionary themes as did their European counterparts (Breslau 2007; Hinkle 1980). It would follow that difference—along with its notions of development and progress—was at the heart of their conceptual framework, too. Extant studies of early American sociological thought would not disagree here, but they treat American sociology's social evolutionism in terms of how it was used to make sense of developmental questions internal to the metropole. Supposedly, early American sociologists were concerned about industrialization, urbanization, the development of capitalism, immigration, class conflict, and the specter of socialism in the United States. We are left to assume that while European sociologists operated within a culture of imperialism, American sociologists escaped it. Hence Collins (1997) forthrightly denies that American sociology had a relationship to the culture of imperialism. Any claim about the "imperialist origins of sociology works best for Britain" but not for the United States (1561). Collins's denial is therefore similar to that of traditional American historiography. Just as traditional historians see the United States as "exceptional" for presumably never having been an "empire" (Go 2007), so too would Collins treat the early sociologists as exceptional for being untouched by the culture of imperialism.

There can be little doubt that American sociology was concerned with development and progress in the United States or that the early sociologists addressed questions of industrialization, urbanization, class conflict, and other pressing domestic matters. But a look at some of their introductory sociology courses should compel us to pause. At Chicago, Albion Small reported that the texts he assigned were primarily for "indicating comparisons and connections between present society and lower levels of culture." As examples, he listed Edward Westermarck's *Origin and Development of Moral Ideas* and Hutton Webster's *Primitive Secret Societies* (Cooley et al. 1912: 634). Charles Cooley's introductory sociology class at Michigan contained lectures on "the public mind in primitive society." Edward Ross's course began with the "origin of man" and proceeded to the "origin and characteristics of races" and "race geography" (633). Ulysses Weatherly's introduction to sociology at Indiana discussed the "origin and history of races-racial geography," the "nature of primitive groups," and the "formation of tribes, races, peoples, nations" (634). These curricula belie the notion that early sociologists were fundamentally concerned with internal domestic issues. It suggests that they, like their European counterparts, were interested in comparisons between societies and peoples around the world.

Even a cursory look at some of the early sociologists' key works discloses that American sociology was interested in global difference. W. I. Thomas's first book was not at all about the United States or even Europe. His *Source Book for Social Origins* was an examination of what he called "savage society" (Thomas 1909a). His articles in the *AJS* were similarly oriented, replete with references to "savage" or "less developed" peoples around the world (Thomas 1905a, 1905b, 1909b). Long before he published his famous work on the Polish peasant—which was indeed about immigration to the United States—Thomas was primarily concerned with matters beyond the United States and Europe. Consider, too, Edward Ross's widely popular *Social Control* ([1901] 1969). By the 1960s, many considered this work to be "one of the classics of the discipline" (ix). As such, we would expect *Social Control* to exemplify the concerns of early American sociology. Specifically, if we were to go by traditional accounts, we would expect it to be about domestic issues particular to the United States. Hence Weinberg, Hinkle, and Hinkle in 1969 put Ross's theory of social control within the context of class conflict in the United States and related domestic questions like urbanization (Hinkle and Hinkle 1969: xxxvii–xxxix). But much of the text is at odds with such a reading. In laying out the purpose of the study, Ross writes: "it is the purpose of this inquiry to ascertain how men of the West-European breed are brought to live closely together, and to associate their efforts with that degree of harmony we see about us" ([1901] 1969: 3). Ross here intimates a comparative perspective between the "West-European breed" and some unspecified Other. In the next sentences, the Other is made transparent. He contrasts the "dolichocephalic blonds of the West," the "Tueton," or the "restless, striving, doing Aryan" with "the passive, unambitious Hindoos" (3). Ross's theory of social control thus depended on a global frame. To be sure, his theory of social control involved classifying different types of control, from "personal control" to the form of "individualistic" social control evident in modern societies (Ross 1897: 243). According to Ross, the former type of control marks an earlier stage of development, and to bring the point home Ross did not look to premodern Europe but rather to the Khonda, the Ostiaks, the Damaras, the Bedouins, and various other examples of the "Asiatic and African races" (240).

American sociologists' evolutionary interests, like those of their European counterparts, therefore entailed a vital interest in global difference. To be sure, much of their work shared the presumption of their European precursors and contemporaries—namely, that historical difference was to be understood by sociospatial difference. According to W. I. Thomas, comparisons across societies provided the best evidence of past development: "tribal society is virtually delayed civilization, and the savages are a sort of contemporaneous ancestry" (1909b: 153). Elsewhere he stressed: "In the very fact that they have not become like us we may hope to find the laws of social physics which raised us above them" (1896: 441; 1908: 117–118). Giddings likewise predicated his cross-societal comparisons on the notion that "there still survive, in various parts of the world, savage and barbarian communities of such varied stages of social organization that every form of social composition may still be observed and comparatively studied in actually existing communities" (1909: 190). Furthermore, such presumptions and their associated focus on global difference were critical to these writers' vision of what sociology is and should be about. In "The Data of Sociology," Lester Ward insisted that the study of "society . . . in its most embryonic stages and among the least developed races" constitutes "one of the most important fields of research" for sociology (Ward 1896: 746). Similarly, Giddings's method of "systematic induction"—the very basis of his sociological research—was aimed at observing "the great processes of social evolution," but such observations meant comparing contemporaneous societies (Giddings 1904: 172–175; 1909). Giddings even predicated his vision of statistical sociology—which would later be decisive for Columbia University's status in the discipline—on an interest in global difference. While the global-comparative method enables the discovery of "differences in social phenomena that are the bases of scientific classification," quantitative sociology would count such differences and ultimately help to create "a complete scientific theory of natural causation" (174; see also Small 1900a: 516–517). W. I. Thomas even suggested that the discipline of sociology itself was entirely dependent on a hierarchy of difference. He argued that the typical "savage tribe" and other less developed peoples were incapable of sociological reflection (Thomas 1896: 434). Only "advanced" peoples at a "high stage of development" could analyze themselves—that is, adopt a sociological perspective. If the advanced races were those who had the privilege of ruling the earth—as Giddings and others would argue—so too did the advanced races have the privilege of being sociologists.

The point is not to reduce the American sociologists' views to "racism." In fact, the early American sociologists differed in their views about what constituted "race," and they sometimes debated whether "inferior" or "less developed" peoples were inherently inferior as a result of their biological constitution (e.g., Stone 1908: 677; Ward 1903: 30–39; see also Go 2004; Stocking 1968). The point is that these American sociologists were oriented to the global scene as much as, if not more than, the domestic one. But was this really about empire? It is one thing to say that American sociologists were interested in global difference, that their categories were homologous with empire's sociopolitical structure and reproduced imperial epistemology, or that their method was structurally similar to the imperial gaze. It is quite another to suggest that American sociology partook directly of imperial culture, that their theory and methods were dependent on the geopolitical scene, or that they were in the least interested in empire or imperialism itself. It may be that the concern with global or racial difference was simply because they were primarily interested in immigration to the United States and associated issues of racial or ethnic assimilation.

Consider, though, one of the earliest articles in the AJS that theorized "assimilation": Sarah Simons's series "Social Assimilation." Simons's analysis was clearly oriented toward the pressing issue of immigration to the United States. The final piece in the series was devoted to it exclusively (Simons 1901b). However, the majority of Simons's series is not at all about immigration. For Simons, "assimilation" was about not just massive groups of people entering the United States but also colonialism, that is, Anglos and Europeans extending outward to rule foreign peoples. According to Simons, "assimilation" takes two key forms: either imperial conquest or immigration. Fittingly, although the last part of her series is devoted to assimilation in the United States and discusses immigration, all of the other parts refer to imperial processes past and present. Simons argues, for instance, that "civilized society arose in consequence of conquest" and then elaborates on the dynamics of conquest, providing a natural history of assimilation that essentially sequenced imperial state building (Simons 1901a: 793). After conquest, "Exploitation is the dominant note in the treatment of the conquered by the conquerors, and social inequality becomes the principle of organization in the new society" (793–795). Only after this discussion does Simons analyze immigration.[5]

Various other articles in the AJS under the editorship of Albion Small further suggest that American sociology's interest in difference was shaped by the geopolitical context of empire rather than purely domestic concerns like immigration to the United States. As editor, Small published articles from Europeans that dealt exclusively with empires or colonialism. These included Friedrich Ratzel's series "Studies in Political Areas" (1897) about the spatial dynamics of empire; Max Maurenbrecher's "The Moral and Social Tasks of World Politics ('Imperialism')" (1900); James Collier's "The Theory of Colonization" (1905); and J. F. Scheltema's "The Opium Trade in the Dutch East Indies" (1907). If American sociology was not interested in empire, why bother publishing these articles?[6] Giddings, in fact, stated that the imperial world and its associated dynamics should be an object of sociological interest in itself. His 1910 presidential address to the American Sociological Society aimed to specify sociology's role in addressing pressing public issues of the time. In listing the key issues, he mentioned immigration and made an oblique reference to class. But mainly he pointed to global and imperial issues: "To speak for the moment of our own nation, the questions that vex us are of bewildering variety and complexity: questions of territorial expansion and of rule over alien peoples; questions arising out of race conflict within our older continental domain; questions of the restriction of immigration, of the centralization or the distribution of administrative authority, and the concentration or the diffusion of economic power" (Giddings 1911: 580–581). Giddings further noted that "one question that overshadows all others" and with which sociologists should grapple did not have to do with immigration but "Is it War or Peace?" (581). His concern here was the "militarization" of societies and potential war between them. This was in 1910 before the outbreak of World War I. The violence attendant with empire at the turn of the century—from the Boer War to the Spanish-American and Philippine-American wars to the Russian-Japanese conflict—was apparently on Giddings's mind.[7]

Even when empire was not directly the object of sociological concern, American sociologists nonetheless referred to the modern imperial world to buttress their arguments. When Irving King tried to theorize how social change influenced the "emotional life of a people," for example, he stressed that the sociologist should first examine "those peoples to whom custom means a very different thing than to ourselves" (1903: 125–127). His first example was British Malaysia. Similarly, when Cooley attempted to see whether the Social Darwinist concept of "survival of the fittest" stood up to actual "fact," he landed on the affirmative, stating that "change by survival" is "not at all speculation, but the most verifiable thing in the world." His examples included South Africa (where "the rapid development of some clan" has been

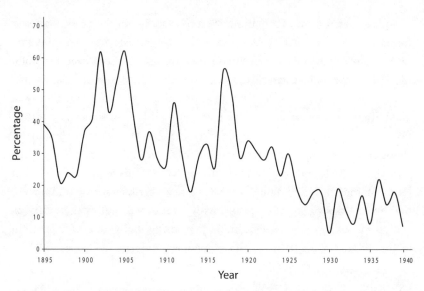

FIG 3.1 · Percentage of articles in the *American Journal of Sociology* with keywords relating to empire and colonialism.

accompanied by the "almost complete suppression of another clan") and the success of European imperialism (Cooley 1897: 64). Albert Keller went so far as to treat colonies as ideal sociological laboratories. In "The Value of the Study of Colonies for Sociology," he suggested that the colonial world provides excellent data for studying difference and development. By examining colonized societies and their peoples, sociologists can "find a rapid and, though imperfect, fairly complete evolution of social forms" (Keller 1906: 418).[8] These references to the imperial world were not uncommon. The mean percentage of articles in the *AJS* that referred to "empires," "imperialism," "colonies," or "colonialism" from 1895 to 1914 was 36 percent with a standard deviation of 12.4 (Figure 3.1). In 1902, the percentage of articles that referred to those keywords reached as high as 60 percent.

The global and imperial, rather than the domestic, clearly drove early American sociologists' interest in difference. This is seen in yet another feature of their work. That is, when they did discuss issues internal to the United States, they did not always abstract them from their global-imperial context. Note Lester Ward's presidential address, "Social Class in Light of Modern Sociological Theory." Given the title, the address was ostensibly invoked by questions of class conflict at home. But for Ward, class conflict was rooted in race conflict and the social relations of empires past and present: he traces the origins of class conflict in modern society to the history of imperial conquests around the globe. Imperial conquests set off the process of class formation: the "conquering race becomes the high caste and the conquered race the low caste." Eventually these two groups, the colonizer and colonized, become social classes: "the simple truth is that the social classes that we find today in the most advanced nations of the world are the outgrowth and natural successors of those primary subdivisions of society, or castes" (Ward 1908: 618). For Ward, class conflict and class struggle were but an offshoot of what he calls "the race struggle": a "universal" struggle wrought by imperial contacts and conquests (Ward 1908: 622). This rendering of class in terms of imperial history and "race struggle" was critical for Ward. It meant that an analysis of social class and its dynamics was not as important as analyses of racial struggles. For him, the primary engine of development in history has been "the struggle of races, peoples, and nations" (1907: 298).[9]

CULTURES OF U.S. IMPERIALISM

If the American sociologists' interest in global difference was not driven by an ultimate interest in the metropole alone but by the geopolitical context of empire, what was the linkage between the broader world and their ideational labor? What mediated the imperial geopolitical order and their theory and research? For some, the answer is simple enough. If American sociologists were interested in global difference and, accordingly, the imperial world, this was only due to intellectual influence from across the Atlantic. Rather than resulting from its own autonomous interests in the imperial world, American sociology's comparative approach resulted from its "provincialism and intellectual dependence upon Britain" (Collins 1997: 1561). It is on this count that Collins rejects any notion that American sociology could have "imperialist origins."

Early American sociology was indeed influenced by European trends.[10] Ward's concept of the "race struggle," for instance, was drawn from the German-language sociologists Gumplowicz and Ratzenhofer (Barnes 1919b: 160–161; Ward 1902a: 650–652; 1902b: 759). Still, to reduce American sociology's concern with difference to European thought alone, as Collins does, begs other questions: Why, for example, did the theme of global difference— and its larger evolutionary framework—resonate with American sociologists? And why would a discourse of racial difference be so critical? Could it not be that the hearty reception to such thought and related discourses of race struggle was shaped by American sociologists' own immediate social context just as much as by their "intellectual dependence" on British and

European thought? A purely intellectualist explanation of the Americans' interests in global difference—and on empire and colonialism—runs the risk of downplaying the larger imperial culture of the United States itself.

It should be remembered first that the United States was a key actor in the new imperialism, too. Having already conquered lands and peoples on the western continent by the postbellum era, the United States began meddling overseas by the turn of the twentieth century. Interventions in Hawaii and Samoa in the early 1890s were the earliest signs; these were followed by a spate of colonial acquisitions in subsequent years. The United States took Hawaii and eastern Samoa. It also seized the Philippines, Puerto Rico, and Guam from Spain as a result of the Spanish-American War. It further established Cuba as a protectorate, seized a string of small islands in the Pacific, and temporarily occupied small states in the Caribbean and Central America. All of this was a continuation of earlier expansion but also a different turn altogether (Burnett and Marshall 2001; Go 2005b; Sparrow 2006). With the new imperialism, the United States became an overseas colonial empire just like its European peers (Go 2005a).

The construction and consolidation of this new American empire had significant repercussions in popular culture at home. There was a veritable imperial frenzy to match the novel reach of America's new overseas imperialism (Hietala 1985; Slotkin 1992). What emerged was an imperial culture mixing jingoism, grandiose visions of global power, and racialized discussions of America's new overseas peoples (Kaplan and Pease 1993). In Washington, senators and statesmen discussed and debated America's standing in the world, its relations with rival powers, and of course what to do with—and how to make sense of—America's newly found colonial subjects. Investigative commissions, military officials, and various other vanguards sent back countless reports and photographs from the ground documenting the new peoples and places. The pages of magazines, journals, and newspapers—voraciously consumed by an ever-widening domestic readership—were replete with images and discussions of America's colonial subjects (Hunt 1987; Thompson 2002). As the *Pittsburgh Dispatch* noted, there was a massive "public thirst" for stories about America's greatness and the "new races under the American flag."[11]

The St. Louis World's Fair of 1904 was but one among many manifestations of this widening American imperial culture (Kramer 2006; Rydell 1984). But the new culture of imperialism also hit academia, as scholars in sociology's sister disciplines quickly partook of it. The American Historical Association responded to the Spanish-American War and its portentous imperialism by organizing a committee in 1898 to conduct a "historical study of colonial dependencies" and holding sessions on colonialism during its 1899 meetings. The American Economic Association appointed a committee on colonies in 1898 and produced a volume entitled *Essays in Colonial Finance*. The American Oriental Society created a special section in 1900 to study America's overseas colonies while pushing Congress to have the work of the Bureau of American Ethnology (traditionally studying Native Americans) extended to the Philippine Islands (Marotta 1983: 128–129; Ng 1994: 129). The *Annals of the American Academy of Political and Social Science*, the *American Political Science Review*, and the *Political Science Quarterly* all included new series or sections of their journals titled "Colonial Government" and "Notes on Colonies." Political scientists such as John W. Burgess at Giddings's Columbia, Woodrow Wilson at Princeton, and Paul S. Reinsch at Wisconsin wrote articles and books on America's new global standing, colonial administration, or the legal and political dimensions of American empire.[12] Lecture series at Stanford, Chicago, Cornell, and Indiana offered insights on colonial policy and the history of imperial expansion, while new courses across various disciplines at Minnesota, Yale, Stanford, and others had titles such as "The Philippines," "Colonial Expansion and System of Administration," "Colonization," "Colonial Government," and "Spanish Legal Institutions with Special Reference to Our Colonial Dependencies" (Ng 1994: 131–133). Many of the academics involved in constructing this imperial knowledge even served overseas in the new colonial states. William Willoughby and Jacob Hollander, political economists at Johns Hopkins, served in high posts in the colonial administration of Puerto Rico, as did Leo S. Rowe, a professor of law at Pennsylvania. Both Willoughby and Rowe produced articles and books on U.S. rule in Puerto Rico and on U.S. colonial rule (Rowe 1904; Willoughby 1905, 1909). Both Dean C. Worcester, professor of zoology at Michigan, and Bernard Moses, professor of history and political science at Berkeley, took up high posts in the Philippines. The head of the first Philippine Commission, charged with the task of going to the islands, reporting on it, and recommending policy to the U.S. government, was Jacob Schurman, president of Cornell University. Albert E. Jenks served as an ethnologist in the colonial administration in the Philippines and helped create the categories for the 1903 Philippine census.[13]

It is hard to imagine that American sociologists were immune to this new imperial culture. To be certain, the very first sociology dissertation was not about America's internal domestic issues or even European imperialism but about Hawaii. Titled "The Making of Hawaii: A Study in Social Evolution," the dissertation earned W. F. Blackman a doctorate from Cornell in 1893, the same year that the Hawaiian monarchy was overthrown by the United States after years of American meddling in the islands (Morgan 1982: 51). In his autobiography, Edward Ross noted that, while at Stanford in 1898, "the Spanish-American War and the gaudy new imperialism gave the public something fresh to think about" (1936: 69). Charles Cooley likewise responded to the imperial frenzy in 1898. He wrote in his journal that the war with Spain, resulting in the acquisition of the Philippines and Puerto Rico, "makes me proud of the race and the American stock" (Ross 1991: 242). And we know that Edward Ross, W. I. Thomas, Franklin Giddings, George Vincent, and Lester Ward were promoting sociology at the Congress of Arts and Science in St. Louis while outside the world's "primitive" peoples were put on display. Furthermore, leading sociologists were embedded in the new networks of imperial knowledge emanating from American universities. The second member of Minnesota's Department of Sociology and Anthropology was Albert E. Jenks, who had been serving in the Philippines and who had also organized the exhibit on the Igorots at the St. Louis fair. The *AJS* reviewed various books penned by their scholarly peers or colonial officials on the new American empire and colonial administration and published articles written by colonial officials returning from the field (e.g., Rowe and Willoughby).[14] Some sociologists even incorporated topics on the American empire into their teaching. At Nebraska, Ross held seminars comparing British rule in India with the U.S. occupation of Cuba and colonialism in the Philippines (Ross 1936: 93). The original sixteen courses in the Department of Sociology and Anthropology at Minnesota included a course on "The Philippine People" (Fine and Severance 1985: 118). At the University of Pennsylvania, Carl Kelsey offered a sociology course called "American Race Problems" that included "studies of the situation in the West Indies, Hawaii, and the Philippines" (Ng 1994: 135).

Firmly embedded within the larger imperial culture and network of imperial knowledge within the United States, America's sociologists did not need to turn to Europe to become interested in empire. In fact, Lester Ward suggested in 1896 that the knowledge acquired from America's imperial apparatus would be better for sociological research than the knowledge culled from the British empire. In his "Contributions to Social Philosophy: The Data of Sociology," Ward argued that ethnological data collected by the United States Bureau of Ethnology was more "scientific" than the data acquired on the "lower races" and subsequently used by British sociologists like Spencer. Therefore the "numerous able and voluminous reports of that bureau [the United States Bureau of Ethnology in the Study of the North American

Indians] constitute an invaluable resource for the sociologist who aims to found the science upon a broad ethnic basis" (Ward 1896: 751). In similar fashion, after the spate of new colonial acquisitions in the wake of 1898, W. I. Thomas suggested that the U.S. empire would continue to offer a fruitful field for sociological research. Reviewing two books on Philippine tribal peoples produced by Jenks and William Allen Reed (who were working under the new Ethnological Survey of the Philippines), Thomas wrote: "No government as such has done so much for the promotion of the early forms of society and the non-civilized races as the government of the United States, and these two volumes of the publications of the Ethnological Survey of the Philippines, we may hope, are the beginning of a series which will be of as much significance to science as the Reports of the Bureau of American Ethnology" (1905b: 273).

Various sociologists in the United States followed these leads, culling examples and data from the American empire for their work. Edward Reuter, a student of Robert Park at Chicago, conducted a study of various "mixed blood peoples" that used data from colonial censuses, military reports, and other official documents on "mixed blood peoples" in various American colonies: the Philippines, Cuba, Puerto Rico, and (the temporarily occupied) Santo Domingo (Reuter 1918: 55–71). Articles in the *AJS* focused exclusively on one or another colonial possession. Albert E. Jenks (1914) wrote about "assimilation" in the Philippines. Samuel MacClintock's "Around the Island of Cebu on Horseback" (1903) recounted the writer's trip around that Philippine island. Fay-Cooper Cole (1916) focused on Filipino culture to theorize animism and spirituality. W. B. Elkin (1902) conducted a demographic analysis of the Hawaiian people, while Ernest J. Reece (1914) studied "Race Mingling in Hawaii." Again, American sociology did not need to rely on Europe for its interest in empire. It was part of a nation that had its own empire, colonies, and colonized peoples.

Even if they did not write exclusively about one American colony or another, sociologists often referred to American colonialism overseas to support and elaborate their arguments. In articulating his theory of the dynamics of social association, Albion Small in 1900 referred not only to the colonial policies of Great Britain but also, as a parallel to Britain's colonial policies, to the ongoing Philippine-American War and "the early policy of our settlers toward the Indians" (1900b: 342–343). In addition, to articulate his notion of multiple causation, Small noted that an analysis of "the present condition of . . . the Philippines" would suitably serve for showing "special combinations" of explanatory forces (Small 1900a: 516–517). Weatherly's *AJS* article on "race and marriage" culled examples from Cuba, Puerto Rico, and the Philippines (Weatherly 1910). Alfred Stone's article on race theory referred to the racial attitudes of American soldiers in the Philippines (Stone 1908: 677–678). Some works even made explicit analogies or connections between pressing domestic issues and imperial issues abroad. W. I. Thomas's work on social psychology spoke of the issues surrounding the "contact of black and white in America" while making comparisons with contacts between Filipinos and Americans under colonialism (Thomas 1905a: 449). Max West's examination of the "Race Question" (1900) lamented the lack of good education for "Negroes" at home and called for special teaching schools where "the students would be chiefly of the darker race." He then suggested that such schools would train teachers who "intend to teach negroes or Indians or Filipinos, in the South or in Alaska, in Puerto Rico or in Hawaii" (254). Paul Monroe's theory of education discussed how education should be used not only to create citizens out of children, or to develop the "intelligence" of women, but also as a means of "raising backwards nations to full membership in the family of nations" (1913: 629). He made special note of the Philippines, where educational measures in the colonial public schools served for him as the "most instructive and creditable" example of the uses of education (Monroe 1913: 631). Albert E. Jenks's article on "assimilation" argued that U.S. imperialism would serve the mission of uplift abroad. American colonialism in the Philippines would help to "develop" the country and provide "sufficient tutelage in the fundamental principles of democracy" (1914: 791).

These and many more references to America's colonies or subject peoples were firmly embedded in America's rising imperial culture, drawing on and articulating with wider imperial discourses circulating in the United States at the time. In theorizing the causes of "race superiority," Edward Ross praised the "self-reliance," enterprising spirit, and technological genius of the Anglo-Saxon, forecasting that "nothing can check its triumphant expansion over the planet" (1901: 75).[15] This kind of discourse had been articulated in the halls of Congress, the jingoist press, and in pulpits across the country to justify American imperialism. Pro-expansionists argued that Anglo-Saxons were destined to "civilize" the world by their imperial hand because of their privileged history and superior traits (Kramer 2003). The sociologists' references also articulated with colonial governmentalities and discourses of administration. William Allen's (1903) theorization of a society's sanitation and health conditions as a mark of superior development was fitting in light of America's programs in the Philippines. Just as his essay was published in the *AJS*, the U.S. Army had engaged in a campaign of confining Filipinos to special villages in a widespread effort to control cholera. And colonial officials had begun reformist programs enlisting American medical doctors to teach the Filipinos better "habits" of sanitation and health (Anderson 1995a, 1995b; Ileto 1988). Similarly, Edward Ross's *AJS* article on "adult recreation as a social problem" theorized recreation in ways that paralleled and drew on American colonial officials' programs for "civilizing" the Filipinos. Just as the American officials aimed to uproot practices like gambling or cockfighting—seen as detrimental for producing efficient labors and good citizens—Ross's theory classified undesirable forms of recreation and suggested that they could be dealt with by a process he called "substitution": the "Filipinos are finding their excitement about the baseball diamond rather than cockpit," whereas "the Igorrotes [*sic*] of Luzon have learned to divert themselves with athletic contests and dancing instead of head-hunting" (1918: 527).

The sociologists' discourse also drew on and partook of heated debates about American empire itself, not least debates between pro-imperialist forces and anti-imperialist activists. The debate between Giddings and Sumner over imperialism is probably well known: Giddings was an ardent pro-imperialist, whereas Sumner took an anti-imperial stance (Giddings 1898; Sumner 1911; see also chapter 1). But several points are worth clarifying. First, the debate was about American imperialism, not European imperialism, as Giddings himself made clear in his 1898 essay "Imperialism?" and his book *Democracy and Empire* (cf. Kennedy and Centeno 2007). Second, amid the debate both Giddings and Sumner landed on arguments that prefigured rather than copied key arguments made by British thinkers. Anticipating the economic theory of imperialism registered by the Briton J. A. Hobson (which in turn influenced Lenin's theory of imperialism), Giddings argued that American imperialism would help the American economy (Giddings 1898: 591–592).[16] Sumner's critique of U.S. imperialism likewise predated Hobson's famous critique of British imperialism and made an argument that Hobson would later make, that is, that imperialism corrupts the imperial country. Taking foreign lands as colonies, Sumner warned in 1896, would mean that the new colonies would "become seats of corruption, which would react on our body politic" (1911: 291). New colonies would demand new expenses on the state and threaten America's "republican institutions" and democracy (Sumner 1911: 292; see also Barnes 1919a: 21). Finally, part and parcel with the debates, Giddings produced a larger theory about America's imperial role in the world and of global social development more broadly. In his 1900 book, *Democracy and Empire*, he theorized the future of imperialism as a benign and necessary one and that it would be led by Americans and Britons who would rule the world by creating a global "democratic empire." In Giddings's view, this was to be a benign global imperial state that was democratic not in the sense that it relied on elections but only in the sense that imperial rulers would benevolently respect local customs and traditions in exchange for "protection" and "order" (1900: 4). For Giddings, this "democratic empire" would be the necessary outcome of social evolution. Tying his claims to his earlier theory of association and resemblance, he posited that human societies were first formed based on racial homogeneity (or "resemblances" based on blood) but that ultimately, through long historical processes of development and interaction, a new unity based on ethics of liberty and law would transcend resemblances of blood. "Those countries which had become most free—namely, England and the United States"—would point the way toward this new unity (Giddings 1900: 9–12).

In short, for Giddings, and for the other American sociologists, American empire was itself of distinct concern. Rather than mirroring or blindly copying European sociological interests, they were interested in empire and imperialism because their own society had become a rising imperial power. Writing in the metropolitan center of that imperial power, and enmeshed in a wider popular culture of imperialism, they could not escape the dilemmas and debates over empire that surrounded them.

IMPERIAL ENDS

In light of all this, it might seem surprising that existing accounts of American sociology elide sociology's imperial orientation. But it is not so surprising when we consider what happened afterward. Traditional accounts of sociology's emergence—which abstract the early sociologists from their wider global context—were written in the decades after World War II. By that time, sociology had allegedly shifted its lens away from the global and imperial and toward the domestic (Connell 1997; Kennedy and Centeno 2007; Steinmetz 2007b; but see also Steinmetz 2009a).[17] Giddings's successors at Columbia realized Giddings's goal of a rigorous quantitative sociology to make Columbia's department unique (Camic and Xie 1994), but the data they used focused more and more on social relations internal to nation-states. Small's and Thomas's successors at Chicago focused on group contact but evacuated the global frame and instead looked at immigrant populations in the United States and developments in American cities (Yu 2001).[18] Sociologists in the 1930s and 1940s conducted studies of foreign societies but focused on their internal developments, for example, examining conditions within particular European states that produced totalitarianism and fascism (Kennedy and Centeno 2007). In the post–World War II period, Parsons's structural-functionalism and associated studies of "modernization" were applied to non-European countries but famously abstracted societal development from its global field (Gilman 2003; Taylor 1996). These trends were general to American sociology, as indexed by the decline in *AJS* articles using the terms "imperialism," "empire," "colonial," or "colonialism."

Explaining exactly why this retreat occurred is beyond the scope of this chapter. Surely the task would demand a consideration of multiple factors, from sociology's shifting place relative to other disciplines to patterns of funding. But keeping in line with the thrust of this chapter, an explanation for sociology's retreat from empire should surely consider the changing geopolitical context. First, anticolonial nationalism grew as never before during the first three decades of the twentieth century. The Japanese victory over Russia (1905) and the Xinhai Revolution in China (1911) signified to the colonial world that nonwhite peoples could determine their own destinies, and colonized elites everywhere became more and more critical of their masters (Furedi 1994: 27–28; Grimal 1978: 36–47). The reinscription of imperial boundaries by the Western powers after World War I further fueled anticolonial nationalism, as colonized groups who had served their colonial masters during the war felt that they were owed political autonomy (Grimal 1978: 4–36). Gandhian populism during the 1920s received global attention and the 1930s depression laid down the socioeconomic conditions for anticolonial protests across Asia, Africa, and the Caribbean (Easton 1964: 366–377; Fraser 1992: 108; Furedi 1994: 10–27; Holland 1985: 1–10).

Second, shifts in opinion about imperialism also occurred in the metropolitan centers themselves. Through the 1920s and 1930s, trade unions and liberals in Britain, France, Germany, and other European powers began to directly challenge the old imperial order, seeing it as no longer viable (Grimal 1978: 11; Howe 2002; Koebner and Schmidt 1964: 221). Many metropolitans in fact blamed imperialism for World War I (Koebner and Schmidt 1964: 281). In the United States, too, the earlier imperial enthusiasm began to subside as the century wore on. Woodrow Wilson had previously been a proud supporter of old-style imperialism and praised America's colonial annexations, but amid World War I he began to raise some doubts. Even before the war, the Democrats' presidential victory in 1912 served as a powerful portent. Unlike the Republican Party, which had unqualifiedly supported U.S. colonialism, the Democratic Party had been more divided. Accordingly, when it took power after 1912, it made new moves—however piecemeal—to slowly devolve political power to Filipinos and Puerto Ricans.

It is not unlikely that this changing geopolitical context had an impact on American sociology, just as it did other sectors of opinion (Connell 1997). At least this was the case for Giddings. Though he had previously believed in the continuance and development of benign democratic empires (a belief "buoyed by the outcome of the Spanish-American war"), and though he had worked to establish American support for a benevolent League of Nations, Giddings eventually became thoroughly disillusioned with the concept of democratic imperialism (Vidich and Lyman 1985: 119). By the time he penned *The Scientific Study of Human Society* ([1924] 1975), he was "no longer so sanguine about democratic empires." The First World War "had dashed many hopes for the spread of American democracy by means of imperialism" (Vidich and Lyman 1985: 124–125). It could be that other sociologists were likewise impacted. Given the rise of anticolonial nationalism, a range of new criticisms of imperialism from different sectors of world society, and the unleashing of imperial violence and war, the sociologists' belief that the earlier turn-of-the-century imperialism would continue unabated, that it would hasten "progress" and the development of subject societies, or that empires would lead to peaceful transnational structures guided by Anglo-Saxon power—all of this must have seemed much less palatable and much more untenable. If early sociology had banked much of its theory and research on the social relations and dynamics of empire, the new global developments as the century wore on likely bankrupted early sociology's imperial interests.

Still, the theoretical underpinnings of the earlier sociological work were not completely overthrown by the analytic retreat from matters imperial. Rather than a fundamental epistemic shift, the legacies of the prior analyses and schemes were carried into postwar American sociology—however in silent form. While statistics as a tool became dominant at Columbia and were used to analyze difference *within* the United States, we have seen that their use had been first promulgated by Giddings in his attempt to better understand global rather than domestic difference. While sociologists inspired by the Chicago School turned to issues of "assimilation" of immigrants into American political culture, we have seen how "assimilation" as a concept had originally been used to apply to the colonial world as much as to the metropole. For Ward, in fact, the only way in which "assimilation" occurs is through conquest of other peoples. In this sense, the concepts associated with the later Chicago School's study of culture contact within the

United States—some of them articulated by W. I. Thomas and Florian Znaniecki in *The Polish Peasant in Europe and America* (1918–1920)—carried the weight of the imperial past. Similarly, the postwar interest in structural-functional "modernization," however applied to postcolonial societies and however internalist, remained analytically homologous with the prior evolutionary perspective on "progress" and "development." Fittingly, modernization theory became tied more and more to American "informal" imperialism and its attempts to develop modern capitalist societies not through colonial rule but through trade, investment, and political aid to developing countries during the Cold War (Gilman 2003; Steinmetz 2007b; Taylor 1996). In short, American sociology shifted away from its imperial and global framework as the twentieth century proceeded. But its new modes of theory and research still carried the traces of a lingering and deep-rooted imperial unconscious.

NOTES

1. On the Congress and the papers there, see Rogers (1905).

2. For a good overview of the institutional development of American sociology, see Morgan (1982).

3. As Collins (1997) notes, although Connell purports to discuss American sociology, most of his examples are from European sociology, and his references to American sociologists mostly include Giddings and Ward. As is apparent in the chapters written by Steinmetz (chapter 1), Semyonov, Mogilner, and Gerasimov (chapter 2), and Santoro (chapter 4), the story looks very different once we extend our gaze to the German and Austrian, Russian, and Italian sociologists.

4. Lyman's analysis of Robert E. Park's writings, fully injected with concerns over imperialism and colonialism, suggests that Du Bois was not alone (Lyman 1992). Kennedy and Centeno (2007) help for thinking about the broad "international" concerns of American sociology in its early years; the only gap in their illuminating study is that they overlook the concerns of imperialism, which are different from simply "international" concerns. For an insightful discussion of the global imagination of historical sociology, see Magubane (2005).

5. Similarly, Weatherly's article in the *AJS* (1910) on the "racial element in assimilation" used examples from the colonial world rather than just examples of immigration to metropoles.

6. Similarly, Becker, in an older content analysis of themes in the *AJS* from 1895 to 1930, found enough content on colonial issues to make it a category for his examination (Becker 1932).

7. To be sure, before these events, Giddings had not listed empire or international conflict as among the "pressing questions of practical policy." In a speech to the American Social Science Association in 1894, he listed mainly domestic

issues as the most important ones for sociological research (Giddings 1894: esp. 146–147).

8. Fittingly, the imperial world was incorporated into some of their teaching. At Columbia, Giddings's lectures on political development were essentially a history of empires (Giddings 1907–1908). Ross gave lectures on "The British Empire" at Stanford in 1899, and at Nebraska he gave a postgraduate seminar on "Colonies and Colonization" (Ross 1936: 71, 93).

9. To be clear, this was not only a matter of immigration for Ward. Vidich and Lyman (1985) take quotes from Ward's *Applied Sociology* to mean he was referring to nonwhite immigration to America, but those quotes make no explicit mention of immigration and instead refer to Western imperial expansion (Ward 1906: 107–108).

10. For starters, see Small's introduction in the inaugural issue of the *AJS* (Small 1895).

11. As quoted in Ng (1994: 125). The literature on America's imperial culture at the time is massive, but see, besides Ng (1994), Kaplan (2005); Kaplan and Pease (1993); and earlier work by May (1968) and Williams (1980).

12. See, for example, Burgess (1899, 1900); Reinsch (1904, 1905, 1907); and Wilson (1901).

13. For more on these academics and officials, see Go (2008a).

14. Some of the writers of those books, along with former colonial officials, also participated at the Congress of Arts and Sciences in St. Louis. They had been invited by Small's organizing committee to discuss such matters as "Colonial Administration" and the "development and history of the colonies" (Rogers 1905).

15. But see Steinmetz (2009a) on Small's anticolonial and antiracist turn after 1910.

16. As Etherington (1984) shows, Lenin's Marxist theory of imperialism drew heavily on Hobson's earlier work published in 1902. In turn, Hobson and Lenin cited American business journals surrounding the Spanish-American War of 1898 for their evidence: in other words, the Marxist theory of imperialism was invented by American businesses urging colonization as a way to deal with overproduction. Etherington, however, overlooks the fact that sociologists such as Giddings published similar ideas before Hobson.

17. It is suggestive that while internalist accounts of early American sociology proliferated beginning in the 1960s, discussions of early American sociology before and surrounding World War II were more cognizant that early American sociology had global and international themes. Becker's (1932) content analysis of *AJS* themes made "colonialism" one of his analytic categories, and Odum's (1951) discussion of early American sociological thought noted how sociology had been concerned with "intercultural relations" on the "international" level and in the context of empire.

18. Though Robert Park became one of these prominent Chicago Schoolers, his journalistic writings at the turn of the century focused on imperialism and race issues in Africa (Lyman 1992).

FOUR

Empire for the Poor

Imperial Dreams and the Quest for an Italian Sociology, 1870s–1950s

MARCO SANTORO

We speak to-day of North American Imperialism, of German Imperialism, of French Imperialism; soon we shall speak of Japanese or Chinese Imperialism.... Imperialism . . . has but one meaning: the effort towards the creation of an Empire by warlike conquest or economic expansion; economics being the modern and attenuated form of the vital struggle. The word Imperialism has then again enlarged its pretensions, and has annexed, so to speak, new verbal provinces. It has been employed in retrospective fashion by M. Guglielmo Ferrero, the eminent Italian sociologist, to characterize the governmental procedure of ancient Rome.

—*THE GERMAN DOCTRINE OF CONQUEST: A FRENCH VIEW*, by E. Seilliere. *With an Essay on M. Seilliere's Philosophy of Imperialism*, by J. M. Hone, 1914

INTRODUCTION

As in other Western countries, in Italy the new intellectual discipline labeled as "sociology" by many of its practitioners as well as its detractors appeared and began its striving for academic recognition in the same juncture that Western imperialism and colonialism were profoundly reshaping global geopolitics (Connell 1997). To be sure, the first publication in Italian including the word "sociology" in its title saw light just four years after the recognition of Italy as an autonomous state (Bertinaria 1865), while the first *corso libero* (i.e., private academic course) of "Social Science" or "Sociology" was established at the University of Turin in 1874, when Italians were still figuring out how to organize their recently unified country. But within a very few years, those same Italians—or a small elite among them—were ready to project their deeply felt nationalistic aspirations for unification out of themselves and beyond the limited boundaries of the peninsula. The social sciences, including the newborn sociology, have been neither alien nor indifferent to these projects—in many ways, indeed, these disciplines directly contributed to their ideation as well as justification.

Chronologically, colonialism and sociology run in parallel in Italy. The first Commissione per le colonie was appointed by the Italian government to study, discuss, and assess the many proposals about colonial expansion already advanced by politicians and scholars in the same year, 1871, that Cesare Lombroso, soon to become the father of the Italian school of criminal sociology, was lecturing on the origins and varieties of the human races (Lombroso 1871).[1] The first Italian colony was established in Africa (at Assab, on the Red Sea) in the same year—1882—that a young Gaetano Mosca, just graduated in law, published his very first article focused on "the factors of nationality" (1882) and a few months after publication of the Italian translation of Herbert Spencer's *The Study of Sociology* (1881; see also Boccardo 1881; Sergi 1881). The first Italian journal consecrated to sociology— the *Rivista di sociologia*, announced by its founding editors as "the second in the world," after the French *Revue international de sociologie*, launched by René Worms—began publishing in 1894, the same year in which France conquered Madagascar, England took Uganda, and Italy tried to conquer, without success, Ethiopia. And the second journal—the long lasting *Rivista italiana di sociologia* (*RIS*) (1897–1921)—was launched just one year after the humiliating defeat of Adwa (1896), which stopped the Italian quest for an African empire for a while.[2] Still, the publication of Vilfredo Pareto's *Trattato di sociologia generale* (1916), the monumental and arguably most influential contribution from Italy to the rising discipline, emerged only five years after the war in which Italy gained Libya from the Ottoman Empire. Interestingly, Libya was declared an Italian colony, and the Dodecanese Islands were recognized as falling under Italy's sphere of influence, just two years after the founding of the first, and short-lived, national sociological association, the Italian Society of Sociology (1910). The discipline finally entered the Italian academic system as an official teaching field in a few undergraduate courses—a process that began in 1924 and was still ongoing in 1936 (Carli 1925a: 193; Castrilli 1941: 14–15)—as the Italian army was fighting against the Libyan resistance and Albania was becoming a de facto Italian protectorate (with Italy playing a key role in endorsing and sustaining the rule of King Zog).[3] Turned Fascist, Italians eventually invaded and conquered Ethiopia, creating the conditions for the establishment of the much longed for Italian Empire (1938), in exactly the same year that a new Italian Society of Sociology was founded and organized thanks to the efforts of the influential statistician, demographer, and sociologist Corrado

Gini, surely the most internationally reputed social scientist of the Fascist era (see Horn 1994; Ipsen 1993) and a strong believer in the necessity of Italian colonial expansion against the will of the established imperial powers.

One does not need much (sociological) imagination to guess that some relation between the developing field of sociology and imperialism as both a doctrine and practice was extant in Italy as it was in France, Great Britain, Germany, and the United States (Connell 1997, 2007; Steinmetz 2009a; see also chapter 3). But which kind of relation(s) exactly? Under which conditions, and with which effects, did these relations work? Which intellectual groups established and cultivated or criticized them? And how did these relations evolve and change in intensity or in direction? Such questions are neither so rhetorical nor so obvious as might seem prima facie.

Indeed, it is the meaning and identity of an "Italian imperialism" that is partly at stake here. Italian imperialism has never been so daring and successful as the British, French, German, or even the U.S. ones (Lenin famously described it as "ragamuffin imperialism," closely following highly influential Italian sources[4]), and this is a circumstance worth considering when assessing the impact of colonialism and imperial politics on Italian sociology (for recent assessments on Italian colonialism, see Andall and Duncan 2005; Ben-Ghiat 2008; Ben-Ghiat and Fuller 2005; Labanca 2002). As the epigraph introducing this chapter suggests, an "Italian imperialism" is something that many will not readily acknowledge, even less readily than the Chinese or Japanese varieties. Even today, when empire and Italy come together, very often the referent is not so much modern imperialism as the memory and legacy of the ancient Roman Empire. The weak symbolic force and reputation of a specifically modern form of Italian imperialism is not, however, a good reason for overlooking colonialism as a cultural matrix of behaviors, institutions, and ideas in contemporary Italy. On the contrary, it is the peculiarities of colonialism and imperialism in modern Italy, the fact of their being so poorly understood or even misrecognized in spite of their roots in ancient history, that are puzzling and deserve investigation.

Still, as a transnational culture, imperialism's influence could have an impact well beyond the limits of its practical implementation in an individual state. This would be enough to justify the study and evaluation of imperialism's impact on Italian culture, too. But this is not all. Imperialism, as we know, can strongly affect intellectual fields, whether it is linked to an aggressive politics of economic and cultural expansion (as in the British or the French cases) or to a defensive politics of internal consolidation and consensus building (as in the Italian case, especially in its liberal phase).

As political and cultural historians have shown in recent years, Italian colonialism differed from other European and U.S. imperialism in a few respects that are worth noting in this context. First, there is the country's backwardness with respect to the other national powers, which not only made prestige instead of economic gain a central concern for both elites and ordinary citizens but also made Italy a nation of emigrants rather than conquerors. Italian colonialism was, in fact, in large part, a response to the phenomenon of mass emigration, and imperialism was more a demographic than an economic or even political strategy. This was a common feature of both liberal and Fascist colonialism. During the Fascist regime, colonies were commonly seen as a means for retrieving emigrated Italians to the motherland—an expectation that merged with the more traditional claiming of foreign lands and seas as a means of economic and political expansion. This "diasporic quality" of the Italian nation calls for a treatment of Italian imperialism that goes beyond linear exchanges between colony and metropole in order to include "relations among the Italian metropole, Italian colonies, and Italians who lived abroad under a variety of national and imperial sovereignties" (Ben-Ghiat 2008: 265).

Another feature that marks Italy off from other colonial powers is the Italian Empire's demise in the wake of Italian defeat in World War II, first through military invasion (both in the metropole and the colonies) and then through diplomatic decision. The demise of the empire in the first years after the war was experienced as an injury to national pride, not only by ex- or neo-Fascists but also by the anti-Fascist political forces, from liberals to leftists, all of whom agreed in their claim to retain their earlier colonies. In fact, Italy not only did not experience any real process of decolonization, but the kind of "external decolonization" (Andall and Duncan 2005) that it had to support—and which prevented Italian from remaining the official language in some of Italy's former colonies—produced a legacy of scorn and humiliation that for many years has made it difficult to have any real debate about the economic, political, and moral costs of Italian imperialism. This lack of discussion and even research is particularly consequential as Italian colonialism, its backwardness and poorness notwithstanding, was often a testing ground for military technologies and colonial violence, especially for the use of chemical and aerial warfare.

The third feature that marks Italian imperialism is the direct heritage of what is for many the first true imperial experience in the history of the Western world, that is, the ancient Roman Empire, seen in both its rise and decline: a cultural and symbolic legacy that impacted not only governing elites and ordinary citizens, fostering their dreams and contributing to their vocabularies of motives and justifications, but also scholars and disciplines—an effect that was understandably stronger and more consequential in Italy than elsewhere. As noticed by a specialist, "perhaps only in Italy was ancient Rome a genuine spur to empire: one of the impulses toward Fascism in politics, and to Italian futurism in the arts, was a sense of humiliation at the degeneration of land of the Caesars into a museum for contemporary foreigners" (Jenkyns 1992: 31; see also Gentile 1999; Visser 1992).

These peculiarities of Italian imperialism call for a specific investigation of its effects on, or better its entanglement with, the Italian social sciences, and with sociology in particular. In Italy, the "big issues" colonial adventures were called on to address and eventually solve were unemployment and emigration, rather than market expansion and resource exploitation. Both topics, unemployment and emigration, are of clear and immediate sociological interest. Also in Italy, imperialism acted on the intellectual field as a source of both moral tensions and knowledge demands (Are 1985; Lanaro 1979). But it additionally worked as a utopian scenario for deeply rooted dreams of renaissance in the name of an ancient imperial greatness, which in the long run proved in fact overshadowing.

As it is clear, what is at stake here is the degree and form of embeddedness of a new and contested discipline in a much larger cultural matrix, roughly identifiable as imperialistic, whose assumptions and cognitive schemata could shape the research practices and modes of knowing of its practitioners (Connell 1997, 2007). Of course, structural influences of this kind could operate even if particular sociologists were—as many indeed were—consciously anti-imperialist or indifferent with respect to colonial policy. It is not simply a matter of individual endorsement or contrast but of systemic or field effects. This chapter thus will not so much dwell at the level of individual intentions (see Steinmetz 2009b) but rather will portray the broader institutional and cultural configuration through which sociology and imperialism got intertwined in the decades in which sociology was developing in Italy, that is, roughly between 1870 and the postwar period, moving from its predisciplinary to disciplinary phases (Goudsblom and Heilbron 2001.)

To formulate more clearly our questions: how, how much, and with what consequences was the emergence of sociology as a discipline in Italy affected by the wider imperial context into which it grew as a national intellectual field among other national fields equally in the making? And what effects did this cultural embeddedness have on Italian sociology as a nationally bounded intellectual as well as academic disciplinary field? Questions like these are seldom if ever addressed by existing histories of Italian sociology, which typically focus on decontextualized intellectual endeavors (and intentions) in the genre of the traditional history of ideas or, increasingly in recent times, on relations between ideas and infranational events and processes, usually marked by dramatic political episodes, such as unification and the rise of the socialist movement or fascism, or by significant intellectual trends, such as the turn toward idealism with the rising star of Benedetto Croce from the dawn of the twentieth century (Bellamy 1987). Even when the focus is on intellectual movements strongly linked to colonialism and imperialism—as nationalism in fact is—attention is firmly given to internal affairs without considering the global context in which they occur. In this perspective, nationalism is seen as related to sociology only as a prelude to the rise of fascism, while its institutional and intellectual links with colonial doctrines and imperialistic culture or policies are largely overlooked, with the result that the histories of Italy and its sociology may look even more peripheral or provincial than they were.

Nevertheless, a careful eye on the sources (both personal and institutional) would surely suggest that imperialism as a doctrine and as a perspective or frame of mind was not absent from the conceptual and intellectual framework of Italian (would-be and actual) sociologists, and that colonial concerns defined all but a small part of their disciplinary agenda. Imperialism surely contributed to shape their general outlook, especially as they needed to locate the present and the national in a longer and wider context—for instance, in encouraging them to look at the glorious Roman history or at contemporary "primitive" societies as sources of data and natural laboratories.

In this chapter I focus on the scholars considered to be the pioneers of Italian sociology and its early practitioners (that is, internationally renowned scholars, including Vilfredo Pareto, Gaetano Mosca, and Enrico Ferri, and lesser-known ones, such as Giuseppe Sergi, Napoleone Colajanni, Achille Loria, Enrico Morselli, Francesco Cosentini, Alfredo Niceforo, Scipio Sighele, Guglielmo Ferrero, Francesco Coletti, Giovanni Lorenzoni, and Corrado Gini) and on articles published in the discipline's main early journal, the RIS (1897–1921). I will thus try to document and assess whether and in which ways colonialism and imperialism as cultural structures and sources of practical concerns were entangled with the practices of social research and social theory that have constituted Italian sociology as an intellectual field and, later, as an academic discipline (on this distinction, see Goudsblom and Heilbron 2001; Heilbron 2004).

A first, necessary step toward this endeavor, however, is a discussion of sociology as it appeared and developed in Italy, a country where "one might suppose that sociology would have had a special warm reception" and "would be extensively cultivated," for "no other country had a more promising tradition in this area of thought" since Machiavelli, Vico, Beccaria, and Romagnosi. But as the writer of these claims had to acknowledge, sociology was in Italy, at least at the time of his writing in the 1930s, "at best a sort of academic stepchild" (Crawford 1948: 554). Contemporary sociologists could have a still more pessimistic view, as Italy is today far from being acknowledged as a center of sociological production—although from Italy comes at least one of the great twentieth-century classics of the discipline, Vilfredo Pareto. So what exactly is "Italian sociology," and how did it come to light, develop, and possibly disappear or decay?

ITALIAN SOCIOLOGY AS AN INTELLECTUAL AND ACADEMIC FIELD

According to Levine (1995: 231), the "most consequential Italian contribution to the sociological tradition" appeared relatively late on the scene, that is, after Marx's reception toward the end of nineteenth century ("it is post-Marxian"). We have to wait, in other words, for the writings of Mosca and Pareto to find, according to Levine, a consequential contribution to sociology in Italy—that is, a contribution whose effect on the sociological tradition could be described as nonnegligible.[5]

Indeed, Marx is hardly the only foreign influence we have to consider if we want to get a full picture of what was really happening in Italy around "sociology" or anything this word could mean in those earlier days. Indeed, Spencer was a much greater influence than Marx on the making of an Italian tradition of sociology. It would be difficult to say what would have been Mosca's and Pareto's contributions to sociology without the heavy influence on Italian culture from Spencer and, in minor tone, Comte and all their followers. Spencer's evolutionism also had an impact through the early reception of Darwin. Even if both Mosca and Pareto set aside this influence when working on their major texts (respectively, *Elementi di scienza politica* and the *Trattato di sociologia generale*), the positivistic and evolutionist mediation was still crucial in their intellectual biographies as well as in their intellectual objectives: to discover the natural laws of social life through historical and ethnographical observation (in the case of Mosca) or through logical-analytical thinking applied to both classical and modern history (in the case of Pareto).[6] Internal sources were at least as important as foreign ones: from Machiavelli to Giambattista Vico, from Gian Domenico Romagnosi to Carlo Cattaneo, early Italian sociologists could rely upon an indigenous tradition of social thought still alive at midcentury and especially strong in the field of politics and economics (including statistics, one of the most cultivated social sciences in nineteenth-century Italy; Patriarca 1995).

Italian sociology was also a much more densely peopled field than any selective reference to a few still reputed scholars would suggest. A look at textbooks and journals published in Italy at the end of the nineteenth century and the early decades of the twentieth would suggest that we need to greatly enlarge the field of Italian sociology well beyond the traditional references to Mosca, Pareto, or even Gramsci—who never identified himself, to be sure, as a sociologist, but was on the contrary very keen to keep distance in his writings from any possible charge of doing the typically positivistic, and often uncultivated, brand of knowledge that was considered sociology in Italy at his time. To be minimally informative and representative of what was indeed the effective status of sociology in Italy at the time, a list of self-claimed Italian sociologists or social scientists who had gained some fame in Italy and abroad—mainly in France but sometimes also in the United States—should include at least criminologists like Lombroso and his followers Ferri, Ferrero, Sighele, and Niceforo (Gibson 2002); the social psychologist Pasquale Rossi; the physician and moral statistician Morselli (the author among other things of an impressive comparative study on suicide, which Durkheim often quotes, albeit critically, in his classic book; Morselli 1879); moral philosophers with strong sociological interests and knowledge, including Cosentini, Icilio Vanni, and Alessandro Groppali; economists such as Loria and Lorenzoni; demographers and criminologists including Colajanni; sui generis Social Darwinists like Michelangelo Vaccaro; and professed statisticians such as Francesco Coletti, Augusto Bosco, Corrado Gini, and Franco Savorgnan, the latter a former student of the Polish-Austrian sociologist Ludwig Gumplowicz. Even if professionally an anthropologist, Giuseppe Sergi (a source of Veblen's leisure class theory) should probably be included in such a list as a central figure in both the reception of Spencerian sociology and in the life of early Italian sociological journals—together with the many scholars who taught in various ways something called "sociology," writing about it (and on it) continuously in the decades between the 1870s and 1940s. Even without an official chair in sociology—to find the first one in Italy we have to look at the period after 1945—many of these scholars contributed to the academic cultivation and possibly legitimation of the new discipline, making it more than a purely intellectual pursuit.

Indeed, it was an early student of Sergi, Alfredo Niceforo—also a follower of Lombroso and Ferri as a criminologist (Gibson 1998)—who represented Italy at the Paris Exposition of 1900 for the field of sociology (Ward 1901). The same Niceforo appears, together with Sighele (the latter also with an excerpt), Rossi, Enrico Ferri, Guglielmo Ferrero, and some others (but, interestingly, neither Pareto nor Michels), among the few Italian scholars quoted or referred to in the "Green Bible" of American sociology, the Park and Burgess textbook first published in 1921. In Sorokin's classic overview of contemporary sociological schools (1928), we find the names of Mosca and Pareto but also Rossi, Vaccaro, Carli, and, above all, Gini, discussed in a long section of an important chapter.[7] If we consider that Italian sociology as an intellectual discipline had at least four dedicated journals between the last decade of the nineteenth and the middle of twentieth century,[8] and that none of them were founded or edited by the three renowned elitists (Mosca, Pareto, Michels) whose contributions to these journals can be counted on fewer than the fingers of two hands, we have an idea of what is missing in the common picture of the "Italian sociological tradition."

As a matter of fact, neither Mosca nor Pareto ever taught sociology—at least in Italy (Pareto taught sociology for a few semesters in Lausanne and held a course in Bologna, on invitation by a local academician, for a few weeks in 1905; Mosca was for all his academic life professor in constitutional law and then history of political thought and only occasionally taught economics). Entered into the Italian university in the 1870s through so-called *corsi liberi*, that is, optional classes that had legal value even if taught by people without a chair in that discipline, sociology became a compulsory teaching field in the new faculties of political sciences promoted by the Fascist regime after 1923. But even in this situation, a scholar such as Michels— who had left socialism to become a fascist devotee if not ideologue (Beetham 1977)—was called on to teach economics and not sociology (although he did give a course in political sociology for one year in Rome, after leaving Switzerland; Michels 1927). During the interwar period, the man who could be identified even abroad as the most influential and authoritative sociologist in Italy, Corrado Gini, was officially a professor in another discipline (statistics) and not an academic sociologist.

Of course, this is not without effect on the analytic construction of something like a sociological "field," conceived of in Bourdieusian terms as a space of intellectual production and competition. It is hard to argue that such a field existed in Italy before the 1950s, especially if we underline the criterion of autonomy as the crucial one for a field to exist (e.g., Bourdieu

2001; Steinmetz 2009b) and identify this autonomy with the presence of an established academic structure, including chairs, professional associations, official educational titles, and, above all, a self-conscious body of practitioners defending the boundaries of their discipline. Assessed from this point of view, sociology in Italy is to be treated more as a subfield of some other established academic field—the economic one, or the statistical one (e.g., Prévost 2002), or maybe the juridical one—or of some recently formed intellectual movement—for example, the eugenic—than as a field in itself, and this until a few decades ago. As a subfield located at the intersection of wider and stronger fields, sociology should probably be conceived of, and studied, as contingent on the crucial events and typical dynamics of other fields. But this would give too much to the latter, be they already established fields like economics or statistics, which entered the Italian academic system in the 1870s, or fashionable and transient ones like eugenics, and would lose something relevant in the history of sociology in Italy. Indeed, there are good reasons to argue that sociology in Italy had a life of its own and that the weak academic infrastructure should not prevent us from seeing it.

What disciplines meant in the context of still relatively undifferentiated knowledge systems is something that cannot be established in advance according to some present (and presentist) criteria. Take, for instance, the case of demography, which like sociology entered the academic system as a fully autonomous discipline only after World War II (even later than sociology). Almost all of the early practitioners of sociology manifested deep interest and devoted strong attention in their work to population issues (see, e.g., Carli 1919; Colajanni 1909; Gini 1912a, 1930a, 1931; Loria 1882; Niceforo 1925; Pareto 1896; Savorgnan 1918; Vanni 1886; Virgilii 1924; see also Fiamingo 1895; Michels 1934; Sorokin 1928). Indeed, the intersection of sociology and demography was so wide in postunification Italy, and the population problem so politically hot, that in the Fascist period the two disciplines, or maybe better the two forms of knowledge, almost merged—a disciplinary fusion made possible by the cyclopic, and encyclopedic, presence of Corrado Gini, the statistician, demographer, and sociologist whose intellectual power during the regime is hard to overrate (Cassata 2006a; Horn 1994; Ipsen 1992). Why Italian scholars—on the left as on the right—were so attracted to the study of population is not difficult to explain: as a country with both an excess of population with respect to economic resources and a strong religious, that is, Catholic, identity, Italy was at the same time marked by heavy emigration flows and deep moral concerns about population control, which expressed itself also in strong and early involvement with the eugenic movement, also from the socialist camp (Bosc 2000; Cassata 2006b; Mantovani 2004). The Italian delegation at the First International Congress of Eugenics (held in London, 1912) witnesses the wide overlap of this intellectual movement with the burgeoning field of sociology in Italy: all but one participant was involved personally in the making of sociology.[9] But what this means in terms of disciplinary autonomy cannot be decided without considering the status of these other forms of knowledge. Indeed, like sociology, demography did not exist in the official topography of academic disciplines, and it was only in 1962— that is, twelve years after the establishment of the first chair in sociology— that a chair in demography was created (and occupied by the foremost student of Gini, i.e., Nora Federici).

Conceiving of sociology as the most general social science, according to the Comtean legacy, was not only very common in Italy (as elsewhere) still in the 1930s but also not the most effective strategy for establishing its autonomy as an academic discipline. Even self-proclaimed and recognized supporters of sociology, such as Raffele Garofalo (the first president of the first Italian association of sociology founded in 1912), thought that sociology as a general science had to become not a specialized discipline to be taught in universities; chairs in sociology would have been redundant (Garofalo 1906). But this would also make sociology an intrinsically expansionist form of knowledge, attracting ambitious and entrepreneurial scholars as well as mavericks and undisciplined intellectuals (or would-be intellectuals).[10]

As many studies have argued in the past, sociology had a troubled existence in Italy. Following a very successful phase (circa 1880–1910)—successful especially in terms of editorial enterprises and intellectual debates—it suffered an apparent decline, which persisted during all of the Fascist period. It was only after World War II—and, we should add, in the context of increasing Italian insertion in the U.S. imperial context—that sociology, so the story goes, really institutionalized itself in Italian university and culture. The first permanent, official chair in sociology dates back only to 1950 (with Pellizzi in Florence), and it is only in the 1960s that a professional sociology emerged in Italy (see Barbano 1998; Barbano and Sola 1985; Treves 1959, 1987). This story has some truth, but it could be accepted only at the price of many simplifications and some negations or neglect. In a certain sense, it is the foundational myth on which current Italian sociology is grounded since the 1950s. What recent studies by sociologists and cultural historians are clearly discovering and arguing is that the seeds of this institutionalization were sown during the Fascist era, with the full consent of the regime (Breschi and Longo 2003; Cassata 2006a; Garzia 1998; Losito and Segre 1991;

Padovan 1999; but see also Lentini 1974, 1983). Suffice to say that both Corrado Gini and Camillo Pellizzi—the two most influential and academically powerful academic scholars active as sociologists in the early years after World War II—were intellectually and politically strongly involved in the Fascist regime, the former as the president of the Istituto nazionale di statistica since its inception in 1926 through 1932, the latter as the president of the Istituto nazionale di cultura fascista, and both as direct and influential advisers of Benito Mussolini. The first permanent chair in the discipline in Italy—that of Pellizzi—originated from the administrative transformation of his early chair in *Storia e dottrina del fascismo* (history and doctrine of fascism) into a chair in sociology, in 1950. Though academically a statistician—that is, a professor of statistics—Gini taught sociology since 1926 and still in 1958, at the Faculty of Statistics he founded in Rome, in the capital's state university (La Sapienza). Visiting professor in the 1930s in the department of sociology of many universities abroad (including Minnesota, Chicago, and Harvard), he was not only the founder of the Società Italiana di sociologia (Italian Society of Sociology) in 1936 but also the president of the renewed Institut international de sociologie (founded by René Worms in 1892) from 1950 to 1962.

As the biography of Gini testifies, the common interpretation of the history of sociology in Italy as a story of progressive decline until an almost complete disappearance under Mussolini is more a myth for the post-Fascist generations than a solid rendering of the life of sociology and social research between the two world wars. In a certain sense, sociology gained stronger support from Mussolini and his administrative machine than it enjoyed under the previous, liberal governments. This is particularly true if we consider sociology as a policy and even public science (Burawoy 2004) rather than as a critical or even professional one.

It is therefore safer to consider sociology in liberal and Fascist Italy as a "field in the making" (Ferguson 1998), that is, as a microcosm without clear boundaries and not very high stakes (no chairs or faculty positions), but where conflicts were fought anyway, and hierarchies built and reproduced, making use of resources often drawn from other fields—the political field included. The degree of autonomy of this field in the making is, as usual, a matter of empirical research, not of theoretical statement, and should be measured and assessed after considering that social scientists contribute with their ideas and programs to the cultural legitimation of political actors, including parties and governments. As we will see, the participation of scholars who identified themselves as sociologists, or were identified as such by their contemporaries or successors, to the forging of national politics—including foreign policies—has been great, much greater that any assessment based only on academic grounds could suggest. At the same time, it is useful to remember that intellectual production is always contingent also on local institutional frameworks and settings and that different frameworks also mean different conditions of intellectual production and intellectual legitimation (Camic 1995; Camic and Gross 2001). This factor of localism should be incorporated into the study of the history of the social sciences not only for explaining differences in the establishment of a certain discipline among different academic institutions in the same country, as Camic did for sociology in the United States (Camic 1995), but also for accounting for different patterns of institutionalization in different countries. It would be naive to judge the status of Italian sociology independently, for example, of a consideration of the institutional structure and functioning of the Italian academic system. Simply put, you cannot in Italy (as in France or Germany, for that matter) establish a chair in whatever discipline if this discipline has not previously been recognized by the government and introduced by law in the official, that is, state-backed, system of disciplines. What you can do is to establish locally the discipline as a secondary or complementary subject within a certain academic institution, say, one of the *facoltà* (that is, schools) at the University of Turin or of Naples, and teach it yourself as a complementary teaching field or give it to some other teacher—including those who have not (yet) won a professorship but have gained the title to act as the Italian equivalent of German *Privatdozent*—that is, *liberi docenti* (private teachers and outside lecturers). This is what almost all the scholars you will find in these pages did.

It would be useful also to distinguish between academic institutionalization and academic cultivation (Shils 1970). Even if not all the scholars who contributed to sociology in Italy were based in the academic system, the vast majority were—even if occupying different chairs. Those who were not academically based in Italy usually held some position, or title, in a foreign university—chiefly among those the Université nouvelle de Bruxelles—or in some cultural institution with strong academic links, such as the Institut international de sociologie in Paris. Many of those scholars were affiliated with some academy, be it locally based or national. Still more important for assessing the status of sociology in Italy, I believe, is that a vast majority of these scholars had positions in political parties and/or in public institutions, including the Parliament and even the government. Many of them were recruited as experts in official committees engaged in different subjects, from statistics to emigration, from justice to agriculture and work. The fact that sociology was not recognized in Italy as a full academic discipline worthy of chairs until after 1945 and as a discipline worthy of special teaching programs and educational credentials until the end of the 1960s, does not mean that sociology in Italy was absent or that it did not matter in the public sphere or academic debate. Indeed, attempts to introduce chairs of sociology had been made many times, even with support from scholars already well established in other disciplines.[11] The fact that these attempts were not successful could mean that the barriers against sociology were higher and stronger in Italy than elsewhere, while the fact that sociology has continued to be practiced, this resistance notwithstanding, could mean that the Italian academic organization of disciplines was loose enough to permit a demographer, a statistician, a moral philosopher, or an economist to practice (and even sometimes to teach) sociology alongside his main discipline. Seen from this point of view, the status of sociology in Italy could be assessed only comparatively—with respect not only to other countries but also to other disciplines in the same country.

Of course, this does not mean to neglect, as Shils put it, that sociology

is more institutionalized where it can be studied as a major subject than where it can be studied only as an adjunct subject, where it has a specialized teaching staff of its own rather than teachers who do it only as a *Nebenfach*, where there are opportunities for the publication of sociological works in sociological journals rather than in journals devoted primarily to other subjects, where there is financial, administrative, and logistic provision for sociological investigation through established institutions rather than from the private resources of the investigator, where there are established and remunerated opportunities for the practice of sociology (teaching and research), and where there is a "demand" for the results of sociological research. (1970: 765)

To become a "major subject" taught by a "specialized staff of its own," Italian sociology—like every discipline and intellectual profession—had to gain the support of the state and possibly of other already established disciplines such as history, philosophy, and law, the greatest and stronger enemies of sociology as an academic discipline in Italy (Bobbio 1969). However, as the history of Italian sociology shows, not all these conditions or factors of institutionalization go together, and it is clearly possible to have journals specialized in sociology and well-established sociological book series, to have financial resources for doing sociological research (or something that could easily be recognized as such) as well as a "demand" for its results, even in the absence of specialized teaching staff or devoted chairs.

Looking at the various ways in which self-proclaimed "sociologists" became consciously and unconsciously entangled with colonial politics and with the colonized populations they studied could be an opportunity also to address with fresh eyes the old question of scientific autonomy and cultural status of sociology in liberal and Fascist Italy.

COLONIALISM, IMPERIALISM, AND ITALIAN SOCIOLOGY

To be sure, imperial and colonial issues were directly addressed, with articles and books visibly and totally devoted to the subject, by only a few of these early practitioners of sociology. Titles like *Politica coloniale* (Colajanni 1891), *Il sentimento imperialista* (Amadori-Virgilij 1905), and *L'imperialismo Italiano* (Michels 1914)—just to quote the most obvious examples—are notable for being exceptions in a large body of sociological production. Although styled in futuristic language and intentionally devoid of any scientific claim, Mario Morasso's *Imperialismo artistico* (1903) could be included in this short list, at least given the peculiar status of the author, a literary man with a brief past as a philosopher of law acquainted with both the German tradition of social research (the same that produced Simmel's seminal essay on the metropolis) and the Italian, that is, Lombroso's, school of criminology (Lanaro 1979: 38–40; Serra Zanetti 1976). A pupil of Lombroso who later became his son-in-law, Guglielmo Ferrero could equally be included, first, as the author of a five-volume narrative of the Roman Empire from its rise to its decline—a work that at the time of its publication knew a clamorous success both in Italy and abroad but that was not enough to help its author gain a chair in the Italian university. Ferrero also authored a book of conferences on (or, better, against) militarism, in which the criticism of the ongoing Italian colonial adventure is embedded in a Spencerian framework centered on the tenet of a necessary evolution from the ancient military society to the modern industrial one (Ferrero 1898, 1902–1907).

Though sociologically informed, Ferrero's and Morasso's writings were barely recognized as sociology by contemporary readers—even if they could be considered as such by a present reader.[12] For this reason I prefer to focus on authors who are more clearly identified as sociologists by their contemporaries.

A physician turned statistician, a discipline he taught at the University of Naples since 1891 (after 1901 as full professor), the Sicilian Napoleone

Colajanni (1847–1921) was a true pioneer of Italian sociology as well as one of the first Italian theorists of socialism (Frétigné 2002, 2007). A harsh critic of Lombroso's school of anthropological criminology, he devoted the greatest part of his work as a sociologist to the development of an alternative criminal sociology emphasizing the causal role of social and political conditions against race and climate. The author of dozens of books —including *Il socialismo* (1885), the monumental *Sociologia criminale* (1889), and *Razze inferiori e razze superiori: Latini e Anglosassoni* (1903)—and hundreds of articles in newspapers, magazines, and scientific journals, Colajanni was a strong and systematic critic of Italian colonialism and imperialism since its inception in the 1880s. Issued in the wake of the very first Italian colonial adventures in Africa and preceded by a series of articles published in a host of "democratic" newspapers, *Politica coloniale* is what would today be seen as an exercise in public sociology. Moving from the idea that colonialism is a form of psychic contagion, a concept he draws from the newly founded science of "social psychology," Colajanni describes, analyzes in its causes and effects, and denounces Italian colonial engagements, insisting on the weakness of this politics as an instrument for solving the problem of overpopulation and unemployment and unmasking the political sophisms and lies that underpin what he called, in a successful formula, an instance of collective brigandage (*brigantaggio collettivo*). A convinced antimilitarist, Colajanni was equally against Marxism, which he conceived as alternative and contrary to democracy, as well as revolutionary unionism. But after the conquest of Libya, he supported the military action and voted in favor of annexation. Two factors were pivotal in this change of mind: the rebirth of national sentiment among Italians and admiration for the Italian army. The parabola of Colajanni and his conversion from opposition and social criticism to a position of institutional alignment centered on governmental reformism developed further with the Balkan crisis, which pushed him toward interventionism. The Russian revolution definitively persuaded Colajanni that only the capitalistic order could guarantee democracy and some freedom. This was the precondition to his sympathy for Fascism and Mussolini, who came to power after Colajanni's death in 1921.

Moving from the same idea of a psychological foundation of a political phenomenon, Giovanni Amadori-Virgilij wrote the first and possibly only (in Italy at least) extended study of imperialism as a sentiment or feeling or even a collective mentality. The author of an earlier book on the primitive forms of the family (1903), Amadori-Virgilij elaborated a comprehensive analysis of imperialism in its most foundational cognitive, emotional, and cultural grounds. England, Germany, and the United States are the countries he focuses on for sustaining with empirical materials his theoretical speculations, whose conclusions read like a plea for imperialism against socialism as the cultural foundation of any nation. Contrary to Colajanni, however, Amadori-Virgilij had no status in the academic world, nor was he a national-level politician, and his book clearly suffered in its impact from the weak reputation of its author and from the contorted and often unintelligible prose in which it is textured.[13] More than the book, however, it is the preface that is worth noting because of its author—Enrico De Marinis, a parliamentary deputy and *libero docente* in philosophy of law at the University of Naples, who happened to be also the first official teacher of a course in sociology in an Italian university—in a chair especially instituted for him by the same minister of public education in 1898. A former member of the Socialist Party and the author of a monumental treatise on sociology intended as a universal or cosmic science (see De Marinis 1901), De Marinis was to become, after leaving the socialists for nationalist liberalism in 1900, one of the foremost supporters of colonialism in Italy, at least among social scientists, first as the president of the Neapolitan società Africana d'Italia (one of the most aggressive organizations in support of imperialistic policy), then as president of the Istituto superiore di studi commerciali, coloniali ed Attuariali, based in Rome, and the collaborator of Minister Tommaso Tittoni for the legal regulation of the recently occupied Somalia (1908), which acted as a base also for the drafting of Libyan charters in 1919.

A place apart in this list of social scientists directly engaged, as critics or analysts, with colonialism in the pre-Fascist era should be granted to Achille Loria and Roberto Michels, without doubt two of the most influential and reputed social scientists working in Italy between the nineteenth and twentieth centuries. Loria was professionally and academically an economist— indeed, one of the most renowned Italian economists at the end of the century—whose eclecticism and intellectual curiosity very often pushed, however, toward sociology, a discipline he taught occasionally, in Padua and in Rome, before joining in 1905 the Faculty of Law in Turin and becoming director of the Laboratorio di economia politica founded by Salvatore Cognetti De Martiis (himself an economist with a strong interest in sociology), which was to become one of the most important academic organizations where social scientists, especially economists and economic historians, were educated in liberal Italy (on Loria as sociologist, see Crawford 1948; and, specifically on his theory of imperialism, Giglio 1973). Loria's interest for the colonies dates back to his very first great work, published in 1889, which set the tenets of his lifelong research on the "economic foundation of society," as the title of one of his most celebrated book says (Loria 1899). In this book—"the most clearly sociological of the series that Loria gave to the world" according to one commentator (Crawford 1948: 569)—Loria elaborates and defends the thesis that all social institutions, and in particular the cultural, normative, or cognitive ones such as law and morality, are organic products of the capitalistic system, which, in its turn, is built on the appropriation of land by the stronger.

Indeed, Loria never wrote a book specifically devoted to imperialist or colonial expansion (this was a duty he reserved to his student, the economist Marco Fanno [1906]), but he wrote about this subject in various places and times, conceiving of it as an important consequence of economic factors—land and capital—which he deeply studied. His interest in colonialism and imperialism was far from occasional, as shown by the continuous presence of these subjects in the various editions of what is arguably his masterpiece, the book *Economia politica* (whose last edition dates to 1945). In a nutshell, Loria's argument with respect to imperialism is the following: no longer finding profits in the metropole, capital—that is, the capitalist class—looks for other places to generate profits. It is at this moment that the colonial phenomenon is born and imperialistic expansion begins. To be sure, Loria is careful to distinguish between colonization and imperialism, as the former refers to population dynamics and the latter to exploitation. While colonization presumes emigration, an economic and industrial phenomenon, imperialism is a military phenomenon that presumes the use of violence. However, like colonization, imperial expansion is the effect of economic conditions having to do with the dynamic of capital, which is "omnipotent and really commands the States" and is therefore able to send armies in a "fantastic riddle of imperialist adventures which have as [their] end the violent appropriation of free lands" (see Loria 1927: 822).

What makes colonialism especially significant for Loria, however, more than its organic link with the dynamic of capitalism, is its methodological contribution to the testing of his own theory, based on the idea that land, and land appropriation more specifically, is the main causal factor in history and in the shaping of societies. Conceived as a variant of the comparative method, the "colonial method" would help scholars to assess the causal impact that land appropriation has in every specific case, through a comparison of the metropolis (where land is completely appropriated) with the colony (where there is still free land). As he explained in a paper delivered at the first congress of the Institut international de sociologie (he was one of its early members), "the social diversity of countries which differs between them only for the element T [land], demonstrates that T is a sociological factor; the social identity of countries which differs only for the element U [the complex of human or psychological elements], demonstrates that U is not a sociological factor." This is what makes colonies so precious:

> In fact, if we compare a colony, as it exists at a certain moment, with the metropole, as it exists in that moment, we are comparing two countries which present a perfect identity in terms of race, religion, culture, intelligence, physical strength, tradition, briefly, all which is related to the human, psychological element, to the U element, and which present on the contrary a difference, even a categorical antithesis with respect to the conditions of production and land appropriation, i.e. the T element; this because in the metropole, land is totally occupied and, in its greatest part cultivated, while in the colony a large portion of land is still free and to be appropriated. (Loria 1898: 142)

Loria's colonial method found its way also into sociology, to become the cornerstone of what a very early Italian dictionary of sociology, probably the first ever published, called *sociologia coloniale*: "that sociological approach or method which consists in the comparative and reciprocally explicative study between phenomena of the colonies and those of the fatherland" (Squillace 1911: 461). The adoption of the "colonial method," we should add, had nothing to do with an appreciation or still worse an acceptance of imperialism as a doctrine and political practice. Indeed, Loria was a convinced pacifist, a collaborator since 1895 of the journal edited by the Società internazionale della pace, directed by Ernesto Teodoro Moneta, winner of a Nobel Peace Prize. Though a student of colonialism, Loria was critical of the *morbus anglius*, considered as a true social sickness, the "fatal corollary of a declined capitalism," able to transform "conquerors into barbarians and conquered into slaves" (1905: 161). Still in 1905, however, Italy seemed to Loria immune to this sickness—an impression that in a few years would have been impossible to maintain.

A theorist and a critic of imperialism, Loria was indeed at the same time a practitioner of and believer in the new science of eugenics imported from Britain, which was cultivated in Italy by both conservative and leftist intellectuals, including Michels (Bosc 2000), offering during the first three decades of the twentieth century one of the main venues through which the discipline of sociology could develop (Cassata 2006b; Mantovani 2004). When an Italian Society of Eugenics was founded in 1919, Loria was among its members. His sympathy for socialism had decreased with the new century—also as a consequence of the strong criticism Marxists had been addressing to his mechanistic and deterministic brand of materialism.[14] And when the war burst out, in 1914, Loria was already in favor of intervention against the central empires, conceived of as a necessary step toward international justice and peace. Apart from these contradictions, which are witness to the cultural complexity of colonialism and imperialism not only as doctrines but as feelings and systems of beliefs, there are good reasons to consider Loria as one of the very first social scientists who devoted themselves, as theorists, to colonialism—a status that even Hobson, arguably the most influential and renown theorist of imperialism, implicitly acknowledged by quoting Loria in two important passages of his seminal book (Hobson [1902] 1965: 54–55) and taking pains to discuss the differences between his theory and Loria's.[15]

Personally very close to the elder Loria, whom he met at the aforementioned Laboratorio, Roberto Michels was a German sociologist and economist, originally of socialist faith, who chose Italy as his adoptive country in 1907, establishing himself first in Turin and then in Rome and Perugia, where he gained the chair of corporative economics in the 1920s in the Fascist faculty of political science, after a period spent as professor of international economics in Switzerland. Globally renowned as the author of one of the first classics of political sociology, *Political Parties* (first edition in German in 1911, in Italian in 1912), Michels devoted a relatively large and scarcely known part of his intensive intellectual work and writing to colonialism and imperialism, from an early article on German imperialism and the Moroccan question (Michels 1906), to *L'imperialismo Italiano* (1914) and *Le colonie Italiane in Isvizzera durante la guerra* (1921), to the concept of the colony in classical Italian economic thought (Michels 1932a) as well as to the related issues of international commerce (Michels 1924, 1934) and nationalism and patriotism (Michels 1929).[16]

Michels's book *L'imperialismo Italiano: Studi politico-demografici* is possibly the broadest and most sustained analysis of Italian colonialism from a sociological point of view ever produced, even if the author is careful not to label his perspective sociological (preferring "historical," "psychological," or "political": even this a clue to the weak symbolic status of sociology in Italy, probably, at least among the audience that Michels hoped to reach with his book). Indeed, what Michels offers here is an explanation of Italian colonial aspirations grounded on three main pillars: demography, economics, and politics. At first glance, the first is the most important, so much as to induce the author to coin the formula "demographic imperialism" to describe—and justify—Italian colonial politics and what he calls "Italy's right to colonization."[17] At the basis of Michels's analysis is the quantitative demonstration of a demographic exuberance that impinges above all on the male population in search of work, making it difficult to find it and inducing people to emigrate abroad. But besides the demographic side, there is the political one: "There exist no people who do not tend automatically toward expansion. There exist no people who do not aim to go beyond its natural borders. There is no constraint, geographical or ethical, which could induce a human race to be content with its own independence. . . . There is no State which does not comprise elements that are ethically heterogeneous and which is therefore not considered, by at least a minimal percentage of the population, as an oppressor" (Michels 1914: 105). What the German-born but naturalized Italian scholar identifies and theorizes through his quantitative and empirical analysis—adding, of course, a good quantity of political realism and sociological imagination to the crude numbers—is an original right to a "politico-demographical colonialism," which Italy as a state with a certain geopolitical position (in the Mediterranean Sea) and an exuberant demographic composition gained with its previous struggle for unification as an autonomous nation. This is what explains, and makes acceptable, to Michels the socialist and pacifist a claim that at first sight had shocked him. Was not Italy the country of the national principle? The nation of the right to autodetermination? How was it possible that Italians, after fighting for their liberty, in a few years had changed their position and were fighting to suppress the freedom of other peoples? Conceived of in this manner, as the necessary effect of a "logical concatenation, which from the simple objective contemplation of the Italian demography brings fatally to the postulate of the creation of colonies" (Michels 1914: 94), Italian imperialism was not only understandable but also legitimate, and there was no reason to mask it under some other label. Italian imperialism was sui generis because of its peculiar causes and forms. But that was all. Against those who negated the imperialistic character of Italian expansionist politics by insisting on its defensive motive and its emotionally charged source, on its spiritual and not utilitarian or materialistic nature, Michels claimed an objective and positive understanding: "Italian imperialism is imperialistic because it instinctively aspires, albeit in small quantities, to a domination which goes beyond its own national and linguistic territory" (xvii).

The most direct contribution that Gaetano Mosca, the other champion of Italian elitism and "the first major figure of modern Italian social theory" according to Levine (1995: 235), made to the analysis of colonialism was not an extended study but a collection of newspaper articles. Published the same year as the conquest of Libya, *Italia e Libia. Considerazioni politiche* (Mosca 1912) is a booklet that witnesses the expertise Mosca had in colonial matters—an expertise that brought him to a charge as *sottosegretario di stato alle colonie*, from 1914 till 1916, in the government led by Antonio Salandra, a conservative politician who was also a professor of law and as a young man the translator of the first Italian edition of Spencer's *Principles of Sociology* (1887). As a deputy, Mosca continued to intervene in colonial issues even after his formal displacement as *sottoministro*, through a series of discourses that reveal his great cultural authority and expertise (see Mosca 2003 for a collection of his parliamentary speeches).

Indeed, the liberal conservative Mosca was far from being a strong supporter of imperialism, or of Italian imperialism above all. His engagement with colonial policy was more an effect of his being a politician and a student of politics than of being an imperialist intellectual or scholar. From a scholarly point of view, his positions were relatively distant from those of the classical imperialist. He was critical of racial as well as geographical determinism. His criticism of race as an interpretive and especially explicative category is one of the main tenets of his plea for a truly scientific political science—even if his criticism weakened with time.[18] He was skeptical also of evolutionism as a paradigm for the social sciences. His favored method, the only one he thought could guarantee a scientific study of social and political life, was "historical"—a label general enough to include also more ethnographical approaches. Indeed, his trust in the same possibility of a science of politics or of the social life was based on the accumulation and availability, at the end of the nineteenth century, of enough knowledge about a vast array of societies—possibly all of humanity—to make finally possible the discovery and individuation of truly general, universal, and constant human trends. In Mosca's words:

> Exact knowledge of physical geography, ethnology and comparative philology, which shed light on the origins and blood ties of nations; prehistory, which has revealed the ancientness of the human species and of certain civilizations; the interpretation of hieroglyphic, cuneiform and ancient Hindu alphabets, which has unveiled the mysteries of Oriental civilizations now extinct—all these were conquests of the nineteenth century. During the same century the mists that enveloped the history of China, Japan, and other nations of the Far East were at least partially cleared away and the records of ancient American civilizations were in part discovered, in part more accurately

studied. Finally during that century comparative statistical studies first came into general use, facilitating knowledge of conditions among faraway peoples. There can be no doubt about it: where the student of the social sciences could once only guess, he now has the means to observe and the instruments and the materials to demonstrate. (1939: 41–42)

As this excerpt suggests, Mosca was well aware of the crucial epistemic contribution given by an imperialistic gaze—a gaze encompassing both Western and Eastern countries—to a sound historical knowledge. Contrary to his contemporaries, Durkheim included, Mosca, however, did not think the simpler the better, that is, that a focus on the most "primitive" or "savages" societies could offer, because of their elementary nature, a more precise and essential knowledge of social life in general. On the contrary, it was on the "large political organisms" that the social scientist had to focus his research if he wanted to find the most general and constant human facts. This would make ethnographic reports on savage societies and tribes—especially those written by travelers and explorers—less useful as sources of knowledge than many contemporary sociologists believed. His criticism of sociology's common faith in ethnography is worth quoting, as it sheds light, I believe, on a more generalized suspicion Italian social scientists had for this kind of source, possibly as a consequence in part of the lack of colonial possessions where it was possible for them to directly engage themselves as participant observers of "savages," in part also—as the references to documents like the Twelve Tables or the Code of Rothari make clear—due to the hegemonic juridical epistemic culture (recall that Mosca and most of the earlier Italian social scientists, including demographers and statisticians, studied at the faculty of law).

In our day there prevails, or at least down to a very recent day there prevailed, in social research a tendency to give special attention to the simpler and more primitive political organizations. Some scholars go as far back as possible and scrupulously analyze animal societies, tracking down in beehives, anthills and the lairs of quadrupeds and quadrumanes the earliest origins of the social sentiments that find their complete expression in the great political organisms of men. The majority keep to the organizations of savage tribes, and all circumstances relating to such peoples are noted and recorded. The narratives of travellers who have lived among savages have so acquired special importance, and quotations from them fill modern volumes on sociology. We do not say that such studies are useless, it is hard to find any application of the human intelligence that is completely unfruitful. But certainly they do not seem the best adapted to furnishing sound materials for the social sciences in general and for political science in particular. First of all, the narratives of travellers are as a rule more subjective, more contradictory, less trustworthy than the accounts of historians, and they are less subject to checking by documents and monuments. An individual who finds himself among people who belong to a very different civilization from the one to which he is accustomed generally views them from certain special points of view, and so may readily be misled. . . . If one is looking for light on the real social conditions of a given people, an authentic document such as the Laws of Manu, the fragments of the Twelve Tables or the Code of Rothari is worth much more than the reports of any number of modern travellers. . . . Psychological social forces cannot develop, and cannot find scope, except in large political organisms, in aggregates, that is, where numerous groups of human beings are brought together in a moral and political union. In the primitive group, in the tribe of fifty or a hundred individuals, the political problem hardly exists, and therefore cannot be studied. (Mosca 1939: 47–48)

A truly scientific social science could hardly exist anyway if one were not able "to lift one's judgment above the beliefs and opinions which are current in one's time or peculiar to the social or national type to which one belongs," and this could come, Mosca argued, only "with the study of many social facts, with a broad and thorough knowledge of history, not, certainly, of the history of a single period or a single nation but so far as we possibly can *the history of mankind as a whole*" (1939: 47, italics mine).

Following his method, Mosca devotes considerable attention in his work to historical political systems, and among them traditional empires have a prominent place. China, India, Japan, Turkey, ancient Egypt, and even the pre-Columbian Mexican and Peruvian empires are among his favorite historical examples, together of course with ancient Rome in both its republican and imperial variants—one of the tropes indeed of Italian political and social studies since Machiavelli at least.

A fair reading of the *Elementi di scienza politica*, without any doubt the masterpiece of this Sicilian pioneer of the social sciences, gives us few reasons to think of Mosca as an expert in colonial issues and an active agent of colonial politics—which indeed he was to become in the following years.

It is true that in his writing he makes use of many sources that could hardly exist without the spread of an imperialistic culture, as it is also true that in his case studies figure not only historical empires and colonies (e.g., the Greek colonies in Sicily and even the British colonies in India or Australia). But it is also true that neither imperialism nor colonialism are addressed as research topics and that even their names are difficult to find in the five hundred pages that make up the book. Indeed, we could suppose that faithful to his claim to be the first, or among the first, to argue for an objective, scientific approach to politics, Mosca never explicitly takes a position with respect to hot political issues that could not be approached from a sound knowledge of facts. Colonialism was clearly a very hot issue in fin de siècle Italy, for the average Italian as well as for the social scientist Mosca: suffice it to say that his masterpiece was published at the end of 1895, just a few months before the Adwa defeat in Abyssinia, and that the man politically responsible for that authentic disaster in Italian political history was another Sicilian, the authoritarian and for many observers reactionary Francesco Crispi (a former follower of Garibaldi), who was also the direct competitor of Mosca's political friend and patron, Antonio Di Rudinì, prime minister in 1891 and again in 1896, after Crispi's defeat. From his correspondence with his friend Guglielmo Ferrero (Lombroso's son-in-law), we know that he did not fail to speculate on both the U.S. overseas expansion in the aftermath of the Spanish-American War and the development of European spheres of influence in China.

However, what Mosca was not explicitly proposing in those years would soon be suggested by some of his most enthusiastic readers, among them the early representatives of the Italian nationalist movement, for whom Mosca was, together with Pareto, a crucial intellectual resource in their claims for a strong politics of power and an expansionist engagement of Italian government, especially in Africa. The historical, political, and cultural linkages between Italian nationalism and the theory of the elites are well known. We will talk about them while discussing Pareto, who was more available than Mosca for instrumentalization by nationalist programs and projects.

Mosca's open, public engagement in colonial issues finally became apparent in 1911, when the nationalist campaigns had already conquered a major part of the Italian people, and the idea of a new colonial expedition that could vindicate Adwa's defeat was spread even among the traditional enemies of colonialism, the socialist movement.[19] Even in this situation, however, the conservative Mosca was far from expressing generalized and enthusiastic support. On the contrary, he publicly expressed his worries about Italy's colonial engagement in Africa, warning against all propagandistic claims of an easy and certain victory against the Ottoman Empire for control of Libya. His position was not that of the humanitarian, nor of the convinced anti-imperialist, but of the political adviser who wanted to make clear which problems this engagement would create for the Italian government and its citizens. In other words, it was again as a detached observer of political things that Mosca entered the field of colonial politics, offering the nation his scholarly competence and sensitivity. His engagement was not as an academic man in front of his scholarly readership or audience, however, but as a public intellectual actively acting as opinion maker as a writer in newspapers.

An anomalous and in many ways insulated figure, a jurist and sociologist, is Michele Angelo Vaccaro, the author of a few sociological books that had some success in their time and gave him a reputation as a sociologist also outside Italy (see, for instance, Barnes and Becker 1938; Crawford 1948; Michels 1930; Sorokin 1928). Outstanding among them is *La lotta per l'esistenza*, published originally in 1886. What Vaccaro has in mind is a law of progress according to which mankind would become ever more pacific as an effect of selection and adaptation and above all as a consequence of cultural progress (and rationalization) in war and conflict management. Full of examples taken from ethnographic research and travelers' memoirs, the book is an exemplar of the revisions that Social Darwinism underwent at the time in Italy as an effect of religious faith and a diffused humanitarianism. It is worth noting, however, that imperialism and colonialism are completely absent from the analysis of social progress that Vaccaro attempts in this and other books. Both are addressed, however, in a text—more a political intervention than a sociological study—Vaccaro published during the war, on the problem of peace and the future arrangement of the world (Vaccaro 1917), where he moves from his idea of war as a principle of selection not of the best but of the worst, to a critique of imperialism, especially the German variety. Not progress but regression and degeneration is to Vaccaro what the current world war was showing—and it is interesting that he read that war as an immediate consequence of "the colonial fever and imperialism" that had hit the "great nations of Europe" (7). If this makes Crawford's assessment of Vaccaro as a wishful thinker and tender-minded a bit superficial, it is not enough to make him a sociologist of empire and colonialism. What makes Vaccaro interesting for us is his indirect involvement in colonial affairs as the special secretary of Francesco Crispi—the main inspirer of the early Italian colonial politics—when Crispi was prime minister in the 1880s and the early 1890s. It was a personal relationship that was based, it seems, in a true devotion to a man and politician Vaccaro was still eager to praise and celebrate in the 1930s when the new regime of Mussolini was transforming the infamous liberal (and ex-Garibaldine) prime minister into a hero of the new "Great Italy," if not a forerunner of the same Fascism (see Vaccaro 1927).

A few texts of a more ethnographic if not autobiographical character should also be mentioned at this point. Totally forgotten or neglected by historians of Italian sociology, these texts are witness of a phase in the development of the social sciences in Italy in which the quest for an empirical and positive understanding of social life was not segregated from the idea of a subjective participation in the same life. We find here autobiographical texts like *In Tripolitania* by Giuseppe Alongi, a police officer who contributed in the last two decades of the nineteenth century important studies in criminal sociology on both the Mafia and camorra (Alongi 1890, 1904) before being appointed as *questore* of Tripoli in 1911. The author of a book on social revolutions in Sicily, Gaspare Nicotri (1910) published in 1912 another book of ethnographical records taken during his travel across the new colony of Libya (Nicotri 1912). Neither Alongi nor Nicotri could be identified as professional sociologists, even if they wrote sociological texts and participated in the sociological culture of their days (indeed, Nicotri was also head of the sociological department of the Università popolare in Palermo, one of the many popular schools established in Italy by the Socialist Party to foster adult education; Michels 1930).

Central among these writers is a true academician, Francesco Coletti, whose book *La Tripolitiana settentrionale e la sua vita sociale studiate dal vero* was published in 1923 after he collected and integrated materials in great part already issued in 1913, in an official publication promoted by the Italian government. A specialist in agrarian economics and a pupil of Loria, among others, Coletti practiced what would be called today (but sometimes even at his times) rural sociology. Officially a professor of statistics and then demography, Coletti was the author of books and articles on emigration (Coletti 1899, 1912)[20] as well as on agrarian contracts and rural social and racial stratification (Coletti 1908). As the main scientist responsible for the parliamentary investigation into the farmers in southern Italy and Sicily (1910) and the secretary of the Società degli agricoltori Italiani, he was asked in 1913 by the minister of the colonies to participate in an agronomic survey on the recently conquered Tripolitania (a region of Libya) with the special mission of studying the social aspects of indigenous economic life. What emerges from his published materials, beside a relatively developed ethnographic imagination, is an attitude that could be labeled both humanistic and colonialist, grounded on the feeling of there being a civilizing mission to fulfill and the sense of ethnic superiority, culturally based and paternalistic in its manifestations—not so different after all from what he showed in his many writings on Italian *contadini* (farmers). A supporter of irredentism during the war, Coletti's entanglement with imperial politics become still more apparent, though always measured, with the advent of the Fascist regime, whose demographic and rural policies he supported and legitimated with his expertise and knowledge (see Coletti 1918, 1926).

COLONIALISM AND IMPERIALISM IN THE *RIVISTA ITALIANA DI SOCIOLOGIA*

Loria, Michels, Mosca, Colajanni, Amadori-Virgilij, De Marinis, Vaccaro, and Coletti are the social scholars with clearly identifiable sociological links who wrote about colonialism and imperialistic politics in the pre-Fascist period more systematically and openly. Compared with the many practitioners of the new science, including well-known ones such as Pareto or influential ones such as Ferri and Niceforo, this could look like a weak presence, attesting to the relative marginality of colonial and imperial concerns in the formation of Italian sociology.

But a discipline is organized also in terms of institutions other than books. Journals are among the most influential disciplinary institutions that have contributed to the development of sociology, offering a venue for publication but also a public space for debate and confrontation. Italian sociology has a long and rich tradition of periodical publications, starting from the *Rivista di sociologia*, founded in 1894 in Palermo by a small group of academics and free intellectuals,[21] which included Giuseppe Fiamingo, the author of a few studies on animal sociology and of the first international assessment of the status of sociology in Italy (issued in the columns of the *American Journal of Sociology*: see Fiamingo 1895); the Social Darwinist Giuseppe Vadalà-Papale, professor of law in a Sicilian university; and above all Filippo Virgilii, a Tuscan-based statistician whose interest for the new social science was apparent in his teaching (e.g., Virgilii 1898) and in part in his writing and research (Virgilii 1916, 1917). A specialist in emigration and population, Virgilii also wrote extensively in the following years on colonies—a topic, as we know, strongly related in Italy to geographic mobility and population dynamics (e.g., Virgilii 1892, 1919, 1924)—even supporting the colonial policies and imperial ambitions of the regime (Virgilii 1927, 1937).[22] In its second year, the editorial board was joined by the physical anthropologist Giuseppe Sergi, holder of one of the very first Italian chairs in anthropology (first in Bologna and then in Rome), possibly one of the most authoritative students of the human races and eugenics in Europe, a pioneer in the measurement of the human body, and a firm supporter of a biological understanding of social life, mainly applied to the study of African populations, especially those of the Horn of Africa, which Sergi identified in an influential book against the common anthropological opinion as the cradle of Western civilization (Sergi 1895; see also Sorgoni 2003).

More strategic as a place to look for instances of imperial entanglements in the sociological community is, however, the journal that succeeded the *Rivista* after its demise in 1896. Founded in 1897 in Rome—surely a more central place than Palermo, also for the potential links with the political and administrative world of the capital on which it could capitalize in terms of networks and resources—the RIS was managed by a group of scholars led by Guido Cavaglieri and Augusto Bosco, the former a jurist, the latter a statistician, and represented for twenty-five years the single most important institution in the burgeoning field of sociology in Italy. Here Pareto published his first sociological essays—a few of them later included in revised form in his *Trattato*—and internationally reputed voices, from Tönnies to Gumplowicz to Durkheim, found their first Italian translations, reception, and reviews there (see Garzia 1992). Like the Durkheimian *Année sociologique*, the RIS was mainly a journal of book reviews, although original essays were also featured in each issue.

Between 1897 and 1921, this small team of hardworking scholars edited 102 issues comprising 658 essays and 3,106 reviews, for a total of 17,421 pages. In purely quantitative terms, the RIS overcame even the *Année sociologique* as an international survey of each year's publications in or relevant to sociology. As in the celebrated French journal, modern industrial society was of interest to the editorial board of the *Rivista*. But also as in the *Année sociologique*, this represented just a small segment of the total concerns of the journal, which included ancient and medieval societies, Oriental and Roman law, primitive economic and legal systems, colonial rule, and general surveys of human history. What is more striking from our point of view is the central place that international or even global relations and processes occupy in the journal, as an even cursory reading of its tables of contents clearly shows.

Just to give a glimpse, the first issue of the journal comprised articles on the theory of population (by Loria), suicide (by Durkheim), and sociology as a field (by Pareto) but also on ancient China (by the Florentine Sinologist Carlo Puini), on barbarians and the fall of the Roman Empire (by the Russian sociologist J. Novicow), and on the origins of human societies (by L. Gumplowicz).

In the second issue, besides articles on methodological and epistemological matters, there were texts by the Finnish sociologist Edward Alexander Westermarck on the legal condition of the black slaves in the United States (this is the opening essay) and by the Italian historian Ettore Ciccotti on war and peace in ancient Athens. In the third issue there were papers on social evolution (by M. A. Vaccaro), anthroposociology (by G. de Lapouge, one of the founders of this discipline whose entanglement with imperialism is well known), and immigration in the United States (by the Belgian E. Levasseur).

Indeed, what sociology meant to the editors of the *Rivista* was something apparently very far from our current conception of it as a science of modernity. To be sure, articles on industrialization, technology, bureaucracy, democratic regimes, and so on were not absent, nor were articles on progress— the topic chosen for the eighth meeting of the Institut international de sociologie (an association that almost all the major Italian sociologists of the time joined) held in Rome in October 1912, to which the journal devoted in 1911 an entire preparatory issue with contributions by influential scholars including Enrico Morselli, Corrado Gini, Achille Loria, Rodolfo Benini, Francesco Coletti, Alfredo Niceforo, Franco Savorgnan, Michele Angelo Vaccaro, Raffaele Garofalo, Vincenzo Miceli, and the managing editor of the journal, Guido Cavaglieri. The bulk of the research material featured in the journal did not concern modernity as such, however, except at best as one stage in a much larger civilization process, the latter being the real focus of Italian sociologists of the time.

This appears clearly from the thematic organization the journal gave to the review of publications, which included as principal subsections, besides one devoted to general sociology, the history and critique of social doctrines, the history of social institutions, and the history of civilizing processes. These were the topics that, according to the editors, "comprise what most properly concerns our science: namely, the study of social phenomena in their entirety and of the theories that endeavor to explain them; the critical and historical study of those theories and doctrines, as already adumbrated by philosophers, historians and economists before sociology become established; and *the study of the social institutions of various peoples, which is the only positive basis for our research*" (Bosco and Cavaglieri 1897, p. 1, note 1, italics mine).

These more strategic topics were followed by anthropology and ethnography ("with special regard to primitive societies"), demography and social psychology, social economics, ethics, legal science, and political science. Only after these, two further subsections were devoted to "new social experiences and to the many economic and moral problems now confronting the civil nations": social movements and contemporary social issues. Last but possibly not least, we find listed subsections devoted to philosophy and contemporary science, supplemented since 1904 by a new section on the methodology of the social sciences.

Not surprisingly, many of the authors contributing articles and reviews were professors and scholars practicing in disciplines already institutionalized and distinct from sociology. Among them was the aforementioned Carlo Puini, one of the most outstanding Orientalists in Italy (contributing articles on ancient China, Tibet, Buddhism, Japan, and the inequality among races); Giuseppe Mazzarella, a Sicilian jurist specializing in legal ethnology (contributing twenty-four articles mainly on ancient Indian law); and the economic historian Gino Luzzatto (contributing on medieval commerce and the communes). Gennaro Mondaini and Enrico Catellani, the former a specialist in colonial history and the latter a student of international relations, were also among the habitual contributors. Their published texts focus on topics that range from public law in the new Africa to national rivalries in European Turkey, from the formation of international groups in the Extreme Orient to the economic development of Australasia. It is in an article by Mondaini—who succeeded De Marinis in 1910 as president of the Istituto superiore di studi commerciali e coloniali—that we find the first sustained analysis in the journal of the contents and objectives of *sociologia coloniale* (colonial sociology), conceived of as an "autonomous branch of an essentially theoretical discipline as is sociology" (Mondaini 1906: 45, note). The presence of scholars such as Mondaini and Catellani looks less surprising if we know that one of the coeditors of the journal, Augusto Bosco, was also strongly involved in the colonial culture of the time, as a member of both the Istituto coloniale italiano and of the editorial board of *La rivista coloniale*, official journal of the same institute (cf. Aquarone 1977; Lanaro 1979: 74, note). A statistician, Bosco was not only the author of a series of studies in comparative statistics on migration, homicide, and the family, but also—as his necrology emphasizes (Cavaglieri 1906)—a passionate traveler who took notes during his many voyages, including those in the Italian colonies (he was one of the few academics attending the Colonial Congress of Asmara in 1905, where the Istituto coloniale was first conceived (Aquarone 1977; Monina 2002).

One year later, an article on "the economic factors of colonial expansion" by a young economist graduated in Turin and destined to a brilliant academic career, exposed the guidelines of a socially grounded economic theory of colonialism that developed organically some of Loria's early insights on the subject (Fanno 1907). Together with Coletti's article on the principles of an economic theory of emigration (1899), this is possibly the theoretically most ambitious text published by the journal—not considering, of course, Pareto's contributions to general sociology.

As a turning point in Italian colonial history, we could expect the war of Libya to have strongly affected the contents of the journal, but this was not the case, suggesting a certain degree of autonomy of the sociological community with respect to contingent political events. Or even a certain lack of expertise on this front—indeed, the contribution of sociologists to knowledge of this region was relatively small, as even the writings of Mosca witness, with their scanty references to national intellectual production (and the contextual description of the German geographer Gerhard Rohlfs as the main source of Italians' knowledge of this part of Africa). In 1911 the First Universal Races Congress was held at the University of London, with the participation of J. A. Hobson, Ferdinand Tönnies, Franz Boas, and W. E. B. Du Bois. Italy was represented by Giuseppe Sergi—whose paper was also published in Italian in the *Rivista*—but the list of Italian scholars supporting the congress is much longer and includes Cavaglieri (as editor of the RIS), Colajanni, Ferrero, Ferri, Garofalo (as president of the International Institute of Sociology), Loria, Mazzarella, Miceli, Mondaini (also as editor of the RIS), Catellani, Sighele, Squillace, and Vaccaro. Absent in the list of supporters but referred to many times in the final bibliography is Alfredo Niceforo (Spiller 1911; on the congress, see Holton 2002 and Rich 1984).

After the entry of Italy into World War I, in which a few of the collaborators on the journal served as officers (among them Gini), and the premature death of Cavaglieri in 1917, with the journal now being edited by the anthropologist Giuseppe Sergi, the imperial gaze became still more explicit, as manifested in articles on colonial possessions in places such as Dalmatia, Abyssinia, and Tigray. Notwithstanding, the typical stance of the journal was far from imperialist, especially if this would mean the tension toward the building of large political unities, an objective Italians had trouble even imagining for themselves. As Sergi claimed in 1916, in an article characteristically titled "Sociologia e nazionalità":

The national autonomy of the small States, which got established in different ways, with industries and wealth of their own, with trades and mines, even with colonies, represents great civil progress in the world; and if Europe could attain her ideal in the confederation of States, this international union would mainly have value for the small

States, because they represent pacific States and do not have ambition of conquest or expansion. Powerful and gigantic states like Russia, Germany and Austria-Hungary in the same confederation would be dangerous, as they represent a past: states which are not really nations, but conglomerates of different nations, like the ancient empires. Only the true nations, even if formed by fractions as with the Slavs, Bohemians, Croatians, Serbians, and Slovenians, have the means of advancing and of becoming rich in peace, and in the hoped confederation, like Switzerland. . . . An empire like the Roman, or that of Charlemagne or Charles V, today is an anachronism, and would mark political and social regression, a danger to the freedom of peoples and the loss of their independence. (1916: 6–7)

Three years later, in an article on the colonial possessions and international justice, Sergi confirmed his anti-imperialist stance while acknowledging the contribution to civil progress that a measured colonialism by small states, like Italy, could offer (Sergi 1919).[23] This does not mean that the scholars aggregated around the journal were pacifists or convinced supporters of the virtues of internationalism: no sociologist faithful to positive science could seriously believe in the practicability of programs like Woodrow Wilson's (cf. Niceforo 1919, with reference to Cosentini 1919).

We have focused until now on direct, explicit engagements by sociologists or sociological venues with imperial politics and colonial concerns. In this manner we have obtained a sufficiently detailed picture of the set of entanglements of the rising discipline with imperialistic culture, while assessing the potential contributions sociologists made to the rise and nourishment, and maybe direction, of a colonial conscience in liberal Italy. But imperialism and colonialism as a more general cultural matrix and imagery can impact, as we know, the production of (sociological) knowledge in more indirect and subtle ways—that is, through a certain anthropological doctrine, or the support of a policy orientation, or even the acceptance of a documentary source at face value.

Influences in this sense are indeed easy to identify for the entire pre-Fascist period of disciplinary development—mainly thanks to the strong presence of a tradition of anthropologically based criminal sociology. This was a sociological enterprise keen on comparisons with supposedly inferior people—a general category that included for many observers, even self-claimed sociologists, not only tribesmen or bushmen but also people living in the barbarian past of Europe as well as in contemporary southern regions of Italy, for example, Sicily, Campania (i.e., Naples), Calabria, and Sardinia (even Corsica, French now but for a long time Italian). An ethnographic gaze was in a certain sense co-essential, intrinsic to Italian sociology since its inception, even when directed to clearly internal, national issues. In a certain sense, the very first colonial gaze of Italian sociology was a reflexive one, directed to the same Italy, or better to its southern part, identified as "Other" (Moe 2002; Schneider 1998).

IMPERIALISM IN ONE COUNTRY: CRIMINAL SOCIOLOGY AND THE "ORIENTALIZATION" OF *MEZZOGIORNO*

However strange it may appear to current practitioners of sociology, the inclusion of scholars such as the now infamous Lombroso and some of his most influential disciples and collaborators has much to recommend itself in a survey of early Italian sociology, especially if we are interested in assessing its imperial concerns and resonances. This inclusion depends not only on the high intellectual reputation, in Italy and abroad (e.g., Petit 2007), gained by Lombroso in his lifetime but also and above all on his lasting though forgotten contribution—both direct and indirect—to the diffusion and institutionalization of the social sciences, among them sociology.

Lombroso and his followers—who make up a veritable collaborative circle (Farrell 2003) from which energies and effervescence spurt—played a crucial part in this story. A disciple and collaborator of Lombroso and a central fellow member of the early tribe of criminal anthropologists, Alfredo Niceforo, was chosen to represent Italian sociology at the Paris Exposition in 1900 (Ward 1901). Another close collaborator of Lombroso, the baron Raffaele Garofalo, a lawyer and professor of law in Rome, was a vigorous promoter and representative of sociology in liberal Italy and was elected as president of the first Italian sociological association (Società Italiana di sociologia), founded in 1910, and as president of the Institut internationale de sociologie. The author of a seminal book on criminology, Garofalo played a part in colonial matters, being personally involved in the legal regulation of the new Italian colonial possessions through his participation as both an expert and a political representative (he was also a parliamentary deputy) to the drafting of the penal code for the Eritrean colony (Garofalo 1908, 1909a, 1909b), a code that was subsequently extended to Libya in 1919 (Cianferotti 1984). Interestingly, Garofalo grounded his argument for the adoption of strong penalties against African natives (stronger than those against Italians) as a means for expressing and supporting the prestige of the white race on the results of "all of the congresses in colonial sociology" (1909a: 5). As we will see, the links between Lombroso and the burgeoning field of Italian sociology were many and deeply consequential.

A physician by formation and a practicing doctor before gaining a professorship in psychiatry and anthropology at the University of Pavia and then in legal medicine and psychiatry at the University of Turin, Lombroso (1835–1909) clamorously entered into intellectual debate with the publication in 1876 of his seminal book *L'uomo delinquente*, arguably one of the few books that could be envisioned as founding charter for a new discipline— criminology. Probably invented by Garofalo, the label "criminology" was an alternative to that favored by Lombroso, "criminal anthropology," and was chosen to emphasize that humans, rather than positive laws, were the most convenient object of study for explaining crime. Although "criminology" did not succeed as the common designation for the new research field until the 1920s, its main substance has to be traced back to Lombroso and his firm belief that crime is a natural phenomenon that could be studied and explained with empirical, objective methods.

The main thrust of *L'uomo delinquente* —which went through five editions in twenty years, raising its length from the original 250 pages to almost 2,000—is relatively familiar but is worth being recalled in this context. Briefly, Lombroso argued that most criminals were atavistic residues or returns on the evolutionary scale, resembling not only animals (or even plants) but—more persuasively—primitive people. He grounded his argument on data on bodily measurements and observations of anomalies such as flat noses, large ears, and small heads—all features, according to Lombroso, typical of apes or savages. This is how Lombroso himself narrated the development of his approach and his first ideas on the subject:

> I began dimly to realize that the a priori studies on crime in the abstract, hitherto pursued by jurists, especially in Italy, with singular acumen, should be superseded by the direct analytical study of the criminal, compared with normal individuals and the insane. I, therefore, began to study criminals in the Italian prisons, and, amongst others, I made the acquaintance of the famous brigand Vilella. This man possessed such extraordinary agility, that he had been known to scale steep mountain heights bearing a sheep on his shoulders. His cynical effrontery was such that he openly boasted of his crimes. On his death one cold grey November morning, I was deputed to make the post-mortem, and on laying open the skull I found on the occipital

part, exactly on the spot where a spine is found in the normal skull, a distinct depression which I named median occipital fossa, because of its situation precisely in the middle of the occiput as in inferior animals, especially rodents. This depression, as in the case of animals, was correlated with the hypertrophy of the vermis, known in birds as the middle cerebellum. This was not merely an idea, but a revelation. At the sight of that skull, I seemed to see all of a sudden, lighted up as a vast plain under a flaming sky, the problem of the nature of the criminal—an atavistic being who reproduces in his person the ferocious instincts of primitive humanity and the inferior animals. Thus were explained anatomically the enormous jaws, high cheek-bones, prominent superciliary arches, solitary lines in the palms, extreme size of the orbits, handle-shaped or sessile ears found in criminals, savages, and apes, insensibility to pain, extremely acute sight, tattooing, excessive idleness, love of orgies, and the irresistible craving for evil for its own sake, the desire not only to extinguish life in the victim, but to mutilate the corpse, tear its flesh, and drink its blood. I was further encouraged in this bold hypothesis by the results of my studies on Verzeni, a criminal convicted of sadism and rape, who showed the cannibalistic instincts of primitive anthropophagites and the ferocity of beasts of prey. (1911a: xiv–xv)

As a cultivated man who had studied in Vienna as well as in Italy, Lombroso clearly drew also on the popularity of Darwin to elaborate an evolutionary scale that ranked certain individuals and categories as more successful in the struggle for existence than others: noncriminals over criminals, first, but also men over women (the subject of many studies and especially one written with his disciple and son-in-law, Guglielmo Ferrero, the future author of a successful series of books on the rise and fall of the Roman Empire, soon translated also in the United States and praised, among others, by President Roosevelt; Lombroso and Ferrero 1893), and of course white over nonwhite, especially black. However, Darwin was not the only source of Lombroso's thought, as even a rapid scan of his most famous and seminal book soon reveals. Apart from the deep influence of his master, Paolo Marzolo—a physician who devoted himself to linguistic studies and elaborated an evolutionary theory that presumed, on the basis of linguistic dynamics, the regression to early stages of civilization—Lombroso found suggestions and methods in scholars including the materialist physiologist Ernst Haeckel, the phrenologist Franz Joseph Gall, and the pathologist B. A.

Morel—the latter author of a theory that assumed that social diseases like alcoholism or syphilis could cause physical as well as moral "degeneration" in even normal people (see Pick 1989). But it was mainly through the work of evolutionary anthropologists and sociologists such as Charles Letourneau— the author of *L'evolution de la morale et sociologie après l'ethnographie*—and their local followers that Lombroso could define his standards for assessing the degree of primitiveness or "atavism" of the criminal born. The following excerpt from the American translation of a compendium of his theories Lombroso wrote for Anglophone readers makes clear the kind of reasoning underpinning criminal anthropology:

> The types of civilization which man has hitherto produced, according to Guglielmo Ferrero, are two: the type characterized by violence, and that characterized by fraud. They are distinguished by the form which the struggle for existence takes. In the primitive civilization the struggle is carried on purely by force, and wealth and power are achieved by arms, at the expense either of foreigners or of weaker fellow-citizens. Commercial competition between two peoples is carried on through armies and fleets, that is to say, by the violent expulsion of competitors from coveted markets. Judicial contests are decided by the duel. In the civilization characterized by fraud, on the other hand, the struggle for existence is carried on by cunning and deceit, and the wager of battle is replaced by legal chicanery; political power is obtained, no longer at the point of the sword, but by money; money is extracted from the pockets of others by tricks and mysterious maneuvers, such as the operations of the stock-exchange. The commercial warfare is carried on through the perfection of the means of production, but still more through the perfection of the art of deceit, the skill acquired in giving the purchaser the impression that he is getting a good bargain. To the first type there belong Corsica, part of Sardinia, Montenegro, the Italian cities of the Middle Ages, and in general nearly all primitive civilizations. To the second type, on the other hand, belong all the modern civilized nations, that is to say, those among whom the capitalistic regime has reached its complete development. The distinction between the two types is not, however, so absolute in reality as it is in theory, for characteristics belonging to the two different types are often found mixed together in the same society.
>
> How since pathology, in the social field as in the physical, follows in the pathway of physiology, we discover these same two means of

contest in the criminal world. As a matter of fact, there are two forms of criminality manifesting themselves in our day side by side: atavistic criminality, which is a return on the part of certain individuals of morbid constitution to the violent means of the struggle for existence now suppressed by civilization, such as homicide, robbery, and rape; and "evolutive" criminality, which is no less perverted in intent but more civilized in the means employed, for in place of violence it uses trickery and deceit. Into the first class of criminals fall only a few individuals, fatally predisposed to crime; into the second any one may come who has not a character strong enough to resist the evil influences in his environment. (1911b: 45)

As the notion of atavism was the intellectual cornerstone of the entire Lombrosian conceptual framework, accepted even by his students and followers as the pillar of the edifice of criminal anthropology, we could easily argue that the whole Italian school of criminology was constructed and nurtured by the comparative tools offered by the imperial system—a system in which Italians were still not participating in political terms, however, even if they could apparently enjoy the intellectual resources it provided. However instructive and suggestive it could be, this is not the most intriguing conclusion we can draw from an exploration of the imperial resonances of the Italian positive school of criminology. More than from an imaginary, purely intellectual imperial system, functioning as a source of data and tools, it is though the particular gaze they applied to their surrounding social reality in Italy that Lombroso and his followers could be labeled as vehicles, or *Träger*, of a truly imperialistic culture in a country not yet endowed with an empire.

The name "anthropology" chosen for defining the new intellectual project is revealing. Even if intended as usual in the mid-nineteenth century as the study of the biological constitution of individual humans—as physical rather than cultural and social anthropology—the kind of anthropology practiced by Lombroso had inscribed in it the division of labor that grounds the relations between sociology and anthropology, where the latter is intended as the discipline specialized in the study of the primitive and colonial subjects. Indeed, the human individuals measured by Lombroso were not randomly selected but chosen in specific environments and places: prisons, poor neighborhoods, asylums. Lombroso devoted himself to the anthropological study of the criminals, prostitutes, brigands, and even the revolutionary, but not, for instance, the professionals, functionaries, or even the shopkeepers. Like the savages, criminals and prostitutes could be legitimately subjected to the anthropological gaze—something Lombroso never extended to "normal," that is, middle- and upper-class citizens, or to working-class people, unless they were insane or ill.

From criminal anthropology to criminal sociology there is indeed just one step—a step taken by the most successful of Lombroso's followers and colleagues, Enrico Ferri, whose *Criminal Sociology* was published in Italian in 1892, French in 1893, and English in 1899. A lawyer and professor of law, Ferri was less keen to measure bodies and skulls and much more open to acknowledging the influence of geographical and even social factors in the making of the criminal. But even if not so committed to the idea of the born delinquent, and inclined toward Lamarckism, he still considered this notion a useful category for accounting for a part at least of the criminal population, that of habitual criminals (and recidivists). Still, the working of the evolutionary scheme of thought inscribed in both Darwinism and Spencerianism (and mediated by Lombroso) is apparent even in his criticism of apparently modern juridical institutions, such as the jury:

> Now the jury belongs to the domain of social pathology, for it is essentially contrary to the law of the specialization of functions, according to which every organ which becomes more adapted to a given task is no longer adapted to any other. It is only in the lower organisms that the same tissue or organ can perform different functions, whilst in the vertebrates the stomach can only serve for digestion, the lungs for oxygenation, and so on. *Similarly in primitive societies*, each individual is soldier, hunter, tiller of the soil, &c., whilst with the progress of social evolution every man performs his special function, and becomes unfitted for other labors. In the jury we have a return to the primitive confusion of social functions, by giving to any chance comer, who may be an excellent laborer, or artist, a very delicate judicial function, for which he has no capacity to-day, and will have no available experience to-morrow. (Ferri 1899: 196, italics mine)

Despite being the author of a few sociological texts of international circulation, vice president of the Institut international de sociologie (in 1895), and teacher of criminal sociology in several universities (from Bruxelles to Rome), Ferri remained relatively detached from the circles of would-be or self-identified sociologists.[24] But it was Ferri who wanted sociology to be taught in his new School of Applied Law and Criminal Justice, which he founded at the University of Rome in 1912. It is not surprising that he invited his former student Alfredo Niceforo, a criminal anthropologist himself, to teach it.

As one of the most reputed and strategically positioned Italian sociologists in the first half of the twentieth century, now almost forgotten but still read and celebrated in the 1960s, Niceforo is one of the most prominent exponents in Italy of an approach to the study of social life grounded on the conceptual couple—the tenet of the imperial worldview—of progress and difference. His first book on Sardinia's delinquency with its atavistic causes and manifestations made his name famous well beyond academic circles (Niceforo 1897). But it was through books like *Italia barbara contemporanea* (1898), *Italiani del nord e Italiani del sud* (1901), and *Forza e ricchezza: studi sulla vita fisica ed economica delle classi sociali* (1901) that his reputation as a sociologist developed at the beginning of the twentieth century. Member of the Société de sociologie de Paris and of the Institut international de sociologie, professor at l'Université nouvelle de Bruxelles and *Privatdozent* at the University of Lausanne (where Pareto had been teaching economics since 1893 and sociology since 1897), representative of Italy at the congress on sociological education held at the Exposition universelle in Paris in 1901 (Ward 1901), and president of the Italian consultative committee of the First International Congress on Eugenics (held in London in 1912), Niceforo was probably the purest fruit of the Lombrosian school in sociology before winning a chair in statistics in 1914 (a discipline he taught in Turin, Messina, Naples, and finally Rome). His research on civilization and progress, and especially on their measurement, had a resonance well beyond Italy, as Park and Burgess (1924: 1003) attest.

How the colonial imagery impinged on his sociological research is demonstrated by the following excerpt from one of his most provocative early books, *Italia barbara contemporanea* (Contemporary Barbarian Italy), where southern Italy is clearly equated to the colonies of imperial powers:

> Italy—let's state this frankly—has in the *Mezzogiorno* and the isles [i.e., Sicily and Sardinia] true regions which are less civilized and less evolved than the rest of the peninsula; regions where that which is still primitive and savage manifests itself with degrees of great or lesser intensity, but that all show a fatal and painful social inferiority. Travel in [these] lands, scan the statistics . . . , study the history of those places, and after doing all this, if you are free of any prejudice or any partisan spirit, I'm sure you will say: Here modern Italy has a high mission to fulfill and a great colony to civilize. (Niceforo 1898: 6)[25]

With his subsequent research program on the "anthropology of the poor" (praised among others by Michels, who introduced Niceforo's main book on the topic to a German-speaking readership: see Michels 1910), Niceforo made even more clear the embeddedness of his socio-anthropology in a wider imperialistic culture: so diverse, so "other" did the poor classes of modern societies appear to him that he conceptualized them as a race as such (Niceforo 1906, 1907). What Lombroso the humanitarian socialist had resisted, the second generation of the Lombrosian school accomplished, extending the main tenets of the master's theory to their most ethnocentric conclusions.

A SOCIOLOGY FOR THE EMPIRE: FROM PARETO TO GINI

Less eager to adopt racial explanations than the criminal anthropologists, scholars such as Mosca and Michels—both usual hosts at Lombroso's salon and very close to his collaborative circle—were very sensitive to civilization differentials. A former believer in the necessity of free trade and a minimal state, an open critic of early Italian colonial adventures, and a neoclassical economist, the third and most influential of the Italian elitists, Vilfredo Pareto, would have slowly changed his mind, becoming at the same time not only a sociologist but also a sympathizer of nationalism (including its protectionist policies) and a moderate supporter of the nascent Fascism regime.[26]

The elitists' attitude toward empire was far from being homogeneous. A firm supporter of colonial policies after 1914 (and breaking with his former mentor Max Weber also as a consequence of his support of Italian imperialistic claims),[27] Michels was the only one who openly devoted his sociological skills to the study of Italian imperialism, grounding its analysis and explanation (and even justification) on the endemic excess of population and the economic and political needs of a people weakened by unemployment, emigration, and a declining international prestige. Less as a social scientist than as a public intellectual and a politician, Mosca participated in the imperial culture of his age—offering his expertise and advice from the columns of newspapers, in governmental positions, and during parliamentary debates.

Far from any direct political engagement, suspicious toward any militant posture, Pareto apparently approached imperialism—as any other social phenomenon—only from a "logical-experimental" perspective. His disappointment with imperial politics is apparent in the manner in which he discusses the doctrine of a split between civilized and savage people as a distinction between "superior" and "inferior" races, with the political corollary of the "right" of the former group to command and control the latter.

What this doctrine doesn't notice, for Pareto, is that no right exists if there is no way to enforce it—making any claim to a civilizing mission a simple mask and excuse for military domination:

> There is on our globe not even a small portion of land that has not been conquered by the sword and where the occupying peoples have not preserved themselves by force. If Negroes were stronger than Europeans, it would be Negroes who had shared Europe, not Europeans Africa. That people who attribute to themselves the title of "civilized" claim to have the right to conquer other peoples whom they like to define as "not civilized" is completely ridiculous; or better, that right is nothing but force. Until Europeans become stronger than Chinese, they will impose their will; but if the Chinese should become stronger than Europeans, the positions will be reversed, and it is not probable at all that humanitarian declarations could be opposed to an army with any efficiency. (Pareto [1902] 1951: 27)

If imperialism as a doctrine of civilizing mission was, in Pareto's eyes, just one among many masks or justifications developed for hiding the true primordial sentiments of conquest and control that really make history and drive social action and social systems, historical empires—both ancient and modern—were one of his more frequent experimental laboratories used to test his interpretations or theories of human conduct. It is not only the ancient Roman Empire—one of the most frequent historical-institutional references in Pareto's writings—but also the Persian Empire, the Egyptian, the ancient Mexican and Incas, up to the modern British, German, and American ones: all historical empires are present in Pareto's knowledge and sociological imagination and explained in terms of force and struggle as the true motors of human life. As an early reader and admirer of writers such as Lubbock (the author of *Prehistoric Times and the Origins of Civilization*), Buckle (*Histoire de la civilization en Angleterre*), Spencer, Bagehot, and, of course, Darwin (whose Italian followers were concentrated in Turin and Florence, the two cities in which Pareto studied and lived in Italy), this is not surprising.

But an imperialistic culture, even if more implicit than explicitly exhibited, surrounds and underpins Pareto's whole system of thought. Comparison among people and societies is at the core of Pareto's claimed scientific, that is, objective method:

> A marked advance has been made in the study of physiology and anatomy by the introduction of the comparative method. It may even be

asserted that it is impossible to understand human physiology and anatomy unless comparison is made between man and other animals. An analogous method of studying the physiology of the social organism leads to equally important results. *It is by comparing civilized with savage society that modern sociologists,* following the traditions of inductive politics which have come down to us from Aristotle, have been able to lay the basis for a new science, whose progress during our century has been truly remarkable. The same method of study applied to the details of the organization of society ought also to be productive of great results. (1893: 677, italics mine)[28]

Even if rarely noticed, Pareto was heavily influenced by the socio-anthropological school of writers including Otto Ammon and especially Vacher de Lapouge, the author of *Les selections humaines.* It is to their studies of human variety and racial differentiation that Pareto explicitly moves for his own doctrine of social heterogeneity—one of the pillars of his whole sociological system and the basis for his concept of "the elite" and therefore also for his theory of the circulation of elites or aristocracies.[29] Critical of the race concept because of its claims to an objective foundation it had not (yet) received, Pareto is strongly persuaded of a natural differentiation among humans, which makes social inequality a much better starting point for a truly scientific social science than any humanitarian assumption of universal equality. There is undoubtedly a tension in Pareto's work between a skeptical attitude toward the knowledge claims of current research on race differentials and his firm persuasion of a constitutive human inequality, which easily moves him toward racial shores. This was, after all, what made his work and name appealing to extreme nationalists (and imperialists) such as the writers and journalists Enrico Corradini and Giuseppe Prezzolini and to Mussolini—who happened to attend Pareto's lessons while exiled in Switzerland. The imperialistic aura of Pareto's work, apparent in his theories and in their assumptions, his political declarations and tastes notwithstanding, is what makes the author of *Mind and Society* a major contributor to the development and intellectual justification of a colonial conscience in Italy, as well as a possible ideologue of the imperialistic claims some Italian circles have been advancing since the beginning of the century, reaching the climax in the Fascist regime (on Pareto's influence on early Italian nationalists, see Drake 1981). The postmortem fortune of Pareto as a Fascist forerunner and theorist of a realist conception of society and political life, which was perfectly aligned with Fascism's doctrine, is well known (see Borkenau 1931; Stewart 1928).

Paradoxically less involved than the two other elitists in the Italian political arena, Pareto was, however, possibly the most political source of inspiration and legitimation for the nationalist movement—a milieu in which it was possible to find a few other sociologists, such as Sighele (a student of Ferri and a pupil of Lombroso) and the maverick Filippo Carli, a curious and interesting figure of the practical intellectual who devoted his studies and brilliant mind to things as apparently different as local industrial development in Brescia (a northern Italian city near Milan, where he was in charge of the local Chamber of Commerce for more than two decades), the elaboration of nationalistic policies and programs (Carli 1919), and the demographic causes and the economic costs of the world war (Carli 1921). He cultivated sociology as a private docent and as the author of dozens of articles and, above all, of two sociological textbooks (Carli 1925a, 1925b), before being nominated to full professor of corporative economics during the Fascist regime (Lanaro 1979).

But Pareto had also a more positive, that is, factual if not analytical, understanding of imperialism as a certain kind of politics or, better, a certain mode of conduct in foreign affairs, as evidenced in the following excerpt from his grand sociological treatise, in which the Italian scholar discusses the way the U.S. president Woodrow Wilson behaves with respect to postrevolutionary Mexico on behalf of U.S. trusts in the oil sector:

> Late in the year 1913, Huerta was President of Mexico. The government of the United States was showing itself intensely hostile to him, while the English Government, which had begun by befriending him, was now deserting him, just to avoid difficulties with the United States. The conflict at bottom was exclusively a matter of business interests. While he was President of Mexico in 1900, Porfirio Diaz had granted oil rights over an extensive territory to Henry Clay Pierce, and Pierce had sold them to the very powerful Standard Oil Company. An English concern, the Eagle Oil Company (Compania Mexicana de Petroleo Aguila) had come to be a competitor of the Standard Oil. President Madero succeeded Diaz. He had favoured the American company and not without personal profit and had thought of decreeing a nullification of the concessions to the English concern. Huerta, on the contrary, confirmed them, and that made him the object of wrath on the part of the Standard Oil, of the Standard Oil's friends and customers, and of other American companies or trusts, which were all desirous of exploiting Mexico with the help of the

United States Government. Wilson, the President of the United States, said nothing of all that. He said that he could not recognize Huerta because Huerta had not been "regularly" elected, and he showed great indignation that Huerta had come into power through a revolution, so violating the sacrosanct dogma of election by popular vote. In that way Wilson was substantially defending American trusts abroad, though at home he was posing as an enemy of the trusts. That is not all. *Wilson had been elected as a pacifist and an anti-imperialist.* In trying to intervene in Mexico he entered upon a policy that spelled war and imperialism. There is no way of determining whether he was or was not conscious of the inconsistency. On the one hand it is hard to admit that he alone was ignorant of what everyone else knew about the rapacious designs of American trusts upon Mexico; *and if the attempt to force a government of American choice upon an independent country like Mexico is not imperialism, it is hard to imagine what imperialism could be.* (Pareto 1935: §2267,[2] italics mine)

What this sketchy discussion of Paretian sociology and its imperialistic underpinnings makes clear, I hope, together with our previous discussions of Lombrosians and elitist social scientists, is that when Mussolini went to power in order to change the parliamentary regime with a newly conceived and organized totalitarian one, most if not all the elements composing the regime's imperialistic ideology were already extant, fabricated and propagated by an ongoing intellectual debate and by the scientific production and circulation of ideas well established in Italy since the liberal age. The Paretian doctrine of the circulation of the elites had indeed only to merge with a larger theory of national development grounded on demographic pressures (as explained by Michels) to generate a theoretically based justification for a politics of colonial and imperial expansion like Mussolini's.

Pivotal in this endeavor was an energetic, talented, and prolific scholar, an academic entrepreneur who was able to organize and substantially control, within a few years, what was surviving of the sociological field in Italy after the closing of the most important sociological journal (RIS), in 1921, and the death of Pareto, in 1923. I am referring to the influential and authoritative statistician and demographer Corrado Gini, one of the major intellectual technocrats who contributed to building the totalitarian state, whose impact on Italian (and not only Italian) sociology, though currently minimized if not neglected, was extraordinary during the interwar period and the first years following World War II. A review and discussion of Gini's work and main ideas in the field of sociology and demography—two disciplines that were strongly linked in the hands of Gini and his compact school—clearly show the relevance of colonialism and an imperialist gaze in shaping sociology (both as an idea and as a set of practices) in midcentury Italy. Gini's deep interest in sociological matters can be traced back to his law thesis, published in 1907 as *Il sesso dal punto di vista statistico* (Sex from a Statistical Point of View), an attempt to determine the statistical law of the sex ratio of birth, which made use of a vast array of statistical sources from Europe, America, and Oceania.[30] Even if clearly a different kind of text than Veblen's or Thomas's almost contemporaneous books on sex, *Il sesso* displays the sociological mind of Gini, even as a statistician. Already in this early work his cosmopolitan gaze is well in evidence in terms of transnational comparisons and scattered references to "primitive societies," documented by ethnographical investigations. As we will see, this interest in primitiveness never disappeared and was only reinforced by Italy's subsequent colonial experiences.

It was in 1911—the same year the Italian government decided to attack the Ottoman Empire as a necessary step for the satisfaction of her colonial ambitions in the Mediterranean—that Gini showed his availability, and ability, to enlarge his scholarly gaze from statistics to a more generally intended social science, focused on what would remain his principal theoretical subject for more than thirty years, the evolution of nations or, more precisely, the rising and declining of national groups. A nationalist by persuasion, though not an active member of the nationalist movement and then party, Gini advanced in this early text (1911) the main tenets of a general evolutionary theory of societies, which merges demography, biology, and Spencerian sociology—supplemented in the following years by a series of new insights mainly taken from Pareto and biochemistry, the latter being the discipline that according to Gini could give a new life to the old organicism. Gini labeled his new organicistic social theory "neo-organicism" (1936).

Originally given as a lecture in 1911 in Trieste, which was still part of the Austrian Empire at the time, this early text gives a succinct but clear picture of Gini's sociological theory, whose tenets and contours he never changed but only refined and empirically tried to support, remaining faithful throughout his life to his juvenile vision—more an indication of a certain intellectual inertia than the effect of a solid and sound approach. His doctrine of the cyclic evolution of nations as the backbone of universal history was set forth and publicly explained in a lecture in Chicago in 1929, part of a cycle devoted to population issues and organized by the Harris Foundation. It is apparent from the following excerpt from this lecturer how global, and racially grounded, was his gaze:

The more closely we study primitive races the more evident it becomes that they are often undergoing a decline in numbers, which, in some cases at least, has proceeded, or anyhow begun, independently from all contact with higher races. In some of these cases the populations concerned are those to whom nature has not been niggardly in providing the means of subsistence, as, for example, in the case of the natives of the Amazon Basin, whose gradual extinction in an environment noted for its luxuriant fauna and flora contrasts with the prosperous demographic conditions of the inhabitants of the Andes, so much less favored by nature. The slow growth, or even the decline, of some peoples contrasts with the intensive expansion of other races, who, as in the case of the Slavs and the Chinese, have overrun vast territories in a few centuries. If we do not succeed to document with the statistics the whole cycle of the population, it is only due to the fact that the statistics are yet young and, like a young baby, have not the experience of a full year but only of one season. But history, tradition, and archaeology allow us to follow in Egypt, in Mesopotamia, in Greece, and in Rome the entire development of the cycle, "the period of the great year," of which Etruscan tradition speaks. The Etruscan sages, Plutarch tells us, learned precisely that there are several races of men, the one different from the other, in life and customs, and that God has allotted to each its time, which is limited to the period of the "great year," after which there happens the renovation of the world and the change in the human races. Someone went even so far as to think that the extension of such a period cannot only be recognized but can even be measured for the Mediterranean civilizations (to which belong the Egyptian, the Greek, the Roman, and those of modern Europe), for those of the Near East (to which belong the Babylonian and Assyrian, the Persian, the Etruscan, the Jewish, and the Arabian), and also for those of India and of Mexico, with the result that the periods would be of an analogous duration in the various parts of the world and, for these and other reasons, they would appear to be due to human nature more than to the environment. Moreover, recent research seems to show that the same parabola described by a people as a whole is also described by the families who compose it; in their case also, and not only in that of royal families and those belonging to the aristocracy and the upper classes, but also in families belonging to the bourgeoisie and to the peasantry, a phase of vigorous growth is followed by one of more or less rapid exhaustion. (Gini 1930a: 5–6)

At the core of Gini's theory of the cyclical rise and fall of populations was the assumption (which was empirically supported) of differential fertility rates among social classes—a tenet that clearly gave a strong sociological flavor to the model. As soon as the dominant class reduced its reproductive capacity (as a consequence for Gini of the natural weakening of the germinal plasma and not of psychologically based choices), new positions opened in the dominant field, creating opportunities for ascension for members of the prolific lower classes. This would generate an exchange of positions between people from the lower and upper classes, which Gini labeled "social metabolism" in order to differentiate it from the Paretian circulation of elites: indeed, it was not a circulation for Gini but a true replacement of the superior elder (in terms of achieved social position) with the inferior younger that could regenerate social life. What happens inside each society among classes occurs also at the international level (which demographically is always composed of populations): not classes but nations are here the main actors, however.

This general model of the rise and decline of nations, conceived as organic populations that replicated in their history the life cycle of the social classes and at the individual organism, was easily expanded and adjusted, in the second half of the 1930s, by Gini and his followers in order to account for the imperialistic expansion of Italy (together with Germany and Japan). In this context, Italy was explicitly conceived of as a perfect instance of the young nation accomplishing its natural, and therefore necessary, cycle of development, moving toward its expansionist stage as its population was also expanding (i.e., increasing)—something that both Gini and Mussolini strongly desired and encouraged, the former through texts, calculations, and theories, the latter through policies, incentives, and laws. If this was not occurring as it should be, with the timing and the rates of achievement it deserved, it was due only to opposition from the old and demographically declining nations, which were still controlling imperial power on a global scale, that is, Britain and France (Gini 1938, 1941a, 1941b; N. Federici 1938, 1942a, 1942b; Fortunati 1940). War would have been the ultimate, natural, and inevitable solution if this opposition had not peacefully finished.

In a certain way, we can say that Gini has been concerned with empire throughout his adult life, as both a demographer and a sociologist (the two disciplines being strongly intertwined in his mind and hands). Indeed, Gini had an imperial perspective not only as a theorist of national development but also as an empirical researcher. His entanglement with empire is especially apparent in the many expeditions he directed as the president and leading scholar of the Comitato Italiano per lo studio delle popolazioni, a research organization he founded in 1928 with public funds that produced in a few years a remarkable set of investigations in colonial regions, including Ethiopia, Tripolitania, and Albania, and publications, both articles and monographs, on the demographic aspects of ancient and "primitive" or underdeveloped societies, such as Mexico before the Spanish conquest, Bantu society, and Indian migrations (see, e.g., Camavitto 1935; Gini and Federici 1943; Mukerij 1936; Sonnabend 1935; see also Federici 1950 for a review of ethnographic investigations on colonies).[31] Identifiable much more as a physical than as a cultural or social anthropologist, especially interested in the measurement and comparison of bodies (in this he was clearly an heir to Lombroso and Sergi), Gini sometimes acted also as a social ethnographer, especially in the field of leisure (e.g., games), and published his ethnological observations and ethnological speculations in international sociological journals such as *Rural Sociology* (Gini 1939). As a theorist, beyond his critical readings of books by Kroeber and Malinowski, he focused his attention on primitiveness and cultural diffusion, undoubtedly his main subject matters in the field of cultural analysis (e.g., Gini 1940, 1949).

His conception of primitiveness is worth considering, as it shows how distant Gini was from the crude forms of racism accepted by such influential Fascist ethnologists as Lindo Cipriani. In brief, for Gini primitiveness is not an inferior condition necessarily rooted in nature (as in physical anthropology) but a stage all people, that is, populations or societies, have to experience in their life cycle. Surely, primitive societies are backward—Gini is very explicit about this—in terms of technical progress and wealth accumulation but not morally or in the artistic sense. However, not all populations are equally able to develop, as some of them have crystallized and have only become elderly: they are senescent societies, without any possibility of developing further. Other societies are young and therefore primitive and still have resources to grow and develop—like the Bantu for Gini.

As a spokesman for Fascism and as an internationally renowned theorist of the demographic (e.g., Gini 1927b) and colonial politics (e.g., Gini 1941b) of Fascism, Gini would seem the perfect exemplar of the heteronomous scholar, whose research, topic selection, and arguments are contingent on the political field (Steinmetz 2009b). Things may be more complicated, however. With an independent mind and temperament, Gini had no easy relationships even with Mussolini, whose strong interest and even passion for population issues and statistical data are well known (Horn 1994; Ipsen 1992). Gini's claims to autonomy as a president of the Instituto nazionale di statistica (ISTAT)—an autonomy that was intended to be both intellectual and organizational—were strong and continuous and ultimately caused his withdrawal from office and substitution with another demographer (one closely related to Gini, however), the statistician and sociologist Franco Savorgnan, author of a few interesting sociological studies on aristocracy and on war (Savorgnan 1918, 1921). Savorgnan had studied in Austria with Gumplowicz, whom he always considered as his mentor (see Strassoldo 1988 and Weiler 2003).

Gini's autonomy from empire is not easy to assess, for the simple reason that his imperial gaze preceded and partly contributed to the Italian imperial programs in a manner that makes it difficult to decide when the scholar was dependent on government and vice versa (in Mussolini's case). Interestingly, sociology was able to enter the academic system on institutional grounds, that is, independently of the goodwill of interested scholars, precisely under the Fascist regime, that is, under the political system that made the greatest effort to create an Italian Empire that could revive the splendor of the ancient Roman Empire and gain a "place in the sun" for Italy. Crafted, or at least offered, as a scientific basis for Fascism, Gini's sociology acquired in the late 1920s and 1930s a visibility and political relevance that were previously negated. If this political link was an ambivalent resource for sociology as an intellectual discipline with scientific pretensions, it was clearly also a significant and potentially highly strategic resource for its academic legitimation—at least in an academic system strongly controlled and ruled by the state, like the Italian one.

It is not by chance that the strongest identity as a sociologist was attributed during Fascist rule to Gini, who, although a statistician, had considerable cultural and social capital and symbolic capital specific enough to the field of sociology to be granted a degree in sociology *ad honorem* by the University of Geneva and to be invited by the acknowledged sociologist Sorokin as a visiting professor to the Sociology Department at the University of Minnesota and later at Harvard (where Gini had Robert K. Merton as an assistant).[32] This reminds us that each national field is embedded in a wider transnational field in which resources also flow in the form of symbolic capital. The reputation of Gini as a sociologist was well established in 1935, when the whole Italian delegation to the International Congress of Sociology was not only led by Gini but where his own theory provided the general framework of all of the papers presented (see especially Levi della Vida 1935 and Michels 1935). In 1950 the international fame of Gini as a sociologist was such that he could be elected president of the Institut international de sociologie, an office he held until 1963, contributing to the development of that organization and to its difficult negotiations with the new International Sociological Association, founded and promoted by the United Nations Educational, Scientific, and Cultural Organization as a democratic and liberal alternative to Gini's institute, which was considered with some reason as strongly compromised by both fascism and racism. This official role helps to explain why Gini—even if he had a chair in statistics—could still serve as an official member of sociological committees in the early 1960s, when sociological chairs and public competitions for their acquisition were eventually established also in Italy.

In sum, if Gini shaped and sold his social theory in the 1920s as a scientific basis for Fascism, including colonial politics, there are good reasons to think the relationship was bidirectional. After all, what he offered the regime was a social theory that had already been formulated, in its main lines, in the 1910s. Gini contributed a sociology to Fascism—a sociology that could fit Fascism's loose totalitarian ideology and expansionist programs. By the same token, Fascism contributed to sociology's legitimation as an intellectual and academic discipline, and not just as instrumental or strategic knowledge for the regime, through Fascist educational and cultural policies that granted sociology a space to develop and to work inside the state apparatus.

It was only after the conquest of Ethiopia and the proclamation of the empire in 1938 that sociology as a teaching subject was linked officially to the colonial world. As "general and colonial sociology," the discipline was intended to offer the main tenets of a sociological education useful for professional statisticians employed in public, meaning state, offices, including the national ISTAT. Under this label, and within the corresponding framework, the discipline was still taught in the faculties of statistics at the end of the 1950s and possibly in the 1960s, and in Rome directly by the influential statistician Gini (1954, 1957).[33] Fifteen years after the end of the Italian Empire and the demise of any colonial possession, Italian youth engaged in the study of sociology in the Italian university —something that happened typically at that time in the faculties of statistics—still had colonies and colonization among their subjects.

Even if the degree of autonomy of sociology as a form of knowledge during the reign of Fascism could not be overrated, and surely suffered from many interferences, censures, and still more important reactions, it should be noticed that the international intellectual reputation of Gini—that is, his social, cultural, scientific, and academic capital—was sufficiently high and independent of local political approbation to guarantee him an intellectual autonomy that caused him troubles with Mussolini. More than a direct influence of Fascism on the intellectual work of Gini, we should think of their relation as one of intellectual affinity and mutual exploitation. Before, and more than being a Fascist, Gini was always a nationalist, believing in the natural inequalities of men, and he was strongly devoted to his intellectual work, with an equally strong belief in science.

More important in this context, the imperialistic underpinnings of sociology during the rule of Fascism were deeply rooted in a nationalistic political culture that emerged during the last two decades of the nineteenth century, as a "natural" development of Risorgimento's national consciousness and a correlate to irredentism, and which was sufficiently strong and diffuse to mark a whole generation of self-proclaiming sociologists, Gini included but not alone.

CONCLUSIONS

In Italy sociology entered in its disciplinary stage only after the end of World War II, that is, after the country had lost its colonies in the wake of defeat against the Allies and the debacle of the Fascist regime. This does not mean that Italy—and Italians—also lost their imperial ambitions and colonial desires. Indeed, in the early postwar years all the political forces at work for creating a democracy from the ruins of Fascism agreed on the importance of a colonial appendix and pressured the international community in the hope of preserving imperial control of Ethiopia, Somalia, and Libya. Unsuccessful as it was—in fact, only Somalia was left under a temporary Italian protectorate, definitively ended in 1950—this political consensus among forces as different as the Christian[34] and Communist parties reveals the strength of imperial culture in Italy, the last and possibly the least powerful of the Western countries to enter the imperial struggle.

The entanglement of Italian social sciences—including sociology—with empire, imperialism, and colonialism, was a significant one since 1870, that is, since the early movements of both a sociological culture and of colonial politics, whose articulations I have tried to document. Let me resume the main evidence of this entanglement.

The birth of sociology in Italy was inevitably strongly linked to the process of nation building, on the one hand, and economic modernization, for example, national industrialization, on the other. Misery and crime were undoubtedly the two main social problems Italian governments had to address after unification, and the rising social sciences found in them both a research object and a source of legitimation, not only intellectual but also political. Not by chance, almost all the pioneers of sociology in Italy were politically engaged and active in political parties or even as representatives in public institutions. As deputies, senators, or ministers and not only as university professors, early sociologists were easily pressured or pulled to address political issues, and this alone could account for their massive involvement, sometimes as supporters and sometimes as critics, in the imperialistic project that the new state began to cultivate within a few years of its birth. But other factors should be considered for explaining the imperial entanglement of Italian sociology since its beginning.

The first is the strong influence the physician-turned-anthropologist Cesare Lombroso enjoyed in the first decades of the new state, especially after the publication of his *L'uomo delinquente* in 1876. Around Lombroso a true school coalesced, from which a new discipline was born: criminal anthropology. As a spin-off of this discipline, criminal sociology enjoyed intellectual success in the last years of the nineteenth century and beginning of the twentieth, expanding from Italy into America, both Latin and Northern. Independent of their personal beliefs and political engagements—the school has always been relatively loose especially with respect to political orientations, including their positions toward colonial policies—Lombroso and his followers contributed to the development and spread of an imperial political unconscious with their same arguments and theses, based as they were on a more or less crystalline faith in the natural inequalities of humans, usually founded in biology, as well as in the virtues of (Western) civilization against what they saw as an incipient and always possible danger of degeneration into savageness and primitiveness. Indeed, when not openly projected beyond the national frontiers as a rationale for imperialistic missions, this concern for *barbarie* as a negative social condition to be stopped and overcome by any means, including physical force (i.e., through the police and army), worked as a doctrinal means for drawing strong boundaries between the normal and the insane or deviant, the latter being a delinquent, one who was mad, a prostitute, or the inhabitant of one of the many "criminal zones" that made up southern Italy—especially the barbarous regions of Sardinia, Sicily, and Calabria. Indeed, before being entangled with imperialism as political doctrine and practice, Italian sociology contributed and participated in an imperial consciousness and culture through its strong identification with criminology, especially that naturalistic version that made the "Italian school" famous all over the world and which strongly affected the understanding of the Italian "Southern question" (*questione meridionale*; Petit 2007; Schneider 1998).

Far from being confined to the Lombrosians, whose influence and success was declining already in the first decade of the new century, this naturalistic, biologic approach to the study and explanation of social processes and problems affected a large segment of Italian scholars in the social sciences, especially if concerned with the study of population—indeed, one of the true obsessions of Italian social sciences since their beginning.

Italian sociologists contributed further to this alchemy with politically charged interventions from well-established positions in the public sphere. The elitist triad represents this triple option. Whereas Pareto worked theoretically on the development of a general sociology whose tenets could be easily appropriated by the incipient nationalist intelligentsia (mainly composed of literary men in search of sociological insights), Michels contributed to an imperialistic legitimation of Italy's involvement in international affairs with his empirical studies on emigration and the poor classes. As an editorialist in influential newspapers, then as a *sottosegretario di stato* to the colonies (that is, as assistant to the minister for colonies, between 1914 and 1916), and at last as a deputy in Parliament, Gaetano Mosca often took positions on colonial issues, sometimes warning against colonial moves, sometimes applauding the government for the success of its enterprises, sometimes advising on legal and political aspects of colonization. Far from being an isolated case, Mosca was only the tip of the iceberg of a deep entanglement of sociologists with imperialistic agencies that lasted for almost fifty years and found in Corrado Gini—head of the Italian national institute of statistics, close counselor of Mussolini on demographic issues, practitioner of colonial demography, and professor of colonial sociology in Rome—its climax.

Of course, not all sociologists in pre-Fascist Italy were nationalist and pro-imperialism. A big tradition of left, socialist sociology also emerged starting in the 1880s, Napoleone Colajanni being the most prolific and possibly most influential exponent. But the idealized legacy of the Roman Empire, and especially the prospect of a national renaissance through sustained and "virile" international engagement, had an impact well beyond nationalist circles, and colonial policies in the end were supported—albeit with some concerns and worries about their implementation—even by left, radical scholars as a solution to the "social question."

Indeed, we can even suggest that one of the main reasons for the neglect of "classical" Italian sociology in current understandings of the discipline is precisely because of its earlier cosmopolitan gaze (which contrasts with the "methodological nationalism" grounding modern sociology) and at the same time—paradoxically—because of its resonance with and embeddedness in a nationalistic culture deeply rooted in a country of only recent unification, and for this reason easily transformable and translatable into imperialistic terms (Lanaro 1979). Crucial elements of that culture—or at least of certain versions of it—like the idea of a natural, that is, essential, difference among groups and races, as well as organic analogies, were easily transferable into sociological writings, while positivistic enthusiasm and zeal could promote, support, and legitimate attempts to ground (the study of) social behavior on biological, even biometric, and statistical foundations.

Of course, the still renowned Mosca and Pareto were embedded in this wide culture and contributed in some way to its propagation and diffusion. However, it is true that their work resonates also with other more liberal and intellectual concerns. This could explain their survival in the contemporary canon—along with the perception of their possible (but always sociologically suspect) greater degree of "genius." But as we have seen, even Mosca was far from being alien to colonialism, while Pareto—albeit distant from any political involvement at the time of his sociological studies after the economic ones—contributed with his theories and models (variously interpreted and even distorted) to the almost scientific legitimation of imperial concerns and dreams during the Fascist regime. Empire was really a generalized common reference for all of these scholars.

NOTES

1. On the composition, mission, and activities of this Committee for Colonies, see Brunialti (1897: 538–541). The first Italian society of anthropology and ethnology was also founded in 1871: see Clemente et al. (1985) and Fedele and Baldi (1988). Anthropology gained academic legitimation in the 1870s, with the first chairs granted to Paolo Mantegazza in Florence (1869), Giustiniano Nicolucci in Naples (1880), and Giuseppe Sergi in Rome (1883). The latter was a strong supporter also of sociology and an active player in the Italian sociological field still in 1920. Among the students of Mantegazza worth noting is Enrico Morselli, another influential actor in the sociological field. See, in general, on this early phase of Italian sociology, Santoro (1992) (especially focused on the relationships between the juridical field and the emerging field of sociology), Burgalassi (1996) and above all Barbano and Sola (1985).

2. On Adwa and its political consequences and meanings, see Mennasemay (1997) and Triulzi (2003).

3. On the Italian penetration of Albania, with bibliographical references, see chapter 13.

4. Michels (1914: 92), quoting the nationalist writer and poet Enrico Corradini.

5. Reading the history of sociology in Italy in this manner, however, it is almost impossible to escape from an apparent paradox that Levine himself acknowledges, that, notwithstanding its late beginning, the Italian contribution "draws on a longer trajectory of history and culture than any other for its ultimate source of inspiration" (1995: 231). Niccolò Machiavelli and Giovan Battista Vico are the original sources identified by Levine at the beginning of the specific Italian sociological tradition. But these two are not alone—nor in many ways the most crucial. Indeed, the paradoxical nature of the Italian contribution to sociology envisioned by Levine would be solved if only he had more carefully searched in the sources of this national tradition and above all in the structure of the Italian sociological field, a task that would have added more material and nuances to his insightful but substantially misleading reconstruction. In order to understand the Italian sociological tradition, we need a much wider horizon than that offered by the reference to Marx in one camp and Machiavelli and Vico in the other. As noticed by R. W. Connell (with explicit, critical reference to Levine), no national tradition is really alone, as each one is always embedded in a flow of exchanges and links with other traditions. Italian sociology is no exception to this general rule.

6. Before and more than being influenced by Marx, many of the Italian socialist sociologists of the last decades of the nineteenth century—Enrico Ferri, Achille Loria, and Napoleone Colajanni—had been exposed to the influence of Spencerian and Darwinian evolutionism or alternatively to German idealism (Hegel's heritage was exceptionally strong in Naples, where Antonio Labriola, the most respected of Italian Marxists, studied). Even Gramsci had been strongly influenced by the champion of Italian idealism, Benedetto Croce, before joining the socialist cause and eventually cofounding the Italian Communist Party. And his early academic studies in the field of linguistics and glottology would represent a strong "cultural" (i.e., superstructural in Marxist language) influence also on his materialism.

7. Interestingly enough, Sorokin's main source in his monumental compilation—including his classification into schools—was an early book by an Italian sociologist, Fausto Squillace, author of one of the very first historical treatises of sociology as a discipline, which was translated and available also in German and Spanish (Squillace 1902).

8. They are *Rivista di sociologia* (1894–1896), *Rivista Italiana di sociologia* (1897–1921), *La scienza sociale* (1898–1910), and *Rivista di sociologia* (1927–1935), to which we can add, as journals in the human and social sciences devoted also to sociological studies, the *Rivista di filosofia scientifica* (1881–1890), which was the major venue and laboratory of Italian positivism, the *Rassegna di science sociali e politiche* (1883–1895), the *Archivio di psichiatria, scienze penali e antropologia criminale* (founded in 1880 by Lombroso), *La scuola positiva* (founded by Ferri, especially important for criminal sociology), *Genus* (founded by Gini, since 1934), and the Catholic *Rivista internazionale di science sociali e discipline ausiliarie* (since 1893). There were also a

few journals, usually short-lived, devoted to other disciplines (e.g., art or medicine) but including in their names the word "sociology." For an overview and brief notices about the aforementioned journals, see Becker (1938), Michels (1930), Squillace (1911), and, more recently, Barbano and Sola (1985: 192–196) and Pusceddu (1989) on the *Rivista di sociologia*, Rossi (1988) on the *Rivista di filosofia scientifica*, and Roggero (1990) and Garzia (1992) on the *Rivista Italiana di sociologia*.

9. The following Italian scholars contributed a paper to the congress: Achille Loria, Roberto Michels, Enrico Morselli, Giuseppe Sergi, Corrado Gini, Alfredo, Niceforo, Raffaele Garofalo, and Antonio Marro. All but one, Marro, were or would have been active also as sociologists, contributing to sociological journals, teaching sociology, or publishing sociological works. See Eugenics Education Society (1912).

10. Consider the case of Pareto. It is doubtless he had in mind something like a "field of sociology" when he decided to enter it with his research and teaching. His criticism of other works—and their authors—was a crucial precondition of his project to devote the last part of his intellectual life to writing a treatise on sociology—together with the ongoing belief that economics, the discipline he studied and taught, did not exhaust the study of human action and that a more general knowledge should be developed for this aim. It is true that his late entry into the field was not subordinated to anything other than his decision to enter (as a star professor in economics and a rentier, he had no status or income constraints). But the same could be said of economics, an already academically established field that he entered without any title, apart from his own writings and his social and intellectual relations. Even if anybody as a private citizen could write and publish on sociology in those years or even found and edit a sociological journal, having an identity as a sociologist was at least in part conditional on its acceptance and acknowledgment by potential pairs, even in a field not yet fully institutionalized as was the case at the time in Italy. Like Pareto, Gini also arrived in sociology through other disciplines—in his case, statistics and demography. Unlike Pareto, he never stopped to cultivate these other disciplines. But it is clear that sociology had a special appeal to him as a generalized, and generalizable, knowledge in which all the results of the special disciplines could find a synthesis and a scientific systematization. If there were many statisticians around him, few would also be sociologists like him.

11. The most significant of these attempts was made in 1906, when a petition signed by almost sixty scholars, including such influential ones as Loria and Morselli, was presented to the minister of education asking for the establishment of chairs in sociology in the Italian university system. What is of interest for us is that the promoter of the petition was a *libero docente* at the University of Florence, Ugo Matteucci, who in 1913–1914 would have taught a course in colonial studies (Matteucci 1913).

12. Indeed, what Ferrero wrote would today be called a sociological history of the Roman civilization. This is one of the reasons professional historians of Rome did not recognize him as one of their own.

13. The reading is difficult also because of the author's efforts to coin new terms: in fact, his references to the literature are very scanty, mainly limited to Pasquale

Rossi's contributions to collective psychology. Even if not declared as sources or quoted, Durkheim or at least the Durkheimian school is also in the air.

14. Gramsci would have synthesized these criticisms with the negatively connoted neologism of *lorianesimo*, a label that could identify those intellectual postures looking for novelties and originality at every cost and more concerned with the literary value than with the conceptual soundness of texts.

15. It may be worthwhile to recall that Loria had a nonnegligible impact on American economic historians, especially Frederick J. Turner (Benson 1950). On Loria's theory of land determinism, see Crawford (1948) and Rabbeno (1892). Ugo Rabbeno was an economist like Loria, sensitive to sociological issues (he wrote a series of books on cooperation described by the author as contributions to "economic sociology") who devoted himself in the last years of his brief career to the study of commercial policies and land colonization, the subject of his last book, which was published posthumously and edited by Loria (Rabbeno 1898).

16. Michels's lasting interest in colonialism as a scholarly object is apparent in one of his last works, published in German (1932b), and by his participation in the colonial congresses of the 1930s (he was among the speakers of the first Italian Congress of Colonial Studies, held in Florence in 1931). In 1917 Michels discussed the Roman legacy in Italian colonialism (1917).

17. The Italian marriage of migration and colonialism had in any case already been celebrated in 1899 by the then young economist Luigi Einaudi, himself based in Turin and future colleague and friend of Michels. His *Un principe mercante: studio dell'espansione coloniale Italiana* (A Merchant Prince: A Study of Italian Colonial Expansion; cf. Einaudi 1899) was a landmark in his long intellectual and professional career (which in 1948 would bring him to the first presidency of the Italian Republic). To convey the excitement of Italy's worldwide expansion at the turn of the century, particularly in Latin America, Einaudi chose to narrate the life and success of one Italian businessman, Enrico Dell'Acqua. With his title, Einaudi wanted to revive the glory of Italy's medieval past, comparing Dell'Acqua to the princes of Venice, Genoa, and Milan. Whereas Crispi had promoted the myth of the ancient Roman Empire, Einaudi was establishing the alternative colonial myth of Italy's wealthy medieval republics. In his book, Einaudi praised what he claimed to be Italy's true imperialism, that is, the pacific colonization of lands through creative entrepreneurship and work. The link between emigration and colonialism was, however, far from new and was one of the main topics of the earlier studies (usually from an economic point of view) on colonialism in Italy: see, for example, Boccardo (1864) and Carpi (1874). Colonies in these early studies usually referred, however, to "colonization" rather than "colonialism" (see chapter 1)—not the outcome of aggressive colonial politics but the pacific entry and establishment of persons and families in another country for work motives, sometimes with the support of a state's diplomacy.

18. In the second edition of his *Elementi*, Mosca added a footnote where he admitted that his criticism of the racial factor—interpreted as "ethnological coefficient"— was too strong when he wrote the book in 1894. Interestingly, the second edition

dates to 1923, that is, eleven years after the conquest of Libya, nine years after Mosca's engagement in colonial governance, one year after the rise of Fascism to power, and the same year he was nominated by government as senator of the *Regno*. In this second edition of his masterpiece, Mosca devoted a whole new essay to the history and criticism of racial doctrines, in an almost completely forgotten (and never quoted or referred to in secondary literature) memory he delivered to the Accademia dei Lincei. See Mosca (1933).

19. This included the most renowned and respected socialist thinker in Italy, the philosopher Antonio Labriola (Bellamy 1987: 185). It is worth noting that Labriola, though critical toward positivism and sociology, devoted a few courses to this subject at the University of Naples, where he was professor of moral philosophy.

20. He developed in particular a theory of the psychology of the emigrant, whose major statement was published in a sociological journal (Coletti 1899).

21. On this journal see Pusceddu (1989: 75–98). Mainly devoted to the discussion of epistemological issues, the journal gave little space to analysis of substantive topics. This was in line with the initial assumption that sociology was "a philosophy of social facts." Among the most interesting articles are Ferrari (1896), which, while discussing the organismic analogy, advances a theoretical hypothesis on the cycle of expansion and decline of nations—an ancient topic that would be revived in the following years by Corrado Gini (1912b, 1930a, 1930b). See also Ferrari (1898), which explicitly addresses the question of colonialism as a stage in the political cycle of nations.

22. Virgilii wrote also on the war and its economic and demographic consequences (e.g., 1916, 1919). Still active in the 1940s, Filippo Virgilii was one of the three scholars engaged in the sociological field to participate in the Congress of Colonial Studies, held at Florence in 1931 (the others were Niceforo and Michels; Gini was on the scientific committee). On Virgilii as a statistician and social researcher, see Marucco (2001).

23. On this "measured colonialism," see also Sergi's contribution to the Races Congress of 1911, Sergi (1911).

24. On Ferri as a Spencerian Marxist, see Beck (2005). On his incipient imperialism, see Aquarone (1977: 314–315), who attributes it to his travels in Latin America in 1908 for lecturing (after he left the editorship of the socialist newspaper *L'Avanti*) and to a strong sense of patriotism. Ferri's ideological acceptance of an imperialistic stance emerged during the Libyan war. In the 1920s Ferri joined the Fascist cause and became an enthusiastic admirer of Mussolini.

25. The negative representation of southern Italy as "Africa" was indeed a common move in some intellectual and political circles since unification: see Moe (2001).

26. Pareto was the only one of the elitists to teach sociology with continuity. But Pareto taught it in Switzerland (at the University of Lausanne), where he arrived in 1893 to succeed Walras. However, Pareto's presence as a sociologist in Italy has always been strong. His first articles on the subject were published in RIS, and his large treatise was written and published originally in Italian. In 1906 Pareto held a course on sociology at the faculty of law of the University of Bologna, invited by the economist Tullio Martello—possibly the venue where Gini, who had just

graduated in the same university and faculty, first began developing his sociological theory.

27. On the complex relationships between Weber and Michels, see Mommsen (1981).

28. Comparisons were also frequent in Pareto's writing for conveying ideas about his own country, surrounding them with a sort of exotic aura, as this excerpt from the same text illustrates: "There is no place in Italy for a citizen who, to preserve his independence, refuses to be a party to political patronage. He finds himself in about the same position as a Hindoo who has no caste. He is an outlaw, a man whom everyone can attack" (1893: 705).

29. On the positivistic and evolutionary roots of Pareto's sociology, see Bucolo (1980) and Nye (1986).

30. In 1914 Gini proposed his income inequality ratio, which is still the most used income inequality index worldwide.

31. Gini also published an original textbook about how to collect statistical data on "primitive" populations, which was still used in teaching during the 1950s (Gini 1941c).

32. At Harvard Gini gave two courses, mainly based on his recently issued (in a new edition) *Prime linee di patologia economica* (1935), which Merton reviewed positively in the first issue of *American Sociological Review*. Merton acted for a while as a supporter of Gini in the States, providing reviews for his and his collaborators' books. In exchange, Gini offered advice to Merton about his career and research topics (Santoro forthcoming).

33. The attribute "colonial" was abolished only in 1968.

34. This includes one of its leaders, Luigi Sturzo, himself a sociologist, and the founder, with Giuseppe Toniolo, of a "Catholic sociology" in Italy. Their contribution to sociology is not addressed in this chapter, but colonialism and empire were not absent from their intellectual and moral horizons, and their entanglement with both passed through the idea of a civilizing mission that could introduce colonized societies—including, of course, Muslim ones—to the true religion and the true God. See, for example, Toniolo (1905).

FIVE

German Sociology and Empire
From Internal Colonization to Overseas Colonization and Back Again
ANDREW ZIMMERMAN

The legacy of German sociology today is bound to a reading of Max Weber as a hermeneutic sociologist, whose methodology of *Verstehen* is commonly regarded as tempering nomothetic social sciences with an allegedly milder, more flexible search for "ideal types." Weber's work is thus counterposed to the supposedly positivistic sociology of Emile Durkheim, the impermissibly abstract theories of British and Austrian economists, and the "determinism" attributed to Karl Marx.[1] While the opposition between German warmth and the cold, ratiocinating West can be traced back much further, one of its most proximate origins in German sociology is the first part of Norbert Elias's 1939 *Civilizing Process*, "On the Sociogenesis of the Concepts 'Civilization' and 'Culture.'" "Whereas the concept of civilization [*Zivilization*]," according to Elias, "has the function of giving expression to the continuously expansionist tendency of colonizing groups, the concept of *Kultur* mirrors the self-consciousness of a nation which had constantly to seek out and constitute its boundaries anew, in a political as well as a spiritual sense, and again and again had to ask itself: 'What is really our identity?'" (2000: 7). Elias acknowledges the special prominence that World War I and the Versailles annexations gave this antithesis between France and England as colonizing bearers of civilization and Germany as colonial victim defending its culture. He also describes European overseas colonization in Africa and the Pacific as part of a civilizing process, doomed to undermine itself because it would ultimately give to the colonized that thing—civilization—whose erstwhile lack was supposed to have justified European colonial rule (Elias 2000: 385–386).

Elias traces the national antithesis of culture and civilization to eighteenth-century social conflicts between aristocracy and bourgeoisie and points to Immanuel Kant's 1784 "Idea for a Universal History with a Cosmopolitan Intent" as an early example of the antithesis. "Cultivated [*cultiviert*] to a high degree by art and science," Elias quotes from Kant, "we are civilized [*civilisiert*] to the point where we are overburdened with all sorts of decency and decorum." Elias continues his citation from Kant: "The idea of morality is a part of culture [*Cultur*]. But the application of this idea, which amounts to little more than the apparently ethical [*Sittenähnliche*] in the love of honor and in outward decency, amounts only to mere civilizing [*Civilisirung*]."

Elias leaves out a sentence occurring between the two he quotes, a sentence in which Kant expresses one of the main theses of his essay: "Still very much is lacking for us to consider ourselves already moral [*schon moralisirt*]." What, specifically, Kant finds lacking is, famously, a "civil society that generally administers the law" (*allgemein das Recht verwaltenden bürgerlichen Gesellschaft*) that would straighten, in the translation Isaiah Berlin made famous, "the crooked timber of humanity." "Man," according to Kant, "has need of a master" who would force nations to end their wasteful conflicts, much as the "savage was reluctantly forced to give up his brutal freedom and seek peace and security in a lawful constitution" (1784: 23–26). In his essay, Kant calls for precisely that form of colonization that would emerge at the Berlin West Africa conference a century later: colonization justified in the name of internationalism, humanity, civilization, and peace. This "in the name of" meant that states able to project military power overseas conquered and ruled regions in which these universal goods were supposed to be lacking. For Kant, the civilizing process required coercion and state authority.

Elias in fact elides Germany's modern colonial expansion when he writes that Germany, unlike other European powers, enjoyed its most "vigorous expansion . . . in the Middle Ages," thereafter "diminishing slowly but steadily . . . hemmed in on all sides" (1978: 21–22). As a native of Breslau (Wroclaw), the capital of Silesia, in a Polish province taken by Prussia in 1741, Elias might have known better about the modern movements of Germany's frontiers; similarly, Germany enjoyed, before the caesura of 1919 noted by Elias, an overseas empire significant in its own right and regarded as a model by colonial powers including Britain, France, and Belgium (Zimmerman 2010). The tension between the primitive and the rationalized, seen in German sociologists from Ferdinand Tönnies to Georg Simmel to Max Weber to Jürgen Habermas, emerged in the decades before World War I in conjunction with practical discussions among national economists about internal colonization in the German East and overseas colonization in German Africa. These national economists not only founded the discipline of sociology in Germany but also shaped the discipline in the United States through, perhaps most important, Robert E. Park and the Chicago School (Zimmerman 2010). Although not every German sociologist supported German colonial efforts, colonialism nonetheless sustained the emergent discipline intellectually and institutionally. Traces of German colonialism thus remain present in much German sociology.

German sociology gained its first institutional foothold in the Verein für Sozialpolitik (Social Policy Association), an organization of academic economists offering advice to the German state on, among other topics, methods of colonizing the German Empire, that is, on settling those territories claimed by the German Imperial State with populations identified as German.[2] This included expelling Poles from, or subordinating them in, the eastern parts of Prussia but, just as important, preventing German workers from leaving the region. The Prussian king Frederick the Great, who had conquered Elias's native Silesia, took the Polish province of West Prussia at the first partition of Poland in 1772, uniting territorially Brandenburg and East Prussia. Frederick's successor annexed Posen to Prussia in the second partition of Poland in 1793. A century later, Posen and West Prussia would become the focus of what Prussian officials would call "internal colonization."

Even before the Prussian state began its "depolonizing" efforts in these two provinces, German social scientists turned their attention to territorial settlement as a means of controlling German workers. Friedrich Wilhelm III of Prussia, advised by his chief minister, Baron Karl vom Stein, had ended bound labor in his kingdom by decreeing in October 1807 that, after 1810, "there will only be free people" in Prussia (Conze 1957: 102–105; Gray 1986; Knapp 1927; Koselleck 1975; Schissler 1978). The liberation of serfs was part of the so-called Prussian reform movement, a program of administrative and economic modernization designed to restore the territory, status, and power that the kingdom had possessed before its defeat by Napoleon's army in 1807. As in the U.S. South half a century later, declaring labor free without reforming land ownership not only left the gross inequalities of unfree labor in place but in many ways increased the economic power of former lords. The net result of the liberation of serfs was an expansion of capitalist agriculture in the east under conditions of de facto unfreedom.

In the second half of the nineteenth century, agricultural and urban workers alike cast off enough extraeconomic constraints to occasion anxiety among social scientists and others committed to preserving the political and economic status quo. German agricultural laborers sought the freedom and prosperity only promised by their formal emancipation in a mass exodus from the land of their former masters. In the century between the defeat of Napoleon and the beginning of World War I, approximately 5.5 million Germans moved to the United States, more than a third of them from the eastern territories (Bade 1980). Added to this overseas migration out of the German east was a mass internal migration of the descendants of dependent farmers to industrial employment in eastern Germany. Between 1880 and 1910, two million individuals left eastern Germany for other regions within Germany (Tipton 1974: 959). A German Employment Law (*Gewerbeordnung*) of 1869 granted urban workers a degree of freedom by limiting—although not eliminating—the use of penal sanctions to bolster the authority of employers (Landmann 1907; see also Steinfeld 2001).

The Verein für Sozialpolitik was founded in 1872 by a group of economists concerned that the transition to free labor—obviously limited though it was—would lead to political and social disorder and especially to social democracy.[3] These economists, who included Gustav Schmoller, Georg Friedrich Knapp, Lujo Brentano, Adolf Wagner, and, two decades later, Max Weber, rejected the laissez-faire, classical political economy associated with Adam Smith in favor of state socialism. Members of the Verein für Sozialpolitik dubbed the classical economists the "Manchester School" and dismissed them as "abstract and unhistorical" in contrast to their own "realistic" approach (e.g., Brentano 1871). Free traders, for their part, chided the economists in the Verein für Sozialpolitik, with its academic leadership, as "socialists of the lectern" (the German term was *Kathedersozialisten*) (Oppenheim 1872). The approach taken by economists in the Verein für Sozialpolitik represented a venerable academic mainstream in Germany, a direction associated with the economist Friedrich List, whose 1841 *National System of Political Economy* criticized followers of Adam Smith for ignoring the distinct positions of nations in international economies in their pell-mell endorsement of free trade. The state socialism of the Verein für Sozialpolitik was formed in reaction to the social democracy of the workers' movement. Like Marx and Friedrich Engels, German Social Democrats embraced a libertarian socialism that emerged out of classical political economy, or "Manchesterism." Social democracy demanded an end to the exploitation of labor by capitalists, not the handouts and paternalistic control from a bourgeois state that the Verein demanded. Indeed, Bismarck, surely the most powerful enemy of socialism in Germany, informed Schmoller the year after the organization's founding that he himself was a *Katheder-Sozialist* (cited in Lindenfeld

1997: 226). Thanks to the high regard Bismarck and other high Prussian officials held for the Verein für Sozialpolitik, Knapp, Schmoller, and Brentano received appointments at the new university in Strasbourg. Strasbourg, in Alsace-Lorraine, had been taken from France during the 1870–1871 Franco-Prussian War, and its university was to show off the German Empire that had emerged out of that conflict.

For the Verein für Sozialpolitik, the end of serfdom and the gradual decline of manorial control demanded new forms of labor coercion suited to an era of free labor. Georg Friedrich Knapp, perhaps the greatest historian of German agriculture and one of the founders of the Verein für Sozialpolitik, framed this problem as one of finding a capitalist replacement for feudal labor relations. Knapp's principal work on free labor, his 1887 *Liberation of the Serfs (Bauernbefreiung)*, criticized those liberals who assumed that, with the abolition of serfdom in Prussia, the free market would work out labor relations automatically (Knapp 1927). Knapp often lamented that the social science of the eighteenth century had condemned serfdom without thinking about "a replacement" for it (Knapp 1925: 137). "Every age has its task," Gustav Schmoller wrote in a review of *Liberation of the Serfs*: "the century 1750–1850 had the obligation to save and liberate the peasants. The century 1850–1950 stands before the even greater task of elevating the working class and reconciling it to our economic order." Schmoller elaborated the political implications of Knapp's historical research, noting that a kind of re-peasantization of the working class could prevent the spread of social democracy after the decline of "patriarchal relations" and calling for mass settlement of workers on smallholds in the Prussian East (Schmoller 1888, quoted in Harnisch 1993: 127).

The Prussian state followed the recommendations of the Verein für Sozialpolitik to sponsor rural smallholding when, in 1886, the Ministry of Agriculture set up a Settlement Commission (Ansiedlungskomission). Since 1881 the Verein had been calling for "the preservation and strengthening of the rural middle class" (1883: v). In 1883–1884 the Verein had published a three-volume work and held a conference on rural conditions in Germany. Participants at the conference made various proposals for using land ownership as a bulwark against social democracy (Verein für Sozialpolitik 1884). In 1886 the Verein published a volume on the state-sponsored settlement of small farmers, which it dubbed "internal colonization," and discussed the topic at its annual meeting (Sombart-Ermsleben 1887: 77). In the volume, Schmoller described the "building, settling, agricultural activity" that distinguished "internal colonization" from the territorial conquest of "external colonization." Internal colonization amounted, in Schmoller's words, to the "definitive settling [*Sesshaftwerdung*] of a people" and "the transition to agriculture." Agriculture, for Schmoller, involved also the advance of "higher moral, intellectual, and technical civilization" and therefore represented an "earnest struggle with the opposing natural forces, with the traditional morals and customs of one's own people and with hostile or recalcitrant elements of foreign peoples" (1886: 1–2).

The Prussian Settlement Commission embraced smallholding primarily to Germanize predominantly Polish areas in the kingdom. The Settlement Commission divided large estates into small plots for German settlers in order "to strengthen the German element in the provinces of West Prussia and Posen against Polonizing efforts" (quoted in Knapp 1925: 138). Anxieties in the Prussian state, as well as among the members of the Verein für Sozialpolitik, increased after 1890, when seasonal workers began arriving in large numbers from Russian and Austrian Poland. The increasing presence of Polish migrant workers made the question of proletarianization and polonization identical for many German elites. In the 1880s, the Verein für Sozialpolitik had found the anti-Polish politics of the Settlement Commission irrelevant to the real problem of proletarianization. In the 1890s, the Verein increasingly made the racial concerns of the Settlement Commission its own. Schmoller and Knapp, two of the central figures in the Verein, had long viewed free agricultural labor in the United States through racial categories, finding the race of black farmers as important as elites in the American South themselves did. In the late 1880s, Knapp began studying black labor in Africa and the New World as comparative cases for his study of the transition from bound to free labor in Germany. In Africa and the New World, as in Germany, labor discipline could never, for Knapp, be achieved by freedom, and thus emancipation required new modes of regulation. Writing on the "Negro question" in the New World, especially in Spanish and Portuguese colonies, Knapp argued that "Negro slavery" was simply a solution to "the worker question on the large-scale agricultural-industrial business of the plantation" that took advantage of the fact that, at the time, Blacks were a race that "stood outside the law of nations [*Völkerrecht*]" (1891: 15).

For Knapp, antiblack racism functioned as a labor coercive regime that could replace slavery as a means of maintaining a plantation labor force. Knapp already detected a tendency toward forced labor or even slavery in the common complaint that the "Negro" was lazy and did not like to work— when in fact, he noted, it was only the case that Negroes did not wish to work for European plantations. Knapp expressed the hope that German rulers of Africa would find methods at least more humane than slavery for extracting labor from their colonial subjects (Knapp 1891: 14–16). In a 1900 lecture, Knapp elaborated the role of racism in New World plantation production, noting that the United States had abandoned slavery but still used racism to control black labor. "The Negro cannot lose the marks of his race; he remains subordinated, even when he becomes a Christian and a free man, and is restricted to lower jobs. . . . Under these circumstances, it is economically possible to free slaves without ruining the plantation. . . . There remains just one final question: that of the racially alien proletariat."[4] It seems that Knapp saw race and racism not as a general feature of labor organization but rather as one of the myriad ways that labor could be controlled in specific economic conjunctures. He does not seem to have concerned himself with the questions of race in Germany itself, although he did lay the groundwork for bringing racism to German agrarian sociology.

It was none other than Max Weber who finally made race a central concern of German sociology, bringing the racism of the Settlement Commission to the center of discussions in the Verein für Sozialpolitik about the control of free labor when he joined the organization in 1890. The young Weber first encountered Poles when the reserve unit in which he served was transferred from Alsace to Posen in 1888. Bismarck had proposed, as one of a number of anti-Polish measures to supplement internal colonization, transferring predominantly German military units to Polish areas, and perhaps this explains the relocation of Weber's own unit.[5] At the end of his first year's service in that eastern province, Weber toured some of the estates set up by the Prussian Settlement Commission. "From that time on," Marianne Weber would later recall, "he felt one of the most important political problems was the winning of the East by a policy of settlement" (Marianne Weber 1975: 146–147).[6] Weber's hatred for Poles continued throughout his life, beginning with his involvement with the Verein für Sozialpolitik, where he alone saw internal colonization primarily as a fight against Poles rather than as a means of preventing proletarianization. In 1896, at the founding meeting of the National Social Party, one of the many new "social parties" offering a patriotic and religious alternative to the Social Democrats, Weber attacked his friend Friedrich Naumann, the leader of the party, for his insufficient hostility to Poles. Naumann should not protest, Weber claimed, against "reducing the Poles to second-class citizens of Germany." In fact, Weber maintained, "the opposite is true: we were the first to make the Poles into humans" (Max Weber 1971: 28–29). In 1899 Weber resigned from the Pan-German League, explaining that, although he supported the aims and leaders of the organization, he believed it did not work with sufficient diligence against Poles in Germany, yielding to the interests of agrarian capitalists in cheap migrant labor.[7] Weber's genius was to develop his anti-Polish racism into a theory of culture, race, and class that continues to this day to shape European and American social thought.

Weber agreed with other members of the Verein that capitalist agriculture had freed rural workers from paternal authority, increasing the freedom of those who remained on the land and improving the standards of living for those who left the land for industrial employment. Like other members of the Verein, Weber worried that this new freedom and prosperity would lead to rural proletarianization, class conflict, and the growth of social democracy. To these social and political anxieties, Weber added cultural and racial concerns of his own. German farmers who left the land were being replaced, Weber claimed, with a "rapidly growing mass of foreign laborers with lower standards of living." The advantages for landlords of these migrant workers stemmed not only from their lower wages and the ease of controlling such "precariously employed foreigners" but also because they did not need to be supported in the winter when there was no work for them anyway. The Prussian East had, through what Weber identified as its typical patriarchal forms of authority, preserved the "military virtue" of the rural population and "created the political might of the nation" (Max Weber 1892: 793, 795, 803–804). Weber worried that German workers would be influenced by the low standards of the Polish workers with whom they had to compete. "It is not possible," Weber explained, "to allow two nations with different bodily constitutions—differently constructed stomachs . . . —to compete freely as workers in the same area." German workers could only compete with Poles, Weber explained, by descending a "cultural step [Kulturstufe]." Weber thus called for the "absolute exclusion of the Russian-Polish workers from the German East" (1924a: 456–457). When Weber assumed a professorship at the University of Freiburg in 1895, his inaugural address that May presented the struggle between Germans and Poles in Prussia as an "economic struggle for existence" shaped by the "physical and mental race differences [Rassendifferenzen] between nationalities." The Polish farmer was winning the economic struggle with the German, Weber explained, "not despite but rather because [of] his low physical and mental habits" (1971: 2, 4, 8). Weber added racist and nationalist anxieties to the prevailing view in the Verein für Sozialpolitik that the increased personal liberty and higher living standards offered by capitalism were not worth the political dangers they brought. He acknowledged that the racist nationalism he advocated presented a political logic that contradicted the logic of the free market, explaining that "the economic policy of a German state, as well as the scale of values of the German economist can ... only be German" (13). Weber seems to have persuaded his colleagues of the social scientific validity of his racism. According to Knapp, Weber's contributions on the topic made the members of the Verein realize that "our expertise has come to an end, and we must start to learn all over again" (1925: 125).

For Max Weber, Polish workers migrated to the West not so much for wages as to break with their subordination in "the entire ensemble of family and familiar environment." In fact, Weber speculated, if the miserable living conditions and long working hours of Polish seasonal migrants were accounted for, their wages would not amount to any more than those of Poles who remained in the east. The migrant was pushed not by pecuniary motives but rather by a "dark urge for personal freedom" (Max Weber 1924a: 492–493). Weber worried that the "swarm of eastern Nomads" would bring German workers down to the cultural level of the "Polish proletariat" in those eastern regions where Germans did not, as they did in Saxony, "look down with contempt on the low standard of living" of these seasonal migrants (Max Weber 1924a: 457, 448). Max Sering, a professor of agricultural economics at the University of Berlin, agreed with Weber that Polish seasonal workers were motivated less by economic gain than by a desire for "increased independence" and "personal respect." It was, Sering explained, "the ideal of freedom and human dignity" spread—"often in a crude form"—to the "lowest social levels" (1893: 13). Sering hoped his research would help the Prussian state to satisfy the new "feelings of independence of the worker" by encouraging smallhold farming. The state could thereby encourage a "social order that lessens the current differences of property and the opposition of classes and removes the causes of the depopulation of the East." Sering meant, of course, the de-Germanization of the East, for there was no shortage of Poles willing to work in Prussia. Settlement would make Polish migrant labor unnecessary, keep Germans settled in the East, and make a "protective barrier for the state against the external and internal enemy" (14–16, 280).

Schmoller soon followed Weber in bringing race to the center of his understanding of historical economics. Schmoller began his 1900 textbook, *Outline of General Economics* (*Grundriß der allgemeinen Volkswirtschaftslehre*), by connecting labor, morality, and civilizational progress to set the groundwork for a racial political economy. Labor, for Schmoller, was human activity that "followed moral-rational ends with consistent effort." In more backward societies, according to Schmoller, only the weak, primarily women and slaves, did heavy work. "It is a great progress," wrote Schmoller, echoing a prevailing sentiment among German and other European colonial thinkers, "when free men also begin to walk behind the plow." "The process of educating individuals, societies, and humanity as a whole to work," he continued, is "an upward path; everything that forces or encourages work ... contains elements of economic and moral, bodily and spiritual schooling." Humanity, for Schmoller, was no abstract concept, and he faulted the political and economic sciences of the eighteenth century for ignoring "the laws of national character." In addition to racial "inherited properties," individuals were also, according to Schmoller, shaped by "the influence of the great spiritual fluid ... that surrounds them, that affects them through imitation, education, and social interaction." "Economics makes sound judgments when it proceeds not merely from abstract humans or even from just their economic activity, but rather when it attends to the varieties of racial types" (1900: 38–39, 140–145). To correct earlier economists' inattention to racial and national characteristics, Schmoller offered his students an overview of the "lowest races," beginning with the "Negro" of Africa and America (Schmoller 1900: 149–150). In his famous *Methodenstreit* with Austrian economists, Schmoller had similarly argued for such social and historical specificity against the abstractions of classical political economy. For Schmoller, as for Weber, race made a real difference in economics, and the particular historicism that differentiated German economists from their Austrian or British counterparts gave prominence to race.

After the turn of the century, Schmoller led many of his colleagues in the Verein für Sozialpolitik in contributing directly to the development of colonialism in Africa. With the turn toward economic development and the control of labor in the inland regions of Africa, sociology displaced ethnography as the leading colonial human science (Zimmerman 2001).[8] This was especially true in Togo and Tanzania, the German colonies that, before World War I, had won admiration from all other colonial powers as model colonies, rational alternatives to the brutality of the Congo (Zimmerman 2005, 2006b. 2010). Schmoller's first direct intervention in colonial planning began with a comment at the First German Colonial Congress, in October 1902. During a debate about the comparative benefits of indigenous smallhold farming and European-run plantations in Africa, Schmoller offered that the question had already been discussed at length among national economists such as himself. Schmoller agreed with many colonial thinkers that European-run capital-intensive plantations using "indigenous or imported laborers of lower races" would produce more than small farms would.

He maintained, nonetheless, as he and his colleagues in the Verein für Sozialpolitik had in the case of German agriculture, that smallholding should be encouraged for political reasons. The state, missionaries, and "all farsighted friends of the colonies," Schmoller held, should encourage indigenous smallholding for the "entire mental and economic development of the natives," for the "future of the conquered lower races" (1902). In Africa, as in Germany, smallhold farming would bolster the political authority of economic elites by disciplining workers.

The debate about smallholding versus plantation agriculture was the major political economic issue in German tropical Africa. It is no surprise, given the extent to which members of the Verein für Sozialpolitik involved themselves in similar issues around internal colonization in Prussia, that many became active supporters of a German colonial secretary who supported both colonial smallholding and the role of social science in forming colonial policy. In 1907 Schmoller led a group of German social scientists, including Knapp, Max Sering, and Adolf Wagner, in forming a "Colonial-Political Action Committee" (CPAC) (see Grimmer-Solem 2003a and 2007). This committee was to organize scientists, artists, writers, and the "liberal professions" to support the German "Volk" against the "petty and anti-nationalistic [*unnational denkende*] majority in the Reichstag," the Catholic Center Party members who criticized German colonial policy.[9] Since 1905 Catholic missionaries in Togo had sent numerous reports of colonial atrocities to the Center Party, which the young deputy Matthias Erzberger and others publicized (Epstein 1959).[10] Major wars against Africans in German East Africa and in German Southwest Africa required large colonial expenditures but offered no hope of correspondingly large profits. The Center Party increasingly excoriated the government of Chancellor Bernhard von Bülow on colonial issues.

Schmoller and his CPAC colleagues worked closely with the new colonial director, Bernhard Dernburg, to defend the colonial enterprise against criticism in the Reichstag. The CPAC supported a view of colonialism that emerged from the smallholder model worked out in the meetings of Colonial Congresses and elsewhere. The CPAC maintained, in a pamphlet it distributed gratis to a German public dismayed by expensive colonial wars and individual colonial scandals, that the time had come for a reinvigorated colonialism. The old colonialism of arm's-length trade gave insufficient control over indigenous labor and did not allow for "the regulation and improvement of production." With the "education of the Negro to work" and increasing control over African labor, Germany would, the pamphlet promised, soon produce enough cotton to cover all its needs, making its textile industry totally independent from U.S. growers (Kolonialpolitischen Aktionskomité 1907: 6–7, 20–21). In pursuit of this cotton project, Germans in Togo consulted with Booker T. Washington and employed Tuskegee Institute graduates and faculty. Washington, in turn, worked closely with German-trained sociologists W. E. B. Du Bois and Robert E. Park (Zimmerman 2010). The CPAC collaborated with Dernburg in the campaign leading up to the January 1907 elections for the new Reichstag.

Dernburg made his most famous speech during the campaign, his call for "scientific colonization," at a forum sponsored by the CPAC for an audience of scientists and artists at the Berlin Academy of Music in January of 1907. After a brief introduction by Schmoller, Dernburg took the podium, reminding his audience that Germany, as the "nation of thinkers and poets," had long led other nations in the humanities and social sciences and had more recently taken the lead in applied science and technology. These areas were, the colonial director explained, "the modern means of developing foreign parts of the world, raising up lower cultures, and improving the conditions of life for Blacks and Whites" (Schmoller et al. 1907: 5). The CPAC distributed the text of Dernburg's speech to every public school teacher and to nonsocialist workers' organizations.[11] Later during the symposium, the Verein für Sozialpolitik member Max Sering took the podium to remind his audience of the problems resulting from the dependence of the world economy on primary materials produced in tropical regions "inhabited by races unable to create a legal order" without "political domination by civilized people" (Schmoller et al. 1907: 30).

After the 1907 elections delivered a Reichstag friendly to Germany's overseas empire, Dernburg set about consolidating the colonial policy advocated by Schmoller and others in the CPAC. Dernburg had the Colonial Office fund a Colonial Institute in Hamburg, building on already existing institutes for tropical medicine and botany and an ethnographic museum in the Hanseatic port, as well as on the city's importance in the trade with Africa.[12] At the Hamburg Institute, as Erik Grimmer-Solem (2007) has described, Schmoller's student Karl Rathgen continued his teacher's efforts at applying the social sciences to practical questions of overseas colonization.

Max Weber was less interested in overseas colonialism than Schmoller and others in the Verein für Sozialpolitik were. He did, however, continue to develop the racial thinking that emerged from German internal colonization, generalizing it through comparison with the case of African Americans, which he observed during a 1904 trip to the United States to lecture at the International Congress of Arts and Science, part of the Universal Exposition at St. Louis (Scaff 1998a,1998b, 2011). At the St. Louis Congress, Weber offered his own expertise on, and political engagement with, agricultural labor and German-Polish ethnic relations in Prussia as an example, and even a warning, to Americans dealing with rural labor and racial conflict. For Weber, rural society could not exist in a "developed capitalistic culture," which necessarily treated agriculture like any other capitalist undertaking, with the landlord functioning as "a capitalist like others" and laborers "of exactly the same class as other proletarians." The rural problem, for Weber, was therefore how a rural community could be created and preserved within, and against, capitalism. As aristocrats became capitalists, European civilization lost what Weber imagined as economically independent bearers of traditional culture. As peasants became proletarians, they turned increasingly to social democracy, weakening the political power of the state and destabilizing the social order. Although the abundance of land in the United States meant that the nation would not face a rural question for years to come, the ethnic issues in German agriculture did parallel the situation in the United States.

Under conditions of capitalist competition, Weber remarked, "the peasant's struggle for existence" often led to "economic selection in favor of the most frugal, i.e., those most lacking culture." Thus in Germany, Polish farmers proved more economically attractive than Germans, a situation that was economically rational but "completely contrary" to "the advance of culture toward the east, during the Middle Ages, founded upon the superiority of the older and higher culture." Weber saw analogous tendencies in the United States, with the growing numbers of African American–owned farms and African American migration into cities. The "present difficult social problems of the South" arose, for Weber, more from ethnicity—presumably he meant black-white relations—than from economics. Furthermore, the "enormous immigration of uncivilized elements from eastern Europe," for Weber, similarly threatened "the expansive power of the Anglo-Saxon-German settlement of the rural districts." There might eventually arise, Weber warned, "a rural population" that "could not be assimilated by the historically transmitted culture of this country," a culture Weber described as "the great creation of the Anglo-Saxon spirit." Americans should look to German policy toward ethnic Poles, for "the greater part of the problems for whose solution we [Germans] are now working will approach America within but a few generations; the way in which they will be solved will determine the character of the future culture of this continent" (Max Weber 1906: 725–726 , 733, 730, 745–746).

Weber soon complemented his German lessons for America with American lessons for Germany. After the St. Louis Congress, Max Weber, along with his wife, Marianne, made a tour of the southern states, where both studied the situation of African Americans to draw lessons for Germany and for their own scholarly work. The couple visited Booker T. Washington's Tuskegee Institute, which, Marianne later recalled, "probably moved them more than anything else on their trip" (Marianne Weber 1975: 295). For Marianne, the "Negro school was truly worth the day's travel," vividly presenting "a piece of the life struggle and idealistic efforts that we had [only] read about in books."[13] As Max Weber explained the Tuskegee program to his mother, "no one is permitted to do only intellectual work. The purpose is the training of farmers; 'conquest of the soil' is a definite ideal."[14] Perhaps Weber had learned to regard farming as "conquest of the soil" from the Prussian Settlement Commission, which did indeed see smallholding by Germans as a means of conquering the Polish East.

After his visit to the United States, African Americans became a central example for Weber as he developed a cultural-racial economics, culminating in his *Sociology of Religion* (1922), the text that incorporated a revised version of his *Protestant Ethic and the Spirit of Capitalism*. Weber had met W. E. B. Du Bois at the St. Louis conference and, after returning to Germany, solicited from the Atlanta University sociologist an article for the journal of the Verein für Sozialpolitik on the "Negro Question in the United States" (1906). While Du Bois's article clearly condemned the racist division of labor it described, the material it presented was of obvious interest to those interested in preserving such a division of labor. In his methodological writings for the study of the "psychophysics of industrial labor" carried out by the Verein für Sozialpolitik beginning in 1907, Weber used the example of African Americans to encourage his colleagues to study the economic efficiency of "ethnic, cultural, professional, and social groups" for various industrial employments, much as one might consider "the profitability of a variety of coal, ore, or other 'raw material'" (Max Weber 1924b: 68, 123, 125–126). Although it would be difficult, he acknowledged, to distinguish "differences 'inherited' in a biological sense" and "differences in tradition," Weber insisted on the existence, "in principle," of "inheritable differences ... in ... nervous and psychic constitution" that influence "the varying tempo, steadiness, and certainty of reaction," which, in turn, influence the "'disciplinability' [*Disziplinierbarkeit*] necessary for heavy industry" (1924a: 27–28). While the study was to consider only various groups of German workers, the possibility of such varying qualities of labor across groups obtained plausibility,

Weber repeatedly stressed, from the example of "American Negroes" (1924b: 247–252).

Weber regularly speculated that the divergent economic capacities that he identified among various ethnic groups rested ultimately on biological race but held that, for the time being, he could connect these only to a range of factors with more obvious social implications, including religion, culture, and level of civilization. These were, in any case, nearly as permanent as biological race. In the *Protestant Ethic* and the sociology of economic culture that emerged from it, Weber accorded religion this role. Religion had served Weber as a proxy variable for race in his 1895 Freiburg address, where he assumed that in West Prussia Protestants were German and Catholics were Polish in order to use census data on religion to draw conclusions about, as he put it, "physical and mental race differences" (Max Weber 1971: 2–3). In his *Sociology of Religion*, however, religion represented the ideas of the "bearers of civilization [*Kulturträger*]." His comparative study of the economic ethics of Protestantism, Confucianism, Hinduism, and Islam thus aimed to explain why whole regions did not achieve the rational, capitalist economics of Protestant civilizations. As in his earlier writings, Weber left open the possibility that civilizational differences resulted from biological race, noting, indeed, that he was "personally and subjectively predisposed to attribute great importance to the meaning of biological heredity" but that "racial-neurology and -psychology" were not yet developed enough yet to carry out such a study (Max Weber 1922, 1: 12, 14–15).

Weber's *Sociology of Religion* proposed an economic theory based on ethnic or cultural groupings rather than on the individual rationality of classical economics. Although widespread, popular understandings of the *Protestant Ethic*, the first volume of the *Sociology of Religion*, hold it to be a theory of investors, it is, in fact, a theory of devotion to profession, a theory of labor. This is quite explicit in the work itself and provides an answer to the questions about the control of free labor that the Verein für Sozialpolitik had been asking since the 1890s. Weber's theory of capitalism is no theory of capitalists but rather of a "rational-capitalist organization of (formally) free labor" that comprised workers, managers, and owners (Max Weber 1922, 1: 7). The central feature of capitalism was, for Weber, the unquestioning commitment to profession (*Beruf*), whether as a worker, an employee, or a "credit worthy man of honor" (62). As is well known, this ultimately irrational asceticism emerged from explicitly theological motivations but became unconscious compulsions as the external technical apparatus of industry replaced the internal motivations of the Protestant ethic. Humans were stuck, famously, in a "shell hard as steel" (Talcott Parson's "iron cage"), possibly not to be released until "the last ton of fossil fuel has been consumed" and the material apparatus of capitalism collapses (Max Weber 1922, 1: 202–204). As long as fossil fuel remained available and the apparatus of capitalism continued to function, Weber and his colleagues at the Verein für Sozialpolitik could lay to rest their concerns about the ill effects of free labor within Germany and worry instead about preventing corruption by Polish and other inferior workers. Employers could select workers from racial and ethnic groups whose specific competences met their needs, just as, as Weber explained in the *Psychophysik*, they selected specific varieties of coal or other raw materials. Weber's *Protestant Ethic*, a theory of race and free labor, was perhaps the most important early text of a sociology that continues to inform empire even to this day, in which white supremacist elites differentiate the globe into a patchwork of ethnically homogeneous regions for various forms of exploitation and in which racism masquerades as a fear—and sometimes even a celebration—of cultural difference (Zimmerman 2006a).

Like Schmoller, Weber rejected the abstractions of classical economics and sought instead a cultural explanation of economic behavior, a cultural explanation that emerged from, and functioned as, a racial explanation. Scholars often cite Max Weber's debate with the now infamous Social Darwinist Alfred Ploetz to suggest that the Heidelberg national economist opposed racism (for exceptions to this, see Manasse 1947 and Marianne Weber 1975). In fact, the debate indicates the importance race played in Weber's thought and the sociological, rather than biological, nature of his racism. At the first German Sociological Congress in 1910, Alfred Ploetz presented, at the request of the organizers, his position on the relation of race (*Rasse*) and society (*Gesellschaft*). While recognizing that races depend on society to survive, Ploetz also endorsed the prevailing Social Darwinistic fears that social welfare policies and Christian charity would undermine natural selection by allowing inferior individuals to survive. Race, Ploetz asserted, ultimately trumped society in both normative and explanatory importance. Werner Sombart led the ensuing discussion, which, though challenging Ploetz's lecture in ways that had the speaker repeatedly interjecting shouts of "Nein!," concluded that practically nobody at the congress, and certainly not his "friend Max Weber, whom he personally knows quite well" rejected "biology." "Quite true!" exclaimed Weber from the audience.

In fact, Weber never rejected the explanatory role of race, self-consciously keeping the question open in many of his writings and suggesting that race played an important, if not all-determining, role in many social phenomena.

Weber disagreed with Ploetz that social welfare policies and Christianity worked against natural selection, but he did not dispute the role of natural selection in human society. Weber and Ploetz, who had each spent time in the southern United States, disagreed about the origin of antiblack racism and on the reasons for what both perceived as black inferiority. For Ploetz racism came from a "racial instinct," whereas for Weber it came from "the old feudal contempt for labor" that emerged as Americans embraced European aristocratic values. While agreeing that black people in America usually smelled worse than white people, the two men disagreed about the origin of this smell: for Ploetz, the smell was biological; for Weber, it resulted from a habitual neglect of bathing. Weber argued that much black inferiority came from the limitations on education and social advancement placed on them by white racists and cited W. E. B. Du Bois as "the most important sociological scholar anywhere in the Southern States" (Ploetz et al. 1911). Yet Du Bois exemplified not African Americans for Max Weber or his wife, Marianne, but rather one of the "half-Negroes, quarter-Negroes, and one hundredth part Negroes whom no non-American can distinguish from whites" (Marianne Weber 1975: 296). Weber rejected the biologism of Ploetz and of the American "one-drop rule" but in doing so worked out a social and economic racism that, in fact, has played an important role in the creation of global inequalities and domination in the colonial and postcolonial periods.

· · ·

THE ANNEXATIONS OF GERMAN colonial and domestic territory following World War I reconfigured the relationship of German social science to imperialism. British colonial reformers such as E. D. Morel of the Congo Reform Association and John H. Harris of the Aborigines Protection Society, who had once advocated transferring the Belgian Congo to Germany, now either placed Germany in the position of Belgium as bad colonizer justifying its own, allegedly good, colonial practices or were marginalized from public discourse (Harris [1912] 1968: 87–90, 294–303; Louis 1967: 35). The jurist Carl Schmitt, meanwhile, began to work out what is perhaps still the most profound critique of colonial sovereignty, as he contemplated a new imperialism in which "one no longer speaks of annexation" but rather of "freedom and the right to self determination of the lesser peoples and nations" (1988: 30). Schmitt initiated his critique of imperialist sovereignty with this 1925 discussion of "the Rhineland as object of international policy" but gradually expanded it to a critique of liberalism as imperialism, first in his 1932 *Concept of the Political*. "War is condemned," Schmitt wrote, "but executions, sanctions, punitive expeditions, pacifications, protection of treaties, international police, and measures to assure peace remain. The adversary is thus no longer called an enemy but a disturber of peace" (1996: 79). Schmitt could have been describing the process by which President Clinton and both Presidents Bush, often with the full cooperation of the "international community," laid waste to, and finally occupied, Iraq—carrying out mass destruction, paradoxically, in order to preserve humanity from "weapons of mass destruction." He also might have been describing the North Atlantic Treaty Organization (NATO) bombing of Serbia or, indeed, the whole bloody history of liberal wars for humanity, beginning, perhaps with the founding of the Congo Free State. Indeed, Schmitt's 1950 *Nomos of the Earth* expanded his critique to include the whole span of modern imperialism, from the Monroe Doctrine and the Berlin West Africa Conference to the postwar international order (Schmitt 1950).

More recently, Jürgen Habermas has brought Weber into a critique of capitalist modernity in order to offer a theory of "communicative action" as "an alternative to the philosophy of history on which earlier critical theory relied"—Habermas, presumably, means Marxism—"but which is no longer tenable" (1984, 2: 397). With his turn to Weber, Habermas, symptomatically, brought a colonial anthropology to the center of critical theory. Where Max Horkheimer and Theodor Adorno (1972) had used Homer's *Odyssey* to explain the dialectic between myth and enlightenment, Habermas used the colonial ethnography of E. E. Evans-Pritchard and others. For Habermas, modern thought emerges through the rejection of the mythical thought, not of classical antiquity, but of "tribal societies." This mythical thought Habermas finds characterized by a *"confusion between nature and culture"* that "signifies . . . a—by our lights—deficient differentiation between *language and world*; that is, between speech as the medium of communication and that about which understanding can be reached in linguistic communication." The failure to distinguish between culture and external nature also leads, Habermas tells us, to that lack of "the *internal* world or of subjectivity" (1984, 1: 48–49, 51). Where Horkheimer and Adorno had looked to classical antiquity for the mythical, Habermas looked to a colonialist ethnography that found lack in the other, a lack, for Habermas, of the very language and subjectivity that was required for the communicative action he advocates. Habermas displays here precisely the imperialist logocentrism analyzed by Jacques Derrida (1976; see also Young 1990).

Habermas develops a critique of this imperialist modernity as, in an uncanny echo of the Prussian Settlement Commission of the previous century, "internal colonization" (1984, 2: 335). Because, as Weber had pointed out in the famous preface to his *Sociology of Religion* (1922), the various "sectors" of Occidental rationality, such as art, economics, or politics, develop separately, they each become reified specializations, separated from what Habermas calls the "lifeworld," everyday subjective life. In capitalist modernity, the lifeworld thus "sees itself thrown back on traditions whose claims to validity have already been suspended." The various expert systems then "make their way into the lifeworld from the outside—like colonial masters coming into a tribal society—and force a process of assimilation upon it" (Habermas 1984, 2: 355). Critical theory as a theory of communicative action would, presumably, teach our "tribal" lifeworld to speak, giving it the language and subjectivity that, in Habermas's interpretation of the ethnographic record, tribal societies lack.

After 2003, Habermas developed a critique of American imperialism in Iraq that, like E. D. Morel's criticisms of the Belgian Congo a century before, preserves and even develops the liberal terminology of imperialism by, ironically, criticizing the most gruesome deeds of this very imperialism. A widely disseminated 2003 essay, written by Habermas but signed also by Derrida, calls for a "core Europe"—Germany, France, and the Benelux countries—to assume concerted leadership in foreign policy, but also in values, both as a counterweight to the U.S. empire and as a check on the governments of Spain and Poland, which cooperated with the American invasion (Derrida and Habermas 2006). Habermas criticized the 2003 invasion primarily because it was illegal according to international law, since it was neither approved by the United Nations Security Council nor a response to an immediate threat to the United States. Confronted by an interviewer with his support for the similarly illegal NATO bombing of Serbia, Habermas pointed both to the presumed danger of genocide in Kosovo—a presumption evidently more justifiable than the presumption of "weapons of mass destruction in Iraq"—and also to the fact that the NATO bombing was carried out by liberal states that respect human rights. The so-called coalition of the willing that invaded Iraq in 2003, by contrast, "split the West and included states that systematically violate human rights, such as Uzbekistan and Taylor's Liberia" (Habermas 2006: 86). Only nations that respect international law, it seems, may violate it and then only in order to preserve it.

There could hardly be a better illustration of Carl Schmitt's Hobbesian insight that the definitive act of sovereignty is not the creation or upholding of the law but rather the declaration of the state of exception (*Ausnahmezustand*), the suspension of the law (Schmitt 1922). At least since the Berlin West Africa Conference, imperialism has always acted as a corrective to some violation of the very humanity it claims to represent. After the atrocities of the Belgian Congo, imperial rule could begin to provide the violations that it would itself then correct, both the Iraq War and the liberal response to that war being only the last two iterations of this long cycle, this permanent state of exception. Habermas explicitly sets up Kant's "Idea for a Universal History with a Cosmopolitan Intent" as a foil to Carl Schmitt's skepticism of international law, and especially law against war, as an occasion, in fact, for permanent war. He rightly points out that Schmitt's critique is also based on his own concept of an imperialism of *Größräume*, which Schmitt saw as a justification for German continental imperialism in the Nazi period (Habermas 2006: 188–193). Yet we are left here with a dispute between empires, each one masquerading as a critique of imperialism.

. . .

ONE LONG-STANDING PROBLEMATIC OF German sociology, from Schmoller to Habermas, has been a dialectic of liberation and constraint inherent in the modern, conceived as a break from the feudal, the Oriental, the mythical, or the "tribal." German sociologists, even apart from National Socialism, have not always been partisans of the liberation side of this dialectic. German sociology, I have tried to show, emerged from real colonial engagements that were repressed, but not deactivated, after World War I. The discipline emerged as an attempt by German economists, led by Gustav Schmoller, to check what they regarded as the deleterious political effects of even those meager economic freedoms that rural and urban workers gained for themselves or were granted by the state in the nineteenth century. The smallholding that these social scientists advocated meshed with the programs of "internal colonization" of the Prussian state, designed to Germanize the Polish territories captured by Prussia in the previous century. Guided by Max Weber, German social scientists adopted the anti-Polish racism of the Prussian state, developing a cultural-racial economics of control that Schmoller and others used to assist German colonial control in Africa. Especially through Max Weber's sociology of religion, this cultural-racial economics, which had emerged in collaboration with German policies of internal and overseas colonialism, became a general cultural economics whose racist origins have generally been obscured. The German defeat in World War I led to the erasure of this colonial history of German sociology, as the victors at Versailles recast Germany as brutal—and therefore unscientific—colonial villain, and vanquished Germans recast themselves as colonial victims. While the jurist Carl Schmitt developed a penetrating critique of the very categories of colonial sovereignty, prominent German social scientists, including Norbert Elias and Jürgen Habermas, preserved the colonial problem of cultural difference and political economic control while obscuring the real military, political, and economic engagements from which this problem emerged. It can be a collaborative task of historians and theorists to return to the colonial origins of sociology—and not only in Germany—to reactivate the political struggles from which these discourses of repression came into being and to take up again the discourses of liberation that they obscured.

NOTES

1. For Weber versus Durkheim, see Berger (1963). The historical school of economics, of which Weber himself was a very young member, conventionally contrasted itself with British and Austrian economics. Talcott Parsons has done more than any other to draw attention to this opposition of Weber and Marx.

2. Much of what follows is adapted from Zimmerman (2010), which has more extensive references to primary and secondary literature than is possible in the short space of this essay.

3. Especially helpful for my account of the Verein für Sozialpolitik has been Grimmer-Solem (2003b).

4. Knapp, Notes on US History and Slavery, July 30, 1900, Nachlass Knapp, Geheimes Staatsarchiv, Preußischer Kulturbesitz, Berlin, Germany (GStA PK). VI. HA, K. II, Bl. 41–43.

5. Vertrauliche Besprechung des Königlichen Staatsministeriums, January 10, 1886, GStA PK, I. HA Rep. 90 A, Nr. 3742, Bl. 1–2.

6. This biography, written by Weber's widow, has been unjustly excoriated. Yet Marianne Weber's portrayal of her late husband's political engagement is confirmed by his own published work. See also Mommsen (1984).

7. Max Weber to the Pan-German League, April 22, 1899, cited in Marianne Weber (1975: 224–225).

8. George Steinmetz (2007), by contrast, has argued for the preeminence of ethnographic discourse, which he conceives broadly, beyond the disciplinary field of German ethnography, in the German colonial project. Steinmetz builds his argument on case studies of Namibia, Samoa, and Tsingtao, and the difference in interpretation may reflect simply the difference in cases considered.

9. Professor Dr. E. Struve, Geschaeftsfuehrer, Geschaeftsbericht des Kolonialpolitischen Aktionskomitee's, n.d., GStA VI. HA Nachlass Schmoller, Nr. 13, Koloniapolitisches Aktionskomitee, Bd. II, Bl. 277–293. On the membership, see Mitgliederverzeichnis des Kolonialpolitischen Aktionskomité, January 1907, Nachlass Schmoller, GStA PK VI. HA, Nr. 13, Koloniapolitisches Aktionskomitee, Bd. II, Bl. 101–113.

10. As John Lowry (2006) has shown, Africans themselves, in Togo as well as Tanzania, Namibia, and Cameroon, thus played a role in the Reichstag dissolution of 1906–1907.

11. Kolonialpolitischen Aktionskomité, Printed circular letters from Schmoller, January 17, 1907 and January 18, 1907, Nachlass Schmoller, Bl. 76–77.

12. Dernburg to Hamburg Senat, July 12, 1907 (copy), "Einrichtung eines Kolonialinstitutes in Hamburg," Staatsarchiv, Hamburg, Germany, 364–366, A I 1, Bl. 61–65.

13. Marianne Weber (Asheville, NC) to her mother, October 12, 1904, Nachlass Weber, GStA PK, VI Nr. 6, Bl. 56–58.

14. Max Weber (Asheville, NC) to his mother, October 13, 1904, Nachlass Weber, Bl. 52–55.

SIX

The Durkheimian School and Colonialism
Exploring the Constitutive Paradox
FUYUKI KURASAWA

Like all scholarly disciplines, Western sociology is grounded in a foundational myth that shapes its self-understanding and fuels its developmental narratives. The institutionalization of the field in the late nineteenth century in Europe and North America formalized an already implicit division of intellectual labor along neat geographical (and, it was assumed, civilizational) lines between sociological and anthropological sciences, with the former devoting itself to modern societies of the North Atlantic region and the latter concerning itself with "primitive" societies in the rest of the world (which, depending on the formulation, could include or exclude the "Orient"). An essential element of sociology's foundational myth and of the widespread belief in the discipline's *sui generis* origins, this division of labor was naturalized while the imperial worldview that generated it was rarely made explicit (Connell 1997); indeed, one could rewrite the story in a coherent and convincing fashion by stating that, *grosso modo*, colonizing societies were the objects of sociological research, and colonized territories were the preserve of its anthropological counterpart.

By now, such a rewriting is familiar to anthropologists, whose self-critique of their discipline for its intimate involvement in empire was inaugurated a few decades ago in the Francophone and Anglo-American worlds (Asad 1973; Leiris 1966; Said 1989; Wolf 1982), eventually begetting a reflexive turn that has utterly reconfigured ethnological practices and analytical schemes (Clifford and Marcus 1986; Marcus and Fischer 1986).[1] However, it remains an alien exercise for most sociologists, who aside from world-systems theorists, have left unexamined the political and cultural underpinnings of the geographical split mentioned above. This conventional lacuna is closely related to sociology's "methodological nationalism" (Beck 2006), that is, its tendency to view societies as culturally and territorially discrete entities corresponding to nation-state boundaries and thereby to consistently neglect structurally based transnational processes and relations of power—capitalism and imperialism chief among them (Calhoun 1995; Wallerstein 1991; Wolf 1982). Furthermore, by contrast to anthropology, sociological work has been largely immune to the influence of postcolonialism, a paradigm that foregrounds the modalities of colonial discourse and representation and their ties to the exercise of Western imperial power; in part because of its emergence out of literary and cultural studies, postcolonial theory has not always meshed seamlessly with the social scientific inclination to concentrate on the historical and comparative dimensions of the functioning of European colonialism's economic system and sociopolitical institutions.

At the same time, the condemnation of sociology for its virtual silence regarding colonialism (Bhambra 2007; Magubane 2005) is belied by the existence of several sociological writings that have engaged with processes of colonization of non-Western societies (Calhoun 2006; Go 2000a, 2007; Kurasawa 2004; Lardinois 2007; Saada 2002, 2005; Steinmetz 2007a). And if there is any part of the sociological edifice that complicates the discipline's relationship to empire, it is that of the Durkheimian School, which encompassed an exceptional group of researchers revolving around Emile Durkheim and Marcel Mauss in the last few years of the nineteenth century and the early decades of the twentieth century.[2] At first glance, the Durkheimians appear to be a poor expository case, for they seem to embody the problem of sociology's colonial blindness and, more generally, of Western social science's imperialist worldview. Despite the fact that their writings, in aggregate and substantive terms, were anything but Eurocentric because they were skewed much more heavily toward coverage of non-Western parts of the globe than of the North Atlantic region, they engaged with the political reality of empire only in a very circumscribed manner.[3] Nevertheless, in this chapter, I want to explore this complication by framing it as a constitutive paradox that can be succinctly presented in the following terms: the Durkheimian School simultaneously presumed empire as a global political system and undermined some of its key ideological tenets. As I understand it here, this paradox is a productive dialectic composed of a set of analytical tensions that structure the Durkheimians' writings, and through which these writings can be read. In addition, it is constitutive in the sense of being at the core of the Durkheimian School's body of work (rather than a peripheral or minor theme) and to the extent that it exists as a condition of possibility for this work. To put it bluntly, the Durkheimian School's writings could not have existed without this paradox. And, importantly, this chapter does not seek to transcend such tensions, since the Durkheimians left them unresolved by keeping them in play—with the evaluative ambivalence thereby entailed—thus supplying a more fruitful and hermeneutically dense way of thinking about the convoluted relationship between sociology and empire.

In order to contextualize the general argument, the chapter begins by locating the Durkheimian School within French intellectual and disciplinary traditions, emphasizing the dialectic between Enlightenment and Romantic currents of thought about the non-Western world and the entwining of sociological and anthropological forms of knowledge. The rest of the chapter unpacks the aforementioned constitutive paradox, for once it is recognized, what matters is to understand how it operates and what are its effects. Accordingly, I want to argue that three manifestations of this paradox exist, which correspond to qualitatively distinct kinds of sociological involvement in colonialism that are routinely conflated in discussions of the Euro-American social sciences' imperialist logic: systemic benefit, willing participation, and ideological legitimation. The chapter's second section investigates the most straightforward of these manifestations, namely, the fact that the European colonial project was the taken-for-granted geopolitical context from which the Durkheimians derived systemic gains in the form of institutional resources and empirical material for the formulation of their conceptual apparatus. In the third part, I want to analyze the ambiguities of Durkheim and Mauss being directly implicated in empire, since their readiness to link ethnographic research to French colonial governance stands in contrast to their questioning of colonialism's violence and threatening of cultural diversity. The chapter closes with a discussion of the third modality of involvement, ideological legitimation, by teasing out the various dimensions of the Durkheimian School's concurrent failure to problematize many of the intellectual cornerstones of European imperialism and, more interesting, its subtle undermining of such cornerstones by recasting commonplace understandings of French republicanism, civilization, cognitive structures, and evolutionism.

SITUATING THE DURKHEIMIAN SCHOOL

Before tackling the three facets of the constitutive paradox found at the heart of the Durkheimians' work, I want to locate their writings within traditions of thought in France. Specifically, much of the Durkheimian School's work was informed by the dialectic between Enlightenment and Romanticism that has characterized encounters with the non-Western world in French intellectual circles. Undoubtedly, two opposing strands of Enlightenment thinking marked Durkheim, Mauss, and the other members of the school. Derived from the Marquis de Condorcet and Auguste Comte, inter alia, the first of these currents coalesced around a theory of modernization anchored in a stagelike, unilinear, and teleological conception of human progress that eventually gave birth to social evolutionism, with its hierarchical ranking of societies or peoples and positioning of them along a chronological continuum.[4] More significant for the Durkheimian School is a second strand of Enlightenment thought that—borrowing Bourdieu's (1990) characterization of Claude Lévi-Strauss—we can identify as "scientific humanism": "Needless to say, in such a context [the Algerian War], in which the problem of racism arose, at every moment, as a question of life or death, a book like Lévi-Strauss's *Race and History* (1952) was much more than an intellectual argument against evolutionism. But it is harder to communicate the intellectual and emotional impact of seeing American Indian mythologies analysed as a language containing its own reason and *raison d'être*" (2). As both Bourdieu and Lévi-Strauss recognized, it was the Durkheimians who laid the foundations for scientific humanism by virtue of their efforts to shift social scientific inquiry away from universal models of human evolution, with their ethnocentric and arbitrary character, toward systematic, comparative investigations of cultural patterns and structures that are present in varying yet equally valid forms within and between societies.

While these Enlightenment approaches invariably defined French perspectives on cultural alterity, they were partially counteracted by a Romantic exoticism designed to problematize the existing social order in Europe. Montaigne's "Of Cannibals," Montesquieu's *Persian Letters*, and Rousseau's *Discourse on the Origins of Inequality* are but three of the better-known works that posited the "primitive" and the "Orient" as alternative worlds and mythological devices through which to effect a critique of many of the central cultural assumptions and institutional arrangements undergirding modern European civilization. As Lévi-Strauss has observed, "In France, from Montaigne on, social philosophy was nearly always linked to social criticism. The gathering of social data was to provide arguments against the social order. It is true that modern sociology was born for the purpose of rebuilding French society after the destruction wrought, first by the French Revolution, and later by the Prussian War. But behind Comte and Durkheim, there are Diderot, Rousseau and Montaigne. In France, sociology will remain the offspring of these first attempts at anthropological thinking" (1971: 505). To place Durkheim or Mauss under the banner of Romanticism would be a gross overstatement, but their interest in "primitive" rituals and belief systems as sources of collective effervescence and societal vitality served as a driving inspiration for a variety of French avant-garde aesthetic movements animated by a Romantic primitivism. Accordingly, in the interwar period, both the Collège de sociologie (which included Georges Bataille, Roger Caillois, and Michel Leiris) and the surrealist movement (led by André Breton) discovered in the Durkheimian School's ethnographically rich studies—on religion, the gift economy, magic, and sacrifice, among other "exotic" topics—the raw materials out of which to forge their sweeping dismissals of a modern West infected by a cult of rationalism, rampant individualism, and the stifling effects of civilized life; as collective alter egos, "primitive" cultures embodied a valuing of the sacred and a spirit of social transgression that could revive creativity and imagination in a moribund Europe living in the shadows of a lingering fin de siècle malaise and the collective disillusionment and devastation that followed from the Great War (Hollier 1988; Kurasawa 2003; Richman 2002).[5]

Lévi-Strauss's quotation draws attention to the other French intellectual propensity within which the Durkheimian School should be located, the interdependence of sociological and anthropological modes of thought. For Durkheim, Mauss, and the other contributors to L'année sociologique, ethnographic research on non-Western societies—notably, indigenous peoples of North America and Oceania—was an essential component of the discipline of sociology; in fact, as already mentioned, it comprised the largest part of the school's scholarly output and could not be severed from its sociological framework without compromising the Durkheimian project in toto. A case in point is The Elementary Forms of Religious Life, Durkheim's late magnum opus, where his diagnosis of a moral crisis in the modern Euro-American world prompted him to examine symbolically mediated religious beliefs and practices among Australian Aboriginal groups, in an attempt to discover the social origins of morality. Furthermore, the Durkheimians' blending of sociological and anthropological knowledge was cemented through their use of a protostructuralist epistemology, whereby they identified a finite set of formal configurations of elements and analyzed relations of similarity and difference across the components of particular objects of study (e.g., institutions, worldviews, and rituals), which were treated as social wholes.[6]

Having briefly explained the position of the Durkheimian project within French intellectual and disciplinary milieus, I now want to discuss the first component of the constitutive paradox that concerns us here, namely, the systemic benefits springing from colonial domination—symbolic and material advantages that the Durkheimian School derived from the structures of empire as a whole rather than from deliberate or willful action on the part of its members. What is striking is that, for the Durkheimians, the global political and economic dynamics that fueled European imperialism existed for the most part at the margins of their work, a structural context that was unspoken and thereby apparently taken as self-evident rather than problematized in and of itself. This was the case despite the fact that the processes of "discovery" and subjugation of non-Western societies were essential to the Durkheimians' capacity to create the sorts of sociological knowledge that could aim for intercultural rigor and comprehensiveness. Of course, taking a step back, the very possibility of holding such aspirations of generating a compendium of a large array of forms of collective life and modes of social organization from all parts of the globe was itself an expression of the imperial worldview of a nation-state and continent that possessed the material resources, military means, and economic imperatives to gain and retain access to, and control over, vast swaths of the planet.

Once established across the world, the machinery of colonial administration was defined by the use of a vast panoply of religious and governmental mechanisms to rule over, and collect information about, indigenous populations. Beginning in the nineteenth century, travelers' tales that delineated the age of "exploration" of Asia, Oceania, Africa, and the Americas were eventually replaced by modes of knowledge production that tied the exercise of imperial power to the provision of detailed representations and descriptive accounts of "native" ways of acting and thinking. Emblematized by the figures of the colonial administrator, the missionary, and the anthropologist, the domains of government, religion, and science all yielded sets of findings about colonized peoples that formed one of the indispensable empirical backbones of Durkheimian research. In other words, the apparatus of colonialism rendered distant societies and groups scientifically knowable for this branch of French sociology.

One could go so far as to say that the Durkheimian School's entire conceptual framework and its diagnosis of modernity are constructed through the comparative lens that empire supplied, since the juxtaposition of modernity and primitiveness (corresponding to that between imperial powers and some of their colonial territories) was a fundamental distinction that facilitated the discovery of European societies' peculiarities. For instance, it was in the "primitive" lifeworlds of the indigenous populations of the South and Northwest Pacific, among others, that embodied modes of social organization that enframed and subsumed the realm of economic activity and where, consequently, production and exchange relations were subordinated to a collective morality that viewed them primarily as social transactions invoking notions of reciprocity and mutual obligation. Such "primitive" sociocentrism toward the economic sphere enabled Durkheim and Mauss to relativize, via intercultural comparison, the supremacy and universalism of the market and of the utilitarian figure of the self-maximizing individual (*homo economicus*), which they contended were the results of historically and culturally specific socioeconomic configurations attributable to the predominance of industrialism and capitalism in the West (Durkheim 1957: 10–13; 1984: xxxii–xxxiv; Mauss, 1988). Similarly, the Kabyle of Algeria and the Iroquois of Canada represented key instances of segmentary societies characterized by similarity (through ties of kinship or locality) and thus embodied what Durkheim designated as mechanical solidarity (Durkheim 1984: 127–128) by contrast to its organic counterpart produced by a complex division of social labor in which specialized actors were functionally interdependent. Unstated by Durkheim was the geopolitical backdrop of French colonialism that made his familiarity with both of these cases of mechanical solidarity possible—a backdrop defined by processes of dispossession of land and violent subjugation of local populations in North Africa and North America (Connell 1997: 1517–1518). For its part, British control over the Australian territory and suppression of its aboriginal peoples created the conditions under which Spencer and Gillen's explorations and ethnographies of the indigenous societies of Central Australia could take place, which, in turn, became the empirical basis of *The Elementary Forms of Religious Life*. Accordingly, Durkheim could evoke the collective vibrancy of "primitive" universes, with their ritualized performances of the sacredness of society, against the moral malaise that afflicted a secularized modern Europe (Durkheim 1995).

A COMPLICITY WITH COLONIALISM?

Given that imperialism was a leading dynamic of European modernity in the late nineteenth and early twentieth centuries, the Durkheimian School's omission of it in scholarly writings and absence of a comprehensive political stance toward it represent glaring omissions that contribute to the constitutive paradox to which I want to draw attention. Undoubtedly, part of the explanation lies in the particularities of the Durkheimians' analytical perspective. Despite their seminal argument about civilizations as legitimate objects of study, their work on modern Europe displayed many of the signs of an aforementioned methodological nationalism; for the most part, France was treated as a self-contained nation-state, without a consideration of how its development and contemporary predicament were intimately tied to a capitalist and geopolitical expansionism aimed at appropriating territories, labor, and natural resources overseas. In addition, the Durkheimian neglect of political sociology (Favre 1983) meant that neither national nor global political structures or actors were accorded adequate weight in their own right. Durkheim did examine the domestic state to the extent that republican ideology informed French civil society through mechanisms of social integration and regulation, whether in the domains of education, civic associations, or shared belief systems. At the same time, he, Mauss, and the members of the Durkheimian School did not concern themselves with the internal dynamics or discourses of the French state, where colonialism would have appeared as one of the pillars of the republican national project, or with the scene of international politics, where imperial rivalry and confrontation between European metropolitan powers would have been a striking feature.

The Durkheimian School's silent complicity with empire can also be attributed to its strategy of disciplinary institutionalization prior to World War I, since what it sought was to establish and have recognized the still-fledgling field of sociological inquiry in French academic circles by promoting its scientificity. Sociology was to become the authoritative science of society, built on objective methodological devices and findings that were unsullied by political positions or value judgments. As such, the Durkheimians' manifold public engagements and activities on behalf of the left in France—which found expression in their political journalism[7]—were kept strictly at bay from their scholarly research lest they compromise the latter's scientific legitimacy (Karady 1983: 74). Nonetheless, most notably during the interwar period, Mauss blatantly contradicted this apolitical orientation in his efforts to promote ethnology, and ethnographic research more specifically, as a practical form of knowledge that was at the service of the French state in its colonies, by helping to train colonial administrators about "native" populations and thereby contribute to more enlightened governance over them through better understanding (Fournier 2005: 166–167, 237, 277; Mauss 1969b: 432).[8] From this vantage point, it becomes impossible to deny that Mauss was converting ethnological scholarship into a tool for the exercise of imperial power, one that participated directly in regimes of oppression of colonized societies.

What, then, can account for this inconsistency? Returning to the question of institutionalization noted above, Mauss, Paul Rivet, and other Durkheimians were preoccupied with drumming up public and political support for ethnology by presenting it as practical science whose studies of "primitive" cultures could be applied to refine technologies of colonial governmentality. To an extent, this instrumentalization of anthropological research in the name of empire can be interpreted as a mode of strategic action intended to counter the decline of Durkheimian sociology in the interwar years (Heilbron 1984) by lobbying and striving to secure funding for institutional sites where such research could be pursued in France, which was seen as lagging behind other Western nations in anthropological infrastructure.[9] Conversely, the Durkheimians perceived colonialism as a propitious context for the collection of ethnographic data, something that had been accomplished by British colonial personnel taught to record their observations of indigenous customs and mores (and how to do so) before these permanently vanished (Mauss 1969b: 426). Yet the Durkheimians' endeavors to incorporate such administrators into the ethnographic undertaking and expose them to the ethnological truism of appreciation for the richness, diversity, and fragility of all human communities—and thus to produce a kinder, gentler imperialism imbued with the self-appointed responsibility to preserve the cultures of non-Western subjects under French rule— smacks of a misguided paternalism and accommodationism, whereby the "natives" can best be protected by reforming the colonial system instead of abolishing it altogether and granting colonized peoples the right to political self-determination. This position additionally betrays a culturalist idealism, that is to say, a culturally sensitive form of wishful thinking that improbably believes that an "enlightened" version of French colonialism can be decoupled from its structural realities, whether these be intensive exploitation of indigenous populations via coercive regimes of labor (slavery, indentured, etc.) or their incorporation into market relations, or yet again the use of military power, state coercion, and culturally assimilationist policies to conquer and govern overseas territories and their inhabitants—none of which, it should be pointed out, is apt to assist in the tasks of cultural protectionism and preservationism that the Durkheimian School claimed for itself.

More intriguing, perhaps, is the possibility that the Durkheimians did not believe that collaborating with French colonial regimes compromised their standpoint of apolitical, objectivist scientism, since they seemingly held a depoliticized conception of colonialism. Because the latter was taken for granted and its raison d'être as a system of global domination never came under scrutiny, it was reduced to a technical matter of administration rather than a political question per se; for the Durkheimian School, then, the crucial issue would not have been whether France and other European states should possess empires but, given the existence of such empires, how they should treat "natives" and how their beliefs, rites, and material artifacts could be conserved for posterity.

This is not to say that the Durkheimians were merely willing accomplices in or apologists for the reproduction of the French Empire. Mauss, for one, was critical of colonialism's globally homogenizing and Westernizing effects, which threatened the very survival of what he perceived to be already fragile societies and peoples. Driven by the core ethnological principle of sustaining cultural pluralism to simultaneously cultivate and demonstrate humankind's breadth, Mauss lamented the fact that the foreseeable disappearance of many "primitive" ways of acting and thinking (traditions, myths, rituals, knowledges, and so on), as a result of the violent and misguided imposition of a more materially powerful metropolitan culture, would irreversibly impoverish humanity (Mauss 1969b: 432–433, 1969e: 445–446). Further, he held that the hybridization produced by the forced blending of cultures on the colonial terrain was damaging to the authenticity and health of materially weaker "primitive" societies.[10] Yet, tellingly in light of the Durkheimian School's depoliticization of empire, the vulnerability and potential loss of "primitive" cultures were presented as a metaphysical destiny and tragic fate, not a consequence of imperialism's destruction of indigenous institutions and belief systems—policies that were particularly nefarious because of the strongly assimilationist orientation of French colonial policies. Hence, neither Mauss nor his Durkheimian colleagues pondered the crux of the matter: the effort to save "primitive" peoples through colonialism, whether "enlightened" or otherwise disposed, was precisely what had wreaked so much damage on the societies of North America, Africa, Asia, and Oceania, fomenting the seeds of resistance and revolt from which would spring, in due course, national liberation movements throughout the global south.

Conversely, as an active and publicly visible member of the socialist movement in France (notably of the Section Française de l'internationale ouvrière, or SFIO), Mauss wrote a series of journalistic tracts denouncing French imperial policies in Morocco, where corruption and generalized incompetence on the part of the colonial administration ran rampant.

Importantly, this condemnation was not so much inspired by anti-imperialism or a belief in the right to self-determination of colonized populations as it was a class-based polemic against the rapaciousness and ineptitude of the French bourgeoisie (which controlled the levers of the domestic state and its colonial proxies). Also significant in Mauss's stance was his commitment to pacifism and socialist internationalism, for he followed leaders of the SFIO in dreading the prospect that rising tensions and conflict between European powers over control of the Moroccan territory would degenerate into a global imperial war with incalculable repercussions (Fournier 2005: 168–169; Mauss 1997).[11]

For his part, in a compelling section of *Moral Education*, Durkheim established a parallel between the presence of corporal punishment in the French educational system and the existence of violence in colonial sites. Anomie was believed to be the source of both of these pathological phenomena, for the weakness of moral regulation and the absence of a collective counterpower in either the classroom or the colony fostered something akin to megalomania on the part of the superordinate party; without moral bounds, the teacher's and the colonizer's power could rapidly deteriorate into an uncontrolled and abusive use of force for its own sake against an infantilized subordinate group (students or colonized subjects).

> Wherever two populations, two groups of people having unequal cultures, come into continuous contact with one another, certain feelings develop that prompt the more cultivated group—or that which deems itself such—to do violence to the other. This is currently the case in colonies and countries of all kinds where representatives of European civilization find themselves involved with underdeveloped peoples. Although it is useless and involves great dangers for those who abandon themselves to it, exposing themselves to formidable reprisals, this violence almost inevitably breaks out. Hence that kind of bloody foolhardiness that seizes the explorer in connection with races he deems inferior. (Durkheim 1973: 192–193)

Later in the same section, Durkheim raises the potential of European public opinion, experiencing revulsion or at least troubled by the brutality of colonial regimes, acting as a counterforce to unbridled violence (Durkheim 1973: 196).

However minor in stature they may be, these passages from Mauss's and Durkheim's work reveal the paradoxical nature of their participation in the political project of colonialism: their attempts to insert Durkheimian ethnology in the machinery of colonial governance and their problematizing of its violent "excesses" could not but make them interpret empire as a self-evident system for the world order.

ERODING THE CIVILIZING MISSION'S IDEOLOGICAL LEGITIMACY

In this, the last section of the chapter, I want to examine the final aspect of the constitutive paradox of the Durkheimian School's engagement with colonialism, namely, the fact that its failure to interrogate European imperialism and partial complicity with it was simultaneously accompanied by an undermining of many of its intellectual premises, which were themselves grounded in Europe's self-understanding as a civilizational zenith (and the consequent inferiority of "primitive" societies) as well as the normalized ethnocentrism of the Euro-American human sciences. Without overstating the critical nature of the Durkheimians' contributions to these matters, it behooves us to appreciate the extent to which they contested what were in most instances late nineteenth and early twentieth century *doxa* about non-Western peoples.

The first aspect of ideological legitimation of colonialism that could begin to be questioned through Durkheimian arguments was its articulation to a particular conception of French republicanism. To be clear, the Durkheimians were centrally concerned with the cultural sustainability and moral vitality of secular republican institutions to reinvigorate postrevolutionary French society (e.g., public education and intermediary bodies), doing little to advance what we could consider to be a postcolonial analysis of the constitution of the republican worldview via warfare and territorial conquest (whether the Napoleonic campaigns in Europe or imperialist invasions overseas). At the same time, I want to argue that Durkheim's remarks about the universalist and cosmopolitan orientation of the French national character—which finds its prototypical expression in Cartesian rationalism—and its tendency to speak in the name of humanity yet not always act accordingly (Durkheim 1973: 278) is suggestive of a tension at the core of the French model of colonialism. On the one hand, born out of the Enlightenment and the revolution itself, this model was organized around the notion of France's civilizing mission, whereby the nation had a duty to expand the reach of the principles of liberty, equality, and solidarity to even the most remote, "uncivilized" corners of the world. The tension between the assimilationist and civically segregationist tendencies of French republicanism meant that overseas colonies could be treated both as geographical outposts of the motherland and as alien territories, with colonial subjects being either remade into Frenchmen and -women via governmental strategies of coercion and socialization or, more often than not, kept captive in their "native" condition through legal codification and inscription (Lustick 1993; Saada 2002; Steinmetz 2005a: 347–348; chapter 15).

On the other hand, as grounded in the liberal doctrine of natural rights, republican ideology recognized that human beings were intrinsically free and equal, which, at least in principle, could support the collective right of political self-determination of all peoples and thereby undercut the imperial project. As previously mentioned, the Durkheimian School never explicitly advocated such a position, and it inverted natural right doctrine (with its attribution of inherent moral ideals in a mythical state of nature) in asserting that society was both the source and guarantor of the tenets of individual liberty and equality (Durkheim 1960, 1965, 1970b). However, the Durkheimian School's writings put into question the French republic's universalism and assimilationism, out of which its colonial adventures could be justified, by demonstrating that "primitive" societies were already civilized and possessed sophisticated ways of thinking about the world. Hence, following Durkheimian thinking, we can straightforwardly arrive at the conclusion that such societies did not require the "gifts" of French civilization or Cartesianism, nor did its inhabitants need to be converted into French citizens.

These statements need to be further elaborated, beginning with the concept of civilization on which much colonial rhetoric drew. What should be remembered is that Enlightenment and postrevolutionary discourse in France was imbued with a singular and evaluative usage of "civilization," to which was grafted a teleological understanding of humankind's developmental progress; the "civilizing process" (Elias 2000) enabled advancement from savagery and barbarism through the use of reason. The French model of a civilized organization of society and of sociocultural mores and beliefs was thus uniform and normative in design, necessarily entailing a comparative judgment of other societies' cultural worth in relation to it—prompting the German Romantics, notably Johann Gottfried Herder, to contest it by proposing a vernacular idea of *Kultur* grounded in local customs and valuing cultural particularism over abstraction and universalism (Herder [1784] 1966). In turn, France's *mission civilisatrice* became the humanist vehicle through which "natives" were to be "benignly" rescued from their self-incurred state of darkness, which actually involved colonial regimes implementing culturally destructive policies on domestic populations (whether in the form of the suppression of indigenous ways of living and languages or the establishment of socializing institutions geared toward metropolitan assimilation).

Durkheim and Mauss's innovation consisted in stripping the idea of civilization of its normativity in order to transform it into an analytical concept whose utility was derived from its capacity to enable researchers to regroup, compare, and contrast institutional configurations and ways of life that transcend the political bounds of the nation-state, rather than from its ranking of the hierarchical worth of societies or peoples (Durkheim and Mauss 1969b). This resignification of civilization engenders two critical moves. First, it performs an intercultural relativization of the universalist pretensions of the dominant narrative of a singular civilizational model and moral system, which according to Durkheim and Mauss, is the product of an ethnocentric arbitrariness that falsely generalizes or naturalizes what is familiar and close at hand; French or European civilization is but one variant among others, which all develop a valid morality suited to their social structure: "This notion of an increasing gain, of an intellectual and material good shared by a humanity that is becoming more and more reasonable, is, we sincerely believe, based in fact. It can allow us to appreciate civilizations sociologically, the contributions of a nation to a civilization, without needing to exercise value judgments, either about nations, civilizations, or *Civilization*. For the latter, no more than progress, does not necessarily lead to the good or to happiness" (Mauss 1969c: 478–479).[12] Furthermore, in a lengthy footnote to *The Rules of Sociological Method*, Durkheim explicitly rejects the hierarchical cataloging of cultures according to their supposed degree of civilization. Such taxonomies are based on criteria too complex or variable to be of any lasting usefulness, to say nothing of the fact that they are unable to take into account the specificities of each society (Durkheim 1927: 109fn1). Concurrently, this resignification pluralizes the usage of "civilization," to the extent that it becomes an analytical framework applicable to Euro-American and non-Western settings alike.[13] Hence, Durkheim and Mauss write about a multiplicity of civilizations and moral systems, which are of equal standing despite containing vastly different modes of social organization and having adopted widely varying developmental paths over time.[14] Such recognition of and esteem for a plurality of civilizational models implicitly counters the rhetoric of a civilizing mission; if non-Western civilizations already exist, and did so prior to their European "discovery," the cultural rationale for the colonial enterprise becomes very tenuous indeed.

Another area where the Durkheimians challenged colonialism's intellectual moorings was in discussions regarding human rationality. Although strongly disputed by Romanticism, the established account of the European Enlightenment was one in which the transition from the "Dark Ages" to modernity enabled human reason to blossom in a manner and to an extent that were geographically unique and historically unprecedented. Cartesian logic and the scientific spirit were cited as being among the highest achievements of French and/or European civilization, distinctive attributes as well as indicators of comparative advancement in relation to the rest of the world. As already noted, this self-conception was commonly employed to validate imperialism, given that the latter could be presented as a humanist endeavor to free the human mind by sweeping away the cobwebs of superstition and ignorance and thereby bestow the gift of rationality on all peoples of the earth.

In French intellectual circles of the late nineteenth and early twentieth centuries, this Enlightenment-based self-understanding—when coupled with the unstated backdrop of empire—nurtured spirited debates about the relationship of modern and "primitive" systems of thought. By far the most widespread view consisted of an incommensurability thesis, according to which an ontological rupture existed between the two radically divergent forms of thinking; the best-known advocate of this position, Lucien Lévy-Bruhl, considered the "primitive" mind to be a prelogical, "mystic" alter ego to its modern counterpart, incompatible with the latter because operating outside of the rules of rationalism and abstraction (Lévy-Bruhl 1923, [1910] 1966).

Throughout their writings, Durkheim and Mauss set about to refute such pervasive claims about the absence of "primitive" rationality and the consequent thesis of necessary intercultural incommensurability. Underpinned by their commitment to a form of scientific humanism, they asserted that it was more valuable to seek to understand the functioning of various civilizations' systems of thought than to evaluate their worth; in fact, the latter exercise was bound to be a subjective one betraying ethnocentric biases and obscuring rigorous comparative analysis. In a protostructuralist move that I previously evoked, the Durkheimians aimed to demonstrate that modern and "primitive" worldviews possessed an identical foundational structure, based on the shared taxonomical rules of binary distinction between similarity and difference as well as hierarchical organization of elements (Durkheim and Mauss 1969a: 82–84). Furthermore, both of these worldviews contain systems of classification of the world that, though substantively different, were bound together by the same formal principle, namely, that their origins reflect their respective societies' or civilizations' modes of social organization and collective consciousness.

Significantly, then, the Durkheimian School distinguishes between "primitive" and "modern" taxonomical systems, yet dismisses naturalizing or ontologizing explanations of their differences, with their hierarchical tenor, in favor of social constructivist arguments. Being collectively oriented and simpler in their composition, "primitive" societies tend to employ more "affective" and imprecise classificatory schemes, which blur the boundaries between categories (sacred and profane, reality and myth, natural and cultural, and so forth) because they are holistic—that is, primarily seeking to explain how particular elements are integrated into the whole (Durkheim and Mauss 1969a: 13–19, 78–81). By contrast, given the individualism and complexity of modern societies, their taxonomical models are rigorous and atomistic in their drive to establish consistent categorizations and disaggregate reality into its component parts to analyze them in isolation from one another. If we resist the ethnocentric tendency to use the latter framework to normatively evaluate the former (and find it wanting), we can grasp the fact that, far from being utterly alien because seemingly arbitrary and contradictory, "primitive" thinking contains an endogenous logic and set of taxonomical rules. Conversely, the Durkheimians claimed, modern societies were much closer to their "primitive" counterparts than was conventionally believed because they themselves were not fully rationalized, whereas no chasm separated scientific from religious thought (Durkheim 1995: 240; Mauss 1969c: 563–564, 1969d: 126–127). Therefore, "primitive" thinking cannot be considered prelogical, for whatever distinguishes it from the modern mind are differences in degree, not in kind; the two possess different, though cognitively equivalent, rationalities.

As one of the dominant paradigms within the Euro-American human sciences at the end of the nineteenth and beginning of the twentieth centuries, social evolutionism represents the last of colonialism's ideological undergirdings to be questioned by the Durkheimians. Formulated by Herbert Spencer, among others, social evolutionary theory not only posited societal or civilizational progress over time—something already present in ideas of development and modernization—but claimed to establish causal relations between earlier and later stages of human history on the basis of biological laws and organicist metaphors (notably, "natural selection" and "survival of the fittest"). Accordingly, spatial distance and cultural variations were made to correspond to different temporalities along a unilinear evolutionary continuum, establishing a hierarchical "denial of coevalness" between societies (Fabian 1983); inexorably moving forward and the most advanced, the modern European world was contrasted to archaic non-Western peoples, who were to stagnate at the stage of humanity's childhood in perpetuity.[15] From such premises, themselves stimulated by European colonialism, flow obvious strategies of justification of imperial conquest of "lower" races and cultures, which are condemned to extinction because of their organic weakness and evolutionary backwardness.

The Durkheimian School's stance toward social evolutionism was ambiguous, yet I would argue that a gradual problematization of it occurred over time. Durkheim's initial body of work contained strong evidence of evolutionary theory's impact on his thinking, which appeared to subscribe to customary assumptions (inherited from his intellectual predecessors and contemporaries) about "primitive" societies as primordial, chronologically antecedent, and, consequently, inferior (Durkheim 1984: 126–128). His Latin thesis went so far as to reproach Montesquieu's *Spirit of Laws* for failing to superimpose an evolutionary framework of progress onto his political taxonomy of "species of government" (Durkheim 1960: 57–60). At the same time, his early writings were already critical of some of evolutionism's major tenets: its assumption (rather than demonstration) of a tenuous causal relationship between earlier and later stages of human progress; its assertion of the existence of a singular trajectory of progress applicable to all cultures, which patently violated the Durkheimians' aforementioned ideal of human pluralism; and a teleological view of history, according to which modernity constituted the final (or most advanced) stage toward which every society was intrinsically moving (Durkheim 1927: 144–147, 169–171; 1970a: 89–90; 1975: 79–80).

Under the influence of Mauss and other ethnologically minded members of the school, Durkheim's later work moved even further away from social evolutionism. If he retains notions of simplicity and complexity to characterize societies on the basis of the degree of differentiation and interdependence between their components, Durkheim does not attribute any evaluative weight to these attributes. Rather, they function as protostructuralist heuristic devices, since the study of more basic social configurations allows the researcher to readily extrapolate formal relations between elements present in all societies without passing judgment on the value of any of them; that "primitive" societies were functionally simple did not imply that they were normatively inferior, nor was superiority associated with their functionally complex modern counterparts. Additionally, while the Durkheimian School accepted the idea of intrasocietal evolution—a society's historical development from a simpler to a more complex mode of social organization—it did not extend such a conceit to an intersocietal scale. Consequently, it never devised a universal evolutionary chain or "scale of civilization" (Tylor 1974:

24) along which societies were positioned according to their corresponding stages of development. Cross-culturally and historically, "primitive" societies did not represent humankind's origins, nor were they prior versions of their modern equivalents, for all peoples existed in the same temporality (Durkheim 1960: 58; 1995: 1–3, 45; Lukes 1985: 519; Schnapper 1998b: 102–107). As Lévi-Strauss explains in his commenting on Mauss: "When he [Mauss] follows Durkheim in refusing to dissociate sociology and anthropology, it is not because he sees in primitive societies early stages of social evolution. They are needed, not because they are earlier, but because they exhibit social phenomena under simpler forms. As he once told this writer, it is easier to study the digestive process in the oyster than in man; but this does not mean that the higher vertebrates were formerly shell-fishes" (1971: 527). Ultimately, the Durkheimians reoriented intercultural analysis from evolutionism's vertical axis of ranking of civilizational progress toward a perspectivist, horizontal axis designed to identify the functional specificities of various societal structures. Put differently, rather than contributing to an evolutionary model of culture that would study non-Western societies as a means to return analytically to Western civilization's past, they were concerned with examining how such societies organized their symbolic and material orders as exemplars of the diversity of sociocultural configurations around the world.

CONCLUSION

I have claimed that the Durkheimian School exemplifies Euro-American sociology's fraught engagement with empire, which can usefully be explained through the concept of a constitutive paradox within its body of work. Indeed, the Durkheimians' writings reveal a productive tension between two opposing currents: the self-evident standing of European colonialism, which appears as a structural backdrop that they never directly contest, on the one hand; and their problematization of some of its central ideological foundations and sources of justification, on the other. Analytically speaking, this creative dialectic's constituent power stems from the fact that it was inescapable and irresolvable for the Durkheimian School, whose investigations and theorizing could not but perpetually set it into play. The Durkheimians' seeming acceptance of empire as a political system of global domination, or at least their taking it for granted, facilitated the institutional recognition of sociology and ethnology as scientific disciplines in France. In turn, academic recognition made possible the ascription of scholarly validity on the intercultural orientation of the Durkheimian School's research program—which ignored the unstated division of intellectual labor between sociologists and anthropologists, itself a colonial inheritance—and on its challenging many of European imperialism's core intellectual assumptions. Concurrently, such questioning could not have occurred without Durkheim, Mauss, and other members of the school having access to knowledge of "primitive" societies and ethnographic material acquired in and through processes of colonization, whose structural roots remained unchallenged. These opposing tendencies cannot be severed from each other without obscuring the complexity and richness of the Durkheimian legacy.

Put differently, then, this chapter made the case that the Durkheimian School simultaneously left colonialism intact as a political system by never scrutinizing its organization of relations of power in the world order, yet sapped it of much of its sociocultural legitimacy by weakening the premises on which it stood: French republicanism's universalism and assimilationism, the idea of civilization, the superiority of modern rationalism, and social evolutionary theory. Moreover, I explored three aspects of the Durkheimian School's interface with empire in which our constitutive paradox is present, namely, through systemic benefits, direct involvement, and intellectual disputation.

Surely, there existed no better institutional embodiment of this constitutive paradox than the Musée de l'homme, inaugurated in Paris on the occasion of the 1937 World Fair largely as a result of the efforts of members of the Durkheimian School (most notably, Mauss and Paul Rivet). Indeed, the Musée had a humanist and universalist mission, that of displaying the wealth of humankind's diversity and of simultaneously making a case for the unity and equality of the world's cultures. Designed to counter the ethnocentric and racist currents of thought that were sweeping through Europe in the interwar period, it was particularly concerned with demonstrating the aesthetic sophistication and cultural richness of the peoples of Oceania, Asia, and Africa, whose material objects were accorded a treatment conventionally reserved for classical Euro-American "masterpieces." At the same time, however, the Musée's collection—itself inherited from the Musée d'ethnographie du Trocadéro—largely consisted of the spoils of the French Empire, artifacts amassed in the metropole after being appropriated and pillaged by "explorers," researchers, and colonial administrations in numerous overseas territories. The Musée remained silent about this reality, that of the imperial origins of its exhibits, but just as significantly never explicitly scrutinized colonialism as a system of global domination and hierarchical differentiation between populations (Conklin 2002). As a result, it left uncontested the socio-economic and political conditions that subjugated, destroyed, and rendered inferior the very societies whose cultures it was determined to preserve and elevate on the same plane as those of the North Atlantic region; apparently, the commitment to intercultural egalitarianism and the cultivation of pluralism did not necessarily go hand in hand with recognizing the universal right to political and economic self-determination.

To those imprudent readers who, imbued with a sense of condescension toward the past, might be tempted to conclude that such blind spots have long since been overcome in the contemporary human sciences, a word of warning is in order. Since being inaugurated in 2006, the ostensible replacement for the Musée de l'homme, the Musée du quai Branly, has hardly resolved the questions that plagued its predecessor; in fact, the more recent iteration's truncated postcolonial sensibilities may well be more troubling, in that they do little to interrogate the imperial origins of the museum's collection, the latter's continued spatial segregation from Euro-American art and cultural artifacts—which, in Paris, are found at the Louvre, the Musée d'Orsay, and the Centre Pompidou, among others—and the primitivist modes of presentation of its displays. Hence, the character of sociology's constitutive paradox may well have shifted a century after the Durkheimian School contributed to it, but its traces remain with us; our predicament is to inherit scholarly tools born out of empire. To be reflexive about such a reality implies neither ignoring it for the sake of disciplinary "normality" nor seeking to reject these tools in the name of a sociological tabula rasa. The task ahead, then, is the activation of a critical ambivalence that foregrounds, and works through, this paradoxical legacy.

NOTES

Research and writing of this chapter were made possible by a Standard Research Grant from the Social Sciences and Humanities Research Council of Canada. I would like to thank Peter Mallory for the excellence and timeliness of his research assistance.

1. These critiques have underscored the fact that European imperialism provided the political conditions required for much fieldwork in anthropology and that the discipline was complicit with colonialism by either bolstering the latter's racialist ideology or collaborating with colonial regimes (or, at the very least, failing to put them into question).

2. The Durkheimian School also included Henri Beuchat, Célestin Bouglé, Paul Fauconnet, Maurice Halbwachs, Henri Hubert, and Robert Hertz, among others

(Besnard 1979, 1983). For the purposes of this chapter, however, only Durkheim's and Mauss's work will be considered. Although the influence of the Durkheimians in French intellectual circles is now widely recognized, their institutional strength and numbers were most significant prior to World War I and declined rapidly in the interwar period (Heilbron 1984).

3. Indeed, Connell (1997: 1516) mentions that only about 28 percent of the content of *L'année sociologique*—the flagship journal of the Durkheimians—concerned contemporary Euro-American societies.

4. Condorcet's *Sketch for a Historical Picture of the Progress of the Human Mind* posited nine stages of human development, whereas Comte argued that human-kind moved from theological to metaphysical to positive states (Comte [1830–1842] 1975; Condorcet [1795] 1955).

5. Ironically, although the Durkheimians' writings may well have served as a vital source of avant-garde aesthetic inspiration in the interwar years in France, their academic prestige had simultaneously declined and their generational renewal was flagging (Heilbron 1984).

6. In recent times, Bourdieu represents the most accomplished heir to this French penchant for intermingling sociology and anthropology, for his early ethnographic work in Algeria (Bourdieu 1962, 1979; Bourdieu and Sayad 1964) provided a perspective from outside through which he could estrange the *doxa* of French society and thereby lay bare the latter's mechanisms of structural domination (Calhoun 2006).

7. For instance, Durkheim intervened in favor of Captain Dreyfus in the infamous Dreyfus affair that consumed France in the late nineteenth and early twentieth centuries (Durkheim 1970b), and Mauss was a cofounder of the socialist newspaper *L'humanité* (to which he was a regular contributor) (Karady 1983: 74). To get a sense of the full array of Mauss's political journalism, see his *Political Writings* edited by Marcel Fournier (Mauss 1997).

8. Accordingly, the first series of the *L'année sociologique* contained several summaries and reviews of books on colonized societies and colonialism itself. I would like to thank George Steinmetz for drawing my attention to this fact.

9. Eventually, this led to the creation of the Institut d'ethnologie in 1925 (whose founders were Mauss, Paul Rivet, and Lucien Lévy-Bruhl) and the Musée de l'homme in 1937 (founded by Rivet).

10. Of course, this reveals Mauss's conception of cultures as essentialized and discrete wholes.

11. As Fournier (2005: 169) writes: "The socialists' position remained ambiguous: the SFIO did not ratify the protectorate the French imposed but it also did not adopt the principle of withdrawal [from Morocco]. Among militants, antimilitarism took precedence over anticolonialism, and if the French policy in Morocco was denounced, it was done in the name of pacifism. This is why, with the end of the Moroccan crisis, the socialist critique of French imperialism in Morocco diminished in frequency and intensity."

12. The translation is my own, while the emphasis is in the original.

13. For instance, they give the examples of Christian, Mediterranean, and Northwest American (which would include indigenous societies of the Pacific Northwest of North America) civilizations (Durkheim and Mauss 1969b: 453). In "Les civilisations: éléments et formes," Mauss supplies many other instances of civilizations from Africa, Asia, and Oceania (Mauss 1969c).

14. On this topic, a section of *The Evolution of Educational Thought* is worth quoting at some length: "Far from being immutable, humanity is in fact involved in an interminable process of evolution, disintegration and reconstruction; far from being a unity, it is in fact infinite in its variety, with regard to both time and place.... The view that there is one single moral system valid for all men at all times is no longer tenable. History teaches us that there are as many different moral systems as there are types of society; and this diversity is not the product of some mysterious blindness which has prevented men from seeing the true needs of their nature. It is, rather, simply an expression of the great diversity in the circumstances under which collective living takes place. As a result those sentiments which we would dearly like to believe are the most deeply rooted in man's congenital make-up have been wholly unknown to a host of societies" (Durkheim 1977: 324–325). In his discussion of Montesquieu, Durkheim makes a similar point by rejecting universal and uniform laws of social organization, arguing instead that societies adopt a variety of structures and belief systems as are suited and appropriate for their conditions of collective life (Durkheim 1960: 16–18).

15. Thus, in Victorian Britain, both the populist anthropological mythologies of Frazer's *Golden Bough* and Tylor's more scientific studies could characterize "primitive" cultures as ancestral and fated to disappear (Frazer 1922: 263; Tylor 1974: 410).

PART II
CURRENT SOCIOLOGICAL THEORIES OF EMPIRE

SEVEN

The Recent Intensification of
American Economic and Military Imperialism
Are They Connected?

MICHAEL MANN

Most Americans deny they have or ever have had an empire. So too did many nineteenth-century British people, for whom the term also possessed negative connotations. The Japanese preferred the label Greater East Asia Co-Prosperity Sphere for their empire. All preferred to say they were spreading freedom through the world. That the British and Japanese claims seem now ludicrous might make us skeptical of American denials too. But the frequency of empire denial makes it essential to define empire. The word derives from the Latin *imperium*, the power wielded by a general commanding an army and a magistrate armed with law—a combination of political and military power. Modern usage adds a geographical element—power exercised over a peripheral by a core. Thus my definition: an empire is a centralized, hierarchical system of rule acquired and maintained by coercion through which a core dominates peripheries, serves as the intermediary for their main interactions, and channels resources from and between the peripheries. As Motyl says (2001: 4), an empire is like a rimless wheel: the peripheries communicate to and through the core but not directly to each other, so that the core controls the flow of all major resources. All roads led to Rome, all gold flowed to Cadiz, all five-year plans were made in Moscow, while today imperial authority flows from two cities, Washington (the capital of the country) and New York (the capital of capital).

Obviously, empires have been varied. I distinguish five types of domination by cores over peripheries, of which the first four are imperial. The five constitute a descending hierarchy of domination. These are, of course, ideal types.

1 · DIRECT EMPIRE: territories are conquered and then politically incorporated into the realm of the core. Once institutionalized, fairly uniform political institutions radiate outward from center to periphery. Roman law came to govern all, and integration of provincial economies occurred. Finally, the empire completes a "disappearing act" when the conquered peoples become ideologically incorporated, acquiring a "Roman" or "Han Chinese" identity, for example. Americans achieved this at the beginning of their imperial expansion, conquering (and mainly exterminating) the natives of North America and conquering and assimilating formerly French, Spanish, and Mexican subjects. From the 1890s they also achieved this in Hawaii and Puerto Rico. But these were the last such ventures.

2 · INDIRECT EMPIRE: the claim of political sovereignty by the imperial core, while the rulers of the periphery retain autonomy and in practice negotiate the rules of the game with the imperial authorities. As Lord Cromer said of British rule, "We do not govern Egypt, we only govern the governors of Egypt" (Al-Sayyid 1968: 68). Americans attempted this in the Philippines from 1898, but massive resistance forced a partial climbdown. Badly burned, the United States did not subsequently attempt indirect empire other than in strictly temporary circumstances.

These first two types involve colonies, unlike those that follow. So when Americans say they have had no empire, they mean they have not had colonies. That has been correct since 1900, except for a short period in defeated countries of World War II.

3 · INFORMAL EMPIRE occurs where peripheral rulers retain sovereignty but with their autonomy constrained by intimidation from the imperial core. John Gallagher and Ronald Robinson (1953: 2–3) developed the concept for the British Empire. Robinson (1984: 48) summarized it as "coercion or diplomacy exerted for purposes of imposing free trading conditions on a weaker society against its will; foreign loans, diplomatic and military support to weak states in return for economic concessions or political alliance; direct intervention or influence from the export-import sector in the domestic politics of weak states on behalf of foreign trading and strategic interests; and lastly, the case of foreign bankers and merchants annexing sectors of the domestic economy of a weak state." However, I clarify the notion of "coercion" by distinguishing two types of military and one type of economic coercion used in informal empire.

3A · INFORMAL EMPIRE THROUGH MILITARY INTERVENTIONS. Here military force is threatened and occasionally deployed in short, sharp military interventions. The gunboat cannot conquer or rule, but it administers pain by shelling ports and landing marines to force a change of policy on the local regime. The European empires, the United States, and Japan all jointly administered such pain to China in the late nineteenth and early twentieth centuries through "unequal treaties" supervised by controlling Chinese customs revenues and budgets reinforced by intermittent military interventions. The United States did it in its own hemisphere with "Dollar Diplomacy." Between 1898 and 1930 there were thirty-one such military interventions by the United States, one a year. This was direct military intimidation but without colonies. There was also a burst after World War II, with massive military interventions in Korea and Vietnam, minor ones in other countries, and the establishment of a global network of military bases aimed at intimidating enemies and neutral states in the Cold War. Another burst has been proceeding since 2001.

3B · INFORMAL EMPIRE THROUGH MILITARY PROXIES. In the 1930s, the United States subcontracted military coercion to sovereign local despots backed by a local comprador class who supported U.S. foreign policy and interests in return for a promise from the Americans of nonintervention and economic and military aid. "He may be a son of a bitch, but he's our son of a bitch" was Cordell Hull's supposed expression. In the post–World War II period, the United States added more covert, deniable military operations of its own, especially through the newly formed CIA. Thus Saddam Hussein used to be our "son of a bitch" but was never acknowledged openly to be so. Israel is our major current son of a bitch (though its government is not despotic over Jews). These are less direct forms of military intimidation.

So far all these types of empire have involved substantial doses of military power.

4 · ECONOMIC IMPERIALISM. Here "empire" remains informal, but an important line has been crossed: military has been replaced by economic coercion. In the second half of the nineteenth century, Britain turned toward more purely economic coercion in Asia and the Americas. Take Argentina. Its trade with Britain was more crucial to it, since it contributed only about 10 percent of Britain's trade, whereas Britain received over 50 percent of Argentina's. Britain also provided the vast bulk of its investment capital. Argentina tried to diversify and reduce its dependence on Britain by raising more capital in New York, Paris, and Berlin, but it failed. Britain could say to the Argentine government, "You adopt this policy, or we will strangle your economy." Britain actually did apply devastating sanctions on Peru in 1876, which helped persuade Argentina to become something of a client state in matters of concern to Britain. Today comparable policies are

called "structural adjustment"—purely economic interventions in peripheral economies by international institutions in which the United States has the predominant power.

This is a borderline case of imperialism. The peripheral country is "free" to say no, but the deterrents are powerful—the denial of foreign investment and perhaps of foreign trade. Sanctions are involved, yet there is no military force. The term "economic imperialism," a qualified form of imperialism, seems appropriate here. Yet if it is applied routinely, it might become institutionalized and so begin to blur into my final type of domination, which is not imperial.

5 · HEGEMONY is used here in the Gramscian sense of routinized leadership by the core over peripheral sovereign states, which is regarded by them as "normal."[1] Because hegemony is built into peripheral everyday social practices, it needs little coercion. Whereas indirect and informal empire and economic imperialism all result in local clients feeling constrained to serve the imperial master, they see themselves as deferring voluntarily to a hegemon, accepting its rules of the game as natural. Hegemony involves more than Joseph Nye's notion of "soft power." He defines this purely in terms of ideological power, as "the ability to get what you want through attraction rather than coercion or payments. It arises from the attractiveness of a country's culture, political ideals, and policies" (Nye 2004: x). This seems naive. The United States could not command other states merely by offering attractive values and policies. Sweden or Canada cannot. The United States differs because some of its practices are built into the everyday lives of others, compelling them to act in certain ways, as those of Sweden or Canada are not.

"Dollar seigniorage" is an example of hegemony. The rule of the dollar results in foreigners investing in the United States at extremely low rates of interest, benefiting Americans disproportionately. Yet foreigners might see this as simply what they do with export surpluses. Also during the Cold War period, other Western governments accepted U.S. leadership as legitimate because they needed the United States to defend it against communism. And hegemony will do a "disappearing act" if its benefits allow peripheral states to become autonomous of the hegemon. The Americans brought economic benefits to their client states in Europe and East Asia, and within about a decade those states became mostly autonomous of the United States. American hegemony transmuted into mutual interdependence, which means no domination at all.

The most obvious feature of American domination in the post–World War II period has been variety across both space and time. Over Europe domination has been hegemonic, not imperial (except for the initial occupation of West Germany), transmuting into mutual dependence. East Asia initially saw a mixture of indirect empire and informal empire through military intervention—the United States fought major wars in Korea and Vietnam to defend its client states and there were many lesser interventions. However, this domination became more benign over time, and hegemony now predominates. Latin America and the Middle East have intermittently witnessed informal empire through military intervention or proxies. These have recently declined in Latin America but increased in the Middle East. American domination has thus been a great mixture of types, like the British Empire before it, though with no long-term colonies. The United States also tended to descend through my ideal types into milder forms of domination—until recently (as we shall see). Conversely, as Chalmers Johnson (2000, 2005) has argued, the global spread of a U.S. military base network might be a new imperial substitute for colonies, enforcing compliance without formal occupation of territory. Beside it, the former network of British naval bases pales in comparison. So there is and has long been an American Empire.

THE NEW ECONOMIC IMPERIALISM, 1970–1995: DOLLAR SEIGNIORAGE

The world benefited from American hegemony over the postwar economy. The world economy boomed in the 1950s and 1960s, boosted first by U.S. growth, then European, then Japanese. The dollar was the reserve currency, backed by gold. This was a lower tariff regime than in the interwar period, which also boosted trade. All continents shared to some extent in growth. Though the Bretton Woods system gave the United States privileges, it was administered by multilateral agreements between states, allowing them to implement their own development plans and to "repress" international flows of capital. This part of American domination was more hegemony than imperialism. But then came crisis. A slowdown at the end of the 1960s took the form of "stagflation," which Keynesian countercyclical policies seemed only to worsen. The prices of export commodities on which poorer countries depended were falling, creating balance of payments difficulties that their Import Substitution Programs could not resolve. The sharp hike in oil prices in 1973 worsened their problems.

The Bretton Woods financial system collapsed between 1968 and 1971. The slowdown, plus U.S. deficits compounded by spending in Vietnam, and increasing financial volatility all meant that the financial "repression" necessary for the Bretton Woods system was faltering. This forced a shift from pegged to floating exchange rates, with the dollar being taken off the gold standard. The United States was importing and spending abroad much more than it was exporting, resulting in big American deficits. Since the dollar was at first still on the gold standard, this resulted at the end of the 1960s in a run on its gold. Fort Knox was being emptied. This seemed at the time to be a threat to American power. The United States might conceivably have gone the way of Britain in the 1940s: after the gold disappeared, the United States might have been forced to sell off its investments abroad to pay for its military activity abroad. Foreigners might have also used their surplus dollars to buy up American industries, as Americans had done in Britain. But after some arm-twisting by U.S. diplomats, the major central banks agreed as a stopgap measure to stop converting their dollars into gold, thereby sacrificing their immediate economic interest to the common good produced by American global responsibilities. At this point neither they nor the U.S. administration realized how costly this would become. This informal mutual restraint held the line until August 1971, when President Nixon took the dollar off the gold standard—to save his war, his expansionary economic policies, and his reelection chances (Kunz 1997: 192–222). The reasons were domestic plus Vietnam, not a premeditated drive for economic imperialism.

The dollar remained the reserve currency. The only use for surplus U.S. dollars held abroad was now to invest them in the United States. As most were held by central banks, they bought U.S. Treasury notes in bulk, which lowered their interest rate. U.S. adventures abroad could now be financed by foreigners, despite American current account deficits, and at a very low interest rate. The alternative, the foreigners felt, was worse: disruption of the world's monetary system, weakening U.S. resolve to defend them, and a fall in the value of the dollar, making U.S. exports cheaper than their own. Hudson (2003: 20) concludes, "This unique ability of the U.S. government to borrow from foreign central banks rather than from its own citizens is one of the economic miracles of modern times." Such economic imperialism meant that U.S. governments were free of the balance of payments constraints faced by other states. Americans could spend more on social services, fight in Vietnam, and consume more, all at the same time. This held off the European challenge in the "real economy," as it was later to hold off the Japanese and then the Chinese challenge. American officials had hit on this only as a short-term solution to what they saw as a crisis. However, with hindsight, for the United States it was not a crisis at all but an opportunity to enhance its "seigniorage" over the world economy.

But this imperial intensification also involved a shift of power toward private, transnational finance capital. The sharp rise in oil prices in the autumn of 1973 generated an increase in the dollar earnings of oil states too big to be absorbed into their own economies. These "petro-dollars" had to be recycled into productive investment in the rest of the world. The Europeans and the Japanese favored doing this through central banks and the International Monetary Fund (IMF). The United States, backed by Britain, insisted that it be done mainly by private banks. The United States had more influence with the oil sheikhs and abolished restrictions on funds flowing in and out of the States. The French socialist government of the early 1980s tried to hold on to its Keynesian control of capital accumulation, but the Reagan administration defeated it through high dollar and interest rates. Europe caved in. As its states adopted fixed exchange rates and free movement of capital, they surrendered control of monetary policy to Europe's financial markets. Though Japan held on, preserving its arcane statism while expanding its influence over East Asia, the Bretton Woods system of financial "repression" was effectively ended. No military force was involved, only the exploitation of an already existing dollar seigniorage.

So this was not only American economic imperialism. It also shifted power from the interstate level to the transnational-market level. A state's credit now depended less on agreements between central banks and the IMF than on private international financial markets run on neoliberal principles. In 1981 the Reagan administration gave Wall Street the same offshore unregulated status enjoyed by the City of London. Gowan (1999: ch. 3; cf. Soederberg 2004) calls this "the Dollar-Wall Street Regime," since it gave the U.S. government and American financiers far more power over the world's monetary and financial relations than had the Bretton Woods regime. But finance capital in Europe and Japan also got more power. The new system also involved greater global instability, for the end of financial repression has made for wilder swings in the value of the dollar, reinforcing unprecedented volatility in the world economy, forcing other states to hold larger reserves in dollars. Though many emphasize the inherent instability and risks of such arrangements, the alternative of moving away from having the dollar as the reserve currency still seems riskier to the players. It is partially legitimate, a hybrid form of economic imperialism/hegemony.

STRUCTURAL ADJUSTMENT PROGRAMS

The second intensification aimed more at the global south. Being perceived as coercion, it is clearly economic imperialism. The Organization of Petroleum Exporting Countries (OPEC) oil price rise made European and especially American banks awash with petro-dollars, since the oil producers could not absorb all their increased profits. U.S. banks, newly freed from investing in Treasury notes, were flooded with funds. This generated an "over-accumulation" crisis, a mass of liquid wealth unable to find sufficient avenues of productive investment (perhaps the first time the Hobson/Lenin explanation of imperialism had some truth). Now the banks became more interested in the South, offering low (sometimes effectively negative) interest rates to southern countries, which borrowed massively to finance their sagging economies. Then in 1979 the United States suddenly tripled its interest rates, for domestic reasons. Others had to follow U.S. rates upward. A southern debt crisis ensued, resulting in intensified economic imperialism. This had not been planned. It was again the unintended consequences of action, deriving from the fact that power relations within capitalist markets are essentially diffuse in nature, while state power is authoritative and in this case reactive.

The World Bank and the IMF now became a key part of the new economic imperialism as they shifted their main focus from the North to the South. Their core activity became "structural adjustment programs," the cutting edge of an economic imperialism all the more effective because its practitioners sincerely believed it was merely rational economics, a reflection of economic reality, and therefore good for everyone concerned. Indeed, it did reflect more market-, inflation-, debt-, and finance-driven economic realities.

Led by the U.S. Treasury, the banks exemplified the "Washington Consensus" (though they also represented the wisdom of Wall Street in New York, the city of London, and finance capital everywhere). These banks would bail out the indebted countries, agreeing to "restructure" their loans in return for deep economic reforms—an austerity program of cutting central and local government spending, imposing high interest rates, stabilizing the currency, privatizing state-owned enterprises, abolishing tariffs, freeing labor markets from union restrictions, and opening up local capital markets and business ownership to foreign business.

This was imperialism since it amounted to a massive intervention in the periphery. The enforcement of the loan terms exacted by the core would restructure the peripheral economy, weaken its government, and increase its dependence on the states and foreign capital of the core. But, again, it was not merely state imperialism. Though led by American power, it was diffuse collective domination by "northern" transnational and financial capital—the same condominium I noted for dollar seigniorage. But this also involved multilateral agreements between the states of the North. Though the United

States was the leading actor, it was flanked and usually backed by other big northern economic powers. The IMF and World Bank governing boards are made up of representatives of states, and indeed the more financially reactionary body, the IMF, is never headed by an American. The United States is the main imperial enforcer, but this is in the common interests of a multilateral and class-fractional coalition. Coercion was strictly economic—no gunboats were used. The peripheral state remained sovereign and could in principle reject the loan offer, though the consequence might be bankruptcy, future higher interest rates, and even possible exclusion from the international economy. It was an offer that most third world governments felt they could not refuse. In any case, most governments rather like getting money.

The full dosage was administered only to the periphery. Though neoliberalism also imposed austerity on workers in the North, U.S. administrations would never dare impose the full program on Americans, though their debts dwarfed those of all other countries. It would have been electoral suicide. European representatives in the international banks were also endorsing policies abroad that they would never impose on their own countries, since it would have grossly flouted the norms of their more community-oriented Christian and Social Democracies. Of course, the decision makers were actually bankers, conservative economists, and corporate lawyers. Austerity was in the interests of their friends and relations, since it would get their loans repaid and they could acquire foreign assets at bargain prices. Because they made the common human error of equating their own interests with the good of humanity, they genuinely believed in the ability of structural adjustment to bring wealth and freedom to all. Indeed, having denuded states of the periphery of their powers of intervention and redistribution, they could also promote the spread of a democracy powerless to achieve social goals—that is, "low-intensity democracy" (see Robinson 1996, though he uses the confusing term "polyarchy").

As in all informal imperialism, structural adjustment required cooperation from local elites who often welcomed "conditionality" since it enabled them to introduce reforms they wanted while deflecting local criticism onto external "villains" (Vreeland 2003: 126, 153). The programs were usually unpopular, the core opposition coming from organized labor and those dependent on the state. Democratic governments were more reluctant to sign up, and most programs were introduced by authoritarian regimes, which made the IMF appear to favor dictatorships over democracies, just as the United States did politically and militarily in this period (Biersteker 1992: 114–116; Vreeland 2003; 90–102). Some even see the demise of

Import Substitution Industrialization (ISI) as driven by politics on the periphery, not in the core. They say ISI had so empowered workers that military coups needed buttressing by the new economics. General Pinochet in Chile, a fervent class warrior, introduced the most rigorous reforms, followed by the military regimes of Uruguay, Argentina, and Turkey, all repressing protest by unions and nongovernmental organizations against dismantling ISI policies (Weaver 2000: 141–144). As experienced, structural adjustment did not seem like freedom.

IMF and World Bank programs contained many elements with different effects. Overall, they enabled debt repayment—the main goal of the creditors—and they tended to further countries' integration into the global economy, shrink budget deficits, and end hyperinflation—all beneficial effects. If the state in question were incompetent or corrupt (and many were), cutting it back might also do some good, though perhaps only if the incompetent or incorrupt were not in charge of the program. But the programs tended also to redistribute from the poor to the rich, from labor to capital, and from local to foreign capital. Overall, they widened inequality. The financial reforms that were prominent from the 1980s also increased inflows of short-term foreign capital, which tended to destabilize the economy while allowing northern businesses and banks, especially American ones, to buy up local economic assets at bargain prices.

The bottom line was supposed to be economic growth that might in the long run justify what neoliberals themselves admitted were short-term side effects. Unfortunately, growth rarely materialized. Vreeland examined 135 countries that in total between 1952 and 1990 were subjected to one thousand years under IMF programs. Controlling for many intervening variables, he found that the more assistance they received, the worse they did. The cost of tutelage was on average 1.6 percent less economic growth per annum, a sizable amount. When he repeated the analysis on a different (and perhaps less reliable) data set for the 1990s, he got 1.4 percent less growth (Vreeland 2003: 123–130).

Given such a poor record, why would states persist with the programs? Countries with strong states and cohesive civil societies might be able to take decisive macroeconomic action themselves, which would avoid the need to go to the banks. Vreeland (2003: 134–151) notes that most loan-recipient states were dominated by oligarchies who benefited from redistribution from labor to capital. He calculates that since the share of labor in national income dropped an average of 7 percent, capital made a net gain, despite the overall gross domestic product (GDP) slowdown. IMF programs benefited the rich and harmed the masses. They seemed deliberately designed that way (says Hutchinson 2001). This was also happening under neoliberal programs within the United States and Britain. Market forces unrestrained by states typically favor those who can bring more resources to markets—though inequality may also be widened by predatory states. As in the past, economic imperialism also benefited the comprador class. Now it also benefited the private financiers who usually supplement IMF loans. Since the IMF sees their loans as crucial to its packages, it defers to "bank-friendly conditions," to get loans repaid and to gain control over foreign financial sectors (Gould 2003). IMF and World Bank loans are more likely to be given to, and the loan conditions are less likely to be enforced on, states that are heavily indebted to U.S. banks, receiving official U.S. aid, or voting at the United Nations with the United States—or indeed France (Oatley and Yackee 2004; Stone 2004). The two banks represent overlapping but not identical interests, and northern capitalist and American state imperialisms sometimes tug in conflicting directions.

East Asia was at first spared structural adjustment. But after the "Asian crisis" of 1997, its economies became more vulnerable. The U.S. Treasury, pressured by American financial firms, pressured the IMF to pressure the South Korean authorities to open up the country's financial sector to foreigners. The United States prevailed, and foreigners were allowed to establish bank subsidiaries and brokerage houses in Korea in 1998. Though the IMF believed this was the right thing to do, U.S. motives had been more self-interested. "Lobbying by American financial services firms, which wanted to crack the Korean market, was the driving force behind the Treasury's pressure on Korea," says Blustein (2001). IMF officials had become cynical about such "ulterior motives," "focussed more on serving US interests than Korea's, in particular . . . greater opportunities for foreign brokerage firms." One said, "The US saw this as an opportunity, as they did in many countries, to crack open all these things that for years have bothered them." In most IMF crisis negotiations, the United States pursued the toughest neoliberal line. It also shot down a Japanese attempt to lead a rival East Asian financial consortium to solve the crisis (Blustein 2001: 143–145, 164–170). An imperial power does not like collective organization on the periphery. Here the U.S. government and American financial corporations were pursuing identical informal imperialism through structural adjustment. Yet this offensive may have ground to a halt, as the East Asian economies have resumed earlier policies of financial repression, somewhat amended.

Britain had pursued in the second half of the nineteenth century a genuine free trade imperialism. It insisted (by force if necessary) that peripheral countries open up their trade, while opening up its own in return. This advantaged the British who had a technological lead, producing goods more cheaply, wiping out the artisanal industries of the periphery. The other imperial powers, including the United States, practiced phony free trade imperialism, opening up peripheral markets while keeping their own protected. Today half-free trade imperialism, led by the United States, is a mixture of the two.

The main international organization trying to open up markets and lower tariff protection was the General Agreement on Tariffs and Trade (GATT), which later became the World Trade Organization (WTO). In the 1970s, like the two banks, it was turning away from a focus on northern economies toward opening up the markets of the South. Its reach was widening, extending freer trade beyond agriculture and manufacturing into services, especially financial services and intellectual property rights. But its grasp was also deepening, as its rulings became backed by a body of international law restraining the North as well as the South. By the twenty-first century, protectionism, such as President George W. Bush's steel tariffs, received heavy fines, while the Europeans' ban on genetically modified crops is likely to get the same punishment. This reflected and reinforced the power shift occurring within northern capitalism, diminishing the power of sectors favoring protection and increasing those favoring liberalization, especially finance.

But the impact of the WTO has been more dramatic on the South. Its main responsibility is to press for free trade. The interest of all countries is to free up the markets of others but not their own. This is especially so for poor countries who know that the rich countries (including the United States) became rich by initially protecting their infant industries, repressing finance, and subsidizing exports. The poor would benefit most by retaining such powers while gaining access to rich countries' markets (if the American Empire really did have a mission to develop the world, it would agree to this, but not surprisingly this is not so). The second-best solution for the poor countries would be free trade for all, since their lower-cost agriculture and low-end manufacturing could enable them to export more. But the WTO pressures them to open up their markets while the rich countries protect their agriculture, which is almost the worst possible regime for them and the most imperialistic. Despite an ostensibly democratic constitution (unlike the two banks), the WTO has been dominated by the rich countries, organized as the "Quad"—the United States, the European Union, Japan, and Canada—so that the gain in relative economic strength by Europe and Japan against the United States resulted less in rivalry than a degree of collaborative northern imperialism. Poorer countries complained about lack of transparency; closed-door, late-night sessions; late release of meeting transcripts; and exclusion from the decisive "green-room" meetings. Countries refusing to support Quad initiatives were placed on a blacklist of unfriendly states, and some had their preferential trade agreements suspended. Jawara and Kwa (2003: 295) say, "Favorite instruments are the promise of benefits under the African Growth and Opportunity Act (by the US . . .), limited concessions on trade restrictions directed toward individual countries (notably on textiles), debt reduction (e.g., the sudden completion of Tanzania's long-overdue debt reduction under the Heavily Indebted Poor Countries (HIPC) initiative soon after Doha) and aid (offered to Pakistan, for example). Many of the promises were fulfilled; others either were quietly forgotten or turned out to be worthless." This coercion was strictly economic—no gunboats sail under the WTO flag—and confined to offering or withdrawing economic benefits.

The greatest achievement of this offensive was the 1994 Agreement on Trade-Related Aspects of Intellectual Property Rights (TRIPS). This protected the patent rights of inventors and the copyrights of writers, musicians, and artists—obviously useful to struggling creative individuals. But TRIPS also tended to shift control of commercially viable creativity and public knowledge into the realm of transnational corporations (Drahos and Braithwaite 2002). Its biggest beneficiaries are big pharmaceutical companies, whose malign influence on AIDS has been widely noted. Their patented drugs against AIDS are too highly priced to be used widely in poor countries—they are often sold at higher prices there than in the corporation's home country. Thus, thousands, perhaps millions, die. "Generic" drugs costing a fraction of the price can be produced by poorer countries, especially by India, but TRIPS prevented their sale. TRIPS kept a northern lock on creativity in cutting-edge technologies, making it harder for others to move into these high-profit fields. The North registers over 90 percent of the world's patents. TRIPS had largely resulted from corporate lobbying. Sell (2002: 171–172; cf. Drahos and Braithwaite 2002: 72–73, 114–119) says that TRIPS was "a significant instance of global rule-making by a small handful of well-connected corporate players and their governments." The chief executives of "powerful American-based multi-national companies" with "superb access to the top levels of policy-making both at domestic and multilateral levels" became the founding members of an "Intellectual Property Committee," which lobbied for TRIPS within GATT. This was a triumph for the Quad states and their big corporations, working together.

But they had exceeded their power. There has been a backlash and some amendments to TRIPS. Resentment over this and other issues boiled over at the Seattle Ministerial Meetings in 1999, which broke up in disarray. After bitter, lengthy negotiations, some breaches of TRIPS were allowed. In 2003 an agreement allowed developing countries to import generic drugs for the treatment of diseases that are "public health threats," though the verification procedures are long and costly. The United States had also suffered reverses within the Organization for Economic Cooperation and Development, failing to commit the organization to end members' controls over capital accounts and financial services movements and to permit complete freedom of foreign corporations to set up foreign branches and buy up local companies to the point where they could dominate local product markets. In 1998, France, followed by others, refused to sign. The United States then turned to the WTO and secured a provisional commitment at Singapore in 2003 to pursue more open investment, financial competition, transparency, and government procurement. This would include an agreement to liberalize financial services to the point where foreign financiers would have identical rights to locals. But this also provoked opposition, as it was perceived as informal imperialism.

The disputes continue. The Doha Development Round of WTO negotiations has been blocked for seven years and may be disintegrating. The United States, Japan, and the EU have taken turns to block progress on agriculture, the item of greatest concern to poor countries. The entry of China (pushed by the United States) has added a large ally to India, Brazil, and the other members of the G-20 organization formed at the Cancun meeting in 2003. Collective organization by the South is a direct challenge to American/northern imperialism, aided in the northern streets by an alliance of protectionists and antiglobalists or alternative globalists, environmentalists, feminists, indigenous peoples, and others—for the new imperialism affects them too. Their power to disrupt and to command media attention at the beginning of the twenty-first century has forced the WTO and the World Bank to make big rhetorical shifts and smaller shifts in actual policy (Aaronson 2001; Rabinovitch 2004). It may not be good news that the WTO is stalled, since poor countries might benefit from freer trade. But it is a sign of collective resistance on the periphery to economic imperialism.

The United States and the EU sought to counter this by making more bilateral and regional agreements with poorer countries. This is the traditional imperial tactic: peripheral countries will communicate with the core but not with each other (Smith 2000: 333). But recently resurgent Latin American leftists have stalled the U.S. plan for the Free Trade Area of the Americas. It is too early to know whether the balance of power has shifted against American and northern capitalist imperialism, but this intensification of economic imperialism may have ceased.

But the three arms of the new economic imperialism did work for the United States, reversing its relative economic decline. By 2000 it had 28 percent of the world's GDP, an increase from 22–24 percent in 1970. Yet the continued rise of China and India will in the long run lead to relative American decline, though finance capital and the dollar, increasingly supported by the Chinese economy, may ensure that a lesser hegemony survives, though of a peculiar debt-dominated kind. The United States continues to operate as the hub of the world's financial markets. In 2003, 83 percent of the $3 trillion daily foreign exchange dealing involved the U.S. dollar, 59 percent of world foreign exchange reserves were held in U.S. dollars, and U.S. government bonds comprised over half of all world bonds. The United States needs this to continue financing its ever-increasing trade and budget deficits. Americans' debts to foreigners probably totaled over $2.7 trillion, over a quarter of its GDP, and so the United States requires an inflow of about $2 billion per day to pay for it. Thus the United States must first keep capital markets open and prevent any return elsewhere to policies of "national development" involving capital controls. It continues to push financial neoliberalism, which is vital to maintain present American economic and fiscal policies (Soederberg 2004: 125). Second, foreigners must want to invest in the United States, rather than elsewhere. Despite many voices saying this cannot continue, it does. Now it is less the Japanese, more the Chinese who are propping up the dollar. The American and Chinese economies are now strongly interdependent, both needing the cooperation of the other in present financial arrangements. The arrangement seems likely to continue for a while, unless protectionism within the United States destroys it.

Is this beginning to resemble British financial hegemony of a century ago, which was kept going by a multilateral collaborative effort among the biggest national economies (Eichengreen 1996)? This would mean slow but graceful American relative economic decline, cushioned by a successor consortium of capitalist powers, plus China. But the rise and fall of the new American militarism has been anything but graceful.

INFORMAL EMPIRE THROUGH MILITARY INTERVENTION, 1990–2006

The collapse of the Soviet Union left an enormous American military pre-ponderance in the world, with almost half the entire world's military bud-get. No other empire had ever remotely approached such superiority. The administrations of George H. W. Bush and Bill Clinton gradually ex-tended the range of U.S. military interventions against enemies they called "rogue states." The lesson of the invasion of Panama in 1989 was as-sumed to be that success would result from launching interventions of overwhelming force. It was followed by a much bigger intervention in Iraq in 1991 and then by major air strikes in Yugoslavia. The results seemed encouraging—and were contrasted to the disastrous intervention in Soma-lia, which was attempted with few military resources. The United Nations seemed compliant, accepting American leadership in these ventures. Russia and China barely demurred, showing no interest in "balancing" U.S. power. Nor did the Europeans. Clinton staffers coined the phrase "multilateralism if we can, unilateralism if we must," though American generals chafed (probably correctly) at the "crippling" restraints placed on them by the mul-tilateral NATO command structure in the Yugoslav campaign. Many Ameri-can politicians vowed not to repeat the experience (e.g., Wesley Clark 2001: 203). Many liberals were complicit in this military intensification, seduced by "humanitarian interventionism" into believing they could improve the world by force.

The new military imperialism was an escalation in the sense that it involved bigger interventions from the outset (Vietnam had seen "mission creep"). There was also a big jump forward with the foreign policy of Bush the Younger. The administration could build on a certain consensus in U.S. policy in the Middle East, for earlier administrations had also threatened military action against any power interfering with the free flow of oil to the West. Eisenhower and Reagan had done so, though it was the liberal Carter who had propounded this as a formal "doctrine." The Middle East has been considered a critical strategic area for the United States, and intervention, including military intervention, has been viewed as a necessary policy tool. Much of the opposition to the war on Iraq came from centrist establishment figures such as Brent Scowcroft or Zbigniew Brzezinsky, who objected to the way it was conducted rather than that it was attempted at all. Since Sad-dam had for so long blocked American interests, establishment opposition to the war was actually quite muted. The Democratic leadership struggled to find an alternative, since it had placed sanctions on Saddam and formally called for his overthrow.

But the way this war was conducted was very different. As I showed in *Incoherent Empire* (Mann 2003), quite different this time was the unilateralism, the lack of interest in and absence of significant allies on the ground in Iraq, apart from Kurdish forces in the North. In all previous interventions since World War II, the United States could count on significant local allies (usually the upper classes and most of the military of the country, though in the former Yugoslavia it was Croatian and Bosnian forces against Serbs). This absence, not the size of the U.S. forces, was what guaranteed disaster in Iraq. The decision revealed American military arrogance, the assumption that its armed forces could conquer, pacify, and begin to rule a country, all very quickly, before handing over to whatever local supplicants then emerged, who would be backed by permanent U.S. bases in the country. We know that this is what Donald Rumsfeld obstinately believed, while Paul Wolfowitz testified to Congress that it would all be paid for with Iraqi oil money. Such overconfidence produced catastrophe, as I predicted.

This marked a reversal of the historic drift of American imperialism toward milder forms of domination. Now the United States was escalating back up the hierarchy of domination, from informal imperialism through proxies toward massive military intervention. Iraq is the culmination of this process. Around 150,000 American troops have been occupying Iraq for the last four years and no fewer than fourteen U.S. "enduring bases" (the Pentagon's term) are currently under construction there. The Iraqi venture breaches the upper limits of the "informal empire through military intervention" subtype, for it is a semicolonial form of rule. At the same time, threats to repeat the military medicine were made against Syria, North Korea, and Iran. The threats against Iran continue. The administration also used its proxy state, Israel, to invade Lebanon in 2006 in a fruitless quest to destroy Hezbollah and further intimidate Syria and Iran. The so-called war on terror seemed to neoconservatives to be repeating the successes of 1898 and 1944–1945: temporary colonies would create client, perhaps even democratic regimes (Boot 2002). This is clearly imperial escalation.

But were the two imperial intensifications, economic and military, closely linked? In one sense they obviously were, as its economic domination allows the United States to afford its enormous military without overtaxing Americans. Foreigners have essentially paid for it through dollar seigniorage—and sometimes by more direct means, as in the Gulf War of 1991. There is also a sense in which they are bound together within the American tradition of liberalism-become-neoliberalism. That has almost unfailingly equated political freedoms with the economic freedom of the entrepreneur. Both strands were present in the intensification of economic imperialism, and to a lesser extent, both were present in the military imperialism. But have the two ventures been part of the same imperial strategy?

World-systems theorists say "yes." They produce a systemic explanation: the United States chose military aggression to reverse relative economic decline, as they claim previous failing hegemons also did (Harvey 2003; Wallerstein 2003). Their claim to historical analogy is false, since the British became less aggressive as they declined. But it might still be true of the Americans. The most suggestive evidence comes in the form of a map showing that each of the wars since 1991 (the Gulf War, Bosnia/Kosovo, Afghanistan, and Iraq in 2003) has resulted in more U.S. bases ringing the oil and natural gas fields of the Middle East and the Caucasus. It might seem that there has been a consistency to U.S. policy. If the United States can no longer rely on its coercive powers within economic markets, perhaps it is turning to military power to ensure its energy needs. There are indeed some who think this way in Washington.

But there are problems with this argument. In the first place, as I showed above, there was no relative decline in American economic power between 1970 and 2000—no market or gross national product share decline needing new military solutions. Indeed, the intensification of structural adjustment and dollar seigniorage increased the power of American economic imperialism. This raises the possibility that there is a grand, unified American strategy, not to stem decline, but to increase American dominance by both economic and military means, and indeed this seems to have been the view of some in the administration. Men such as Dick Cheney and Rumsfeld seem not to have been motivated primarily by any of the stated reasons for the invasion of Iraq (terrorism, weapons of mass destruction, and the spread of democracy). For them these were pretexts, acceptable to the public. Their real goal was to finally subdue the Middle East by force. Saddam was chosen not because he was a powerful threat but because he would be easy meat. Other "rogue states" might then cave in; if not, they would be confronted too (Gordon and Trainor 2006). The administration would never call this imperialism, but such a grand strategy was obviously exactly that.

However, Cheney, Rumsfeld, and other hawks have shown little interest in economic imperialism. In general, the economic and military strategies were pushed by different actors, both internationally and within the United States. As I have emphasized, economic intensification was pushed multilaterally, not only by the United States, but also by other northern states and by finance capital more generally. Yet U.S. military imperialism was pushed unilaterally, from Washington. Only Tony Blair can be plausibly cast as a foreigner with any influence over U.S. military imperialism, and that influence disappeared in late 2002 once the second UN Resolution on the invasion of Iraq was not secured.

Moreover, different administrations, parties, and interest groups pushed the two policies. The Clinton administration focused on international trade and finance and was strongly supported by major capitalist interest groups. As a cultural liberal, Clinton was perceived as actually being antimilitarist, an image strengthened by his initiative to give more rights to gays in the military. In "harder" aspects of foreign policy, his administration drifted, split between cautious "realists" versus "globalists" or "aggressive multilateralists," who saw the core of America's new mission as humanitarian interventionism. Both sides chafed at Clinton's inability to choose any goals, which they said derived from his lack of interest in both their agendas. Bombing from a safe distance became Clinton's forte in both Yugoslavia and Iraq, while lobbing a few cruise missiles in the general direction of Osama Bin Laden completed the "harder" side of his foreign policy (Hyland 1999). It was not very aggressive.

Madeleine Albright, one of the "aggressive multilateralists" in the administration, says that she despairingly asked a pertinent question of Joint Chiefs Chairman Colin Powell in 1995: "What are you saving this superb military for, Colin, if we can't use it?" (Albright and Woodward 2003:182). But the question was asked much more persistently by out-of-office Republicans, and it was already being answered aggressively in their policy documents written from 1993 onward. When the administration of Bush the Younger came to power in 2001, its foreign and defense policy was overwhelmingly staffed by those often labeled "neoconservatives" (Bacevich 2002; Daalder and Lindsay 2003; Gordon and Trainor, 2006; J. Mann 2004; Packer 2005). Their policy was based on a particular reading of twentieth-century history. In the words of Donald Kagan, when adversaries "read strength and a strong will, they tend to retreat and subside. When they read weakness and timidity, they take risks." "Strong will" referred to World War II and the Cold War, "weakness" referred to the 1990s—to Bush the Elder as well as Clinton—and to policies like not marching on Baghdad in 1991, appeasing North Korea, allowing Iraq to manipulate sanctions, and ignoring China's human rights violations. But the neocons also drew on the tropes of Munich appeasement of Hitlerian evil and Hitler's ultimate defeat, generating an eschatological rhetoric of good and evil. Since Roosevelt, a progressive Democrat, had embarrassed them, Winston Churchill (appropriately a great imperialist) became their hero.

Their arguments brought them support from the conservative religious side in America's "culture wars." I confess to not fully understanding how the religious right, which had been hitherto obsessed by domestic moral issues, came to support a militaristic foreign policy (few of them actually believe that the Jews must occupy the Temple Mount to prepare for the Second Coming of Christ). But they did so, and in the process added a degree of chiliasm to imperialism: good must triumph over evil, God over the devil. Through the 1980s and the 1990s, the Republican Party was captured by various rightist factions: the religious right in moral matters; business conservatives rolling back regulation, unions, and progressive taxation; and last, the foreign policy hawks. Since President George W. Bush himself seemed to endorse all their views—perhaps he was the only one who did so—each was given a rather free hand in their own sphere.

In foreign policy no satisfactory label can fully encapsulate the various hawkish actors of the Bush administration. The term "neoconservative" has been widely used to refer to those hawks who seemed to root their aggressive foreign policies in a strongly ideological vision. Though neoconservatives also have domestic policies, their main impact has been on foreign policy, and Irving Kristol declared that above all else neoconservatives like himself call for a revival of patriotism, a powerful military, and a very expansionist foreign policy. This seems to me to equal imperialism, though only some of them would accept the label. Kristol and others, including Richard Perle, Paul Wolfowitz, and Douglas Feith, have proclaimed a mission to spread freedom, American style, across the world by military expansion—power with a moral purpose. Their critics, stressing their ideology, say this is often with scant attention to inconvenient facts on the ground—"Feith-based analysis" was the jibe of George Tenet, Bush's CIA chief. This ideological form of imperialism was especially evident among intellectuals who did not have administration posts, such as the staff of the *Weekly Standard* (Kristol is its editor) or the American Enterprise Institute. Other hawks, especially those at the top of the administration, principally Vice President Dick Cheney and Defense Secretary Donald Rumsfeld, have seemed rather less ideological, more hard-nosed. Their main mission was to increase American power across the world, though (like all imperialists) they also thought this would be a force for the general good. Some call them "assertive nationalists" rather than neoconservatives. Since they had been career administrators, not intellectuals, it may be simply that they had never publicly revealed their ideology. As they seemed to share the unreal fantasies of "faith-based analysis," and since they made such enormous mistakes, we cannot call them pragmatists or realists. As for the president himself, it is difficult to categorize this inarticulate man who is said by insiders to be highly active in policy formation. In his own inimitable and simple way, he is more of an ideologist than a pragmatist.

But since they all shared enormous faith in American power, which overwhelmed realistic analysis of any other power configurations in play, we should simply call them imperialists. They proposed slashing and burning their way across the world in order to see it reborn in the American image, which would be for the better, of course. They might differ in the relative weights they gave to the different parts of the slash–burn–rebirth triad, but they all had enormous confidence in possessing the military means to achieve it. Of course, they themselves hate the term imperialist, but this would just be another example of their ability to deny reality.

They reversed the priorities of the Clinton administration. While militarism pervades the writings of the intellectuals among them, they are silent on international economic issues, which seem to interest them not at all. The essays edited by *Weekly Standard* stalwarts Kagan and Kristol (2000) contain only one economic recommendation: to double the military budget. Richard Perle seems to have never paid any attention to issues of trade or economics (according to Weisman's 2007 biography). Kristol gave only "two cheers" for capitalism—it promotes freedom and wealth for most people, but capitalist markets and consumer economies, he said, are empty of meaning and morality. He, like other self-described neoconservatives, favors a much stronger state than do neoliberals (though some have pointed out that to impose neoliberalism in reality requires a powerful state). We will find in Iraq that the imperialists shared a particular affinity with neoliberals, but that derived more from their slash–burn–rebirth geopolitics than from economic principles.

But the imperialists knew they were few in numbers. They saw enemies everywhere they looked, inside the administration as well as among liberals and Muslims. In the book written by Perle and David Frum (the man who coined the phrase "axis of evil"), all Muslim states are seen as hostile and in need of overthowing, but so too are the Pentagon, the CIA, and especially the State Department seen as hostile, in need of total restructuring (Frum and Perle 2003: 194–228). The imperialists, who controlled the top of the administration, had the power to dismiss or sideline generals and CIA officers who merely counseled caution. They did this freely and found others who would do their bidding, though both the officer corps and the agency were on the whole unhappy about the policies they were asked to implement

(Gordon and Trainor 2006; Tenet 2007). With little purchase within the State Department, they could not do the same there, so they ignored State Department advice and marginalized its presence in Iraq. Disgusted with the CIA and other intelligence agencies, they set up their own Office of Special Plans operating out of Cheney's office, providing them with intelligence reports that confirmed their own ideological predilections. Conspiracy theorists can have a field day here, since this was indeed a conspiracy, a few key players acting secretively, doctoring intelligence, concealing their motives, and seducing Americans with scaremongering and false information. In the final analysis, it is difficult to know whether these were deliberate lies or sincere fantasy laced with "the ends justifies the means" rationalizations. We are all capable of both.

There was therefore also a shift of departmental powers as Bush the Younger replaced Clinton. The Pentagon rose above both State and Treasury in influence in the White House, and the office of the vice president also rose in importance. Treasury and Commerce openly continued Clinton trade policies, continuing the shift more toward bilateral free trade agreements, but this seemed rather separate from "harder" foreign policy. The civilian heads of the Pentagon, who had never fought in a war, dominated foreign policy but secretively. So different parts of the state were involved in the two intensifications, using very different methods.

However, despite their narrow base, the imperialist could operate within a broader myth then current in the Republican Party and cultivated electorally, that President Reagan had boldly led Americans to destroy the "evil empire," the Soviet Union (this denied agency to Soviet citizens themselves). This dwarfed older memories of military hubris in Vietnam, in which only the dove-ish secretary of state Colin Powell and his dove-ish deputy Dick Armitage among the leading policymakers had actually fought. As many liberals had been caught up in the "humanitarian interventions" of the 1990s, they were ill equipped to oppose new interventions clothed in an equally moral mission. So there was relatively little opposition from the political classes to the imperialists.

If we consider broader public support, we should not expect mass support or opposition for the economic and military intensifications. Foreign policy is rarely perceived as striking at the direct interests of most people. I have written elsewhere of how the formulation of foreign policy, far more than domestic policy, tends to be dominated by political elites and particularistic pressure groups (Mann 1988). The workings of international finance are arcane, and there is little popular consciousness of them in the United States (there is more in Argentina). Americans are largely unaware of the negative effects that structural adjustment programs might have on those on whom they are imposed. In opinion polls Americans exaggerate the extent of U.S. foreign aid programs by a factor of over ten (Mann 2003: 80). Few Americans have even the slightest idea that foreigners might be funding their credit card debts. More Americans are mobilized by trade issues, for free trade versus protectionism is a well-established debate in American politics, involving major pressure groups. There is a large literature by political scientists on the domestic political support for protectionism versus free trade. This identifies labor pressure groups as persistent protectionists, while business divides according to whether its interests lie internationally or domestically—the latter being more likely under certain conditions to be protectionist. Overall, as in many other countries, the political right tends to favor freer trade, and the left is more protectionist, though in the United States this is crosscut by the tendency for Congress to be more protectionist than the president. Perceived economic interests, mediated by pressure groups, are generally behind such economic policy issues, and finance capital and multinational enterprises have tended to be the main group pushing for economic imperial intensification. This is familiar interest-group politics and rather rationalistic.

When it comes to war, things become different. Once again it begins with public indifference to the process by which an international crisis develops. And again, some particular interest groups constituted exceptions. American Jews play a major role in U.S. policy in the Middle East, as do oil companies. Jews have played an important diffuse role in U.S. militarism by contributing negative views of Arabs in general. Some imperialists in the administration—men including Richard Perle, Douglas Feith, and Elliot Abrams—also favored overthrowing Saddam because it would be good for Israel (Packer 2005). It is difficult to know how important this pressure was.

But during wars, unlike in international economic affairs, public opinion often comes to play a major role. Once a crisis has erupted, and if the United States threatens and then actually fights the perceived enemy, popular nationalist emotions tend to erupt without parallel in matters of international political economy. The political leadership wraps itself in the flag, stresses the danger to the country, and manipulates information flows. Administrations also perceive electoral utility in a "good war." It may also feel it has just cause for war, or it may invent enemy "atrocities." Most often it exaggerates a real threat by trading on racist or other stereotypes of alien foreigners and exploiting its monopoly of the means of domestic communication regarding far-off lands. Hitler invented Polish attacks on Germans along the border;

Bush the Younger invented links between Al Qaeda and Saddam Hussein. In 1964 the United States invented the second Gulf of Tonkin "incident," though not the first one, yet greatly exaggerated their significance in justifying military aggression. The Japanese government justified Pearl Harbor as a response to the "strangulation" of Japan by U.S. trade and oil embargoes, and this metaphor was only an exaggeration of the real practices of Western informal imperialism. Saddam Hussein was a cruel dictator, and he might have had a few weapons of mass destruction (though I doubted it). He did not have links to terrorists, but how could many Americans know this? The administration greatly exaggerated his threat to the world, and skeptics (like me) were listened to by very few people and denounced as unpatriotic. Reason will not prevail over regimes manipulating such emotions in such contexts.

This popular support has dangerous rhythms for administrations. At first most people rally round the flag and believe almost all that their leaders claim. If the enemy backs down or the war is quickly won, the emotional intensity dies down, but the legitimacy of the regime is enhanced and elections can be won—as Margaret Thatcher proved over the Falklands/Malvinas. If war endures longer, the emotional commitment will gradually diminish. If war seems to be going badly, the response will vary according to whether the war is perceived as being in genuine defense of the homeland or whether it was a war "of choice," where one can subsequently choose to desist without dire consequences for the homeland. Thus, even when things seemed very bad, the commitment of the British, Russian, German, and Japanese populations in World War II remained strong, whereas Americans in the period 1898–1902 could choose to engage and then disengage from imperial wars, and they could also turn against engagement in Vietnam. They also did so over Iraq.

It is now proved by many sources within both the civilian and military administrations that the hawks wanted to invade Iraq and that inside the Bush administration some plans were made for such an invasion before September 2001 (e.g., Clarke 2004; Gordon and Trainor 2006; Tenet 2007; Woodward 2004). Until September 11, 2001, the imperialists doubted that this would be popular among Americans. But 9/11 was an incident without precedent in American history. There was shock and outrage among Americans, as indeed there was to a lesser extent abroad. Revenge was the dominant popular emotion, and it was very powerful. George Tenet recounts that the day after 9/11, he ran into Richard Perle, head of the Defense Policy Board, outside the White House. Perle immediately said: "Iraq has to pay a price for what happened yesterday. They bear responsibility." This, says

Tenet, despite the fact that "the intelligence then and now" showed "no evidence of Iraqi complicity" in the 9/11 attacks. The vice president urged the Cabinet that this provided the opportunity to hit Iraq, but he was overruled because revenge strictly required hitting Afghanistan, and most of the world's governments agreed. The Afghan operation then seemed for a while to go well, reinforcing the case for also hitting Iraq. Internal opposition evaporated as Colin Powell, seen as a skeptic within the administration, abased himself to give a transparently false case for Saddam's weapons of mass destruction at the United Nations. We were asked to believe in chemical weapons trucks with canvas walls whipping up contaminating dust as they trundled across the desert. Nonetheless, this case was fed to the American public almost without criticism by politicians or the media. Despite quite sizable antiwar demonstrations in major U.S. cities, 70 percent of Americans initially agreed that "going to war in Iraq was the right thing to do." Similar numbers believed that Saddam Hussein had close ties to Al Qaeda, had weapons of mass destruction that could hit the United States, and had been involved in the planning of the attack of 9/11—all ridiculous, but who ever said that reason governed human conduct?

Underlying these responses was Americans' overconfidence in their country's military strength, paralleling that of the administration itself. The memory of Vietnam had been obliterated by triumphs against the Soviet Union and lesser enemies in the 1990s, followed by seeming Afghan success (in reality, it is far from that). Few expected that Iraq would be a difficult war. They did not think it would last long and they did not think they themselves would be asked to make any significant sacrifices. They were imbued with what I described (initially in the context of Britain's war over the Falklands/Malvinas Islands) as "spectator-sport militarism," enthusiastically cheering on one's team from the sidelines but without any other expenditure of effort (Mann 1988). The emotions were forcefully expressed but did not lie deep, and if one's team performs poorly, one can desert it.

The Bush administration seemed aware of the dangers inherent in such sentiments and took preventive actions. To better control information flow, it "embedded" reporters within U.S. military units. It banned publicity for returning coffins and funerals of service personnel. It refused to publish figures of Iraqi casualties, which previous administrations had done. It refused to contemplate conscription, as had happened in Vietnam. Americans would not sacrifice in this far-off cause. Despite all these precautions, with the occupation failing so lamentably in its objectives, public opinion soured. Support for the war halved, to around 30 percent by late summer 2007. It had been a war of choice, and most Americans now chose to end it. Public opinion, like the Bush administration, had not endorsed military intensification out of a sense of weakness or decline, as world-systems theory has it, but out of a sense of overweening pride in strength. But the public accepted its mistake much quicker, it seems.

And so we come to Iraq, its oil, and American motives. Iraq has either the biggest or the second-biggest oil reserves in the world. Obviously, this was a war about oil, but it was not just about Iraqi oil. If Iraq had not had oil, there might have been no war. But the fact that its neighbors were also major oil producers made this war almost certain. Cheney's Energy Task Force had stated clearly in 2001 before the invasion that Saddam Hussein was the greatest obstacle to the "free flow" of oil in the region. One might think that the best way to get rid of the obstacle was to befriend him, since he had every incentive to sell it and Americans to buy it. Note, however, that the United States is actually less dependent on Middle Eastern oil than are the Europeans, the Chinese, or the Japanese. These other nations secure their access to it through peaceful multilateral agreements. But obviously relations with Saddam had degenerated too far for kissing and making up. In any case, U.S. oil politics had never gone strictly along market lines. Geopolitics had always gotten in the way. The United States had for a time done a deal with Saddam, but that had been geopolitical, lining him up as an ally against another major oil producer, Iran. Now the United States was the ally of Saudi Arabia and the Gulf States, geopolitically aligned against both Iraq and Iran. Saddam was publicly taunting the United States, yet he was by now a much easier military target than Iran, for he had been enfeebled by the 1991 Gulf War and the following ten years of sanctions. Saddam was picked on not because of any weapons of mass destruction or support of terrorism or even because of any threat he might pose to anyone other than Iraqis. Nor was he even picked on mainly for his oil. He was picked on not because of his strength but because of his weakness. He could be rolled over as a fearsome demonstration to the rest of the Middle East of U.S. military power. Iraq would be stage one in a takeover of the Middle East, to secure all its oil, to protect Israel from harm, and to intimidate Russia and China. This was the slash-and-burn, but it would be followed by the rebirth of the Middle East as its Muslim states became peaceful, democratic, and Israel-tolerant, under American tutelage. Gordon and Trainor (2006) show from their interviews that this was the policy Centcom officers thought they were being asked to follow. It would project American military imperialism on an unprecedented scale

But its first stage was Iraq, and Iraq's oil was the biggest immediate prize. In 2001 Cheney's Energy Task Force drew up detailed maps of the Iraqi oil fields and lists of fields controlled by non-American companies. These documents were leaked and are available on the Internet. There were also several meetings that year between the task force and American and British oil industry chiefs. Most of the Americans later denied this before a 2005 congressional committee though the Republican chair of the committee had been careful not to put them under oath for the session. This was a wise precaution, as it seems they were lying: leaked Secret Service documents of who was admitted to the White House confirm the meetings, while the former head of Conoco has admitted attending one of them.

But what exactly was said there? Were the oilmen told of a possible upcoming invasion two years before it happened? That would seem very risky, endangering the secrecy of the operation. But we just do not know. Many critics of the war jump to the conclusion that it was a mutual conspiracy between the administration and the oil industry or even that the United States invaded Iraq at the behest of the oil industry. But the information available so far indicates a more complex picture. There were two rival plans, the imperialists supporting one, the oil magnates the other. There is no evidence that oil companies led the way toward military intervention. The impetus came from the imperialists. However, once the oilmen knew the administration was bent on invasion, they hastened to state their preference.

The oilmen did not like the policy proposed by the administration. It had originated in a document full of neoliberal sentiments, "Moving the Iraqi Economy from Recovery to Sustainable Growth," produced by the Treasury Department and USAID. This became the main direct connection between economic and military imperialism. The policy was concretized in 2003 by the U.S. consultancy firm BearingPoint into a structural adjustment program similar to those I discussed earlier. Paul Bremer, the administrator of the Coalition Provisional Authority (for fourteen months the dictator of Iraq) wrote much of this into his draft "Orders," which became Iraq's laws during his reign. The draft included the privatization of oil, along with all other state industries. Foreigners could own it all, and they might actually have done so, since few Iraqis could have afforded to buy large tranches of a state-owned industry. But the imperialists had another more important motive. They expected that when order did return, the private oil companies freed from state regulation would begin pumping as much oil as they could. This would cause the global price of oil to fall, and they hoped this would then cause OPEC and particularly Saudi Arabia to totter. The neocons wanted to use Iraqi oil as a geopolitical tool against both Iran and Saudi Arabia, slashing and burning their way through the Middle East, destroying existing despotic regimes, and then seeing the region born again as some mixture of American domination and democracy (Frum and Perle 2003 frankly avow this motive, stressing democratization, while Juhazs 2006 sees it as a conspiracy and stresses domination). Though this was a neoliberal plan, it was subordinated to an imperial slash–burn–rebirth mission.

But the major oil companies were horrified. Any collapse in prices would also slash their profits, and they were appalled by the notion that the United States might undermine OPEC. So they devised another plan, completed in January 2004, with the help of Amy Jaffe, a staffer of the James Baker Institute in Texas (which had also hosted Cheney's 2001 task force). As Jaffe said, "I'm not sure that if I'm the chair of an American company, and you put me on a lie detector test, I would say that high prices are bad for me or my company." In fact, through the State Department, the oil companies stalled Bremer's privatization program by placing a former CEO of Shell Oil USA, Philip Carroll, as head of Iraqi oil resources. As he later told the British Broadcasting Corporation (BBC), "There was to be no privatization of Iraqi oil resources or facilities while I was involved." Oil was exempted from privatization in Bremer's orders. Carroll said he saw slash-and-burn privatization as pure ideology, failing to perceive the regional strategic vision behind it. The oil industry's rival plan, spearheaded by Carroll, was to form a single nationalized Iraqi Oil Company, which would then act as a responsible member of OPEC. This was pitting imperialists seeking radical change against industry conservatives who wanted to keep things as they were (see Greg Palast's BBC Newsnight Report, March 17, 2005). And since this was big oil, the imperialists had met their match. In practice, a stalemate resulted, between these two plans and also between the conflicting interests of the Shia, Sunni, and Kurdish communities in Iraq. No final allocation of oil has even now been approved.

This confirms that it was not immediate oil profit that initiated the Iraq invasion but longer-term regional strategic visions—naturally involving oil. But these were the visions of the imperialists within the administration, not of the oil industry, which remained conservative in its approach, favoring continuity and stability, not the slash–burn–rebirth mission of the neocons.

Those favoring a more conspiratorial capitalist interpretation of the invasion than mine also cite the interlocks and the payoff between the administration, especially Cheney, and oil maintenance and construction corporations like Halliburton, Bechtel, and Parsons. Juhazs (2006) notes that 150 U.S. corporations made $50 billion profit out of three years' work of rebuilding Iraq, with Halliburton easily the biggest beneficiary at $12 billion. But each major oil corporation makes as much or more profit in a single year than Halliburton did in three. It may be that Cheney's connections with Halliburton or George Schultz's with Bechtel got the contract for their respective firms rather than another. And it would be hoped that the administration had indeed at some point consulted construction companies about the costs of rebuilding, especially given the likely extent of American bombing. But has a war ever been instigated by construction firms hoping to profit from its devastation? This would be a strikingly irrational subordination of American national and capitalist interests to a small fraction of politically connected capital. The larger U.S. military-industrial complex is also active in lobbying for the maintenance and renewal of America's massive military (Johnson 2005), but it rarely lobbies for war, and there is no evidence it did so here. It seems that the war was led from within the administration and not at the behest of powerful outside pressure groups, except for the Israel lobby.

The final contrast between the two imperialisms is that where economic imperialism was patient, calculative, rational, and successful, military imperialism was impatient, ideological, and irrational. Economic imperialism intensified gradually, step by step, as it dawned on U.S. and capitalist policymakers what new powers they possessed. The evolving policies were clearly geared to the interests of the United States in general, as seen through the lens of particular American capitalist groups. The policies worked, bringing success for the United States and for those capitalists. In contrast, military intensification was ideologically germinated and premeditated well in advance, riding roughshod over real terrains, awaiting only the opportunity provided by 9/11. It was buttressed by faith in the "American century," which had been won by conjoined economic and military power—an imperialism that dared not speak its name. Within the administration this was set amid a sweeping view of modern history. This ideology, religious in tone more than content, overrode any serious knowledge of the regions in which the interventions were to be made.

It is an imperial policy as misguided as Japanese imperial policy was after about 1936. The ring of U.S. bases around the oil does not actually bring any more oil. These bases serve little real purpose. They have not even influenced a bit player, President Karimov of Uzbekistan, to moderate his repression. In response to U.S. pressure, he asked American troops to leave his country. So have the Saudis. The bases do not protect U.S. clients but destabilize them. The U.S. bases cannot pacify Iraq nor even extract as much Iraqi oil as Saddam did. The bases grew up as part of a global strategy of defense against the rival Soviet and Chinese empires. Then they seemed to promise an informal military empire, capable of punishing "rogue states" and of intimidating Russia and China. Yet Iran and North Korea have already shown this to be bluff. They are acquiring nuclear weapons while the United States is tied down in Iraq and Afghanistan. The intervention in Iraq and Lebanon continue to strengthen the regional power of Iran, a bizarre outcome, since earlier the United States had successfully used Iraq under Saddam Hussein to balance Iran. Neither intervention has worked to secure economic or strategic interests. They add much instability to their region, and they have added more international terrorists to the world, the opposite of what empire and hegemony are supposed to do.

The policy of unilateral preemptive military interventions is an irrational failure. Many insiders in the CIA and State told the administration that beforehand. So did most Middle Eastern experts and some pundits like myself. But the neocons did it nonetheless—and then purged their CIA and State critics—because of a militarism that is their political raison d'être. They feel that turning back would be an admission of failure and probably the end of their political influence. That was also the view of the Japanese militarists in the late 1930s. When almost all the army planners were advising an end to Japanese expansionism, since no matter how many colonies Japan conquered, it would still depend crucially on American- and British-controlled markets, the Tokyo leadership sacked them and ignored their advice. In the end their goal had become merely to hold on to their political power or go down fighting (Snyder 1991: ch. 4). As in Japan then, the American neocons are buttressed by Snyder's "myths of empire" strongly rooted in American institutions and culture, especially in the Republican Party and its base—though not in most of American capitalism.

There has therefore been rather little connection between those two types of imperial intensification, though originally they had been closely linked. American economic strength provides the resources for its militarism, while its military position at the end of World War II had also guaranteed its economic strength. There was also some linkage between the two through neoliberalism, since Iraq was subjected to a structural adjustment program. Yet as I noted, this has not yet included Iraq's major resource, oil, and the neoliberalism in Iraq was less a set of economic principles than a slash–burn–rebirth imperial sense of mission that would be anathema to economists. The connection today is of a weaker kind: two distinct conservative interest groups have agreed to a trade-off within the administration and the Republican Party—you can have your policy if we can have ours. But they show little interest in the other's policies, and indeed the economic imperialists did better under Clinton and the Democrats.

This example demonstrates that societies are not systems, and states are not cohesive. In fact, they are both a bit of a mess, full of contradictions, muddles, mistakes—like the lives of humans in general. Societies are not a complete mess, for they contain relatively enduring and powerful social structures. But these are plural, with logics that are distinct. The four sources of social power—ideological, economic, military, and political—have their own institutions, their own logic of development, even while also being entwined with each other. There is no overall system or functionality. Military cannot be reduced to economic power, nor vice versa, nor are they both cogs in a single system moving in a single direction. American global militarism and American-led global capitalism have been pushed by different power groups in different directions and with very different results. On the one hand, some American power actors successfully developed new forms of global economic imperialism/hegemony. On the other hand, different American actors have been blinded by military imperialism. Whereas American economic imperialism exhibits shrewd, self-interested opportunism—human beings operating at what is probably their highest level of rationality—American military imperialism exhibits ideological, self-destructive folly—probably their highest level of irrationality.

In the long run there will inevitably be further relative American decline. Eichengreen (2006) has given the most believable future scenario. He suggests that the burden of U.S. debt will eventually undermine dollar seigniorage, with Asian and Middle Eastern banks finally pulling the plug by switching much of their savings elsewhere. Good economic management might still preserve the dollar as a reserve currency, but by 2020 or 2040 it might share this status with the euro. The latter date would truly validate the notion of an "American century." Such a shift would make unsustainable the present level of American military spending. Eichengreen's judgment is relatively favorable toward the United States. But who knows how much faster this ludicrously counterproductive "war on terror" will drag down the United States—and, of course, the Middle East. In the long run, in both origins and destination, American economic and military imperialism are closely linked. But in the meantime, they seem not to be.

NOTES

1. Therefore, I am not using it in the political science or international relations theory senses of either domination more generally or global or regional domination by a single power, nor in Doyle's (1986: 40) sense of a dominance exercised only over foreign and not domestic policy.

EIGHT

The Empire's New Laws
Terrorism and the New Security Empire after 9/11
KIM LANE SCHEPPELE

Empires are not what they used to be. In the classic days of empire, countries at the core of power and influence in the world physically conquered and directly managed peripheral territories. But the ham-handed treatment of the locals by colonial powers eventually resulted in a backlash—to the point where it is impossible for any powerful state to attempt that sort of direct control anymore. The long-distance manipulation of substantial resources and populations has not diminished, however. It is being handled in new ways through different institutions. But just as the older forms of empire were always caught in the logics of the local as the conquered territories pressed back against the center, the newer form is also predictably less universal than it claims to be and also subject to local appropriation for local purposes. Nowhere is this more visible than in the contemporary "global war on terror."

This chapter explores the role of law in the construction of contemporary imperial reach. While the story of the role of law in economic globalization is well known, this chapter will explore a newly created body of law—global security law—that was developed quickly in response to the attacks on the United States on September 11, 2001. Global security law was created by a series of remarkable resolutions passed by the United Nations Security Council after 9/11, resolutions mandating that all member states of the United Nations change their domestic laws to fight the "global war on terror" (GWOT) in parallel ways.

In its scope and ambition, the new global security law rivals the legal infrastructure of economic globalization. But because of its connections with the national logics of national security, this new international legal frame operates to enhance the powers of states, to change the balance of power between states, to alter the power relations internal to national governments, and to give these national governments far more direct power over both their nationals and residents. In the development of global security law, the "international community" (and for that, read the United States and other veto-bearing powers on the Security Council) outsourced the GWOT to national governments around the world. National governments, as I will show, picked up the GWOT as an opportunity to rearrange their own domestic architecture in ways that benefited national executives by strengthening their powers relative to others in their domestic sphere. Because the interests of powerful countries in the Security Council could be linked to the fate of national executives around the world (including those in the veto-bearing states themselves), compliance with the new global security law has been extraordinarily high.

The astonishingly rapid changes of national laws around the world in response to changes in international law could have occurred only if the central mechanisms driving the change were capable of being presented in two contradictory ways for two different sorts of states.

First, for states whose commitment to international law is part of their own deep devotion to the rule of law as a basic principle of state legitimacy, new draconian antiterrorism laws could be portrayed as necessary in order for the state to remain compliant with international law. But for international law to underwrite these national laws, the identities of the core states at the center of the new imperial web had to be disguised in the fiction that the UN acts on behalf of a global community of agreement. In practice, the five veto-bearing permanent members of the Security Council—the United States, United Kingdom, France, Russia, and China—can act together with some combination of rotating states in the Security Council to become "the international community" on whose behalf the new law is being created, while the vast majority of states to whom this new law applies have never been consulted and it is far from clear that they or their populations would have consented if they had been. International law has traditionally been binding on a state only if it consents to be bound, but the newly realized ability of the UN Security Council to "legislate" through passing binding resolutions has upended this first principle of state consent. Not surprisingly, then, "the international community" is often framed as the author of these new mandates, as if there is a new democratic demos that includes all states, especially the international-law-compliant ones, so that the consent of some of them represents the consent of all of them.

Second, for states of a more nationalist bent who believe that international law is a threat to sovereignty, antiterrorism laws can be presented to national publics as purely national ideas driven by national self-interest. The very fact that sovereignty-anxious states were being compelled to comply with the directives of the Security Council could be disguised in the fiction that these states retained their sovereign law-making authority because, after all, they wrote their own domestic laws in front of their own domestic publics. (This is the lawmakers' version of "Look, Ma—no [foreign] hands!" as a device for demonstrating independence.) The fact that these national statutes *also* complied with international law did not have to be mentioned in the domestic debates, if that would have derailed the process. As a result, the conduct of some states in passing antiterrorism laws and joining the global antiterrorism campaign was often reframed nationally (and nationalistically) to domestic constituencies as required by "national interest."

These two fictions—that international law represents the international community and that antiterrorism law primarily serves national interests—have combined to create a common global framework underwritten by a dual rationale. Depending on which route a state took to introducing its domestic antiterrorism law, either an international consensus or the retention of domestic sovereignty was used as the victorious argument. National executives who found one of these rationales unconvincing in their domestic space could always use the other one to achieve the same result. But they both led to the same policy and to the same level of international coordination. Taken together, these two strategies of legitimation have produced a concerted, cooperative antiterrorism campaign that has united most countries in the world in a common template of action. As a result, the Security Council resolutions have managed to achieve overwhelming compliance of states as they develop policy along remarkably similar lines. This does not look like old-fashioned imperialism because the mechanisms of coordination are different. But in its ability to control a large periphery from the small number of core states, the new global security law reproduces some of the same effects.

There are many reasons to think of these changes in an "imperial" frame. In particular, the new coordination between core and peripheral states operates in practice in much the same way as old colonial logics did. As in the old empires, core states use peripheral states to extract scarce resources that are not in the direct possession of the core states by binding this extraction to a discipline that benefits the core states. In old-fashioned empire, material resources were generally the object of extraction. In the new empire, "terrorists" are produced and relocated as the core transmission belt of empire. Either way, the center gets from the periphery what the center needs.

In addition, in new as well as in the old empires, the disciplinary logics of control have worked to discipline populations in both the center and the periphery. In the old empires, the control radiating out from the center could often be used by peripheral leaders for local advantage out in their bailiwicks because these local leaders would be backed up with power from the center. At the same time, these disciplinary logics of control could be used by leaders at the center against segments of their own populations, because the power of leaders at the center was built up by their enhanced control over the periphery.

In the new empires, one can see the same dynamics at work. Local leaders in the periphery benefit from being part of the imperial project, just as national leaders in the core states are able to use this security project effectively for transnational control and for localized repression. As in the old empires, states at the core define the interests, options, and strategies of the peripheral states. In so doing, they transform themselves as well because they too are part of this system in which a coordinated international project creates roles for all states. In the new empire, the global war on terror has created security regimes at the core as well as at the periphery, and the leaders of both sorts of states gain power from their ability to work with each other.

In short, both old and new empires create a method for generating core control over crucial internationally dispersed resources. And both old and new empires are able to sustain themselves because leaders at all levels benefit from imperial structures. In this chapter, I will explain and explore these new legal changes to show how the new imperial reach operates in ways that will look familiar.

OLD AND NEW IMPERIAL LOGICS

Theorizing the new empires began with reconsidering the classic ones. Postcolonial studies bequeathed to the current examination of empires more nuanced understandings of how classic empires operated.[1] By contrast with traditional studies emphasizing the centrality of both economic extraction to empire and the interdependency of both center and periphery in the common project of colonialism, the field of postcolonial studies has shown how activities at the managed, and integrated, often uncomfortably, into the universalizing aspirations of modernizing imperial powers.[2] Of course, the economic rationales for colonialism were always central in practice to European powers. But the project of colonialism affected many more realms than the purely economic one, shaping as it did ideas of the nation and its Other, of social similarity and difference, and of modernity itself.[3] Eventually, colonialism turned on itself, as concepts and categories developed for managing the differences between metropole and colony came to be mapped directly onto the domestic populations of the metropole.[4] The study of classic colonial projects (plural because there were enormous differences among them) reveal that imperial reach always affects the core as well as the periphery and that local variation across an imperial expanse is the norm rather than the exception. One would imagine, of course, that new forms of empire would reveal something of the same logics of cultural flux, local adaptation, and increasing interdependence of social, cultural, and political forms between metropole and colony.

Over the several decades before 9/11, the new economic globalization had increasingly substituted its own logics for territorial domination as the primary organizing principle of the international realm, leading many analysts to talk of a new form of empire. In this new theory of empire, imperial power is still a meaningful organizing force, but this power is organized differently than under the older form of empire. Nation-states are no longer the primary players in the world system, reaching out to control bits of territory that they remake in their own image as colonies. Instead, corporations and other transnational economic formations (international financial institutions, networked labor organizations, and international regulators, for example) have replaced states as the central agents of structuration and change.[5] In the new economic empire that emerged after World War II and accelerated in its growth from the 1980s on, deterritorialized law has substituted for territorialized politics as the central organizing device that manages disparate flows.

Saskia Sassen argued this "dislodging of national capabilities" through economic globalization destabilized states both in theory, as states have simply become less important for understanding global change, and in practice, as they control less and less of relevance to their own populations.[6] Understanding the rise and fall of nation-states through the variable assembly of territory, authority, and rights, Sassen places law at the core of the exercise of power in both its national and postnational forms. From World War II onward, international economic law—expressed through the Bretton Woods agreement and subsequent trade regimes—drove much of the change. This international law not only made possible new forms of transnational power and control, but it also redistributed power within the state as well, as national executives increasingly represented their countries on a world stage and accumulated domestic power as a result.[7]

For Michael Hardt and Antonio Negri, the new form of empire has also rested centrally on a new legal formation, though they see a different law in play. For them, the United Nations has been "a new center of normative production that can play a sovereign judicial role"[8] because it could mediate between nation-states and a genuinely supranational center in determining the legitimacy of the use of force. In the post–Cold War world, the UN appeared as the center of a form of "governance without government," "consensus under a supreme authority of ordering."[9] Empire was "formed not on the basis of force itself but on the basis of the capacity to present force as being in the service of right and peace. . . . Empire is not born of its own will but rather it is *called* into being and constituted on the basis of its capacity to resolve conflicts."[10] And how did this new international legal formation achieve this centrality? Even before 9/11, Hardt and Negri pointed to the dominance of fear as the "primary mechanism of control that fills the society of the spectacle."[11]

After 9/11, however, globalization theory has remained surprisingly undisturbed, despite the enormous changes in the world system that 9/11 produced. Of course, 9/11 figures somewhat in the new writing on globalization; its effects are too large to ignore. But most globalization theorists see the post-9/11 changes as affecting primarily the policy of the United States and those particular places, such as Afghanistan and Iraq, where shooting wars were started. Saskia Sassen, for example, sees the American strategy after 9/11 as a descent into nonlegal exceptionalism and secrecy within the United States,[12] but she sees no broader implications of these events. The forces of globalization continue to act as they did before 9/11, with a bit of U.S. exceptionalism around the margins. After 9/11, Hardt and Negri discovered that there could be a "state of war within Empire, and there is no end to it in sight."[13] But they wrongly analyzed these new developments as "suspending the international rule of law," because the state of exception—which they interpret with Carl Schmitt as the space of no law[14]—has become the rule instead.[15] Looking primarily at the most visible manifestations of the shooting wars in Afghanistan and Iraq, both launched without formal Security Council approval in advance, Hardt and Negri pronounced: "The modern legal framework for declaring and conducting war no longer holds."[16] Nonetheless, they noted: "Law has always been a privileged domain for recognizing and establishing control over the common."[17] And they proceeded to explore the sort of democratic possibilities generated by the new economic globalization as if 9/11 itself were an odd peripheral event.

But have globalized economic processes really been so unaffected by 9/11 and its new empire of fear? As George Steinmetz has convincingly shown, it is hard to argue that strong states have disappeared when they are busily spying on and arresting their own citizens in the name of the war on terror.[18] What I will show in the rest of this chapter is that states generally, and not just the United States, have seized back power that had been formally ceded to transnational economic institutions, interrupting the previously relatively unimpeded international economic flows. New security barriers have blocked the flows of capital, people, goods, and services. The political field has reasserted its control over the economic sphere while national governments—newly reempowered but also working through transnational institutions—have made a comeback. In short, fear of terrorist attack has caused new barriers to appear within the formerly limitless international economic sphere and those barriers track the old-fashioned limits of the nation-state. Politics has displaced economics again as the central locus of international power.

The new globalization literature, most written or imagined before 9/11, focused on the new economic empires that come with globalization, but they were too quick to count states out as key players on the world stage. Looking back at the end of the Cold War before a new global antagonism took its place, we can see the 1990s as a period when powerful states felt that their territories and populations were not seriously threatened in a violent way. Now that states have a clear enemy (even though that enemy does not take the form of particular other nation-states), they are willing to use the substantial resources still at their command—armies and heavy weapons but also intelligence agencies and new forms of global surveillance—to parry the threat. For a brief window between 1989 and 2001, the world system could appear to be governed primarily by transnational economic forces that ignored state borders because the international political system and its fortifications of boundaries were relatively stable.

But there was a lot in economic globalization that strengthened state power even as globalization theorists claimed that states were being undermined and replaced by global economic forces. In particular, the triumph of economic globalization allowed states to recast as "inevitable" the polarizing effects of free markets. What had once been visible political decisions to refuse the demands for equality of particular parts of the population could now be portrayed as the inescapable results of economic "laws" that had nothing to do with politics at all. Repressing a population by force is a far more costly thing for a state to do than to leave disadvantaged groups to their fates under free markets whose control could be portrayed as beyond the reach of states.[19] Economic globalization theorists may have mistaken the support that powerful states gave to the new economic formations for helplessness in the face of inevitable change.

Since September 11, however, powerful states have been reasserting themselves as the key players in the international system, wielding forces that have already dominated economic globalization as the organizing principle of this new world order and will no doubt do so for some time to come. Both the physical territory and the set of interests embodied in the idea of "national security" are protected by national armies, massive stocks of weapons, and transnational institutions that do not transcend states but that provide a forum for relations among states. With such resources, political and even military domination of a threatening periphery by the threatened center is still quite possible, even in an era of economic globalization that has been thought to have fundamentally weakened nation-states.

The period from 1989 to 2001, therefore, looks in retrospect not like the coming of a permanent new world order of global economic flows but as the period between world-ordering wars in which states were confident enough to let other international actors play in what had been for centuries—and is once again—state space. Since 9/11, the "global war on terror" reveals a desire for the centers of "civilization"—which see themselves as the targets of this new global terror—to control the peripheries from which the threats come. We are already seeing that economic globalization can be reined in when powerful states assert the once-again-dominant need to protect their territory.

As we rethink this new security empire, however, we need to recall not just the analyses of economic globalization but the lessons learned from postcolonial studies. In particular, we know now that empires maintain themselves not just through the successful ability to extract what they need from their colonies but also through the ability to control the intellectual management of difference that the juxtaposition of metropole and periphery suggests. Old-fashioned empires discovered that imperial ideology affected all concerned and that both core and colony were shaped by their interdependence. As we will see, when the metropole wants crucial things crucially enough from the periphery, this gives the periphery some power over the way that the demands are met. And as will be no surprise given what we know about old-fashioned empire, the metropole will reproduce within itself the very differences it tries hard to project onto the periphery. In many ways, then, we will recognize in the new security empire many of the strategies and tactics developed by old-fashioned empires.

THE LEGAL ARCHITECTURE OF THE NEW IMPERIALISM

Law has always been central to the operation of empire. Old-fashioned colonial empires operated through *administrative law* as their signature legal form. Administrative law was developed as part of the domestic law of the imperial power and then was extended in a command-and-control way directly to imperially administered territories. Often the colonized and colonizing states were linked through a system of bureaucratic rotation of officials from center to periphery and back again, as well as by a movement of legal decisions on appeal from the colonized to the colonizing state for correction, consolidation, and certification. Old empires operated through the direct legal administration of conquered territories from the center through the mechanism of administrative law. Of course, administrative law had to deal with a variety of internal contradictions: how the universalizing ideology of modern law could nonetheless inscribe forms of difference between core and peripheral populations, how the regularization of procedure provided some legal protection to those whose control was to be ensured through these procedures. And administrative law was meaningfully supplemented in many colonial systems by the adaptation of indigenous law to colonial rule as well, to the point where many colonized people were seemingly unaffected by the legal changes colonialism brought. But administrative law was internal to the operation of empire, however local the law in the colonies often seemed to be, and it bound core and peripheral formations in a common logic of legality. Law was, in many ways, the language through which the different levels of state power spoke to each other.

The new security empire is also coordinated through law, but, by contrast, through a new form of *international law*. International law is forged in transnational institutions and then put out for adoption by target states. Target states adopt the new international law through rules of lawmaking designed within their own state apparatus to adapt international command to local legality. States incorporate international law into domestic law without appearing to lose sovereignty over their own territories, populations, or resources because the effective legal procedure for adopting new law, in the end, is the law of their own state. In this way, the cross-border movement of international law appears more voluntary than old-fashioned colonial administrative law, but it still contains many of the same tensions between universalizing aspirations and distinct local adaptations. Laws enacted in different local political contexts from a common template will ultimately have as many differences as similarities.

Until 9/11, international norms virtually always required the consent of the state to bind that state. Treaties require the consent of each "state party" to become law for each state. The long-standing practice of many states could create customary international law for all states, though a practice of deviating from the common conduct of other states could undermine the strength of common norms. But the norms of customary international law have developed over decades, even centuries, of compliant conduct on the part of many states in the world system, compliant conduct that looks quite like consent. Without a prior history of long-standing custom or an explicit treaty regime, there was virtually no other way to create international law. There was, in common understanding, no international legislature that could create binding new legal norms overnight without the separate consent of each state.

Since the United Nations was established, however, the Security Council has had the power to pass resolutions by using its "Chapter VII" authority (named for the part of the UN Charter that gives the power), and all member states of the United Nations are then required to comply with these resolutions. Essentially, this is an outgrowth of treaty mechanisms; member states of the UN signed the UN Charter, and it is this underlying consent that gives rise to the obligation to follow Chapter VII resolutions of the Security Council.

The Chapter VII power of the Security Council, however, was rarely used for anything that required substantial general adjustments of domestic law in member states—and certainly for nothing that approached a common legislative template for states to adopt—between the time that the Security Council was set up at the end of World War II and the end of the Cold War. That was because the five veto-bearing permanent members (the United States, UK, France, Russia, and China) rarely agreed on much.[20] But once the wall came down, literally and figuratively, between the first and second world war, the Security Council has used this old power in new ways. After 9/11, when the veto-bearing members could justly feel either that they were all potential targets of transnational terrorism or that they stood to gain from acting as though they were, the Security Council has been able to pass resolutions under its Chapter VII authority that have created a detailed new security framework—instant international law that all states must adopt regardless of whether they have explicitly or implicitly consented. What is astonishing and novel about this new framework is that it has been established through Security Council resolutions that look and act like international legislation. Giving general legislative powers to the Security Council was clearly not what most states thought they were doing in signing the UN Charter.

Starting with Security Council Resolution 1373 and continuing through a set of other supplementary resolutions dealing with "threats to international peace and security" (the threshold requirement that allows the Security Council to act), the core states of the world system have been able to require both themselves and also less powerful states to adopt new international security law as part of their domestic law. Since then, nearly every country in the world has changed its laws after 9/11 to comply with this new security framework, some with but most without explicit public reference to the fact that they were required to do so by virtue of their membership in the United Nations.

Resolution 1373 passed the Security Council at UN Headquarters in New York City within three weeks of the 9/11 attacks, while the still-smoldering ruins of the World Trade Center were only a few miles away. Though the resolution was apparently introduced at the behest of the U.S. government, the official record does not indicate the initiating state. Moreover, the official record is silent on the negotiations leading up to the passage of the resolution. All we know is that it passed unanimously on September 28, 2001, at 10 PM without any recorded debate in a session that officially lasted five minutes.[21] More legislative in character than anything that the Security Council had previously attempted, Resolution 1373 (and later associated resolutions like 1390, 1456, 1535, 1566, and 1624) invoked the Security Council's Chapter VII authority under the United Nations Charter to deal with the problem of terrorism, meaning that the resolution immediately became legally binding on all member states of the UN as soon as it was passed.

What did Resolution 1373 require of states? The core elements of the resolution required states to

1 criminalize terrorism as a separate offense in national criminal codes (along with associated crimes of attempt, conspiracy, and material support—expanded in 2005 in Resolution 1624 to include incitement to terrorism), with harsher punishments attached to terrorism-related offenses than to common crimes.

2 disrupt terrorism financing within and between countries, demanding that states develop strategies for immediately freezing the assets of anyone who was placed on UN watch lists as a suspect in terrorist activity.

3 detect terrorists and their plots before such plots could materialize, through the development of new strategies for uncovering information about these plots and through sharing information acquired through these new methods across agencies within a government and across national boundaries.

4 crack down on the flow of migrants, refugees, and asylum seekers so that terrorists could not use the system of legal transnational migration to assist their planning and to carry out their attacks.

But this framework omitted some crucial safeguards that it might have been wise to include. The resolution included no official definition of terrorism, leaving this highly charged subject to each state to work out on its own terms. And the Security Council did not provide for the maintenance of any particular human rights standards as states complied with this resolution. In fact, for the first several years, the Security Council Web site explicitly said that monitoring of human rights in the course of the antiterrorism campaign was to be left to other UN bodies because this was not the central mission of the Security Council.

To give the resolution teeth, the Security Council created a Counter-Terrorism Committee (CTC) with the mandate to track national compliance with these directives and to intervene aggressively in responding to the national reports that countries were required to submit, indicating what they had done to fight terrorism. First, the CTC monitored national reports showing that domestic laws had been changed. Then, the CTC required countries to provide statistics to show that they had been using these laws. (For example, how many terrorism arrests have been made? Or how many assets connected to terrorists have been frozen?) Eventually, CTC staff members made site visits to particular countries to ensure that their conduct tracked their reports.[22]

Compliance has been extraordinary—or at least states have eagerly claimed to follow along. All but five of the member states of the UN filed compliance reports with the CTC of the Security Council; many countries submitted four or five reports before the CTC stopped publishing them in 2006.[23] Virtually all of the reports claim that their states have made changes in their laws to comply with the resolution.

States ranging from Brunei to Vietnam criminalized terrorism by using definitions that appeared to sweep in the entire domestic opposition.[24] Even the United States and Canada criminalized terrorism in controversial ways, by adding definitions of terrorism that were markedly different than other crimes within each of these systems. The United States, for example, does not require standard mens rea (intent) for a terrorism offense; now it requires that an act only "appear to be intended" to cause terror.[25] Canadian law now requires that, to count as terrorist, a criminal act be committed with a particular political or religious motivation,[26] states of mind into which Canadian law typically avoids inquiring.[27] Other countries, particularly Arab states, criminalized terrorism while exempting freedom fighters.[28] States that tried to push back by refusing to criminalize terrorism, such as Mexico, were repeatedly urged to comply by the CTC, and Mexico eventually gave in, creating a crime for which the minimum sentence was eighteen years.[29] The worry in all of these cases is that the new terrorism crimes have given tremendous prosecutorial discretion to national executives, who can use the vaguely worded and highly punitive laws to suppress domestic dissent or to selectively target domestic Muslim populations.

In the area of freezing assets, states have also generally been very willing to comply. Resolution 1373 requires states to "immediately" freeze the assets of individuals and groups on the UN Security Council Sanctions Committee watch list for terrorism.[30] States including France, Spain, Bulgaria, and Brazil created "automatic" procedures through which the mere listing of an individual or group on the UN Sanctions Committee watch list generated an order to all domestic financial institutions to freeze the assets of those listed.[31] Venezuela and Mexico attempted to push back, claiming that they could not freeze assets without evidence that the persons or groups had broken a law, but the Security Council refused to provide such information. Eventually, even Venezuela and Mexico caved in to the pressure and found ways to freeze assets immediately without individualized evidence.[32] These asset-freeze procedures generally bypass domestic and regional human rights guarantees that no one will be deprived of property without a hearing or other formal procedure.

With respect to the obligation to prevent terror cells from developing on the territory of sovereign states, here too states have shown a readiness to take action in compliance with Resolution 1373. Some states, including the United States, Argentina, and Spain, have created counterterrorism centers that bring national police, regional police, and military intelligence units together in a common organization with the aim of discovering domestic

terror cells.[33] Other states have created special terrorism police.[34] New surveillance technologies, for example, communications-intercept capacity, have
been implemented in the name of the war on terror.[35] While much of this sort
of compliance is hidden in the webs of affiliation among national security
agencies, it is clear even from public reports to the CTC that surveillance of
potential terrorists, and no doubt many others, has increased worldwide.

Finally, with respect to monitoring the use of the system of international
migration by potential terrorists, states have also reported high levels of
compliance to the CTC. The tightening up of asylum policies to exclude
potential terrorists has clearly had a drastic effect throughout the European
Union[36] and within the United States as well.[37]

Resolution 1373 and the antiterrorism campaign that it represents seem
to be having effects on the ground. But how do we know that these many
new laws and seemingly correlated effects are part of a new imperial reach?
Why do states comply?

A TALE OF TWO COUNTRIES

To see how the new global empire works, we need to look in more depth at
particular places. Given the worldwide expanse of the new global security
empire, one could look almost anywhere and expect to see its effects. But it
helps to look at places that are consequential not only for what is happening
within their own borders but because they are crucial in the global anti-
terrorism campaign, for it is here where one would expect the results of the
new imperial formations to be most important. As a result, we will consider
Russia and Pakistan after 9/11 and the ways in which their far-reaching domestic changes can be seen as part of the global anti-terrorism campaign.

Russia is a state that is in some ways at the center of the new imperial web
and in some ways at its periphery. It has a veto on the Security Council and
is a large state accustomed to being a superpower. Nonetheless, Russia had
fallen on hard times after the collapse of the Soviet Union in 1991. A decade
of economic chaos, population decline, internal conflict, and failing institutions had turned Russia into a shell of its former self by the time of 9/11. In
addition, Russia had been fighting a domestic civil war against an Islamic
republic and had for years alleged that foreign fighters wanted to yoke this
struggle to a global program. Even before 9/11, Russia had been the target of
numerous terrorist bombings. The new global security crisis after 9/11 presented Russia with a chance to be a player on the world stage again and to
trade its influence on the Security Council for being given a freer hand in

restructuring its domestic politics to fight its domestic terrorism problem without external criticism.

Pakistan, by contrast, is a peripheral state in the world system but a crucial state in the global anti-terrorism campaign. It was clear almost immediately after 9/11 that Pakistan would be one of the crucial sources of terrorists that core states wanted to capture because its state support for the Taliban and its proximity to the location from which the attacks came meant that it was likely to have many terrorism suspects within its borders. The global anti-terrorism campaign, therefore, required that Pakistan become a compliant fighter of terrorism in much the same way as the earlier forms of colonialism required South Asia to become a compliant producer of other goods that the imperial powers needed. Pakistan, like Afghanistan, could easily have come under attack for "harboring terrorists," had it failed to comply. No surprise, then, that Pakistan became a willing player in the global anti-terrorism campaign on the terms demanded by the "international community." Pakistan's willingness to do the bidding of the core states, particularly the United States, has created domestic problems for its weak leadership, which is on the way to becoming another casualty of the global anti-terrorism campaign. And so to the national stories.

RUSSIA

Terrorism was not new to Russia on 9/11.[38] When the Soviet Union dissolved itself in 1991 and a plethora of new states was created in its place, Russia entered a decade of economic chaos punctuated by terrorist attacks. Most of the terrorist attacks within Russia itself were blamed on Chechen nationalists, whose attempts to free themselves from Russian rule resulted in two civil wars in Chechnya.[39] Chechnya is a Muslim republic within Russia, home to an ethnically and linguistically distinct population whose leaders sought independence from Russia as soon as the Soviet Union began to splinter. To bring the Chechen conflict to broader national attention within Russia over more than a decade, Chechen nationalists took hostages in hospitals, theaters, and schools throughout Russia, bombed the Moscow subway on several occasions, brought down airplanes, and sent suicide bombers into crowds in the Russian capital.[40] At the time of 9/11, Russia had a terrorism problem, but it was generally thought, by Russians and others, to be primarily Russian in origin.

Before 9/11, the Chechen wars were greeted with near-universal international condemnation. The First Chechen War, from 1994 to 1996, was characterized by brutal human rights violations on the part of the Russian military in Chechnya, a brutality matched only by the fighting tactics of the Chechen rebels. The Second Chechen War, which began in 1999 and which reached a gradual if fragile peace by 2007, was just as brutal. Grozny, the capital city, was completely leveled by indiscriminate bombing by Russian forces. Reports of horrific abuses committed on all sides filtered out, though the situation was so dangerous for journalists that little reporting of the war occurred from any quarter.[41] The human rights community issued a string of strong condemnations; many countries around the world—the United States included—heavily criticized the human rights abuses that Russia committed in Chechnya.

As Russian forces laid waste to Chechnya, Chechen nationalists launched terrorist attacks throughout Russia. In June 1995, 1,500 hospital patients in the Russian village of Budennovsk were taken hostage, and in January 1996, 3,400 hospital patients were taken hostage in Dagestan. The escaping terrorists, taking human shields from among the patients in both cases, were chased, but mostly it was the hostage patients who were killed. In September 1999, two apartment buildings in Moscow and several more in other Russian cities were blown up over the course of twelve days, killing three hundred people.[42] In August 2000, a bomb exploded at the busy Pushkin Square Metro station, killing eight people only a few blocks from the Kremlin. By the time of 9/11, Russians were well aware of terrorism and eager for their government to do something about it.

Russian president Vladimir Putin was one of the first international leaders to express sympathy with the United States on 9/11. In a telegram sent that day to American president George Bush, Putin noted: "We understand your grief and your pain only too well. The Russians have experienced the fear of terror themselves. There is no doubt that such inhuman actions should not go unpunished. The entire international community should rally together in the struggle against terrorism."[43] Soon thereafter, Russian foreign minister Igor Ivanov made the point even clearer: "Russia hopes that Washington will now change its critical attitude to its campaign in Chechnya. The problem of international terrorism did not arise on September 11, but two years ago when residential houses were blown up in Moscow. In other words, the terrorists have made Russians and Americans friends in misfortune. Now we may find it easier to understand each other."[44]

Not surprisingly, Russia was an eager supporter of Security Council Resolution 1373 when it was proposed later that month. As a veto-bearing member of the council, Russia could have rejected it. But instead, Russia clearly saw an opportunity for it to fold its "Chechen problem" into the global anti-terrorism campaign. A global anti-terrorism campaign suited its domestic agendas perfectly. As one Russian commentator put it at the time of the Security Council debate, "The Americans will have to drop those double standards. . . . You can't continue saying that an Islamic militant who kills Americans is a terrorist, while one who kills Russians is some kind of freedom fighter. We expect that to change."[45]

On the day before the Security Council resolution passed, President George Bush publicly endorsed Russia's war in Chechnya by saying that the Chechen rebels were linked to the terrorist network that had been responsible for 9/11.[46] The timing of the American declaration that Chechnya was part of the global anti-terrorism campaign suggests that this was the price Russia cleverly extracted for its support of Resolution 1373.

In reporting to the CTC on its compliance with 1373, Russia condemned terrorism in the strongest possible terms and pronounced its eager willingness to work with the UN in its global campaign. In its first report to the committee, Russia proudly listed its extensive pre-9/11 antiterrorism laws as proof of its commitment to fight terrorism. Though these laws had once generated concern from human rights advocates because they gave broad permission to the state to engage in "counterterrorism operations" (which included the entire Second Chechen War, fought by interior ministry troops as a "counterterrorism operation"), these laws now became an internationally approved part of the global anti-terrorism campaign, forwarded as Russia's efforts to comply with Resolution 1373. As a further sign that Russia fully supported Resolution 1373 and its approach to fighting terrorism, President Putin issued an *ukaz* (decree) called "On Measures to Implement United Nations Security Council Resolution 1373 of 28 September 2001," repeating Resolution 1373 practically word for word, making the entire resolution Russian law on the order of the Russian president.[47]

Though it managed to get its campaign in Chechnya considered part of the global anti-terrorism campaign, this did not end the Chechen war or the terrorist attacks. Instead, terrorist attacks increased in audacity and moved closer to the centers of power in Russia. In October 2002, a Chechen group took nearly one thousand people hostage in a theater in Moscow; 130 performers and theatergoers as well as all of the hostage takers died during the "rescue." In July 2003, two suicide bombers blew themselves up at an outdoor rock concert in Moscow, killing fifteen people in addition to themselves. Several times that summer, suicide bombers were apprehended in central Moscow before they could detonate their charges. At the end of the summer, a suicide bomber in North Ossetia killed fifty people at a military hospital. In December 2003, a suicide bomber blew herself up across the street from the Kremlin, taking five lives along with her own—and this the day after a commuter train in Stavropol had been bombed, killing another forty-two people. In February 2004, the Moscow subway was bombed and thirty people were killed. In June 2004, a shoot-out in Dagestan left ninety-two dead at the interior ministry. In July of that year, three were killed in bus bombings in Voronezh. In August 2004, two airliners leaving Moscow for different cities in Siberia were blown up in midair by suicide bombers, leaving eighty-nine people dead. Later that month, another subway bombing in Moscow caused ten more deaths.[48]

And then there was Beslan. On the first day of school in September 2004, 1,500 students, parents, and teachers were taken hostage in Middle School #1 in a small village in the Russian region of North Ossetia. After three days during which the hostages were held in the stifling gymnasium of the school without food or water, a terrorist bomb was accidentally detonated, triggering the security forces' storming of the school. In the chaos, more than three hundred people died, 150 of them schoolchildren. Russians were shocked. Despite all of the terrorist attacks that had occurred before then, Beslan had an overwhelming public effect because children had been the primary target. Finally, something had to be done about terrorism.

The hostage taking at Beslan spurred Russia to go to the Security Council to get a counterterrorism resolution of its own. Resolution 1566, passed on October 4, 2004,[49] called on states to extradite any person who had facilitated terrorist acts of any kind. Given that Russia believed that Chechen nationalists who were plotting these attacks had been given refuge in Western Europe, the resolution was seen in Russia as a victory for their domestic fight against terrorism. Moreover, the resolution constituted a new committee of the Security Council with the mandate to consider expanding the terrorism watch list of the UN Sanctions Committee to go beyond Al Qaeda and Taliban members, the groups to whom sanctions had previously been limited. While no other groups or individuals have been listed since this resolution was passed, Russia clearly wanted the ability to argue that Chechen fighters should be part of the UN's campaign against terror.

At home, content before Beslan to fight terrorism domestically with the means that had been at his disposal before 9/11, President Vladimir Putin proposed a far-reaching domestic antiterrorism plan in September 2004 that went well beyond what Resolution 1373 envisioned for national law.[50] Putin proposed increasing the "vertical of power" within Russia, which meant strengthening the power of the executive through the complex system of Russian federalism. He proposed that he himself be allowed to appoint regional governors, instead of allowing elections to accomplish the task. In addition, he proposed that the national parliament be made more effective, so that it could act more decisively to fight terrorism. He proposed that all single-member districts in the Duma be eliminated, replacing a mixed system of election with a system in which all representatives had to stand for election on party lists in pure proportional representation. Both of these elements of his new antiterrorism strategy passed the parliament against the backdrop of a panic about terrorism. These new laws had the effect of strengthening Putin within his own domestic context and giving him broader powers against both the regions and the parliament for purposes that went well beyond fighting terrorism.

Although the restructuring of the Russian regional governments and parliament had not been on the CTC's wish list of things they wanted states to do, Russia had been pressed for some years by the CTC to enact a new law on terrorism that would broaden the offenses that could be punished in domestic criminal law and that would clarify further how terrorism would be fought as a domestic legal matter. After Beslan, Russia was more than ready to comply. The law against terrorism that passed the parliament in March 2006 defines terrorism as "the ideology of violence and the practice of influencing the adoption of a decision by state power bodies, local self-government bodies or international organizations connected with frightening the population and (or) other forms of unlawful violent actions."[51] While the previous law on terrorism required "violence" as an element of terrorism, the present law allows the state to act based on ideology alone. In addition, the new law permits counterterrorism operations that involve the unlimited monitoring of telephone and other communications, the unlimited searching of property, the commandeering of private vehicles and other resources, and the uses of military forces to fight terrorism—all with no legal authorization other than the order of the director of the operation. In reporting to the CTC in June 2006, the Russian government not only took pride in this new law but also indicated that it was at work on a new project that would enable it to filter the Internet so that it could take down all sites justifying and encouraging terrorism,[52] in order to better comply with Resolution 1624 of the Security Council, requiring states to take steps to prohibit incitement to terrorism. Of course, the ability to filter the Internet is useful beyond the terrorism context for any state that wants to keep better track of what its population is up to.

The draconian measures to change the shape of government and to put new repressive antiterrorism policies in place did not prevent more terrorist attacks. In November 2009, the elite Nevsky Express train between Moscow and St. Petersburg was blown up by a terrorist bomb, killing twenty-seven people. In March 2010, massive bomb blasts in two busy Moscow subway stations killed forty people and wounded another hundred. In January 2011, Domodedovo Airport, a newly renovated hub for international flights, was the target of another terrorist attack in which thirty-seven people died. In the summer of 2011, authorities claimed to have averted a massive terrorist strike in the center of Moscow. At that point, the security services noted that "169 'terrorist' crimes had been recorded in Russia this year [by July 2011], 110 of them in the North Caucasus province of Dagestan. [In addition,] 95 law enforcement and security agents had been killed and more than 200 wounded fighting militants this year."[53]

It was widely thought that Putin had taken the terrorism portfolio with him to the prime minister's job, which he had moved into when term limits forced him out of the presidency in 2008. As a result, when Dmitri Medvedev took over the Russian presidency from Vladimir Putin in March 2008, the terrorism policies already in place continued. As Medvedev's tenure as president progressed, however, talk of differences between his position and that of his predecessor grew. In response to the Moscow Metro bombings and the Domodevovo Airport attacks, Medvedev signed new antiterrorism laws, but they were nowhere near as draconian as those that had been enacted while Putin was president. (However, it is hard to be so draconian a second time once all of the obvious draconian things had already been done.) Medvedev instituted a color-coded terrorism alert scheme, imitating the U.S. system that was about to be dismantled. And he suggested that a new terrorism law should allow terrorism suspects to be tried outside the region where the terrorist attack occurred, both to prevent witnesses from being intimidated and to prevent overwrought juries from overreacting. But these are hardly the responses that Putin had to terrorism. No government reorganizations, sweeping new antiterror laws, or punitive excesses have been proposed by Medvedev. Medvedev seemed to be more interested in getting the system that was already in place to fight terror to work effectively.

From this account, we can see that Russia, particularly during the years of Putin's presidency, used its power on the Security Council to leverage the international community's support for the Russian fight against global terrorism, which is how the Chechen conflict was portrayed. Because Russia is one of the core states on the Security Council, it has shared the power to shape how the global anti-terrorism campaign is structured. But because Russia also has elements of a peripheral state—it has been subject to criticism from other states for its human rights violations and "managed" democracy—Russia has been able to use the global anti-terrorism campaign as a general legitimating cover for many of the domestic projects it would have been more heavily criticized for adopting were they not framed as part of the fight against terrorism. Along the way, Putin personally used the global anti-terrorism campaign to consolidate his own power within Russia by using it to achieve domestic reforms that put more power into his hands. Russia was therefore able to increase its power relative to other states, to concentrate power domestically in the hands of the executive, and to exercise more untrammeled powers over its own citizens and nationals through signing onto the global anti-terrorism campaign. While Dimitri Medvedev was less prone to overreaction (or opportunism) than Vladimir Putin was as president, none of the antiterrorism policies that Putin put into place have been rolled back. Russia remains a power that has used international antiterrorism policies to strengthen the hand of the president and executive branch and to weaken both other branches and human rights.

PAKISTAN

Since the time of its independence in 1948, Pakistan has lurched between fragile democratic governments and tougher military dictatorships.[54] During the 1990s, however, Pakistan seemed to be developing a relatively stable two-party democracy in which power changed hands peacefully on a regular basis. But lurking behind this apparently peaceful facade were two destabilizing elements. First, the military and security services in Pakistan have been very powerful and deeply political from the country's founding, so civilian politics are always conducted in the shadow of the garrison. Second, although the country has a moderate, middle-class base that is capable of sustaining both the rule of law and democratic institutions, more radical Islamic groups have always existed around the margins, not fully governable from within ordinary democratic politics. These two elements are intertwined. The military and security services have been able to preserve their power in part by selectively supporting radical Islamic elements to do their bidding.

Because Pakistan sees itself as locked in continual struggle against India, primarily for control of the disputed province of Kashmir but also in a more existential way, the radical Islamic elements within Pakistan have been stoked by the military and security services in order to destabilize Indian control over Kashmir, to launch occasional terrorist attacks against India, and to create buffer zones for Pakistan in the region, evidenced most obviously in the Pakistani security services support for the Taliban in Afghanistan. Because Pakistan had tested its first nuclear weapon in 1999 and launched a new campaign against India in Kashmir shortly thereafter, the country was under international sanctions at the time of 9/11.

Pakistan had been struggling with internal terrorism of its own before 9/11. In January 1997, a pipe bomb was detonated at the district court in Lahore, just as members of a radical Sunni organization were brought there for trial. The blast killed twenty-three people and wounded another fifty-five. The investigation identified a member of a radical Shia organization as the bomber and, in the clamor for public revenge, the Anti-Terrorism Act of 1997 was introduced by the government of Nawaz Sharif, who had just been returned to power in a landslide election the month after the terrorist attack.

Pakistan had coped with a great deal of sectarian violence before this without the draconian measures of the 1997 Anti-Terrorism Act, so the radical quality of this law stood out against the otherwise moderate Pakistani legal landscape. Terrorism was defined broadly in this new law as the commission of a long list of criminal acts with the motivation "to strike terror in the people, or any section of the people, or to alienate any section of the people or to adversely affect harmony among different sections of the people."[55] The definition of terrorism meant that almost any strong oppositional movement could be seen as adversely affecting the harmony of political life or alienating sections of the people from the government. The act also introduced special antiterrorism courts that could quickly put terrorism suspects on trial without the procedural niceties of the ordinary courts. In the wrong hands, these antiterrorism courts could be a powerful political tool for consolidating power.

The Lahore pipe bomber was tried before one of these new courts and given the death sentence. When the Pakistani Supreme Court heard the final appeal, it upheld the conviction and the death penalty but struck down sections of the 1997 Anti-Terrorism Act as unconstitutional because the new antiterrorism courts failed to guarantee both independence of the judges and a route of appeal through the regular courts.[56] The Nawaz Sharif government modified the law narrowly to comply with the Supreme Court's decision but left the rest of the antiterrorism law in place.

As it turns out, however, the Anti-Terrorism Law was not enough to control new sectarian violence spinning out of control. The murder of a key politician in the Sindh Province in the fall of 1998 caused radical unrest. First in Sindh and then throughout the whole of Pakistan, a new Pakistan

Armed Forces (Acting in Aid of Civil Power) Ordinance was introduced to quell disturbances.[57] The new law was able to create military courts very like the ones struck down earlier by the Pakistani Supreme Court in its review of the antiterrorism law. Not fooled, the Pakistani Supreme Court nullified this new law in its entirety in a unanimous decision ringing with support for the ordinary rule of law.[58] The Nawaz Sharif government capitulated to the court.

Against this backdrop, the military coup that brought Pervez Musharraf to power later that year could be portrayed as providing the strong hand needed to deal with domestic unrest. At first, broad swaths of the moderate Pakistani middle class were relieved, as Musharraf promised an end to both the "civil commotion" and the corruption that had plagued the Nawaz Sharif government. Though Musharraf suspended the constitution, he promulgated a Provisional (Constitutional) Order in which he announced that "Pakistan shall . . . be governed, as nearly as may be, in accordance with the constitution."[59] The Pakistani Supreme Court, called upon as it always is during military coups to pronounce on the legitimacy of the new regime, said that the coup had been occasioned by necessity, thereby giving Musharraf legal permission to do what he did. But the Court also gave Musharraf a deadline to return Pakistan to civilian and democratic rule within three years.[60]

Musharraf's consolidation of control rested on retooling the antiterrorism law. Introducing many political crimes into the law (e.g., conspiracy to commit an offense against the state), Musharraf then charged Nawaz Sharif himself with having committed terrorism and brought him before the newly refitted antiterrorism courts. Before the case could be decided, the government struck a deal with the former prime minister, permitting him to go into exile. With his opponent gone, Musharraf then began to use the antiterrorism courts to handle all cases involving political opposition to his government. In August 2001, more amendments to the antiterrorism act permitted two radical Islamist groups to be listed as threats to the state and hundreds of their members were arrested.[61]

When 9/11 occurred, Pakistan was a peripheral state that had been marginalized by international sanctions. But it was clearly one of the Security Council's most pressing targets precisely because it was at the top of the list of U.S. concern. As it prepared to attack Afghanistan in the fall of 2001, the United States demanded that Pakistan cut its support for the Taliban government of Afghanistan and join the American campaign against Afghanistan by lending airspace, security support, and a willingness to tamp down Islamist reaction to what was about to occur. Although Musharraf made it appear that cutting support to the Taliban was a high price to pay, much of the Pakistani military elite had apparently been looking for an excuse to do so for some time.[62] In addition, Musharraf could point to his antiterrorism laws as early proof of his dedication to the cause. As a result, the "antiterrorism campaign" that had been waged largely against Musharraf's (and earlier Nawaz Sharif's) political opponents suddenly turned out to be useful in legitimating Pakistan's domestic policies before the world. When Resolution 1373 passed, Musharraf could brandish the antiterrorism law and his selective crackdown on Islamist groups in the summer of 2001 to say that he was already on board with the global anti-terrorism campaign.

In its first report to the Counter-Terrorism Committee, Pakistan began by saying: "Being itself a victim of terrorism for over [the] last two decades, Pakistan . . . [enacted] the Anti-Terrorism Act in 1997 which was later amended in August 2001. Under this Act, special courts have been established for speedy trial of those involved in terrorist activities."[63] The banning of weapons (mostly to get them out of the hands of Musharraf's opponents) was also portrayed as part of the global anti-terrorism campaign, with the first Pakistani CTC report proudly announcing 21,163 raids on those suspected of having illegal weapons.[64] Never mind that all of the raids occurred after Musharraf's coup and before 9/11. Pakistan threw itself into the global anti-terrorism campaign, bragging to the CTC about the many repressive measures taken by Musharraf to consolidate military control after 1999 as part of the fight against terrorism.

Musharraf's strategy worked. With his apparently eager cooperation in the global anti-terrorism campaign, money began to flow to Pakistan from the United States, international financial institutions, and other countries that had previously sanctioned Pakistan for its development of nuclear weapons. Just in the fall of 2001 alone, the U.S. Congress first suspended duties on Pakistani textile imports to the United States[65] and then gave President Bush authorization to waive the usual ban on providing direct assistance to countries whose "duly elected head of government was deposed by decree or military coup."[66] By the end of 2007, Pakistan had received about $10 billion in U.S. direct assistance, most directed toward Pakistan's military and security services.[67]

Musharraf's strategy worked in another way as well. Faced with the Supreme Court deadline of three years before he had to return the country to civilian and democratic rule, Musharraf was able to use his participation in the global anti-terrorism campaign to take the country on a different course. Before 9/11 diverted him, Musharraf had started the process of democratization by holding elections for 102 district governments in the summer of 2001. He promised to hold provincial and national elections in a phased sequence over the following two years.[68] But by early 2002, his commitment to giving up power was already starting to fade. In April 2002, he held a referendum to ask the Pakistani people whether they would give him five more years as president. Official reports indicated that on more than 50 percent turnout, Musharraf had won 97.7 percent of the vote.[69] Emboldened by this, he permitted provincial elections to take place in October 2002, but in an atmosphere where the military suppressed the moderate political parties both by preventing their leaders from returning to the country and by blocking their rallies in the name of national security. The military blatantly supported their own faction of the Pakistani Muslim League instead. The strategy backfired, however, and radical Islamist parties, traditionally outvoted by the moderate parties, gained surprising power in a number of areas of the country, consolidating their control in two of Pakistan's four provinces.[70] By the end of the promised round of elections, Pakistan was in the hands of more radical elements than it had been before 9/11.

From quite early on, it became clear that Musharraf intended to use the global support he got for his participation in the global anti-terrorism campaign to entrench himself and the military and to use antiterrorism law as a framework for doing so. In the fall of 2001, after the Security Council passed Resolution 1373 requiring that states take action to fight terrorism, Musharraf promulgated the Anti-Terrorism (Amendment) Ordinance 2001, which brought into Pakistani law many elements of the Security Council program. It expanded the range of terrorism crimes, permitted the government to designate individuals and organizations as affiliated with terrorism and to block all of their transactions as well as to freeze their assets, and to ban all public statements made by anyone so labeled.[71] The government also created forty-one new antiterrorism courts that fall to demonstrate that they were doing all they could to fight terrorism.[72]

In January 2002, the antiterrorism act was amended again to change the panel of judges in the antiterrorism courts to include military judges on every panel. This was done against the backdrop of the Daniel Pearl case, since his accused killers were being tried at the time in a Pakistani antiterrorism court.[73] Another amendment to the antiterrorism act in October 2002 gave the government the power to detain and hold for one year without charges anyone suspected of being a terrorist. Human rights organizations have reported on the extraordinary number of detentions and disappearances since this amendment of the antiterrorism law went into effect.[74]

Issued under his military authority as a Legal Framework Order in August 2002, Musharraf announced his intention to bring back the power of the president to dissolve any civilian government at will and to create a National Security Council of military advisers who would govern with the president.[75] A package of constitutional amendments passed the Pakistani parliament in December 2003 and entrenched the power of the president to dissolve parliaments.[76] Although Musharraf promised that he would step down in 2004 as a condition of getting the Pakistani parliament to pass this amendment, he avoided doing so when the time came. In the meantime, he kept increasing the severity of the antiterrorism laws, authorizing life sentences for anyone who assisted terrorists and increasing the punishments for all other terrorism offenses as well.

In 2007, Musharraf put himself back before the voters again to renew the five-year term of office he had been granted in 2002. Although he won election again, the election was clouded by a pending case before the Supreme Court of Pakistan, in which his ability to hold the office of chief of the military and civilian president at the same time was challenged. The Supreme Court put off its decision until after the election. But after hearing behind the scenes that the Court was preparing to rule against him, denying him his new term of office unless he gave up his military post, Musharraf struck first. Declaring martial law on Friday November 2, 2007, after learning the decision would be handed down the following Monday, he inveighed against "extremist elements," once again using his antiterrorism campaign to cloak his efforts to stay in power. While the motivation for the state of emergency seemed to have been to avoid the court decision against him, Musharraf claimed that the emergency was necessary because of the increase in terrorist attacks within the country and the need to restore peace.

In the state of emergency, Musharraf suspended the constitution and declared that a number of specific fundamental rights were no longer protected. He put the defiant judges of the Supreme Court under house arrest and packed the courts with supporters who swore an oath under the new Provisional (Constitutional) Order that replaced the constitution for the duration of the emergency. He then amended the constitution in multiple ways to further entrench his power. These actions and Musharraf's new immunity from legal challenge bore witness to the nonnormalcy of the situation in Pakistan. While he may have been primarily attempting to keep himself in power, the cover he used was antiterrorism.

Eventually, Musharraf's campaign against the judges led to his undoing. Popular support for Chief Justice Iftikhar Chaudhry brought tens of thousands of Pakistanis into the streets demanding his release. Only after a great deal of international pressure, and after he extracted a guarantee that the courts would not rule against him, did Musharraf lift martial law, declaring parliamentary elections for 2008 and appearing to the world to return things to normal. The assassination of Benazir Bhutto in late 2007 during a political rally in the run-up to the election exposed either the inability of the government to actually control "extremist elements" or the cooperation between extremist elements and members of the Pakistani military and security services, depending on the explanation one accepts. In the February 2008 elections, the political party of the late Benazir Bhutto won the most votes, and her husband Asif Ali Zadari became president with Yousuf Raza Gilani as prime minister.

The security situation in Pakistan continued to worsen after Musharraf stepped down and it appeared in the immediate aftermath that the fragile new civilian government was barely able to protect its own population, let alone do anything to contribute to the international fight against terrorism. Unlike Musharraf, who had used the antiterrorism campaign to strengthen his position in power, neither Zadari nor Gilani consolidated control in the same way, by dealing themselves new powers with antiterrorism law. They have by and large not deployed the antiterror campaign to shore up their domestic political standing. Though Zadari signed a new law that increased the interrogation period for suspected terrorists from thirty to ninety days in October 2009,[77] he struggled to contain the growing threats to his own people from attacks by insurgents often linked to terrorist organizations. When Osama bin Laden was killed by U.S. forces that had raided Bin Laden's Pakistani compound without notifying Pakistani authorities, the ability of the government to contribute much of anything at all to the global antiterrorism campaign was called into question.

That said, most of the antiterrorism legal framework put into place by Musharraf for his own purposes remains in place. Regardless of how draconian it was, however, the framework has not worked to stop Pakistan's slide into civil war. In 2009 alone, thousands of Pakistanis were abducted and killed. That year, fully eighty-seven suicide attacks were recorded in the country, resulting in 1,299 deaths and several thousand injuries.[78]

In 2010, the parliament passed a constitutional amendment that reversed the earlier constitutional amendment adopted by Musharraf so that now the president may not dissolve the parliament at will any longer.[79] Pakistan signed several important international human rights agreements, though it did nothing to bring them into domestic law. It appeared that the new government was taking some substantial, if largely symbolic steps, to return its antiterrorism policy to a constitutional footing. In the meantime, however, the slide into chaos continued for Pakistan.

From this account, we can see that Pakistan quickly turned repressive measures instituted by Musharraf to seize and maintain power into a public demonstration of its commitment to fight terrorism. Pakistan's eager support for the global anti-terrorism campaign right and the UN Security Council–led international initiatives after 9/11 succeeded in getting sanctions against it removed, clearing the way for important resources to flow to the Pakistani military (which, after all, was Musharraf's main base of support). This support also gave Musharraf cover to put in place a whole series of decrees, laws, and even constitutional amendments that appeared to be part of an antiterrorism campaign but that had as their main effect keeping him in power. The Security Council and its central member, the United States, were happy with the bargain—Pakistan's cooperation in the global anti-terrorism campaign was secured in exchange for the "international community's" support of Musharraf.

Of course, after Musharraf stepped down, this bargain looks less advantageous for all because the security situation has worsened both for Pakistani citizens and for the global campaign against terror. But the Security Council and the United States are in an awkward position. Given the increasing radicalism of Islamist forces in the tribal areas of Pakistan and their increasingly bold incursions into parts of Pakistan where once the population felt safe, the position of Pakistan in the global anti-terrorism campaign is one of the most urgent issues the Security Council and the United States face. Pakistan may have created a huge infrastructure for fighting terrorism with international approval, but it now seems unable to control its own domestic threats any longer.

THE INTERNATIONAL STATE OF EMERGENCY

The new international legal framework developed since 9/11 permits control of the periphery by the center much as old-fashioned imperial administrative law did for an earlier form of colonial empire. After 9/11, the United States wanted to be able to seek out terrorists wherever they were located, but the United States needed the cooperation of the states in which such terrorists were located. The United States initiated the antiterror campaign in the Security Council to create a worldwide web of legal interdiction. For various reasons, the other permanent five member states supported this campaign, as did all other states that happened to be on the Security Council when the 9/11 attacks struck. The result was the creation of global security law as a device to enable the states that feared terrorist attack to work through the states that were the primary producers of terrorists to neutralize the threat. Although the United States was the primary mover, it could not have accomplished this project alone.

But, as we know now from postcolonial studies, all empires are precarious. They rest on the guarantee that imperial power will be exercised in ways that benefit powerful locals so that they continue to support the center. In both old and new empires, this often involves the transfer of resources from the center outward, as well as the legitimation by the core of the (sometimes dodgy) practices at the periphery. These transfers and legitimation practices are performed in exchange for the production and transfer of other scarce resources (in this case, crackdowns on terrorists) from the periphery back to the core. The new security empire has much in common with the old empire of material extraction, except now the center provides support for and legitimation of governments in exchange for the governments at the periphery searching out and disabling terrorists.

As with the old-fashioned system of administrative control, the new international law links powerful and less powerful states in a global embrace to accomplish ends dictated in large measure by the powerful states but with local agendas that adapt the central mandates for local purposes. As we have seen in the cases of Russia and Pakistan, the new imperial reach ends in an only partial grasp.

The new system of imperial control, however, hides the hands of influence more effectively than in previous imperial formations. In the vast majority of states that changed their laws after 9/11 to fit this new legal frame, it was not apparent to much of the population that the domestic legal changes were made in concert with an internationally coordinated campaign that had the United States at the center of it or that those changes were offered up as evidence that the peripheral state was going along with American demands. Instead, these domestic legal changes were often generated by local campaigns of fear, portrayed as crucial for domestic national (often nationalistic) security and offered as examples of heightened sovereignty of nation-states. Moreover, insofar as Security Council resolutions require the veto-bearing members to go along with the new campaign on terrorism, this gave particularly sweet opportunities for states with seats on the council to take some benefits for themselves.

As with the old imperial administrative law, however, the new global security law operates primarily by permitting strong states to shape some of the content of the internal legal systems of weak states, which is enough to achieve the goals of the powerful states as long as the peripheral regimes seem to be doing the jobs they have been delegated. In the new empire, international institutions have given all states marching orders (or license) about how states should change their domestic laws to combat terrorism. States have complied with these new international mandates at a quite astonishing rate, but that is at least in part because the domestic executives who have pushed the changes in peripheral states often themselves have something quite directly to gain in terms of enhanced power and room to maneuver. Just as old colonial elites often stood to gain personally and institutionally from being the enforcers of colonial law, so do the new antiterror elites in peripheral states stand to gain from their compliance with global security law.

The new international law requires all states to take radical steps to criminalize terrorism, to curb terrorist threats at home, and to act as barriers to the transnational flows of people and money involved in terrorism. Not surprisingly, these domestic actions have had repressive effects on particular domestic populations at both center and periphery as well as on the expression of political dissent and on the budding constitutional structures of rights protection in many states. If traditional empires involved the repression of far-flung populations directly at the behest of a core of powerful states, then the new empire is surprisingly like the old. But there is a difference. The states that are the targets of this new form of empire never lose their sovereignty and in fact may not appear to be acting in concert with the core imperial states at all. The new empire is managed through international law, and that means that the agents behind the new empire appear only as the "international community." The compliant acts in this new empire appear only to be "following the law." The agency behind this law is disguised.

This new international order encourages the concentration of powers in the hands of national executives around the world while it limits procedural protections for those suspected of being terrorists, infringes a wide variety of rights, and makes the category of "noncitizen" a more fragile and dangerous one everywhere. It therefore has all of the hallmarks of a state of emergency. But this state of emergency exists not just in one country; it is multiplied across the whole field of nation-states and results in parallel emergencies coordinated centrally as part of a global campaign. Of course, some states in the world order never guaranteed their citizens constitutional protections anyhow; now they have a free pass to continue not to do so as long as these states say that they are fighting terrorism. For those states that did have a robust constitutional order with separation of powers, due process, and rights protections, however, the post-9/11 international legal order creates pressures to abandon key elements of constitutionalism, especially for vulnerable sectors of their populations.

The new form of empire is now a transnational legal order that coordinates parallel states of emergencies in a new global war to create an international state of emergency.

NOTES

This article is current as of August 2011. Developments occurring after that date are not reflected in this account.

1. For a review, see Frederick Cooper and Ann Laura Stoler, "Between Metropole and Colony: Rethinking a Research Agenda." Pp. 1–56 in Frederick Cooper and Ann Laura Stoler (eds.), *Tensions of Empire: Colonial Cultures in the Bourgeois World* (Berkeley: University of California Press, 1997).

2. Dipesh Chakrabarty, *Provincializing Europe: Postcolonial Thought and Historical Difference* (Princeton, N.J.: Princeton University Press, 2000).

3. Arjun Appadurai, *Modernity at Large: Cultural Dimensions of Globalization* (Minneapolis: University of Minnesota Press, 1996); Uday S. Mehta, "Liberal Strategies of Exclusion." Pp. 59–86 in *Tensions of Empire: Colonial Cultures in the Bourgeois World* (Berkeley: University of California Press, 1997).

4. John Comaroff and Jean Comaroff, "Homemade Hegemony." Pp. 265–285 in *Ethnography and the Historical Imagination* (Boulder, Colo.: Westview Press, 1992); Thomas Holt, *The Problem of Freedom: Race, Labor, and Politics in Jamaica and Britain, 1832–1938* (Baltimore, Md.: Johns Hopkins University Press, 1990).

5. For the anxieties of scholarship around these issues, see Arjun Appadurai (ed.), *Globalization* (Durham, N.C.: Duke University Press, 2001).

6. Saskia Sassen, *Territory, Authority, Rights: From Medieval to Global Assemblages* (Princeton, N.J.: Princeton University Press, 2006).

7. Ibid., 168–179.

8. Michael Hardt and Antonio Negri, *Empire* (Cambridge, Mass.: Harvard University Press, 2000), 5–6.

9. Ibid., 14.

10. Ibid., 15.

11. Ibid., 323.

12. Sassen, *Territory, Authority, Rights*, 148–184.

13. Michael Hardt and Antonio Negri, *Multitude* (New York: Penguin Books, 2004), 4.

14. Carl Schmitt, *Political Theology* (1922, translated by George Schwab, Cambridge, Mass.: MIT Press, 1985).

15. Hardt and Negri, *Multitude*, 7.

16. Ibid., 22.

17. Ibid., 202.

18. George Steinmetz, "The State of Emergency and the Revival of American Imperialism: Toward an Authoritarian Post-Fordism," *Public Culture* 15, no. 2 (2003b): 323–345.

19. Kim Lane Scheppele, "A *Realpolitik* Defense of Social Rights," *University of Texas Law Review* 82, no. 7 (2004): 1921–1961.

20. Erika de Wet, *The Chapter VII Powers of the United Nations Security Council* (Portland, Ore.: Hart Publishing, 2004).

21. The public record on the debate over Resolution 1373 can be found at http://daccessdds.un.org/doc/UNDOC/PRO/N01/557/31/PDF/N0155731.pdf?OpenElement.

22. The work plans of the CTC can be found at http://www.un.org/en/sc/ctc/resources/work.html.

23. Country reports are available at http://www.un.org/en/sc/ctc/resources/1373.html. In the notes that follow, the cited reports of states to the Security Council can be found at this site.

24. Brunei Darussalam, CTC Report, June 14, 2002, S/2002/682. Vietnam, CTC report, January 31, 2003, S/2003/128.

25. 50 U.S.C. §2331.

26. Bill C-36, 49–50 Eliz. II Part II.1.83.01 (1) (2001).

27. Kent Roach, *September 11: Consequences for Canada* (Montreal: McGill-Queens University Press, 2003), 25–28.

28. Yemen, CTC report March 2, 2002. Yemen copied language from the Arab Convention on the Suppression of Terrorism, 1998, part 1, translated at http://www.al-bab.com/arab/docs/league/terrorism98.htm.

29. Mexico, CTC Report, August 1, 2002, S/2002/877 at 10; Mexico, CTC Report, September 10, 2003, S/2003/869.

30. For the structure and jurisdiction of the Resolution 1267 Sanctions Committee, see http://www.un.org/sc/committees/1267/index.shtml.

31. France, CTC Report, July 10, 2003, S/2003/270 at 8; Spain, CTC Report, June 9, 2003, S/2003/628; Bulgaria, CTC Report, June 9, 2003, S/2003/692 at 3; Brazil, CTC Report, July 19, 2002, S/2002/796 at 7; Brazil, CTC Report, March 21, 2003, S/2003/356 at 17.

32. Mexico, CTC Report, August 1, 2002, S/2002/877 at 9; Mexico, CTC Report, September 10, 2003, W/2003/869; Venezuela, CTC Report, July 30, 2003, S/2003/774.

33. United States, CTC Report, June 17, 2002, S/2002/674; Argentina, CTC Report, September 13, 2003, S/2002/1023; Spain, CTC Report, June 29, 2004, S/2004/523 at 10.

34. Yemen, CTC Report, March 7, 2002.

35. New Zealand: Telecommunications (Interception Capability) Act, 2004 No. 19. Art. 13.

36. Anneliese Baldaccini and Elspeth Guild (eds.), *Terrorism and the Foreigner: A Decade of Tension around the Rule of Law in Europe* (Leiden: Brill Publishers, 2006).

37. Jennifer Ludden, "Anti-Terrorism Laws Impeding Asylum Seekers," *National Public Radio*, All Things Considered, January 25, 2006.

38. My information about Russia comes from having lived there for most of 2003, from visiting frequently before and since, from interviewing lawyers and judges, and from following the daily press there, in addition to the sources explicitly cited.

39. Kim Lane Scheppele, "'We Forgot about the Ditches': Russian Constitutional Impatience and the Challenge of Terrorism," *Drake Law Review* 53 (2005): 963–1027.

40. Ibid.

41. A number of Western journalists were kidnapped and killed, as were international aid workers. When aid agencies and international reporters pulled out, the Chechen war sank to new levels of invisibility to the outside world.

42. The pedigree of these bombings is contested. Russian officials blamed Chechens; opposition figures blamed the Russian government itself, which, they say, planted the bombs to have a pretext for engaging the Second Chechen War. Some evidence supports each position, but after 9/11 most international opinion came down with the Russian government and blamed the Chechens.

43. "Vladimir Putin Sends Telegram of Sympathy to the United States," RIA Novosti Newswire, September 11, 2001.

44. Alexander Shumilin, "Comrades in Misfortune," *Izvestia*, September 20, 2001, p. 2.

45. Grigory Bondarevsky, quoted in Fred Weir, "Russia Backs American-Led War on Terrorism but Wary of Joining It," Canadian Press Newswire, September 23, 2001.

46. Roland Watson and Vanora Bennett, "Bush Sides with Putin against Chechen Rebels," *The Times* (London), September 27, 2001.

47. Russia, CTC Report, January 18, 2002, S/2001/1284/Add.1.

48. Scheppele, "'We Forgot about the Ditches,'" 1008–1020.

49. S/Res/1566 (2004).

50. Peter Baker, "Putin Moves to Centralize Authority: Plan Would Restrict Elections in Russia," *Washington Post*, September 14, 2004, p. A1.

51. Federal Law No. 35-FZ of March 6, 2006 on Counteraction of Terrorism, Art. 3(1).

52. Russia, CTC Report, June 30, 2006, S/2006/446.

53. Steve Gutterman, "Russia Says Authorities Have Averted a 'Large Terrorist Attack' in Moscow," Reuters News Service, July 18, 2011, reposted at http://www .huffingtonpost.com/2011/07/18/russia-moscow-terrorist-attack-averted_n_901831 .html.

54. The information from this section is based on extensive reading of the daily press in Pakistan, on working through laws and court cases, and on some interviews with Pakistani lawyers, as well as on the sources explicitly listed.

55. Anti-Terrorism Act, 1997 (August 20, 1997), PLD 1997 Central Statutes, available at http://www.fia.gov.pk/ata.htm.

56. *Mehram Ali v. Pakistan*, PLD 1998 SC 1445.

57. Charles H. Kennedy, "The Creation and Development of Pakistan's Anti-Terrorism Regime, 1997–2002." Pp. 387–411 in Satu P. Limaye, Mohan Malik, and

Robert Wirsing (eds.), *Religious Radicalism and Security in South Asia* (Honolulu, Hawaii: Asia-Pacific Center for Security Studies, 2004).

58. *Liaquat Hussain v. Pakistan*, PLD 1999 SC 504.

59. Provisional Constitutional Order No. 1 of 1999 (October 14, 1999), PLD 1999 Central Statutes 446.

60. *Zafar Ali Shah v. Pervez Musharraf,* Chief Executive of Pakistan, PLD 2000 SC 869.

61. Kennedy, "Creation and Development of Pakistan's Anti-Terrorism Regime," 403–404.

62. Ibid., 405.

63. Pakistan, CTC Report, January 10, 2002, S/2001/1310 at 3.

64. Ibid., 7.

65. Pakistan Emergency Economic Development and Trade Support Act, S. 1675, 107th Cong. § 2 (2001).

66. Pub. L. No. 107-57, 115 Stat. 403.

67. Glenn Kessler, "Democracy Gets Small Portion of U.S. Aid; Documents Show Much of the Money Helps Entity Controlled by Musharraf," *Washington Post,* January 6, 2008, p. A17.

68. Terence Cushing, "Pakistan's General Pervez Musharraf: Deceitful Dictator or Father of Democracy?" *Pennsylvania State International Law Review* 21 (2003): 621–647.

69. Ibid., 631.

70. Aqil Shah, "Pakistan's 'Armored' Democracy," *Journal of Democracy* 14, no. 4 (2003): 26–40.

71. Saba Noor, *Evolution of Counter-Terrorism Legislation in Pakistan, US Institute for Peace* (2008), available at san-pips.com/download.php?f=69.pdf.

72. Ibid., 11.

73. Kennedy, "Creation and Development of Pakistan's Anti-Terrorism Regime," 408–409.

74. Amnesty International, *Pakistan: Human Rights Ignored in the "War on Terror"* (AI Index: ASA 33/036/2006), available at http://lib.ohchr.org/HRBodies/UPR/Documents/Session2/PK/AI_PAK_UPR_S2_2008anx_asa330362006.pdf.

75. Osama Siddique, "The Jurisprudence of Dissolutions: Presidential Power to Dissolve Assemblies under the Pakistani Constitution and Its Discontents," *Arizona Journal of International and Comparative Law* 23 (2006): 615–715.

76. Seventeenth Amendment to the Pakistani Constitution (December 2003).

77. Amnesty International, *Annual Report: Pakistan 2010*, available at http://www.amnestyusa.org/research/reports/annual-report-pakistan-2010.

78. Ibid.

79. Human Rights Watch, *Pakistan 2011*, report available at http://www.hrw.org/en/world-report-2011/pakistan.

NINE

Empires and Nations

Convergence or Divergence?

KRISHAN KUMAR

Imperialism is becoming everyday . . . more and more the faith of a nation.
—LORD CURZON, Viceroy of India, 1898 (in Mehta 1999: 5)

Our Empire is not an Empire at all in the ordinary sense of the word. It does not consist of a congeries of nations held together by force, but in the main of one nation, as much as if it were no Empire but an ordinary state.
—J. R. SEELEY ([1883] 1971: 44)

The nationalist idea has a peculiar appeal because of the way in which it asks people to celebrate *themselves* rather than anything beyond them.
—JOHN BREUILLY (2000: 217)

NATION VERSUS EMPIRE

It has long been the conventional wisdom that nations and empires are rivals, sworn enemies. The principle of nationalism is homogeneity, often seen in ethnic terms. Nations strive to embody, or to produce, a common culture. They express a radical egalitarianism: all members of the nation are in principle equal; all partake of the common national "soul." Nations, moreover, are intensely particularistic. Although they do not deny the existence of other nations, or their right to cultivate their ways, they are generally concerned only with their own way, convinced that it is superior to the ways of all other nations. Nationalists, as John Breuilly suggests above, are highly inward looking. They tend to celebrate themselves—"we English," "we Germans," "we French"—simply for their good fortune in being who they are, rather than for any cause or purpose in the world that might justify their existence.

Empires, by contrast, appear to exhibit principles antithetical to those of nations. They are multiethnic or multinational. Far from having or seeking a common culture, they stress the heterogeneity of cultures, especially that between the elite and the local cultures. Empires are hierarchical, opposed in principle to egalitarianism. The lines of solidarity are vertical, between subject and ruler, not, as in nations, horizontal, between equal citizens or fellow members of the same ethnic group. Empires finally aspire to universalism, not to particularism. As with China or Rome, they see themselves as being at the center of the known world, the source of civilization itself, and the carrier of the civilizing process to all the corners of the globe. Far from celebrating merely themselves, they tend to see themselves as the instruments of larger purposes in the world, generally of a moral or religious character. Toward nationalism they are contemptuous, thinking of it as something petty and self-centered. "I am not nacional [*sic*]; that is something for children," declared the Count-Duke Olivares of imperial Spain, in an expression typical of the imperial mentality (in Eliott 1984: 74).[1]

A powerful statement of what Benedict Anderson in his *Imagined Communities* calls "the inner incompatibility of empire and nation" (2006: 93) is to be found in an equally famous study of nationalism, Ernest Gellner's *Nations and Nationalism*. For Gellner empires—seen as essentially premodern in type—belong to what he calls "agro-literate" society, the central fact of which is that "everything in it militates against the definition of political units in terms of cultural boundaries" (1983: 11; see also Breuilly 2000: 198–199; Gellner 1998: 14–24). Power and culture belong to different realms. Crucially, the culture of the elites—often cosmopolitan or international in character—is sharply differentiated from the myriad local cultures of the subordinate strata in the empire. Modern empires, such as the Soviet empire, perpetuate this division, which is why for Gellner they are inherently unstable in a world in which nationalism is the dominant principle.

For nationalism, argues Gellner, closes what in modernity becomes an increasingly intolerable gap between power and culture, state and nation. It insists that only political units in which rulers and ruled share the same culture are legitimate. Its ideal is one state, one culture—which is to say, its ideal is the "nation-state," since it conceives of the nation essentially in terms of a shared culture. In the eyes of nationalists, for rulers of a political unit to belong to a nation other than that of the majority of the ruled "constitutes a quite outstandingly intolerable breach of political propriety" (Gellner 1983: 1). What, to nationalists, could possibly justify the existence of an entity such as the British Empire, in which a handful of British ruled over millions of Indians, Africans, and others, all of whom contained within themselves the seeds of potential nationhood?

In pitting nation against empire, Anderson and Gellner work within a tradition that stretches back to the eighteenth-century European Enlightenment. Anthony Pagden has drawn attention to the thought in particular of Johannn Gottfried Herder, one of the fathers of European nationalism, in "setting up the unalterable opposition of nations and empires." "For Herder, the concept of a people, a *Volk*, and the concept of empire, were simply incompatible. Sooner or later all the world's empires were destined to collapse back into their constituent parts," seen as peoples or nations (Pagden 2003: 131–132; see also Muthu 2003: 210–258; Pagden 1994: 172–188). "Nothing," declared Herder, "appears so directly opposite to the end of government as the unnatural enlargement of states, the wild mixture of various kinds of humans and nations under one sceptre" (in Muthu 2003: 248). This view became a commonplace of nineteenth-century liberal thought as it increasingly allied itself with the national principle. Even those liberals, such as Lord Macaulay and John Stuart Mill, who defended empire accepted that nationality was the "natural" principle and that empires could be justified only insofar as they were leading "backward" peoples toward independent nationhood (Mehta 1999: 77–114; Pitts 2005: 123–162).

The history of the relations between nations and empires in the past two centuries would seem to bear out the truth of this view of difference and divergence. For what has that history been but one of a revolt against empire in the name of nationality? In the wake of World War I, the great continental land empires, commonly denounced as the "prison-houses of nations"—the Russian, the German, the Austro-Hungarian, and the Ottoman empires— all came crashing down, to be replaced by independent nation-states that were widely regarded as their legitimate heirs. The victorious allies' charter of 1918, President Woodrow Wilson's Fourteen Points, loudly proclaimed the triumph of the principle of nationality over that of dynastic empire (Ferguson 2005: 172–173; Hobsbawm 1994: 31; Kappeler 2001: 213; Seton-Watson 1964: 19–23).

Later came the turn of the oceanic or overseas empires of the French, the Dutch, and the British. In a spectacular series of "wars of national liberation," their colonies claimed and enforced their independence on the basis of the nationalist doctrine that had become the norm of the international system. It became common to speak of the movement "from empire to nation" (e.g., Emerson 1960) to sum up this postwar experience. Moreover, the breakup of these empires too had partly been the result of a cataclysmic war,

World War II, and as with the previous war, there was official endorsement of the nationality principle in the United Nations' Universal Declaration of Human Rights of 1948 ("everyone has the right to a nationality"). Later still, in 1989, the "informal colonies" of the Soviet Empire in Eastern Europe declared their independence, followed swiftly thereafter by similar actions among the various national republics or "internal colonies" of the Soviet Union itself (though, as Gellner rightly noted [1998: 57], it was not nationalism itself that brought down the Soviet Union).

The collapse of the Soviet Union in 1991 seemed to set the seal on the long-drawn-out encounter between nation and empire. Despite much talk about the new "American Empire," it was clear that formal empire in the classic sense had for the time being at least reached a certain historic terminus (the announcement of the "end of history" and similar claims that liberal democracy had triumphed in the world were some kind of recognition of this). The opprobrium that had, with increasing force since World War II, gathered around the terms "empire" and "imperialism" seemed now to hold sway everywhere. No state called itself an empire anymore; only its enemies did so. If indeed there was or is an American Empire, as Niall Ferguson argued, it was "an empire in denial," an empire that practiced "the imperialism of anti-imperialism," an empire that "dare not speak its name" (Ferguson 2005: xxii, 6, 61–104; cf. Teschke 2006: 137).[2]

NATIONS AS EMPIRES

But there is another way of telling the story of the relation between nation and empire. In this account, nation and empire are not so much opposed as acknowledged to be alternative or complementary expressions of the same phenomenon of power. Empires can be nations writ large, nations empires under another name.

The great historian Sir Lewis Namier once said that "religion is a sixteenth-century word for nationalism" (quoted in MacLachlan 1996: 15). This seems to be a typical case of a secular thinker's refusal to accept the sincerity or authenticity of the participants' own protestations. The sixteenth-century conflicts that tore apart most European societies were indeed "wars of religion," and any attempt to convert or reduce them to nationalist (or even "protonationalist") conflicts seems, pace Anthony Marx (2003), highly anachronistic.[3] But what is insightful in Namier's comment is the recognition that nationalism can take a variety of forms and expressions, and that "imperial nationalism" therefore may not be as contradictory as it first sounds.

In the first place, it is important to note that many early modern states—those that later evolved into nation-states—saw themselves as empires. David Armitage (2000: 29–32), among others, has stressed that in the sixteenth and seventeenth centuries especially, the term "empire" was often used in its original (Roman) sense of sovereignty or supreme authority, rather than in its later—and more common modern—meaning of rule over a multiplicity of lands and peoples.[4] This allowed many absolutist monarchies, such as the French, and even small city-states, such as Milan under the Visconti Dukes, to declare themselves empires. For English speakers, the best-known example of this is the famous pronouncement in Henry VIII's Act in Restraint of Appeals of 1533 that "this realm of England is an empire, entire of itself." By this was meant that the king of England acknowledged no superiors in his realm, that his rule was sovereign or absolute, and that there could be no appeal to a higher power, such as the pope or the Holy Roman emperor (Ullmann 1979).[5] Here then was an assertion of empire as sovereignty or self-sufficient authority very similar to one of the central claims of the nation-state.

There was a further way in which empire and (nation-) state might overlap. Many of the early modern states were what have been called "composite monarchies" or "multiple kingdoms"—states, that is, such as Spain or Britain, where one monarch might rule over several territories.[6] Thus Spain—leaving aside what we might think of as its more classically imperial possessions in the New World and elsewhere—contained Castilians, Catalans, Basques, and others, in their several territories; Britain, with the accession of James I in 1603, and more firmly with the Act of Union of 1707, was a composite state made up of English, Welsh, Scottish, and Irish subjects of the monarch (Armitage 2000: 22–23; Eliott 1992; Koenigsberger 1987; Russell 1995). Such states, in other words, contained that variety and plurality of peoples and lands that empire connoted, both classically and in modern times. Whether therefore the stress was on sovereignty or multiple rule, state and empire were conjoint terms for much of the early modern period—as found in the writings of Bodin, Hobbes, Grotius, and Spinoza (Armitage 2000: 14–23; Koebner 1961: 52; Pagden 1995: 13–14).

But there is an even more compelling consideration that might lead us to see convergence rather than divergence between (nation-) states and empires. Most nation-states, or what became nation-states, are, like most empires, the result of conquest and colonization. The later ideology of nationalism of course disguises this unpalatable fact, as it exhibits amnesia about many other aspects of the violent origins of nations (Marx 2003: 29–32). The rise of nationalist historiography in the nineteenth century drove a wedge between "domestic" and "extraterritorial" history, between the nation-state and empire—both the territorial empires that had preceded it and the extra-European empires that were constructed across the globe in the eighteenth and nineteenth centuries. Nevertheless, as David Armitage says, "the nation-state as it had been precipitated out of a system of aggressively competing nations . . . functioned as 'the empire *manqué*'"—within Europe itself as much as beyond it (Armitage 2000: 14).

Robert Bartlett (1993) has given the classic account of how European states were formed by a process of "conquest, colonization and cultural change," in the High Middle Ages, between 950 and 1350. From their heartlands in the old Carolingian lands—modern France and western Germany—Frankish and Norman knights swept westward, eastward, and southward. Normans conquered England and went on to take Wales and Ireland. They put enormous pressure on the Scots, forcing them, on pain of survival, to adapt to Anglo-Norman culture and institutions. In the East, Germans cleared the forests, established new towns, and settled in old ones—such as Prague—in large numbers, opening the way to the eventual incorporation of these lands in Prussia and other German states. Burgundian families established their rule in Portugal and León-Castile and spearheaded the Christian Reconquest of Andalucia from the Moors.[7] The Normans conquered Sicily and from this base spread the ways and institutions of Latin Christianity throughout the southern Mediterranean and many parts of the Levant (aided by the Crusading movement that established the Crusader kingdom of Jerusalem). In this massive centrifugal movement, a uniform system of town charters, commercial law, coinage, language (Latin), educational, and ecclesiastical institutions came into being in a huge swath stretching from the Baltic to the eastern Mediterranean. "Europe, the initiator of one of the world's major processes of conquest, colonization and cultural transformation, was also the product of one" (Bartlett 1993: 314).

This dynamic process of conquest and colonization meant that the states and kingdoms that were established in medieval and early modern Europe nearly all had the appearance of empires. England, for instance, once united by the Norman Conquest of 1066, went on in its turn—largely at first under Norman auspices—to "unite" (that is, conquer) the peoples of Wales, Ireland, and eventually Scotland, into another state, the United Kingdom, and another nation, the British.[8] Observing that "many of the most successful nation states of the present started life as empires," Niall Ferguson asks, "what is the modern United Kingdom of Great Britain and Northern Ireland if not the legatee of an earlier English imperialism" (2005: xii)? Just as Europe itself, so too England began its great colonizing venture in the world with an initial act of "internal colonization," the construction of an "inner empire" of Great Britain that became the launching pad for the creation of an "outer empire" of "Greater Britain" overseas (cf. Cooper 2005b: 172; Kumar 2003: 60–88).

France achieved nationhood by a process of conquest launched by the Capetian kings from their base in the Île-de-France and leading eventually to the forcible incorporation of Brittany, Burgundy, Languedoc, Normandy, Gascony, Aquitaine, Provence, and several other once proud and independent principalities of the Carolingian successor kingdoms of West Francia, East Francia, and Lotharingia. At the point at which, in 987, Hugh Capet became king of West Francia, the kingdom, says Colin Jones, "looked more like a collection of potential future states than a single, unitary one" (1999: 75). It took several hundred years, and the suppression of many internal rebellions, for the French kings to weld together the disparate territories of their "inner empire" (Collins 1995). Even the great centralizing influence of the French Revolution still left much to be done, at least in the countryside, where the majority of the people lived. According to Eugen Weber (1976), it was only in the late nineteenth century that the process seriously began of turning peasants of many tongues and disparate traditions into Frenchmen and Frenchwomen. Rogers Brubaker points out that the idea of *la mission civilisatrice*, usually applied to justify France's overseas empire, initially had reference to the civilizing mission of the French state in relation to its own domestic inhabitants. This "internal *mission civilisatrice*" was to be carried out by the *instituteurs*, the school teachers, "whose mission was to *institute* the nation" (Brubaker 1992: 11). As Eugen Weber says, "the famous hexagon [i.e., France in its current form] can itself be seen as a colonial empire shaped over the centuries: a complex of territories conquered, annexed, and integrated in a political and administrative whole, many of them with strongly developed national or regional personalities, some of them with traditions that were specifically un- or anti-French" (1976: 485; see also Kuzio 2002: 32).[9]

Spain shows even more clearly the pattern of unification through conquest—the more so as it remains in several respects still incomplete, with a persistent Basque separatist movement and intermittent calls for independence emanating from Catalonia. From the time of the union of the kingdoms of Aragon and Castile in 1469, Spanish monarchs engaged in a strenuous and only partly successful effort to bring adjacent territories into a single state and to form a Spanish nation.[10] That the process was tortuous, marked by frequent rebellions and civil wars, is made clear in the comment of an eighteenth-century Spanish civil servant, Olavide, that Spain was "a body composed of other smaller bodies separated, and in opposition to one another, which oppress and despise each other and are in a continuous state of civil war.... Modern Spain can be considered as a body without energy ... a monstrous Republic formed of little republics which confront each other" (in Carr 2000: 6).

Spain, France, and England/Britain are the countries most regularly invoked in the literature on nationalism as early, well-formed nation-states (see, e.g., A. Smith 1991: 55). It is salutary to remember, then, how much of conquest and colonization there was in the formation of these nation-states and how imperfectly the word "nation," with its suggestion of consensus, community, and homogeneity, sums up the resulting product. "Spain," "France," "Britain," and their respective nations were the result of the more or less forcible integration of neighboring lands and peoples by dominant groups whose institutions and culture often differed considerably from those of the conquered peoples. This pattern has often been noted for later examples of nation building. For example, it was common to say, in the nineteenth century and later, that "Germany" was made by Prussian conquest of the other German states; less commonly, but perhaps equally accurately, it might be said that "Italy" was made by the Piedmontese conquest of the other Italian states (which explains the famous remark of Massimo d'Azeglio in 1868, that "we have made Italy, now we must make Italians"). And it has frequently been pointed out that many of the "new nations" of Africa and Asia are so only in name, that they are artificial creations, the result largely of the wars and political maneuverings of the former imperial powers. What we need to stress is that this pattern is not simply typical of latecomers to nation building but has been the norm since the very earliest examples. Many "nation-states," to put it another way, are empires in miniature; they have been formed as empires have usually been formed. There is in that sense an inescapably imperial dimension to the nation-state.[11]

EMPIRES AS NATIONS: "IMPERIAL NATIONALISM"

If nations have often been conceived and constructed as empires, might the reverse also be true? If nations can be seen as mini-empires, can empires be seen as large nations? Does imperialism converge with nationalism? What are the degrees—and limits—of this convergence?

Anthony Smith has in several places (e.g., 1986, 2004) argued that all nations are constituted by "core" *ethnies*, around which may cohere other ethnic groups in subordinate roles. In the English case, for instance, it is impossible to ignore the contribution over the centuries of Norwegians, Normans, Huguenots, Scots, Welsh, Irish, Jews, Indians, Afro-Caribbeans, and other ethnicities to that mix we call "Englishness." But it is equally clear that, by about the sixteenth century at the latest, there had emerged something like an English nation (which is—*pace* Greenfeld [1992]—quite a different matter from saying that we can find English *nationalism* in this period). The English language, for one thing, had by then come into its own, supremely with the works of Shakespeare, Marlowe, Spenser, and others. Protestantism was beginning to do its work, especially in its nonconformist forms. Parliament and the common law were already beginning to be acknowledged as emblems of the national culture. This was the beginning of something like "racial Anglo-Saxonism," to use Reginald Horsman's (1981) term, though it had little of the biological character ascribed to it in its nineteenth-century guise. It does mean, though, that by this time a distinctive and dominant *ethnie* had emerged in England, setting the terms and conditions within which later groups were invited to find, or to force, a place (for other examples, see Kaufmann 2004). It is this core *ethnie* that lends its peculiar qualities to the nation; it is this group that defines the "national character," difficult as it always is to enumerate its attributes precisely.

Can we not say something similar about empires? Most empires are constructed by a particular people—the Romans, the Spanish, the English/British, the French, the Russians, the Turks, and so forth. It is they who name it and oversee its development. Whatever their numbers, it is they who tend to define its character. They are, we may say, the "state-bearing" peoples of the empire. And, just as a particular ethnic group might come to identify itself with the nation it creates, so a particular people or nation might come to identify itself with the empire it founds. Nations and empires, we have said, tend to think of their purpose or destiny in the world in different terms, the one more inner, the other more outward looking. But it seems fair to say that in both cases we can discern a group or groups that identify with their creation and derive their sense of their collective identity from it.

I have elsewhere (Kumar 2000, 2003: 30–35) argued that we can call the sense of identity of imperial peoples a kind of "imperial" or "missionary nationalism." There is, I agree, a double danger in so doing. In the first place, the ideology of nationalism does not emerge until the late eighteenth century, and it is therefore anachronistic and misleading to speak of nationalism in any form before that time. Since empires for the most part clearly predate the age of nationalism—even if they persist well into it—we obviously need to specify clearly what we might mean by "imperial nationalism." In the second place, for all the suggestive parallels, empires are not nations (and nations are not empires), as we shall see. Hence to speak of imperial nationalism runs the risk of confusing two entities—nations and empires—that for most purposes need to be kept separate.

The reason for nevertheless thinking that "imperial nationalism" might be a useful concept is the gain that comes from seeing two disparate phenomena from a common vantage point. Like nationalists in relation to their nation, imperialists feel that there is something special or unique about their empire. It has a mission or purpose in the world. This may, again as with nationalists, endow imperial peoples with a sense of their own superiority, a feeling of inherent goodness as of a people specially chosen to carry out a task (cf. Smith 2003).[12] Imperialists, like nationalists, are true believers.

What are the causes or missions that have given imperial peoples a sense of their collective identity? For most Europeans, the pattern was set by the Romans, with their belief that they were giving nothing less than civilization—Roman laws, Roman institutions, Roman culture—to the world. Hence it was possible for the Romans to identify their empire with the whole known world, the *orbis terrarum*. Later European empires, from the Holy Roman Empire onward, repeated the claim, to an almost wearying degree, though the content might vary depending on the particular place or time. Thus although the Spaniards, like most imperialists, saw themselves in the image of Rome, it was as a Catholic power that they saw their mission, in Europe and in the New World (a role intensified with the Protestant Reformation). The Austrian Habsburgs took up the torch from their Spanish cousins, putting themselves not just at the head of the Counter-Reformation but also—as the *Östmark* or *Österreich*—seeing themselves as the defenders of European civilization on its eastern flank, against the threat of the infidel Turks. The Russians, proclaiming Moscow the "Third Rome" and themselves the legatees of the doomed Byzantines, aspired to continue the struggle for orthodoxy in the world. A similar resolve, but for a contrary cause, animated the English when as "the Protestant nation" they attempted to lead the Protestant crusade in Europe and the New World, especially against the machinations of the Catholic powers of Spain and France. The French, for their own part, having first hitched their empire to the Catholic cause, after their Great Revolution of 1789 and the turn toward republicanism, increasingly came to identify French imperialism with *la mission civilisatrice* (as, in the later phases of the British Empire, did the British). This too, in its own terms, was the mission of the

Russians in their second or Soviet Empire, the spreading of reason and science to the benighted in the form of communism. In this renewed emphasis, begun with the Romans, on the mission to civilize and enlighten, the wheel had come full circle.[13]

Merely to list these causes or missions is to cast doubt on the analogy between nationalism and imperialism. Nationalist causes are not typically like these. For some time in the early nineteenth century, when a form of liberal nationalism flourished under the banner of Giuseppe Mazzini and his followers, nationalism did indeed ally itself with the noble causes of spreading freedom and enlightenment in the world (Alter 1994: 19–23, 39–65). But the period that followed, the period of "organic nationalism," showed another face of nationalism: one that was vindictive and intolerant toward rivals, one that trumpeted the power and glory of particular nations, one that asked its citizens to die for the nation whatever the cause it chose to embrace. The Nazis' celebration of the Teutonic or Aryan peoples, in and for themselves, indicated the logical endpoint of this type of nationalism (Alter 1994: 26–38; Hobsbawm 1992: 101–130).

Imperialist ideologies are universalistic, not particularistic. That difference has to be borne in mind. Imperial peoples do not, unlike nationalists, celebrate themselves; they celebrate the causes of which they are the agents or carriers. It is from this that they derive their sense of themselves and their place in the world. But the parallel with nationalism is still instructive. In both cases we see the attempt to effect a fusion, a symbiosis almost, between a people and a political entity. Imperial nationalism plays down membership of a "mere nation," with its tendency toward self-congratulation and self-importance; but it does so in order to insist on a higher form of nationalism, one that justifies the nation in terms of its commitment to a cause that goes beyond the nation.

It is somewhat ironic, in view of this, that the greatest apparent convergence between imperialism and nationalism is to be found in the very period—from the 1870s to World War I—in which nationalism threw off its liberal mantle and presented itself in the guise of naked power seeking. The historian Wolfgang Mommsen speaks of "the deformation of national politics" in this period: "The idea of the nation state progressively lost those elements which in the first half of the nineteenth century had made it an emancipatory ideology, directed against the arbitrary rule of princes and small aristocratic elites, and an intellectual weapon in the campaign for constitutional government. Instead it came to be associated with the power-status of the established national culture, and the imposition of its values on ethnic or cultural minorities both within and beyond the body politic was now considered essential" (Mommsen 1990: 215; see also Mommsen 1978).

Mommsen sees this deformation as directly connected to the "high imperialism" of the times, when the great powers—in particular Britain, France, and Germany—competed for dominance on the world stage through the acquisition of larger and larger territorial empires (Mommsen 1990: 212). This was the view too of another liberal thinker, J. A. Hobson, the great critic of imperialism, who saw imperialism as "a debasement of . . . genuine nationalism, by attempts to overflow its natural banks and absorb the near or distant territory of reluctant and unassimilable peoples" ([1902] 1988: 6). For Hobson as for other liberal thinkers, nationality still appeared the natural and desirable principle—a "plain highway to internationalism"— with imperialism a "perversion of its nature and purpose" (11).

Such a position has seemed too kind to nationalism, in the view of other thinkers. For them nationalism is inherently imperialistic, just as it was inevitable at this time that imperialism would take the form of nationalist rivalries. Imperialism is then seen not so much as a perversion as a more or less natural extension of a power-seeking nationalism; in its turn, the nation comes to conceive of itself in the image of empire, the traditional emblem of grandeur and the supreme expression of Great Power status. "Imperialism and nationalism," says Christopher Bayly, "were part of the same phenomenon. . . . The rise of exclusive nationalisms, grasping and using the powers of the new and more interventionist state, was the critical force propelling both the new imperialism and the hardening of the boundaries between majority and assumed 'ethnic' populations across the world. . . . Imperialism and nationalism reacted on each other to redivide the world and its people" (2004: 230, 242–243).[14]

Once again, therefore, the ground between empire and nation, imperialism and nationalism, seems to crumble and disappear. If nations can be seen as empires, then empires, especially modern empires, can seem no more than nations writ large. The British Empire, or "Greater Britain" as some termed it, is in this view no more than the expression of British nationalism, the desire to expand the British presence and power in the world (see, e.g., Seeley [1883] 1971); the French Empire, partly in rivalry with Britain, the expression of a wounded French nationalism in the wake of the crushing defeat at the hands of Prussia in 1871 (see Schivelbusch 2004: 103–187). Imperialism appears as hypertrophied nationalism, perhaps, but nationalism nonetheless, expressing its ultimate logic and tendency.

EMPIRE AND NATION: CONTINUING ANTAGONISMS AND TENSIONS

Is this then the conclusion? Are Gellner, Anderson, and so many others wrong in drawing such a sharp distinction between the principle of empire and that of the nation? Is imperialism simply nationalism under another name?

It would surely be premature, not to say facile, so to conclude. Ann Laura Stoler and Frederick Cooper, reacting against the centrality accorded to the nation-state in conceptions of European history since the eighteenth century, rightly warn that "it is not clear that simply considering empire as an extension of nation will get to the root of the problem" (1997: 22). No more, perhaps, than reversing this procedure and seeing nations as extensions of empires or as empires in miniature. We have to respect nations and empires for their differences as well as their admitted similarities. Nations are not empires and empires are not nations, whatever the gains in looking for parallels and commonalities.

Max Weber once observed that while all "Great Powers" tend, for reasons of prestige, to be imperialist and "expansive," this was not the case with all nations, some of which sought their principles and sense of national pride from within themselves. "Not all political structures are equally 'expansive.' They do not all strive for an outward expansion of their power, or keep their force in readiness for acquiring political power over other territories and communities by incorporating them or making them dependent. Hence, as structures of power, political organizations vary in the extent to which they are turned outward" (Weber 1978: 910). Britain, France, and Germany might feel the need for empire but not so Switzerland or Norway.

This perception might be one way of considering the fact that empire and nation can, at different times, alternate in the striving of states. In the early modern period, the examples of the Spanish and Portuguese empires made it seem that empire was the only way of establishing one's presence in the world. The British, Dutch, and French hurried to imitate the imperial style of those countries, with a considerable measure of success. Later, in the nineteenth century, as the national principle gained in strength, nation-state formation seemed to offer a more fulfilling, as well as for many a more practicable, option. This was especially so in the case of smaller or weaker countries, such as Italy, Poland, Ireland, Norway, and the Slav peoples of the Habsburg empire. Here empire was the enemy, not the goal.

But nationalism, rather than imperialism, was not just for small or weak countries. The tension between nation and empire could often be seen within the same country, including some of the most powerful, at the same time. Britain in the nineteenth century had its "Little Englanders" who, especially after the loss of the North American colonies, felt that empire was ruinous to British commerce and corrupting in its moral and political effects at home. The way forward was for Britain to renounce imperial entanglements and to exert its influence by the example of its peaceful and prosperous existence as one nation among others (see, e.g., Gott 1989; Thornton 1968: 1–56).[15] In France, after the loss of Alsace-Lorraine following the Franco-Prussian War of 1871, there was a bitter struggle between the imperialists, keen on matching Britain's imperial power, and the nationalists who felt that it was essential to France's national honor to recover the lost provinces and for whom empire was a crippling distraction (Baumgart 1982: 55–68; Schivelbusch 2004: 176–187).

Nationalism and imperialism could therefore, despite their similarities, point in very different directions. A world of nations, accepting the particularities of different peoples and promoting the cultivation of unique national cultures, was quite different from a world of competing empires, each intent on reforming the world in its own image. J. A. Hobson, the best-known writer on modern imperialism and one who was fully alive to the connections between nationalism and imperialism, nevertheless felt the need to make it plain at the very outset of his study that the kind of imperialism that was collusive with nationalism was of a very novel and highly untypical kind. It was novel and untypical because it took the form of competing nations, each striving to magnify their empires; whereas the true principle of empire was unitary and universal.

> The notion of a number of competing empires is essentially modern. The root idea of empire in the ancient and the medieval world was that of a federation of States, under a hegemony, covering in general terms the entire known recognized world, such as was held by Rome under the so-called *pax Romana*. When Roman citizens, with full civic rights, were found all over the explored world, in Africa and Asia, as well as in Gaul and Britain, Imperialism contained a genuine element of internationalism. With the fall of Rome this conception of a single empire wielding political authority over the civilized world did not disappear. On the contrary, it survived all the fluctuations of the Holy Roman Empire. Even after the definite split between the Eastern and Western sections had taken place at the close of the fourth century, the theory of a single state, divided for administrative purposes, survived. Beneath every cleavage or antagonism, and notwithstanding the severance of many independent kingdoms and provinces, this

ideal unity of the empire lived. It formed the conscious avowed ideal of Charlemagne. . . . Rudolf of Habsburg not merely revived the idea, but laboured to realize it through Central Europe, while his descendant Charles V gave a very real meaning to the term by gathering under the unity of his imperial rule the territories of Austria, Germany, Spain, the Netherlands, Sicily and Naples. In later ages this dream of a European Empire animated the policy of Peter the Great, Catherine, and Napoleon. (Hobson [1902] 1988: 8–9)

There is not much to add to this masterly sketch, merely to say that its accuracy has been confirmed by most later studies of the imperial idea (see, e.g., Folz 1969; Muldoon 1999; Münkler 2005). Hobson goes on to say that the "internationalism of empire" was continued, with diminishing force, in the "humane cosmopolitanism" of the Enlightenment and the French Revolution, only to "wither before the powerful revival of nationalism" in the nineteenth century. Nationalism properly understood and practiced, he continued to believe, was not in necessary contradiction with internationalism. But linked to an aggressive and competitive imperialism, which transforms "the wholesome stimulative rivalry of varied national types into the cut-throat struggle of competing empires," it threatened "the peace and progress of mankind" (Hobson [1902] 1988: 10–12).[16] Hobson saw no hope, or even necessity, of reviving the universal empire. He was no liberal imperialist. But he was clear about what had been the consequence of the degeneration of both the national and the imperial ideal. They came to feed off each other, turning their backs on the promise of their respective principles.

The recent revival of interest in empire has, no doubt, many sources. But one surely has to do with concerns over the recent excesses of nationalism, in the former Soviet Union and Yugoslavia, as well as in many areas of the Middle East, Asia, and Africa. Already in the mid-nineteenth century, when nationalism was only just getting into its stride, Lord Dalberg-Acton warned against the oppressive and exclusive principle of nationality, which, "by making the State and nation commensurate with each other in theory . . . reduces practically to a subject condition all other nationalities that may be within the boundary" ([1862] 1996: 36).[17] Against this he defended both the British and the Austrian empires as bastions of liberty. Something similar has recently been said by a historian of the Russian Empire, Andreas Kappeler. "Studying the history of multi-ethnic empires," he says, "can serve to remind us that there are alternative principles with regard to the structure of states and societies" and can "also clarify the problematical nature of the (ethnically restricted) nation state." Kappeler thinks that "as in the successor states of the Habsburg Empire there may even come a time when people will idealize and look back nostalgically at the Russian multi-ethnic empire whose geographical borders and intellectual horizons far exceeded those of the ethnic nation states" (2001: 3, 392).[18]

There is a certain amount of nostalgia around, no doubt, as when certain enthusiasts for the European Union talk about a "revived Habsburg Empire" or when people look back admiringly to the *millet* system of the Ottoman Empire as some kind of model for our "multicultural" societies. There are even those who see in the earlier empires some presage of present-day globalization and praise, for instance, the *pax Britannica* of the British Empire as an exemplar of a possible world order (see, e.g., Ferguson 2004). One can dispute all of these, if one chooses to. But there can surely be no doubt that empires have much to teach us about many of the problems that preoccupy us today: multiculturalism, transnationalism, diasporas, the nation-state in an era of globalization, multinational corporations, and the possibilities of supranational organization. Empires are, almost by definition, multicultural, multiethnic, and even multinational. They have been created by and in turn the cause of vast migrations of people across the globe. They preceded the nation-state and they, or something like them, may well succeed it. None of these features, it need hardly be said, apply to nations; empires and nations, for all the interesting ways in which they overlap, do in the end belong to different worlds.

Not only that, but it can be argued that these worlds have interacted with each other for much longer than we are inclined to think. The nineteenth century is often labeled the "era of nationalism," but we need to remember that empire persisted well into the twentieth century and that it is only with the end of the great overseas European empires in the 1950s and 1960s that the nation-state really came into its own. The nineteenth century, as several thinkers have stressed, was a world of empires as much as, perhaps more than, it was of the new nation-state (Cooper 2005b: 171; Ferguson 2005: xi–xiii). What were the dominant actors on the world stage—Britain, France, Russia, the Ottomans, Austria-Hungary, Germany, China, Japan, perhaps also America—but empires?[19] Not until after World War II was the hold of empire on the world loosened, and even then it was given a significant renewal with the expansion of the Soviet Union's "informal" empire in Eastern Europe. "In the 1960s," says Frederick Cooper, "a world of nation-states finally came into being, over three centuries after the peace of Westphalia, 180 years after the French and American revolutions, and 40 years after the Wilsonian assertions of national self-determination" (2005b: 190).

It might also be worth observing that this "world of nation-states" was closely supervised by two superpowers, the United States and the Soviet Union, both of whom while denying the fact acted very much like the empires of old. Even the demise of the Soviet Union in 1991 still left one "lonely superpower" (Huntington 1999) to carry on the imperial task of policing the world. The future of this venture remains highly uncertain; but even if it does not succeed, it is highly unlikely that an anarchical world of nation-states will be the outcome. The world is too tightly intermeshed for the major nations to accept such an arrangement. Nationalism, said Ernest Renan over a century ago, is "the law of the age in which we live." But, he predicted, "nations are not something eternal. They have had their beginnings, they shall have their end" ([1882] 2001: 175). What is even more remarkable to contemplate is not just the end of nations but the possibility that nations, or at least nation-states, never really had the world to themselves, even for a relatively short period. They have always lived in the shadow of empire.

All this should make us rethink our common notions of the presumed sequence "from empire to nation" or of an "age of nations" succeeding an "age of empire." Nations and empires, as Frederick Cooper (2005b) stresses, have been variable forms of the political imagination throughout the recent period—at least since 1800, to go back no further. They have coexisted with and mutually influenced each other, even to the point where the same state might act or appear at one time as an empire, at another as a nation-state. China and the United States—both ambiguous cases of empire in the literature—are two obvious examples of this (see, e.g., Osterhammel 1986), but one could say the same thing about Britain or France. Nations and empires are different ways of conceiving the world as well as the collective self, but that has not prevented each of them from being regarded at various times as alternative possibilities, depending on their perceived fitness for the occasion.

As ideological formations, nations and nationalism may well have occupied center stage in the modern world order, at least in the last two centuries. But empires have also been part of that order. Their disappearance has been relatively recent, and the signs of their existence are still all around us, not least in the large populations from the former empires that are now part of the life of most major Western cities. If empires belong to history, it is to that aspect of history that has an inescapable afterlife. "The empires of our time were short-lived, but they have altered the world for ever," says a character in V. S. Naipaul's novel *The Mimic Men* ([1967] 1985: 32); "their passing away is their least significant feature."[20]

NOTES

A different version of this chapter previously appeared as "Nation-States as Empires, Empires as Nation-States," *Theory and Society* 39 (2010): 119–143.

1. Max Weber made a similar point in his contrast between the "striving for prestige" characteristic of "Great Powers" and mere "national pride": "such pride can be highly developed, as is the case among the Swiss and the Norwegians, yet it may actually be strictly isolationist and free from pretensions to political prestige" (1978: 911).

2. One of the best accounts of the "American Empire"—which she calls the "empire of capital" (Wood 2005)—recognizes the difference between this form of empire and the historic instances of empire, though Wood finds the origins of this new kind of imperialism in aspects of earlier British rule, for instance, over Ireland. See also on this Mann (2003) and Steinmetz (2005a); and for an excellent collection of essays comparing America with other forms of empire, see Calhoun et al. (2006b).

3. I have similar objections to the discussion, which closely parallels Marx's and on which Marx draws, in Gorski (2000). See Kumar (2005).

4. See also Pagden (1995: 12–13). Koebner (1961: 18–64) emphasizes the importance of the Italian humanists in restoring the original meaning of "lawful authority" to the term "empire," thus allowing those states outside the Holy Roman Empire—which had more or less monopolized the concept of *imperium* during the Middle Ages—to declare themselves empires. It is worth emphasizing nevertheless that the more modern meaning of empire can also be found in the classical period. Both the sense of empire as sovereign rule and its application to rule over a variety of peoples can be found in Roman usage from a relatively early time (Koebner 1961: 4–6, 11–16; Lichtheim 1974: 24–26; Richardson 1991: 1; Woolf 2001: 313).

5. The general form of the argument that, like the emperor in his empire, the king was emperor in his own kingdom (*rex in regno suo erat imperator*) had long been deployed by the canon layers, especially in France, against the universalist claims of the Holy Roman Empire. See Folz (1969: 156–157, 160); Muldoon (1999: 143, 146).

6. Some scholars have wished to distinguish between "composite monarchies" and "multiple kingdoms." Thus seventeenth-century England can be said to be a composite monarchy because, with particular laws for such counties as Kent and the County Palatine of Chester, it "did not have a single uniform system of law characteristic of the single state"; whereas James VI and I, as king of England, Scotland, and Ireland, ruled over a multiple kingdom, the kingdom that he—but not the English or Scottish parliaments—termed "Britain." Conrad Russell, who makes this distinction, argues that "all multiple kingdoms are composite monarchies, but not all composite monarchies are multiple kingdoms" (1995: 133; see also Armitage 2000: 22). While the distinction may be useful for certain purposes, it is not one that has found favor with most commentators, who tend to use "composite monarchy" and "multiple kingdoms" more or less as synonyms. See, for example, Pocock (2005).

It should hardly need pointing out that medieval states, even more than early modern ones, were composite monarchies and to that extent approximated to empires. As Muldoon says, giving the example of the twelfth-century English Angevin monarchy, with its extensive territories in England, Wales, Ireland, France, and elsewhere: "All the major medieval kingdoms, consisting as they did of a conglomeration of dynastic lands, were empires whether or not anyone chose to employ the term" (1999: 142).

7. "The Frankish warriors came to see themselves as men 'to whom God has given victory as a fief.' They anticipated an expansionary future and developed what can only be called an expansionary mentality." By the late Middle Ages they provided kings and queens for 80 percent of European kingdoms. "The penetration of the British Isles by French knights, the participation of the Burgundian aristocracy in the wars of the Reconquest and the dominance of Franks in the crusading ventures of the eastern Mediterranean had resulted in the establishment of new Frankish dynasties from Scotland to Cyprus" (Bartlett 1993: 43, 90).

8. The Scots, it is true, unlike the Welsh and Irish, were never formally conquered by the English; but there is no doubt that the Union with Scotland in 1707 had strong elements of a shotgun marriage about it; everyone knew that England was prepared to invade if the Scottish parliament rejected the union (see Kumar 2003: 135–136 and references there).

9. The idea that France is a nation formed by conquest was clear to Ernest Renan. He reminds us of that uncomfortable fact in the context of his famous observation that "forgetfulness, and I shall even say historical error, form an essential factor in the creation of a nation." The French, like all other nations, forget, and must forget, that "unity is ever achieved by brutality. The union of Northern and Southern France was the result of an extermination, and of a reign of terror that lasted for nearly a hundred years" (Renan [1882] 2001: 166).

10. The imperial ambitions of Castille were clear even before the union with Aragon in the fifteenth century. "Iberian unity, which remained a central political objective of the Christian kings as they moved south from Leon, found expression in terms of the recovery of the ancient Roman province of Hispania. In 1077 Alfonso VI was already using the title 'imperator constitutus super omnes Ispaniae nationes,' and in 1135 his successor Alfonso VII actually had himself crowned 'Hispaniae Imperator'" (Pagden 1995: 41).

11. For some interesting reflections on the imperial dimension of the nation-state, with special reference to France, "the most talked-about model of the nation-state," see Stoler and Cooper (1997: 22–23).

12. Cf. Max Weber, who links the "prestige interests" of the Great Powers—which generally takes the form of a drive toward imperial expansion—with "the legend of a providential 'mission,'" which he sees as a manifestation of "the idea of a nation." Just as with empire, then, "those to whom the representatives of the [national] idea zealously turned were expected to shoulder this mission" (Weber 1978: 925).

13. For these examples, see Kumar (2000) and the references therein. For a good discussion of the Christianizing mission, differently conceived, of the Spanish and British in the Americas, see Elliott (2006: 57–87, 184–218).

14. The view of an association between imperialism and nationalism is a longstanding one—almost, one might say, the traditional one, at least for this period (see, e.g., Schumpeter [1919] 1951). With the rise of Italian, German, and Japanese

fascism in the 1920s and 1930s, generally seen as a form of extreme nationalism and expressing itself in distinctly imperialistic form, the affinity between imperialism and nationalism seemed to many only too obvious. See on this especially Arendt (1958: 123–302) and Kohn (1932: 49–76). Several more recent writers take a similar view: see Armitage (2000: 14); Hobsbawm (1987: 158–161); Lichtheim (1974: 81); Pagden (2003: 132–138); and Zimmer (2003: 35–38). D. K. Fieldhouse remarks that "the rise of the imperialist ideology, this belief that colonies were an essential attribute of any great nation, is one of the most astonishing facts of the period [1870–1914]." It was also, he says, "an international creed, with beliefs that seemed to differ very little from one country to another." He cites the German nationalist the historian Heinrich von Treitschke, in 1879: "Every virile people has established colonial power. . . . All great nations in the fulness of their strength have desired to set their mark upon barbarian lands and those who fail to participate in this great rivalry will play a pitiable role in the future to come. The colonizing impulse has become a vital question for every great nation" (Fieldhouse 1961: 207). Bernard Porter quotes Finland's president Paasikivi in 1940, "Alle Grossmächte sind imperialistisch" in support of the view that "nations turn to empire-building when they are large and powerful" (2004: 310).

The Marxist view of imperialism, which sees it as the "highest stage" of capitalism, also tends to go along with this view, since Lenin and others regarded imperialism as the necessary expression of the rivalry of the leading nation-states of the period as they competed for markets. But in the long run Lenin thought that nationalism, especially in the colonial world, would turn against imperialism and become the agency of its destruction. See on this Mommsen (1982: 29–65).

15. A characteristic expression of the Little Englanders was William Cobbett's: "It is my business, and the business of every Englishman, to take care of England, and England alone. . . . It is not our business to run about the world to look after people to set free; it is our business to look after ourselves" (in Gott 1989: 94).

16. "While co-existent nationalities," says Hobson, "are capable of mutual aid involving no direct antagonism of interest, co-existent empires following each its own imperial career of territorial aggrandisement are natural necessary enemies" ([1902] 1988: 12).

17. A number of recent works have restated this point about the exclusionary, and potentially murderous, tendency of nationalism—for example, Mann (2005), Marx (2003), and Wimmer (2002).

18. It is worth remembering that one of the first and most influential works in the revival of nationalist theory, Elie Kedourie's *Nationalism* (1961), was a passionate protest against nationalism and that a later work (Kedourie 1971) by Kedourie explicitly compares nations and empires, to the decided detriment of the former. See for a discussion of Kedourie's views, O'Leary (2002). There are also decidedly positive readings of empire in several recent works, particularly those concerned with "the American Empire" (e.g., Ferguson 2004, 2005: esp. 24–26).

19. Eric Hobsbawm has remarked that "the era from 1875 to 1914 may be called the Age of Empire not only because it developed a new kind of imperialism, but also for

a much more old-fashioned reason. It was probably the period of modern world history in which the number of rulers officially calling themselves, or regarded by western diplomats as deserving the title of, 'emperors' was at its maximum." As Hobsbawm notes, the title was claimed not just by the rulers of Germany, Austria, Russia, Turkey, and Britain but also by those of China, Japan, Persia, Ethiopia, and Morocco (Hobsbawm 1987: 56–57).

20. Cf. the remarks of Bernard Cohn and Nicholas Dirks in emphasizing the wide-ranging imperial legacies in the contemporary world: "Colonialism played an active role in the cultural project of legitimation and in the technological development of new forms of state power. Colonialism also left active legacies in the form of the modal Western states, in the constitution of postcolonial relations between the West and the third world, and in the new histories and states that have been constructed in the twentieth century. Colonialism is too important a subject to be relegated either to the history of nineteenth century Europe on the one hand or to the negative nationalisms of third world studies on the other." Just as the European nation-state "was predicated on its own colonial experience," so too third-world nationalism was a "response to colonial experience [which] reproduced (though with crucial differences) the European experience" (Cohn and Dirks 1988: 229).

TEN

The New Surgical Colonialism
China, Africa, and Oil
ALBERT J. BERGESEN

INTRODUCTION

Imagine a developed country seeking to extract raw materials in the developing world by investing in resource extraction projects that pay low wages, with no benefits, plus working long hours. Now what if the exploited labor belonged to the country doing the extraction? You would probably say, wait a minute here; let me see if I have this right: exploiting their own to exploit others. I am confused, you say. I agree it is confusing, and the picture is not entirely clear, nor is it well theorized, but there does seem to be some anecdotal evidence suggesting we may be entering a new twenty-first-century phase of neocolonial relations that are qualitatively different from what the world system has seen before.

Let us get more specific. I am referring here to economic and political relations between China and Africa, which, though complex and in flux, are nonetheless raising questions, such as whether China's growing trade, aid, and investment in Africa is anything like a new form of neocolonialism (Economy 2006; Economy and Monaghan 2006; French 2006; Frynas and Paulo 2006; Junger 2007; Keet 2007; Young 2007; Zweig and Jianhai 2005). Others agree that there is a neocolonial quality to China-Africa economic relations but that they are the product of Western neoliberal attitudes and practices that have crept into China's domestic economy. Marks, for instance, argues that "the march of neoliberalism within China and its impact on the Chinese people has advanced hand-in-hand with China's growing imperialist role abroad" (quoted in Young 2007: 3). Some defend China's African relationship (Sautman and Hairong forthcoming), and still others note the geopolitics of global resource extraction that might have prompted China's activity in Africa.

"As the Chinese look around the world to see where they can invest," Jeffrey Bader, of the Brookings Institution, explains about China's grim hold on Sudan, "they see that the international oil companies have basically locked up most of the good reserves, and they don't have the technological ability to compete. So they look at the niches. And the niches often are places like Iran and Burma and Sudan. Only 23 percent of the world's known oil reserves are open for ownership by foreign oil companies, so China's fighting for a piece of that 23 percent. And Sudan is one of those countries where you can still get a piece" (Junger 2007: 5).

While the precise nature of this emerging relationship is not entirely clear, we can nonetheless entertain some ideas about why this might not be another instance of the older neoliberal Washington Consensus model but perhaps something like a newer Beijing Consensus model that points toward the future of twenty-first-century neocolonialism.

CHINA IN AFRICA

To begin with there seems to be agreement that "China's voracious demand for energy to feed its booming economy has led it to seek oil supplies from African countries including Sudan, Chad, Nigeria, Angola, Algeria, Gabon, Equatorial Guinea, and the republic of Congo. The U.S. energy information administration says China accounted for 40% of the total growth in global demand for oil in the last four years; in 2003 it surpassed Japan as the world's second largest oil consumer, after the United States" (Pan 2007: 1). Second, with this new requirement for raw materials, "Beijing estimates its consumption will amount to 450 million tons in 2020, 60 percent of which would be imports. It seems that the United States and China are competing to secure access for the oil riches of Africa" (Frynas and Paulo 2006: 238). Africa is now responsible for more than a quarter of China's oil imports, and China has become Africa's third most important trading partner, behind the United States and France and ahead of Great Britain. This relationship is broader than just oil. "More than 800 Chinese companies are reportedly operating in 49 African countries, and Chinese trade with Africa was said to surpass US $50 billion in 2006—a five fold increase from five years ago" (Frynas and Paulo 2006: 231). This in turn has led to the further suggestion that we might be revisiting a second Scramble for Africa or a "new scramble for African oil" (Frynas and Paulo 2006).

With such a new Scramble for Africa, serious questions are raised about neocolonial and dependency relations arising from China's need for African raw materials. China, for instance, takes 64 percent of Angola's oil, in a country where 90 percent of their government expenses come from such oil revenues (Pan 2007: 2). Although there are obvious analogies with earlier Western forms of neo-imperial resource extraction relations, the China-Africa relation seems, in some essential way, to have introduced new twists into the more well-documented neoliberal, neocolonial, or dependency-based North-South relationship. If there is such a neo-neocolonial form of exploiting foreign natural resources—and again this is early and speculative—it might be called something like surgical colonialism.

SURGICAL COLONIALISM

By surgical colonialism I mean resource extraction by a foreign power that involves a minimum of local disruption, making the extraction almost surgical in nature. The concept is best understood within the history of earlier waves of colonialism, which appear over time to have become ever more moderated in their degree of local disruption, reaching a point of what could be called surgicality going into the twenty-first century. Bergesen and Schoenberg (1980) noted that the history of the modern world system since the sixteenth century (Wallerstein 1974–1989) has been characterized by two waves of colonialism.

The length of colonial expansion lessens from the first wave, led by Spain and Portugal and centered in the Americas, to the second wave, led by Britain and France, centered in Africa, India, and Southeast Asia. Along with time of duration lessening, there is also less local disruption in the process of resource extraction. Colonial Wave 1 saw the most severe disruption: enslavement of Africans and the use of indigenous peoples to work in silver and gold mines in Mexico, Peru, and Bolivia; resettlement of Europeans in colonial areas; disruption of local forms of governance; and forced conversion to the culture and religious beliefs of the colonials. Colonial Wave 2, though, was more moderate in disruption. Slavery had been abolished; there was often more co-option of local political elites, and core religious beliefs were often spread by persuasion and conversion. Finally, colonial rulers went home when the second wave ended. It is in this historical context that we must situate the present set of emerging Chinese economic practices to obtain raw materials from Africa. If, as the literature suggests, this might be but another wave, or another Scramble for Africa, then we must ask how it is similar yet different from the earlier two waves.

Though obviously different from the first two waves, this new wave seems different from the more recent neocolonial practices of the West in important ways. If such neoliberalism centered, in part, on states agreeing to a number of externally imposed conditions for aid or economic transactions, such as transparency, good governance, respect for human rights, and so forth, then even that obligation is removed in the successor Beijing Consensus, where noninterference in local affairs is a cornerstone of Beijing's economic ties to the developing world. Consider the example of a loan to Angola:

> The loan allowed Angola to spurn an International Monetary Fund offer that would have required guarantees of transparency and responsible governance. In exchange, China gets 40,000 barrels per day of crude oil and has a guarantee that 70 percent of associated construction contracts will go to Chinese businesses. In a country where local industry is struggling to gain momentum after nearly three decades of civil war, it was a devastating blow. Now thousands of imported Chinese workers are constructing office buildings, apartment complexes, hospitals, schools, highways, railroads, and an airport in Angola. They even use imported Chinese cement. (Junger 2007: 8)

But the emerging Beijing Consensus is more than just the absence of interference from IMF-imposed loan conditions. That is, it is not just the absence of negatives but the presence of what could be called positives (development aid) as well. This feature is probably a continuation of Western policies of attaching aid projects for infrastructure development to economic access, but Beijing certainly seems to do it to a much greater extent than had occurred in earlier Western relations.

> The Chinese say to these countries, "Look, roads will help your economy, so let's build a road, and we'll provide most of the money for it. . . . The rest of the loan is then provided by Chinese banks and secured against future oil revenues from the country. The road-building contracts go to Chinese construction firms with Chinese engineers, workers, and equipment. . . . The construction materials come on Chinese ships and are moved on Chinese trucks and Chinese equipment that use Chinese-made rubber gaskets. The Chinese Embassy

in Chad is totally self-contained—they even grow their own vegeta-
bles." (Junger 2007: 3, 8)

Aid, of course, is not devoid of resource extraction contracts:

> Giving money away in Africa is good business: it is a continent rich in
> resources and desperately lacking in everything else, and once an in-
> dustrialized country is in there it can insert itself into almost every
> part of the economy. Let's say that China lends an African country a
> billion dollars that will be secured by future oil revenues. To produce
> those revenues, the Chinese stipulate that the oil infrastructure—
> pipelines, wells, offshore rigs, roads—must be built by their firms,
> which either have been written into the loan contract or can underbid
> everyone else because they are effectively state-owned. (Bids from
> Chinese construction firms regularly come in at 25 percent below
> those of Western rivals.) The construction work is also financed by oil
> revenues, but it hardly matters to China whether the original loan is
> paid off, because it now owns a huge chunk of the country's future oil
> revenues—a much more lucrative enterprise than simply calling in
> loan payments. (Junger 2007: 132)

When commentators say, "they will come in and provide everything that
surrounds the development of the country" (Economy 2006: 3), or when
in Angola, "Beijing has secured a major stake in future oil production
with a $2 billion package of loans and aid that includes funds for Chinese
companies to build railroads, schools, roads, hospitals, bridges, and
offices; lay a fiber-optic network; and train Angolan telecommunication
workers" (Pan 2007: 5), we are speaking of some kind of not only "full-on
supplier" but also a tremendous amount of expenditure to obtain natural
resources.

This is reminiscent of classic Western aid packages, and as such there is
nothing new in the practice of "offering poor countries comprehensive and
exploitative trade deals combined with aid" (Pan 2007: 3). In this regard,
perhaps we are just witnessing degrees of change and not new forms of
North-South relationships, but consider the following commentary:

> According to experts, Chinese construction firms regularly underbid
> Western rivals by importing cheap Chinese workers and slicing their
> profit margins to as little as 3 percent. . . . Even in small business ven-
> tures, the Chinese are hard to compete with. A Taiwanese restaurant
> owner in Chad . . . admits he hires Chinese workers because they are

so cheap. "I would rather take Taiwanese workers, but I can't," he explains. "They take a month vacation every six months and want to be paid $2,000 a month. The Chinese don't take vacations and will work for $700 or $800 a month. Chinese merchants are everywhere now—in Angola, in Niger, in Congo. They're able to undercut locals because all their goods come from China." (Junger 2007: 3)

What is involved here is bidding on projects below cost, and that can be done only with subsidies, and that appears with state-owned enterprises, which in turn suggests something about nominally socialist states in the twenty-first century possessing distinct advantages in the world capitalist system. "International oil companies will only invest in an oil and gas field if it is of commercial significance in order to justify the investment required for such operations. On the other hand, the Chinese do not have those concerns while bidding for oil and gas licenses because they are government funded companies" (oil company executive quoted in Frynas and Paulo 2006: 244). This is a general practice, and there have been complaints about dumping steel on European and American markets, along with the under-bidding for oil and development contracts in Africa. "Chinese companies have exported round the world at prices that do not reflect costs" (Marsh and Bounds 2007). To have prices that do not reflect costs is to be outside the bounds of the capitalist free market process, which means to have an advantage over private multinational Western enterprises. And that raises the irony that socialist state enterprises now command, in Africa at least, a comparative advantage over privately owned capitalist firms, where prices have to more often reflect costs.

Is this a new economic model or just a momentary instance of a country so flush with cash that it can afford to underwrite the success of its enterprises to guarantee their entry into competitive markets and thereby guarantee their access to oil and other raw materials? Who knows, but let us assume that this is reflective of a new global development led by the newest and most dramatically growing economy of the twenty-first century. It stands to reason that if China is becoming the world's lead economy, it should take the lead in new forms of North-South neocolonial relations, unless one wants to argue that the most dominant have finally given up their differential advantage over weaker states and more vulnerable developing countries. If this is something of a new form, its comparative advantage in Africa at least is dramatic and successful. But there are also a number of larger theoretical questions this phenomenon raises.

It is clear that the manner in which resources from developing zones of the world system are extracted to be used by more developed areas is in constant flux. From the brute force of the early centuries to the seeming surgical nature of extraction today, strategies continue to evolve that take into account the state of the world from the previous wave inherited and the capacities of new great powers coming online. Following the first wave of colonialism centered in the Americas and led by Spain and Portugal, settler colonies where the colonizers' culture, religion, and even ethnic-racial origin mix with that of the colonized, largely disappears. The second wave of the later nineteenth century, focused more on Africa, India, and Southeast Asia and led more by Britain and France, was more one of political occupation, and with its termination in the 1960s, the world system now constitutes its own global polity populated with sovereign nation-states, a point noted by world polity theorists (Meyer et al. 1997).

In terms of resource extraction, the penetration of the rich into the soil of the poor for their raw materials takes an even more indirect form. At first it was captured in notions of export and import dependence along with foreign investment dependence and the notion of neocolonialism. More recently the terminology has turned to neoliberalism—the imposition by fiat of free market policies for developing countries by international financial institutions such as the IMF and World Bank. It has been summed up as the Washington Consensus, where the idea is that IMF loans require local states to alter domestic economic policies according to the wishes of private multinational enterprises, which in prevailing morality is considered an interference with their national right of economic sovereignty.

But critiques of the Washington Consensus/neoliberalism say little about Beijing's relations with Africa or about the possibility of a post–Washington Consensus in the form of the newer, and more aggressive, Beijing Consensus. The new China-Africa relations do not involve private multinationals or private banks and financial institutions or adherence to constraints from international institutions such as the IMF. Instead the new Beijing Consensus is built on just the opposite: state enterprises, state banks and financial institutions, and a policy of noninterference. There are also new additions to the model. There are prices that do not reflect market costs, making them all but necessary for developing countries to accept, and as such outbidding private Western multinationals, and with a similar price advantage, there are more extensive aid packages for infrastructure development. For example, "[a] planned deal between China and the Democratic Republic of China would tie up mineral resources in exchange for $5b in infrastructure projects and loans. A preliminary agreement was signed this week just as an IMF mission landed in Kinshasa to review progress towards the resumption of budget support for the Congo. IMF, World Bank and African Development Bank officials seem to have been caught off guard by the scale and timing of China's plans. . . . It will give China a distinct advantage in the Congolese copper belt" (Wallis and Bream 2007: 10).

Finally, there is the exploitation of labor but, importantly, not that of the developing country. "Legal and illegal Chinese immigrants are moving to Africa by the hundreds of thousands to work in extractive industries, construction and manufacturing" (Economy and Monaghan 2006), such that "historically, Chinese cooperation projects . . . have involved the importation of massive Chinese work brigades who do almost all the work and deliver a turn-key finished product" (French 2006: 131). It is another component of the surgical nature of the new North-South relations. These are competitive advantages that cannot be met by Western enterprises in Africa; hence, the advantage goes to China, the new economy within the global system and the new pioneer in ways to extract raw materials from weaker countries. This is obviously different from Spain in Mexico, from Britain in India, and, the more one thinks about it, from Euro-American multinationals under a neoliberal regime dubbed the Washington Consensus.

Given that critical thinking focuses on the Washington Consensus model, let me try a mind experiment to dramatize what might be different about the emerging Beijing Consensus model. Imagine a representative of the Beijing Consensus making the following argument about the superiority of the new post-Western way of managing resource extraction from the developing world.

In the past, resource extraction was done on the backs of the host country's labor force with a maximum amount of social disruption. Think of the history of Western colonial relations with the global South. Now think of China in Africa today; this obviously is not seventeenth-century Spain in Latin America enslaving indigenous people to work in Mexican and Bolivian silver mines or the extraction of gold from upper Peru. Nor is it even the Scramble for Africa in the late nineteenth century. We do not treat the Congolese like the Belgians did; why, it's not even the Washington Consensus of global neoliberal investment policies. We do not push our policies on local governments. We fully believe in noninterference. What happens in Darfur stays in Darfur. And we do not impose those constraints on using our aid imposed by the World Bank or International Monetary Fund. We do none of that. Think about it. Our state firms bid lower than those private Western capitalist multinationals. So we work for less. We provide, with the same sort of low-cost loans, development aid and infrastructure projects as well. Some would say we are exploiting Africa; not at all.

Here is the clincher: if, God forbid, there are colonial costs, like exploiting labor, well, we assume them ourselves. That's right, we assume the colonial costs ourselves. We exploit our own labor—we pay our people below-market prices for labor, provide poor benefits, housing, and so forth. This is historical and turns the tables on past core-periphery practices of the larger capitalist world system. For the first time, the exploiter will exploit himself, and further, to make sure there is no mess or social disruption made in getting the oil, copper, gold, diamonds, iron, and uranium we need, we will build—below cost—and completely finance, manage, and use our own labor (and even our own cement) to build hospitals, schools, sports stadiums, rail lines, highways, apartment buildings, government buildings. In short this is a neo-neocolonial extraction process that is purely surgical in nature. You won't even know we are there. In, out. Our money, our technology, our firms, our labor, our banking, and we even leave you better off then when we started—as we build you lots of infrastructure you didn't have before. What do you have to lose: some oil or minerals. OK. But we pay for them, and we leave more infrastructure than when we arrived. You will be untouched in the traditional sense of colonial disruption, or imperial relations, or even the newer dependency-type relations, or those neoliberal IMF and World Bank–enforced regulations. We won't impose any of those on you. None. We believe in your sovereignty and noninterference. We aren't meddling neocolonials. We don't impose our value system on your organic natural way of doing things.

The point of this admittedly dramatized and exaggerated monologue is that critical thinking remains wedded to a critique of the present, which in the fluidity of the evolving world system is a critique of the past. What I want to suggest here is that the world is changing. America—and the neoliberal Washington Consensus critique—is part of the past. The Beijing Consensus suggests something about the future, about emerging twenty-first-century North-South relations of surgical exploitation—and as such not only a new developmental stage in core-periphery relations but facts on the ground that challenge our way of thinking about a number of topics.

For one, Western critical thinking for the past couple of hundred years has focused on a distinction between the individual and the collective or the private and the public. In economic life, in a line of thinking from Marx and Lenin through *dependencia* theory and present critical writings on neoliberalist economic policies, the private firm has been the problem and the public or state the solution. It was, and still is today, the bedrock assumption that private multinationals outside state control can engage in varieties of predatory and unscrupulous economic practices. While an earlier zeal to nationalize production seems to have passed, the moral sentiment that the public management of production is morally preferable to the private remains a key element of faith for the left. In its contemporary form, the problem is the private multinational and its financial agents, like the IMF or World Bank. The solution remains collective public management.

But what we see today seems the opposite, at least in the African case focused on here. What is most competitive, most cutthroat, most purely instrumental and devoid of moral foundation, is not the private firm but public state enterprises. To leave the local alone, to not interfere when the local is Darfur, or the military in Burma/Myanmar, or repressive African regimes, alters the moral significance of the noninterference mantra of the Beijing Consensus. That the meddling IMF wants transparency, good governance principles, and environmental protection, while the public/state does not care one way or the other seems to violate the prime assumption that what is private is what goes wrong, and what is public and the state is what is right.

Indeed, the appearance of new economic powers such as China in world affairs has marginalized the Western-driven economic model based on externally imposed conditionalities ranging from the respect for human rights and good governance to liberal economic reform in exchange for financial assistance. Energy-hungry nations such as India, Brazil, South Korea, Malaysia, and China have proven more supportive and have provided loans, debt relief, scholarships, training, and military hardware without political or economic conditionalities, in exchange for a foothold in the oil business. In turn, incumbent African leaders have identified Chinese unconditional financial resources, cheap products, and know-how as an important tool to fend off pressure for political and economic reform from international organizations such as the IMF and Western governments (Frynas and Paulo 2006: 239).

SOCIALISM AND CAPITALISM

At the deepest level of theorizing lies the sociological sense of history and its developmental patterns. I do not think anyone still believes in the Marxian notion of mechanical stages of economic development, yet it is also true that no successor model has appeared, and the advent of a successful socialist state as the lead economy within the capitalist world economy poses problems worth contemplating. For many China is now de facto capitalist, and with socialist utopia again pushed into the future, no one speaks of existing socialist states anymore. Yet it is the case, and something that has to be faced, that their central economic enterprises, from oil companies and construction firms to those in banking and shipbuilding, are state owned. This is not the time for being a stickler on definitions, and I fully realize the ambiguity of the present situation, yet it is more the case that the Chinese means of production are owned by the state than by private capital, and so on some grounds a designation of at least something socialist seems appropriate. But this then runs into the reality of China in Africa, where the better, if you will capitalist, competitor is, of all things, the socialist enterprise. One after another, the oil lease, development contract, or infrastructure project goes to the Beijing state enterprise, not to the private Western multinational. If it was the private capitalist firm that lowered prices by cutting or suppressing wages, it is now the state-owned enterprise that relies on low-wage Chinese labor.

Admittedly, something like national self-exploitation sounds like a silly concept—more Nietzschean and Freudian than Marxian—yet it is, in some way not as yet fully understood and certainly not fully theorized, part and parcel of the new way of doing things in Africa. It helps create the surgical quality of the new Beijing Consensus. Low wages, yes; poor working conditions, yes; no insurance, yes; but we import our own people and treat them this way rather than, or along with, how we treat locals.

Again, the challenge, at its core, is to the most primal assumptions in radical Western theory: the antiprogressive nature of the private and the unregulated and the progressive nature of the public and therefore the regulated, which practically becomes the state. When the state is welfare, protection for minority rights, public services, democratic institutions, public services, and so forth, then the state as progressivity makes sense.

But when it is state plus firm then it gets complicated. If it remained a domestic fusion, it is not clear how the Western critical mind would react. Given earlier endorsements of the Soviet planned economy and collectivized/national production in China, things might not seem so contradictory. But with state-owned enterprises we get a lethal mix of the historically positive (the state) and negative (the business firm) in the Western moral imagination. And when it is such a state firm that is doing capitalism better than the private capitalist Western firm, then, well, the crisis in the moral significance of the private and the public is upon us. The irony only deepens, for given the conditions of global capitalism, socialism as in the Chinese enterprise example may be the next phase of capitalist development. It is as if historical development has outrun the scope of social theory.

Let us put this issue in its historical context. In very general terms, the original capitalist firm was the family firm, often an inventor plus a finance person. That entity expanded into the modern multiunit corporation, which then morphed into the multinational corporation, and now, we seem to be on the cusp of the state firm, or the socialist multinational corporation. In theory, the production unit was the private entity devoid of social controls. Those were provided by the regulatory nature of the state, which by evolution or revolution was to tame the ravenous nature of the private accumulator and replace it with public accumulation and distribution for need and use. In moral principle that assumption underlies the critique of neoliberalism, which is, about the freedom of private capital to go and do what it wants independent of state control. In this model, the private is the danger, the exploiter, the extractor of resources, and the public is the counterweight. It may turn out to have been a nineteenth- and twentieth-century moral model that arose in opposition to the rise of the capitalist firm and private accumulation. It may be outdated in the twenty-first century, for how applicable is this moral model to exploitation and resource extraction of the most dynamic growth engine of early twenty-first-century world capitalism—China? I would suggest not very helpful at all. For here the accumulator is the state, with its companies, or firms, or enterprises. Here the absence of labor organizing and unions is tied to the presence of the accumulating state, not the absence of state interference in the economy. Here the overseas search for raw materials, using whatever means works, is now led by the state-owned oil companies, not the private ones. Here the financing for these firms is from state-owned banks, and the development projects to facilitate the resource extraction agreement in the first place is also by state-owned firms, their banks, their technicians, and even their labor. The emerging Beijing Consensus may be the historical successor to the present Washington Consensus just as it is evident that East Asia is the historical successor to North America as the center of the capitalist world economy.

The theoretical contradictions are worth contemplating. It is only social-ism (state-owned enterprises) that allows success in capitalist competition, for they can suppress waves and underbid. That is the pooling of capital at the state level, plus government-owned banks and lending institutions allow below-market bidding. Ironically, it is the social firms' commercial success that makes the socialist state flush with cash, which then allows under-bidding of private firms. That the most aggressive and successful enterprises are socialist state-owned ones and that private, purportedly capitalist enter-prises not owned by Western states are at a disadvantage because of said privateness is a data crisis for received critical theory.

Who is prepared to acknowledge that to be private, Western, and multi-national, with IMF and World Bank backing, is to be disadvantaged in the capitalist world economy? And who is prepared to argue that to be govern-ment owned by a socialist state, without IMF and World Bank pressures, to willfully not exploit local labor but to exploit one's own, to not disrupt local arrangements and not interfere in local politics, to recognize the local and abhor the global, is to be the most successful new model of resource extrac-tion by the global rich and powerful over the global poor and weak? It is not just Western productive advantage that is falling behind, but Western criti-cal thinking seems head-in-the-sand fixated on America, the declining heg-emon, at the expense of the emerging successor hegemon of China and its developing Beijing Consensus worldview.

RETHINKING EMPIRE

Surgical imperialism, should there be such a phenomenon, has mystified crit-ics of North-South relations because of both the transitional period we are in and the inner globological workings of global geopolitics. By transitional I mean the simultaneous economic decline of the United States and the ascent of China. Think of the last wave of the powerful exploitation of the weak's natural resources in a geopolitical fashion, the 1875–1914 second wave of colo-nialism. The United States at that time was the ascending power and accord-ingly had few colonial holdings compared with the British Empire, on which the sun never set. In today's third empire cycle, China plays the role of the United States and America of Britain. In those pre-1914 years all eyes were on the British Empire, as today upon the American Empire. America as empire is the dominant discourse. Then to speak of America rising and Britain de-clining would have been less popular than to focus on the pros and cons of the British Empire. It is a debate repeated today, with pro arguments about bringing democracy to the Middle East, rooting out terrorism, providing aid to failed states, keeping the sea lanes open for the flow of oil, and so forth.

By the end of the nineteenth century, Britain was in economic decline vis-à-vis the United States, and empire, or more formal geopolitical exercises of power/control, was a defensive necessity to pressure what came earlier with the more organic economic trade imperium. What this means is that economic colonialism and military colonial interventions don't always advance at the same time. The economic expansions abroad and the geopolitical sense of British and American vital interests follow, naturally enough. There are also periodic interventions to maintain the expanded global trade or economic sphere of influence. This was classically observed by Gallagher and Robinson (1953), and it descriptively works for both mid-nineteenth-century Britain and 1945–1975 America. This, though, becomes more formalized and ossified in the period of economic decline that follows, Britain in 1875–1914 and America from 1975 to present, because the economy shrinks, leaving spheres of previous influence in a more fragile condition, hence open to challengers (both locals and other great powers), revolts, revolutions, failed states, and other forms of instability. To maintain what was, as what is, formal political-military influence is required, and that took the form of colonialism then and American overseas bases and troop deployments today.

The decline of the famed British and American empires is the product not of imperial overreach (Kennedy 1987) but of economic shrinkage. On the surface the phenomena look the same, but their inner dynamics are different and can be seen in the following stages. First, economic ascendance involves trade relations expanding into new overseas areas beyond the extant political-military reach of the rising country. This was the world Admiral Mahan saw for the United States at the turn of the twentieth century when he recommended the expansion of American sea power to match the growing global scope of American trade and economic power. This dynamic is diagrammed below, as Stage 1 where economic expansion overseas outpaces military overseas expansion:

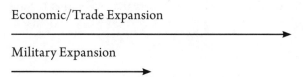

Economic/Trade Expansion

Military Expansion

Stage 1, for instance, would describe the condition of China in the early twenty-first century. Actually, if the term "overreach" is to be employed, it is better as economic or trade overreach, not imperial, military, or colonial overreach.

What surges beyond bounds is trade relations, not colonial relations. Next, with Stage 2 we see a military expansion to protect expanded trade relations. This was the case with the expansion of the British and American navies to cover their earlier "trade overreach," and many predict that China will follow the same path of military extension to protect trade routes and their import of oil and other raw materials. The new equilibrium is diagrammed below:

Economic/Trade Expansion

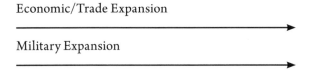

Military Expansion

This yields a state of trade–military equilibrium and is perhaps the epoch of the imperialism of free trade: military use to keep lanes of commerce, foreign markets, and sources of raw materials open to the hegemon's expanding economic base. This perhaps described mid-nineteenth-century Britain and 1945–1975 America. Stage 2 has yet to begin for China.

This brings us to Stage 3, which on the surface looks like imperial overreach but is actually economic shrinkage accompanying the hegemon's economic decline. This looks as follows:

Economic/Trade Expansion

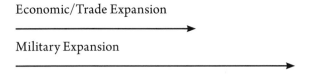

Military Expansion

Stage 3 in and of itself is military expansion, colonialism, empire, and so forth. But when we compare it with Stage 2 we can see that it is not so much the military that has expanded as the trade and economic that have pulled back, leaving the military in places where there is less economic presence, backing, or underwriting; hence it looks more like sheer military adventurism, expansion, and so forth. There is some change, of course—more formal basing and control—but this is a shoring-up exercise, not a new departure. Empire is a formalization of the exercise of power that was earlier the imperialism of free trade.

FROM EMPIRE TO GREAT POWER WAR

Empire is not, though, the last state of a cycle of hegemonic dominance. That is war over hegemonic succession, and in viewing the early twenty-first century as one of American imperial overreach critics unwittingly mystify the real geopolitical reality. There are four stages in the cycle of hegemonic domination: ascent, dominance, decline, and succession struggle. We can briefly identify each.

HEGEMONIC ASCENT

From the point of view of different countries, ascent and decline occur in the same historical period and are associated with two modes of colonialism/imperialism. The extant but declining hegemon tries to hold on to spheres of interest that were established earlier by trade overreach and were earlier maintained by periodic interventions, as described by the Gallagher and Robinson (1953) thesis. From informal to formal empire is the usual specification. But what must be remembered is that the formal is not an inevitability but the direct consequence of the hegemon's economic and trade decline, hence a geopolitical shrinkage of previous informal influence, which requires to maintain the same geospheres of influence a more formal military deployment—what is popularly called colonialism or empire. Britain had the most extensive colonial holdings at the end of the nineteenth century and was simultaneously the economic power in decline, whereas with the least holdings was the hegemon ascending, the United States, and with more, but less than Britain, the challenger that would be left out, Germany. Today the hegemon in decline is the United States; it has the most formalized holdings in the form of overseas bases, troop deployments, and so forth. Earlier the United States was in ascension and accordingly had fewer such bases. Today China is the ascender and has even fewer bases but, important to observe, pioneers the next mode of global dominance relations: the surgical imperialism idea. Note the sequence: Britain had formal colonial occupation; the United States slides to bases and troop deployments; China slides even further to aid packages, development projects, noninterference, use of, and perhaps exploitation of, their own labor, and of course the use of their own capital and technology. But these are but surface or placeholder changes, for the underlying dynamic is the same from the point of view of both the declining and ascending. Whether through formal occupation or military bases, the decliner is trying to hold on to a slipping hegemony; left out of the major resource sources, but struggling with new techniques to get in, the ascenders are pioneering new modalities of resources extraction by the globally powerful from the globally weak. Earlier Britain held India; today the United States holds or influences Saudi Arabia and the Middle East; earlier the United States nibbled around the edge of British holdings with Puerto Rico, Panama, the Philippines, and Guam;

today China works Africa and the edges of American holdings with influence in Sudan, Chad, Angola, and Myanmar. It is the same dynamic and the same underlying process, just different surface manifestations.

Note that Europe and Russia are not in this picture of overseas holdings nor is either considered the rising hegemon. Like Germany earlier, the EU-Russian bloc will be largely left out of the new Scramble for Africa, and their resultant resentment will grow, making the Eurasian heartland a potentially resentful area.

HEGEMONIC DOMINANCE: IMPERIALISM OF FREE TRADE

This is the height of hegemonic presence, where a state obtains what it wants with economic advantage (trade, production) and as such does not need formal political-military settlements overseas. The first colonial cycle, led by Spain and Portugal, was more "sociological" in the nature of its effects on its holdings: new settlers, new religions, new social relations, and so forth. The second colonial cycle, led by Britain and France, was more "political" as it was more a domination of political occupation, where one ruled or administered but did not move to, live with, or marry into, as earlier. Now, with the third wave, on the defensive side we see domination that is more "military": bases, flyover agreements, port-of-call agreements, and so forth. Here we see a purely globological dynamic as both the declining hegemon's domination is slighter (military presence versus political occupation or settlement) and the ascender's new form is also slighter (the surgical imperialism concept).

HEGEMONIC DECLINE

The third stage is what we commonly call empire or imperialism. It is Britain in the period 1875–1914 and the United States from 1975 to present. Aspects of this have been discussed throughout this chapter, and so I want to skip to the fourth stage, Great Power war.

HEGEMONIC SUCCESSION STRUGGLE: GREAT POWER WAR

Colonialism or imperialism is not just dominance of the global weak; it is also competition and struggle between the global powerful in and around succession to the declining hegemon. First and foremost there is a correlation between colonialism and Great Power war. But upon closer examination, the rivalry of colonial expansion appears to precede the violence of Great Power wars. As is well known, the wave of late nineteenth-century colonialism was followed by the Great Power war of 1914. But this phenomenon is perhaps a more general globological feature of the world system as a whole, where the two peaks in number of colonies established precede the peaks in number of battle deaths.

Colonial rivalry, though, is not just for raw materials but involves national identities, security concerns, and spheres of influence—held and desired—that are activated and put into play. It involves risers, fallers, and the left out. Last time around Britain was a faller, the United States the riser, and Germany the left out. It is the left out that attempts, as a last resort, to restructure the hegemon's international system to break out of its encirclement, by colonial outpost, sea power, and the larger global web of the hegemon's power. During earlier periods of free trade imperialism/colonialism and economic expansion, worries about encirclement and spheres of influence are less of an issue for the left out zones. In effect, given generalized prosperity, they too benefit. Europe did quite well in the post-1945 years. But given decline, the rise of new powers, and areas taken, held, and so forth (Middle East, Africa) by the old decliner and new ascender plus their natural spheres of influence (United States: South America, Canada; China: Southeast Asia), there is little left for the left out EU-Russia zone.

Boxed out of the colonial holdings the last time around, it was Germany that reacted with force to break up the system (in World War I). Britain, the extant hegemon, did not start either world war. Now it is EU/Russia that is surrounded or boxed in by the United States', the declining hegemon and China, the ascending hegemon who now control the Americas, Asia, and Africa, leaving Europe and Russia nothing but themselves. It is a powerful bloc with European industry plus Russian raw materials, but it is a globally boxed-in zone, hence resentful, and the predicted initiators of a breakout move to disrupt the hegemonic succession process from North America to East Asia, which, if it continues unchallenged, will bypass Europe and Russia. With no economic challenge possible, their only option is a military challenge. The Napoleonic strategy of France was in response to the forthcoming transition from Spanish to British hegemony. It failed, of course, as did Germany (1914–1945), but that does not mean that the next left out zone will not again try to break out or disrupt the hegemonic succession process once again. The Europe-Russia bloc will attempt to disrupt this transition. World War III will be initiated by Europe and Russia, not the United States. This is because the old hegemons in decline defensively engage in holding on—what we now call colonialism or imperialism—but from their point of view they are holding on to what they feel is theirs. Ascending hegemons profit from the world as it is and can see the coming passage of power. They do not want to break up the system either. It will, as it is, deliver them hegemony.

The United States did not initiate World War I or II; China, Japan, and East Asia will not initiate World War III. Like the United States the last time around, China and Japan are profiting from the status quo, for the overhead costs of global security are in the hands of the declining hegemon, helping to ensure both its further decline and the ascendance of East Asia.

Who is left to initiate World War III? Canada, Latin America, Southeast Asia, Africa, the Middle East? They are all too small to start a world war—but Europe and Russia are another story. Economically powerful (like Germany before) yet boxed in geopolitically when the new scramble for influence is on and the world economy stagnating, they become the zone of global resentment, and at some point, they react and strategically calculate that a breakout maneuver, an attempt to break the global hegemonic transition from North America to East Asia, is their prime hope. All of this sounds way too intentional. Agreed. On the ground, the globological dynamics will manifest as triggering incidents, accidents, and so forth, like Princip, Sarajevo, and Archduke Ferdinand the first time around. As I understand it, no one saw World War I coming, and although there is periodic talk of the 1914 analogy, or pre-1914 conditions, the continued emphasis on American Empire as the prime source of future global instability seems seriously misplaced. Again, aging hegemons do not initiate system-changing conflicts. They, mistakenly, feel that the system is theirs and works for them. And the rising powers are profiting from the way it is. Discontent comes from neither risers nor decliners but from the resentful left out. I think that happened in the past, and I fear it will happen again in the future.

PART III

HISTORICAL STUDIES OF COLONIALISM *&* EMPIRE

ELEVEN

Nation and Empire in the French Context
EMMANUELLE SAADA

In the sociological tradition, the modern nation-state is often described as the historical product of political liberalism, with France as its most fully realized example. Nowhere else in the world, this tradition tells us, have the boundaries of population, territory, and state apparatus converged so completely. This thesis is grounded in a powerful claim of reciprocity: in the French case, the nation as an "imagined community" is the product of the state (through cultural, political, and social policies producing the nation) while the state is the emanation of the sovereign nation (Schnapper 1998a).

Yet to a great extent France has also been, throughout most of its history, an empire-state (Cooper 2005a; Wilder 2005). This was true long before the Revolution. From the thirteenth century on, the French crown expanded through the conquest or annexation of neighboring regions and overseas territories, most notably in the Americas. This trajectory was not interrupted by the collapse of the ancien régime: in the early nineteenth century, Napoleon established one of the largest continental empires in European history. Subsequent regimes, from the Restoration to the Third Republic, built a new overseas empire, with strongholds in Africa, Southeast Asia, and the Pacific region, second in surface area only to the British Empire. These external acquisitions were paralleled by an ongoing process of "internal colonization": the regions of Savoy and Nice became French only in 1860, thirty years after the conquest of Algiers. In the decades preceding World War I, these two processes generated very similar questions in metropolitan France and throughout the empire: respectively, how to make "peasants" and "indigenous people" into Frenchmen (Colonna 1975; Weber 1976).

It is common to date the end of the French Empire to the 1950s and early 1960s. The independence of Algeria in 1962—until then the most important extraterritorial possession in economic, symbolic, and political terms—marked the endpoint of an era of French imperialism. Nonetheless, a few territories, some dating back to the colonization efforts in the seventeenth century, still remain under French sovereignty. This is the case of Guadeloupe, Martinique, Guyana, and Réunion, which became Overseas Departments (*Départments d'Outre-mer*) in 1946. This is also the case of New Caledonia, French Polynesia, Commores Islands, Saint-Pierre and Miquelon, French Austral and Antarctic Territories, and Wallis and Futuna Islands, which have kept a looser connection with metropolitan France as overseas territories (*territoires d'outre-mer*). By this measure, France is still an empire both within and without its national borders. The alliance formed in the 1970s between *Kanak* (New Caledonian) and Corsican independence movements was one sign of a continued connection between internal and external forms of colonialism (Lebovics 2004).

France thus offers a unique observation point for the sociological study of empires: it is a country endowed with the objective characteristics of an empire-state and the political imagination of a nation-state. It is a great "case" for unpacking the intricate relationships between national and imperial forms of political domination and, thus, for furthering our sociological understanding of both.

But this characterization calls for at least one cautionary remark and one preliminary question. First, the caution: we must be aware of the possibility that highlighting the uniqueness of the French case can obscure more than it reveals. National typologies of imperial formations often implicitly reaffirm the analytical preeminence of the "nation" over "empire" by showing how specific national traits have been translated into imperial formations. Comparative approaches, which have generally focused on the colonial projects of Great Britain and France, have often ignored the enormous colonial variations within each empire (the same goes for the German case; see Steinmetz 2007) and confused more or less coherent official accounts of imperial projects produced in metropolitan centers with actual local policies. Contrasts between "British indirect rule" and the supposedly centralized administrative practices of the French case are a common example of this generalizing impulse. Among the risks of such an approach is the tendency to diminish the complex historical dynamics that constantly transformed the European projects over the course of empire (for an analysis of such intraempire transformation, see Conklin 1997). Moreover, these attempts at characterizing "national imperial styles" overlook that the politics of comparison were central to colonial practices themselves (Stoler and Cooper 1997); often, they were used to legitimize specific policies in a context of European competition over the best way to colonize (Dimier 2004). Comparison is not only an analytical device for the historian; it was also an ideological tool for colonial actors.

COLONIAL VARIATIONS

French colonial historians have traditionally specialized in the study of distinctive areas and fixed periods. They have been more interested in specific colonial situations than in imperial logics and have insisted on the variations within the French imperial project. Nearly all draw a distinction between two main phases of the French colonial empire. The first was located primarily in the Americas and, to a much lesser extent, the west coast of Africa (Senegal), the Indian Ocean (Bourbon Island, known today as Réunion Island, and Ile de France, known today as Mauritius) and the Indian peninsula (with a few possessions along the coasts). This early phase began in the seventeenth century and survived until the defeat of Napoleon in 1815. It was built primarily on the institution of slavery, which fueled colonial economies and imperial strategies (African territories were conquered mostly to facilitate the slave trade). The second colonial empire dates to 1830 with the conquest of Algiers. At its high point in the early 1920s, it encompassed territories in Africa, the Pacific Ocean, and Asia.

The definitive abolition of slavery in French territories in 1848 is an often-cited turning point in this periodization: by granting citizenship to former slaves, the French state put the "old colonies" of the New World and of its few possessions on the west coast of Africa and in India on a different political trajectory than the territories conquered in the nineteenth and early twentieth centuries. Slavery, the "peculiar institution" of the first colonial empire, was replaced by modern colonial domination—the economic, political, and cultural domination of indigenous subjects.

The difference between the two empires eventually became part of the official rhetoric of colonization and provided a rationale for the conquest of sub-Saharan Africa as a way of purging it of indigenous forms of slavery. After 1848, legal, economic, and cultural "assimilation" prevailed in the old colonies and led to their formal incorporation as French departments in 1946 (Mam-Lam-Fouck 2006). In the colonies of the second empire, in contrast, the French state implemented a range of strategies to ensure their continued differentiation from the metropolitan center.

The vast territories conquered after 1830 in Africa, the Pacific Ocean, and Asia were thus treated very differently than the earlier acquisitions. Throughout the nineteenth and early twentieth centuries, consequently, the French empire was divided sociologically and politically along several major lines and was very heterogeneous across them.

The empire comprised departments, colonies, protectorates, and other forms of rule. These had diverse legal and administrative statuses, reflecting in part the evolution of the legal theories of sovereignty and a change in policies at the turn of the century from "assimilation" to a looser link of "association" (Betts 1961). Administrators (and, later, historians) also distinguished between "settler colonies" (*colonies de peuplement*) and "exploitative colonies" (*colonie d'exploitation*), with significant implications on forms of governance and the organization of colonial society (Elkins and Pedersen 2005; Stoler 1989).

Algeria was the model of full political integration. After 1848, it was governed as a set of three departments that were constitutionally part of the French territory. Most possessions in Africa, the Pacific Ocean, and Asia, conversely, were colonies. These were administered by a relatively centralized institution, the Ministère des colonies (created in 1894), although it too admitted significant diversity in its procedures and practices along geographical lines. Some territories in Indochina (Tonkin, Annam, Laos) and North Africa (Tunisia and Morocco) were protectorates: the former sovereign powers were officially maintained but in reality greatly limited by French interventions. Finally, in 1919, the League of Nations gave France a mandate over a number of former German and Ottoman territories (Togo, Cameroon, Lebanon, Syria): French rule in these territories was ostensibly limited and supervised by the international organization but in reality was much more pervasive.

Another major factor of variation was the range of imperial objectives in play, from diplomatic competition with other European powers—especially England (Tocqueville 2001)—to maneuvering for military advantage (often in the form of *points d'appui*, or strategic harbors for the navy), to land speculation, to the more gradual exploitation of agricultural and mineral wealth.

In some places, colonization also was seen as a mean of resolving the prevalent "social question" that preoccupied fast-industrializing France (Ageron 1978). Throughout the nineteenth century, Algeria and New Caledonia became home to exiles of the "dangerous classes" of France (Chevalier 1973). Participants in Parisian revolutionary movements were sent to Algeria in 1848 and New Caledonia in 1871. The inhabitants of Alsace and Lorraine who fled German occupation after the 1870 war were also directed toward Algeria, which was represented as a "new France" (Stora 1999).

New Caledonia was notable as a laboratory for attempts to rehabilitate criminals, especially recidivists who were considered "unfit" for French society. These often found themselves shipped to New Caledonian prisons. Upon release, they were often denied return passage to France and ultimately made up a large part of the islands' farming population. As in Algeria, farming on conquered land was a deliberate social and political strategy for strengthening the French presence, rehabilitating social outcasts, and, more broadly, accommodating populations displaced by industrialization (Merle 1995). Algeria and New Caledonia were distinctive colonies in these regards and were the only territories with sizable populations from France.

The colonization of sub-Saharan Africa and of the Indochinese peninsula was very different, both in its underlying rationale and its practice. Unlike in Algeria and New Caledonia, which were considered settlement colonies, conquests in Africa and Asia were pursued primarily for political and economic reasons. At first, international political considerations were paramount: France was very much a competitor in the "Scramble for Africa," the competition for African colonies among European powers. France also had ambitions to conquer parts of China and saw the Vietnamese empire as a first step toward that goal. Securing mineral and food supplies was also an explicit goal of late nineteenth-century conquests.

The *mission civilisatrice* proclaimed by the governments of the Third Republic provided a powerful ideological framework for these efforts—even though the concrete implementation of this program was limited and quickly challenged by the local colonial state (Conklin 1997). Also important was the Saint-Simonian notion that territorial expansion was an occasion for national renewal, capable of fostering demographic, economic, and cultural progress (Leroy-Beaulieu 1874). The Prussian victory over France in 1870, the subsequent occupation of Alsace and Lorraine, general demographic decline, and the prolonged economic crisis of the late nineteenth century fueled this colonial ideology.

Finally, a major goal of colonization in Africa and Asia was the extraction of local natural resources and the intensive production of agricultural goods for metropolitan use. Exploitation of the local workforce and the maintenance of order were central objectives of colonial agents, albeit sometimes contradictory (Berman 1984). In the territories colonized under these auspices, the French presence was limited both in number and scope: the French population was composed mostly of members of the military, public administration, and industrial or commercial enterprises.

This difference between "settlement" and "exploitation" profoundly shaped the composition of colonial societies. In the latter colonies, the ratio of men to women was much higher—as were turnover rates as military, administrative, and commercial personnel rotated back to France. The age balance also skewed younger, reflecting the dominance of the military and other short-term personnel. These differences dramatically impacted the colonizers' relationship with indigenous societies: gender imbalances drove sexual liaisons across the colonizer-indigenous divide (Clancy-Smith and Gouda 1998; Stoler 2002). Where European families were more numerous, intimate contacts between colonizers and colonized were more limited and less open. As a result, the reproduction of colonial society—a central focus of imperial strategists and colonial administrators—implied very different challenges from one colony to the next (Stoler and Cooper 1997).

The nature of the colonial project also had repercussions on governing styles. In Algeria, the extensive occupation of the land by large and small enterprises implied massive expropriation and relocation of the population. In New Caledonia, this process led to the creation of reservations for the indigenous Kanak. These two territories were the sites of the most extensive strategies of control—they were "total" in the sense that colonial rule targeted all aspects of daily life (Sayad 2004: 64). In other territories, the exercise of colonial power was less ubiquitous but no less violent in its efforts to crush local resistance. As Frederick Cooper described it, drawing on Foucault, such exercise of power was less "capillary" and more "arterial" (Cooper 1994: 1553).

Another principle of differentiation and—in some respects—fragmentation within the French Empire resulted from the variations among representations of indigenous populations. By the end of the nineteenth century, French anthropologists had devised a complex "evolutionary scale" that justified the relationship between European colonizers and the diverse subjects of French and other European empires. European culture sat at the top of the scale, as the ultimate standard of civilization. Next were the Annamites of Indochina, favorably regarded because of their "superior" "ancient civilization," with its close ties to China. Algerians came next, with a strong and often politically instrumentalized distinction between the superior village-dwelling Berbers or *Kabyle* (who, it was claimed, were related to the original Gaul population of France) and the nomadic "Arabs" (Lorcin 1995). Widely described as belonging to the white race,

Algerians were considered "educable" barbarians rather than complete "savages" (Le Cour Grandmaison 2005). West Africans occupied a lower position on this scale and were often represented with childish traits. Lowest in rank were the Kanak of New Caledonia, who were widely depicted as true savages (Bensa 1988).

These representations justified but also shaped the local exercise of colonial domination. The Vietnamese enjoyed a higher degree of administrative autonomy relative to other colonized groups largely because of the notion that they were "superior" to other peoples and therefore capable of exercising greater privileges. Colonial rule in New Caledonia, in contrast, was characterized by intense violence, spatial segregation, contempt for cultural institutions, and the absence of public education—a situation supported by the common view that the Kanak were barely human (Salaün 2005).

The interplay between representations and colonial policies was complex and evolving. This hierarchy of peoples predated colonialism. It was a product of the increasingly global consciousness of the eighteenth century and relied on travelers, explorers, and conquerors for data (on the German case, see Steinmetz 2007a). In the latter part of the nineteenth century, these theories were developed into an elaborate "racial science" under the leadership of Paul Broca and the Paris Anthropological Society. This science was informed in large part by the accounts of local colonial agents and, especially, the considerable body of amateur ethnographers in the colonial service. Anthropological accounts, in turn, became the reference texts for new colonial personnel, creating a feedback loop that embedded racial science in the full range of colonial practices (Sibeud 2002; Steinmetz 2007a).

The administrative categories to describe subjugated people also changed over time, reflecting the transformation of modes of domination. This is very clear in the Algerian case, where the first occupiers of Algiers developed a very loose set of categories that mixed national and religious principles of differentiation. Early French rule did not have a clear approach to relations between colonizers and colonized but rather adjusted to a quickly changing situation. In 1830, it included the indigenous population into decision making. On July 6, 1830 (the day after the official capitulation of Algiers), the general-in-chief, Comte de Bourmont, created a commission to "study the needs and resources of the country and the institutions to be changed or maintained." This group was made up of a "mix of notables, from the different indigenous castes and the French population, who will perform the different functions necessary to civil society."[1] In the same spirit, an 1832 ordinance organizing the justice system in Algeria mentions the different "nations" making up the Regency. This relatively inclusive approach disappeared over time, and rigid distinctions between "indigenous subjects" and "citizens" became the basis of colonial rule, for reasons that we will explore later.

The different indigenous responses to French rule were another important determinant of variations within the empire. Local cultures responded differently to French presence, depending on their political imagination and social organization. These differences were extensively documented by the French administration, which drew "racial maps" that indicated populations more or less amenable to colonization and played favorites in an effort to leverage local power bases—a practice known in the colonial administration as "race politics" (Bazin 1985).

IMPERIAL FORCES

Early representations of the empire tended to mirror the diversity of circumstances and solutions. The process of conquest was haphazard and did not have a preconceived plan. The word "empire" itself was rarely used in French discourse before the turn of the century (Saada 2012a). The vision of empire as a single, unified entity was largely the product of the twentieth century, forged between the wars and especially during World War II, when French resistance to the German occupation had to fall back on the overseas territories (Ageron 1997). As an administrative and political concept, empire became ubiquitous in colonial administrative and political discourses only in the 1930s.

This unification occurred across several fields of practice. The turn of the century saw the emergence of the notion of a "colonial science" that drew specialists from a range of disciplines (anthropology, sociology, ethnography, geography, medicine, law, and administrative science). Supported by international organizations such as the International Colonial Institute (located in Brussels), colonial science found an institutional home first in the École coloniale (founded in 1889 to educate the highest ranks of colonial administration) and later in the Académie des sciences d'outre-mer (Academy of Overseas Sciences), created in 1923 and modeled after other prestigious French institutions of knowledge. In 1920, the Ministry of Colonies underwent a major internal reorganization: its several units were no longer divided by continent but rather by cross-regional subjects (economic development, health and welfare, law, political affairs, and so on). Over time, colonial administrators became correspondingly more specialized. After World

War II, technical competence in these subject fields became more highly valued than general knowledge of particular regions (though the École coloniale maintained distinct curricula for sub-Saharan Africa, including Madagascar, and the Asia-Pacific region).[2] Colonial administrators tended to remain within the zone for which they had been trained. But other circuits of material and symbolic goods developed over time and translated the idea of empire into a lived experience. Law was the field of theory and practice that was most important for the production of the empire as a relatively homogeneous social space (Saada 2002). Although most laws passed by the French parliament were not automatically applicable to the colonies, the tendency to unify legal dispositions through codification was very strong. In the late nineteenth century, "colonial law" began to emerge as a distinctive field. It was taught in law schools and discussed in specialized law journals. The same was true of colonial case law: legal decisions made in one territory became models for others.[3] The highest French courts in the civil domain (*cour de cassation*) and in public law (*conseil d'etat*) were also the supreme judges in colonial matters: their decisions contributed greatly to the production of an empire of law (Saada 2007). In this context, law often served as a means of translating between localized "social problems" and "major colonial questions." It offered a universalizing language and circuits for the diffusion of ways of framing and resolving colonial problems.

In addition, the circulation of personnel, colonial representations, technologies of power, and legal norms meant that strategies and practices of colonial domination traveled from one place to the other. This is especially true for the production of population categories, modalities of "group making," and legal definitions. In this domain, Algeria served as the main "laboratory" for imperial policies applied throughout the empire and was the source of many of its basic forms. The legal and political construction of the "indigenous subject"—the central element of the politics of colonial difference—was the most important of these.

The unifying forces within French imperialism have often been neglected by colonial historians, who tend to focus on developments within a particular region. Colonial historiography has been deeply marked by such analytical divisions. As already mentioned, the chronological division between the pre- and post-1830 empires has been fundamental, as has the distinction between "slavery" and "colonialism." In both cases, however, the continuities run deep. This appears clearly in the deliberations of the Commission for the Abolition of Slavery, established in February 1848 to draft the decree of abolition of slavery (April 27, 1848). Many of the commissioners wanted the decree to include a grant of full citizenship to the former slaves. The Algerian case, however, raised particular difficulties (Girollet 2000). The status of indigenous Algerians was by no means clear—it would be another thirty years before the category of the *indigène* or "subject" of the empire received fuller legal clarification. In the meantime, abolition plus citizenship implied that freed Algerian slaves would gain more rights than their indigenous masters. Faced with this "absurd" outcome, the commissioners opted to avoid all mention of citizenship in the general decree of abolition. This choice would reverberate through decades of subsequent debate about the differences between "citizens" and "indigenous subjects" in the colonies.

OPERATORS OF COLONIAL DIFFERENCE

Until World War II, the defining element of the "colonial politics of difference" was the opposition between "citizens" and "indigenous subjects" (*citoyen* versus *sujet*). Political subordination was the primary goal: subjects could only elect local representatives with limited decision power; in some territories, they had no forms of representation at all. But the distinction anchored myriad other forms of subordination in everyday life. Subjects paid a variety of special taxes, among them "the head tax" (*impôt de capitation*) reminiscent of feudal times. In most territories, they were obligated to work for the government without compensation (*corvée*). Subjection also implied a submission to long lists of rules regulating behavior and relationships with the colonizer. Called *Code de l'indigénat* (indigenous penal code), this disciplinary system was first developed in 1881 in Algeria and later exported to other French territories (Le Cour Grandmaison 2010; Merle 2002). It consisted of a list of crimes specific to indigenous populations, such as the refusal to pay taxes or perform *corvée*, subversive activities against the colonial order, and public manifestations of a "lack of respect" for colonial authority (Saada 2002). Some crimes were specific to particular regions: in New Caledonia, the *Code de l'indigénat* punished walking naked outside the reservation; coming to the capital city, Nouméa, after the curfew; or entering a European home without being invited (Merle 2002). Local administrators were empowered to judge and punish those crimes, ignoring the constitutional principle of the separation of powers.

The code reinforced broader differences in the legal norms pertaining to private lives of citizens and subjects. French citizens followed the French civil code while indigenous populations were subjected to colonial jurists' interpretations of "local customs" in such matters as marriage, inheritance, and contracts. Indigenous subjects were also subjected to special surveillance techniques and could not travel outside the administrative boundaries of their communities without an internal passport. To a large extent, this was the ancestor of the "identity card" that later became central to French administrative and police procedures: in this and other cases, metropolitan technologies of power owed a great deal to colonial experiences (About and Denis 2010).

Finally, subject status meant diminished access to employment, educational opportunities, and participation in the army: all of these crucial national institutions were highly segregated. The higher ranks of colonial administration were closed to *indigènes* until the late 1920s.

Taken together, these distinctions describe a system of legal pluralism in the colonies that departed radically from the revolutionary ideal of producing the nation through a unique system of norms and laws (Bell 2001). Although partly a pragmatic expression of the limits of colonial power, this pluralism eventually acquired a rationale in late nineteenth-century evolutionary theories of law, analogous to the anthropological accounts of racial capacities for civilization. Specific legal systems belonged to different stages on the "civilization scale" and could not be successfully interposed.

NATIONHOOD AND CITIZENSHIP

The distinction between subject and citizen also hinged on an increasingly elaborate distinction between nationality and citizenship (*nationalité* and *citoyenneté*). Until the Lamine-Gueye law after World War II, indigenous subjects were French nationals—they were legally part of the French state and subject to its sovereignty. But they did not enjoy the full range of rights associated with the notion of citizenship.[4]

This was not simply a difference in the scope of rights accorded different peoples—rather, nationality and citizenship belonged to different fields of practice. Toward the mid-nineteenth century, nationalité became the central concept for describing the legal link between an individual and the state. This linkage began to be the object of intense debate among French legal theorists and politicians. This scrutiny culminated in 1889 with the passage of the *Code de la nationalité*, which defined Frenchness as a complex combination of place of birth (*jus soli*) and descent (*jus sanguinis*) (Brubaker 1992).

Citoyenneté, in contrast, was a concept rooted in the affirmation of popular sovereignty against monarchic rule—a critical principle of the French Revolution. But in the nineteenth century this principle played a diminishing role as a legal concept, losing clarity and significance: the numerous constitutions of the period omitted it entirely (Lochak 1991). Rather, it became a political concept—object of constant debates about the rights and obligations of participation in the policy but with little presence in law.

Despite this disappearance, the longer arc of French liberalism involved a slow conflation of two concepts. Nationality increasingly carried with it a number of political and social rights: "universal" male suffrage in 1848 and its extension to women in 1944 and—beginning in the late nineteenth century—the growing range of social welfare programs linked to nationality are milestones of this process.

The colonial division of nationality from citizenship ran contrary to this "triumph of the citizen" in nineteenth-century France (Rosanvallon 1992). It points to the deep but often overlooked connection between citizenship and civility in the drawing of the boundaries of the French nation—a connection that was explicitly translated as a link between race and citizenship in the empire.

THE ALGERIAN LABORATORY

The "indigenous subject" was not a ready-made concept in 1830: rather, it was the result of a slow process of adjustment by local colonial power to shifting conditions of domination in the second part of the nineteenth century. Of course, the forms of rule over indigenous inhabitants have long been scrutinized by colonial administrators and legal theorists. During the old regime, the successive *Codes noirs* (black codes), regulating relationships between masters and slaves, were the most significant attempt to establish coherent categories of colonial rule. In 1685 and again in 1723, the codes declared slaves to be "personal property." The French Revolution produced a radical change in both the theory and practice of colonization and set the terms of a debate that would span the next two centuries. Political rights were granted to "free men of color" in 1792. Slavery was abolished in 1794. Both decisions, heavily influenced by slave uprisings and diverse forms of political expression (Dubois 2004), were rescinded by the First Empire. The Restoration and the July monarchy in the first half of the nineteenth century proved to be more liberal and witnessed the reemergence of an abolitionist movement. Although this movement was rather timid compared with that of Great Britain and—by that point—applied to a much reduced overseas empire, equal rights for "free people of color" were granted in 1833.

With the conquest of Algiers in 1830, new questions emerged that were linked no longer to slavery but to the management of indigenous populations with developed political and social institutions and corresponding capacities to resist French conquest and rule. In the treaty of the capitulation of Algiers, the French state pledged not to undermine the "freedom of its inhabitants of all classes, their religions, their property, their businesses and industries." It pledged further "to respect [the Algerians'] wives." This precedent proved decisive in the construction of the category of indigène. For the next thirty years, the exact degree of "Frenchness" of the Algerians was the subject of ongoing political and legal controversies. In 1862, the French court in Algiers decided that Algerians were "French but not in the same way as the French people born on old French soil." More precision was given by a law in 1865 that specified that indigenous people, "Muslim" and "Israelite" alike, were French nationals without being citizens and that they retained their original "personal status"—that is, their traditional legal condition defined by customary law. The distinction between "subject" and "citizen" was thus rooted not in participation in the political sphere but in the norms applicable in the private sphere—or, to put it in Norbert Elias's terms, in participation in a specific *civilization* (Elias 2000).

A few short years later, this uniform approach to legal pluralism came to an end. In 1870, the Crémieux decree determined that Algerian Jews had a "higher capacity" to "assimilate to French civilization" and on this basis granted them full citizenship. Collective exceptions of this kind were infrequent, however, and generally confined to the old colonies. In Guadeloupe, Martinique, Réunion, and French Guyana, former slaves had been granted full citizenship rights in 1848, upon the second abolition of slavery. That same year, voting rights were given to the inhabitants of the old coastal French establishments of Senegal and India. In 1916, in the midst of World War I, and in an attempt to recruit more soldiers, the inhabitants of the "four communes of Senegal" (Dakar, Saint-Louis, Rufisque, and Gorée) were declared full French citizens, without having to give up their personal status, defined by Islamic law (Diouf 2000). Elsewhere, the distinction between citizens and subjects spread from Algeria to most territories of the empire.

IMPERIAL NATIONHOOD

While rigid colonial divisions emerged in Algeria and elsewhere, nationality had become the object of intense political and legal scrutiny in metropolitan France in the 1870s and 1880s (Brubaker 1992). These debates led to the 1889 law that defined French nationality as transmitted through filiation and, in the absence of this criterion, by birth on the French territory and socialization in France. A child born of foreign parents who immigrated to

France was considered to be French at the age of majority—if he or she had lived in France for at least five years during the "formative" period of his or her life.[5] This text, which still broadly defines French nationality, was initially applied to the "old colonies" and to Algeria—with the caveat in the latter case that it did not change the condition of indigenous peoples. After much debate, the law was extended on this basis to other colonies in 1897. The privileges of birth on "French soil," described by the principle of jus soli, were suspended in this colonial application of the law. Racial and "civilizational" differences between indigenous peoples and the mostly European foreigners present in France figured prominently in this suspension. Indigenous children had to be "assimilated" to the local populations because they did "not belong to the European race, the white race" and were not like those foreigners "whose civilization and degree of social progress correspond to ours" (Solus 1927: 59.)

Here race served both as a practical criterion and a founding principle for the distinction between populations. Race was understood by colonial administrators and legal theorists less as a biological reality than as a cultural one based on the characteristics of distinct civilizations (Stoler 2002). It was also a political concept that mapped international relations of power. In Indochina, for example, the populations considered "assimilable" to French civilization were the (non-French) Europeans and the Japanese—both resident in the peninsula in small numbers. Chinese people, in contrast, were numerous but had the status of indigenous subjects until 1930, when pressure from the Chinese government produced an agreement to treat Chinese as foreigners "assimilated to Europeans" (Nanking Treaty, 1930).

RACE AND LAW

At the end of the nineteenth century, jurists and administrators justified the exclusion of indigenous people from citizenship on the basis of two claims: first, they argued that there was an organic link between private norms of behavior and public participation to the polity, that is, between civility and citizenship (Rosanvallon 1992); second, they defended a strong articulation between race and law.

Both assertions expressed the social evolutionism prevalent in contemporary legal thought: colonial legal theorists, in particular, insisted on the deep connection between social norms, defined by civil law, political organization, and stages in the civilizing process. In this context, participation in French civilization (defined as a complex set of behaviors in the private sphere—civility) was a precondition to the exercise of citizenship rights.

For example, in Algeria and sub-Saharan Africa, colonial jurists and state actors repeated ad nauseam that followers of Islamic law could not participate in the French polity and deliberate about rules that they refused to abide by in their own domestic space (Dareste 1916). In this context, polygamy and more broadly norms regulating domestic organization and gender relations were considered defining features of civilization. These norms became the subjects of repeated and intense judicial scrutiny in the context of individual applications for French citizenship (Blévis 2003).

Colonial legal doctrine considered that each legal system was the product of a civilization and, more fundamentally, a race. Indigenous people had to remain subjects because they could not change civilizations, any more than they could change their race. One consequence of this argument was that the French civil code, far from being the monument to universal logic and reason that its original authors claimed, became a kind of "customary law" for the "French indigenous person."

This had consequences for French citizens as well. In Algeria, French citizens who converted to Islam were not allowed to acquire the legal status of "Muslim indigenous people." Marriages contracted under Islamic law, in this context, were considered invalid. Conversely, Algerian converts to Christianity—a significant group among the Kabyle—remained barred from full citizenship and were legally defined by the oxymoronic category of "Christian Muslim indigenous person."

IMPOSSIBLE ASSIMILATION

These connections between civility and citizenship and between race and legal systems contributed to a dramatic shift in the meaning of "assimilation." In the years following the Revolution, assimilation had strong universalistic implications and was exemplified by the export of French institutions to the colonies. Law—and more generally civil and political rights—was believed to have civilizing power. The promulgation of the French civil code on the coast of Senegal in 1830, the 1833 law granting equality to "free people of color," and the granting of voting rights to former slaves in 1848 were prominent expressions of this idea.

By the late nineteenth century, assimilation signified something rather different: a predominantly individual process of adopting and incorporating the traits of French civilization (Lewis 1962). Legal theorists strongly criticized the artificial imposition of institutions appropriate only to the French "milieu." In 1848, "assimilation theory had prevailed. Race distinctions were ignored. Nobody understood how difficult it was to treat a Muslim or a Hindu exactly like a French person from France" (Dareste 1916: 7). The president of the Colonial Sociological Congress held in Paris in 1900 opened the meeting with a cry of "No assimilation! This is the motto that we need to follow in all matters: law, administration and politics. It is the main principle of all colonial sociology" (*Congrès international de sociologie coloniale* 1901: 237).

Here participation in the French polity was not defined by the voluntary adhesion to a common political project, as it was during the Revolution, but by an individual process of internationalization of "French ways." French thinkers imposed further conditions on this process. It was not sufficient to want to assimilate—individual will was not enough and came under suspicion (Girault 1929). Nor was formal education in the French system adequate, since the "imprint" left by the familial milieu in the first years of life would always prevail (Mérimée 1931: 66–67).

Instead, assimilation was supposed to be a process of unconscious absorption of French civilization through imitation. In their reasoning, French colonial theorists drew heavily on late nineteenth-century neo-Lamarckian theories that established a strong connection between "race," "civilization," and "milieu" (Rabinow 1989). These implied that individuals are the product of an organic relationship with their material and social environment. "Milieu" is dialectically linked to "heredity" and "soil" to the "blood." This vision takes us far from the Durkheimian conception of socialization as the result of state institutions (Durkheim 1956)—a view often wrongly represented as the cornerstone of French Republican ideology (Beaud and Noiriel 1990).

The earlier history of inclusiveness and in particular the successful grant of citizenship to former slaves in 1848 was a historical anomaly in this context and produced a correspondingly new interpretation of slavery. Colonial theorists argued that the long and often intimate interactions between masters and slaves in the colonies of the Americas had "initiated" the African populations to French civilization (Billiard 1899: 8). Perversely, slavery came to be seen as a historical condition for assimilation and for political and civil equality.

Although the sources of this fundamental shift in thinking were varied and complex, it owed much to colonial Realpolitik—to the adaptation of colonial strategies to the realities of colonial rule. In Algeria and elsewhere, colonial administrators were constrained by scarce personnel and resources. They governed populations that were numerically superior and largely hostile. In this context, the colonial state had to appropriate "traditional rule" in order to maintain order (Amselle 2003).

Assimilation as a process of adoption of French norms and cultural practices survived the end of empire and remains central to the politics, administration, and legal practices surrounding foreigners and immigration in France. It can be argued that it is one of the most vivid legacies of the colonial experience. The concept, directly descended from colonial practices, still explicitly figures in the civil code in the provisions regulating naturalization. The foreigner who wants to become French needs to "prove his or her assimilation to the French community, notably through the knowledge of the French language and of the rights and duties conferred by French citizenship." He or she is subjected to examination by the French administration during an "assimilation interview." More broadly, the notion of assimilation and its correlate, "integration," are central to the discourse of immigration, past and present. As in colonial times, it often refers to behavior in the private sphere that is considered the defining feature of French civilization. The particulars of gender relations and domestic organization figure prominently among them.

NATIONAL MODELS AND EMPIRE

In the sociological tradition and in French political rhetoric, France is often represented as the most accomplished example of the civic nation, where belonging is based on adherence to a common political project. This is usually contrasted to the German ethnic conception of the nation. Quoting Rogers Brubaker, a recent proponent of this argument, "if the French understanding of nationhood has been state-centered and assimilationist, the German understanding has been Volk-centered and differentialist" (Brubaker 1992: 1). In making this judgment, sociologists and historians have relied especially on differences in the ascription of citizenship and the naturalization of foreigners in the two countries: in Germany, relatively low rates of naturalization and the ascription of citizenship based on jus sanguinis (on descent) were viewed as evidence of the closure of the German polity. Elements of jus soli in French law—ascription of citizenship based on place of birth (or at majority)—provided evidence of the civic character of the French nation.

Within this tradition, the colonial case has been the subject of diverse interpretations. Often it is considered as an exception. Dominique Schnapper, a prominent sociologist of citizenship, has notably dismissed the colonial case as a "legal monster." For Schnapper, the colonial case was an unsustainable exception to the construction of modern citizenship and should thereby be discounted in attempts to understand the larger process (Schnapper 1998a: 125–126). Brubaker, for his part, made use of the colonial case as a proof of the strength of the civic model of the nation, with an emphasis on the "mission libératrice and civilisatrice" (1992: 11).[6] These contradictory interpretations of the colonial case suggest either a problem with the model or a misunderstanding of the colonial situation. The history sketched in this essay suggests that both are at work.

Some more recent efforts to describe the colonial dissociation of citizenship and nationality have embraced the notion of "colonial contradictions" in the French Republic (Bancel, Blanchard, and Vergès 2003). In the wake of the 2005 riots in France, this critique has focused on the denunciation of hypocrisy in French republican ideology—universalistic in the metropole and differentialist with respect to the empire and its immigrants. A wide range of academic and popular publications linked together current forms of social discrimination, political disenfranchisement, and the rather problematic notion of "colonial heritage" (Bancel, Blanchard, and Lemaire 2003). Though a step forward compared with the previous neglect of the empire and its aftermath, this approach and its central descriptive tool, the notion of "contradiction," are problematic (Saada 2006; Wilder 2005). There was no such neat division, and "contradictions" abounded in the metropolitan space (the exclusion of women, people with mental disorders, criminals). While largely critical of the sociological model of the French nation, such analysis is also limited by its reversal of that model's terms. Denouncing the contradictions of "the French Republic," it assumes the existence and agency of this historical abstraction. In many ways, the Foucauldian notion of "problematization" takes us further than "contradiction" (Foucault 1994), in the sense that imperial rule "poses a problem" for French political discourses and practices more than it contradicts them. It allows us to see that the colonial dissociation of nationality and citizenship does not "contradict" the French model of the nation but reveals deep tensions within it. Most notably, it directs our attention to the importance of race within French definitions of the nation and of the articulation between civility and citizenship in the metropole as well as in the colonies (Saada 2012b). Rethinking the opposition of civic and ethnic nations is one obvious result of this critique, as is—more broadly—a de-emphasis of national models in favor of a more historically grounded analysis of power relations.

NOTES

1. July 6, 1830, arrêté. Quoted by Pinson de Ménerville (1884: 5).

2. Because Algeria was composed of fully integrated French departments and Tunisia and Morocco were protectorates, state employees in these territories were not part of the colonial administration per se.

3. This did not apply to Algeria (which, as part of France, had a specific legal system and legislation). Nor did it apply to the protectorates of Morocco and Tunisia, which had kept most of their previous judicial institutions.

4. To a considerable extent, the 1946 Lamine-Gueye law and the constitution of the Fourth Republic that granted "French citizenship" to all inhabitants of the French Empire did not really put an end to this distinction, insofar as they reproduced the colonial divide through the opposition between "local law citizen" and "common law citizen" (*citoyen de statut de droit local* and *citoyen de statut de droit commun*) and through the institution of correspondingly separate electoral bodies.

5. Another important disposition was that a person born in France of foreign parents themselves born on the French territory would be French at birth (Brubaker 1992).

6. Brubaker overlooked the fact, however, that in the German colonies up until around 1910 the *jus sanguinis* did not apply, insofar as indigenous women marrying German men in the colonies, along with their children, were classified as "white" or "European" under colonial law (Steinmetz 2007a). In this respect, colonial law was not in fact decisive proof of a clear difference between France and Germany.

TWELVE

Empire and Developmentalism in Colonial India

CHANDAN GOWDA

The conceptual architecture of "development" is a powerful intellectual and political legacy of colonial empires of the nineteenth and early twentieth centuries. An overwhelming consensus that newly decolonizing societies embraced the idea of development in the post–World War II era has resulted in scant scholarly attention to this historical phenomenon. Harry Truman's 1949 presidential address, which declared the obligation of the Western countries toward the "underdeveloped areas" of the world, is usually seen as the originary moment of development discourse (Escobar 1995; Esteva 2010). Historians have also noted that the British and French used the discourse of development to legitimize their colonial rule in the 1940s and that it subsequently found official endorsement in decolonizing states (Cooper and Packard 1997: 7). The intellectual lineage of development as a state-supported discourse extends further back in time. By reconstructing the conceptual foundations of the elite's development imagination in the state of Mysore in South India between the late nineteenth century and the end of colonial rule in the mid-twentieth century, this chapter recuperates a powerful intellectual legacy of nineteenth-century colonialism, which later attracted academic prestige in the guise of modernization theory.[1]

HISTORICAL BACKGROUND

Two-fifths of the territory of British India consisted of "Native" or "Indian" states whose rulers had formally pledged their loyalty to the colonial power in return for limited political autonomy in running their administrative affairs. This colonial strategy of extracting political compliance along with annual financial and military tributes from local rulers in exchange for semiautonomy in administering their states is better known as the strategy of indirect rule (Fisher 1991). Under the scheme of indirect rule, the British warded off the threat of political rebellion from the native rulers, ensured a steady revenue supply for themselves, and saved on the costs of administering those states directly.[2]

After fifty years of direct colonial rule between 1831 and 1881, the British restored a descendant of the previous ruling family as the ruler of the state and brought Mysore under indirect rule.[3] Mysore's territory was the third largest among the Native States in colonial India. In 1900, its population was around five million, 90 percent of whom lived in agricultural villages. The state's political elite consisted of the maharaja (monarch), his dewan (prime minister), and civil servants in charge of administering the eighteen departments; the state's decision-making authority was concentrated in them.

The state elite of Mysore initiated numerous programs of economic development within the space of institutional semiautonomy opened up by indirect colonial rule. The political scientist James Manor notes that the monarchs and prime ministers of Mysore were "heroes in the eyes of nationalists throughout India . . . since they provided evidence of how splendidly Indians could govern themselves" (1978: 13). An analysis of the elite's discourse of development in Mysore reveals its intellectual lineage. Further, it clarifies the centrality of the colonial-imperial context within which "development" became attractive for the state elite in Mysore.

An exclusive focus on Mysore is not to suggest a Mysorean exceptionalism or the autochthonous origin of its elite's discourses. The discursive field pertaining to development was not uniquely contained within Mysore; in fact, many of the certitudes in elite thought were part of the discursive traffic across British India and outside. According to the historian David Ludden the foundations of India's "development regime" were laid between the early and late nineteenth century (Ludden 1992: 253–261; also, Ludden 2005). The massive knowledge accumulated by the British in the form of land surveys, maps, censuses, ethnographic documentation, and crop, soil, irrigation, and mineral data formed the basis of standardized instruments of rule and the centralization of the colonial state's administrative functions. Sugata Bose clarifies that while the techniques for producing macroeconomic statistical knowledge were in place by the early nineteenth century, the idiom of nationalist development became manifest only toward the late nineteenth century (Bose 1998: 47–48).[4] Nationalist economic thought was largely the creation of figures such as, among others, Dadabhai Naoroji, M. G. Ranade, R. C. Dutt, and G. K. Gokhale, who had found the economic thought of Adam Smith, John Stuart Mill, and David Ricardo attractive but not suited to economic conditions in colonial India (Ganguli 1977: 56–85). The intellectual influence of John Stuart Mill and Herbert Spencer on the dewans of Mysore has been recorded (Chandrasekhara 1981: 195; Gundappa [1971] 1997: 15). A few of them were personally associated with nationalist economic thinkers outside Mysore, including Ranade and Gokhale (Chandrasekhara 1981: 182).[5]

The word "development" surfaces in the Mysore elite's political vocabulary in the late nineteenth century with reference to economic matters. In 1881, Dewan Rangacharlu stated: "The development of the various industries on which the prosperity of the country is dependent equally demands our consideration" (AOD [1881–1899] 1914: 7). In 1886, Dewan Seshadri Iyer noted that the high-ranking nations of his day had "considered heavy protection duties not too high a price to pay for the fostering of new industries and have reaped their reward in the rapid development of their mineral wealth" (AOD [1881–1899] 1914: 100). In the early twentieth century, "development" continued to primarily signify a concern with economic issues. In 1918, Dewan Visvesvaraya, who later wrote *Planned Economy for India* (1936), a pioneering book on planning in India, observed: "Every progressive nation . . . is aiming to secure for itself better organization, greater cooperation from its people, improved methods of manufacture, cheap supply of raw materials and increased enterprise in trade. The developments we have undertaken in Mysore are in consonance with the trend of this new thought. . . . We have in a small way educated the people to the importance of economic development" (AOD [1913–1938] 1938: 48).

Often synonymous with economic development, "development" was a subcomponent of a more expansive concept of progress. This becomes evident in Dewan Visvesvaraya's declaration: "Progress, if it is to be sustained, should be many-sided; but, in the present state of the country, economic progress with which we are concerned demands our chief attention" ([1914b] 1917: 152). However, as we shall see, a seemingly economic concept such as development was embedded in a conceptual schema pertaining to "noneconomic" realms.[6]

My archive consists mainly of the political elite's speeches delivered at the Mysore Representative Assembly (MRA), the Mysore Legislative Council (MLC), the Mysore Economic Conference (MEC), state exhibitions, and other institutional fora in Mysore over six decades.[7] In restricting focus on

the elite's discourses of development, I have been guided by the methodological strategy Kwame Anthony Appiah uses in his conceptual history of
race in the United States. He explains that the social practice of "semantic
deference" justified his decision to examine Thomas Jefferson's writings on
race in order to recover the meaning of race in the United States in the late
eighteenth and nineteenth centuries (Appiah 1996: 41). Many technical
terms, Appiah explains, become popular linguistic currency even when their
meanings are not clearly understood by most users. When asked to clarify
the precise meaning of such technical terms, like "race" in Jefferson's time,
nonspecialists are likely to point to specialists for help (Appiah 1996: 42).
An analogous sociocultural predicament of semantic deference can be presumed to obtain among nonspecialists in Mysore in relation to the discourse of development.

   In addition to venues such as the MRA, the MLC, and the exhibitions, the
elite frequently delivered speeches at schools and professional associations,
at the inaugural ceremonies of new hospitals, hostels, electric and water facilities, and other infrastructural facilities. On many an occasion, a speaker
would cite from predecessors' speeches, rendering an intertextual continuity in the space of development discourse. Collections of these speeches were
published and distributed to various offices and libraries, both inside and
outside Mysore. Also, local newspapers frequently carried excerpts from
them. An examination of the elite speeches and writings on development
across six decades reveals the consistent operation of four key discourses:
neomercantilism, utilitarianism, social evolutionism, and orientalism.[8] Despite the frequent interarticulation among these discourses, they are analytically distinguishable. This exercise in identifying the chief discursive strands
is not to view them as reified entities. These discourses often reinforced their
self-validity while being in a dynamic relationship with historical processes
and acquiring new valence through new textual affinities.[9]

NEOMERCANTILISM

Historians have noted the key influence of the neomercantilist writings
of Friedrich List (1789–1846) on nationalist economic thought in late nine-
teenth- and early twentieth-century India.[10] B. N. Ganguli, the economist
and historian, has pointed out that "the principal focus of attention" of the
nineteenth-century Indian intellectuals was "the anti-*laissez faire* doctrines
of List" (1977: 24). Another historian has also observed that the "macroeconomics" of this period was based less in classical economic theory than
in "the ideas of the German Historical School and particularly of Friedrich

List" from whose work the economic nationalists drew "the basic arguments for infant industry protection" (Datta 1978: 3–6). Ranade, one of the most influential among the first generation of nationalist economists in India, formulated "an approach to Indian development along the lines enunciated by List" (Chakravarty 1997: 46).

List, a key neomercantilist, was the "first universally read opponent of free trade in the 19th century" (Heckscher 1935: 325). His nation-centered theory of economic development that was to guide state policy in his native Germany, which he considered to be backward in relation to Britain, had found admirers even in post-Restoration Japan (Cumings 1999b: 61). In *The National System of Political Economy* published in German in 1841 and in English in 1856, List had proposed an economic theory that presumed the economy of a nation-state as its unit of analysis in opposition to Adam Smith's argument that "'political' or *national* economy must be replaced by 'cosmopolitical or world-wide economy'" (List [1841] 1904: 98; italics in the original). He argued that Smith's advocacy of a worldwide laissez-faire would allow an already dominant economic power such as England to become the most powerful nation in the world, to the detriment of countries such as France, Germany, and Italy (List [1841] 1904: 103).[11] His prescription that the states in backward countries should actively shield and foster their "infant industries" through the imposition of tariffs on imports from industrially advanced countries had tremendous appeal to Indian economic thinkers, who urged the British to espouse a similar obligation toward industry in India (Gokhale 1962: 335; Ranade 1900: 9–23).[12] List's model of a protectionist, autarkic national economy was also presupposed in the Mysore elite's model of development.[13] An economist at the University of Mysore has recorded the appeal of List's protectionist ideas in colonial India: "The infant-industry argument . . . has been immortalized by Friedrich List. It has gained so much popularity as to be exalted to the level of an axiom" (Balakrishna 1940: 240).[14]

List presumed colonialism as being a permanent political-economic feature in the world; indeed, for him, the possession of colonies was a sign of a developed national economy (List [1841] 1904: 142, 145). Although List used the example of India to demonstrate how Britain had adopted protectionist policies to safeguard its own "cotton and silk manufactories" (34–36), his prescription of state-directed industrial development was exclusively for the "civilized" countries and not for the "barbarous and half-civilised countries of Central and South America, of Asia and Africa" (153). A dubious environmental determinism secured List's theoretical proposition that restricted the option of industrial development and the right to colonize to "civilized" countries.[15] Despite List's theoretical endorsement of European colonialism, it is ironic that Indian nationalist economists should find inspiration in this "false prophet" (Ganguli 1977: 79). In a good illustration of a creative editorial relationship that many Indian intellectuals had with Western thinkers who built theoretical models exclusively for Western countries, economists such as Ranade, Gokhale, and R. C. Dutt strategically appropriated those parts of List's theory that were useful for their arguments while rejecting those they found to be unacceptable.[16] Ranade, for instance, argued that List's theory of environmental determinism was a contingent, not a transhistorical fact (Ranade 1900: 24). Dutt borrowed from List's discussion of the exploitative economic policies of the British in colonial India and moved on to affirm, contra List, the capacity of Indians to exercise historical agency in developing their manufacturing abilities (Dutt [1901] 1970: 208–209).

In addition to the basic presumption of a national economy, other mercantilist tenets guided the Mysore elite's imagination of development. Chief among them was a calculated economic orientation toward the population. The early mercantilists of the seventeenth century harbored "a fanatical desire to increase population" as that was a source of wealth-generating labor (Heckscher 1935: 158).[17] Although this view lost force consequent to the ascendance of the Malthusian caution toward population increase, rapid technological innovations in the mid-nineteenth century, which suggested an unlimited capacity to manage the needs of a growing population, tempered the Malthusian demographic alarmism (Jagirdar 1963: 139). Indeed, an anti-Malthusian view of population was an important component of List's economic philosophy, which affirmed the power of machine technology to sustain demographic expansion (List [1841] 1905: 142).

The Mysore elite also shared this view of population as an important constituent of a nation's productive powers. Although they did not favor a large population,[18] they viewed it as an economic asset that could be harnessed to increase the state's wealth. An early instance of this view is found in Dewan Rangacharlu's annual address to the MRA in 1882: "Now England . . . supplies the greater portion of the world with cloth and other manufactures. [This is] . . . the result of numerous individual men devoting their intelligence to effect small discoveries and improvements from day to day in their several occupations which in their aggregate produce such marvelous wealth and general prosperity. What then may not be accomplished if the large population in this country once entered on a similar career of progress" (AOD [1881–1889] 1914: 20). In this view, the local population consisted of potentially useful individuals, whose contributions in the aggregate would result in enormous prosperity and wealth for the country. Each individual is seen as a member of a national community of potential producers with a significant economic role to perform in aid of the country's progress. Another illustration of this attitude is also contained in Dewan Visvesvarya's address to the MEC in 1915: "Our town-population, which is less than one-tenth of the total population, is inadequate for industrial needs and should be increased to one-fifth" ([1915a] 1917: 239).

In the early decades of the twentieth century, the elite made explicit reference to Mysore's connectedness with a worldwide system of economic transactions. The economic consequences of World War I and the Great Depression had been felt in Mysore too. The elite's preference now was for an economy that would be as self-reliant as possible amid vulnerability to international economic trends. Although the mercantilist image of a state-protected autarkic economy was harder to sustain as an empirical possibility, the state elite continued to imagine the nation as a body of producers and consumers, whose interests were reconciled in the functioning of a national economy (Ismail [1933] 1936: 245; Visvesvaraya [1914a] 1917: 205).

UTILITARIANISM

Eric Stokes has provided a detailed account of the important relation of utilitarian philosophy to the formation of British colonial policies in India (Stokes [1959] 1992). Jeremy Bentham and James Mill were key figures in this historical episode. For them, a government could achieve the key utilitarian objective of maximizing happiness by securing the institution of private property and allowing each individual to pursue his self-interest. An ideal political system "reconciled liberty and security and laid on individual action no further restraint than was beneficial," whereby "happiness would be . . . 'maximized'" (Stokes 1959: 67). Whereas Mill perceived "the device of representative democracy" as ensuring a steady check on any possibilities of despotism in England, he ruled it out as an option for India where oriental despotism was inherent to its political institutions" (Stokes 1958: 68). Since Mill expected the utilitarian colonial government to successfully transform a backward civilization such as India, colonial paternalism did not appear a violation of the utilitarian ideal of minimal government. And a pedagogic relationship between the colonial state and the colonized was justified on the grounds that the former better understood "the 'real' and long-term interests" of the latter (Iyer 1960: 13). In Mysore, the ruler and his bureaucrats assumed a similar paternalist relationship with the local subjects.

The utilitarian model of government had appeared to be politically valid for the Mysore elite all through the nineteenth century. In 1874, Dewan Rangacharlu had affirmed: "In this utilitarian age, . . . social institutions can only hope to stand by their capacity to meet the wants of the people" ([1874] 1988: 8). The rulers of Mysore in the late nineteenth and early twentieth centuries had been educated in the principles of utilitarian moral philosophy (Sastri 1937: 17–18). In keeping with classic utilitarianism, which evaluated the merits of action through the conceptual yardstick of happiness, they often declared that the objective of their government was to secure the happiness of their subjects. In 1907, for instance, the ruler declared: "It shall ever be my aim and ambition in life to do all that lies in me to promote the progress and the prosperity of my beautiful State, and the happiness of my beloved people" (Wadiyar [1907] 1934: 44).[19]

In elaborating their moral philosophy, utilitarians deployed the concept of utility to evaluate the desirable consequences of action, with an aim toward undermining "those definitions of social purpose which excluded the interests of the majority of people, or in one sense of all people such as definitions of value in terms of an existing order or in terms of a god" (Williams 1983: 327). This concept of utility was gradually absorbed—without its ethical content—across other domains of thought, such as neoclassical economic models, rational choice theory, and, more generally, a capitalist business ethos (Biervert and Wieland 1993: 93–115). Although utilitarianism surfaced in the elite discourses in its original avatar as moral philosophy, its instrumental version appeared more frequently. An orientation toward the world solely based on considerations of utility is exemplified in concepts such as waste, efficiency, productivity, and energy, which extended analytical leverage in the elite's calibration of the desired means of economic development.

The state elite used the concept of waste to identify instances of loss of economic value.[20] A reductionist understanding of the world as solely a resource to be exploited, this perceptual attitude united various issues under a common metric of value. Peasants who worked only a part of the year, illiteracy, lack of awareness of "the ways of the civilized," improper business ideals, unconcern with one's health—all of these were seen as so many instances of waste from the vantage point of an economism that presupposed these matters to be connected with fostering a national economy. The concept of efficiency is integrally linked to the definition of waste; indeed, to be efficient is not to be wasteful. Increasing agricultural and industrial productivity was also a constant concern among the state elite, who frequently asserted that increase of industrial production was the "main object of the economic policy of every country" (AOD [1913–1938] 1938: 49). Attesting to the dominance of concepts from the natural sciences in interpreting socio-economic institutions, "energy" also surfaced frequently in the elite articulations of development.[21] An attribute perceived to be present in all individuals, it could be channeled into useful activities, that is, activities that aided in the development of the state.

ORIENTALISM

Essentialist characterizations such as the lazy native, fatalistic peasant, ill effects of tropical climate on the characters of Indians, and the inherently despotic nature of Indian rulers served to uphold the backwardness of Indians and the necessity therefore of a colonial civilizing mission.[22] The Mysore state elite's interests in development found an anchor in such an orientalist regime of representation.

Edward Said used the term "orientalism" to refer to the complex discursive apparatus that posited an essential ontological difference between societies of the East and the West or the analogous binary of the Orient and the Occident. This discursive apparatus, he argued, was produced and sustained as a result of the West's colonial and imperial dominance in the world (Said 1978).[23] The discourse of orientalism would be more durable, of course, when the oriental subjects themselves acknowledged its validity and identified themselves through it.

The historian Ronald Inden has noted that the British utilitarians, the European Indologists, and the Evangelicals of the nineteenth century were agreed that India had an "other-worldly or spiritual orientation," which meant that its civilizational essence had a religious basis (Inden 1990: 85).[24] Inden's main observation is that the Indological objectification of Hinduism as a religion that privileged the "'imagination' and the 'passions' rather than 'reason' and the 'will'" was ultimately a post-Enlightenment exercise of defining Europe as the home of transcendent Reason (Inden 1990: 89). Indological views of Hinduism as a religion that had degenerated from the seventh century onward informed nineteenth-century colonial clichés about the stagnant and unchanging nature of India (Inden 1990: 117–122). Further, as Michael Adas has argued, scientific and technological progress came to be perceived as a sign of civilizational and racial superiority in the late nineteenth century: "By the last decades of the nineteenth century, British colonizers—whether missionaries, explorers, or government officials—tended to measure 'evolutionary distance' in terms of technological development" (1989: 310).

From the vantage point of these orientalist discourses, the political, economic, and cultural institutions of Mysore appeared a deviation from their counterparts in the occidentalized West—if the West was modern, scientific, efficient, energetic, and progressive, then Mysore was traditional, nonscientific, inefficient, unenergetic, and backward. The state elite frequently alluded to Europe as the home of modern civilization while viewing India as a decadent, religiously oriented civilization. Addressing students at the Maharani's Girl School in 1883, Dewan Seshadri Iyer conveyed a robust optimism on the transformations under way in India: "The old Aryan civilization of the east, after centuries of decay and degeneration, now shows signs of healthy revival by contact with the more modern civilization of the west" (cited in Chandrasekhara 1981: 104). Two decades later, Sri Kantirava Narasimharaja Wadiyar, the monarch's brother, reminisced about his recently concluded visit to Europe: "the high state of civilization, and the steady and ready state of progress the West maintains, as compared with the lethargy and conservatism of the East, cannot but produce a most striking impression upon the mind of any visitor from our land" ([1913] 1942: 30). Dewan Visvesvaraya deplored the otherworldly orientation of Hindus, which did not provide favorable grounds for a relationship of command to existing resources, unlike the secular, materialist orientation to the world seen to exist in Western countries (Visvesvaraya [1913b] 1917: 63). More than two decades later, Dewan Mirza Ismail would remark that Europe had been "the creator of modern civilization" ([1936] 1942: 39).

The Mysore elite's acceptance of the spurious orientalist claims was selective. For instance, their visions of development did not engage with representations of Indians as cunning and deceitful. A probable reason for this avoidance, in addition to the paramount consideration of self-respect, is that these did not seem meaningful variables for explaining economic backwardness in Mysore. However, the elite concurred that the local subjects were indisposed toward industrial discipline and valorized the importance of modern technology.[25]

The power of orientalism can also be seen in the symbolic significance of Japan for the elite. Japan was an inspiration for the Mysore state elite as it had proved that an Eastern society could achieve progress. The editor of a Mysore weekly noted: "Japan is an oriental country which has marched forward with the West, and a country which has done it within the shortest space of time.... Mysore may not be Japan but it has nothing to lose by envying Japan, studying Japan and by following Japan!" (Josyer 1930: 47). Japan was objectified as a country that had disproved myths about the backwardness of Eastern societies. Invocations of its success by almost every dewan of Mysore were therefore often a rhetorical prelude for proclaiming Mysore's potential capacity for success (Banerji [1925] 1926: 1158–1159; Urs [1917] 1953: 189–190). The perceived commonality between the two societies was their location in the Orient.[26]

In formulating development programs, the state elite accepted the validity of the orientalist stereotypes about Indians but believed that their moral and political responsibility consisted in overcoming them. This political imperative became evident in the Dewan Rangacharlu's speech in 1882, which signaled the importance of the founding of MRA for refuting a common orientalist allegation: "The universal satisfaction with which it [the news of the MRA's founding] has been received throughout Southern India, and I believe, in other parts of India . . . refutes the assumption often made that they are not yet prepared for self-government" (AOD [1881–1899] 1914: 11). In 1922, another dewan declared that an electric power installation built by local engineers proved the illegitimacy of the orientalist charge of the inefficiency of Indians (Banerji [1922] 1926: 323).

European modernity subscribed to a perception of the world that was "locally grounded in a way that implied its universality and concealed its particularism" (Bauman 1992: 12). Such a possibility did not obtain in Mysore, where the state elite's espousal of the universalist ideal of economic progress was unaccompanied by the concealment of local particularism. In fact, orientalist discourses heightened the visibility of the local particulars as so many obstacles for achieving economic modernity. In the elite's attempts of overcoming the perceived cultural obstacles and developing Mysore, their relationship with their fellow Mysoreans mirrored the colonizer's relationship with themselves and shared the tutelary impulses of the colonial civilizing mission.

SOCIAL EVOLUTIONISM

The mode of historical consciousness that embeds the elite's development thought in Mysore corresponded to the discourse of social evolutionism.[27] Though, unlike the historical models associated with figures such as Comte or Marx, which purported to have discovered invariant laws of sociohistorical evolution, the elite shared only a broad theoretical conviction that development involved the inevitable and desirable transition of agrarian societies to industrial ones.

In 1882, Dewan Rangacharlu conveyed that the state was "most anxious" to "rouse" "the people" toward "industrial enterprise and progress" (AOD [1881–1899] 1914: 20). Thirty-one years later, Dewan Visvesvaraya asserted:

"If we want to know in what direction to move, we must compare ourselves with, and be guided by the experience of, progressive countries" ([1913b] 1917: 63). In 1941, a distinguished Mysore intellectual identified three phases in the state's "modern political history": "Bureaucracy" (1831–1881), "Consolidation and Development" (1881–1922), and "Popular Awakening" (post-1922) (Gundappa [1941] 1998: 448–449). Analogizing these historical phases, respectively, to the sprouting of a bud and its subsequent transformation into a flower and then a fruit, he explained that these "three steps" were "innate to a country's history" (Gundappa [1941] 1998: 449). He considered a social evolutionist conception of time to be a country's *svabhava*, a Sanskrit term designating an essential or intrinsic nature.

The elite's evolutionist thought frequently found metaphorical analogues for progress and backwardness in select images of Western and non-Western societies. In their comparativist orientation, which underlined the deficiency of local institutions, numerous local features were held up for comparison with those presumed to exist in the West: the native doctors in Mysore were secretive while those in the West openly discussed their findings; the local peasants did not keep proper accounts of expenditure while their counterparts in the West did; the local landholding patterns were fragmentary and irregularly shaped unlike those in the West; the per capita newspaper consumption was higher in the West; and so on.

The elite's certitudes of social evolutionism were embodied in powerful binarisms such as tradition versus modernity, the religious versus the secular, and agriculture versus industry. In each of these binaries, the latter term was valorized at the expense of the former term. The devalorization of the reified categories of tradition, religion, and agriculture, each of which appeared to work to the detriment of creating a modern society in Mysore, occurred from the smug conviction in a unilinear historical evolution.

Among their many acts of historical reification, the British orientalist discourses had located the causes of India's backwardness in the unchanging nature of its tradition. Also, the image of a changeless, self-regulating Indian village, which was a repository of obstacles to modern civilization, anchored discussions of rural India among the colonial officials and the state elite alike. Louis Dumont, the social anthropologist, attributed the idea of a village as a self-contained political and economic unit to Thomas Munro, the early nineteenth-century British colonial administrator. Munro depicted the village as "a kind of little republic," that is, a self-contained social structural entity, with an internal division of labor and political arrangement that persevered, since "the age of Menu [*sic*],"[28] amid the shifting vicissitudes in macropolitical regimes (Dumont 1966: 71). Henry Maine's influential works, *Ancient Law* and *Village Communities in the East and West*, also emphasized heavily the communitarian aspects of Indian villages, disavowing the importance of caste or political forces outside the village. Maine's writings, Dumont argues, have to be contextualized in relation to his own conviction that Indian villages were the counterpart of Teutonic villages and to the hegemony of social evolutionist thought in nineteenth-century Europe.[29]

The state elite, too, objectified "tradition" and "villages" as historically unchanging entities that proved a hindrance for their attempts at bringing economic development to Mysore. Speaking at the MRA in 1882, Dewan Rangacharlu said: "When all the world around is working marvelous progress, the 200 millions of people in the country cannot much longer continue in their long sleep, simply following the traditions of their ancestors of 2,000 years ago" (AOD [1881–1899] 1914: 20). Three decades later, Dewan Visvesvaraya claimed that the peasant had to be "weaned" from "the powerful influence of tradition, indifference to change and belief in fatalism," as that would make him show "more activity," which was "better for the country" ([1913a] 1917: 91). In 1931, Dewan Mirza Ismail stressed the need to depart from "traditional ruts in which [India] moved through centuries of time" and partake in the comforts of modern civilization (Ismail [1931] 1936: 67).

In the elite's evolutionist vision of development, agriculture was a sector sure to become marginal in the future. An economy dominated by agriculture seemed a profound imperfection. Ranade had sharply stated: "The sole dependence on Agriculture has been the weak point of all Asiatic civilization" ([1890] 1990: 296). The chronopolitics underlying the elite's view of agriculture becomes obvious in Dewan Visvesvaraya's words: "Occupation and production in the country are chiefly confined to the most primitive of professions in the world, *viz.*, agriculture" ([1915b] 1917: 296). The Department of Agriculture's 1926 *Report on the Progress of Agriculture in Mysore* (RPA) declared its main concern to be that of raising the condition of the Mysore village "in the fullness of time, to the level of the urban life of England or America" (RPA 1926: 144).

The state elite perceived a commonality between Mysore and the Western world on a deracinated plane of temporal progress. In this social evolutionist orientation, civilizational differences were temporal in nature, and as such they could be reconciled in history. A senior bureaucrat clarified this orientation: "Villages are the stronghold of conservatism all the world over and ours are no exception to the rule" (Rao 1915: 52). In his *Reconstructing*

India, Dewan Visvesvaraya wrote: "The Indian peasant is not essentially different from his fellow in other lands" (1920: 175). A temporal conception of civilizational difference enabled this self-universalizing gesture. However, on the plane of orientalist discourse, which posited an essential ontological difference between the Occident and the Orient, the elite indulged in acts of self-particularization. The numerous occasions in which they felt that the local subjects were fatalistic and otherworldly oriented illustrate this self-particularizing tendency. The elite's representations of a collective self-image of a backward people departicularized local cultural differences in favor of a unified, abstract subject of development, denying any contradictions between their interests in development and those of the nonelite.

DEVELOPMENT AND THE REALM OF THE SOCIAL

In the elite's vision of development, the field of the economy as a space for state intervention was purified of the realm of the social.[30] Dewan Visvesvaraya, for instance, clarified that though "progress" was "many sided," "economic progress" demanded the state's "chief attention" ([1914b] 1917: 152).

In 1926, Krishnaraja Wadiyar IV, the ruler of Mysore, pointed out that the "historic past" mattered for "*any* reconstruction of our social, political or religious polity" ([1926] 1934: 253; emphasis added). The omission of the economy from the list of domains that could be reconstructed only with the aid of the "historic past" is significant; it was perceived as separate from the social, political, and religious realms. Further, the economy was reified as an acultural domain unavailable as a space of intervention for traditional knowledge. This separation of the realm of the social from the economic and the areas of activity gathered under the former are explained in Dewan Visvesvaraya's address to the MRA in 1918:

> All the activities not deliberately classed as administrative or economic may be said to fall under "civic and social." Their object is, as the name implies, to train the citizens to become good citizens and good members of society. It is proposed, by means of a special organization, to spread among the people of the country a knowledge of literature, art, culture, manners and morals; to inculcate habits of discipline, orderliness, loyalty to the Sovereign, love of country and spirit of service; to reform social customs and practices by raising the status of women, improving marriage customs and elevating the backward and the depressed classes; to create opportunities to every one

according to his station in life, to bring up healthy families, to live in clean and sanitary dwellings and to help in building up well-planned and beautiful villages and towns; and generally to enable the non-official public to co-operate with Government and with one another in the general uplift of the masses of the population in all parts of the State. (*AOD* [1913–1938] 1938: 49)

Issues of caste and gender, among others, were perceived to belong to the realm of the social.

Clearly, the elite saw little value in Indian culture from their viewpoint of economic development. As the naturalized model of a modern economy was located within the coordinates of industrial standards of efficiency and discipline, the habits of Mysoreans appeared an unhelpful attribute, a problem. "Tradition" and "Religion," which appeared as obstacles in the elite's envisioning of economic development, signified positive content in relation to putatively social issues, such as language, spirituality, and so on. Indeed, there was enormous self-pride among the elite in past literary and spiritual achievements. However, even positive articulations of the components of the social could not sidestep the power of the development discourse. The need to "combine the best of the West and the best of the East" was a frequent response in Mysore (Wadiyar [1921] 1934: 192).

THE COHABITATION OF DISCREPANT DISCOURSES

The discourse of development occasionally became translated into the terms of locally prevalent Indian philosophical discourses. A historian in Mysore noted that the concept of "good government" was a "happy translation" of the ancient *dharma* [moral duty] of rulers" (Sastri 1937: 16). Exemplifying an anachronistic historical method, he retrofitted to the past a concept that had emerged from a different spatiotemporal formation; in asserting the historical primacy and originality of "good government" within the traditions of dharma, he conferred on an older concept new referential content and assimilated it to a new discursive register.[31] The two discourses rest on different conceptions of self and community. Whereas the discourse of development presumed a secular, atomistic conception of the individual self, the discourse of dharma posited a distinctly nonsecular, nonindividuated conception of the self. The latter's conception of the self often presumes the presence of divine agency in human activities. The two models of the self and its orientation to the world are therefore at sharp variance with each other. In the political arena, for example, the copresence of the two discrepant kinds of discourse is obvious. One set of justificatory bases of the maharaja's authority lay in Indian philosophical discourses of *Raja Dharma* (king's moral duty), which saw his rule as possessing a "sacral quality" (Richards 1998: 2). Discourses on kingship in South Asia drew from "Hindu," Islamic, Jaina, and other philosophical traditions, which had varying ontologies of political authority. However, even this heterogeneity, according to historian J. F. Richards, will permit us to identify "a numinous or sacral quality, however defined" in conceptions of kingly authority. Another shared point of view was that "kings are somehow necessary for the protection of the people through the maintenance of the moral order or dharma" (Heesterman 1998: 14).

A second set of justificatory bases for Mysore's ruler drew from the discourse of political democracy, whereby he staked his claim to authority in the name of the people. Powerful accusations of oriental despotism imposed great pressures on the ruler to demonstrate his ability to be otherwise, which meant discharging the necessary functions of a modern representative government.[32]

The state elite's embrace of the discourse of representative government is announced in the order announcing the formation of the MRA in 1881, which stated that "*the interests of the Government are identical with those of the people*" (Rao 1891: 106; emphasis in the original). Again, the maharaja asserted in an address to the MLC: "The happiness of the people is both the happiness and the vindication of the Government" (Wadiyar [1924] 1934: 232).

The ruler's message to the MLC in 1939 affirmed the importance for the state to espouse both the Indian and Western political philosophies: "I pray that you may succeed in evolving a scheme that will blend Western ideas of progress with our own traditions of Satya [Truth] and Dharma [Morality]" (cited in Srikantaiya 1941: 193). This note powerfully illustrates the ruler's inability to be indifferent to the "Western ideas of progress" alongside which the Indian ideals of Satya and Dharma *had* to coexist. The latter could provide only an ethical orientation to the world, whereas the former were accompanied by instrumental knowledge, whose value for building a modern economy was all too evident. This chapter has focused mainly on "Western ideas of progress," toward which the state elite could not exercise the liberty of being indifferent.

A NOTE ON CASTE AND GENDER

Although issues of caste inequality were mostly viewed as social and not economic issues,[33] the need to ameliorate the social and economic conditions of "lower" castes found institutional expression in 1918 when the state decided to grant members of "backward" and "depressed" castes preferential allotment in state employment and educational institutions. Women were not represented in the Mysore state bureaucracy. They were allowed to vote and contest the MRA and MLC elections only in 1927. In 1939, the Second Committee on Constitutional Reforms reserved eleven seats for women in these legislative fora. Although the issue of women figured prominently with respect to the age of marriage, that was perceived to be a social and not an economic issue. The levels of fervor seen in the elite attempts at developing the economy, however, are not similarly present with respect to the reform of institutional practices related to caste discrimination, child marriage, or widow remarriage. Their caution in this regard derived from both a pragmatic interest of not antagonizing local power structures and a social conservatism. For instance, during the MRA discussions on the desirability of introducing a penal measure to discourage child marriage in Mysore in 1932, Dewan Mirza Ismail favored state nonintervention in a manner characteristic of his predecessors (Ismail [1932] 1936: 125). His adoption of a gradualist and incrementalist approach to the issue of social reform is in stark contrast to his zeal for adopting Western economic practices to hasten local economic progress. For our purposes of isolating the elements constituting the development thought of the Mysore elite, it is sufficient to note that the institution of caste became another object for the state's technical intervention in the form of reserving positions in state employment and in educational institutions. The power of the state to define the valid modes of official address on the subject of caste justice is also crucial to note. In 1920, a delegation of the "untouchable" castes submitted a petition to Dewan Kantaraj Urs, claiming state assistance for their betterment. Their discursive strategies of self-presentation and seeking state redress reflect the power of the state-validated discourses of history and modern development: "We are an ancient community with a civilization, philosophy and history of which we reasonably feel proud. We are confident also that our social condition will automatically improve with the improvement of our economic condition. Our foremost need is education—more education—universal education" (cited in Urs [1920] 1953: 276–277). Demands for social justice in relation to caste inequity came to be expressed within the terms of the state's development discourse.

DISCOURSE INTERRUPTED

The political elite's self-location within the parameters of development discourse indicates the latter's power in only one conversational sphere, albeit a powerful one backed by state power. The discourse of development proliferated in theoretical and nontheoretical forms: newspaper reports, school curricula, jokes, metaphors, caricatures, gossip, tall tales, and other constituents of the fabric of everyday conversations in various social spheres. The oppositions and skepticism it elicited in these spheres do not permit us to view its social career in Mysore as being unambiguously triumphant. For instance, an anonymous article in a local newspaper chided the state for not curbing the flow of people into the cities, which had "denuded" the villages of its inhabitants:

A bold peasantry, their country's pride,
When once destroy'd, can never be supplied.

So sang Goldsmith a hundred years ago, and what was true in his day, is equally true in the present time. (Anonymous 1921)

Although official discourses displayed conviction in the need for bringing Mysore within the ambit of industrial modernity, instances of dissent and skepticism did surface within them. For example, official discussions occasionally expressed apprehension about the negative consequences of increasing industrialization on rural realities in Mysore. However, such occasional caution did not destabilize the authority of the discourse of development.

The violence and tragedy of colonial intellectual politics becomes obvious in the Mysore political elite's visions of their backwardness and development. In the context of powerful colonial accusations of civilizational weakness, the elite's view of their moral-political competence came to rest on a sociohistorical ontology embedded in the discursive infrastructure of colonialism. Seduced by the conceptual armor of colonial empire, the elite concept of development vacillated between a self-universalizing and self-particularizing gesture, where the terms of the universal and the particular were themselves founded on dominant European discourses. These modes of elite self-identification not only occasioned pathos but also summoned the grounds of political agency. Their epic claims of self-failure and self-uplift, directed both to an imagined West and a home audience in Mysore and elsewhere in colonial India, extended justificatory premises for the state's development interventions from above.

Under conditions of political semiautonomy that enabled the elite to function as ethical actors, they endorsed a model of development that had emerged from European intellectual formations. This instance of knowledge seduction involved a nonreflexivity about the conceptual foundations of development discourse. Gandhi and saints such as Ramakrishna

Paramahamsa, Ramana Maharishi, and Narayana Guru, to name a few who lived during the period of Mysore's indirect rule, elaborated conceptions of the self and community that sidestepped the protocols of colonial knowledge.[34] This chapter has strived to affirm the ethical importance of knowledge reflexivity for a politics of liberation. Interventions that seek to achieve freedom need to work with a heightened understanding of, and wakefulness to, the ethical, political, and epistemic specificities of the moral-cultural universes they wish to work in and not seek anchor in destructive a priori models of development masquerading as universal science.

Timeline of British imperialism in India and modern Mysore

1619   The East India Company (EIC) obtains permission from
              Jahangir, the Mughal emperor, to trade in India.

1619–1757   The EIC expands its trading interests in India. The cities of
              Bombay, Madras, and Calcutta emerge as major commercial
              centers.

1757   The EIC win the Battle of Plassey and take political control
              over Bengal. With a clear ambition toward the political
              subjugation of India, which consisted of many independent
              and vassal states, the EIC vanquished or subjugated most of its
              political rivals in the subcontinent by the mid-nineteenth
              century.

1857   A series of armed rebellions against the British break out all
              over North India. The British termed this episode the "Sepoy
              Mutiny" while the Indian nationalists later referred to it as the
              "First War of Indian Independence."

1858   Following the subjugation of the armed rebellions, Queen
              Victoria abolishes the EIC and brings India under the Imperial
              Crown.

1885   The Indian National Congress (INC) is founded to provide an
              organizational front for the nationalist struggle against
              colonial rule.

1920   Mahatma Gandhi launches the Non-Co-operation
              Movement.

1942   The INC launches the Quit India Movement.

1947   British rule ends in India, and the subcontinent is "vivi-
              sected," in Gandhi's words, into India and
              Pakistan.

MYSORE

1766–1769   First Anglo-Mysore War. Hyder Ali, the ruler of Mysore,
              successfully defeats the combined military attack of the

British, the rulers of Western India, and the neighboring kingdom of Hyderabad.

1780–1784   Second Anglo-Mysore War. Tipu Sultan, Hyder Ali's son, counters another attack by the same group of allies. Without a clear victor, the Treaty of Mangalore, which preserves the status quo prior to the war, is drawn.

1789–1792   Third Anglo-Mysore War. A defeated Tipu Sultan signs the Treaty of Srirangapatnam, which results in the loss of half of Mysore's territory to the British and its local allies.

1799   Fourth Anglo-Mysore War. With the support of its allies, the British kill Tipu Sultan and overcome their most formidable obstacle to colonial expansion in southern India. They install Krishnaraja Wadiyar III, a member of the erstwhile Wadiyar dynasty, as ruler of Mysore.

1831   The British defeat a militant rebellion at Nagar and assume direct political control over Mysore, which lasts until 1881.

1881   Mysore is brought under Indirect Rule again, and a member from the Wadiyar family is made the maharaja of Mysore.

1902–1940   During the political tenure of Maharaja Sri Krishnaraja Wadiyar IV and the spirited prime ministers such as Sir M. Visvesvaraya and Sir Mirza Ismail, Krishnarajasagar Dam (1911–1932), the first hydro-electric project in India, and major institutions such as Mysore Bank (1913), Mysore University (1916), and Mysore Chamber of Commerce (1916) come into being.

1947   Mysore joins the newly independent Indian Union.

NOTES

This chapter draws from my dissertation (Gowda 2007). Research for this chapter was supported by grants from the American Institute of Indian Studies; National Science Foundation Grant SES-0326942; and the Rackham Graduate School, International Institute, and the Department of Sociology at the University of Michigan. I would like to express gratitude to the following individuals for their valuable comments on this chapter: Jeffery Paige, George Steinmetz, Sumathi Ramaswamy, Lee Schlesinger, Julia Adams, and Ou-Byung Chae.

1. For a discussion of the ideas of development among the Latin American elite in the nineteenth century, see Baud (1998) and Gootenberg (1993).

2. The Indian states have not received sufficient attention from historians of South Asia possibly due to the organization of the colonial official archive itself, which has documented British India more extensively than the Indian states. The absence of anticolonial nationalist movements in the Indian states is another possible reason.

3. During British direct rule, the various chief commissioners, who were in charge of administering Mysore, introduced apparatuses of modern bureaucracy. Although British political control was resented, the state elite viewed the introduction of bureaucracy as a positive contribution (Rangacharlu [1874] 1988: 9). These historical details and the practice of colonial rule are explained in more detail in chapter 2 of my dissertation (Gowda 2007).

4. The nationalist movement that emerged in British India did not elicit broad-based support in Mysore until the late 1930s. The discourses of development found in Mysore, therefore, do not neatly overlap with those of Indian economic nationalism. This chapter does not elaborate the implications of this tension for reasons for space. Contrary acts of national identification with India and Mysore are found in official discourses in Mysore. Mysore was sometimes referred to as a "nation" and Indians from outside the state were occasionally referred to as "foreigners" and "aliens." In the early twentieth century, however, the Mysore elite and the educated nonelite viewed themselves as belonging to the larger national-political entity of India. For instance, the Maharaja affirmed at the Mysore Legislative Council: "We, in Mysore, form, as it were, a nation within a nation (Wadiyar [1924] 1934: 231)."

5. Explicit acknowledgment of intellectual affiliation with economic nationalists in the writings of the Mysore state elite is rare. The most plausible reason for this has to be the power of the colonial political arrangements within which Mysore was situated. The state's formal assent to function without any antagonism toward the British colonial interests made it difficult for the political elite to be openly critical—unlike the economic nationalists in British India—of the colonial mechanisms that thwarted their political freedom.

6. Occasionally, development was taken to be synonymous with the multidimensional concept of progress. The ruler's inaugural address at the reconstituted Mysore Legislative Council in 1924 is illustrative in this regard: "The ceremony which I am performing to-day is thus a step in a continuous and well-ordered process of development, which has been going on for forty years" (Wadiyar [1924] 1934: 232).

7. Founded in 1881, the MRA was a purely deliberative body without powers of legislation, which consisted of state-nominated agriculturists and landlords. The MLC, which was formed in 1907 as a body with limited powers of legislation, consisted of state-nominated members. The MEC was founded in 1911 to function as a forum for entrepreneurial individuals to discuss issues related to economic progress in Mysore.

8. The influential theories of modernization elaborated by sociologists such as Daniel Lerner, Alex Inkeles, and David McLellan in the 1960s and 1970s are a codified amalgam of these four discourses.

9. For instance, although Mysore wanted to become economically self-reliant as early as 1881, this interest was conceptually repositioned within the politics of the *swadeshi* movement in subsequent decades. Emerging in the province of Bengal in 1905, with the aim of making India economically self-reliant, the *swadeshi* movement demanded boycotting the consumption of imported articles in favor of locally produced ones. Although the term "swadeshi" did not come into official use immediately in 1905 in Mysore, the state's discourse of economic self-reliance interarticulated with that of swadeshi. In 1933, Dewan Mirza Ismail claimed that Mysore had promoted swadeshi seven years before the term came into use: "It is now forty-five years since the State of Mysore began to promote *Swadeshi* enterprises through the means of this Exhibition" ([1933] 1936: 241–242).

10. Influential in Western Europe between the sixteenth and the late eighteenth centuries, the economic doctrine of mercantilism corresponded to the emergence and consolidation of the nation-state model in Europe. Briefly stated, it advocated measures to secure the economic and political interests of the nation-state at a time of frequent wars. In order to meet the rising expenditure on civil administration and military needs, mercantilists favored the acquisition of precious metals, like gold, as they were readily accepted for economic transactions. This objective could be best achieved by encouraging exports and discouraging imports through protective tariffs. The publication of Adam Smith's *The Wealth of Nations* and its widespread success undermined the theoretical appeal of mercantilism. Smith's model of the universal economy did not favor the imposition of artificial obstacles to protect a nation's interests.

11. A historian has noted that List played an important role in recasting "the spatial assumptions of classical economic paradigms [which] conceived the division of labor and markets as abstract configurations with no specific spatial extension" (Goswami 2004: 216).

12. Urging the British to impose a duty on sugar imported from Java, which posed a "serious competition" to the sugar industry in India, G. K. Gokhale, the famous nationalist politician and economist, said: "Sir, the great German economist, List, points out in one place what happens when a country like India comes into the vortex of universal competition. He says that when a country, industrially backward, . . . comes into the vortex of universal competition—competition with countries which use steam and machinery and the latest researches of science in their production—the first effect is to sweep off local industries, and the country is thrust back on agriculture. . . . I certainly would strongly advocate that the Government of India should follow this advice of List" (1962: 335).

13. I am referring only to the elite's objectification of the image of a national economy. The British had imposed many imperial restrictions in Mysore. For example, the British had an exclusive right over excise duties on salt (*AOD* [1881–1899] 1914: 2). Also, they assumed control over the postal system in 1886 (*AOD* [1881–1899] 1914: 61).

14. For a brief elaboration of List's infant industry argument and its influence on development economics, see Shafaeddin (2005: 42–61).

15. List proposed a twofold classification of countries based on their location either in the "torrid zone" or the "temperate zone," wherein the countries in the former category were naturally situated to specialize in agriculture and those in the latter were well positioned to develop their manufacturing potential. Further, the "mental and social development" and the "political power," which would accrue to the countries of the temperate zone would enable them to develop colonial relations with the countries of "inferior civilization" in the torrid zone.

16. Another instance of such a strategic discursive appropriation occurred with John Stuart Mill's ideas of liberty and representative democracy, which were immensely popular among educated Indians in colonial India: "In his essay, *On Liberty*, John Stuart Mill had carefully stated that its doctrines were only meant to apply to those countries which were sufficiently advanced in civilization to be capable of settling their affairs by rational discussion. . . . But although he himself refused to apply the teachings of Liberty or Representative Government to India, a few Radical Liberals and a growing body of educated Indians made no such limitations" (Stokes [1959] 1992: 298; also Mehta 1999: 97–106).

17. In his influential essay on governmentality, Foucault (1991) singled out the state interest in population as marking a shift from the pastoral model of exercising power to a governmental one in Western Europe. I have not engaged the discussions of colonial governmentality here as they recenter the state; Foucault's key observation that governmentality was both individualizing and totalizing aimed precisely to decenter the state and reveal the workings of power in nonstate spheres, such as the consolidation of statistics, demography, and medical science, among others, as scientific disciplines. In colonized societies like Mysore, the state worked with this knowledge without corresponding institutional reinforcements from "civil society," so to speak.

18. With the assistance of the Rockefeller Foundation, Mysore became the first state in India to carry out a birth control experiment in 1927.

19. It is likely that the utilitarian concept of "happiness" resonated with older political discourses concerning a ruler's responsibility for the well-being of his subjects. Still, the fact that British tutors had educated the rulers of Mysore in "the theory and practice of government, the reading of modern history and science [and] the principles of jurisprudence and methods of revenue administration" (Srikantaiya 1941: 184) affords strong grounds for seeing the invocations of "happiness" as more properly belonging to the discursive order of utilitarianism.

20. The concept of waste itself has an old intellectual lineage. The concept was important for utilitarians including Jeremy Bentham and John Locke. "Waste" provided a conceptual anchor for Locke's argument against the law of entropy, which held that the materials of nature could be transformed only from usable to nonusable state. Locke claimed that "everything in nature was waste until man took hold of it and transformed it into usable forms, [and] that the world and history were progressing from chaos to order" (Stokes 1995: 125). Waste broadly came to be seen as the antithesis of the quality of being productive in the late eighteenth and early nineteenth centuries. Adam Smith used the term to refer to uncultivated land, for example.

21. Philip Mirowski's (1989) study shows the conceptual intimacy between economics and physics.

22. British orientalism in colonial India was not a straightforward enterprise of producing inferior representations of Indians. Indeed, the officials of the East India Company, influenced by the universal humanism of the eighteenth-century *philosophes*, identified a glorious tradition in ancient India. Scholars such as William Jones and officials including Warren Hastings expressed deep admiration for the literary and other artistic achievements in classical India (Hutchins 1967; Kopf 1969: 22–42; Metcalf 1994: 9–15). It has to be remembered that such romantic projections of the Indian past jostled with the theses of oriental despotism and the historical degeneration of Indians (Metcalf 1994: 15). The romantic attitude waned with the growing prominence of scientific racism and evangelical zeal in England in the mid-nineteenth century.

23. It has been remarked that Said's argument gives overwhelming agency to the Western societies in their powers of defining the Orient. How did the Orient respond to its representation by the West? There is no single answer to this question. While the Mysore political elite, for example, accepted the historical validity of many orientalist claims about Indian history and society, some of the most important saints in India in the late nineteenth and twentieth centuries, such as Ramakrishna Paramahamsa and Ramana Maharshi, stayed outside the intellectual gambit of orientalism.

24. As these scholars also perceived "caste" to be a central institution in India, Hinduism was privileged over Islam or other religions as a site for deeper investigation into the foundations of Indian civilization. The inapplicability of the Semitic concept of "religion" in the South Asian context has long been noted with a view to guard against objectifications of a monolithic Hinduism.

25. In addition to its use as a means of transport and communication, Dewan Rangacharlu favored the building of local railways "also to train up Natives in the working of Railways and of the engines and machinery connected with them; and thereby also diffuse the practice of handling machinery amongst the people" (AOD [1881–1899] 1914: 17).

26. In 1916 and 1919, Mysore sent two official delegations to Japan to learn about its administrative and economic policies (Banerji [1923] 1926: 690). In addition to periodic visits by students of Mysore, members of a Merchant's Deputation from Mysore also visited Japan in 1916–1917. The Mysore Economic Conference, a state organization founded in 1913 to promote local economic investment, was modeled on the Japanese Investigation Commission (Hettne 1978). The Village Improvement Scheme, a major scheme that aimed at making the local peasants "productive" and compiling extensive statistical knowledge about rural society in Mysore, was also modeled on a parallel Japanese scheme.

27. It is well known that eighteenth- and nineteenth-century European conceptions of progress were marked by the telos of industrial modernity. The notion of history as a progressive, linear sequence of events in time is the contribution of Christian eschatology, which viewed history as a series of events testifying to the continuous perfectibility of humans (Löwith 1949: 182–190). Thinkers of the French

Enlightenment, such as Voltaire, Condorcet, and Comte, detached the concept of historical progress from its theological moorings and rendered it secular (Löwith 1949: 60–114).

28. The "time of Manu" is used to mean ancient times. Manu is often considered to be the author of *Manusmriti*, one of the eighteen *Dharmashastras*, which are texts of moral codes composed somewhere between 200 BC and 200 AD. But scholarly opinion considers the authorship to be a misattribution to a nonexistent figure and recognizes the *Manusmriti* to be the joint work of many writers.

29. It is well known that Marx developed his idea of primitive communism based on Maine's book, *Village Communities in the East and West*. Dumont argues that Maine's criticisms of the utilitarian concept of human agency, based on his observations on Indian village life, had an influence on Talcott Parsons as well.

30. Karl Polanyi and Louis Dumont have pointed out that "the economy" as a realm independent of the political and religious fields is an invention of capitalist literature.

31. Indeed, this is the dilemma marking appropriations of the past by professional historians, who seek to understand diverse places and times through methodological devices belonging to the order of post-Enlightenment secular rationality. One of the most compelling arguments against the universality of Enlightenment thought has been made through an unmasking of the monopolistic authority of modern historiography to explain and interpret any and all pasts (Chakrabarty 1992; Nandy 1983, 1995).

32. In *The Native Princes of India*, published in 1875, C. U. Aitchison, a British official, complained that the governments of Indian states were: "personal Governments, where the preponderance of good over evil depends less on opportunity than on the character of the Chiefs and their Ministers. Perhaps in another generation . . . the doctrine that the King exists for the people will no longer sound strange in the ears of the Native princes" (quoted in Sastri 1932: 211).

33. Occasionally, the state elite saw caste purely in terms of an economism: as we saw earlier, Dewan Visvesvaraya considered caste disputes a "waste of mental energy." In appealing to the members of the MRA for the necessity of state aid for the uplift of the untouchable castes, Sir Kantaraj Urs said: "I submit that, apart from bare considerations of humanity, it is a great economic loss to the State that such a large body of our fellow-subjects should be left in such a helpless condition" (AOD [1913–1938] 1938: 80).

34. The works of the philosopher Ramachandra Gandhi illuminate the political relevance of these figures. See, for example, Gandhi (1984, 2005).

THIRTEEN

Building the Cities of Empire

Urban Planning in the Colonial Cities of Italy's Fascist Empire

BESNIK PULA

INTRODUCTION

Anyone reared in the postcolonial sensibilities of American academe can easily be struck by the delight with which average citizens of Albania's capital, Tirana, express admiration for the squares and buildings laid out and erected by Italian builders and funded largely by Italian capital in the 1930s and 1940s. No doubt, the impressively large Skënderbeg Square at the center of the city, the neoclassical buildings that are home to ministries and other government offices, and the modernist structures that house the public university—all a legacy of Albania's domination by Italy in the era between the two world wars—contrast sharply with the drab and mostly unimpressive architecture of the five decades of socialist rule that followed in the postwar era. The architectural differences continue thus to signify the failure of the socialist state to live up to its promises of progress and modernization, compared with what the Italians had seemingly been capable of accomplishing within a much shorter period. But more than this contrast between two historical epochs, the layout of Tirana's center, with vast open space and wide boulevards reminiscent of something that could have been thought up by a Le Corbusier (who, incidentally, declined the offer to design Tirana's urban layout back in the 1930s, opting for Algiers instead), and the stock of Italian-made buildings, aligned against the old mosque and the few surviving Ottoman-era structures of old Tirana, become exceptionally important for an intellectual culture that has become fixated, since the fall of the communist regime, on a seemingly irresolvable contradiction over "civilizational" orientations, questioning whether and to what extent Albania has, is, and will be finally departing the "East" and embracing the "West" (Sulstarova 2006).

Contrast this relationship with the past with another society with a shared history of Italian dominance during the same period. The object that symbolizes the Italian colonial period for most Ethiopians is the thousand-year-old Aksum obelisk, a commemorative monument to the ancient Ethiopian empire, seized in 1937 under Mussolini's orders and installed in Rome as a trophy of colonial conquest. Only recently has the Italian government fulfilled its formal promise of returning the obelisk, which had been an object of contention between the two states ever since Ethiopia regained independence.[1] It is notable how, in both cases, the built environment signifies vastly distinct colonial legacies of the very same colonial power. In one case, the Italian colonial past represents a certain political and cultural connection to the West; in the other, the theft of the obelisk demonstrates that colonialism was motivated by racism and intended little more than the repression of native culture. But in both cases, the built environment, more than representing a mere collection of physical constructs with aesthetic value, functions as a central object of contention in the construction and reconstruction of postcolonial legacies, cultural identities, and the meaning of past and present political struggles.[2]

Developments such as these have motivated researchers to question the ideological, institutional, and political goals and motivations that stood behind colonial interventions into the built environment. No doubt, the rise and institutionalization of professional urban planning during the early twentieth century meant that the possibility for such interventions became much more likely and systematic. The importance of demonstrating the superiority of the civilization of the colonizer took the form of, as one Italian architect stated in the mid-1930s, the need to impose culture not only through laws but also through buildings.[3] As one of the significant features of modern-era colonialism that has recently received the attention of scholars, colonial urbanism becomes an important way of understanding colonialism and its legacy in the full range of its dimensions.

This brings us to the general question posed by this chapter: in what ways did colonial urban planning, that is, the use of city design as a tool of social policy, operate as a mechanism of domination, and what explains its variation over different colonial contexts? While existing research cast the colonial city as a social machine employed by colonial rulers to maintain social and physical boundaries between colonizer and colonized, my goal here is to illustrate, by way of comparison, that the social and symbolic function of colonial urbanism diverged across colonial contexts with the institutional and ideological form that empire building took in each context. In the case of Italian colonialism, I show how policies of colonial urbanism and architecture reflected the distinct ideological and institutional ways in which Italy's dominant elites sought to represent their empire and mobilize colonial subjects into the project of Italian empire building. In Ethiopia, Italian empire was intended and carried out as a project of direct domination and subjugation of what was seen as a racially inferior population, whom empire would "civilize." Defined by the colonial "rule of difference" (Chatterjee 1993; see also Steinmetz 2007b), Ethiopians were treated as legally subordinate and the country administratively reorganized and annexed to existing colonies Eritrea and Somalia. In Albania, by contrast, Italy's empire was described as a "community," defined by its goal of universalizing Fascist social order offering underdeveloped societies a path to modernization that was both rapid and protected against what Fascist ideologues claimed to be the degeneracies of liberal and communist alternatives. Italy's political domination of Albania was disguised by such gestures as giving Albanians formal equal citizenship rights, supporting Albanian irredentism and enlarging the state's territory, and establishing institutions for the study and promotion of Albanian culture. As a component of colonial policy, colonial urban planning reflected these goals. While city design in Ethiopia was intended to promote racial divisions, in Albania public architecture was intended to convey the triumph of Albanian nationalism under Italian empire.

Why compare Ethiopia and Albania? In comparison to Italy's longer, pre-Fascist era colonies in Libya and Eritrea, both Ethiopia and Albania were conquered and ruled by Italy within roughly the same time frame (Ethiopia, 1935–1941; Albania, 1939–1943). Yet Italian colonial urbanism in these two colonies catered to radically different goals: Italian urban planners in Addis Ababa sought to radically refashion the city as the capital of the newly established Italian East Africa and create distinctly segregated Italian and native zones and urban facilities, while in Tirana, even while Italians settled in the city in significant numbers, Italian urban planners sought to reinforce the image of an Albanian (albeit Fascistized) national capital. Even as Italian architects and urban planners jostled to join the imperial bandwagon and convinced the government to set up an Office of Colonial Urbanism in charge of designing colonial cities and settlements in Italian East Africa, Tirana was intended more as a showcase of "Fascist style" and seen outside the context of colonial urbanism per se. Plans of "ethnic zoning" were never contemplated there, while racial segregation constituted the basis of all planning in Italian East Africa. This chapter is concerned with accounting for this divergence in Italian colonial urbanism, by situating the role of architects and urban planners within the overall framework of the Italian imperial enterprise.

This leads us to the question of the broader significance of colonial urbanism and its relevance as a feature of modern colonialism. Colonialism, as King (1990) points out, was constituted but also expressed by the structure, organization, and layout of colonial cities and settlements. While even early modern colonies exhibited certain patterns of settlement and spatial division between settlers and natives (Ross and Telkamp 1985), modern colonial states were among the first to develop the institutional means of direct intervention into urban environments through detailed planning and centralized control of architecture and city layout. Even Le Corbusier, the infamous architect who vigorously promoted planning methods in Europe and the United States during the interwar era, was able to realize most of his plans not in any European capital but in Algiers, the capital of colonial Algeria (Lamprakos 1992). For a long time, such interventions into the built environment were interpreted by sociologists as resulting from global processes of "modernization" (Davis 1955; Light 1983) or, alternatively, of the gradual integration of European colonies into the world capitalist system (Castells 1977; Chase-Dunn and Smith 1984; Smith 1996). Only a small number of sociologists developed an interest in explaining the actual content of colonial urban policies and the consequences of such interventions for the structure, layout, and social dynamics of colonial cities. Pioneering research in the field focused on the processes leading to the development of "dual-city" morphologies (Abu-Lughod 1965, 1980) and the cultural consequences of colonial urbanism (King 1976). However, even while the emphasis on local historical dynamics in such studies transcended the theoretical limits of world-systems theory and its epistemological privileging of global structural forces, those studies nonetheless still retained an ambiguous relationship with that theoretical approach. In King's case, this led to an advocacy of a theoretical approach to the study of colonial cities that amalgamated a number of distinct theories and methodologies with no clear emphasis in causal structures (King 1990; D. Smith 1991).[4] In his later work as well, King (1995, 2004) is unable to resolve the contradictions between his dual emphasis on cultural factors and colonial discourses and his holding on to a position that advocates the causal primacy of the global capitalist market in urban development, including the determination of architectural forms. King's theoretical conundrum may be symptomatic both of the marginal position of colonial urban studies within sociology and the need to attach colonial urban studies to shifting dominant paradigms in urban sociology. Dominant approaches in urban sociology, conversely, have scantly considered colonial cities as objects of analysis (Orum and Chen 2002).

King's more recent work incorporates the growing interest in colonial urbanism of disciplines such as anthropology and architectural history. Less under the sway of theoretical paradigms in urban sociology and under the more direct influence of postcolonial theory and Foucault's critical analysis of power, the study of colonial urbanism in these disciplines interprets colonial urbanism as a component part of colonial discourse. Such discourse-oriented approaches see the origins of colonial urbanism as part and parcel of the transformations of a technologically oriented modernity that sought to turn the city itself into a "regulator of modern society" (Rabinow 1989), as a consequence of planners intending to demonstrate the possibilities of urban planning by using colonies as sites of experimentation (Wright 1991), while others have analyzed colonial architectural forms as physical inscriptions of the discourse of colonial difference (Metcalf 1989). Architectural historians have distinguished their work from social analysts by their emphasis on the "physical frame of things" and urban "spatial characteristics," even if their intended analysis is the embeddedness of architectural practice in relations of power (Çelik 1997: 2). However, as the critical theoretical work of Lefebvre ([1974] 1991) argues, any analytical separation of social dynamics and spatial features, in particular the social use and representation of urban space, may be untenable (see also Gregory and Urry 1985). In any event, renewed research into colonial urbanism by other disciplines has exposed the limits of the economistically driven analyses of urban development that have dominated urban sociology, and the specific need to examine colonial urban formations as historical objects in their own right. More than mere symptoms of anonymous structural forces, historically based research has shown the implication of urban planning and architecture with colonial discourse and its "rule of difference" in the production of colonial urban space. Economistic analyses of colonial urban development fall flat particularly in the case of Italian colonial urbanism, which produced few economic benefits to the Italian state and Italian capitalists, while Italy's entire colonial endeavor proved to be disastrous from an economic perspective (Larebo 1994; Mack Smith 1976). Specific focus on urban layout and architectural form, objects of analysis that sociologists have typically shied away from, and the demonstration of their contentious social functions and semiotic values for colonial administrators, metropolitan publics, and colonized subjects bring to light the need to study colonial cities as more than mere physical amalgamations of buildings and as specific kinds of cultural products that provide broader insights into the institutions and dynamics of colonial domination.

While substantial research has been carried out by historians on French and British colonial architecture and urbanism (Metcalf 1989; Wright 1991), interest in Italian colonial urbanism is much more recent and in relation to the Fascist period commonly linked to Fascism's general ideological and political relationship with urbanism. Fascist ideology had an uneasy and at times antagonistic attitude toward urbanization, driven primarily by its conservative inclinations toward a managed and controlled industrialization that would preserve the agrarian character of society. Ironically, however, the period of Fascist rule in Italy was characterized by massive projects of urban transformation both within Italy and abroad (Kostof 1973, 1994; Mioni 1986). In Italy, this included the building of over eighty new planned urban settlements (Ghirardo 1989), as well as the transformation of existing cities, including the capital, Rome. Rome in particular was a prominent site of Fascist-era urban transformation, which included systematic demolitions to make way for expansive boulevards and squares that served as the backdrop to Fascism's mass spectacles and the rising to prominence of Roman-era ruins.[5]

Fascist-era urbanism extended into Italy's colonies as well. For example, Tripoli, which had been under Italian control since 1911, had few architectural or planning interventions during the liberal era. However, with the rise of the Fascist regime, Tripoli underwent significant changes in urban layout and public architecture (Von Henneberg 1994). Similar transformations were effected in Eritrea and Somalia. However, it was after Ethiopia's conquest that Italian architects and planners developed their most ambitious plans (Fuller 2007; Gresleri, Massaretti, and Zagnoni 1993). With references to Roman ruins and the regeneration of the ancient empire, colonial urbanism became a constitutive feature of Italian overseas expansion, to an extent that (given its short life span) perhaps exceeded those of other Western colonial empires. In what follows, this chapter examines the discursive sources and the institutional structures that determined Italy's vastly divergent urban planning goals in two colonies, Albania and Ethiopia, and particularly their respective capitals, Tirana and Addis Ababa.

BUILDING ITALY'S FASCIST EMPIRE: ITALIAN EXPANSION IN AFRICA
AND THE EASTERN ADRIATIC COAST, 1935–1943

Like Germany and Belgium, Italy was a relative latecomer to the colonial fray. But whereas Germany lost all its overseas possessions after 1919, Italy continued to maintain a presence in the territories of present-day Eritrea (which, first occupied in 1860, was Italy's oldest colony), Somalia (occupied in 1889 and reoccupied in 1905), and Libya (occupied in 1911). These colonies persisted as Italy transformed from a liberal into a fascist state beginning with Mussolini's takeover in 1922, and Italian overseas expansion resumed once again with the invasion of Ethiopia in 1935. After the completion of Ethiopia's conquest in 1936 and the forced dethroning of Ethiopia's native ruler, the Italian government consolidated Eritrea, Somalia, and Ethiopia into a single entity called *Africa Orientale Italiana* (Italian East Africa) and officially proclaimed Italy an empire, which it celebrated rhetorically as part of Italy's destiny to resurrect the ancient Roman Empire (Falasca-Zamponi 1997). In early 1939, prior to the commencement of the major hostilities of World War II, Italy invaded Albania and substituted the country's native king with Italy's own ruling monarchy to claim a "protectorate" over the country. The entry of Britain into war and the Italian army's defeat in Greece in 1941 ended Mussolini's dream of imperial expansion by way of retracing the Mediterranean path of the Roman Empire. Albania, however, remained occupied by Italy until the fall of the Fascist regime in 1943.

Efforts to recount the much neglected—and, according to many, much repressed—history of Italian overseas expansion and colonialism, spurred the publication of Italian-language monographs on the topic beginning some four decades ago.[6] But the topic has only in recent years received greater attention in English-language research (Ben-Ghiat and Fuller 2005; Palumbo 2003b). However, the growing research on Italian colonialism has almost exclusively focused on Italy's colonial experience in Africa, ignoring Italian expansion along the eastern Adriatic.[7] Regretfully, this neglect in the historical literature has largely reproduced the geographic and historical division between colonial and noncolonial territory according to the official designations of the Fascist regime, while also limiting our understanding of the range of various social and political formations that constituted Italy's modern empire. For Italy's Fascist government, all of its conquered territorial possessions were considered part of its "Imperial Community," though all parts carried different designations, juridical statuses, and were administered under different lines of authority. Thus, while Italy's African territories were officially known as colonies, Albania, Italy's largest "colonial" possession in Europe, was ambiguously preserved as an autonomous entity incorporated under a "personal union" with the Italian ruling monarchy.[8] This included an internal administrative difference as well: Italian East Africa fell under the jurisdiction of the Ministry for Colonies, while Albania's administration was handled by a special department within the Foreign Ministry. Moreover, Albania's administrative structure was largely preserved, with the exception of the Albanian crown, which was assumed by Italy's House of Savoy, and with certain institutional modifications intended to mold Albania into a Fascist state.[9] Fascist officials continually insisted that the union between Italy and Albania represented a union between two sovereign and self-ruling states. But while the shell of a sovereign state was preserved in Albania, Rome, in addition to handpicking loyalists to lead the government, set up a parallel civil-military administration that was under its own direction and maintained a deep presence within all of Albania's administrative bodies (Agani 2002: 166–186; Fischer 1999). Rome also dissolved the Albanian army and Albania's Foreign Ministry and imposed a customs union.

In terms more specific to colonial policy, the difference between Italy's African colonies and Albania was constituted primarily by the fact that the "Italianization" of Africa was expected to occur mainly through a policy of demographic colonization that maintained a racial difference with natives (Labanca 2003). In Albania, however, mass cultural assimilation was also seen as a viable policy direction. That this latter goal was entertained with all seriousness by the Italian government is made clear in the written records of Italy's foreign minister Galeazzo Ciano, the strongest proponent of Albania's occupation, who indicated in 1937 the possibility of Italy's demographic and cultural "absorption" of Albania, using as a point of reference the descendants of Albanians in southern Italy who had migrated there from Albania during the fifteenth and sixteenth centuries:

> I have persuaded the Duce to give 60 millions to Albania over the next four years, for works of various kinds. My visit to Tirana convinced me of the necessity for taking good care of this sector of the front. We must create stable centers of Italian influence there. Who knows what the future may have in store? We must be ready to seize the opportunities which will present themselves. We are not going to withdraw this time, as we did in 1920 [when Albanian insurgents forced the Italian military out of the port city of Vlora]. In the south we have absorbed several hundred thousand Albanians. Why shouldn't the same thing happen on the other side of the entrance to the Adriatic? (1953: 4)

In the weeks prior to the military conquest of April 1939, Ciano argued that up to two million Italians could be settled in Albania, whose existing population barely exceeded one million (Fischer 1999: 9–10).[10] Moreover, colonization projects were attempted before Italy's formal occupation. Beginning in 1926, the Italian-controlled Ente Italiana agricolo Albania (EIAA) began a project of settlement of Italians on agricultural lands in western Albania. Although the initial numbers of colonists were small, by 1939 EIAA had settled some hundreds of Italians, mostly poor peasants, and planned greater expansion (Miho 1976).[11] After occupation, Rome also stepped up its ideological efforts directed at the Albanian population. Reflecting the belief in the possibility of mass acculturation, a high National Fascist Party (Partito nazionale fascista [PNF]) official asserted the need for Albanians to become "fascistized, Italianized and de-Balkanized" (quoted in Koka 1985: 65). Cultural assimilation, it seemed, would include as a first step political and ideological conversion, a belief shared both by Ciano and by leaders of the PNF. Thus, in addition to setting up an Italian civilian and military administration parallel to the existing government headed by locals, the PNF directed efforts toward organizing an Albanian Fascist Party with local leaders in order to build a mass following among Albanians.[12] The PNF also extended its system of *Dopolavoros* of after-work socialization for workers and its Fascist youth organization to Albania. Fascist salutes and uniforms were also introduced to bolster Albania's new Fascist identity.

An American legal scholar of the period had termed Italy's legal and institutional treatment of Albania as one reflecting the establishment of a "vassal state" (Kempner 1941), but given the features of military occupation, direct control over the political apparatus, economic penetration, and the long-term intentions to colonize and Italianize the country, a colonial situation did indeed emerge, though one lacking the explicit racial features of non-European colonies (Balandier 1966). Put in terms of a more formal analysis, the relationship that emerged between Italy and Albania after 1939 matches, according to the comparative historical definition of colonialism developed by Osterhammel, a situation in which "an entire society is robbed of its historical line of development, *externally manipulated* and transformed according to the needs and interests of colonial rulers" (1997: 15; emphasis in original).[13] While lacking the "rule of difference," which defined European colonies in Africa and Asia, the goal and practice of colonization distinguishes Albania from other Axis "vassal states" in eastern Europe, where friendly governments were put into place but no goals of cultural assimilation were carried out or intended.[14] More important, Italy was the only Axis state to extend its territorial control in both Africa and Europe, confronting it with the unique challenge of reconciling classic forms of colonialism in Africa with territorial expansion in Europe.

In this sense, it may be useful to speak of two distinct historical types of Italian colonialism and their respective types of "colonial situations": the "classic" colonial situation of *racial colonialism*, where political and social dominance was marked by the legal, social, and institutional division and segregation of colonizer and colonized according to an officially sanctioned racial hierarchy, and *paternalist-assimilationist colonialism*, defined primarily by military and political domination of a colonizing state over a colonized society, with the goal of remaking native culture to conform to the image of its own. There is another level at which the latter type of colonialism differs from the former. In Albania the Italians not only were able to take advantage of local intraelite conflicts to draw "collaborators" into political institutions and the bureaucratic apparatus but also used Fascist ideology to attract an intellectual following among part of Albania's cultural elites, who partook in the new regime and wrote favorably about Italy's imperial project. This, in effect, turned colonial subjects not only into mere servants of empire but gave them an active symbolic stake in articulating the scope, relevance, and virtues of empire (Pula 2008). This feature may also be considered one of the distinguishing marks of what I am terming paternalist-assimilationist colonialism, in that the form of colonial subjectivity is not constituted by rigid and biologically defined boundaries of race but becomes one in which cultural difference is secondary to the proclaimed sociopolitical universalism of the imperial project.[15] Certainly, the fact that a single imperial state engaged in two very distinct types of colonial projects shows the movement between tension and complementarity of the ideological (Fascist) and cultural (nationally and culturally Italian) strands of discourse articulating the goals of Italy's imperial expansion. Scholars of Italian colonialism, perhaps due to their exclusive focus on Africa, have usually missed this tension within Fascist Italy's imperial project, tending to see Fascism mainly as a more militant version of Italian nationalism. However, the experience of Albania shows how Fascism (the claimed ideological universal) and Italian cultural nationalism (a particular identity within a realm of competing nations) served as very different kinds of justifications for Italy's overseas expansion, while each aspect becomes more or less salient in different colonial contexts. The comparative analysis in this chapter provides one possible understanding of this divergence lying at the heart of Italy's imperial project.

THE INTERNATIONAL IMPERIAL FIELD AND VARIATION IN FORMS OF
ITALIAN COLONIAL RULE

The geographic extent of Italy's Fascist empire may partly account for the variation in forms of rule Italians introduced in their African and European colonies. The internal dynamics of colonial states were largely responsible for the kinds of policies pursued by colonial administrators (Steinmetz 2007b, 2008a). Rather than mere administrative apparatuses carrying out the will of metropolitan elites, colonial states functioned as semiautonomous fields that contained struggles between dominant factions largely centered around proper insight into the culture of the colonized, with significant consequences for colonial policy.[16] But colonial state formation is also characterized by particular administrative structures, and at this level Italian rule in Italian East Africa and Albania differed in significant ways, providing different opportunities and participatory possibilities for the colonized in the colonial state and the project of empire more broadly.[17] The administrative form of the colonial state determines the *ontological* sense in which the colonized is treated as a juridical subject: as an *object* of colonial administration, or as *subjects* who are conceded a limited political and ideological space, producing a certain *civil society of the colonized*.[18] Put in other terms, the difference lies in granting colonial subjects a subordinate citizenship within empire (as in the case of Albania), as opposed to a complete exclusion from citizenship, an exclusion that is justified and framed around racial terms (as in Ethiopia).[19]

But why did the structures of respective colonial states differ to such a radical degree? As discussed above, precolonial differences in the internal political organization of each state do not sufficiently account for the path pursued by Italian occupiers in both cases, as both Ethiopia and Albania functioned as relatively centralized states in the period prior to Italian conquest. Yet proponents of Italian expansion believed that Italy enjoyed a much freer hand in remaking Ethiopia politically and administratively than it did Albania, where the administrative bodies of the preoccupation sovereign state were largely preserved. I suggest that one of the significant causes of difference was not only internal to the Italian state but resulted from a historically earlier division of the geography of imperialism, a structure of causation that, at the global level of European colonial practice, had separated Africa from Europe's periphery (and the Balkans in particular) as two distinct contexts of European imperial practice. The historically constituted cultural and political geography of imperial conquest and domination is significant to the extent that it narrowed the field of choices for practices of colonialism, especially since, at the time of Italy's drive toward overseas expansion in the late 1930s, colonialism had long moved beyond being a "zone of contact" with foreign cultures and had consolidated into a long-standing field of practice for powerful European states. Since its origins, the modern interstate system has been characterized by a system of territorial acquisition and administration that was regulated on an ad hoc basis by an emerging body of international norms (Tilly 1990). These rules conferred distinct statuses on European and non-European territories and their relationship with the rising system of sovereign states.

Since its establishment as a unified nation-state in the mid-nineteenth century, Italy had continuous strategic interests in both the Balkans and Africa, having an active interest in the territorial reorganizations in the Balkans during the Ottoman Empire's dissolution in the early twentieth century (including the possibility, proposed by a number of Italian political leaders of the era, of annexing parts of the eastern Adriatic Coast), while competing with other European states to expand its colonial possessions in Africa. There were also differing structures of competition between imperial states in these two parts of the world, distinguishing the stakes involved. In Africa, Italy was competing with the British and French empires for expanding control of resource-rich land and strategic ports, while competition in the Balkans pitted it more directly, until their disintegration in 1919, with the territorial empires of Austria-Hungary, Germany, Russia, and the Ottomans, as well as the expansionary states of the Balkans (in particular Serbia, Greece, and Bulgaria). After its unification in 1859, Italy quickly gained a role in the so-called Congress system that succeeded the post-Napoleonic Concert of Europe and was an active participant in the Congress of Berlin in 1878, which tackled the "Eastern Question," as well as in the Conference of Ambassadors in London in 1913, which recognized Istanbul's loss of the vast part of its European territories and also granted independence to Albania. As an international system, turn-of-the-century imperialism was organized around stakes, norms, and principles that differed significantly in distinct geopolitical zones of imperial domination. In Africa, Italian domination was exercised through conquest and direct rule, while in postindependence Albania, Italian influence until 1939 was pursued mainly through diplomatic treaties and political pressures (Pastorelli 1967, 1970).

Italy's division of spheres of imperial competition was reflected not only in its international behavior but also in the form of internal organization of overseas rule within the Italian metropolitan state after its conquests of Ethiopia and Albania (e.g., the handling of colonial administration by different ministries, the different legal statuses accorded to conquered territories, and the manner of their annexation), as well as the realm of practices within the colonies. The global European practice of late imperialism, I argue, was embedded within a historical geography of conquest, domination, and global spatial (and thus social and cultural) regulation, and this normative framework that sustained a world of colonial empires was reflected in the legal and institutional practices of Italy's colonial rule.

Schmitt ([1950] 2003) uses the concept of *nomos* to refer to the practices of global spatial organization that were historically sanctified and expressed in the evolving norms and structure of international law, based on a system of mutual recognition by ruling sovereigns and regulating international political practices.[20] Drawing from the historical origins of the *jus publicum Europaeum* in the practices of land acquisition in the absolutist era, Schmitt analyzes the historical rise of a Eurocentric world set around the European interstate system and spatially divided between the territories of *dominium*, that is, land legally held and ruled by mutually recognized sovereigns, and the "free space" of non-European territories, as space open to European conquest. This division is also reflected in the legal character of interstate conflict. In the tradition of jus publicum Europaeum, Europe was considered a *theatrum bellum* (theater of war), in which the conduct of war and conquest itself became a regulated affair, developing such instruments as diplomatic negotiations, peace treaties, rules of warfare, and neutrality. War was "a relation among equally sovereign persons," in which the enemy constituted one who demanded defeat and subjection but not annihilation (Schmitt [1950] 2003: 142–143), constituting what Schmitt terms a rationalization and "bracketing" of war. The system therefore defined the stakes of inter-European conflict and regulated its conduct and established mechanisms to restore balance to the international (European) order after conflict. But European expansion beyond Europe required the development of new, distinct rules that were applicable to extra-European space, where rulers were typically not recognized as equal sovereigns (Young 1994). During the nineteenth century, the resulting spatial division of the world led the jus publicum Europaeum to recognize five basic types of territories: (sovereign) state territory, colonies, protectorates, "exotic countries with European extraterritoriality," and free occupiable land (Schmitt [1950] 2003: 184). The disintegration of the jus publicum Europaeum, in Schmitt's view, came after 1885, prompted partly by the crisis that ensued over the United States' unprecedented decision to recognize the Congo Society as an independent state. The recognition and entry of new sovereigns within the Eurocentric system, the rising power of the United States as a challenger to European hegemony (as well as its particular hegemony in the Western Hemisphere), and the increasing division of the world into *Großräume*, or spheres of influence particular to individual powerful states, led the Eurocentric order into crisis and eventual disintegration.[21] Beginning in 1919 with the Paris Peace Conference, one that according to Schmitt could not be characterized as a "*European* conference in terms of its representatives and subjects, but only in terms of its object and theme" ([1950] 2003: 240; emphasis in original), the way was opened for a universalized international law, though one that would stand on extremely shoddy grounds for much of the first half of the twentieth century.

In retrospect, we can say that it is within this disintegrating world political order that Fascist Italy attempted to increase its stake in its claim of being a colonial power on the global scale. However, what Schmitt sees as the disintegration of the European system after 1919 may instead represent a protracted crisis; the underlying principles of the jus publicum Europaeum had yet to be fully challenged and perhaps would not be until after the establishment of the United Nations and decolonization, when a universal system of international law based on a globally diffuse system of sovereign states was established. In any event, in spite of the increasing number of new states joining the international system after 1919, as well as attempts to build collective international security arrangements with institutions such as the League of Nations, the basic terrestrial divisions of the jus publicum Europaeum had not been fully displaced. In fact, as data collected by Bergesen and Schoenberg (1980) show, in the era between the two world wars, European overseas control continued to expand. To claim thus that the European system disintegrated after 1919, as Schmitt suggests, may be somewhat overstated, even if its old principles had been deeply challenged by the rising new international order. In addition, the fledgling European system based on the League of Nations was directly challenged beginning in the 1930s, when Japan, Germany, and Italy engaged in a series of acts of aggression throughout the world. However, these events remain curiously unexamined by Schmitt.[22]

From this perspective, one can argue that Italy's approach to its African and European territorial conquests (and its respective populations) may partly be reflective of the continuing hold of the old division between dominium and free territory, corresponding with (a claim not made by Schmitt) an anthropological division of the world into civilized, semicivilized, and uncivilized (Harvey 2001).[23] That such geographically based civilizational rankings informed the hierarchy of peoples within Rome's "Imperial Community" and their corresponding administrative structures is illustrated by the manner in which Fascist ideologues theorized the emerging imperial political formation. Thus, one Fascist theorist described the Imperial Community as "a new complex political organism, a *corpus misticum* consisting of diverse parts." The parts of the Imperial Community, however, exist within a hierarchy: "first come Italy and Albania; second in importance, but not equal to the Italo-Albanian union, are Libya and the Aegean possessions; and finally, in a different position, is Italian East Africa." The ordering was accounted by "differences in geographic positions, races, and levels of civil development of their various populations, *differences which correspond to their respective juridical status within the Imperial Community*" (Ambrosini 1940: 63; emphasis added).[24] Prior political history was of no relevance to this geographic hierarchy of civilization, which furnished the basis of legal hierarchy as well. It ignored the facts that Ethiopia had been an internationally recognized independent state, a member of the League of Nations, and self-ruling for a much longer period than Albania. Situating Italy's aggression on Ethiopia within Schmitt's analysis of the crisis of the jus publicum Europaeum, the mode in which Italian political elites justified expansion in Ethiopia may be indicative of the Italian state's attempts to reopen the possibilities of new colonial conquests in Africa by reinforcing the orthodox spatial division between sovereign and nonsovereign space and thus nullify the attempts by the League of Nations to establish a universal rights-based system of interstate relations applying to all member states.[25] In addition, Italy's engagement in what amounts to a colonial project in Europe may be reflective of the contradictions faced by the Italian government itself, feeling the need to engage in various legal, political, and diplomatic machinations so as to rid Albania of its political autonomy while maintaining the shell of a nominally sovereign state and claim Albania as an equal in the "Imperial Community."

While by no means the main explanation, this is one way to start making sense of the radical disjunctures in the administrative forms of Italian overseas rule. In the case of Italian colonialism, understanding the structure of administrative and political institutions helps to contextualize the role of racial and ethnographic discourses in determining the kinds of colonial policies pursued in each colony, which is emphasized by postcolonial scholars (Bhabha 1994b; Said 1978; for a critical evaluation see Steinmetz 2007: 19–71). In the case of Italian colonialism, the problem is compounded by the existence of two divergent forms of discourse informing interpretations of native culture. For example, while there was renewed emphasis on the ethnographic study of Albanians after Italy's occupation, the representations of natives in Ethiopia were quickly monopolized by the discourse of scientific racism that gained prominence in Italy after Ethiopia's occupation. In the late 1930s, Mussolini became more accepting of the racial ideology practiced in Nazi Germany, leading to efforts by the government to extend official recognition to scientific racism and adopt its premise of biological races as a matter of policy. This included the publication of a government-sponsored popular journal on questions of race, efforts by the regime to give prominence to marginal racial scientists, and Mussolini's personal interventions in the debate between Italian racial scientists on the "Aryan" or "Mediterranean" origins of Italians (Gillette 2002). In addition, the period 1938–1940 saw the adoption of a series of racial laws applicable both within Italy and its overseas colonies. In the mainland, these laws mainly targeted Italy's Jewish population, while special measures for Italian East Africa included strict restrictions on misogyny and intensive efforts by the authorities to regulate sexual contact between Italian male colonizers and native women. But while these efforts largely failed, it is notable that such policies were never put into place in Albania (Jacomoni 1965: 170). Misogyny was never perceived as a problem in Albania, even though some tens of thousands of Italians, mostly men, resided in Albania. It is also not the case that particular actors held racist attitudes more than others and that this affected policies such as urban planning: as I show below, the same architect who developed the layout plan for Tirana had done extensive work in Ethiopia, where he strongly advocated racial segregation. Rather than attitudes on race, the structure of colonial administration and its institutions placed limits on the types of categorizations that could be effectively put into use in colonial policy, including urban planning. This includes the treatment of African territories and populations as the proper space of racial colonialism, while an intense cultural and ideological imperialism—even in combination with policies of colonization—constituted a proper technique of rule for Europe's periphery.[26] The ambitions of Italian colonial urban planners and architects came to represent this distinction in the types of urban layouts it sought and the architectural forms it proposed and partly implemented in the two colonial contexts.

URBAN PLANNING IN TIRANA AND ADDIS ABABA: THE FASCISTIZED CAPITAL AND THE "CITY OF EMPIRE"

The remainder of this chapter examines Italian colonial urban policy by comparing urban planning in Tirana and Addis Ababa, both intended plans as well as those carried out. Planners advocated a policy of "ethnic zoning" in Ethiopia, intended to physically segregate urban areas and settlements between Italian colonists and natives; in Tirana, Italian planners continued the project of building a city that was intended to stand as a symbol of Fascist modernity, even while bearing symbols of Albanian national identity. In Ethiopia, urban planners and architects advocated racial divisions even before the rise of scientific racism into official dogma, while in Albania, architectural form came to be inspired by more romantic ethnographic representations of Albanian ethnic identity. Thus, the growing influence of scientific racism did not displace earlier ethnographic frames that cast Italians and Albanians as sharing "ancient ties" dating from the Roman era. The fact that racial discourse did not apply to Albanians as forcefully as to Italy's African colonial subjects meant that older ethnographic representations served as the basis on which the Italian colonial state could veer ambiguously between a paternalistic project of political domination and a project of cultural assimilation. Within Italy's political field, these two poles were represented by the foreign minister, Ciano, who saw Albania in geostrategic terms and advocated assimilation, and Italy's highest official in Albania, Francesco Jacomoni, who advocated a paternalistic role for Italians as protectors of Albanian cultural identity.[27] In this context, architectural form shifted toward Jacomoni's position in seeking to imitate native forms, most prominently in the case of the design for the Casa di Fascio.

Italian architects commenced work in both Ethiopia and Albania very soon after Italy's takeover, and construction also followed soon after plans were set. The urban structures and layouts envisioned for both Addis Ababa and Tirana in terms of city form are strikingly similar. Both were modeled according to the rationalism and monumentalism of the City Beautiful movement of the 1920s and 1930s (Hall 2001), with an imposing central district and boulevards that radiate outward toward the periphery. However, while the design of the overall city layout was similar, Addis Ababa's plan included a detailed designation of city spaces intended for Italians and others for natives. The initiative to plan newly conquered colonial cities in Africa in accordance with racial principles had issued directly from a group of influential Italian architects and planners and predated the official rise of scientific racism. After the completion of Ethiopia's conquest in 1936, colonial urbanism came to occupy center stage in many of the debates among Italian planners.[28] The dominant view among planners was the need to develop a general plan for the entire empire, which would include the planning of old and new settlements in newly conquered lands, and the establishment by the state of an Office of Colonial Urbanism (Ufficio urbanistico coloniale), staffed by planners to manage its implementation. While debating

the type of urban and architectural forms to be adopted, the extent of development, and whether it would be based on the preservation of existing
structures or the complete transformation of urban environments, and in
choosing between modernist, neoclassical, or experimental architectural
forms inspired by "traditional" native architecture, planners coalesced
around the notion that Italian colonial architecture must be characterized
by a monumentalism that followed in the footsteps of the great works of the
Romans, whose empire official Fascist discourse claimed to be reconstitut-
ing in modern guise. In addition, planners maintained a strong position regarding the undesirability of African culture as serving as a guide or inspiration for urban and architectural design. Being a territory inhabited by a
"fully primitive" population, according to architect Luigi Piccinato writing
in 1931 (quoted in Boralevi 1986: 245), and given the stated need to sharply
distinguish Italian civilization from that of the colonized, Italian planners
moved toward the position of an Italian "civilizing mission" that intended to
mobilize planning as a tool to exhibit the superiority of Italian culture (Fuller
1988) but also to help accomplish the project of colonization by setting up
the necessary infrastructure for massive Italian settlement, which was projected to follow the conquest. Treading this general path, the First National
Congress of Urbanism, held in 1937 in Rome, issued a concluding statement
that strongly advised that Italian colonial planning take as one of its key guid-
ing principles the "clear separation of Italian and indigenous quarters"
(quoted in Boralevi 1986: 247). As Boralevi notes, the principle of ethnic
zoning was embraced quite quickly by Italian planners as it became constitutive of the urban layout plan for Addis Ababa, produced a short five months
after the conquest of the country. According to the general scheme for the
city issued by the colonial government's planners in 1937, Addis Ababa
would consist of four districts: a political district, a commercial district, and
two separate residential districts, one reserved for Ethiopians, the other for
Italians, further subdivided into residential quarters for colonial administrators and another for workers. The racial division of the city was maintained in subsequent updates of the plan, even as construction of new city
areas by Italian firms was taking place and as Addis Ababa was designated
the capital of Italy's African empire (Boralevi 1986). While notions of racial
segregation predated the regime's acceptance of scientific racism as an official doctrine, the concept of "ethnic zoning" was made legitimate and given
scientific credence by the doctrines of scientific racism. "Ethnic zoning," as
carried out by Italian planners in Ethiopia, thus applied only to the division
between Italian colonists and native Ethiopians and did not include further

subdivisions between the many ethnic and linguistic groups that inhabited Addis Ababa. In fact, Italian colonial governments did not make significant attempts to establish formal divisions between Ethiopia's various ethnic groups, underlining the primacy of racial division in Italian policy and the strong impact of racial discourse on shaping Italian colonial policy in Africa (Barrera 2003).

In actuality, policing the racial boundaries envisioned by Italian urban planners and colonial administrators was much more problematic. Among the phenomena that irked Italy's colonial administrators and unsettled their plans of maintaining racial boundaries was the growing practice of miscegenation. Both popular colonial fantasies of sexual domination of exoticized native women that were depicted in Italian imagery of the African colonial world as well as the fact that a disproportionate share of settlers in Africa were male contributed to the growing practice of miscegenation and interracial marriage (*madamismo*), leading Rome to adopt a series of measures banning interracial relationships and denying citizenship to offspring (Barrera 2005; Pickering-Iazzi 2003). At the same time, Italian economic policy in Ethiopia, which was tied to its policy of massive settlement of Italian workers and peasants, was failing spectacularly, proving unable to maintain a steady Italian presence in the colony and unable to fulfill Rome's ambitious plans of turning Ethiopia into an economically profitable enterprise (Larebo 1994; Pankhurst 2001). In Addis Ababa, the grandiose plans of Italian planners of transforming the city into an imperial capital came only to partial realization, with Italian residential quarters only partially completed and the failing colonial economy casting many Italian colonists into conditions of poverty, in some cases even worse than those of natives. While harboring grandiose plans of resurrecting a Roman Empire in the Mediterranean, which would leave its lasting imprint through imposing architectural works, Rome's colonial policy proved to be little more than a short-lived, brutal, militaristic adventure, with many of its designs for Addis Ababa and other colonial settlements remaining little more than blueprints.

The debates on colonial urbanism among planners and architects in the late 1930s did not include Albania, an exclusion that continued in the period after conquest, showing how even among architects Albania registered as a universe very much apart from the "primitive" and racially divided world of African colonialism. Racial discourse was never capable of furnishing a basis for Italian elites in their policy decisions on Albania, and thus urban planning in Albania became less concerned with the spatial ordering of social groups and took on a more explicitly ideological function. Far from being intended as a manifestation of racial superiority, urban planning in Tirana sought to monumentalize the alleged achievements of Fascism and the Fascist Imperial Community, while paying tribute to local culture and national identity. One of the reasons for this distinct emphasis may be that Italian planners and architects had been involved in Tirana's construction since the late 1920s, when Italian political and economic influence first began its exertion in Albania. Hence, even before the Italian military disembarked on the Albanian shore in April 1939, the layout for Tirana had already been heavily shaped by Italian planners. Tirana had become the official capital of the newly independent Albanian state only in 1924. At the time, with a population of about 30,000, it was only one among a number of the country's urban centers dispersed throughout the country, while the port of Durrës served as an administrative center in the period immediately after independence (Duka 1997). With the establishment of the regime of Ahmet Zogu in 1924, among the policies the government pursued was the development of Tirana, in order to fashion the city more like a large European national capital. Most of the construction of the Albanian capital's main square and central boulevard during the 1920s and 1930s was paid for by Italian loans. As a result, Italian architects, construction firms, and workers performed much of the work, while Italian architects designed the city's master plan. By 1939, a significant portion of Tirana's new central district was already completed, including Skënderbeg Square (named in commemoration of the medieval Albanian notable who resisted the Ottomans), and two portions of the central boulevard, one part of which was aptly named after Mussolini. The central square and boulevard contrasted strongly with the rest of the small and narrow structures of the former Ottoman town, to the point where it prompted one European observer to sarcastically note, after a visit in Tirana, that he saw "a boulevard without a city" (quoted in Aliaj, Lulo, and Myftiu 2003: 38). However, while the original master plan, drawn up by Italian architect Armando Brasini in 1925, proposed the development of an imposing (and, in the original plan, walled) "Roman island" at the center of the old Ottoman town, very much like Italian planners had done in separating the "old" and "new" city in Tripoli, the new plan of 1939 contemplated no such division and instead proposed an integrated city with a center that would feature a combination of neoclassical, modernist, "Fascist-style" architecture and native (pre-Ottoman) forms (Gresleri 1993).

In addition to the revised master plan for the city, the establishment of the Luogotenenza, representing the Italian civil-military component of

FIG 13.1 · The Casa di Fascio, now housing the Polytechnic University of Tirana, and its square on the end of Tirana's main boulevard, completed in 1942 (photo by author).

Albania's governing structure, led to a series of new regulations for urban design being put into place. Among others, the local government of Tirana established an agency charged with approving the architectural plan of every new private construction, down to the smallest corner kiosk. As Jacomoni (1965) notes in his memoirs, the influx of Italian capital led to a construction boom, and according to his (likely exaggerated) count, for the short period of Italian rule, Tirana saw the construction of seven hundred new private residential and commercial units. In any event, within a few years after Albania's occupation, Tirana grew by about thirty-five thousand inhabitants, while its territory nearly doubled (Aliaj, Lulo, and Myftiu 2003: 45). In addition, according to one estimate, by 1943 some thirty thousand of Tirana's residents were Italian.[29] Facts such as these led Aliaj, Lulo, and Myftiu to characterize the years of Italian occupation as one of the periods of Tirana's fastest growth.

Among the key architects to participate in the planning of the city layout was Gherardo Bosio, a renowned Florentine architect who had volunteered to fight in Ethiopia and remained there after the occupation to produce a number of urban plans for the empire. Bosio wrote extensively on colonial urban planning and had developed the plans for the Ethiopian towns of Gondar, Dessié, and Gimma. In his work on Africa, Bosio advocated strict divisions between native and Italian zones, including not only areas of residence but also separate commercial districts and even traffic patterns so as to ensure that contact between the two groups within the city remain limited to the most necessary interactions (Boralevi 1986; Fuller 1988). However, the principle of clear ethnic demarcation of city zones was not suggested in Bosio's plan for Tirana, even if Italian planners had full control over the direction of city planning and the Luogotenenza controlled the funds that would finance the ensuing construction of public buildings. Moreover, Bosio was commissioned to design the new political and cultural complex to stand at the apex of Tirana's central boulevard, which had been renamed Viale Impero. The complex, which would include a stadium, a theater, and various administrative offices, included the Casa di Fascio, a distinct structure that would stand in contrast to the robust rationalist design of the other buildings within the complex because it would be intended to architecturally represent Albanian national identity. Bosio based the design of the building on the image of the *kulla*, the tower-like structure found in the Albanian highlands, whose population was romanticized for their archaic way of life by ethnographers such as Baldacci. The appropriation of the kulla was intended not merely to adorn a modern building but as an enlarged replica strategically situated within the center of the city to shape the city's identity, as well as represent Fascism's promise of rapid modernization.[30] The effort, moreover, to modernize architectural forms that predated Ottoman conquest (and the city's own Ottoman heritage) from a specific ethnographic repertoire of "Albanian traditionalism" meant that city design served as a tool to continue the Albanian nationalist project of constructing an Albanian national identity, even if such construction was being carried out by an agent of empire. The design also played into the official discourse of regeneration of ancient civilization by way of modern empire, including a return to the supposed "ancient ties" between the Romans and the ancestors of the Albanians, a view that had been propounded by Albanophile scholars such as Baldacci, Bernardy, and Mustilli.[31] The discourse of ancient ties also cohered with a number of Albanian supporters of the Italian Fascist empire, who echoed this view and frequently referred to Italians as "big brothers" and Mussolini as Albania's savior (Pula 2008). The construction of the Casa di Fascio symbolized Fascism's seemingly mystical creative powers

FIG 13.2 · Picture of Iballja clansmen in the region of Puka in the
northern Albanian highlands, taken by Austrian scholar Baron Franz Nopsca
in 1905. The building in the background is an example of a stone-built
kulla dwelling, which Bosio imitated in his design for the Casa di
Fascio (photo courtesy of Robert Elsie).

to regenerate and renew, transplanting the primordiality of "Albanian-
ness" represented by the traditional domicile of Albania's highlands into
modern form and made by the Casa into a "home" for Fascism's claimed
status as a universal force. The Casa thus complemented the ideology of
Fascist empire and Albania's existence as a national community within
the fold of Rome while also functioning as a symbol of Albania's modernizing aspirations, which Rome claimed to be in the process of realizing. It
could be therefore said that Tirana's city design reflected the way in which
Italy's empire projected itself into Albania: a historical endeavor intended
to expand imperial control by aggrandizing native culture and manipulating nationalist sentiment, all the while opening the space for Fascistiza-
tion and "Italianization" and creating a relationship of subordination to the
greater power of Rome. It is unclear from the existing historical record
whether Bosio knowingly tuned his project to the political machinations
devised by Ciano and Mussolini, or whether he acted out of dedication to
his profession and his intellectual interest in foreign culture. However,
given Bosio's reputation and dedication to his profession as an architect,
it seems that the latter is more likely the case (Cresti 1996).

CONCLUSION

The significant consistency between Italian urban planning and the overall institutional and ideological framework of Italian colonialism in Italian East Africa and Albania contexts points to the fact that urban planning cohered deeply with the principles of organization of the entire range of institutions of colonial domination. At the institutional level, the differential treatment of the two territories and their respective populations stemmed partly from earlier European practices of imperial domination and the persisting view among Italy's Fascist elites of the racial inferiority of Africans, bolstered by the rise of scientific racism as an official doctrine of the Fascist state. On the one hand, the legacy of Italian imperial involvement in Albania pushed the Italian government toward the "protectorate" policy and in granting Albania a relatively privileged position within Italy's Imperial Community. Italy's position in Albania was embedded in the system of European territorial acquisition and rule, governed by the nomos of European international legal practice, which had historically privileged Europe as a zone of sovereign state territory and distinguished it from Africa as a zone of free territory open to conquest. Consequently, Italy's Fascist rulers faced few inhibitions in dissolving the state of Ethiopia and creating a new administrative region to be attached to Italy's overseas empire, while devising institutional forms intended to ensure Rome's control and at the same time preserving the semblance of an autonomous state in Albania.

Even while entertaining the goal of demographic colonization of conquered lands with the massive settlement of Italian workers and peasants, Italian urban planning in newly conquered territories nonetheless proceeded on separate tracks. In relation to Ethiopia, Italian architects and planners followed the existing tradition of European colonial urbanism by advocating strict segregation and designed urban layouts based on principles of racial division. Seeking to drastically transform the structure of the city, Italian plans for Addis Ababa included massive redevelopment and division of the city into Italian and native zones, reflecting Ethiopians' exclusion from citizenship. In Albania, the symbolic function of the city was lodged within the framework of Fascism and its universalizing aspirations, with Fascism representing an alternative road to modernity for poorer countries such as Albania. In addition, the weakness of scientific racism and its crass categorical divisions between groups meant that more perspicacious forms of ethnographic representation gained a much more prominent role, including such theses as that of ancient ties between Romans and the ancestors of the Albanians and the regeneration by architecture in the Casa di Fascio of what was seen as an archaic, pre-Ottoman substratum of Albanian culture, inspired by the ethnographic work of Albanophile scholars such as Baldacci. Through such cultural works, Italian domination in Albania claimed to be doing the work of Albanian nationalism, all the while politically and economically subjugating the country and even vaguely entertaining the possibility of mass cultural assimilation.

As other scholars have noted, Italian colonial urbanism was tightly bound to Italy's project of empire, while urban planners enthusiastically embraced Italy's conquest of Ethiopia and the formation of Italian empire. Yet colonial urbanists and architects adjusted urban plans and architectural form in accordance largely with the political and ideological principles that governed each colony. In Ethiopia, urban planning set out to assist the construction of a racially segregated society, while in Albania, urban planning was seen as a tool of modernization and an ideological tool of Fascist empire.

Yet it is important not to reductively treat the works of Italian urban planners as mere instruments of Italian imperial politics. Just as the practice of urban planning itself was deeply enmeshed within the colonial enterprise, Italian urban planners and architects saw in colonial empire the opportunity to demonstrate the social utility and transformative capabilities of their trade. Italian urban planners and architects also saw in colonial empire the opportunity to compete with other European planners and showcase the achievements of Fascist modernity and architecture (Fuller 2007). As Wright (1991) shows, colonial urban layouts and architecture are a consequence of the imperialism of the planning profession just as much as of the political imperialism of states. That planners saw in empire the opportunity of realizing the virtues of their own work is illustrated by Hall's (2001: 198) quote of a letter by British architect Herbert Baker to Edwin Lutyens, on the occasion of their selection by the British India Office to design New Delhi: "It is really a great event in the history of the world and of architecture—that rulers should have the strength and sense to do the right thing. It would only be possible now under a despotism—some day perhaps democracies will follow. . . . It must not be Indian, nor English, nor Roman, but it must be Imperial. In 2000 years there must be an Imperial Lutyens tradition in Indian architecture. . . . Hurrah for despotism!" Such sentiment was shared by Italian architects, who enthusiastically rallied behind empire and sought a role in its project of subjugation. And yet, it is only by situating architectural and urban planning within the divergent structures and ideological goals of different types of colonial states and their geohistorical sites that we understand how the specific hubris of the planning profession came to fit into the overall project of empire.

NOTES

1. The return of the obelisk is no doubt not the only question of colonial restitution. After decades of refusal, in 1995 the Italian government formally admitted that the Italian military had used ammunitions laden with poisonous gas in the Ethiopian war. On the postcolonial significance of the obelisk, see Pickering-Iazzi (2003). See Del Boca (1992, 2003) on the politics of remembrance and suppression of colonialism and empire in Italy.

2. See Doumanis (1997) for an exemplary study on the politics of memory of Fascist empire among its formerly colonized subjects. Like the Greek Dodecanesian islands studied by Doumanis, Albania was spared the large-scale violence that the Italian military inflicted in Africa and benefited from Italian focus on infrastructural development. These have contributed to the historically skewed image of Italians as "good" colonizers, shared in the collective memory of Italians and their former European colonial subjects.

3. The architect Ferdinando Reggiori stated in 1936: "Every people that must export its own civilization, or better yet, 'colonize,' cannot achieve this without imposing through its laws its own buildings" (quoted in Boralevi 1986: 242).

4. In particular, Smith, a world-systems theorist, chastised King for attempting an "interdisciplinary synthesis that would weave together recent threads of urban planning and architecture, 'the new urban sociology,' and global political economy (with a few strands of postmodern embroidery)" (D. Smith 1991: 554).

5. On this particular point, including how medieval buildings were torn down in order to expose older Roman-era ruins that lay under or nearby, see Falasca-Zamponi (1997). Falasca-Zamponi discusses the links between this practice and the Fascist regime's growing emphasis, particularly after the 1935 Ethiopian campaign, on the myth of the resurrection of the Roman Empire and the government's official proclamation of Italy as an empire. On the role of Roman tropes and ruins in Fascist and Nazi politics, see Hell (2010).

6. Most important of these is the pioneering work of Del Boca (1969). On the general neglect of historians to examine the history of Italian colonialism, see Triulzi (1982). For a more recent statement, see Palumbo (2003a) and Labanca (2003).

7. Among the few studies of Italy's non-African colonialism is Doumanis (1997).

8. Fischer (1999) shows how Italian postoccupation policy was to a certain extent intentionally ambiguous as to Albania's legal status. Fearing a diplomatic backlash, Italian policy was intentionally designed to preserve the shell of an independent state while ensuring effective Italian control internally. As for the use of the term "colonial," some historians (including Fischer and most Albanian historians) have used the term to characterize the period of Italian rule in Albania. However, the term is used in a loose sense without drawing out the implications of what such a designation means for the historical practice of modern colonialism more generally.

9. Among the changes included was the renaming of Albania's parliament as the Superior Fascist Corporative Council (to which were added fourteen Italians as deputies) and the establishment of the Central Council of the Corporative Economy to direct economic policy.

10. Throughout the 1920s and 1930s, having become the chief financial backers of the Zog monarchy in Albania, Italian interests had already penetrated Albania deeply. Rome had helped establish and controlled a majority stake in the Bank of Albania and had set up the Societa per lo sviluppo economico di Albania to administer the use of Italian grants and loans in Albania, which effectively put Albania's economic policy under Rome's control. On Rome's economic policies in Albania in the period before occupation, see Fishta (1979, 1989, 1999).

11. The basic idea behind the policy of demographic colonization was to divert the flow of Italian immigration and transform potential immigrants into a population of overseas colonists directed by the state. See Larebo (2005) for a summary of the features and the eventual failure of the policy.

12. This is another distinguishing feature of Italian rule in Albania. In Slovenia, for instance, to which Italian troops were deployed in 1941, the Italians did not attempt to establish a separate Fascist political organization but supported a local pro-Fascist group, the *Domobranci* (Defenders of the Homeland).

13. Albania's case does not fully adhere to Osterhammel's second part of his formal definition of colonialism, which includes the unwillingness of foreign rulers to make cultural compromises with the natives and to preclude assimilation (2005: 15–17). However, the fact that Italian rule in Albania included the possibility of the acculturation of natives may make the colonial relationship no less abominable and may even make it more insidious. In any event, the other significant fact is that the Italian government did see Albania as a *settlement colony* and had tens of thousands of Italians settled there, and not only as an extraneously ruled territory (such as British India) or a friendly political satellite (such as were East European Axis allies Hungary, Romania, and Bulgaria to Nazi Germany).

14. An exception to this may be German-occupied Poland (see Furber 2003).

15. This is a distinguishing feature of Fascism, as it sought to dismantle the traditional liberal gap between public and private, politicizing, from the top down, every facet of individual life and thus legitimizing the state's supervision and intervention in all of them. It is in this sense that Fascism was not only a *political* ideology per se, that is, one that concerned itself only with the particular form of political and economic institutions, but an ideology that subsumed the entire moral character and being of the individual. It is in this context that Mussolini and other Fascist ideologues claimed Fascism to be a *totalitarian* system (Ben-Ghiat 2001; Berezin 1997; Gentile 1996).

16. Steinmetz develops the concept of the colonial state field starting from Bourdieu's field theory (Bourdieu 1984, 1996a, 1999).

17. See Robinson (1972) on the role of native "collaboration" in making colonialism possible.

18. Chatterjee (1993) illustrates such a relation between colonizer and colonized in British-ruled India. For example, early Indian nationalists had no qualms about India's subjection to Britain's empire but rather criticized the failed policies of modernization carried out by the British. It was in a later phase that Indian nationalists turned toward a wholesale rejection of British rule but only after nationalism had succeeded in creating an autonomous cultural space. In Albania, the embrace of

modern empire by a faction of Albanian nationalists occurred after the country's independence from the Ottoman Empire; however, a relatively autonomous cultural space persisted and was even encouraged by the Italians, even if ideologically policed (Pula 2008).

19. This indeed was the case legally as well. With Albania, Rome enacted a policy of dual citizenship and one of free travel, which permitted Albanians and Italians to travel and settle freely throughout both countries (in reality, very few Albanians moved to Italy). Upon the dissolution of Albania's Foreign Ministry, the Italian government issued an order permitting Albanian citizens to seek counsel at Italian embassies: "With express orders by the Duce, no discrimination can be exercised against Albanians who seek help from [our embassies], and enjoy the same rights and duties as Italians, based on the principle of full equality" (quoted in Jacomoni 1965: 161). In Ethiopia, in contrast, Ethiopians were denied the privileges of Italian citizenship.

20. In Schmitt's discussion of *nomos*, a concept he develops against the approach to law found in legal positivism, nomos represents the normative and spatial principles of a system of ordering, the original act of an *ordo ordinans* ("order of ordering"). Nomos is not law itself but rather the set of principles out of which legal order is generated and legitimated as such. "In its original sense," Schmitt writes, "*nomos* is precisely the full immediacy of a legal power not mediated by laws; it is a constitutive historical event—an act of *legitimacy*, whereby the legality of a mere law first is made meaningful" ([1950] 2003: 73; emphasis in original). More specifically, "all subsequent regulations of a written or unwritten kind derive their power from the inner measure of an original, constitutive act of spatial ordering. This original act is nomos. All subsequent developments are either results of and expansions on this act or else redistributions (*anadasmoi*)—either a continuation on the same basis or a disintegration of and a departure from the constitutive act of the spatial order established by [acts such as] land-appropriation, the founding of cities, or colonization" (Schmitt [1950] 2003: 78). Clearly, this is a philosophically realist position that sees particular classes of action as explainable by reference to a particular (or particular set of) historically constituted generative principle(s), rather than a set of empirically independent and unrelated acts.

21. For example, Schmitt notes the increasing distinction made by legal scholars toward the end of the nineteenth century between European and American international law. The growth in the sheer number of independent sovereign states also created turmoil in the system. Thus, Schmitt notes how European jurists failed to notice that the recognition of new states constituted not the *universalization* of the European system of international law but its collapse as a European system per se. Schmitt expresses this in a powerful statement:

Jurists believed that Europe was being complimented by the reception of non-Europeans, and did not notice that, in fact, they were loosening all the foundations of a reception, because the former—good or bad, but in any case conceived of as a concrete order, above all as a spatial order, by a true community of European princely houses, states, and nations—had disappeared. What appeared in its place was no "system" of states, but a collection of states randomly joined together by factual relations—a disorganized mass of more than 50 heterogeneous states, lacking any spatial or spiritual consciousness of what they once had in common, a chaos of reputedly equal and equally sovereign states and their dispersed possessions, in which a common bracketing of war no longer was feasible, and for which not even the concept of "civilization" could provide any concrete homogeneity. (2003: 233–234)

22. The only exception in Schmitt's (2003) book is Italy's invasion of Ethiopia; see subsequent discussion in text. On Schmitt's more explicit writings on Nazi imperialism and the reasons for his avoidance of direct discussion in his 2003 book, see Hell (2009).

23. Harvey discusses Kant's *Geography*, which ranked the world's populations according to a racial scheme. Noting how Kant's geographic knowledge contradicts his better-known writings on universal ethics and cosmopolitanism, Harvey quotes Kant suggesting that "humanity achieves its greatest perfection with the white race. The yellow Indians have somewhat less talent. The negroes are much inferior and some of the peoples of the Americas are well below them" (quoted in Harvey 2001: 210–211). In the case of Albania and the Balkans, Wolff (1994) and Todorova (1997) show how, beginning with Enlightenment thinkers, Europe's eastern and southeastern periphery was consistently seen as an ambiguous intermediate zone between the civilization of the West and the barbarism of the East.

24. Ambrosini further states that "it is only the population of Italian East Africa who are in a state of subjugation, but such that does not exclude the possession of religious and civil rights to participate in local administration and the Empire's economic development." Subjugation was not appropriate for Libya and the Aegean islands "due to each region's respectively advanced stage of civilization," but those populations nonetheless required a treatment that brought all of the kingdom's populations "to the same level." This type of sociopolitical organization, though new in Ambrosini's view, nevertheless "conformed to the Roman tradition" (1940: 63).

25. Schmitt recognizes the failure of the *jus publicum Europaeum* to be replaced by a new nomos, chiefly by the failure of states to "bracket" war. Schmitt discusses this failure using the League of Nations' inability to preserve the rights of Ethiopia, a member state, after Italy's aggression, when the League eventually legitimized the complete annihilation of the state's political identity and recognized its annexation by Italy and transformation into Italian East Africa. Conversely, Mussolini justified Italian expansion on the basis of being "denied" its "right" to "a place in the sun" like other colonial empires (Mack Smith 1976). Such rhetoric ghastly contradicted the League's goal of establishing a rights-based collective body of international governance but also demonstrated the internal contradiction between such a system and the fact that a number of European states continued to maintain the status of colonial empires.

26. On the distinction between colonialism and imperialism, see Osterhammel (2005) and chapter 1 of the present volume.

27. It is significant in this sense how views of Albania within the Italian metropolitan and colonial administration differed. Most telling is how Jacomoni takes issue with Italy's foreign minister Ciano for writing, in his personal diary, that the assumption of Albania's crown by the House of Savoy meant the end of Albania's independence. Jacomoni instead argues that the "union" between Italy and Albania represented a relationship of equals (1965: 153–168). Ciano, conversely, was concerned with maintaining the appearance of an independent state, while ensuring that the Italian government had a free hand in exercising control within the country, including picking the leadership (Fischer 1999: 5–58).

28. These debates are reported at length in Boralevi (1986) and Fuller (1988).

29. No definitive numbers on Italian settlement in Albania exist. Fischer (1999) states that upon the collapse of the Fascist regime in 1943, 30,000 Italians lived in Tirana alone. Statistics cited by Misha (1970) indicate that in the period 1940–1941, over 51,000 Italian laborers came to Albania and 44,250 left, while between 1942 and 1943 the number of Italian workers fluctuated anywhere between 7,000 and 13,000, based on the reports used. In the period 1939–1940, official figures cited by Misha suggest that approximately 190,000 individuals entered and 150,000 departed Albania through its main port, Durrës.

30. Italian architects had done similar work of adapting native forms to modern architecture in Africa as well, particularly Libya, but nowhere, according to my research, did they place symbols of national culture so centrally within a city.

31. In his magisterial and influential volume *L'Albania*, the anthropologist Baldacci (1929) purported to provide a thorough ethnological study of Albanians, in which he prominently emphasized the ancient Illyrian origins of Albanians and the "ancient ties" existing between Illyrians and Romans. His descriptions particularly focused on the Albanian highlands, from whence Bosio apparently received his inspiration for the *kulla* replica. In any case, the stress on ancient ties between Rome and the Albanians found its way into other publications as well, while racial categories were much less prominent in discussions. Ancient Rome's role in Albania became an explicit topic for the archaeologist Mustilli (1940). Studies by folklorists such as Bernardy (1941) and the publications of the Istituto nazionale di cultura fascista on Albania contained almost no references to racial categories (Ambrosini 1940; Morandi 1942). Ambrosini's historical account situates Albania's membership in the Italian Empire entirely within the historical context of what he describes as continuing historical ties between the two sides of the Adriatic and scantly and only superficially refers to race. The publications of the Centro studi per l'Albania established within the Italian Academy of Sciences were also entirely staffed by ethnologists and linguists with few affinities to the epistemic categories promoted by Italian racial scientists such as Guido Landra, Marcello Ricci, and Lino Businco, who paid little attention to Albania but extensively disseminated racist conceptions of Africa through Rome's Racial Office and its journal, *La difesa della razza* (Pankhurst 2005). The influence of scientific racism on other academic disciplines was also curbed by the unsettled nature of the field, its political instrumentalization by Mussolini, and its inability to become organized around a racial orthodoxy (Gillette 2002).

FOURTEEN

Japanese Colonial Structure in Korea in Comparative Perspective

OU-BYUNG CHAE

INTRODUCTION

This chapter attempts to provide a sociological and historical overview of Japanese colonialism and the colonial situation it created in Korea from a comparative perspective. Except for the late Ottoman Empire, the Japanese colonial empire was the only non-Western colonial empire in the history of modern colonialism. There have been many characterizations to address the historical specificity of non-Western colonialism as marginal, among them "defensive colonialism" (Cumings 1981) and "imperialism of the weak" (Kim 2006) for the Japanese Empire, and "borrowed colonialism" (Deringil 2003) for the Ottoman Empire. While acknowledging the insights of each of these perspectives, in this chapter I am interested in a more comprehensive and sociological picture. If a given colonialism reveals specific characteristics, it may not be limited to the ideology and practice of the colonizer. The colonial situation it creates in a specific colony and the way the colonized react may also reveal these characteristics. We need a larger conceptual device than colonialism and a typology of Japanese colonialism.

This chapter has two objectives. First, I suggest the concept of colonial structure that enables us to holistically understand the mutual implications between colonizer and colonized. Second, I develop a typology of non-Western colonial structure established in Korea by Japanese colonialism and derived from Western "new imperialism" in the late nineteenth century. Characterizing Japanese colonialism as a derivative colonialism, I propose that the structure of the Japanese colonialism can be understood as a triad, whereas Western colonialism was dyadic. In the dyad the colonizer and the

colonized forge a direct relationship; in contrast in the triad the two collectivities do so through the mediation of the third party, that is, "the West,"[1]
as cultural representation.

Let me provide some caveats. By triad I do not intend to particularize
and essentialize the characteristics of Japanese colonialism. Depending on
the researcher's own interest, the possibilities of the construction of various
typologies for the same object are wide open. Western colonialism itself
shows varieties, from which comparisons within a specific empire and
across empires are possible (e.g., Steinmetz 2004). Also, it should be noted
that the Japanese colonialism is not different from the Western one in every
respect. That the colonial state is characterized as "the state *sans* nation"
(Comaroff 1998) and the "rule of difference" (Chatterjee 1993; Steinmetz
2004) is also true of Japanese colonialism. Yet given the commonality of
"colonialism," it can be still meaningful to compare two historical types of
empire. Last, this chapter is primarily interested in developing a typology in
which the focus is placed on collective, political, and stable identities of
social actors rather than fractured and free-floating identities.

COLONIAL STRUCTURE

Colonialism refers to the rule of domination between a minority of alien
invaders and a native population and a form of territorial rule that usurps
sovereignty and enforces the rule of difference through the colonial state
(Osterhammel 2005: 16–17; Steinmetz 2006b: 143). This definition is certainly useful, and I do not question the concept itself. But when it is used
beyond its contextual boundary, it may lose sight of mutually defining and
defined relationships between colonizer and colonized. Colonialism is a term
that reflects the ideologies and practices of the colonizer, and the colonized is
absent in it. Like any other sociological category of collectivities, the identities
and discourses of the colonizer and the colonized are relationally constructed
(Hall 1996; Laclau and Mouffe 1985: 106). While colonialism "conditioned the
reactions of 'dependent' peoples" (Balandier 1966: 34), the colonizer is also
"fabricated like the native; he is made by his function and interests" (Sartre
2001: 44). To properly understand a specific case of colonialism and colonial
situation, we need to look at the relational context in which the colonizer is
involved and the context in which the colonized is constructed.

The distinction between the colonizer and the colonized as a cultural binarism is brought in by the colonial power as an ideological impetus of or justification for its colonial rule, and once introduced, it can be adopted by the

colonized, which taken together reproduce and reinforce it through cultural, economic, and political divides. Sartre was already aware of this in calling colonialism a "system" (2001), and in this chapter, I am working in a similar way but building on the theoretical elaborations of "structure" in recent decades (Bourdieu 1977; Giddens 1984; Sewell 1992, 1996), I capture this systemic character with the concept of colonial structure. More specifically, if we are to follow William Sewell's notion of structure, the colonial structure can basically be understood as having mutually sustaining relationships between cultural schemas, resources, and modes of power (Sewell 1992, 1996). But although colonial *structure* shares this essential feature with other structures in general, as *colonial* structure, it also has its own specific characteristics stemming from the rule of difference, colonialism as a territorial empire, and the systemic character of the mutual implication between colonizer and colonized.

First, power and resource distributions are asymmetrical between colonizer and colonized, and such social reorganization by an alien power creates colonial grievances and leads to perennial system instability (Balandier 1966: 54; Wallerstein 1986: 19). As the infamous colonial administrative terms "native question" (Mamdani 1996) and "native policy" (Steinmetz 2003a) evoke, colonial power often has to address the ingrained problem of colonial resistance through various ideological and institutional apparatuses. Second, the instability of the colonial structure has much to do with colonial cultural schemas, which assume a highly ideological character. A colonial structure characterized as perennially unstable implies that ideologies of legitimation and contestation are already involved in it. In order to legitimize foreign political overrule, the colonial power attempts to infuse the ideology of the colonial state's beneficial role as exemplified in the "civilizing mission" and the "white man's burden," while setting racial and/or cultural boundaries between the two collectivities (Chatterjee 1993: 19–21). The colonized, particularly the native elites, for anticolonial nationalist cause, also deploy ideological strategies to "frame" or "suture" colonial grievances among the masses (Laclau and Mouffe 1985; Tarrow 1998).

As Sewell argues, for the concept of structure to be possible, there must exist a mutually implying and sustaining relationship between the three components. For example, he writes, "schemas are the effects of resources, just as resources are the effects of schemas" (1992: 13). It is clear that the master schema of binary opposition between the two collectivities and their opposing ideologies is the effect of unequal distribution of resources and power. Likewise, the asymmetry and its instability are the effects of colonial and anticolonial ideologies. Colonial structure can then be seen as having asymmetry in resources and power between the two collectivities, which produces not only the schema of binarism but also tension-laden bifurcated ideologies, which in turn reproduce the asymmetry in conflicts.

In the formation of a colonial structure, the identities and ideologies of the colonizer assumed the inferior other. As is well known, orientalist discourses played a crucial role in the colonial expansion (Said 1978), complicated with various psychological mechanisms, such as projection (Fanon 1967). Just as the construction of the colonizer presupposed the existence of the colonized, the construction of the colonized was fundamentally circumscribed by the presence of the colonizer. As Fanon put, "the colonized's first action is reaction" (1967: 36), or as Timothy Mitchell writes, "colonial subjects and their modes of resistance are formed within the organizational terrain of the colonial state" (1988: xi). As ideal types, I suggest that there are two general mechanisms in which the colonized react to colonial power and develop ideological strategies. One is attraction/imitation, which occurs when colonial elites perceive that there is no alternative strategy to pursue and that this is the only possible way to overcome the backwardness of the nation or to preserve it. This strategy is double-edged in the sense that although it contributes to the reproduction of the system through collaboration, it also may operate in a way to undermine the colonial difference the colonizer imposes on the colonized (Bhabha 1994a). The other mechanism is repulsion/rejection, which takes repulsive stands toward colonial cultures and often leads to a search for an alternative ideology that the colonial power does not offer. In contrast to imitation or adaptation, rejection operates to create independent political space within the colonial binarism. It produces heretical discourses and political programs, and from this ideological and political opposition to colonial power, the rejection strategy tries to obtain legitimacy. It attempts to provide an alternative ideological guide through which colonial grievances are interpreted and a concrete political program is created.

With this outline of the colonial structure, below I discuss the colonial structure in Korea established by Japanese colonialism. But first, for comparative purposes, let me briefly outline the general characteristics of the Western colonial structure that I call a dyad.

DYADIC STRUCTURE

Western colonial structure, despite its diversity, can be understood as dyadic when compared with non-Western colonial structure. Simply put, in the dyad the ideologies and political identities of the colonizer and the colonized are formed through the unmediated relationship between them. In Western colonial structure, as is well known, the colonizing power was equipped with the alleged "Western modernity" of the epistemology of linear evolutionism that supposedly culminated in scientific rationality, humanist universality, and capitalist materiality. The self-identity of "Western civilization" was made possible only through the presupposition of the "non-civilized other." The cultural and racial distinction between West and non-West was expressed as "indirect rule" or the rule of "association" that made use of local power and culture in colonial administration. In this model, a certain amount of power and resources was transferred to native elites in the form of self-rule, by which the dyadic structure was decentralized to a certain degree (Mamdani 1996). There were two main reasons why this mode of colonial rule was enforced.

First was economic and political liberalism. As the excentric approach suggests (Robinson 1986), Britain was the hegemon in the imperial order of the mid- to late nineteenth century, and its ideology was the liberalism of free trade. The intervention of free trade imperialism operated according to the principle "by influence if possible, by formal means if necessary" (Gallagher and Robinson 1953). Even when imperialism transformed itself into colonialism through territorial acquisition and building a colonial state, it still attempted to minimize costs by constructing a system of collaboration that made use of native elites. In addition to this economic motivation, liberalism since the eighteenth century justified indirect rule by excluding natives, who were in the stage of "infant" or "subhuman" (Mehta 1997), from liberal principles or by the pretext of respecting the natives' own path of different evolution and their cultures.

Second, the colonial state had to figure out the "native question." Colonialism had to cope with the ingrained legitimacy problem, and the use of the native elite came to be considered as a means to solve this problem. It was devised in two levels. First was the recruitment of the Westernized natives into colonial administration. Although they were the rank and file of the colonial state, their numbers and upward mobility were strictly limited to avoid diminishing colonial difference. Second, most of collaborators were composed of (newly invented) traditional elites (Mamdani 1996; Ranger 1983), as in the roles of chief and caïd in colonial Africa or prince in colonial India. Except for administrative cities and other regions under direct rule, most regions divided by ethnicities and religions were under the control of local elite. This strategy of divide and rule not only appeased them but also purported to repress the rise of nationalism through ethnic divisions.

Although local elites who were accustomed to local identities bestowed by colonial state became an obstacle to the formation of an integrated anti-colonialism, a relatively small number of Westernized elites formed their identities through attraction/imitation and repulsion/rejection vis-à-vis the colonizer's culture. Attraction to the colonizer's culture appeared as strategy of imitation. As far as the colonizer's culture claimed to be modern, the colonized's imitation was also modernism, as ideologically expressed in the national bourgeoisie's liberalism or a socialism that pursued Western universality but at the same time attempted to overcome capitalist modernity. Conversely, the repulsion/rejection couplet rejected modernism by way of repulsive stands to it and often founded alternative identities in the natives' authentic culture, that is, through nativism as an antithesis of modernism. Frantz Fanon characterized this binarism of modernism/nativism as "dual narcissism" (1967). It should be noted that in spite of its explosive impact on anticolonial struggle in the later period of Western colonial rule, the colonized's nativism was still caught in the epistemological horizon of colonial culture. For example, the sense of black supremacy in negritude is the result of the internalization of orientalist binarism of Western colonialism.

To be sure, as many studies on colonial situation show (Fanon 1967; Memmi 1967; Sartre 2001), attraction/imitation and repulsion/rejection are often mixed in reality. Modernist identity formed through identification with Western culture often experienced frustration with colonial discrimination, which then led to founding a nativist identity in which once negatively regarded native culture was transformed into positivity. Moreover, modernism and nativism often formed a fused identity, and they were strategically combined in anticolonial movements (Robinson 1972: 137).[2] This strategy pursues an identity strategy of the "different but modern" (Chakrabarty 1997: 373) that is simultaneously different from and similar to Western modernity.[3] There were plenty of examples: (neo) Mahdism in Sudan, the negritude of Senghor and Cesaire, Nkrumah's consciencism, Arabism, and Gandhism.

TRIADIC STRUCTURE

The discussion so far has depended on theories and concepts distilled from the Western colonial situations. As discussed below, when it comes to the colonial structure in Korea, we should be careful with these theories and concepts. At the level of causal mechanisms, they may hold; but at the level of the empirical, they may need to be reserved. I contend that this was because the relational context in the non-Western colonial situation was wholly different from that in the colonies of Western colonialism. Simmel noted that "the sociological situation between the superordinate and the subordinate is completely changed as soon as a third element is added" (1950: 141). The colonial structure in Korea was a triad to the extent that it was established through the cultural mediation of "the West." In this structure, the colonizer's definition of the colonized and the colonial policy were formed through the mediation of "the West," and so was the reaction of the colonized.

DERIVATIVE COLONIALISM

The triadic structure did not come into existence independently of the dyadic structure. Surely, Japanese colonialism and its spawned colonial structure in Korea had their own distinctive characteristics. Yet as far as it was derived from the worldwide imperial order of Western dyadic structure, it should be understood as a historical formation rather than as an orientalist derivative. In the world historical context, the time when Japan rose as a colonial empire coincided with the period of the Western empires' transition from nonterritorial to territorial empires, triggered by the "partition of Africa" in the 1870s. In this historical conjuncture, Japanese colonialism's derivative character was the outcome of the coworking of attraction/imitation and repulsion/rejection.

First, in empire building as well as modern state building, Western imperialism provided models that the Japanese political elite would adopt. In the era of new imperialism, in the newly rising interstate system, empire building was a prerequisite for the recognition of the nation-state (Duara 2003; Dudden 2005).[4] German law and *Staatswissenschaften* strongly influenced the drafting of the Meiji Constitution, and the restoration of the emperor system followed the Western empires' use of "invented tradition" (Hobsbawm and Ranger 1983). The same was true of the method of colonial expansion. The Japanese political elite used the Western empires' gunboat diplomacy to construct a treaty port system in Korea and fully made use of international law in acquiring Taiwan in 1895 and Korea in 1910.

However, this strategy of imitation is not sufficient to exhaust all the characteristics of Japanese colonialism. To the extent that imitation of the new imperialism was a constitutive mechanism, so was rejection of the West. Japan barely escaped conquest by the Western powers (Peattie 1984: 6), but unequal treaties with them persisted until 1911, when Japan had already colonized Korea. The presence and threat of Western powers awakened the national consciousness of Japan, and it was in no sense in an imitative mode. The Meiji Restoration in 1868 was undertaken in the name of "loyalty to the emperor and repelling the barbarians" by the discontented samurai class under the declining Tokugawa *bakufu* system. While the Western-oriented Itō Hirobumi was present in making the modern state, the nativist Inoue Kowashi added the ideological coloring of Shintoism to the emperor system. Mimicking Western inventions of tradition, the Japanese emperor, as a father of the family-state,[5] was elevated to the status of Confucian monarch. Last, following Western colonial practices, Japanese colonial ideology emphasized the role of "civilization," but it was nonetheless Japan's own rendering of civilization.

Thus Japan's encounter with the West simultaneously entailed senses of attraction and repulsion, which then became the key mechanisms of the production of modern political identities. On the side of attraction/imitation was a force of "civilization and enlightenment" led by Fukuzawa Yukichi, and on the side of repulsion/rejection, there were Asianists represented by Darui Tokichi and Okakura Tenshin. Caught between the two orientations, the formation of Japanese political culture did not evolve in a unitary fashion that exclusively favored either direction. Rather, it was a process of conflicts and of checks and balances (Gluck 1985). This reflects a dilemma for Japan as a newly rising non-Western colonial empire. Japan was doubly engaged with the West and Asia. In relation to the West, Japan had to keep its own identity while demonstrating its ability to satisfy the criteria of Western civilization; in relation to Asia, although Japan could not help remaining in Asia, it also had to distance itself from other "less civilized" Asian countries, such as China and Korea.

However, as far as imperial expansion was concerned, there seemed to be less disagreement. As exemplified by Fukuzawa's argument for *datsu-A* (leaving Asia), imitation of the West or liberalism in Japan aimed at colonial expansion, abandoning hopeless collaborations with neighboring Asian countries. Just as in Western imperial political culture, Japan's liberalism was "inwardly constitutionalism, outwardly imperialism" (Matsuo 1974: vii).[6] Nativist reaction or Asianism as an extension of the former argued for the solidarity of Asia against white encroachment. Asianism was initially developed as an anti-Western imperialist discourse, which was also shared by Chinese and Korean elites. As Japan's economic and military strength rapidly grew, however, a view of Japan's leading role among China, Japan, and Korea emerged within the discourse (Kang 2003), which in turn began to be used for colonial expansion. Asianism motivated and justified colonial subjugation by appealing to the motto of liberating Asia. The liberalist trend survived until the era of *Taishō* democracy (1905–1925), yet it existed primarily in the domain of civil society. Following Western colonial practices, liberalism in Japan preferred indirect colonial rule to assimilation. Liberalism provided a critical voice about assimilationist colonial policies but could not exercise enough power to shape colonial policies. Conversely, Asianism was espoused by ultranationalists whose social backgrounds included not only journalists and intellectuals from civil society but also the military and politicians who were responsible for designing concrete colonial policies.

In the era of new imperialism, the Japanese political culture was formed in simultaneous material imitation and cultural rejection of the West. Modern state formation and empire building took place at the same time, and in this process, imitative and rejective attitudes were gradually incorporated into a body of knowledge known as Asianism. Asianism soon turned from anti-Western or imperial "heterodoxy" to colonial "orthodoxy." Assimilation and direct rule as colonial ideology and policy were extensions of the Japanese political culture of Asianism.[7] As a derivative colonialism, the Japanese imperial culture of staying "antagonistic toward the West, while still remaining modern" (Tanaka 1993: 22) paradoxically resembled the anticolonial strategies in Western colonies.

COLONIAL IDEOLOGY AND POLICY

Japanese colonial ideologies and policies were devised through the cultural mediation of the West. Japan's modern political culture was formed in response to the new imperialism of the West, which was directly mirrored in the rendition of its own colonialism. Within the framework of Asianism, the relationship between the Japanese and the Koreans had to be simultaneously close and distant. In relation to the West, similarity between them should be stressed; as far as Asia was concerned, difference had to justify foreign political overrule. The categories of "race" and "culture" were deployed to realize this task.

In the Asianist discourse, the three countries of China, Japan, and Korea were understood as sharing the same culture and race (*dōbun dōshu*). Yet beyond this, a view of Japan and Korea's closer historical connection by virtue of their shared culture and ancestry (*dōbun dōso*) was proliferated during the time that Korea was colonized. This view was specifically developed as *Nissen dōsoron* (theses on the same ancestry of Japan and Korea),[8] which argued not only that Korea originated from Japan but also that the Japanese emperors substantially ruled over the southern regions of the Korean peninsula for two centuries in ancient times. Thus, long before the annexation of Korea in 1910, it was narrated that ancient Korea had already been the colony of Japan. The culture of ancient Korea was able to blossom thanks to the blessing of the emperors, and for this reason, their languages, customs, and religions were similar to one another. Provided that the Japanese and Koreans shared the same culture and ancestry, the logical implication of Nissen dōsoron was that the annexation of Korea was a natural return to the ancient state of union (Duus 1995: 420; Kita 1910: 69–72). In the era of new imperialism in Asia and Japan's accession to the imperial circle, the slogans of dōbun dōshu and dōbun dōso were emphasized and gained in popularity.

This view was also reflected in the official ideology and policy of the colonial state. It was stated that "in purport, the annexation of Korea is totally different from the cases where the Western nations annexed half-civilized or inferior nations. . . . Since [Japan and Korea are] the same race and culture, and thereby customs are not very different from each other, [their] amalgamation/assimilation under [a] unified nation is never a difficult job to do" (Chōsen sōtokufu 1914: 2). While a racial distinction was made between the white and yellow "man," racial and cultural sameness was emphasized between the Japanese and the Koreans (Iyenaga 1912; Nitobe 1911). Japanese colonialists stressed that since they shared the same racial and cultural origins, it would be self-contradictory and unrealistic to adopt a Western "laissez-faire" (indirect rule) native policy (Saeki 1910: 61–62). So the official line of colonial rule was assimilation (dōka) and direct rule. The ultimate end of colonial rule was the Japanization of Korea.

But as Sartre once put it, "assimilation taken to its extreme meant, quite simply, the ending of colonialism" ([1964] 2001: 46; also see Steinmetz 2003a: 47). While in Western colonialism the contradiction lay in universality and its rule of racial difference, in Japanese colonialism the contradiction revolved around assimilation based on particularistic Asianism and its impossibility. Assimilation was a colonial "fantasy," a desire never to be realized yet constitutive of realities (Žižek 1989). Assimilation had to be proclaimed, yet at the same time some reservations also had to be made in order for colonialism to be possible. What was often expressed as mindo (the level of the people) was low, meaning that political, economic, and social barriers should be discarded gradually (Hara [1919] 1999: 61–65). The extension of the Imperial Constitution to Korea was suspended, and the legal status of Koreans remained undefined throughout the colonial period (Chen 1984: 246).

Here it should be noticed that the Japanese colonial ideology employed a double criterion of culture. As a rejective mode against the West, it essentialized folk or ethnic culture in order to emphasize the Asiatic commonality between Japan and Korea. As an imitative mode toward the West, it made a distinction between itself and the colonized. "Race" is used to differentiate the yellow from the white, Japanese from Western "colonialism."[9] In coexistence with the colonial rule of difference, the slogans of assimilation took different names with growing intensity: *Naichi enchōshugi* (the principle of the extension of Japan) in the 1920s, *Naissen Yuwa* (Japan and Korea in harmony) in the early 1930s, and *Naisen ittai* (Japan and Korea as a single body) beginning in 1936.

When we turn to the dimensions of power and resources, the distinctiveness of Japanese assimilationist direct rule should not be underestimated. Contrary to the retreat of French colonial rule from assimilation to association,[10] the assimilation principle based on regional particularity was reinforced throughout the colonial period as Japan's conflicts with the West sharpened. While direct rule was typically enforced in settler colonies in Africa, Korea was not a settler colony proper. This assimilationist direct rule should also be distinguished from direct rule in nonsettler colonies without an assimilation policy, such as most of the sub-Saharan African colonies and the Punjab region in British India. The colonial state in Korea enjoyed immense autonomy and capacity. The expansionist military clans constituted a major power in Japanese politics after the Restoration, and for security reasons they monopolized the governor-general position in the colonies. All eight governors-general came from the military, and their power was comparable to that of the prime minister in Japan. The governor-general was the supreme commander of the army in Korea, and the administration, legislation, and judicial branches in the colony all belonged to him. The governor-general was directly appointed by the emperor but was not interfered with or directed by the cabinet in Japan.

As in other Western colonies, the colonial authorities were soon faced with the native question. In order for an efficient colonial administration, it was important to induce collaboration from Koreans, and landlords and intellectuals were the candidates. But economic incentives for the landlords and political measures to win the intellectuals were fundamentally different from the partial transference of power to local elites found in the Western colonial structure. In spite of intermittent disturbances, the colonial government attempted to figure out the native question by deepening the asymmetries in power and resource distribution, rather than endowing the natives with self-rule. The immense capacity of the colonial state can be sensed when the ratio of Japanese colonial officials to the Korean population is compared with those in Western colonies in the late 1930s. As Table 14.1

shows, the ratio in Korea, 1/341, is more than ten times greater than those in Western colonies. The sheer size of the colonial state in Korea is also telling. Table 14.2 shows that, including Koreans and except for the Japanese military force in Korea, the number of officials employed in the Government-General of Korea and its affiliated branches in 1934 was 82,377, which constituted a ratio of 1/256 to total population. The number of police personnel (19,326) made up nearly a quarter of all employees, yielding a ratio of 1/1,093 to the

TABLE 14.1 · Ratio of Alien Officials to
Native Population in Various Colonies in the Late 1930s.

Colonies	Alien Officials	Native Population	Ratio
British Nigeria	1,315	20,000,000	1/15,209
Belgian Congo	2,384	9,400,000	1/3,943
French Equatorial Africa	887	3,200,000	1/3,608
French West Africa	3,660	15,000,000	1/4,098
French Vietnam in 1937	2,920[1]	17,000,000	1/5,822
Korea in 1938	64,365[2]	22,000,000	1/341

Source: Chōsen tōkei kyōkai (1939: 39); Cumings (1981: 11–12); Delavignette (1950: 18); Grajdanzev (1978: 79).

1 The number of military personnel is excluded.
2 This also excludes the number of military personnel but includes professions. However, as Grajdanzev notes, there was very little room for professions in Korea outside of government service (1978: 79). There is one more thing to be said about this number. On the basis of the statistics provided by Grajdanzev, Cumings estimates the number as 246,000 in 1937 (1981: 12), which is nearly four times exaggerated. Grajdanzev misleadingly reported the percentage of public and professional services (38.1%) from the total population, not from the occupational one, which is then used by Cumings to estimate the number.

TABLE 14.2 · Ratio of Government-General Employees
to Population in Korea in 1934.

Government-General Employees	Population	Ratio
82,377	21,125,827	1/256
(Police: 19,326)	(Korean: 20,513,804)	1/249
	(Japanese: 561,334)	1/1,093 (police/Korean)

Source: Chōsen sōtokufu (1936: 11–35).

Korean population. Along with this political centralization assisted by effective police surveillance, the colonial state promoted the centralization of resources by introducing a modern taxation system that was enabled by the general cadastral survey (1910–1918) (Kim 2006: 218–219). It can also be contrasted to the lack of a central colonial budget and the weak investment in the "imperialism on the cheap" of the Western colonial structure (Cooper 2005a: 157; also see Cumings 1999a).

THE NATIVES: FOUR REACTIONS

In colonial Korea, as in many other colonies, there existed a variety of activities based on different identities. The butchers' human rights movement, women's movement, and agrarianism are among the examples (Shin and Robinson 1999). In addition, there was a large gray zone that could not clearly be captured either by resistance or collaboration. In this light Prasenjit Duara (1997) suggests the restoration of various alternative narratives repressed by the nationalist one. However, his suggestion paradoxically reveals that certain identities and discourses have been more salient than others during the (post)colonial times. The colonial ideologies and policy and the reactions, identities, and discourses of Korean political elites together constituted a kind of magnetic field, and the mechanisms that formed the major flows in the field were attraction/imitation and repulsion/rejection. Despite their similarities in appearance to their counterparts in the Western colonies, the political identities and discourses produced through these mechanisms should be understood differently, since the relational context from which they originated was different. Just as colonial ideology and policy were formed through the cultural mediation of the West, the ways Korean political elites reacted were mediated through the West. In this section, I briefly sketch four major political or cultural discourses that circulated among Korean intellectuals. They were two modernisms— liberalism and socialism—and two nativist discourses—Asianism and Korean ethnic nationalism.

Modernisms: Liberalism and Socialism

As in other Western colonies, in colonial Korea modernist political identities and discourses were represented by liberalism and socialism. Liberalism refers here to a political orientation that pursued the republican political system and capitalist economy of the West, and socialism includes social democracy and communism. What needs to be considered first is the ways modernism, especially liberalism, was produced. If modernism in the Western colonies was formed through the colonized's imitation of colonial cultures, can we say the same in colonial Korea?

Liberal nationalists emerged via two main routes. Before the colonization, the first generation was created primarily through contact with Christianity and education by mission schools in Korea; this generation later received higher education in the United States and led nationalist movements abroad and in Korea. The second generation of liberalism was mainly composed of the elite who obtained a college education in Japan in the 1900s and the 1910s. They went to Japan for higher education after the annexation, and there they were blessed with the tide of liberalism in Japanese civil society.

The gist of liberalist opposition to colonial rule is well expressed in Rhee Syngman's speech in 1948: "We have never stopped fighting for individual freedom and free republic. Since those who suppressed us ruled by autocracy, our belief in democracy got firmer in our hearts" (*Hansŏng ilbo*, August 16, 1948). As Rhee's recollection succinctly conveys, liberal nationalism stood as a rejection of colonial rule and identification with the third party in the colonial relationship, which was the West. Clearly liberalism was neither colonial ideology nor the official political culture of the metropole. Through the cultural mediation of the West, liberal nationalism was established as an anticolonial ideology that rejected Japan's Asianist imperial cultures and policy of assimilation.

The West, particularly the United States, was often idealized in its general level of civilization, domestic politics, international policies, and even its colonial policies. Anticipating the inevitable clash between Japan and the West in future, the liberal nationalists also attempted to borrow the power of the West for national liberation. These idealized images of the West and tactical anticipation were reflected in the two broad liberal nationalist strategies of obtaining independence through "preparation" and "diplomacy." While liberals in exile put more effort into diplomacy, because of political constraints, domestic liberals were mainly engaged with the projects of preparation. Moreover, if not ideal, the "liberalist" colonial rule—indirect rule or self-rule—and successful nationalist movements in Western colonies were often referred to as desirable and feasible institutions and strategies.

Another major secularist anticolonialism that entered into rivalry with liberalism and even often overwhelmed it was socialism. As in other Western colonies, socialism/communism in Korea was welcomed as an alternative modernist project as well as an anticolonial one. Japan and other Western countries were considered examples of the same category of imperialism, which could be overcome only by means of revolution. As socialism's subsequent development shows, socialists came to question liberal nation-alists' compromising strategies (Kim and Kim 1986: 27–28). Socialism grew quickly in the peninsula during the 1920s and became a major rival to liberal nationalism. Although both originated from the same nationalist problem-atic, because of the rivalry between them and because of selective oppres-sion from the colonial state, they came to occupy the separate identities of "nationalism" and "socialism," and their activities were respectively called the "national movement" and the "social movement" both by themselves and by the colonial government.

As a modernist project, socialism in colonial Korea can be understood in the relational context of the colonial structure. Like the liberalists, socialists were initially attracted to the third pole as ideological source and potential political resource. The Communist International's policy in the early 1920s to support nationalism and encourage bourgeois-democratic revolution as a necessary stage for socialist revolution also resonated with Korean national-ists' intentions. Although they were self-styled socialists, the early commu-nists "had at best a precarious hold upon Marxist doctrine" (Scalapino and Lee 1972: 3). The later generation communists became more theoretically armed, but still the location of socialism in colonial Korea can be under-stood in the context of the triadic structure: they were attracted to industri-alism and cosmopolitanism, rejecting capitalism and its extreme political form, that is, Fascism that rapidly grew in Japan since the early 1930s.

Nativisms: Asianism and Ethnic Nationalism

In colonial Korea, there were two opposing identities that were nativist. One was Asianism that resonated with colonial ideology. The other was ethnic na-tionalism that originated and grew in the process of ideological confrontation to the colonial ideology. Just as the modernisms in colonial Korea originated from a different path from those in Western colonies, so did the nativisms.

The first position was collaborationist. Those who took this position, iden-tifying themselves with the Asianism of Japanese colonialism and conse-quently against Western encroachment on Asia, followed the racial *jus sangui-nis* of the Asian traditional culture of "same culture, same race." To be more precise, their nativism was fused with modernism. From early on, Japan was recognized by the Korean elite as a successful case of "civilization and en-lightenment," and during the colonial period it was perceived as the leader of an alternative modernity that overcame the West's individualism, material-ism, and capitalism. After all, they were caught by Japanese colonialism's project of modernity based on the cultural and racial identity of Asia.

Nativism in the Western colonies and Asianism in colonial Korea are similar to each other in their emphasis on "authentic" tradition as a means to resist the West. However, as we have seen, while nativism in the Western colonies arose against the colonial culture, thereby constituting a dual narcissism with the colonizer's modernism, the Asianism of Korean intellectuals, rejecting the Western way, internalized or ideologically followed the culture of Japanese colonialism. Although they were a minority in number and their political influence was minimal in the beginning, as the "decline of the West" became visible and the Japanese Empire demonstrated its status as a regional hegemon in East Asia during the interwar period, a large number of liberalists converted in the later period of the "total war" (see Young 1998), following the propaganda of *naisen yuwa, naisen ittai,* and "the Great East Asian Co-prosperity Sphere."

As another position that was in sharp contrast to Asianism, ethnic nationalism in Korea found the Korean nation's identity in the glorious past of mystified ancient Korea and attempted to inculcate the nation's cultural tradition and spirituality. It first appeared in the late nineteenth century, but it began to be exploited and widely circulated right after Korea became the protectorate in 1905. Its ideological contents were deepened during the 1910s and the 1920s by historians such as Sin Ch'aeho, and it became an intellectual movement under the reinforced police surveillance of political activities of Koreans since the early 1930s.

Ethnic nationalism in colonial Korea recalls nativism in the Western colonies in the sense that both entered into the relationship of dual narcissism with colonial culture. In the dyadic structure, the nativism of the colonized originated from an attempt to fight the colonizer's orientalism with occidentalist ideological content. However, in this process, nativism internalizes the colonial binarism of racial and cultural differences. By the same token, in the triadic structure, ethnic discourse in colonial Korea attempted to refute the alleged supremacy of the Japanese nation in Asia and thereby resist assimilation. Confronted with the colonial discourse of the distinctive Japanese spirit and its supremacy, Korean intellectuals tried to refute it by demonstrating the supremacy of the Korean spirit and cultural tradition. However, despite its ideological contestation, it did not exist outside colonial discursive formation; it internalized the form of ethnic imagination of the colonial power (Chae forthcoming).

Yet there are two important differences between them. First, while nativism in Western colonies stood as a conscious antithesis of modernism, ethnic nationalism in colonial Korea did not. It was not an ideological revolt but a defensive engagement with direct rule and assimilationism (Em 1999: 345). For example, when assimilationism began to be reinforced in the mid-1930s, An Chaehong, who greatly contributed to the dissemination of the ethnic discourse, stated, "If men and women of Korea somehow have the means and will to tide over the situation at the front line, they should make a dash without hesitation. Otherwise, devote [yourself] to culture! Since political advancement is difficult now, devote [yourself] to culture!" (An 1935: 3). Second, unlike many nativisms in Western colonies, ethnic nationalism in Korea during the colonial period did not exist as a political movement. While nativism in Western colonies, for example, negritude and Gandhism, fueled mass mobilization in the later period of colonial rule, ethnic nationalism in Korea, even as late as the end of the colonial rule, did not exist as a political movement. As intellectual discourse and cultural movement, its circulation was limited mainly to intellectuals. This difference reflects the triadic structure in the imperial order of the dyadic structure. For example, nativism in Africa began to appear in the 1930s and became a leading ideology from the 1940s, which coincided with the rise of Fascism in Europe and Japan. While Fascism's racist romanticism inspired the native elite in British and French colonies in Africa (Arnold 1981: 51–52; Nesbitt 2003), in the same period colonial Korea witnessed the collapse of the secular liberal nationalist movement and the liberalists' conversion to collaboration or submergence into ethnic discourse, as a passive means to resist the encroachment of the "inner space" by reinforced assimilationism.

In sum, as Table 14.3 shows, the four identities in the triadic structure discussed so far apparently resembled those that appeared in the Western colonies, but because of the cultural involvement of the West, they originated from different paths and took different characteristics in relation to the colonial power: similar mechanisms but different actualizations. The colonial structure in Korea had rather complicated relationships among the collectivities involved. "The West" as a third party existed as a cultural representation and did not have a direct relationship with the dimensions of

TABLE 14.3 · Two Ways the Colonized React
to the Colonizer and Different Ideological Outcomes.

Type of Colonialism	Attraction/Imitation	Repulsion/Rejection
Western	Modernism	Nativism
Japanese	Asianism (Nativism)	Modernism

resource and power. However, insofar as the presence of the West was culturally presupposed by the ways resources and power were distributed, it would be legitimate to see the colonial structure in Korea as triadic.

NOTES

1. Rather than a concrete and objectified thing, "the West" in this chapter refers to an abstract image discursively circulated among social actors. This image, which is abstracted from the original context and thus appears as a reified representation, is produced and reproduced through colonialism's orientalist knowledge and the colonized's reaction to it. On this subject, see Chakrabarty (2000); Sakai (1997).

2. As a good example, Nehru as a national bourgeois utilized Gandhi's nativism for anticolonial mobilization and postcolonial state building (Chatterjee 1986).

3. Chatterjee also remarks that "true modernity for the non-European nations would lie in combining the superior material qualities of Western cultures with the spiritual greatness of the East" (1986: 51).

4. As the term "colonialism" carried positive meaning, "empire" also obtained a certain normativity in the global circulation of political discourses. The Great Japanese Empire was named after Western empires—for example, the Great British Empire—and was then even adopted in Korea as the Great Korean Empire (1897–1910).

5. To avoid possible confusion, I would like to make clear that the notion of "family-state" in this essay is different from Julia Adams's notion of "familial state" (2005a). Whereas the former refers to the Japanese nation-state as a family, the latter refers to the patriarchal structure within the Netherlands state.

6. As for liberal strategies of exclusion in Western colonialism, see Mehta (1997).

7. As for a possible flow of ideas from French to Japanese assimilation, Peattie states that there is scant evidence of this and that the Japanese assimilation ideas were distinctively Asian (Peattie 1984: 96). Duus argues that the shift from French assimilation to association lay in the recognition of fundamental differences between colonizer and colonized, whereas Japan's intensified assimilationism was due to the colonizer's firm belief in commonality (Duus 1995: 413).

8. *Nissen dōsoron*'s nascent form can be traced back to *kokugaku* (Japanology) in the eighteenth century, but it became a powerful view at the moment of colonization of Korea (Hatada 1969: 38). There are some disagreements among Nissen dōsoron scholars, but the core of Nissen dōsoron is an inseparable historical relation between the Japanese and the Koreans and the former's superiority over the latter. For a general account of this view, see Kanazawa ([1929] 1978).

9. Inazo Nitobe, who first translated the term "colony" into Japanese and founded a discipline of colonial policy in Japan, typically showed this dualistic attitude toward the West. On the one hand, he urged that in its colonization of Korea, Japan should follow the rules of the game set by Western powers: international law (Dudden 2005). But on the other hand, recognizing the impetus of the Japanese Empire

in the way of warrior (*bushido*), he opined that the colonial policy Japan should pursue in Korea was not the Western way but assimilation (Nitobe 1911).

10. From the early nineteenth century on, French colonialism adopted "assimilation" as an ideal of native policy. But the native policy based on this ideal was soon confronted with political, economic, and military problems. Although the principle of assimilation had been largely ignored in local colonial administration, its efficacy came to be questioned in France at the end of the nineteenth century. Immediately after World War I, "association" took the place of assimilation as the official policy of French colonialism. Ideological influences behind this change were the more "liberal" colonial administration ideas of British indirect rule and Dutch association and "scientific" social evolutionism that acknowledged the different evolutionary paths of different races (Betts 1961). Although not entirely abandoned since then, assimilation was not seriously implemented (Grimal 1978: 60; also see Smith 1981: 99).

FIFTEEN

Native Policy and Colonial State Formation in Pondicherry (India) and Vietnam

Recasting Ethnic Relations, 1870s–1920s

ANNE RAFFIN

A substantial literature seeks to understand the colonial environment as a space of coercion, struggle, and negotiations among groups. One early contribution in this vein by Ranajit Guha conceived of the colonial state as an instrument of domination yet one that did not have to resort to hegemony in order to exercise rule (Guha 1992). Nicolas Dirks's research on the relation between colonialism and culture shows us that colonialism is a cultural project linked to the complicated interrelations between coercion and hegemony (Dirks 1992b 4–5). Frederick Cooper and Ann Stoler (1997) argue that cultural boundaries were maintained through the use of the categories of race, gender, and class. In her study of French Syria and Lebanon, Elizabeth Thompson (2000: 1) notes how clear boundaries were uncommon as colonizers regularly relied on indigenous intermediaries in order to rule. Bargains were made between the state and its mediating agents, which in turn created the terms of membership in the civic order. Indeed, the author analyzes how colonizers, local elites, and the subaltern population together molded the colonial state.

The current study extends the use of such an approach to the French colonial empire, by investigating the complex relation between the rule of law and domination in the colonial context and its subsequent impact on colonized groups' access to resources and privilege. The particular focus here is on state policies and local dynamics of cultural boundaries in two French colonial settings, namely, Pondicherry (India) from the 1870s to 1905 and the Vietnamese cities of Saigon, Hanoi, and Haiphong from 1914 through the 1920s.

The choice of Pondicherry and Vietnam as units of comparison was guided by the desire to investigate how the agents of colonial states in two overseas territories sought to broker different politico-legal frameworks and ideological currents originating from a common metropole and put them into practice. Studying two colonies of a single colonizer allows us to grasp the influence of the French colonial style of the Third Republic in these overseas territories. At the same time, we may see the different ways colonial states and local populations in India and Pondicherry reacted to the experience of such power. The analytical point is to explain how policies of a single metropole, at different points along its own historical trajectory, resulted in contrasting outcomes in the colonies regarding patterns of intergroup relations and colonial state building.[1]

France in the period of the Third Republic (1870–1940) was distinguished by the dialectic link between the consolidation of the republican regime at home and the conquest of the empire abroad. French officials reconciled this contradiction with the ideal of bringing the *mission civilisatrice* to the indigenous populations in an effort to uplift the "inferior races." As part of its emancipatory discourse, France would integrate the colonies into the "greater France" by propagating the universal principles of republicanism— those of unity, liberty, equality, and fraternity. At the heart of this agenda was the belief that natives could be improved, alongside imperial propaganda that nourished a specific sense of a French identity based on grandeur and racism (Chafer and Sackur 2002: 9).

This orientation resulted in a mixture of overseas policies that were more or less emancipatory, more so in the case of India, less so for Indochina. For India, these policies included universal suffrage for Indian natives in 1871 and decentralized local councils in Pondicherry in 1872; for Vietnam, they consisted of the repatriation of Frenchmen from Vietnam to the motherland for the war effort, as well as Governor-General Albert Sarraut's politics of "Franco-Annamese collaboration" after World War I.

In both settings, the effect of the policies was to redraw political and economic boundaries that demarcated group resources and identity among the colonized populations. This led to very different outcomes in the two cases under study.

In Pondicherry, the enlargement of political institutions to include locals did not ultimately lead to the securing of more democratic political procedures. Indeed, Chanemougan, the leader of the upper castes, was able to mobilize the Hindu electors and to co-opt the local institutions. This evolution resulted in the enhancement of the interests of the Brahmanical order.

Chanemougan became a sort of a "king of French India" from 1880 to 1906 as he was able to preserve and reinforce the caste system by using political institutions that were created by the imperial power (J. Weber 1991).

In Vietnam, by contrast, the repatriation of Frenchmen to serve in World War I provoked changing conditions in labor and housing markets in the colonial cities, which in turn led to calls for greater ethnic integration, all of which combined to heighten interethnic tensions. Actions undertaken by the Vietnamese community to assert their economic emancipation from the Chinese resulted in outright interethnic conflicts. However, such incidents were quickly put down by colonial state authorities, and conditions overall never actually became so serious as to challenge the colonial order; rather the status quo was maintained.

In the case of Vietnam, the colonial state institutionalized different degrees of inequality for Chinese and Vietnamese subjects within a framework based on a "rule of colonial difference" (Chatterjee 1993) in which all colonized people were considered inferior to Europeans. Attempts by the metropole, the colonial state, or native groups to alter this triangular balance between the French, Chinese, and Vietnamese did provoke a spectrum of responses from the affected groups that range from coordinated defense to coordinated attack (Tilly 2004). Meanwhile the colonial state reacted to social boundary changes in the housing market and the economic sphere by passing laws and using coercion to defend the long-range interests of the colonizers. The following section details the origins of French colonialism in the two locales and initial efforts by the state to redraw group boundaries.

NATIVE POLICIES: RESHAPING THE COLONIAL STATE AND REVAMPING "CULTURAL DIFFERENCE"

PONDICHERRY: COLONIAL ORIGINS AND REDRAWING GROUP BOUNDARIES DURING THE 1870S

The origins of French colonialism in India were modest. France staked a claim to Pondicherry in 1673, a fishing village located on the southeast Indian coast, partly as the result of the efforts of an ambitious local official who sought to increase his revenues from customs dues. French commercial involvement there expanded at the beginning of the eighteenth century under the guidance of the East India Company, which created dynamic trading posts in Pondicherry, Chandernagor, Mahé, and Masulipatam. Pondicherry gradually evolved into a prosperous trading post and had acquired some 100,000 inhabitants by the mid-eighteenth century (Haudrère 2003).

Ongoing imperial rivalry with Great Britain caused France to surrender the Indian enclaves to her rival and then regain them several times, the final such loss occurring in 1793. However, it was the French Revolution—or more precisely the execution of King Louis XVI—that finally pushed England to declare full-scale war on France. In 1815, the Treaty of Paris granted France five geographically dispersed *comptoirs* (trading posts) in India, including Pondicherry, Mahé, Yanaon, Karikal, and Chandernagor (Aldrich 1996: 23; Miles 1995: 5; J. Weber 1988: 5).

Although social scientists have studied the history of "French India" during the eighteenth century, the golden age of the colony, little has been written on subsequent French colonial experience in the region (Le Teguilly and Moraze 1995: 162). One interesting aspect of nineteenth-century French colonial history in India and the five French-held communes of Senegal, as well as in Martinique, Guadeloupe, Guyana, and Réunion, is how these overseas territories became a political laboratory where boundaries between colonizers and colonized were redrawn (Deschamps 2003: 110). As long-established colonies, Indian subjects in Pondicherry, Karikal, Mahé, Yanaon, and Chandernagore were initially allowed by the decree of March 28, 1848, issued after the Revolution of February in France, to participate in choosing the deputy of India. For a time these colonies were granted representation in the national legislature (Aldrich 1996: 212).

Such formal recognition did not necessarily mean that all subjects understood the terms of political participation, however. For instance, some peasants from the South Indian district of Karikal were under the misapprehension that the act of voting was simply a device to deport them as laborers to the islands of Mayotte or Réunion (Michalon 1990: 40, fn. 101). A top-down implementation of new forms of political participation does not translate automatically into steps toward democratization. The process also necessitates the existence of a sociopolitical culture that enables people to learn about democratic knowledge and practices. In fact, this climate of partial political emancipation for Indian subjects eventually led to violence between castes and outcastes, and French authorities withdrew the legal privileges with the coming of the Second Empire in 1852.[2]

Following this first unsuccessful attempt, universal suffrage was finally implemented throughout French-held India in 1871 and maintained thereafter. Rather than bringing the Indians closer to the colonizers, this entailed the estrangement of many due to the violation of local customs and habits, as Weber has demonstrated. Indeed, how could an outcaste be the equal of a member of a caste? How could anyone reconcile the dictates of

Brahma with the principles laid down by the French Revolution? (J. Weber 1996: 314).

One problem was the electoral lists. If the 1871 right to vote in national elections asserted equality among locals, racial boundaries were maintained through the constitution of different electoral lists for French and Indian voters. In 1884 a third list appeared for the *renonçants*, the Indians who had renounced their legal status as Hindus or Muslims in order to submit to the French civil law decree of September 21, 1881 (Annasse 1975: 58; Clairon 1926: 95–99). The creation of this three-list electoral system was a measure originating from the colonial supreme court (Conseil supérieur des colonies) in response to the renonçants who demanded the right to be registered on the first list with the Europeans. Despite the fact that the Cour de cassation—the main court of last resort in France—settled the case in favor of the renonçants in 1883, the colonial state still refused to grant them this right (Clairon 1926: 121–124).

Local political participation expanded with the creation of the local council and the colonial council in 1872. The colonial council was replaced in 1879 by a general council elected by universal suffrage in which the colonizers occupied the majority of seats (Clairon 1926: 105). French predominance was also retained within both councils, as members were elected by voters who were 50 percent French and 50 percent Indian (Closets d'Errey 1934; J. Weber 1988: 7). The argument in favor of this voting system went as follows: "There was a concern for the minority, the civilizing element, to favor it [that is, the civilizing element], to defend it also against the invasion of the indigenous element of which the spirit of caste keeps its influence on the habits. They were afraid that the Europeans would have to conform to the Hindu population. . . . They were afraid to annihilate the European influence. They had recognized the duty to safeguard the superiority of the principles of our civilization while respecting the laws of the Indians" (Poulain 1894: 3). For the Europeans, caste was perceived as the key marker of the Indian society, one that was incompatible with a modern definition of society (Dirks 1992a: 56–57).

Indeed, embarking on political assimilation for the natives before ensuring their cultural assimilation was viewed by many colonizers as a threat to the civilizing mission because of the central role of the caste system. In principle, such laws allowed the colonized subjects to participate more fully in the life of the political community at the local and national levels. In practice, however, their ethnicity—based on a distinctive shared culture mostly grounded on the caste system from the colonizers' point of view—required control through electoral means. Culturally, locals were perceived as insufficiently French and therefore inferior, so universal suffrage actually created "subjects with electoral vote" rather than French citizens (Michalon 1990: 40).

This quasi-representative political structure was completed with the transplantation of the French administrative division, the *commune*, to the French Indian establishments in 1880. The councils of these ten new communes (*conseils municipaux*)—four located in Pondicherry—were also elected by universal suffrage while the councils, in turn, nominated the mayor who managed the commune (Closets d'Errey 1934).

Considering the bigger picture, it is evident that local colonial authorities in Pondicherry had no other choice but to support respect for native customs; Pondicherry itself was a Lilliputian colony with a weak colonial state that lacked sufficient coercive means to control the population. As the decree of January 6, 1819, stated: "The Indians either Christians, either Moors [Muslims], or gentiles [Hindus] will be judged, as in the past, according to the laws, practices, and customs of their castes."[3] Earlier attempts to undermine local traditions had led to drastic retaliations from the population. For instance, the colonial authorities officially prohibited the Pongal celebration (feast of the harvest) in February 1714, which resulted in the exodus of Pondicherry's Indians to the British territory. The governor Pierre Dulivier was able to secure the return of the merchants and artisans to the French establishment by promising that no other action would officially be decreed against pagan celebrations, even if they occurred on a Sunday (Weber 1988: 139). Ultimately, the French state swore to "respect the religion" of the local population in all its cession treaties, throughout the empire (Saada 2003: 16).

Despite the imperial state-centered assimilationist policies of the 1870s–1880s, the colonial state in Pondicherry chose to maintain respect for traditions, as a means to maintain peace among different local groups and thereby to preserve its semblance of power over the inhabitants. In addition, the majority of colonial officials did not support political boundary-changing measures between what they perceived as "us," the colonizers, and "them," the colonized. A "proper" distance had to be maintained between both groups.

VIETMAN: COLONIAL ORIGINS AND GROUP BOUNDARIES FROM THE EARLY 1900S TO 1920

As part of the larger entity of Indochina, the Vietnamese cities of Hanoi, Haiphong, and Saigon were more recently acquired French possessions—compared with those in India—and were not under any form of republican rule. Vietnamese were subjects, not citizens, and thus remained under the authority of local rules rather than French law. They were excluded from basic rights, such as the right to vote. The French navy had been instrumental in establishing the colony of Indochina during the nineteenth century, and settlers began to arrive in the 1870s. Over time, the French community there became composed of four groups characteristic of all Western colonizing societies: the armed forces, civil servants, the merchant/business community, and missionaries.

Like their counterparts in India, colonial administrators in Vietnam were also ambivalent about the extent to which natives should be assimilated into French culture. A strain of "French colonial reformism" did appear in Vietnam between 1905 and 1928 that gave rise to a new Franco-Vietnamese policy, which became a key theme of colonial discourse after 1911. Such an approach aimed to replace permanent colonial domination with a less pervasive form of long-term French supervision over its "backward" colonies. The policy also cautiously allowed a greater representation of the new local elites within a still-unequal partnership between colonizers and colonized.

Before the end of the nineteenth century, Cochin China managed to secure a Colonial Council, but this body remained under the control of the colonizers and had limited authority. Under the territory's governor-general Albert Sarraut (1911–1914, 1917–1919), several chambers of representatives were created at the provincial level in Tonkin and Annam. However, such institutions were only consultative and their membership was restricted. Over the long term, this limited inclusion of the Vietnamese elites in the running of political affairs reinforced the political status quo, as these elites became identified with the local conservative forces. Vietnamese nationalists described these examples of Franco-Vietnamese collaboration as "reactionary delegations of natives under the influence of the French," and such local perceptions fed the growth of political radicalism in Vietnam during the 1920s (Brocheux and Hémery 2001: 292–295; Buttinger 1967: 87–100; Duiker 1995: 32–33).

The opening of more opportunities to Vietnamese merchants in Hanoi during World War I created social tensions by feeding intergroup competition over both jobs and housing. Integration within the white quarters was the demand of the new indigenous elite, a demand that was to prove unacceptable to the white population of Hanoi. In the Vietnamese case, colonialism created openings at the economic level for some members of the indigenous elite but overall lacked any measure of political integration comparable to what the principles of the Third Republic had triggered among colonials in French India. Vietnam also differed from the Indian colonies in that cultural prejudices were not formally expressed in religious and legal texts; as far as can be determined, Vietnamese elites never petitioned the colonial state for spatial or other forms of segregation between colonizers and Vietnamese.[4]

The colonial state faced again a similar challenge when a group of Vietnamese contested the triangular economic relations among colonizers, Vietnamese, and Chinese from 1919 to the 1920s. At the beginning of the twentieth century, writers such as Gilbert Chieu advanced the idea of substituting Vietnamese for Chinese dominance in economic positions across industry, banking, and commerce, while Vietnamese newspapers such as *Thoi Bao* and *Cong Luan* began to promote the idea of "economic nationalism." Indeed, before World War I, some Vietnamese businessmen attempted to gain entry to professions traditionally held by the Chinese, in commerce generally and in the rice trade in particular. Nguyen Phu Khai, founder of the newspaper *Tribune indigène*, was an outspoken supporter of the idea of economic emancipation for the Vietnamese. He shared these beliefs with Bui Quang Chieu, who founded Vietnam's Constitutionalist Party, and it was this organization that fostered the anti-Chinese campaigns in Vietnam in 1919 (Brocheux 1972: 454). Despite colonial officials' desire to decrease the economic power of the Chinese community, the colonial state would intervene to maintain peace and indirectly to support the economic status quo.

SOCIETAL RESPONSES TO SOCIAL BOUNDARY CHANGES IN PONDICHERRY
FROM CONFLICT TO STATUS QUO

In Pondicherry, universal suffrage and the creation of local councils served to redistribute power among the various groups in society. These political avenues reinforced the power of high-caste Indians who were then able to take over local institutions created by the Third Republic; this in turn undermined the power of the white community. The high-caste power broker Chanemougam and his supporters opposed any measures of the "civilizing mission" that might seek to alter Hindu identity by imposing a presumed equality among Indians. In Pondicherry, the challenges posed by the Third Republic were settled largely by following existing norms, an approach that preserved the "live and let live" basis of a more generalized respect for intergroup differences. Those of lower-caste status were often co-opted by the upper-caste Chanemougam, who stressed the importance of religious identity over political rights, a view in accordance with the high castes' presentation of themselves as a religious moral authority independent of the colonial state. And in truth, locally embedded identities were not so easily displaced by the new, large-scale, more detached social identities fostered by the Third Republic (Tilly 2003: 5).

EDUCATION AND REPUBLICANISM

Some colonial state agents in Pondicherry observed that because locals lacked a sense of political identity or political consciousness, the dominant religious hierarchy served to keep any demands for change in check. In fact, it was the colonial metropole that initiated such changes, by questioning the nature and content of education in its Indian colony. Indeed, the Third Republic paid particular attention to the issue of education, as primary education had become free, lay, and compulsory in 1882 in the metropole. Further, its supporters believed that educational institutions would be the tool that would culturally and therefore politically assimilate citizens and subjects into the imperial nation (Michalon 1990: 111–112). In Pondicherry, the native educational policy of the late nineteenth century supported the creation of diverse types of schools, from public to private ones, which targeted various populations.

The belief that schools could convey a proper political culture to the natives was underlined by the chief of the Service of Public Education. The Service of Public Education linked the question of access to education to broader issues of universal suffrage, as there was a need "to enlighten the masses in order to inculcate in them the notion of civic rights."[5] Proper training and socialization through education was seen as a means of ensuring that locals would acquire sufficient qualifications for the right to vote. As of March 25, 1893, it was decreed that primary instruction would now be compulsory for male and female children of Europeans, for children of those descended from Europeans, and for children of renonçants—all of which meant that the actual number of children to whom this ruling applied was very limited.[6]

As the educational landscape in Pondicherry began to shift, two local discourses collided among colonial state officials. One of these was a universalizing orientation that sought to "uplift" the natives and teach them the imperial language and its way of thinking, while the other was a more restrictive orientation that allowed only for transmitting basic knowledge to the Indians in their local languages.

Accordingly, the school environments embodied both of these tendencies, a reflection of contradictory propensities in the colonial project itself. For instance, in 1895 some local officials observed that "the fusion of the castes exists . . . in all the schools," whereas others commented that in certain cases "the outcasts and the members of the castes have their own special duster and chalk." According to one M. Rassendren, a member of the general council, since all children of all classes could be admitted to public schools regardless of their "cult, caste, color, and origin," the prejudices of caste in education therefore no longer existed. In making this claim, Rassendren, a local, was consciously rejecting the collective identity defined by Hinduism with its code of laws, the *Manu*, while choosing to embrace the egalitarianism of French republicanism.[7]

While the result of native policy was to begin incorporating Indian locals into the education system, the question remains exactly which Indians were so affected. Speaking of these changes, in 1872 the governor of French India claimed that in Pondicherry, "the experience proves daily that the fusion between pagans and Christians is complete on the ground of education . . . in the little seminary of the [Catholic] Mission where Christians and pagans, among which a large number of Brahmins' sons, are admitted without distinction."[8] In fact, embracing Western educational institutions was a means for the upper strata of the indigenous social hierarchy to maintain its Brahminical dominance. According to Srinivas, it was the high-caste Brahmins who were first to leave the village for the town under English colonial rule, having perceived the opportunities a Western education could offer (Srinivas 1996: 86). Further, only the Brahmins as a caste had the right to education, which in the traditional context meant learning the religious texts. The Brahmin caste as a whole was divided into the priestly caste Brahmins (*Vaidika*), whose path was to master the *Vedas*, or religious texts, and the worldly Brahmins (*Laokika*), who embraced secular professions. In Pondicherry and elsewhere, Indian students who were admitted to Western schools were most likely to have come from the high-caste groups.

From the high-caste perspective, access to colonial educational institutions had mixed consequences. On the one hand, a much greater degree of contact with Europeans in these environments meant that anyone from the upper castes would have to perform stricter rites of purification (J. Weber 1988: 514). However, the polluting influence of European outsiders was relative: mingling with those outsiders who enjoyed political and economical power, from which high-caste Indians could benefit, was more acceptable than mixing with the lower castes. High-caste Indians and colonizers were thus able to coexist in this restricted public sphere, since their association did not fundamentally challenge the societal order of separation based on caste hierarchy. Temporarily suspending the boundary between "us" and "them" thus became part of everyday routine (Tilly 2004: 8).

In contrast to this was the Collège Calvé, founded by Calvé Soupraya-chettiar in 1877 to offer primary education to boys of all religions, including Muslims and Hindus of any caste. (Outcastes were still prohibited, however, in accordance with the wishes of the founder.) In 1885, Souprayachettiar's adult children who were running the school decided to hand it over to the colonial authorities, who proceeded to make it accessible to all children, "without distinction of either origins or caste."[9] The officials who dismantled the caste-based school structure were guided in doing so by the policy-making ideas of the Third Republic—to promote education for all children and hence "enlighten" the locals. However, the beneficiaries of this revamped system very often responded in turn by stressing their caste identity. Even some local Frenchmen justified the continued separation of the castes by making reference to the existence of a "caste spirit."

For instance, in 1898, two girls' schools in the district of Pondicherry whose mission was to educate "the most ignorant part of the population" were closed down because of economic considerations. When pupils from these two institutions tried to enroll in schools nearby that catered to girls of caste origins, these schools went on strike in protest. Admitting low-caste or untouchable pupils would not only have posed a threat to the Hindu hierarchy based on notions of impurity but would also have undermined the social and economic advantages attached to those in a higher position.[10] Dumont has observed that in the traditional order, ritual status had primacy over political and economic considerations. In Pondicherry, however, caste status conferred educational advantages, such as access to better schools, which were themselves as significant as any ritual prestige to be had from holding higher rank in caste hierarchy. Hence some members of the higher castes were willing to fight in order to maintain such privilege.

In addition, local beliefs about caste segregation corresponded to the colonial wish to keep the races divided, as both orientations were grounded in ethnocentric ideology. For example, under the governors of Lalande de Calan (1849–1851) and Durand d'Ubraye (1857–1863), the colonial administration unsuccessfully tried to open the Collège colonial to the Indians. The missionaries who ran the school observed: "Despite our opinions, our surveillance and our severities, the indigenous students that we sent to try this adventure were so insulted and soiled by the Europeans that by themselves they gave up the favor which was accorded to them" (J. Weber 1988: 1239–1240).

The Collège colonial was finally opened to the Indian population only in 1878, and hostilities toward indigenous students went on for many years (J. Weber 1996: 245). An anonymous writer in the newspaper Le progrès complained about one incident in 1893 when a local Indian student was beaten up by a *créole* on school grounds, and the headmaster did not intervene. The Indian student was subsequently expelled from the school, despite the fact that he was the one who had been attacked. The Collège colonial justified this action by claiming, among other things, that the dismissed student was "a deceitful boy." In the aftermath of the expulsion, the two boys recruited their respective mates to hold a street fight. The entire episode showed that indigenous education was still a volatile public issue; for the writer, the lack of intervention by the school authorities, as well as their decision to expel the native student, showed that "we do not want to see Indians to progress in secondary education."[11]

The more equalitarian and assimilationist spirit of the Third Republic challenged a hierarchical system that was already in place, a system that continued to confer advantages on its European and créole populations. In Pondicherry, an official republican universalism was too contested and underfunded to be fully realized.

Local administrators continued to vacillate between embracing the principle of assimilation or of separation in educational matters, and their choice to maintain separation was often an indirect means of evading racial and religious tensions and maintaining the privileges of the colonizers, créoles, and especially those of the high castes, who were often able to impose their views.

A FARCE OF THE REPUBLICAN LAW?

The local Pondicherry newspaper *Le progrès* stood in opposition to the high-caste coalition leader Chanemougam and all that he represented, including traditional institutions such as polygamy and the caste system as a whole. In particular, the paper condemned the practice of appointing upholders of such traditions to the position of mayor, a measure that the colonial state regularly supported in the name of the republican values. Writing a series of articles on marriages in Pondicherry, the editor deplored the fact that even Europeans who wed other Europeans sometimes did so through marriage ceremonies that were conducted according to Hindu customs, rather than French law:

> The mayor . . . from the [high] vellâja caste . . . covered with ashes, dung, and other excrements as aromatic as the first ones and still smelling of the cow's urine of which he sprayed his head and throat, before leaving home, will come to prance at City hall. Covered with his whimsical hat which clashes with his tri-colored sash, he will hold off the fiancés, eaters of beef, that the touching or the breathing will taint and will say to

these noble Children . . . : *In the name of the law*—which does not exist for me and that I despise—*I marry you*—senseless people who are not ashamed to come asking an enemy of the law to sanction your union.[12]

In the eyes of Hindus, non-Hindus were even more impure and lower ranking than outcastes since the latter did not belong to the social order. In addition, the fact that colonizers ate meat did not help, because within the traditional frame of reference only outcastes consumed meat; thus impure contact with Europeans was to be avoided. Accordingly, the Hindu mayor protected himself from contamination by smearing himself with dung coming from a sacred cow.

Another example recounts the August 1886 marriage ceremony of two ex-outcastes, who earlier on had become renonçants, in the commune Oulgaret, Pondicherry. The mayor, member of the *retty* (landowners) caste, delegated the task of marrying them to a member of the municipal council who belonged to a lower caste so that the mayor himself could remain untainted by contact with the impure. The mayor called in a Brahmin before reentering city hall in order to purify the room.[13]

In one last example, the marriage of renonçants who formerly were members of castes was performed by a mayor belonging to the *Vannia* (farmers) caste, who did not speak French. He conducted the rites in Tamil, while his secretary translated line by line into French. After relating this story, the newspaper added: "We are asking ourselves if it isn't a mockery . . . to oblige the Renonçants, who speak French, to hear their marriage ceremony in Tamil language and in such a pitiful manner."[14] We can deduce from this that the writer believed that cultural assimilation should precede political integration into the French imperial nation. Journalists of *Le progrès* apprehended the significance of caste only through its ritual purity, in opposition to the republican values of equality and rationality it supposedly represented. Indeed, ritual primacy and economic and political privileges together acted to maintain the position of the high castes.

SOCIETAL RESPONSES TO SOCIAL BOUNDARY CHANGES IN VIETNAM
MAINTAINING SEGREGATION AND THE CHALLENGE OF WORLD WAR I

The dual nature of Hanoi was contested during World War I, when some Vietnamese sought to translate their economic success into social status by resettling in European neighborhoods. They attempted to redraw the boundaries between "French" and "not French" and consequently the advantages attached to belonging to such groups. These Vietnamese actors were in effect demanding a new right, that is, the freedom to choose their own neighborhood. All of this was made possible by the changing economic fortunes of Hanoi's communities brought about by World War I, which greatly enhanced the economic standing of both Vietnamese and Chinese relative to the French. Ensuing was a new indigenous elite that contested the spatial segregation by buying up properties in areas formerly designated as European space. As Vann rightfully underlines, white privilege translated into access to better material goods, particularly in housing: "Colonial urbanization was the inscription of racial differences onto the city" (1999: 175) imposed by the colonial order. However, in the case of Hanoi, wealth was not only in colonial hands but also in those of the Chinese merchant class, which dominated Hanoi's economy. The flourishing Chetty community of traders and usurers also had a share.

What changed the economic balance of power was the French government's repatriation of its citizens overseas for the war effort. Such a situation allowed Chinese merchants and Vietnamese entrepreneurs to take over the economic positions these Frenchmen left behind.

Later when the French returned, many Vietnamese merchants were unwilling to accept the lower-status economic positions they had held prior to the war. Some of them had already bought buildings in the designated white part of the city. The colonial administration responded to what they perceived as such threats by passing laws that tagged some streets as "European only" in architectural style of the houses built there (Vann 1999: 175–182). Indirectly bargaining with the colonial state, this new Vietnamese elite was asserting its power and displaying what Wallman calls an "identity investment" based on its members' economic and political interests (Wallman quoted in Rex 1986: 95). Although one reason for segregation—the inability of the elite to afford housing costs in white neighborhoods—had been removed, it was replaced by another justification, namely, white prejudice, through demands for state intervention in order to maintain racial boundaries (Massey 2002: 351). It should be noted that only the well-to-do Vietnamese were the ones advancing claims for residential access; the Chinese or Indian communities made no comparable demands.

ECONOMIC NATIONALISM

As Donald Horowitz (1985: ch. 4) has observed, a common undertaking of colonial powers was to promulgate the idea of "backward" and "advanced" groups in colonial society. In Vietnam, colonial perceptions or racial hierarchies led some Frenchmen to view Chinese as more necessary and "better" than the indigenous people, as Chinese were perceived as "a counterbalance to the indolence of the Annamites [Vietnamese]" (Ennis 1936: 125). In general, the French needed Chinese commercial expertise, as the latter were more informed about the local conditions than the colonizers (Cheung 2002: 41).

In continuity with the precolonial period was the organization of the Chinese following their places of birth into five dialect entities known as *bangs*, or congregations, each of them accountable to the colonial state for its members' conduct and for payment of taxes, which reinforced the spatial and administrative separation between the locals and the Chinese (Chang 1982: 6–8).

From the beginning of the twentieth century onward, colonial state efforts to dominate the Chinese population were directed basically at dividing Chinese and Vietnamese. This separation and hostility between both communities meant for the French that neither group could be a real political challenge for the colonial power (Cheung 2002: 39). The divide-and-rule strategy did, however, arouse a desire among the Vietnamese for a bigger economic piece of the pie. The idea to substitute Chinese with Vietnamese in economic positions in industries, banking, and commerce emerged at the beginning of the twentieth century and would express itself through Gilbert Chieu's writings, whereas Vietnamese newspapers such as *Thoi Bao* and *Cong Luan* were already promoting "economic nationalism." Nguyen Phu Khai, founder of the newspaper *Tribune indigène*, strongly supported economic emancipation of the Vietnamese (Brocheux 1972: 454). Khai argued that Vietnamese were economically dominated by the Chinese while politically controlled by the French. In order for the country to make progress, it required first economic modernization, in which Vietnamese would play an important role. In fact, as a way of removing the Chinese, the Vietnamese needed to secure the Chinese business spirit, duplicate their frugal spending habits, and enhance their sense of social solidarity (Brocheux 1995: 103).

A public campaign started on August 1, 1919, in Saigon, when regular customers, mostly Vietnamese civil servants, decided to boycott two Chinese-owned cafes over the increased price of coffee. On August 9, Jean Morène in the newspaper *L'opinion*, chronicled the event and called for a general boycott.[15] This article led the local press to discuss the economic position of the Chinese in Vietnam, and the consensus was that "all of them approve the principle [boycott] as a good one if it is used with caution."[16]

Tensions were exacerbated by numerous rumors, including reports that Vietnamese workers had been unfairly dismissed from Chinese rice-processing factories (August 22, 1919); mention of one Chinese correspondent named

Ly-Thien, who had supposedly written an offensive letter in which he referred to Vietnamese as "small savages" and "idiot" (August 29, 1919); a warning that the Chinese from Cholon would be exterminated (September 15, 1919); and the announcement that Chinese were putting crushed glass in rice and cakes.[17] In addition, the native press added fuel to the fire by printing lists of Vietnamese who continued to patronize Chinese establishments and requested local seamen to police such places. This led the colonial state to censor local newspapers.[18]

In Saigon, a number of violent incidents ensued between the Chinese and Vietnamese communities and between the police and the Vietnamese. The movement spread from Saigon to other cities such as Hanoi and Haiphong. In Hanoi, the movement was fomented by students from Southern Vietnam who were returning to the university in September. Peaceful nighttime demonstrations of five hundred to a thousand people began on September 13, 1919, in the commercial area as a means to prevent Vietnamese from patronizing Chinese businesses. The demonstrations became more tense on September 27, when the mostly student crowd booed the police, while some of them were reported to have actually rebelled. Meanwhile, a group of local military medics "aggressively restrained the Vietnamese agents of the police." The colonial state responded by confining students at home, expelling others, dismissing the director of the school the Collège du protectorat, and ordering local troops to stay in their barracks.[19]

In Haiphong the Chinese communities held meetings to protest against Vietnamese obstructions to their businesses. Tense relations continued up to 1927, when violent clashes between the two communities resulted in the death of twelve persons, eleven Chinese and one Vietnamese; one hundred injuries; and widespread destruction of property. Reports of French police attributed these incidents to the fact that the Chinese had taken "pride of place." Not only did they control important sectors of the economy, Chinese workers were also paid higher than the Vietnamese due to what the French perceived as their greater resistance and drive.[20]

The legal status of the Chinese within the French Empire was one factor that created discord. The Vietnamese newspaper *Cong Luan* underlined how Chinese were guests, not subjects, who "received hospitality in our country due to their business" and who could be easily expelled from Vietnam. Chinese living in Indochina were legally defined as "foreign Asian." Hence in symbolic terms they did not actually belong to the imperial nation and were able to remain in the country only in economic partnership with the colonial state in Vietnam, which chose to tolerate them.[21] However, the

Chinese could remain relatively confident of their position since the colonial state needed their economic skills for the colony to function properly and they knew that the French perceived them as more advanced compared with the Vietnamese, whom the French regarded as a backward people.

In the end, the boycott movement died away in the mid-1920s as it was unable to undermine Chinese businesses in any significant way. Rather, it served only to bring a smaller number of Vietnamese into a limited range of new commercial activities (R. B. Smith 1969: 132–136). The French authorities, in turn, took a "hands-off" approach to these actions. As long as the boycott did not lead to outright racial demonstrations, the colonial state hesitated to restrain Vietnamese in their fight against Chinese economic power, since the former were now perceived as partners in the construction of a "Franco-Annamese collaboration," as part of Governor-General Albert Sarraut's political plan for Indochina after the war. State authorities did seek to reduce the economic power of the Chinese within the colony by promoting the economic development of the Vietnamese community but only within legal means.

Ethnically segregated economic activities triggered within this local elite not only a sense of economic inadequacy but perhaps also a sense of political deficiency. The French had promoted better working conditions for the Chinese since the former needed the latter's commercial expertise (Leveau 2003: 121). While from the beginning of colonization some Vietnamese people opposed French rule, others were ready to collaborate with the colonial authorities if they could benefit from such enterprise. Indeed, the promotion of a Vietnamese economic elite and its craving to establish itself within the white elite quarter underscored such collaboration. Scholars of social conflict note that economic inequality among ethnic groups is one of the key causes of intergroup tension.[22] In the present case study, the state's policies at the core—France—and in the periphery—Indochina—boosted the economic rise of Vietnamese merchants and led to heightened animosity between Chinese and Vietnamese and between the Vietnamese elite and the colonizers.

CONCLUSION

We turn now to a synthesis of insights gained by examining both the impact of policies formulated in the metropole and the reactions of the colonial state and the local population in French colonial Vietnam and India, as they gave rise to different social outcomes in the colonies. A comparison of these two cases reveals how state intervention shaped the possibility of ethnic conflict in French colonies.

What were the particular dynamics at work that led to these outcomes? The dual nature of the French state—at the metropolitan and colonial levels—was at the source of the tension. Authorities formulated policies in the metropole for France and parts of the French colonial empire without taking into account the concerns that others in the colonies of Vietnam and Pondicherry perceived as immediate and pressing. The effect of these policies was to redraw boundaries among groups that were in the process of trying to either maintain or increase their privileges.

On top of this, bureaucrats of the colonial state were also pursuing their own local agendas regarding the management of their respective colonies, which further nourished tensions among the various ethnic-racial groups. More precisely, state agencies in the colonies had to respond to changes initiated by the state in the metropole. These included political reforms in Pondicherry and a wartime demand for soldiers in Vietnam. Initiatives for change came from the local population as well, such as attempts by high-caste Indians to preserve their social privileges in India and demands by the Vietnamese for access to white neighborhoods and entry into economic niches dominated by the Chinese.

In Pondicherry, the colonial state responded to the challenges posed by largely following existing norms that sanctioned existing intergroup differences. Yet policies made in the metropole also served to redistribute power among the various groups in society. They did so by reinforcing the power of high-caste Indians who were then able to take over the new local institutions, which in turn undermined the power of the European community. Lower castes generally supported the upper-caste leader Chanemougam, who underlined the importance of religious identity over political rights. Ironically, the move toward partial democratization, which entailed giving more weight to the notion of the "will of all the people" in policy measures regardless of caste, ended up reinforcing stratification according to Hindu religious distinctions and racial differentiation. Occasional countermoves by a weakly repressive colonial state failed to prevent such developments and allowed the local authorities to maintain a hierarchical but peaceful status quo until 1905, when events in French-held India led to the resumption of the so-called caste wars.

Because cultural integration was commonly a condition of political participation throughout the French Empire, political rights were denied to colonized people on the ground of cultural difference. Pondicherry was the one exception to the rule; here, Indians from all religious orientations were granted the right to vote in parliamentary elections.

However, formal political inclusion was not a viable means of making full-fledged citizens out of Indian subjects. The governor of India in the 1880s stressed the impossibility of turning locals into Frenchmen unless the colony decided to teach the French language to all indigenous children, a measure he referred to as "one of the primordial elements of assimilation."[23] In the same vein, Weber observed that assimilation by exporting French institutions rather than transplanting French culture was doomed to failure (J. Weber 1991: 301). In essence, then, despite moves toward electoral democratization, the colonial "rule of difference" was simply reestablished at other sites and through different means. Even more than cultural integration, what would have been required was a set of institutionalized democratic practices among the elites, who would perceive such state institutions as more than just the machinery to protect their personal interests.

In Vietnam, the colonial state managed to oversee a fragile ethnic balance prior to World War I but did a poor job of circumventing ethnic friction both during and immediately after the war. In the case at hand, we see how the core state intervention recalling French citizens from Hanoi created a gap in the triangular relations between the French, Chinese, and Vietnamese and produced tensions between these groups over issues of jobs and housing. This intervention disrupted the complementarities that had previously existed among different racial groups. The exit of the French and the colonial state's support of a new Vietnamese merchant class in Hanoi during World War I led to a redistribution of economic roles and increasing intergroup tension. In particular, contestations occurred between the remaining white community and some of the better-off Vietnamese over access to housing in elite neighborhoods. In 1919, tensions erupted between Chinese and Vietnamese who were competing with one another over control of the local economy in cities such as Hanoi, Saigon, and Haiphong. Both the Chinese and the Vietnamese communities counted on the colonial state to protect their interests. At first, colonial state authorities lent their support to the Vietnamese, whose economic ambitions were part of what was termed the "Franco-Annamese collaboration." Later, however, they opted for more restrained measures when law and order were challenged. Such a change of course led administrators to indirectly support the existing economic status quo.

Unlike the high-caste Indians in Pondicherry, the new Vietnamese elite lacked access to local institutions that could have allowed them to assert their claims to inhabit white neighborhoods. With greater incomes but still excluded from the city machine, the Vietnamese used the only resource available—the community—to assert their new power, by attempting to build houses in a European section of town. However, this channel for change was obstructed when authorities invoked laws requiring that houses in the area had to conform to a European architectural style. Any group making a claim on the colonial state had to work through the existing configuration and conform to the state's rule of difference, and this set powerful limits on the scope and nature of change.

The contrasting legal and cultural situations in these two colonial entities better allows us to reflect on the relation between metropolitan laws, the colonial state, and local subjects. Reconstructing the past is a means of assessing the viability of approaches to managing problems in the present. If long-term social trends persist, their causes are likely to remain (Tilly 2001). In light of recent events in Iraq, we would benefit by looking at the colonial past elsewhere in the world to explore the dilemmas that foreign countries face when they seek to exert control over disparate communities in a precarious political context. And, as the cases here demonstrate, we must also take note of how group identities and allegiances under such conditions are often not easily dismissed.

NOTES

1. On the dramatically differing policies pursued by the German colonizers in their various colonies, and even vis-à-vis different ethnic groups within a single colony, see Steinmetz (2007a).

2. For instance, in July 1848, pariah villages were burnt after the outcastes dared to wear slippers, a privilege of the castes. To maintain peace, the colonial authorities declared that the outcastes wearing slippers would be fined. See J. Weber (1996: 100–102).

3. Bulletin officiel des établissements Français de l'Inde, 1877, p. 539, Record Centre of Pondicherry, Jeewanandapuram, Lawspet, Pondicherry, India [hereafter RCP]. All translations from French to English are mine, unless otherwise noted. Weber (1988: 482, fn. a).

4. However, many ordinary Vietnamese harbored personal attitudes of racial prejudice toward the colonizers, and there was popular resentment toward any example of interracial partnering involving the French and Vietnamese. For instance, Kim Lefèvre (1992) argues that a local woman who shared a life with a Frenchman became dishonored in the eyes of her compatriots, a status that would later prevent her from marrying a Vietnamese man or regaining her honor.

5. Conseil général de l'Inde Française, 1872, p. 329, RCP.

6. Conseil général de l'Inde Française, 1895, p. 100, RCP.

7. Ibid., 156–161. In fact, the *renonçant* Rassendren, a rich Vellaja, supported the Christian Ponnountamby, who fought against the caste system and wanted to replace the *Manu* with the French civil law. By 1890, in order to escape sentencing, Rassendren made an alliance with Chanemougam, who opposed any assimilation to the French culture. See J. Weber (1988: 227–228, 235, 250–253).

8. Conseil colonial, 1872, p. 211, RCP.

9. Conseil général de l'Inde Française, 1885, pp. 204–206, RCP; Conseil local de Pondichéry, 1874, pp. 193–201, RCP.

10. Conseil général de l'Inde Française, 1898, pp. 117–118, RCP.

11. "L'incident du collège" and "L'indigène et l'instruction publique," both in *Le progrès*, May 21, 1893, pp. 150–152.

12. *Le progrès*, July 11, 1886, pp. 890–891.

13. "Pondichéry, le 1er août 1886," *Le progrès*, August 1, 1886, p. 902.

14. "Pondichéry, le 7 novembre 1886," *Le progrès*, November 7, 1886, p. 959.

15. "Boycotteurs, Boycottés," *L'opinion*, August 9, 1919.

16. "Le boycottage," *France-Indochine*, September 24, 1919.

17. Indo, GGI, Série F, box 39827, file 6, Centre des archives d'outre mer, Aix-en-Provence, France (hereafter CAOM); Ly-Thien, "Aux petits Annamites sauvages," *Courrier Saigonnais*, August 29, 1919.

18. Indo, GGI, Série F, box 39827, file 6, CAOM; *Courrier Saigonnais*, September 4, 1919.

19. Report from Marty, Hanoi, November 14, 1919, in Indo, GGI, Série F, box 39827, file 6, CAOM.

20. Indo, GGI, box 64190, file "Tensions entre Vietnamiens et Chinois, 1919," CAOM.

21. "Encore les Chinois," *Cong Luan*, August 5, 1919.

22. For a general summary of the causes of ethnic conflicts, see Jesudason (2001).

23. Conseil général de l'Inde Française, 1884–1885, pp. 5–6, RCP.

SIXTEEN

The Constitution of State/Space and the Limits of "Autonomy" in South Africa and Palestine/Israel

ANDY CLARNO

INTRODUCTION

In both academic literature and popular discourse, the early years of the twenty-first century have witnessed a proliferation of comparisons between Israel and South Africa. Terms such as "Israeli apartheid" and the "Bantu-stanization of the West Bank" have become commonplace. While deeply insightful and politically productive, many of these analyses overlook the fact that contemporary Israel exists in a fundamentally different "world-historical time" than apartheid-era South Africa (Braudel 1980; Mann 1986). In fact, Israel launched the "peace process" that has solidified its reputation as an "apartheid state" at the same time that the system of formal apartheid in South African was being dismantled.

The end of South African apartheid and the beginning of the Middle East "peace process" coincided with and contributed to a fundamental transformation in global power relations during the early 1990s. Ushered in by the fall of the Berlin Wall, the collapse of the Soviet Union, the 1991 Gulf War, and the hegemony of the Washington Consensus, there emerged a "New World Order" marked by corporate globalization, neoliberal economics, and U.S. military domination. To understand this transition, researchers increasingly employ the language of "empire" (Hardt and Negri 2000) and "American empire" (Mann 2003; Steinmetz 2003b, 2005d). The shift in world-historical time constituted by this imperial transition is fundamental for understanding the differences between contemporary Israel and apartheid-era South Africa.

This chapter presents a comparative historical analysis of similar state spatial strategies employed before and after the imperial transition. At different world-historical times, the Israeli and South African states have produced "autonomous" spaces inside the territory over which they exercised sovereignty. In these spaces—"Bantustans" in the language of apartheid, "Area A" in the language of the Oslo Accords—Palestinians and black South Africans could exercise limited "autonomy," "self-government," and perhaps even nominal "independence." The first part of this chapter demonstrates the similarities in these strategies and argues that the production of "spaces of exception" is fundamental to the constitution of sovereignty in colonial-settler states. The second half of the chapter considers the imperial transition as an intervening mechanism in the production of state/space. This transition helps explain four fundamental differences between the Bantustan strategy in South Africa and the enclosure strategy in Palestine/Israel. By analyzing state strategies to produce spaces of exception before and after the imperial transition, I hope to contribute to the analysis of sovereignty in the empire of the early twenty-first century.

THE CONSTITUTION OF STATE/SPACE

Sovereignty implies "space," and what is more it implies a space against which violence, whether latent or overt, is directed—a space established and constituted by violence. —HENRI LEFEBVRE ([1974] 1991: 280)

Henri Lefebvre insists that states do not simply monopolize violence within a given space. On the contrary, sovereignty is constituted and reproduced through the use of violence to produce space. Indeed, Lefebvre notes that "state power endures only by virtue of violence directed towards a space" ([1974] 1991: 280) and refers to space as the "privileged instrument" (2003: 85) of the state in its effort to regulate social relations and reproduce its own authority.

Neil Brenner has recently incorporated this insight into his analysis of the shifting terrain of "state space" (2004; Brenner et al. 2003). Building on the work of Bob Jessop (1990), Brenner draws an analytical distinction between *state spatial projects* that affect the territorial configuration of state institutions (i.e., borders, administrative divisions, and so forth) and *state spatial strategies* for regulating the economy and governing the population (Brenner 2004: 89–94). The analytical distinction, however, does not always correspond to a distinction in practice. As the cases under consideration in this chapter demonstrate, projects to reshape the geography of sovereignty can be strategies of power in and of themselves. I will therefore use the term "state spatial strategies" for efforts to reconfigure space and thereby facilitate the exercise of sovereignty. As Lefebvre notes, such strategies produce not only the space but also the state itself. In other words, they contribute to the constitution of state/space.

A comparative historical analysis of state spatial strategies in South Africa and Palestine/Israel provides evidence for Lefebvre's argument that the use of violence to produce space is integral to state formation and the exercise of sovereignty. Despite different chronologies, South Africa and Israel both emerged from colonial-settler state projects supported by the British Empire. A prominent feature of these projects was the use of violence to displace Africans and Palestinians in order to produce spaces of settler sovereignty. In both cases, the states/spaces were constituted through wars. The Union of South Africa was consolidated through decades of frontier wars and a war between British and Afrikaner colonies. The State of Israel emerged out of war in 1948 and conquered additional territories through war in 1967. These wars produced not only the state itself but also the space of sovereignty—its hierarchies, its fragmentations, and its boundaries.

Rather than focusing on the initial moment of state formation, however, this chapter compares two later efforts to produce state/space. Recognizing that state formation is an ongoing process (Jessop 1990), I explore state spatial strategies employed by contemporary Israel and apartheid-era South Africa. For these states, Palestinians and black South Africans—excluded from citizenship but present and rebellious—constitute "demographic threats" to settler sovereignty. To avert this threat, South Africa and Israel have attempted to produce "autonomous" spaces inside the territories over which they exercise sovereignty.

Through forced removals, home demolitions, land confiscations, the erection of walls, the digging of trenches, and other military operations, South Africa and Israel have concentrated the colonized populations within strictly delimited spaces. In these spaces, black South Africans and Palestinians have been granted "autonomy" or even nominal "independence." But this "autonomy" is severely constrained. In fact, these "autonomous" zones are the materialization of state spatial strategies to enable the continuation of settler sovereignty.

ISRAEL AND SOUTH AFRICA

For nearly forty years, comparative historical researchers have juxtaposed Israel and South Africa. Grounded in the comparative analysis of settler societies, these analyses have focused on ethnic conflict, religion, identity, state formation, and national liberation (Akenson 1992; Greenberg 1980; Greenstein 1995; Jabbour 1970; Younis 2000).

In addition, numerous studies have employed an analogy with South African apartheid to examine political developments in Palestine/Israel. Although some of these comparisons predate the onset of the Oslo process (Benvenisti 1984; Davis 1989), they have gained popularity since the early 1990s, when Israel introduced a new system of control based on permits, checkpoints, closures, and limited self-government for the Palestinian population. While human rights organizations (LAW n.d.) denounced the "Bantustanization" of the West Bank, Edward Said drew attention to the racism and segregation that were entrenching an "Israeli apartheid system" (1996, 2001, 2004). Recent books by Marwan Bishara (2002), Uri Davis (2003), Leila Farsakh (2005), Virginia Tilly (2005), Ali Abunimah (2006), and Joel Kovel (2007) all draw comparisons between contemporary Israel and apartheid-era South Africa. Even Jimmy Carter (2006) is now describing Israeli policies as a "system of apartheid."

Most of these studies point to political similarities between the Palestinian "autonomous areas" in the West Bank and Gaza Strip and the Bantustans in apartheid-era South Africa. They highlight the fragmentation of the West Bank into islands of Palestinian territory, separated from one another and surrounded by Israeli checkpoints, settlements, and bypass roads. They argue that a Palestinian state composed of these isolated enclosures would be both illegitimate (receiving its mandate from the State of Israel rather than the Palestinian electorate) and unviable (remaining politically and economically dependent on Israel). They point to the system of identity documents and permits that the state uses to classify, track, and control the movement of Palestinians. And they reveal the existence of a dual legal system in the occupied territories, with Israeli settlers subject to Israeli civil law and Palestinian residents subject to Israeli military orders.

In groundbreaking work on the system of Palestinian labor migration, Leila Farsakh (2002, 2005) has moved beyond the purely political to analyze "Bantustanization" as a form of economic regulation. In addition to territorial fragmentation, she argues, the Oslo process turned the West Bank and Gaza Strip into "labor reserves" for the Israeli economy. The *Protocol on Economic Relations* that grounded the Oslo process implicitly "recognizes the right of Israel to limit labour flows and to define the conditions under which workers are entitled to enter the Israeli areas" (Farsakh 2005: 160). These protocols helped to legitimize the system of permits and closures deployed by the state to control the movement of Palestinian workers. As a result,

Palestinian workers remain dependent on the Israeli labor market, but their access to that market has become increasingly constrained.

Unfortunately, Farsakh does not account for the neoliberal restructuring that accompanied the Oslo process and contributed to the expulsion of Palestinian workers from the Israeli economy. Neoliberal restructuring is significant not only because of its consequences for Palestinian workers but also for its global impact. Throughout the world, neoliberal restructuring has marked a transition in imperial power relations. In South Africa, this transition contributed to the collapse of the Bantustans and the end of formal apartheid (Bond 2000). But the race and class inequalities that characterized apartheid have grown deeper as a result (Marais 2001). In Palestine/Israel, neoliberal restructuring helped constitute Israel's new strategy of indirect rule through separation and enclosure.[1] Yet none of the existing comparisons consider this transition when analyzing the state spatial strategies deployed by Israel and South Africa.[2]

I will return to this point shortly in order to compare the deployment of similar state spatial strategies before and after the imperial transition. In doing so, I will argue that the transition helps account for four important differences between the South African Bantustans and the Israeli enclosures. Before doing so, however, I will discuss the Bantustans and the enclosures in their respective world historical contexts. My analysis focuses on three dimensions of these state spatial strategies: citizenship, governmentality, and labor regulation. This comparative historical approach demonstrates that the production of "spaces of exception" is constitutive of state/space in colonial-settler states.

BANTUSTANS

Prior to 1948, dozens of "native reserves" scattered throughout South Africa provided a territorial basis for the migrant labor system that supplied African workers to the gold and diamond mines while deterring African urbanization and depressing African wages (Lester 1998; Marks and Rathbone 1982; Wolpe 1972). They also enabled the creation of separate state institutions for European "citizens" and African "subjects." The state governed Africans indirectly through chiefly authorities administering customary law in the reserves (Mamdani 1996).

The Bantustan strategy emerged in the 1950s in response to mounting resistance, international pressure, and the rapid urbanization of black South Africans as a result of the mechanization of agriculture, growing industrial demands for semiskilled labor, and overcrowding in the reserves (Evans 1997). Threatened with a breakdown in the migrant labor system and a "de-tribalized" urban African population that was not subject to the chiefly authorities in the reserves, the government introduced a series of reforms that crystallized into the Bantustan state spatial strategy (No Sizwe 1979). The Bantustan strategy provided a mechanism through which the state attempted to define the boundaries of citizenship, govern the African population, and regulate African labor.

Unlike the reserves, the ten Bantustans were ethnically defined "national homelands." The state created legally defined ethnic categories and assigned all Africans an ethnic identity and citizenship in a corresponding Bantustan (Lester 1998). It also promoted "self-government" and eventual "independence" for the Bantustans. In doing so, the state redefined the population of South Africa as a constellation of national groups and insisted that the policy of "separate development" would allow each nation to develop independently in its own national homeland.

While Europeans had citizenship rights in South Africa, Africans could exercise political rights only in their designated Bantustan (Mamdani 1996). The legal system thus not only distinguished between white "citizens" and African "subjects"; it further divided the African population into distinct "ethnic" groups subject to different Bantustan governments. By producing separate and fragmented African "nations," the Bantustan strategy stripped Africans of their South African citizenship, reinforced indirect rule with nominal sovereignty, challenged racial solidarity with ethnic division, and enabled the claim that whites constituted the single largest "nation" in the country (No Sizwe 1979). In doing so, it sought to ensure the continuation of exclusive settler sovereignty throughout the territory of South Africa.

The tribal councils of the reserves were replaced by governmental structures that symbolized modernity and independence: ministries, legislative assemblies, elections, militaries, postage stamps, and so forth. The devolution of authority augmented the administrative and repressive powers of the Bantustan bureaucracies, which were granted jurisdiction over education, public works, agriculture, welfare, taxation, and local policing. But the South African government retained control over defense, national security, borders, communications, transportation, foreign affairs, currency, and international trade (Butler, Rotberg, and Adams 1977). The state also retained financial control over the Bantustan governments, reserved the right to veto Bantustan legislation, and developed a highly centralized

Department of Native Affairs with increasingly unlimited administrative powers over African life (Beinart 2001; Butler, Rotberg, and Adams 1977; Evans 1997; Hill 1964).

The Bantustan strategy and other apartheid policies were structurally coupled with a centrally managed, racial Fordist economy characterized by rapid industrialization, state support for domestic production, a split labor market, and a welfare system for white workers (Saul and Gelb 1986). The rise of manufacturing generated demands for a permanently urbanized, semiskilled African working class. The state sought to manage the growth of this class through pass-law exemptions and the construction of segregated "townships" on the urban periphery (Hindson 1987). But overcrowding in the Bantustans, the mechanization of agriculture, and growing demands for industrial labor contributed to the rapid urbanization of Africans. This threatened to undermine the Bantustans as rural supports for the migrant labor system that fed the mines.

To combat these trends, the apartheid government created an administrative bureaucracy—the Labor Bureau—to regulate labor from the Bantustans (Evans 1997). Charged with issuing passes to African workers and allocating labor on the basis of regional demand, the Labor Bureau established 797 offices and deployed thousands of agents in the Bantustans and the townships (Greenberg 1980: 97). But a major loophole in the pass laws allowed Africans seventy-two hours to find work and register their contracts with the Labor Bureau upon reaching an urban area (Evans 1997; Lester 1998). As Ivan Evans notes, "the only way to detect Africans without the seventy-two-hour exemption was to demand the document from every African" (1997: 115). This revealed the inefficiency of the pass laws as tools for regulating migrant labor and undermined the work of the Labor Bureau.

As a result, the Bantustans increasingly became a "dumping ground" for the South African government in its attempts to prevent unwanted urbanization. After 1960, the government stopped building African townships on the outskirts of white cities and instead built new townships inside the Bantustans. It also tried to "decentralize" industry to the Bantustans and to promote agricultural production through "betterment" schemes and forced villagization (Hindson 1987). Most important, however, was the policy of forced removals. From 1960 to 1983, at least 3.5 million Africans were forcibly removed to the Bantustans from urban areas, white farms, informal settlements, "black spots," and lands excised from the Bantustans (Platzky and Walker 1985). Hundreds of thousands were also "deported" to the Bantustans each year for violating pass laws and residency restrictions.

The Bantustan state spatial strategy thus sought to reinforce settler sovereignty in South Africa by revoking the citizenship of Africans and declaring them citizens of invented "national homelands." It bolstered the mechanisms of indirect rule through nominal independence and the creation of modern bureaucracies in the Bantustans. And it attempted to stabilize an urban African industrial working class while buttressing the migrant labor system that provided unskilled African workers to the mines. Over time, however, the dominant aspect of the Bantustan strategy became the use of forced removals to combat unregulated African urbanization.

ENCLOSURES

After occupying the West Bank and Gaza Strip in 1967, Israel imposed its sovereignty over these territories and governed them through direct military rule. Despite various proposals for indirect rule and the creation of a Civil Administration for the occupied territories in 1981, the Israeli military continued to directly govern the Palestinian population until the early 1990s. The occupied territories were incorporated into Israel's centrally managed, racial Fordist economy as captive markets and labor reserves. By the late 1980s, nearly 40 percent of Palestinian workers depended on jobs in Israel—primarily unskilled work in the agricultural and construction sectors (Farsakh 2005: 209–210).

During the 1980s, Israeli elites confronted a popular uprising and an economic crisis. High rates of inflation and stagnation, an Arab boycott that restricted foreign investment, and the crisis of global Fordism shook the foundations of Israel's state-centered economy (Shafir and Peled 2000a). As Israel began neoliberal restructuring to confront this crisis, a popular uprising, or intifada, erupted throughout the occupied territories. The conjuncture of these crises led sections of the emerging Israeli business elite to insist that political and economic liberalization would have to go hand in hand. Seeing neoliberalism as the solution to the economic crisis, they argued that Israel could never fully integrate into the global economy as long as conflict with the Palestinians continued (Beinin 2006; Peled 2006; Shafir and Peled 2000b).[3] By the early 1990s, Israel had adopted market-based economic reforms and initiated peace negotiations with the Palestine Liberation Organization. From the outset, therefore, the Oslo "peace process" was coupled with neoliberal restructuring.

These shifts eventually crystallized into a new state spatial strategy for indirect rule through separation and enclosure (Hammami and Tamari

2006; Weizman 2007). In 1991, Israel began requiring Palestinians to obtain military permits to enter Israel or East Jerusalem for any reason. Through the Oslo negotiations, Israel agreed to the establishment of the Palestinian Authority (PA) as a limited self-governing body for Palestinians in parts of the West Bank and Gaza Strip. Israel then fragmented the occupied territories into isolated enclaves by withdrawing its troops from Palestinian population centers and encircling them with military checkpoints, settlements, and bypass roads. The PA was charged with the task of suppressing resistance inside the enclaves (Rabbani 2006). Since the outbreak of the second intifada in 2000, Israel has intensified the enclosure strategy through the extensive use of roadblocks, fences, trenches, and now the "separation barrier" or "Apartheid Wall" in the West Bank.

Like the Bantustans, the enclosure state spatial strategy provides a tool through which the state has sought to define the boundaries of citizenship, govern a rebellious population, and regulate the labor force. First proposed in the early 1970s, the enclosure strategy provides an answer to the principal dilemma that Israel faced after 1967: to retain sovereignty over the occupied territories without providing citizenship rights to the occupied Palestinian population (Weizman 2007: 93–94). It seeks to avert the "demographic threat" to the Jewish state by creating "autonomous" enclaves where Palestinians can claim citizenship. Israeli negotiators have also proposed the enclosures as a solution to the even greater "demographic threat" posed by five million Palestinian refugees insisting on their internationally recognized right to return to the homes from which they were expelled in 1948.

By redeploying its troops to fortified checkpoints on the outskirts of Palestinian cities, Israel transformed the space of confrontation and nullified the effectiveness of the rocks and slings that Palestinians employed during the first intifada. Instead of military patrols, Israel uses permits, checkpoints, curfews, and "closures" to govern the Palestinian population. By varying the intensity of the generalized "closure" of the occupied territories, the military controls Palestinian movement—not only into Israel but also between the various Palestinian enclaves. Watchtowers, video cameras, unmanned drones, and satellites enable constant surveillance of the enclosures. And the military continues to exert its direct control over the enclosures through regular invasions by the army and rule from above by the air force (Weizman 2007).

The Oslo process severed East Jerusalem from the rest of the West Bank and divided the remainder of the West Bank into different areas of jurisdiction. The PA was granted jurisdiction over security affairs in Area A

(18.2 percent of the West Bank) and civilian affairs in Areas A and B (an additional 21.8 percent). Israel retained jurisdiction over security and civilian affairs in the rest of the West Bank as well as East Jerusalem (B'Tselem 2002). A similar division existed in the Gaza Strip until the Israeli "disengagement" in August 2005. Within the scattered enclosures of Area A, the PA is expected to ensure the security of Israel by "confronting all those engaged in terror" ("Performance-based Roadmap" 2003). Israel retains control over external security, borders, and airspace as well as the right to veto Palestinian legislation. The state also collects $60 million a month in value-added taxes and import duties on goods destined for Areas A and B (Pan 2006). Though legally obliged to transfer these funds to the PA, Israel often uses the money as leverage to extract political concessions. However, the PA budget is even more dependent on financial assistance from foreign donor states—roughly $1 billion per year by 2005 (Pan 2006). The PA is thus responsible not only to Israel but also to international powers such as the "Mideast Quartet," composed of the United States, the European Union, Russia, and the United Nations.

The enclosure strategy has been coupled with the simultaneous neoliberal restructuring of the Israeli economy. The reduction of state controls and the liberalization of trade and investment have generated a major transition from a labor-intensive economy centered on production for the domestic market to a high-tech service economy integrated into the circuits of global capitalism (Ram 2000). Free-trade agreements with Jordan and Egypt have enabled Israeli manufacturers to shift production from the occupied territories to free-trade industrial zones in neighboring countries. And economic restructuring on a global scale has contributed to the immigration of over one million Russians and 300,000 migrant workers from China, Romania, and Thailand (Ellman and Laacher 2003). Since the outbreak of the second intifada in 2000, Palestinians have been almost entirely excluded from the Israeli economy. These changes have facilitated enclosure by reducing Israeli demand for Palestinian workers. The economic policies of the PA, which have been largely shaped by the World Bank, call for the construction of export-oriented, free-trade industrial zones to take advantage of the excess Palestinian labor (Lagerquist 2003). But after an initial experiment in the Gaza Strip, even these citadels of neoliberal employment have yet to materialize.

The enclosure state spatial strategy thus addresses the "demographic threat" by providing Palestinians with "citizenship" in "autonomous" (and perhaps eventually "independent") enclaves. It facilitates the government of a rebellious population through indirect rule, control over movement, and spatial fortification. And unlike in South Africa, where apartheid was a strategy for ensuring access to cheap black labor, the new Israeli strategy of enclosure has involved the steady eradication of work for Palestinians.

SPACES OF EXCEPTION

These tribal cocoons called "homelands" are nothing else but sophisticated concentration camps where black people are allowed to "suffer peacefully." —STEVE BIKO (1978: 86)

In his influential theory of sovereignty, Giorgio Agamben (1998, 2003) draws on the work of Carl Schmitt (2003, 2005) to argue that sovereignty is exercised through the decision on exceptions: cases that stand outside the normal operation of the law. According to Schmitt (2005), the sovereign can suspend the law (specifically, the legal protections of political citizenship and legislative checks on executive power) by declaring a "state of exception" and determining what should be done about it. During a state of exception, he argues, "the state remains, whereas law recedes" (Schmitt 2005: 12). Agamben (2003) draws out the ambiguity of such a situation, noting that executive decrees issued during a state of exception have the "force of law" without being laws. For Agamben, the defining characteristic of a state of exception is this ambiguity or "indistinction." It exists outside of the normal legal order but within the purview of the state. Agamben argues that we are increasingly subject to a permanent state of exception because (1) executive decrees have replaced parliamentary legislation (Agamben 2003) and (2) doctors, scientists, security guards, and other private actors have acquired the "sovereign" power to decide whether a life is worthy of being lived (Agamben 1998).

Agamben (1998) uses spatial imagery to highlight his argument: the concentration camp and the "zone of indistinction." With no legal status or citizenship rights to protect them, those confined to a concentration camp exist as "bare life." Anything becomes possible because "power confronts nothing but pure life, without any mediation" (Agamben 1998: 171). For Agamben, the concentration camp is the materialization of a permanent state of exception—a space where the state exists but law recedes. The ambiguity that defines the state of exception is given spatial expression in a zone that is included in the space of sovereignty through its exclusion from the protections of the law. The modern state is constituted through the creation of such "zones of indistinction" that blur the boundaries between sovereign power and the law. These spaces demonstrate that the law exists only through the possibility of its own suspension.

Despite Agamben's use of spatial imagery, his theory of sovereignty is fundamentally nonterritorial. Drawing on the work of Schmitt and Michel Foucault, he replaces a spatial definition of sovereignty with one focused on the decision over life and death. "In modern biopolitics," Agamben argues, "sovereign is he who decides on the value or the nonvalue of life as such" (1998: 142). Discussing euthanasia, eugenics, experimentation on human guinea pigs, and "brain death," Agamben argues that doctors and scientists make sovereign decisions when they determine the threshold beyond which human life becomes "life unworthy of being lived" (1998: 139) and can therefore be terminated without punishment.

Agamben emphasizes the juridical foundations of the concentration camp, which lie in the sovereign declaration of a state of exception. Similarly, he highlights the sovereign decision over life and death within the camp. But he obscures the spatial foundations of the concentration camp.[4] The production of the camp as a space that both contains and disempowers its captives is essential for creating a situation in which power confronts bare life without mediation. Concentration camps are spatial enclosures that enable the state (or other actors) to isolate and divide populations, control movement and access to resources, and repress resistance with violence, death, and destruction. My argument, therefore, is that the production of space makes possible the sovereign decision over life and death.

Returning to the work of Lefebvre provides an important corrective to Agamben's theory of sovereignty. Lefebvre's reminder that "sovereignty implies . . . a space established and constituted by violence" ([1974] 1991: 280) allows for an analysis of the camp as a spatial strategy to facilitate the exercise of sovereignty. Sovereignty operates through the production of what Agamben calls "spaces of exception" (2003). Although spatially distinct and often physically enclosed, these spaces exist in an ambiguous relationship to the state. Excluded from legal protections, they remain subject to sovereign decisions. In their own ways, both Lefebvre and Agamben argue that such spaces are fundamental for the constitution of modern sovereignty.

The state spatial strategies employed by contemporary Israel and apartheid-era South Africa are designed to produce spaces of exception. The Bantustans and enclosures are included in the sovereign space of the state through their exclusion from the protections of the law. Permanently excluded from citizenship, Palestinians and black South Africans are granted an empty form of "autonomy" but remain subject to sovereign decrees, such as administrative proclamations, military laws, and emergency regulations as well as imprisonment, torture, and death. Steve Biko's description of Bantustans as "sophisticated concentration camps where black people are allowed to 'suffer peacefully'" (1978: 86) captures quite well the bare life conditions of the enclosures and the Bantustans: the sovereign permission of a degree of freedom, the racial basis of the exception, and the "peaceful suffering" of those excluded from citizenship. These spaces of exception are fundamental for the continuation of exclusive settler sovereignty. As Lefebvre ([1974] 1991) suggests, the ongoing process of state formation depends on the use of violence to produce space.

SPACES OF EXCEPTION BEFORE AND AFTER THE IMPERIAL TRANSITION

In the first half of this chapter, I have argued that contemporary Israel and apartheid-era South Africa employed very similar state spatial strategies to maintain settler sovereignty throughout the territory under the state's control. By producing spaces of exception, these states excluded parts of their population from legal citizenship while ensuring that they remained subject to the sovereign power of the state. Despite their similarities, however, the Bantustans in South Africa and the enclosures in Palestine/Israel exhibit a number of significant differences. In the second half of this chapter, I will argue that the imperial transition of the late twentieth century can help account for these differences. The imperial transition marks an important discontinuity in world-historical time that separates contemporary Israel from apartheid-era South Africa. Many of the differences between the spaces of exception in South Africa and Palestine/Israel stem from the fact that the Bantustan strategy was deployed before and the enclosure strategy after the imperial transition.

THE IMPERIAL TRANSITION AND THE FIELD OF SOVEREIGNTY

The early 1990s witnessed not only the demise of South African apartheid and the beginning of the Oslo process, but also Desert Storm, the collapse of the Soviet Union, the signing of the North American Free-Trade Agreement (NAFTA), and the Washington Consensus. These shifts marked the rise of the United States as the world's only military superpower, the globalization of corporate domination, and the hegemony of neoliberal economics. According to U.S. president George H. W. Bush, this moment heralded the emergence of a "New World Order."

During the 1990s, critical analysis of these developments emphasized their economic dimensions, especially the global power of multinational corporations and the devastating impact of neoliberal restructuring. In the early years of the twenty-first century, however, this critique has increasingly addressed new forms of imperial power (Ahmad 2004; Hardt and Negri 2000; Harvey 2003; Smith 2005; Steinmetz 2003b, 2005d; Stoler 2006; Tadiar 2004). Moving beyond the economics of neoliberalism, the study of empire highlights shifts in the operation of sovereignty. Despite competing conceptualizations, therefore, these studies have "brought the state back in" to the analysis of contemporary global restructuring (Evans, Rueschemeyer, and Skocpol 1985) or, more precisely, "brought empire back in" to analyses of politics (see chapters 1 and 9 of the present volume).

Ann Stoler proposes the concept of "imperial formation" to highlight the fact that empires are "states of becoming rather than being, macropolities in constant formation" (2006: 135–136). Stoler points out that the United States Empire was considered "new at the turn of the twentieth century, 'new' by Du Bois in 1920, and again by Arendt and others in 1948" (2006: 135). Although the empire itself is not new, she suggests, it has undergone a fundamental reformation since the early 1990s. My analysis of this imperial reformation builds on the work of Michael Hardt and Antonio Negri, Neil Brenner, and Saskia Sassen. I incorporate their insights into a modified version of Pierre Bourdieu's field theory to argue that the imperial transition has reconfigured the "field of sovereignty."

For Bourdieu, a field is an arena in which actors struggle over a particular "field defining" form of capital (Bourdieu [1980] 1990; Bourdieu and Wacquant 1992). A field can therefore be likened to a playing field whose configuration is defined by the set of objective relationships between players. These relations are shaped by the rules of the game and the goals over which the players compete. In a social field, the competition pits forces against one another not only for power within the field but also for power to define the limits of the field and the rules of the game. Drawing on this framework, Julian Go (2008b) has analyzed the imperial projects of Britain and the United States in relation to a shifting field of global power. He argues that transformations in the global field contributed to the tendency of the United States to pursue an informal rather than a formal territorial empire after the end of World War II. My analysis of the "field of sovereignty" builds on his effort to theorize a global field.

Beginning in the seventeenth century, an autonomous "field of sovereignty" began to emerge in Western Europe. The actors in the field were nation-states, and the field-defining form of capital was ultimately the sovereign power to decide on the exception. Because this power was territorially circumscribed, territory itself became a form of capital, and the production of space became a weapon wielded by states in the struggle for sovereignty. The dual principles established by the Treaty of Westphalia in 1648 provided the rules of the game: respect for the territorial integrity of other states and nonintervention in their internal affairs. Because these rules applied only to relations between recognized European states, powerful states built extensive colonial empires to extend their sovereign reach beyond their own borders. During the twentieth century, the final collapse of the Ottoman, Japanese, and various European empires globalized the field of sovereignty by incorporating the newly independent nation-states. Although struggles between the U.S. and Russian empires often made a mockery of its principles, the Westphalian field of sovereignty was institutionalized in the United Nations and soon spanned the globe.

The imperial transition has thoroughly transformed this field. Saskia Sassen (2006) argues that the 1980s inaugurated an epochal shift in the relationship between territory, authority, and rights. She refers to this as a process of "denationalization." The authority of the nation-state has been eroded by the privatization of formerly public functions, the increasing power of multinational corporations, the rise of global financial markets, and the free-trade regime policed by the World Trade Organization (wto). Nongovernmental organizations (ngos) and human rights organizations have begun to play important governmental roles throughout the world. And even within states, the authority of legislative bodies has been depleted by the expansion of executive powers—a tendency also noted by Giorgio Agamben (1998) and George Steinmetz (2003b). Rather than simply a shift in power relations between nation-states, therefore, this process has produced new global "assemblages" that are no longer centered on the nation-state (Sassen 2006).

Similarly, Michael Hardt and Antonio Negri (2000) argue that the emergence of a new capitalist "Empire" has produced a "decentering" or "deterritorialization" of sovereignty. According to them, the new Empire has "smoothed over" national borders and blurred the strict divisions between core and periphery. Whereas earlier forms of imperialism were based on the extension of a state's sovereignty beyond its own borders, imperial sovereignty is now exercised by a hierarchical network of nation-states, multinational corporations, and the structures of global civil society (NGOs, religious institutions, political parties, and others). Atop the imperial "pyramid" stands the United States military, which polices the Empire in the interests of global capital.

In an important challenge to this thesis, Neil Brenner (2004) highlights the dramatic "rescaling of statehood" that has accompanied neoliberalization. Instead of simply being deterritorialized, he argues, sovereignty has been "reterritorialized" at both subnational and supernational scales. Spatial Keynesianism promoted a centralized political authority, a standardized administration, and an equalization of investment throughout the nation-state. Neoliberal restructuring, conversely, has "rescaled" the administrative capacities of the state to regional and municipal bodies that must now compete with one another to attract investment and accumulation (Brenner 2004).

On another front, George Steinmetz (2003b, 2005d) criticizes the concept of sovereignty employed by Hardt and Negri. Differentiating between "regulation" and "sovereignty," Steinmetz acknowledges that imperial regulation during the 1990s was "politically decentered, with movements towards fragmented and overlapping sources of sovereignty" (2003b: 326). Since September 11, 2001, however, it is undeniable that the "United States is the controlling center of a global empire" (Steinmetz 2005d: 340). Steinmetz draws on Schmitt to argue that it is "possible to identify the locus of sovereignty" (2003b: 336) only during an emergency. With no sense of crisis and no clearly defined enemy, it was not easy to identify the United States as the global sovereign during the 1990s. And although the political regulation of its empire may be decentered, the declaration of a global "state of emergency" after 9/11 clearly reveals the global sovereignty of the United States (Steinmetz 2003b: 337).

Returning to the framework of field analysis, I want to argue that the Westphalian field of sovereignty has been reconfigured by the processes that Sassen refers to as "denationalization" and Hardt and Negri term "deterritorialization." Political regulation has been decentered, new actors have entered the field of sovereignty, and the rules of the game have been challenged. The most blatant subversion of the principles of territorial integrity and noninterference is the U.S. invasion of Iraq. Even more fundamental, however, is the establishment of the WTO with the jurisdiction to enforce neoliberal trade agreements without regard to legislation passed by the parliamentary bodies of sovereign states. These free-trade agreements have redistributed power from nation-states to multinational corporations, many of which have now entered the field to vie with states over claims to sovereignty. In many regions of the global South, export-processing zones and "resource extraction enclaves" have come under de facto corporate sovereignty (Ferguson 2006). Perhaps the most important new actors in the field of sovereignty are the private security companies that have grown rapidly throughout the world and the private military companies that have proliferated in the wake of the U.S. war against Iraq.

Yet Brenner's analysis provides an important reminder that state sovereignty has not simply withered away in the face of these destabilizing forces. Instead, states have responded with an array of strategies designed to produce spaces of sovereignty at multiple geographical scales. Aihwa Ong (2006) points to the flexible division of state territories into differentially governed zones. Exceptions to the law allow certain zones to attract capital investment, while exceptions from neoliberalism allow the state to deploy different governmental strategies in other spaces. Brenner (2004) highlights the strategies employed by metropolitan councils to produce competitive regions that will attract foreign investment. He also suggests that the formation of the European Union represents an effort to produce spaces of state sovereignty at the supranational scale (Brenner 1999). The same can be said of the African Union. And the United States has staked its claim to global sovereignty by declaring a state of emergency and producing spaces of exception in Iraq, Afghanistan, Guantanamo Bay, and secret military prisons throughout the world.

Imperial power relations were fundamentally transformed in the late twentieth century as a result of the military dominance of the United States, the unprecedented power of multinational corporations, and the global hegemony of neoliberal economics. The "new" U.S. Empire has been characterized by a decentralization of regulatory power from states to international financial institutions, corporations, and organs of civil society. These shifts reconfigured the Westphalian field, bringing new actors into competition to produce spaces of sovereignty. In the face of these threats, states have reasserted their sovereignty at multiple scales.

STATE/SPACE/EMPIRE

Rather than simply an outgrowth of shifting power relations at the global scale, the imperial transition was constituted by a multiplicity of political, economic, and spatial transformations at local, national, and regional scales. Among the more notable moments in this process were the transitions during the early 1990s in South Africa and Palestine/Israel. In the mid-1980s, both South Africa and Israel were settler states with Fordist economies facing economic crises and popular uprisings. The conjuncture of these crises produced transitions in both states that, from the very beginning, coupled political negotiations with neoliberal restructuring. Although they followed similar economic paths, however, Israel and South Africa embarked on entirely different political transitions. The democratization of the South African state produced a recognizable postcolonial society, while the Israeli state maintained a fundamentally colonial relationship with the occupied Palestinian population.

As I argued above, the Bantustans in apartheid-era South Africa and the enclosures in contemporary Palestine/Israel are the products of similar state spatial strategies. In both cases, the production of "spaces of exception" was a strategy for reinforcing and maintaining exclusive settler sovereignty throughout the territory controlled by the state. But the enclosures currently under construction in Palestine/Israel differ from the South African Bantustans in several crucial ways. To some extent, these differences stem from the divergent histories of identity formation, class formation, and state formation in these two states (Greenstein 1995). This demands that comparative analysis remain attuned to the social embeddedness of state spatial strategies. Still, it is possible to isolate at least four important differences that stem from the fact that the Bantustan strategy was deployed before and the enclosure strategy after the imperial transition of the late twentieth century. Each of these points provides insight into the operation of sovereignty under conditions of globalization and U.S. Empire.

To begin with, shifts in the relationship between the forces of regulation have reconfigured the field of sovereignty. Whereas the field was dominated by nation-states prior to the imperial transition, it has now been opened up to a range of state and nonstate actors that operate at multiple geographical scales. The field has also witnessed the proliferation of strategies to reassert state sovereignty in the face of this competition from nonstate actors.

The Bantustan strategy in South Africa was the product of a state intent on mediating the demands of mining capital, industrial capital, agricultural capital, and a burgeoning Afrikaner nationalist movement. The finances of the Bantustan governments were controlled entirely by the South African state, and all of the institutions involved in regulating the African population were arms of the state: the police, the courts, the Labor Bureau, and the various Bantustan governments. Despite the fact that aspects of the

Bantustan strategy were first developed by British imperial forces, the strategy was produced and enforced by the South African state in conjunction with South African capital. And although South Africa sought to articulate its Bantustan policy with the U.S. imperial project, the United States was never directly involved in governing the African population. Therefore, although the state remained in constant dialogue with imperial power, the Bantustan strategy was developed and deployed at the scale of the nation-state. In fact, when faced with external challenges to the policy of apartheid, the South African government sought refuge in the Westphalian principle of noninterference in the internal affairs of nation-states.

In Palestine/Israel, in contrast, the enclosure strategy was enacted by the Israeli state in close coordination with the United States government and the institutions of global capitalism, particularly the World Bank. The State of Israel is fully integrated into the networks of the U.S. Empire. Stephen Walt and John Mearsheimer (2007) have argued that the Zionist lobby manipulates U.S. politicians into placing Israeli interests above those of the United States. Critics such as Joseph Massad (2006) respond that the United States never acts against its own interests and that Walt and Mearsheimer failed to account for the correspondence of interests between the U.S. Empire and the Zionist lobby. In either case, it is incontrovertible that the U.S. government not only supports but actively coordinates its actions with the Israeli state. The founding documents of the Oslo "peace process" were signed on the White House lawn, U.S. (and European) military teams train Palestinian security forces, and the U.S. veto at the United Nations protects Israel from international condemnation.

In addition to the United States, European states and the representatives of global capital play crucial roles in regulating the Palestinian population. The World Bank helped shape PA economic policy from its inception. As Adel Samara notes, "the PA's economy may be alone in having been designed from its very beginning by the policies and prescriptions of globalizing institutions" (2000: 21). More than one-half of the PA's budget consists of loans and grants made by international "donor" states. As demonstrated by the "financial blockade" imposed on the PA after Hamas won legislative elections in 2006, these states use their financial clout to place pressure on the PA. Until 2007, monitors from the European Union oversaw the border crossing between Egypt and the Gaza Strip (under the supervision and direction of Israeli security personnel). And since 2002, the "Mideast Quartet" has played an important role in controlling the parameters of discussion on the "peace process." All of this demonstrates that the enclosures of the

West Bank are regulated by a network of imperial power coordinated by the United States. The enclosures are governed not by a single state but by a multiplicity of state and nonstate actors—including a plethora of NGOs that operate throughout the West Bank and Gaza Strip.

Yet rather than a stateless process, the Israeli enclosure strategy is geared toward reasserting state power in the face of challenges to its sovereignty. These threats are numerous: a rebellious population demanding independence, an emerging business class seeking autonomy from state control, a "peace process" with the potential to shrink the space of Israeli sovereignty, and an imperial transition reconfiguring the field of sovereignty on a global scale. Confronted with these threats to its sovereignty, the State of Israel has reacted by producing spaces of exception that help ensure the continuation of settler sovereignty throughout Israel/Palestine. The enclosure strategy was pursued by state actors intent on maintaining Israeli sovereignty over the "autonomous" territories and the rebellious Palestinian population. Although present from the beginning, this assertive state strategy became overt after the ascension of Benjamin Netanyahu as prime minister of Israel in 1996. And in October 2000, the state unleashed the full force of its military to crush an outbreak of resistance in the occupied territories. One year before the United States declared its global state of emergency, Israel violently asserted its sovereignty by declaring its own state of emergency. In this state of exception, Israel invaded and besieged Palestinian cities, demolished refugee camps, assassinated leaders, imprisoned activists, and built a giant wall around the cities of the West Bank. This reassertion of state sovereignty in the face of its threatened dissolution is a fundamental aspect of the imperial transition.

The second effect of the imperial transition has been an intensification of individualized technologies of power. As Michel Foucault argues, biopower is always both totalizing and individualizing—exercised through the regulation of the population and the disciplining of individual bodies (Foucault 1978, 1982). But regulation in the empire of the early twenty-first century has involved a rapid advance in the technologies of power focused on the individual. This corresponds to a shift in the dominant discourse of security from "communism" to "terrorism." While the discourse of "communism" produced a fear of the masses, the discourse of "terrorism" is focused on fear of the individual suicide bomber—what Arjun Appadurai calls the "fear of small numbers" (2006). In comparison with the Bantustan strategy, which focused primarily on regulating the population, the Israeli enclosure strategy is much more attuned to the individual.

In South Africa, white fear about black urbanization dominated the 1948 election that inaugurated the apartheid era. Expressed through the racial lens of *swart gevaar* (black peril), this insecurity focused on the fear that white cities would be overrun by large numbers of black people. This dovetailed with the anticommunist discourse of the Cold War era and contributed to claims by the South African government that it stood on the front lines of the battle against communism in Africa. One of the first laws passed by the apartheid regime was the Suppression of Communism Act (1950). Within this context, the Bantustans provided a spatial strategy for governing large numbers of Africans through indirect rule, pass laws, and forced removals. Although the apartheid regime certainly targeted individual activists (such as Nelson Mandela and Steve Biko), its spatial strategies were primarily focused on regulating and containing a large population.

As a strategic response to the first intifada, the reorganization of the Israeli occupation also seeks to contain mass resistance. Fortified checkpoints protect troops from popular mobilizations, and territorial fragmentation has induced a localization of resistance by breaking national networks of solidarity. But the checkpoints and the wall are not only rigged to control large crowds—they also target the individual. The advent of the individual suicide bomber has been countered by a vast array of individualized technologies of power. The Israeli government has compiled extensive state knowledge about each and every Palestinian. By scanning the magnetic identification cards that Palestinians must carry in order to pass through a checkpoint, soldiers can access each person's extensive security records and determine whether to detain, deny, or permit that person to pass. A long and ever-expanding list of individuals who are to be arrested on sight has produced a new category of "wanted" subjects. Embodying this subjectivity, countless Palestinians refuse to even approach the checkpoints out of the fear that their names are on that list. But the individualization of control has reached its limits in preparations for the assassination of political activists—known as "targeted killing" in Orwellian doublespeak: "After a Palestinian is put on the death list, he is followed, sometimes for weeks, by a 'swarm' of various unmanned aircraft. Often, different swarms follow different people simultaneously in different areas of the Gaza Strip. In this way the security services establish the targeted person's daily routines and habits, and maintain continuous visual contact with him until his killing" (Weizman 2007: 241). As this chilling example demonstrates, the security logic in Israel is increasingly driven by the "fear of small numbers" (Appadurai 2006). Similar processes are under way throughout the world, especially as part of the ongoing "war on terror."

The third principal difference between the Bantustans and the enclosures is a "time-space compression" in the operation of sovereignty. According to David Harvey (1990), the transition from Fordism to neoliberalism has entailed an intense period of "time-space compression." Post-Fordist strategies of capital accumulation involve flexible networks of economic production that span the globe and respond instantaneously to new information. Harvey (1990) argues that this time-space compression has also contributed to the emergence of volatile, ephemeral forms of postmodern culture focused on either the simulacra of escape or the security of identity in a shifting world. Building on this insight, I want to suggest that these cases reveal a similar "time-space compression" in the exercise of sovereignty. Compared with the earlier South African strategy, the Israeli strategy has reduced the time horizons of control and transformed a two-dimensional reserve into a three-dimensional enclosure contained from all sides.

In South Africa, the "independent" Bantustans were conceptualized as miniature nation-states, complete with borders and air-space. The borders were secured by joint patrols of the Bantustan military forces and the South African Defense Forces (Grundy 1986: 72). This arrangement applied not only to borders between the Bantustans and South Africa but also to "international" borders such as those that Bophuthatswana shared with Botswana and the Transkei shared with Lesotho. The South African state maintained direct control over underground resources. Through the Bantu Mining Corporation, the state attracted investment by white-owned firms by leasing the right to explore and mine the mineral deposits of the Bantustans (especially Bophuthatswana) (Butler, Rotberg, and Adams 1977: 129, 215–216). The Bantustan governments had no say in the negotiations and received neither royalties nor rents from the mines. "In other words," wrote Steve Biko, "Bantustans only have rights extending to 6 feet below the surface of the land" (1978: 83). This demonstrates the limits to the autonomy of even the "independent" Bantustans.

The Bantustans did, however, gain formal authority over their airspace, as demonstrated by Article 2 of the "Non-Aggression Pacts" between South Africa and each of the Bantustans: "Neither of the parties shall allow its territory or territorial airspace to be used . . . for . . . hostile actions or activities against the other Party" ("Non-Aggression Pact" 1982: 21). In fact, the defense forces of the Transkei and Bophuthatswana each had an air wing, considered vital in the latter for policing a territory composed of numerous scattered enclaves (Cawthra 1986: 127; Heitman 1985: 116–118). These spatial characteristics clearly demarcate the Bantustans as small nation-states whose (quasi-) sovereignty extends vertically to that vague threshold where airspace (and state sovereignty) ends and outer space begins.

The Labor Bureau that regulated the allocation of African labor was a huge, immobile Keynesian bureaucracy. Coordinated from Pretoria by a Central Labor Bureau, the system attempted to coordinate the flow of labor from the Bantustans to white farms, factories, and mines. It based its decisions on data collected from regional and local bureau offices on a biweekly or monthly basis (Evans 1997: 89). The system was thus slow to respond to changing conditions. And the pass laws gave Africans a three-day grace period in which to find work upon reaching an urban area. These mechanisms lacked the flexibility to prevent undocumented African urbanization. As a result, South Africa relied on ad hoc pass raids, deportations, and forced removals to produce separation.

Compared with the Bantustans, the Israeli enclosures reveal an intense time-space compression. Despite mechanisms for "coordination" with the PA, Israel maintains direct control over Palestinian movement through the numerous checkpoints, terminals, and international borders. Within the West Bank, a system of permits, checkpoints, and closures enables the state to instantaneously and flexibly adjust the flow of Palestinians through hundreds of separate checkpoints (Hanieh 2006). All of the territories can be systematically shut down at a moment's notice. Just as easily, one enclosure can be sealed while limited movement continues between the others. Or some individuals can be prevented from passing a checkpoint while others are allowed through.

But the control over horizontal movement is only one aspect of the Israeli enclosures. Israel has developed a sophisticated three-dimensional architecture of control that exploits the verticality of the region (Weizman 2002). Not only does Israel construct Jewish settlements on hilltops surrounding the Palestinian enclosures and watchtowers that overlook Palestinian cities, but a series of tunnels and bridges facilitates the unimpeded movement of Israeli traffic on the segregated road system above and below Palestinian cities. The state also extracts water from the aquifers below the Palestinian enclosures. Through these mechanisms, the state has produced two vertically separate but overlapping spaces in the occupied territories—an open, flexible, and rapidly expanding space for Israeli citizens that exists not only alongside but above the closed, immobile, and shrinking space of the Palestinian enclosures (Weizman 2007).

And unlike in South Africa, Israel has retained control over the airspace above the Palestinian enclosures. In doing so, they have supplied evidence to support Schmitt's claim that airspace "has become the force-field of human power and activity" (2003: 354). According to the *Israeli-Palestinian Interim Agreement on the West Bank and Gaza Strip*, "All aviation activity or use of the airspace by any aerial vehicle in the West Bank and the Gaza Strip shall require prior approval of Israel" (1995: Annex I, Article XIII-4). Continued Israeli control over Palestinian airspace has been a constant condition for Palestinian statehood—from the liberal Geneva Accord to Ariel Sharon's conditions for accepting the so-called Roadmap (Lerner 2004; "Statement from PM's Bureau" 2003). The state makes extensive use of this airspace to control Palestinian life. Satellite imagery and unmanned drones enable constant surveillance. High-speed, low-level flights generate terrifying sonic booms over residential areas. And changes in the rules of engagement have normalized the use of helicopters, rockets, and warplanes against Palestinians. As a result, the Palestinian enclosures have become three-dimensional containers rather than simply walled-off spaces (Weizman 2007). Palestinians half-joke that when the wall is complete, a roof will be added.

As John Collins (2008) points out, however, the intensification of Israeli power has proceeded not only through control over space but also through control over time. Rockets, snipers, and warplanes strike instantaneously. The speed at which these war machines operate contributes to a time compression that precludes the possibility of resistance. "In recent years," Collins points out, "we have seen how attacks can be accelerated further, and also miniaturized, through the use of booby-trapped cell phones that kill in the time it takes to say hello" (562). By deploying the weapon of speed, Israel has collapsed time and completed what Collins refers to as the "*four-dimensional confinement* of the Palestinians" (563). And the state often exerts its control over time not only by accelerating the immediacy of control but also by slowing things down. Waiting for a checkpoint to open or a curfew to be lifted has become routine. Even more, due to the slow pace with which Israel is constructing the wall through the West Bank, some Palestinians have become accustomed to life behind the wall long before others have even begun to feel its effect. This is designed to fragment resistance and produce a slow acquiescence to the presence of the wall.

All of this constitutes an unprecedented time-space compression in the operation of sovereignty. The four-dimensional enclosure of the Palestinians has generated a powerful yet flexible strategy for producing state/space.

The fourth and final difference between the Bantustans and the enclosures has to do with the question of labor. As I demonstrated above, the Bantustans were constructed to secure the migrant labor system as part of South Africa's attempt to regulate a racial Fordist economy. Urban townships and pass-law exemptions helped meet the needs of manufacturing capital for a permanently urbanized, semiskilled African workforce. And forced removals sought to ensure that the urban population did not grow out of control and that mining capital could count on the presence of a low-cost labor reserve in the Bantustans. The economic factor underlying every dimension of state spatial strategy was the need to ensure continued access to cheap African labor.

The Israeli enclosures, conversely, have accelerated the elimination of Palestinian workers from the Israeli economy. A familiar story throughout the world, neoliberalization in Palestine/Israel has produced a "surplus" or "disposable" population: permanently unemployed, too poor to consume, separated from the means of subsistence, and abandoned by the neoliberal state. Record numbers of people face permanent structural unemployment. Mike Davis refers to this as the "late capitalist triage of humanity" (2006). The hemorrhaging of labor in Palestine/Israel is exacerbated by the policy of replacing Palestinians with foreign workers and compounded by the long-standing support within the Zionist movement for economic and political separation. To borrow a phrase from Loïc Wacquant, the enclosures in Palestine/Israel serve "only to warehouse the precarious and deproletarianized fractions" of the Palestinian working class (2002: 53).

As neoliberal restructuring generates surplus populations throughout the world, enclosures have become an increasingly common spatial strategy of regulation. Some enclosures surround the poor and marginalized, as in Palestine/Israel and the U.S. prison system. Others surround the rich and powerful, as in the gated communities and fortress suburbs of São Paulo, Los Angeles, and post-apartheid Johannesburg. At every conceivable scale, from the "Green Zone" in Baghdad to the U.S.-Mexican border, surplus populations and spatial enclosures are coming to define sovereignty in the empire of the early twenty-first century.

CONCLUSION

The state spatial strategies under consideration in this chapter lend support to Lefebvre's thesis that sovereignty implies "a space established and constituted by violence" (1974: 280). The Bantustans and enclosures make possible the continuation of settler sovereignty by containing rebellious populations, excluding them from citizenship, and facilitating their regulation. Although deemed "autonomous" or even "independent," these spaces remain fundamentally within the sovereign space of the settler state. More precisely, it is through the production of these "autonomous" zones that the settler state is able to exercise its sovereignty over them. Bringing Lefebvre into dialogue with Agamben, I refer to these zones as "spaces of exception." They are included in the space of state sovereignty through their exclusion from the protection of the law. These state spatial strategies, therefore, are fundamental to the constitution of both the state and its space—in short, the constitution of state/space.

The enclosures in Palestine/Israel are significant not only for their immediate effects but also for what they reveal about the operation of sovereignty after the recent transition in imperial power relations. By comparing the deployment of similar state spatial strategies before and after the imperial transition, I have attempted to isolate the effects of this transition on the operation of sovereignty. Building on recent theories of empire, I argue that the reformation of the U.S. Empire beginning in the late 1980s reconfigured the field of sovereignty. The rules of the game were changed and new actors entered the field to compete with nation-states over sovereignty. Confronted with threats to their domination of the field, states have developed an arsenal of new strategies to produce spaces of sovereignty at multiple geographic scales. Israel's effort to enclose the Palestinian population represents one such strategy. Compared with the Bantustan strategy in South Africa, Israel's strategy of enclosure stands out for its individualized technologies, its time-space compression, and its enclosure of surplus populations. Perhaps more significantly, it stands out for the regulatory role of diverse imperial actors and the forceful reassertion of sovereignty by the Israeli state. These seemingly contradictory processes are definitive of contemporary imperial sovereignty.

Historical timelines of South Africa and Palestine/Israel

SOUTH AFRICA

1652–1910	*Colonial Era*
1652	Dutch establish colony at the Cape of Good Hope.
1806	British take control over the Cape Colony.
1811–1906	Frontier wars between British, Afrikaners, and Africans.
1836–1840	Afrikaners leave the Cape Colony on the "Great Trek."
1852–1854	Independent Afrikaner republics established.
1867	Diamond mining begins.
1886	Gold mining begins.
1899–1902	South African War between British and Afrikaners.
1910–1948	*Segregation Era*
1910	Colonial republics join together to form the Union of South Africa.
1913	Natives Land Act institutionalizes system of "native reserves."
1923	Native Urban Areas Act tightens urban segregation.
1948–1994	*Apartheid Era*
1948	National Party wins election; apartheid begins.
1950–1953	Major apartheid legislation adopted.
1959	Promotion of Bantu Self-Government Act creates separate "ethnic" homelands.
1960	Sharpeville massacre.
1970	Bantu Homelands Citizenship Act strips Africans of South African citizenship.
1973	Durban strikes.

1976	Soweto uprising; Transkei becomes first "independent" Bantustan.
1986–1990	Pass laws repealed.
1990	Mandela released from prison.
1994–Present	*Postapartheid Era*
1994	African National Congress wins nonracial election; Bantustans dissolved.

PALESTINE/ISRAEL

1880–1917	*Early Zionist Settlement*
1882	First modern Jewish settlement in Palestine.
1897	First Zionist Congress.
1916	Sykes-Pikot Agreement; Arab Revolt against the Ottoman Empire.
1917–1948	*British Mandate*
1917	Balfour Declaration: British support creation of Jewish homeland in Palestine.
1922	League of Nations approves British Mandate for Palestine.
1936–1939	Palestinian "Great Rebellion."
1939–1945	WWII and the Nazi Holocaust.
1947	UN partitions Palestine/Israel.
1947–1948	Civil war begins.
1948–1967	*State-building Era*
1948	British withdraw; Israeli Declaration of Independence; first Arab-Israeli war; explusion of the Palestinians.
1956	Tripartite invasion of Egypt.

1967–1993	*Occupation Era*
1967	Six Day War; Israeli occupation of the West Bank and Gaza Strip begins.
1973	Yom Kippur War/October War.
1978	Camp David Accord.
1982	Israeli invasion of Lebanon.
1985	Israel begins neoliberalization.
1987–1993	Palestinian intifada.
1991	Gulf War; permit system introduced.
1993	Israel initiates closure policy.
1993–Present	*Post-Oslo Era*
1993	Declaration of Principles; beginning of the Oslo "peace process."
1994	Palestinian Authority established.
2000	Second Palestinian intifada.
2002	Construction of the separation wall begins.
2003	"Roadmap to Peace" published.
2005	Israeli "disengagement" from Gaza.

NOTES

1. For an analysis of the relationship between neoliberal restructuring and the political transitions of the 1990s in Palestine/Israel and South Africa, see Clarno (2008).

2. Greenstein (1995) does account for world-historical time, but his analysis is focused on the period prior to 1948.

3. This discourse remains prevalent among sections of the Israeli business elite today. See Remnick (2007).

4. Even Foucault ([1975] 1995, 1980) recognized that the configuration of space is fundamental for the operation of power.

SEVENTEEN

Resistance and the Contradictory Rationalities of State Formation in British Malaya and the American Philippines

DANIEL P. S. GOH

INTRODUCTION

Although most contemporary non-Western countries inherited their states from colonialism, colonial state formation has been an understudied process in historical sociology. In the past decades, neo-Weberian scholars have influentially asserted their state-centered perspective, which is concerned with the relative power of a state versus other social forces in its territory grouped under the rubric of "society" (Evans 1995; Skocpol 1979). But neo-Weberians have carefully avoided the question of colonial state formation. The comparison of empires poses theoretical problems, since they involved a complex of jostling states, institutions, and social groups that defies the state-society framework. The comparison of colonial states also poses methodological issues, since these involved the extension of metropolitan sovereignty into colonial territories through subsidiary state, thereby complicating the independence of the neo-Weberian unit of analysis. Hence, it is often assumed that colonialism involved the imposition of Western state forms on alien societies, that the European state "served as the template for state formation everywhere" (Tilly 1985: 182).

In recent years, however, neo-Weberian analysis has begun to move into the study of colonial state formation, usually as a prelude to the explanation of postcolonial political and economic development (Kohli 2004; Lange 2006). Nonetheless, confronted by the variation of colonial rule, usually dichotomized as indirect patrimonial rule versus direct bureaucratic rule, neo-Weberian scholars have sought explanations. These explanations share the fundamental argument that the political and economic interests of the metropolitan state determined colonial state institutions, moderated by the effectiveness, costs, and risks of implementing these colonial state institutions in the alien context of local societies. In the latter sense, neo-Weberian scholarship has been approaching a rational choice theory of state formation, in which colonial governors, as principals in the bounded colonial game of power and exploitation, were calculative rational actors who enacted the most cost-effective state institutions according to the demands of metropolitan political-economic interests.

The challenge to the neo-Weberian perspective comes from scholars who have brought the insights of cultural studies and postcolonial theory to bear on the sociology of state formation (e.g., Steinmetz 1999, 2007a). Comparative studies of colonial state formation from this alternative perspective have emphasized, instead, the sociocultural logic of state building rather than the political-economic calculations of metropolitan interests (Go 2003b; Steinmetz 2002, 2007a). These studies share the view that governors and other officials not only arrived in the colonies with interest-based frameworks for policymaking but also brought with them beliefs concerning native societies conditioned by their position in the metropolitan sociopolitical field and inflected by cultural categories of interpretation. The traffic of political-cultural contestations in the colony and between the metropole and colony then influenced the direction of colonial policy and thus state formation.

In this essay, I seek to combine both approaches to understand colonial state formation in Malaya and the Philippines. However, I argue for the central role played by resistance in "interfering" in the rationalities of colonial governing, as anticolonial practices that had to be interpreted and dealt with in terms of co-option or suppression by colonial officials in the frames of both political-economic interests and anthropological discourse, therefore creating the possibility of political controversies over native policy. Governors were central in this process, as they wielded extraordinary powers and were expected to exercise strong leadership to bend alien society to metropolitan interests. At the same time, governors often held competing ethnographic views of native groups as a result of their different political positions, social locations, and career biographies in metropolitan society. In the metropole-colony nexus, the governor was the central node where political decisions were negotiated, made, and executed. These justify a methodological focus on governors as key "rational actors" negotiating the rationalities of state building. The cases of state formation in British Malaya from 1895 and the American Philippines from 1898 have been a standing historical puzzle for their contrastive trajectories. As Trocki (1999: 91) notes, British rule in Malaya began with patrimonial protection but ended up defined by the centralized bureaucratic institutions of direct rule, while the Americans sought direct rule in the Philippines to assimilate the Filipinos but ended protecting a neopatrimonial Commonwealth run by mestizo elites. In my analysis, I focus on the contradictory rationalities of state formation caused by resistance and how these created an oscillating pattern of policy shifts by succeeding governors that determined the trajectory of state formation. In each case, the oscillations culminated in political crisis that brought the contradictory rationalities to the surface in the form of surging native resistance and signified the decay of colonialism.

RESISTANCE AND THE RATIONALITIES OF COLONIAL STATE FORMATION

In his comparative-historical study of colonial state formation, Kohli identifies three ideal types of state authority. Neopatrimonial states have "the façade of a modern state," but the lack of distinction between public and private interests leads to weakly centralized state institutions and the patrimonial corruption of rational-legal authority (Kohli 2004: 9). In contrast, cohesive-capitalist states have "centralized and purposive authority structures" that not only are independent of society but also "penetrate deep into the society" to allow the state to effectively pursue developmental objectives (Kohli 2004: 10). In between are fragmented multiclass states that have rational-legal authority structures but in which public authority is fragmented by class conflicts. Kohli's Japanese Korea, like British Malaya, counts as a cohesive-capitalist state, while British Nigeria, like the American Philippines, comes closest to a neopatrimonial state. The British implemented "indirect rule" through traditional rulers to run Nigeria "on the cheap, expending as little energy as possible," while the Japanese built up a centralized state to develop Korea to fit "Japanese needs and interests" (Kohli 2004: 18, 40). The British, lacking specific economic interests in Nigeria, only slightly advanced the agrarian condition, while the Korean masses were proletarianized to serve Japanese agricultural and industrial capital.

The problem with Kohli's approach is that the same neo-Weberian assumption of the metropolitan derivation of colonial state formation is replicated. By analyzing state formation within the frames of metropolitan political-economic interests, "excentric" metropole-colony factors are ignored rather than ruled out (Robinson 1986). The neo-Weberian model thus approaches a rational-choice model of state formation, where interests are taken as the bounded rationality in which governors apply cost-benefit calculations to establish the most efficient institutions relative to the colonial game. As the alternative perspective proposes, one crucial set of excentric factors is sociocultural. Indeed, using the case of Dutch metropolitan-colonial state formation, Adams (1994, 1999) shows that sociocultural factors, gendered and emotive familial ideologies in her case, are often controlled, subsumed, or introduced as historically contingent factors in the explanations of state formation in rational-choice historical sociology. In this respect, Kohli's footnote for the Nigeria case bears interest. Kohli wonders why in the rational deliberations of colonial officials they did not think that the returns of state investment in developing rich agricultural lands would more than compensate for the expenditure and insightfully observes that "it would be far too easy to attribute policy choices to underlying 'interests,' both because 'interests' are not always obvious and because there is always more than one way to pursue 'interests'" (2004: 302).

Steinmetz's (2007a, 2008a) work on colonial state formation in the German colonies of Namibia, Samoa, and Qingdao is instructive. Steinmetz observes that the multivocal character of anthropological discourse allowed for the adoption of different ethnographic perspectives and therefore different native policies. Using Bourdieu's cultural theory, Steinmetz argues that a colonial official's adoption of a particular perspective was influenced by his pursuit of cultural distinction in the colonial field, directed at the metropole-centered conflicts of social class. The ethnographic perspective adopted tends to showcase the colonial official's holding of cultural capital associated with the official's social class. Thus, despite similar metropolitan political-economic interests for the three colonies, the native policies adopted, the political consequences for native groups, and the institutionalization of the state in the three colonies were very different.

In fact, Steinmetz's sociocultural aspects are implicit in Kohli's explanatory narratives. While he does not conceptualize the ethnographic representations and political beliefs of colonial officials, they are implicit when he observes (1) the uniqueness of Japanese imperialism in colonizing states "with whom it shared racial and cultural traits" and the special role played by Japanese technocrat Itō Hirobumi and (2) the role played by archconservative Lord Frederick Lugard in implementing "indirect rule" in Islamic northern Nigeria as it "reflected an anti-industrial bias rooted in their own aristocratic backgrounds and in their sympathy for the local rulers" (Kohli 2004: 32, 312). For Nigeria, Kohli (2004: 313) implies the ethnographic factor in his observation that "Lugard interpreted past practices" in the north to conclude that land was communal for the purposes of colonial land policy. Kohli also notes, "One gets a sense in the historical literature that, on occasion, British rulers in the colonies were still fighting out their own proxy 'class war' (aristocracy vs. the bourgeoisie) in the colonies" (312). In these observations, we begin to get an approximation to Steinmetz's argument that ethnographic discourse and the class background of officials were important to colonialism. If both political-economic and sociocultural rationalities were in play, then the question is how they interacted to influence colonial state formation.

Another crucial element missing in the neo-Weberian approach is native resistance. Teasing out resistance as a determinant factor is critical because, first, it corrects the view that colonial state formation was merely derivative of metropolitan factors. Second, resistance was an irreducible sociological fact in colonialism, and we have to account for it in our theoretical models. Third, if a relationship between resistance and the rationalities of state formation can be shown, then we can build a model that accounts for the interaction of the rationalities. I take native resistance to mean the general strategies and everyday tactics employed by native communities to oppose, defy, and withstand colonial intrusion into their political, economic, and cultural life. Resistance refers not only to armed opposition but also to the diverse practices employed differently by various native groups during the later stages of state formation (Isaacman and Isaacman 1977; Scott 1985), often appearing with collaboration in ambivalent and ambiguous ways because they operate in the political-economic and sociocultural logic of native society (Ortner 1995). For my analysis, resistance is best described as the autonomous undercurrent of subaltern thoughts and practices that had escaped the institutional power of the colonial state and which could mobilize into a nationalist mass movement, manifest as incidents of unrest, or erupt as sudden rebellions. As a corollary, collaboration describes the imperfect and partial co-optation and institutionalization of subaltern practices into the colonial state field.

Resistance is subsumed as a cost factor of metropolitan political-economic considerations in the neo-Weberian approach. Kohli writes with reference to Nigeria, "The British opted not to establish a centralized state that would supplant the power of traditional chiefs because they were simply not prepared to commit the human and material resources for creating an effective central state" (2004: 303–304). But if it were in metropolitan interests to run Nigeria on the cheap, why then did the British spend great sums maintaining the centralized state in India in the same period? Kohli explains the difference by way of the timing of colonialism: a centralized Indian state was critical to British global expansion in the nineteenth century, but by the time the British colonized Nigeria, "they were much 'wiser'" (328). But if the locus of explanation is to remain centered in the metropole, such a shift must be imperial, that is, the British must also have been "wiser" in India. Thus, Kohli (2004: 229) points to a change in Indian policy after the 1857 Mutiny, when the British turned to indirect rule to "ally with and strengthen the position of traditional Indian elites" in the interior. In other words, a rebellious eruption of resistance caused a major shift in imperial policy from direct to indirect rule to deal with the resistance in a cost-effective manner. Lange (2004: 908) is more explicit in his survey of British colonialism, arguing that "the presence of local populations" determined the choice of direct or indirect rule in two ways, by "obstructing access to land and greatly increasing the costs and risks of large-scale settlement" and, citing the 1857 Mutiny, by being "more likely to revolt against invasive forms of colonialism," thereby making themselves "most effectively ruled" through indirect rule.

In the sociocultural approach, resistance is seen as a material force in changing the course of colonial state formation via its impact on the cultural categories of the latter. In Mamdani's work on colonial "decentralized despotism" in Africa, the British and French regimes ethnographically reified authoritarian native culture as the customary authority of "tribes." As a result, the colonial state is bifurcated between a modern legal order that racially distributed liberal rights and co-opted customary authority implemented in the rural areas to hold back the torrents of mass resistance (Mamdani 1996: 16–21, 90–96). Thus, resistance caused a single shift in policy, creating bifurcated colonial states. In my two cases, however, resistance was integral to the oscillating logic of policy shifts, creating the trajectories of colonial state formation that culminated in political crises. As I have argued elsewhere, scholarly pioneers and officials in Malaya and the Philippines were constructing competing ethnographies that transcribed different aspects of resistance into anthropological idioms (Goh 2007a). Colonial officials were actively producing ethnographies to understand resistance. This active cultural transcription of material threats to imperialism created the possibility of contradiction in the rationalities of colonial rule.

The neo-Weberian perspective pins the determinant of colonial state formation on the pragmatic cost-benefit calculation of bureaucratic administration as aligned with metropolitan political-economic interests with regards to the particular colony. The alternative thesis I propose here is that the political-economic and ethnographic rationalities responding to resistance interactively determined colonial state formation. State formation proceeded in a linear fashion when those rationalities were aligned with each other, perhaps as in Kohli's Korea and Nigeria cases. But in situations when the rationalities contradicted each other because of the nature of native resistance, contestations and conflicts over colonial policy generated a trajectory of colonial state formation under different governors. This trajectory is characterized by the oscillation of colonial policies, with succeeding governors reversing their predecessor's policy, sometimes exacerbating the contradictions in the process. The oscillation culminated in imperial controversies where the contradictory rationalities emerged in the form of political crises and led to the decay of colonialism.

Theoretically, I am drawing from Steinmetz's employment of Bourdieu's theory of the political field. In Bourdieu's view, the Western state is racked with symbolic struggle simultaneously taking place with the struggle for political power. The struggle is over the legitimate way to represent the world, the stake being "the monopoly of the elaboration and diffusion of the legitimate principle of division of the social world and, thereby, of the mobilization of groups" (Bourdieu 1991a: 181). For Steinmetz, the metropolitan field of political representation generated the main positions in the field of competition between officials in the colony, who sought to assert the superiority of their cultural distinction by making claims to ethnographic acuity. Here, I take the field of representation as extending from the metropole into the colony, where resistance accentuates the endemic symbolic struggle between different political parties and class factions. In the attempt to determine the principle of division of the colonial world, the interpretation of resistance becomes a lightning rod for the competition between colonial officials over public opinion in the metropole and over political recognition within the imperial bureaucracy. This interpretation is bounded by both the political-economic and ethnographic rationalities. When the policy implications of the differing political-economic and ethnographic rationalities adopted by colonial officials to understand native resistance contradicted each other, contestations over native policy between different factions of officials ensued, creating the field conditions where the mobilization of resistance and the economic problems resulting from collaboration caused oscillations of policy from governor to succeeding governor.

ASSIMILATING FILIPINOS, PROTECTING MALAYS
America's political-economic interests in retaining the Philippines after the 1898 Spanish-American War were, first, to maintain its "open door" free-trade policy in China by using the strategically located islands as its Asian base and,

second, to develop the agriculturally rich islands to supply American manufacturing with crucial raw materials. These interests called for a strong centralized colonial state that would assimilate the Philippines. The "open door"
interest called for the maintenance of political stability, but the second interest tipped the scale in favor of what President William McKinley termed as
"benevolent assimilation." In 1900, the investigatory Philippine Commission
emphatically placed the Philippines in the path of American's westward
expansion by recommending the territorial plan based on the Jeffersonian
scheme of government for the Louisiana Purchase territories, with Congress
possessing the right to veto the local legislature and the president appointing
the chief executives. The commission considered the British Malaya protectorate and British Commonwealth models but rejected them on the basis that
the Filipinos had advanced beyond bonded servitude to a hereditary aristocracy but were too atrophied by despotism to be a self-governing dominion.
The American strand of anthropological discourse saw Anglo-Saxon America
as the culmination of the westward racial march of civilization completing the
circle by returning to its Asian birthplace (Schueller 1998). In this view, it was
American manifest destiny to displace retrograde Old World powers to revive
the stalled civilization of backward natives.

In contrast, the primary interest for British colonialism in Malaya was
strategic and localized, beginning with attempts to stabilize the Perak sul-
tanate. Political stability in the Malay states intertwined with the economic
interests of the adjacent Straits Settlements of Penang, Malacca, and Singapore (see Map 1). Established as free-trade footholds in the Dutch-dominated
archipelago, the Settlements depended on migrant Chinese labor and tin
capital for their economic life. The 1867 Penang riots inaugurated a decade
of political instability along the west coast of Malaya, when Chinese secret
societies allied with different Malay raja factions in interlocking interethnic
alliances running down the coast took their dispute over peninsular tin
mines into the streets. Afraid of spreading unrest, the British intervened
and sought to separate the political from the economic. After a major rebellion in Perak was crushed in 1875, the British perfected the "indirect rule"
system of placing residents in traditional Malay courts to give sultans advice
they were obliged to accept by treaties of protection. This disentangled the
Malay elites from the Chinese tin economy and kept Chinese miners from
getting embroiled in political contests between rajas, who were subdued by
pensions or bureaucratic incorporation. The preservation of customary authority for colonial rule was in line with British anthropological discourse
on the Malays. The famous naturalist Alfred Wallace argued that Malay so-

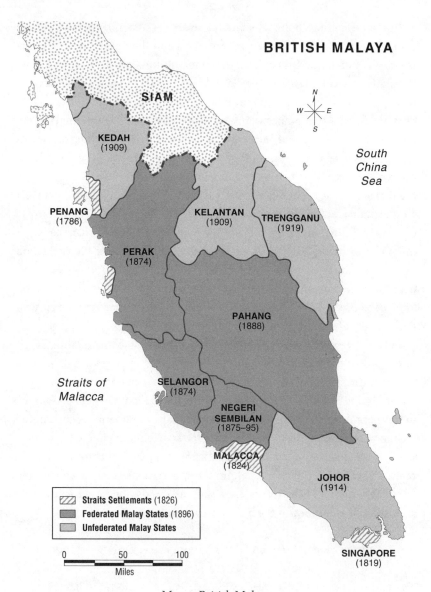

SIAM

KEDAH
(1909)

South
China
Sea

N
W   E
S

PENANG
(1786)

KELANTAN
(1909)

TRENGGANU
(1919)

PERAK
(1874)

PAHANG
(1888)

Straits of
Malacca

SELANGOR
(1874)

NEGERI
SEMBILAN
(1875–95)

MALACCA
(1824)

JOHOR
(1914)

Straits Settlements (1826)
Federated Malay States (1896)
Unfederated Malay States

0   50   100
Miles

SINGAPORE
(1819)

Map 1 · British Malaya.

ciety, like all societies, must obey laws of evolution and pass through "feudalism or servitude, or a despotic paternal government" in "its onward
march from barbarism to civilization" (1986: 264). This was a view that educated generations of colonial officials who sought an ethnographically calibrated government that would preserve and gradually civilize the medieval
Malays.

The metropolitan political-economic interests and anthropological discourses in motivating colonialism in Malaya and the Philippines were diametrically different. This explains the different initial thrust of state formation in the two colonies, with the United States aiming to assimilate Filipinos through centralized rule and the British seeking to protect Malays in residential rule. The Philippines were a grand exercise in American imperial democracy and development, but Malaya was a local affair of keeping the Straits Settlements safe and viable. In their respective anthropological discourses, the Americans aimed to cultivate the Filipinos in their own image, while the British sought to conserve Malay society to allow Malays to grow at their own racial pace. But the interests and discourse were broad enough to accommodate different rationalities. I have argued elsewhere that the larger discourse of medievalism was multivocal enough to allow for vacillation between seeing the natives positively as model medievals and negatively as degenerate medievals, each implying a different political policy (Goh 2007b). The interests discussed above also show ambivalence toward the dual priorities of political stability and economic development. These ambivalences allowed for different interpretations of the best approach to assimilating Filipinos or protecting Malays, of which the most important ones were structured along the lines of conservatism versus technocratism in both cases. This confluence is due to similar American and British metropolitan field conditions in this period, when conservatives were politically dominant but confronted technocrats rising from strong metropolitan state building in the era of post-laissez-faire liberalism. Faced with the varied sociological patterns of resistance and collaboration in the colony, the conservatives saw the solicitation of collaboration and the technocrats saw the imposition of autocratic rule sidelining collaboration as the best approach, respectively.

RESISTANCE AND THE CONSERVATIVE-TECHNOCRAT CONFLICT

The main resistance to American imperialism was the rekindled Filipino nationalist revolution, which the Americans initially supported and then suppressed. When faced with resolute American imperialism, the revolution's mestizo leaders, Western-educated elites occupying the middling professions and lower sectors of the Spanish colonial state, split into three camps. The first group, led by General Emilio Aguinaldo and his revolutionary Filipino peasants, continued to fight. The second group conditionally collaborated, formed the American-backed Federal Party, and sought assimilation as a way to advance their interests as native economic elites. The third group, made up of provincial and Manila political elites, collaborated but sought to undermine colonialism and achieve national independence within the framework of imperial democracy through their Nationalist Party machine. In Malaya, resistance came from immigrant groups whose material force was derived from their importance to the colonial economy. The first group consisted of anti-Qing Chinese secret societies that operated clandestinely as organized crime entities when suppressed. The second group, the Straits Chinese, was made up of conservative Chinese capitalists and their English-educated descendants, who aligned themselves with the empire and sought reluctant British political recognition. The other two groups were Chinese-speaking modernists, who represented diasporic extensions of the nationalist movement in China. One group was aligned with the conservative Kuomintang and sought to negotiate Chinese interests with the colonial state. The other group was clearly anti-imperialist, associated with leftist factions of the nationalist movement. European planters should also be considered as a factor in local resistance, having emerged as an important interest group by the end of the nineteenth century.

In dealing with the varied resistance in the Philippines, the Americans were split along the same lines as in the conflict between mainstream political machines and reformist Progressives that defined U.S. domestic politics in this period (Abinales 2003). The mainstream faction, made up of Republicans and Democrats, offered patronage support to the Filipino elite collaborators, sought a policy of rapprochement with the revolutionaries, and limited land ownership to draw in medium-scale planter capital to partner the collaborators. Conversely, the Progressives, represented by the U.S. Army, career civil servants, and reformist politicians, preferred a hard-line approach to suppress the revolutionaries, discipline the collaborators, and open up the economy with large-scale American capital. Both factions believed their approach was the most rational means for American interests and their ethnographic rationality was the most accurate in American anthropological discourse. The mainstream faction saw the elites as model Westernized students who might be used to achieve political stability and as indigenous mediators of American investments. In contrast, the Progressives saw the elites as degenerate mimics of Spanish caciquism preventing the advancement of the masses, who should be directly civilized by American officials and capital.

In Malaya, the conflict reflected the tension in the concomitant growth of the empire underpinned by the Conservative "new imperialism" of combining indirect rule with the missive of colonial development, and the rise of its welfare state, which bred a professional colonial civil service and a class that saw things in a distinctively technocratic manner (Lloyd 2002). Technocrats not only act to impersonal and functional purposes and formal means-end rationality but also strive for an elevated social distinction that would increase their social position vis-à-vis the governed (Bourdieu 1996b). In the colony, it was already presupposed that the gap between rulers and the governed was natural, that is, racial, thus deepening the technocrat's striving for distinction and his rejection of native collaboration. In Malaya, Conservatives and technocrats interpreted resistance within the frames of metropolitan political-economic interests and anthropological discourse in ways that were rational from their class and political position. The Conservatives tolerated Chinese secret societies and nationalists, co-opted the Straits Chinese in the Settlements, and kept the Chinese separate from the body politic in the states by using the customary authority of Malay rajas, to whom they ethnographically endeared as aristocratic cousins. The Conservatives also sought to work closely with European planters to develop Malaya as an agricultural dominion to displace the economically dominant Chinese. On the other hand, the technocrats tended to treat the Chinese as a dangerous oriental class that must be separated from the body politic by a strong centralized state. For the technocrats, Malay customary authority was a useful constitutional fiction for deepening bureaucratization, in which indirect rule was reworked as a form of colonial constitutional monarchy. Planter interests were treated as a mere factor in overall development favoring British capital.

In both cases, the Conservative-technocrat tussle was evident from the beginning. Appointed in early 1900 to take over pacified provinces, the civil government led by the mainstream faction of Governor, and later U.S. president, William Taft, an Ohio Republican, grew increasingly frustrated with the heavy-handed approach of the Progressive-dominated army. Taft's petitions to the metropolitan government for complete civilian rule with pro-assimilation Filipino elite collaborators were finally answered when an end to the Filipino-American war was declared in July 1902, but the pro-Progressive Theodore Roosevelt metropolitan government allowed the southern Muslim islands of the Philippines to remain in the army's hands as a compromise (see Map 2). In Malaya, after the technocrats led by Governor Cecil Smith and Colonial Secretary William Maxwell, both career colonial civil servants, outlawed and suppressed the powerful Chinese secret societies against the objections of conservative officials in 1890, they turned to federating the Malay protectorates as a step in the centralization of British rule. This sparked a fierce contest in and between London and Singapore that was decided by the incoming Conservative metropolitan government

THE AMERICAN PHILIPPINES

0   100   200

Miles

South China Sea

• Baguio

LUZON

Philippine Sea

Manila

TAYABAS *Bicol Peninsula*

MINDORO

N

W — E

S

SAMAR

VISAYAS

PANAY

Iloilo •

LEYTE

CEBU

NEGROS   **BOHOL**

PALAWAN

Sulu Sea

MINDANAO

Cotabato •

SULU

British North Borneo

Celebes Sea

Map 2 · The American Philippines.

in 1895, when it appointed Charles Mitchell, a colonial military officer cut from the old conservative cloth, as governor. Mitchell modified the federation plan to consolidate Malay customary authority and installed Frank Swettenham, a lower-middle-class colonial officer and aspirant to the planting aristocracy, as resident-general to protect Malay raja and European planter interests from the interests of the Settlements, which was dominated by the Chinese and British technocrats and financiers.

However, these resolutions signified not the end of the tussle but the beginning. The Conservatism-technocratism approaches developed into the contradictory rationalities that drove state formation. When the Conservative collaboration approach was undertaken, political stability was indeed easily achieved, but the native elites or European planters would use state resources for their own material gain and hampered economic development. The latter then affirmed the Progressive view of the mestizo elites as venal caciques in the Philippines and discredited Conservative policy as corrupt in Malaya, thus justifying the hard-line political and instrumental economic approach of the technocrats. Technocrat policies were successful in advancing economic development, but they brought on political instability. The Filipino elites would mobilize against Progressive hard-line rule, disciplining corruption in their own ranks to show that they were good students of imperial democracy, thereby affirming the mainstream ethnographic view and justified the return of the collaboration approach to restore political stability. In Malaya, because the technocrats tended to take repressive measures against Chinese resistance, the ensuing political unrest, with disgruntled planters and Malay aristocrats in tow, swung the position toward Conservative policy. The cycle then began anew and the contradiction deepened, creating the trajectory that defined colonial state formation.

The Progressives made two political comebacks: the first time during the 1904–1905 governorship of Luke Wright, a close Roosevelt associate, who took hard-line action against revolutionary peasant remnants and mestizo elite power (Paredes 1988); and the second time from 1911 to 1913, when Progressive cabinet members of Governor Cameron Forbes, representing the upper chamber of the bicameral legislature, staged a legislative revolt that caused political stalemate with the nationalist-dominated Philippine Assembly (Jenista 1971). Filipino elite graft and pork-barrel politics linked to mainstream Republican collaboration policy preceded both Progressive reactions, involving first the *Federalista* Manila elites and then the *Nacionalista* provincial elites. Each Progressive reaction led to elite mobilization that brought about political instability, which greatly discomforted the metropolitan government and led to the return to the mainstream Republican formula for elite collaboration. In the first Progressive reaction, the Federalistas withdrew cooperation and threatened to unite with the Nationalist Party. Taft, now the metropolitan secretary of war who oversaw the Philippines, removed Wright and appointed James Smith, a conservative Democratic lawyer from California, as governor, who subsequently courted the cleaner Nacionalistas after they won the 1907 Assembly elections. Nacionalista corruption grew under Forbes, scion of the famous business family and Taft's protégé, which led to the second Progressive reaction. The resulting legislative deadlock paved the way for Governor Francis Harrison, a Tammany Hall Democratic congressman appointed by Woodrow Wilson, who won the presidency after Taft and Roosevelt split the Republican vote along mainstream and Progressive lines, to deepen collaboration in his Filipinization policy.

In Malaya, the technocrats made an extended reaction and a short abortive comeback, the first during the 1904–1919 governorships of John Anderson, a rising imperial technocrat, and his successor Arthur Young, who accelerated administrative and political centralization and expanded British protection into five neighboring Malay states; and the second during the 1927–1929 governorship of Hugh Clifford, an eminent imperial statesman who rose through the ranks starting in the Malayan colonial service. The opposition of Swettenham, Anderson's predecessor, to the freeing of indentured Indian labor and mismanagement of labor welfare led to chronic labor shortages, which caused agricultural development to falter to the discredit of Conservative policy. Anderson resolved the economic problems, and Malaya became a major rubber-producing economy. But this came at the price of political instability, as the technocratic hard-line policy could not accommodate the anti-imperialist nationalism that inflamed the Chinese population. Boycotts, strikes, and riots broke out in 1905, 1908, and 1912 and escalated into martial law during the protests of 1919. From 1920 to 1926, Governor Laurence Guillemard, a Conservative political appointee, attempted to solve the problems by reviving Malay elite and Straits Chinese collaboration through his decentralization policy.

Collaboration policies stretched the contradictory rationalities to the limit. Mainstream and Progressive Republican attempts to undermine Filipinization failed because the nationalists organized independence campaigns to the metropole. Congress promised independence and delegated greater powers of government, leaving only the top three executive positions in American hands. Harrison extended Filipinization to the colonial economy by using state resources to develop the agro-industrial ventures of politically connected Filipino elites (Stanley 1974: 202–225, 249–262). American assimilation was thus turned into indirect rule, a protectorate in all but name, in which political stability was achieved at the cost of a centralized colonial state and the price of elite corruption. Conversely, British protection had turned into direct rule, a central government in customary guises, in which rapid economic development came at the price of instability. The decentralization policy attempted to reverse this, but the contradictory rationalities balanced each other in a stalemate. Technocrat and planter opposition bogged down decentralization. Adding to the political turmoil was increasing Malay smallholder discontentment with state restriction of rubber production, which was plagued by widespread corruption because of European planter involvement in implementation. From 1927 to 1929, Clifford tried to reverse decentralization to maintain a strong state to control rising Malay and Chinese restlessness, but the Conservative metropolitan government stopped him and the stalemate continued.

POLITICAL CRISIS AND COLONIAL DECAY

State formation was at a crossroads in both cases in the 1920s, with a number of logical policy options to pursue, each having its own political-economic implications. The Republicans, who returned to power in 1920, could bring Democratic policy to its logical conclusion and grant Filipino commonwealth self-government, or moderate the policy by reviving Taft-era collaboration, or choose the Progressive option of reasserting direct rule. The Labor Party that won power for the first time in Britain in 1929 could achieve political stability by intensifying Conservative decentralization, or proceed with strong state building by backing the technocrats in reversing decentralization, or politically accommodate the Chinese and build a fragmented multiclass state. The technocrat option of strong centralized state building was eventually chosen. Why was the hard-line choice made in both cases? This is more puzzling given that the logical choice, by virtue of political ideology and rationality, of the mainstream Republican administration would be the moderate collaboration policy and that of the radical-liberal Labor administration the Chinese accommodation policy.

First, the explanation partly lies in the relative weakness of the metropolitan administrations. Warren Harding represented American isolationism and therefore deferred to factions with more experience in imperial affairs. Harding sent Cameron Forbes and General Leonard Wood, representing respectively the mainstream and Progressive Republican factions, on a fact-finding mission to the Philippines, which reported that the problem was the venality of mestizo elite neopatrimonialism in the form of the Nationalist Party machine and recommended the resumption of the governor's direct rule authority. This was Wood's idea, who believed a strong Governor General would resolve the situation in the Philippines. In the case of Malaya, the Labor administration was a novice in government and, similarly, deferred to experienced bureaucrats. But even the Colonial Office bureaucrats were locked in stalemate over the acknowledgment of Chinese political claims. In the end, the only agreement was that the Malayan problem was a Chinese one.

Second, in both cases, the eventual decision was made to appoint a governor with strong ethnographic knowledge of resisting native groups. Harding appointed Wood, who was a military commander in Cuba and then Taft's Philippines. The Labor government appointed Cecil Clementi, the governor of Hong Kong and an Oxford-trained Chinese orientalist. Clementi came from a family of colonial officials, which included his uncle Cecil Smith, the technocrat who set the Federation into motion. Wood and Clementi interpreted resistance according to technocratic rationalities, their belief in the correctness of their views further strengthened by their own experience in the colonies. As military governor of Mindanao from 1903 to 1906, Wood brutally crushed Moro resistance in the southern Philippines. When he was governor of Hong Kong, Clementi argued that China was not a nation but a collection of states to justify his military action against anti-imperialists in neighboring Canton.

Third, the contradictory rationalities logically entailed technocrat policies to follow the decentralization and Filipinization policies. The key justification for technocrat policies was economic malaise and corruption that accompanied conservative policy, which gave credence to the technocrat ethnographic views. In Malaya, the botching of rubber restriction because of close planter involvement discredited Conservative policy. In the Philippines, Democratic policy achieved political stability at the cost of the state coming close to bankruptcy in aiding Filipino agro-industrialists. Indeed, both Clementi and Wood successfully solved the economic problems with their hard-line and instrumentally rational approach that brushed aside the collaborators. Clementi successfully implemented the second round of rubber restriction and encouraged native agricultural development, while Wood brought the state back to financial health.

But trapped in the contradictory rationalities induced by the interaction between resistance, interests, and ethnography, political instability followed their successes. To recover the governor's autocratic power, Wood sought to separate the executive and legislative arms fused by Filipinization, micromanaged the government departments, and exercised his veto power freely to reduce the patronage power of the nationalist political machine. Wood then took steps to divest state-financed Filipino enterprises and state-owned corporations to American investors, while seeking to parcel huge tracts of land to American corporations. In response, the nationalists embarked on a campaign of noncooperation, caused legislative deadlocks, mobilized the masses with independence campaigns, and launched independence missions to Congress to discredit Wood's rule through metropolitan publicity. The images the nationalists deployed were militarism and imperialism, contrasting Wood's military background and military aides with Filipino civilian government and democracy. Clementi's approach in Malaya was no less autocratic. Clementi suppressed Chinese political activities, banished vocal nationalists, regulated Chinese immigration, sought to "Malayanize" the Chinese, and brushed aside Straits Chinese collaborators. Under the cover of customary authority, Clementi cultivated the Malay sultans by holding a record total of five durbars to push through a "decentralization" program that would unite the Malay states and Settlements into a single pan-Malayan entity under his executive rule. The sultans, Clementi argued, were a buffer between the British government and the Chinese. This narrow definition of customary authority as exuding from Malay rulers politicized the Malay elite bureaucrats, and they went on to found modern Malay nationalist organizations (Roff 1994: 235–247). Malayan civic groups and planters objected to the veiled centralization while Conservative and liberal officials led by the chief secretary in the Federation objected to Clementi becoming the "fifth sultan." Straits Chinese leaders in the legislatures broke decorum to express deep Chinese discontent. The Malayan Communist Party grew its support among the Chinese masses rapidly in this political climate.

In line with the contradictory rationalities, the ensuing political instability led the metropolitan governments to pursue the conservative policy options of favoring political stability. After Wood's death during his trip back to the United States to obtain unconditional metropolitan support in 1927, mainstream Republican governors were appointed to revive collaboration with the elites to salvage American rule, but they quickly learned that it was no longer tenable because of the nationalists' political stranglehold. When the Democrats returned to power in 1933, American rule was abandoned and the U.S.-Philippines relationship began to move to a postcolonial patron-client statism. The autonomous Philippine Commonwealth was established in 1935, bringing the Democrats' Filipinization policy to a logical conclusion. Clementi's autocratic policy was pursued by disobeying metropolitan directives and presenting the metropole with fait accompli actions and durbar announcements that could not be withdrawn without the loss of British prestige. Clementi's insubordination eventually caused the metropole to remove him. In his stead, Shenton Thomas, a Victorian Conservative with a clerical background, revived Guillemard's decentralization policy and sought Straits Chinese collaboration.

While the contradictory rationalities account for the political instability and its resolution, they do not fully account for the instability developing into crisis proportions. Here we need to return to the strong ethnographic rationality held by Wood and Clementi, which blinded them to political realities and caused them pursued their hard-line policies without compromise or moderation. Because he saw the Chinese as an ancient Oriental race capable of only understanding despotic rule, Clementi failed to see the intricacies of Chinese nationalist resistance and saw the Chinese as posing a monolithic problem. He suppressed the anti-communist Malayan Kuomintang because he saw it as a subversive anti-Manchu secret society rather than a modern political organization, thus creating a political vacuum that the communists filled. Similarly, Wood was in denial that the masses desired independence and acted in ways that reinforced the nationalist portrayal of him as an autocratic imperialist. Thus, when the Nacionalistas legislated twice for a plebiscite on independence, Wood vetoed both bills because he believed that certain results favoring independence would not reflect the people's real desire. In his disdain for the nationalists, Wood unwittingly undermined the only viable opposition to the nationalists. Wood solicited the support of the nascent leftist *Democrata* Party, but this backfired as the Nacionalistas portrayed the Democratas as pro-imperialists, and the latter quickly lost electoral ground.

The contradictory rationalities also cannot fully explain the difference in the tail end of the two trajectories. The Philippine Commonwealth brought the deepening contradictory rationalities to a logical end in the beginning of decolonization, but in Malaya, the contradiction remained at a stalemate and decolonization would have to wait until the 1950s. The key factor lies in the different sociological character of resistance in the two colonies. While the Filipino nationalists were a coalition of Hispanicized elites straddling the urban and rural, agricultural and industrial classes, the Malay elites were traditional aristocrats who lived on state pensions or occupied the lower rungs of the bureaucracy. The Filipino elites were able to exploit the contradictory rationalities by working the democratic levers of the imperial regime, but the patrimonial Malay rajas knew only to make personal representations against technocrats to the Colonial Office, which was itself becoming an established bureaucratic unit. They were unable to exploit the levers of parliamentary democracy and British public opinion. Segregated from the colonial body politic, the Chinese nationalists had little effect on imperial politics, while the Anglicized Straits Chinese leaders had few organic links with the immigrant Chinese masses. Besides, Chinese resistance was fragmented and erupted in different forms and separate incidents. The growth of the Filipino nationalist movement deepened the contradictory rationalities toward decolonization, but spurting Chinese resistance only justified the return of the collaboration approach, which the Malay elites could not exploit to push the contradictory rationalities to a resolution. It was only after Malay nationalism had matured in the postwar years that it became a major factor in bringing the contradictory rationalities to its decolonization conclusion.

CONCLUSION

I have shown that political interpretations of resistance vis-à-vis metropolitan imperial interests and anthropological discourse by colonial officials generated contradictory political-economic and ethnographic rationalities, which caused colonial state building to develop in a trajectory of oscillating policies, shifting between key resistance events and economic problems caused by collaboration. This study disarticulates neo-Weberian theory in several ways. It suggests that the autonomous state operating with formal-legal rationality, held as an ideal type against which all states are evaluated, cannot possibly exist. We cannot get more "rational" in this respect than the cases of colonial technocrats seeking to impose modern state institutions on alien peoples, but as I have shown in the cases of the Wood and Clementi governorships, the formal-legal rationality of their centralization policies was shot through with the sociocultural rationality of their ethnographic views. This goes much further than Skocpol's (1985: 15) caveat that autonomous state actions cannot be disinterested because, at the very least, they reinforce the authority and social status of state officials. In my study, the social interests and cultural beliefs of society appear to go right into the heart of the state to affect key policy decisions that drive the direction of state formation. This puts the relative autonomy of the state and the state-society dichotomy into question. In this light, the state, even cohesive-capitalist states, appears more like an institutional field where social groups stake and contest their claims.

The influence of sociocultural rationality in state building also throws into question the neo-Weberian proposition that the formal rationality of political economy informing modern state formation is the counterpart to the Weberian proposition that the formal rationality of economics is becoming increasingly dominant in the modern world (Levine 2005). In Weberian terms, it seems that the substantive ethnographic rationality implied by Steinmetz's (2007b) study and mine and the substantive patrimonial rationality implied by Adams (2005a) continue to inflect rationalizing modernity not in a peripheral and residual manner but in a significantly constitutive fashion. This criticism applies to rational-choice models of state formation, which tend to induct these values as the irrelevant ends of rational actors whose calculations of means invariably lead to the formation of modern state power and authority as the most efficient means to accomplish those aims. Here, local resistance is reduced to cost and liabilities in the calculations of rational state actors. But as the general failure in accomplishing the original ends of colonial state building expressed in the trajectories and the smaller-scale failures in achieving policy success during each governorship expressed in the oscillation of policies in my two cases show, the calculations of putatively rational state actors were faulty precisely because they were shot through with the "irrationalities" of ethnographic meanings.

In my study, I have taken a leaf from Steinmetz's (2007a) theoretical model, which focuses on the sociopolitical locations of colonial officials and their ethnographic rationalities in driving state formation. However, I have placed resistance as a central factor in the contestations of colonial officials rather than their competition for metropolitan cultural distinctions. The controversial governorships of Wood and Clementi, who had reached the pinnacle of their standing in metropolitan society when they resolutely pursued hard-line policies that threatened to degrade their class-cultural standing, suggest that their experience of resistance was at this moment more important than metropolitan distinctions. More important, resistance produced contradictory rationalities, creating a pattern of oscillating policies that limited the range of possible "rational" policy options and therefore narrowed the field of cultural distinctions and actor motivation. Thus, liberal officials in Malaya were mostly sidelined by the Conservative-technocrat contest, and the Democrats could only deepen mainstream Republican collaboration policy to create a Philippine client state but not pursue substantive democratization befitting Wilsonian ideals. Therein lay the limits to rationality in state formation, when the rationalizations of local resistance to the imposition of domination give rise to contradictions in the very exercise of state power and authority, creating historical modernisms moving to the rhythm of hybrid rationalities that postcolonial societies have inherited.

CHRONOLOGY OF BRITISH COLONIALISM
IN MALAYA

1826	Straits Settlements established with Penang, Singapore, and Malacca under British East India Company rule.
1867	Straits Settlements established as a Crown Colony under direct rule from London. Chinese secret societies riot in Penang.
1867–1874	Chinese secret societies and their Malay chieftain allies fight each other for control of tin mines in peninsular Malaya.
1874	Malay sultanates of Perak and Selangor placed under British protection and administered by British residents reporting to the governor of the Settlements.
1875–1876	Assassination of resident James W. W. Birch leads to the Perak War.
1877–1889	Perak resident Hugh Low stabilizes Perak and establishes indirect rule.
1887–1893	Governorship of Cecil Clementi Smith. Bureaucratic consolidation of British protectorate administration.
1890	Suppression of Chinese secret societies.
1894–1900	Governorship of Charles Mitchell. Promotion of planter colonialism.
1896	Federated Malay States established under the administration of Resident-General Frank Swettenham.
1901–1903	Governorship of Frank Swettenham. Planter economic problems.
1904–1911	Governorship of John Anderson. Centralization reforms.
1909–1919	Unfederated Malay states of Kelantan, Kedah, Perlis (1909), Johor (1914), and Trengganu (1919) come under British protection.
1911–1919	Governorship of Arthur Young. Centralization reforms.

1919	Chinese anti-imperialist boycotts and riots lead to martial law rule in Penang and Singapore.
1920–1927	Governorship of Laurence Guillemard. Decentralization reforms. Rubber restriction controversies.
1927–1929	Governorship of Hugh Clifford. Attempted reversal of decentralization.
1930–1934	Governorship of Cecil Clementi. Centralization reforms. Political crisis.
1934–1942	Governorship of Shenton Thomas. Decentralization revived.
1937	Labor unrest involving Indian and Chinese workers.

CHRONOLOGY OF AMERICAN COLONIALISM IN THE PHILIPPINES

1565–1821	The Philippines ruled as territory of the viceroyalty of New Spain.
1821–1898	The Philippines ruled directly from Madrid.
1896	Philippine revolution begins.
1898	Spanish-American War leads to purchase of the Philippines by the United States.
1899	First Philippine Republic established by revolutionaries under General Emilio Aguinaldo.
1899–1913	Philippine-American War leads to suppression of the Philippine revolution.
1900	First Philippine Commission submits recommendations for civil government. Second Philippine Commission formed to establish civil government. Federal Party formed and supported by Commission.
1902	The United States declares the end of the Philippine-American War. Guerrilla resistance continues.
1901–1903	Governorship of William H. Taft. Cultivation of Federal Party collaborators.

1904–1905	Governorship of Luke E. Wright. Centralization reforms. Federal Party opposes Wright.
1906–1909	Governorship of James F. Smith. Cultivation of Nationalist Party collaborators.
1907	Nationalist Party wins elections for the lower-chamber Philippine Assembly.
1909–1912	Governorship of Cameron Forbes. Cultivation of Nationalist Party collaborators.
1911	American Commissioners stage legislative revolt and deadlock government.
1913–1921	Governorship of Democrat Francis B. Harrison. Filipinization of government. Financial crisis.
1916	U.S. Congress promises eventual independence for the Philippines.
1921–1927	Governorship of Leonard Wood. Reversal of Filipinization. Political crisis.
1923	Nationalists launch noncooperation movement.
1927–1932	Governorships of Henry L. Stimson, Dwight F. Davis, and Theodore Roosevelt Jr. Attempted cultivation of Nationalist Party collaborators.
1932	U.S. Congress grants the Philippines independence after a ten-year transitional Commonwealth government.
1933–1935	Governorship of Democrat Frank Murphy. Preparations for self-rule.
1935	Philippine Commonwealth established.
1935–1942	Peasant unrests in central Luzon.

NOTES

This paper was presented at the Sixteenth International Sociological Association Congress of Sociology, Durban, South Africa, July 23–29, 2006. I would like to thank Rafael Wittek and other participants at the session "Limits of Rationality in Historical Sociology" for their comments.

Conclusion
Understanding Empire
RAEWYN CONNELL

EMPIRE AND SOCIOLOGY

The creation, crisis, and transformation of global empires is one of the basic facts of human social experience in recent time. What was truly the first world war stretched for about four hundred years, and by the end of it the armies of Europe and North America had conquered, or brought under indirect control, almost the whole population of the earth. New ways of living, once unimaginable, are still being generated by global social forces operating on the terrain created by the old empires.

It is logical that sociology, conceived a century and a half ago as the general science of society, should be concerned with empire. That has not always been recognized: the stories told to students about the discipline's history often read as if the sociological imagination were walled up in Europe and North America. The impressive array of studies in this book provides a definitive proof that sociology has not been so narrow-minded.

The narratives in Part 1, tracing the development of the discipline in each of five imperial powers—Russia, France, Italy, Germany, and the United States—show significantly different pathways. But in every case, we can see sociologists involved, from the earliest days of the discipline, with issues about colonization, imperial power, hierarchies of race, "primitive" societies and their contrast with the "advanced," social progress/development, and a host of related questions.

The discipline has, as Steinmetz nicely puts it, many "entanglements" with empire. Indeed there are so many that this must be regarded as one of the formative issues in the making of sociology.

One consequence is the making of sociological theories about empire—explanations of imperialism, classifications of empires, accounts of the dynamics of particular empires. The studies in Part 2 are examples of that kind of sociological reasoning, showing particularly how it can illuminate the contemporary world and the contending strategies of the United States and China.

The case studies in Part 3 provide empirical refinements of the sociology of empires. Here we examine the different trajectories of particular colonies within the one empire, or the contrasts between empires, or sometimes their convergences. In these studies, sociology wrestles with the complexities of countervailing power, the ambiguous role of colonized elites, the dilemmas of imperial managers, the character of the colonial state, and the changing structure of colonial society.

All this adds up to a large, and newly vigorous, branch of sociology. Yet the connection between sociology and empire does not end with the sociology of empire. There is also, if I can put it this way, empire *in* sociology.

Sociology as an organized social practice, an institutionalized formation of knowledge, was created in the imperial centers at the high tide of direct imperial expansion. Sociology drew much of its significant data from the knowledge dividend of empire—from the imperial archive, as Semyonov, Mogilner, and Gerasimov note in their discussion of Kovalevski in chapter 2. As Go (in chapter 2) and Kurasawa (in chapter 6) demonstrate with a wealth of detail, an interest in empire and willingness to appropriate its data were as common among the first generation of sociologists under the presidents as under the czars.

It would be extraordinary if the discipline's concepts were not influenced by this situation. Indeed they were and are. For instance, Zimmerman shows the formative traces of colonization and empire in the thought of Max Weber (see chapter 5). The comparative method that Durkheim saw as the heart of sociology is exactly the colonizer's gaze on the colonized within the epistemology of empire.

Coming forward to recent sociological thought, presumptions of global difference, the centrality of the metropole, and appropriation of the experience of the colonized—that is to say, an imperialist epistemology—underlie the general theories put forward by Coleman, Giddens, and Bourdieu (Connell 2006). Sociology certainly has other possibilities. But the depth to which sociological thought has been shaped by its location in empire should not be forgotten. This is a realm where constant critique is needed.

KNOWLEDGE ABOUT EMPIRE

The discussions of empire in professional sociology exist, of course, in a larger context of public debate and social science. Sociological perspectives are often missing from this wider discourse. Global political economy is a significant case. The pioneering work of Amin (1969), whose *Accumulation on a World Scale* is still valuable forty years on, like the widely read work of David Harvey (2005), rest on a schematic class analysis that misses most of the social dynamics and elides the world of institutions.

Even more strikingly, Hardt and Negri's famous *Empire* (2000), which in the recent literature on globalization uniquely captures the violence, fear, and corruption generated by global power dynamics, deliberately downplays the arena of the social. They argue that the "mediations" provided by civil society are withering away, that institutions from the family to the welfare state are in decline, and that postmodern change is sweeping all of human life into a grand confrontation between Empire and Multitude. Like Negri's earlier work as a radical theorist and activist in Italy, this dispenses with empirical study of the social (Connell 2011). It rules out in advance such sociological innovation as Stacey's (2011) vivid cross-national study of changing family forms and the political struggles around them.

Sociology is needed for an adequate understanding of contemporary empire as much as historical sociology is needed for understanding empires of the past. But whose sociology?

The literature of the sociology of empires, like sociology in general, has mostly been written by white middle-class men in the global North. To make this observation is not a denunciation or a guilt trip. In my view, we should welcome contributions to these issues from any direction, including white middle-class men from the global North. But as sociologists, we should be willing to raise sociology-of-knowledge questions about our own formations of knowledge and join the decolonization of sociology proposed by Gutiérrez Rodríguez, Boatcă, and Costa (2010).

Sociology is part of a global structure of knowledge production, which has a powerful tendency to centralize the theoretical moment of science in the global North and to create intellectual dependence or "extroversion" in the periphery (Hountondji 2002). This hegemonized academic knowledge production is in tension with the social multiplicity of knowledge—opening questions about what Harding (2008) has called "sciences from below."

As sociologists concerned with empire, we have to recognize that knowledge about imperialism is not confined to the imperial powers. The colonized also know what is going on. And the intellectuals of colonized societies work as hard as the intellectuals of the metropole to understand the process—perhaps harder, as it can be a matter of life and death for them.

Several of the studies in this book call attention to the ideas of groups in colonized societies. In chapter 14, Chae speaks of the intellectuals of Korea under Japanese imperial power, drawing on liberal and socialist ideas to contest the occupier's ideology. In chapter 12, Gowda describes the governing elite of one of the princely states in British India, crafting a developmentalist ideology from a position of political weakness. Goh describes the importance of Filipino resistance and collaboration for the shifting strategies of U.S. colonialism in the Philippines (see chapter 17). Beyond these cases is a broad arena of thought about colonialism and contemporary empire that comes from anticolonial struggles, postcolonial critique, peace movements, global feminism, environmental struggles, and more.

The knowledge and ideas that come from these sources is not easily merged with academic sociology. There are deep fissures and contestations here, arising ultimately from the violence and the split culture of empire itself. For this reason, I consider a "field" analysis of the sociology of empire not adequate to the terrain; to put it more bluntly, this would limit our intellectual resources to those conforming to a specific Northern construction of the problems. There is more wealth—and more difficulty—to be found. It is perhaps in the tensions and synergies between differently situated formations of knowledge that we find best possibilities for new understandings of empire.

SOUTHERN THEORISTS OF EMPIRE

Let me give two examples of what is to be found by opening the lens wider: texts that have been accessible for a long time but are little noticed except by area specialists.

The first is a book that was once much better known. It is called *The Three Principles of the People* (San Min Chu I) and is a transcription of lectures delivered in 1924 by Sun Yat-sen—replacing a book whose draft manuscript was destroyed in the civil wars that followed the overthrow of the Qing dynasty. Sun was not an academic social scientist; he was a medical doctor who became a political activist and briefly president of the first Republic of China. In the 1920s, his party, the Kuomintang, was reorganizing and needed a statement of principles. Sun, nearing the end of his life, produced a complex text, part theory and speculation, part commentary on current affairs, part programmatic and organizational.

It is of interest in many ways, the most immediate being that it provides a brilliant conspectus of the world of imperialism in the early twentieth century, as understood by someone who had struggled against both internal and external empire, with many setbacks but also with notable success. Sun discusses population movements, economic domination, interventionist states, rival empires, war, and the disintegrating effect of outside imperialism on culture and politics in China.

Sun is anti-imperialist to the boot heels. But he is also critical of simple-minded anti-Westernism, as seen in the Boxer movement. Sun is respectful of European culture (offering, for instance, a perceptive critique of Rousseau). He develops arguments about how to combine Chinese tradition with European science and technology—long anticipating postcolonial theorists on "hybridity." This includes a concern with social technologies, such as divided-powers constitutions. Sun is also interested in other anticolonial movements, such as Gandhi's noncooperation movement in India.

There is more, including a critique of Marxism that raises issues about embodiment and the natural environment. Sun is no social radical; he has a traditional Chinese intellectual's respect for social hierarchy and is antagonistic to unionism. But he offers an extraordinarily interesting account of social dynamics in the periphery of the European empires, which is worth fresh attention.

My second example, from the following decade, is a very different kind of text. In 1938 Jomo Kenyatta published *Facing Mount Kenya: The Tribal Life of the Gikuyu*. This was a monograph in the style made famous by Malinowski (who contributed a preface) and in sociology by the Chicago School. It covered economic organization, kinship, religion, law, and so on, in an elaborate and sophisticated presentation of a non-European way of life. What made it unique in its day, and still unusual, is that it was a full-scale ethnography written by one of the subjects of the ethnography.

Kenyatta was at the time a leading figure in Gikuyu politics. He had been chosen leader of his age cohort, became general secretary of the Gikuyu Central Association, launched the first Gikuyu journal, and was spokesman for the indigenous people at the colonial government's inquiries on land issues. He became the leader of an independence movement and head of the postcolonial government, but in 1938 that was still in the future. What is really remarkable about *Facing Mount Kenya* is that Kenyatta was able to use the genre of a social-scientific monograph to contest colonialism and thus reverse the usual complicity between social science and colonial administration.

This is not only because he plainly narrates episodes of violence, deception, and greed on the part of the British colonizers, of a kind usually glossed over by ethnography at the time. More profoundly, Kenyatta contests colonialism's disdain for the colonized—the root of all Northern social science's discourse about "primitive," "backward," or "developing" societies—by turning social theory against colonialism. He picks up social-scientific functionalism and says, in effect, here among the colonized we have a fully functioning and well-integrated social system: "On concluding this study it cannot be too strongly emphasised that the various sides of Gikuyu life here described are the parts of an integrated culture. No single part is detachable; each has its context and is fully understandable only in relation to the whole" (p. 309).

But the Europeans—who, Kenyatta observes, cannot even keep the peace in Europe—have set about wrecking this social order for their own purposes, and their guns and railways give them the power to do so. *Facing Mount Kenya* is, among other things, a remarkable literary achievement, a beautiful lament for the social worlds destroyed by global empire. Kenyatta's successors are still struggling with the long-term consequences.

SOUTHERN ISSUES: LAND AND GENDER

One of the issues emphasized by Kenyatta is land. The Gikuyu, following generous local custom, had allowed the new arrivals the temporary use of land—and thus lost it. The British, Kenyatta argues, misinterpreted the Gikuyu land tenure system in other ways too that made it easier to expropriate land, especially the best land—"the land which was, and still is, the soul of the people" (1938: 213).

Here Kenyatta was opening up a major issue about imperialism, which sociological theory almost entirely misses. There is little about the land in mainstream sociology in any period, except in the marginal field of rural sociology. This is not a question of abstract "space" but of actual land (and for that matter sea) with its varied productive capacities and its densely layered social meanings. Anyone who is not familiar with the complex uses and meanings of land for an indigenous people, the way a specific landscape is part of a changing social order, should read Somerville and Perkins's wonderful (2010) *Singing the Coast*, based on the survival of a small indigenous community in eastern Australia.

The seizing of land for occupation by a settler population, driving local people off it and shattering their social structure, is a constitutive operation of settler colonialism, as shown in Sol Plaatje's ([1916] 1982) classic *Native*

Life in South Africa. The process also occurred on a vast scale in North America, Australasia, and the southern cone of South America. As Clarno shows in chapter 16, this process continues to characterize settler colonialism in contemporary Israel.

A somewhat different process, the seizing of land without settlement, transforming colonized populations into plantation workforces, is the main economic basis of exploitation colonialism, from the sugar islands of the West Indies to the rubber plantations of Malaya. As Pula shows in chapter 13, the application of colonial power to urban land is also a feature of empire. The Italians did not get far, but the Spanish and British did, and modern New Delhi and Ciudad México are their legacy. The Chinese regime seems at the moment to be doing it internally, shattering and rebuilding cities such as Guangdong.

As a good ethnographer, Kenyatta also talks about gender relations. He describes kinship, marriage and sexuality, and gender as a factor in politics and economics. Some of this is tough stuff: he acknowledges that Gikuyu women are excluded from government and differentially valued—compensation for the death of a man was ten cows, for a woman three. Kenyatta defends female genital mutilation on the grounds that it makes girls marriageable, declaring the indigenous, not the missionaries, as the authorities on its meaning—a position some big men in postcolonial times also have adopted on gender issues.

Here Kenyatta opened up another important and troubling terrain for the sociology of empire. The literature of this subject is almost wholly written by men, citing other men and rarely women. The topics it mostly deals with—states, elites, geopolitics, macroeconomics, war, conquest, and rule—are coded masculine in metropolitan culture or, to rephrase that, are popularly understood to be men's business. But men often do not notice the gendered character of men's business; and that seems to be true of much of the sociology of empire.

But empire is gendered. There is now a considerable feminist literature pointing this out, both historically and in relation to contemporary empire (Eisenstein 2009; Harcourt 2009). The workforce of conquest was overwhelmingly male. Conquest and land seizure shattered local gender orders, resulting in a centuries-long epidemic of rape and appropriation of women's bodies for domestic labor. Gendered workforces were forcibly created in plantation economies and continue to be created today in *maquiladoras* and export processing zones. Missionaries conducted a worldwide offensive against non-European sexualities and gender arrangements, which is continued today in homophobic pogroms. Is this hard to see? The gender processes are in front of the eyes of any scholar looking at the documentation of colonial societies.

As Ashis Nandy brilliantly showed in *The Intimate Enemy* (1983), empire also affects gender among the colonizers—reshaping images and practices of masculinity. There is growing research on the way colonizing powers set about creating patterns of masculinity among settler communities that were adequate to the task of imperial government, that is, holding subject races down. Morrell's (2001) historical work on colonial Natal is a paradigmatic example. In fact, the whole subject of race relations in empire is inextricably bound up with gender and sexuality. The point is perfectly illustrated by the repressive laws introduced during the colonization of Papua New Guinea: the book by an Australian historian narrating the colonizers' paranoia is pointedly called *"Not a White Woman Safe"* (Inglis 1974).

NEW EMPIRE

A great deal of effort has gone into understanding the structures of global power that crystallized after the independence struggles and decolonization of South and Southeast Asia, northern and southern Africa, and the Pacific island colonies. Rightly so. The historical experience of Latin America showed that formal independence need not mean the end of colonial social structures, nor did it prevent the intrusion of new forms of external power, achieved first by Britain and then by the United States (Cardoso and Faletto 1979).

Though we can get lost in definitional debates, I have no difficulty in seeing the late twentieth-century combination of investment from the metropole, trade dependence, military coercion, one-way cultural influence, and political manipulation as a new form of empire. There are different kinds of empire, as Mann rightly argues in chapter 7, and particular empires have changed structurally in the past. Historians speak of the "second British empire," and certainly the heaven-born bureaucrats of the late nineteenth-century Raj do seem to have operated a different system of power from the robber barons of the old East India Company. Still it was a ruthless empire, based on extremely brutal suppression of the independence movements of 1857. Any tendency to sentimentalize Victoria's empire can be cured by contemplating what the same empire was doing to the indigenous peoples of eastern Australia at the time, to get its hands on wool, grain, and gold (Reynolds 1982).

One of the concerns of this book is whether a new form of empire is currently being constructed. There are certainly pointers that way. Bergesen's description in chapter 10 of Chinese intervention in Africa as "surgical imperialism" is one. This does seem to have different characteristics from the Washington Consensus version of globalization—though the Chinese regime's cold-blooded deals with local oligarchies and dictatorships strongly recall the U.S. regime's deal making during the Cold War.

Clarno's careful comparison of the segregationist practices of the South African and Israeli regimes also suggests significant change. This is not so much in the greater technical resources of the Israelis as jailers of an indigenous population. The selective murder of Palestinian activists can be matched in other cases, such as the Phoenix murder program run by the United States against the National Liberation Front in Vietnam. The novelty is more in the changing economic meaning of the segregation. In the context of global neoliberalism, Clarno argues, the Palestinians are becoming one more surplus population, unemployed and unemployable, rather than the labor force the regime needs. As close-focus studies of Palestinian communities show, the violent disruption of ties to the land, and the social order built on village agriculture, is a key to this situation (Hanafi 2006).

I have been interested in how the "metropole apparatus" of the old imperial centers, that is, the institutionalized capacity of colonizing societies to sustain imperial dominance, has increasingly shifted into transnational space (Connell 2007). In chapter 8, Scheppele identifies one such mechanism: international law in the first decade of the twenty-first century, creating a permanent "state of exception" to facilitate the war on terror, with local regimes using the international agreements to legitimate domestic repression.

If Scheppele is right about law and Clarno is right about the situation of the Palestinians, the combination points to a dynamic in the growth of the international security state, legitimating arbitrary power in relation to populations whom the international economy treats as rubbish people—and who are made landless whether by occupation, war, or economic pressure. The current hostility toward refugees and "illegal immigrants" in the United States, the European Union, and Australia suggests that a popular base for this mechanism is being created in the rich countries.

Empires change, and the change is not necessarily predictable, if Mann's diagnosis of the irrationality at the heart of U.S. military imperialism is right. But we can do a lot to understand what is happening, and that understanding can be an asset for democracy. The sociology of empire, as represented in this book, is opening up profoundly important issues with which social scientists and social movements need to engage.

Bibliography

Aaronson, Susan. 2001. *Taking Trade to the Streets: The Lost History of Public Efforts to Shape Globalization*. Ann Arbor: University of Michigan Press.

Abbott, Andrew, and James T. Sparrow. 2007. "Hot War, Cold War: The Structures of Sociological Action, 1940–1955." Pp. 281–313 in Calhoun (2007).

Abdel-Malek, Anouar. 1971. *Sociologie de l'impérialisme*. Paris: Editions anthropos.

Abend, Gabriel. 2006. "Styles of Sociological Thought: Sociologies, Epistemologies, and the Mexican and U.S. Quests for Truth." *Sociological Theory* 24 (1): 1–41.

Abinales, Patricio. 2003. "Progressive-Machine Conflict in Early-Twentieth-Century U.S. Politics and Colonial-State Building in the Philippines." Pp. 148–81 in Go and Foster (2003).

About, Ilsen, and Vincent Denis. 2010. *Histoire de l'indentification des personnes*. Paris: La découverte.

Abrams, Philip. 1968. *The Origins of British Sociology, 1834–1914: An Essay with Selected Papers*. Chicago: University of Chicago Press.

Abu-Lughod, Janet. 1965. "Tale of Two Cities: The Origins of Modern Cairo." *Comparative Studies in Society and History* 7:429–457.

———. 1980. *Rabat, Urban Apartheid in Morocco*. Princeton, N.J.: Princeton University Press.

Abunimah, Ali. 2006. *One Country: A Bold Proposal to End the Israeli-Palestinian Impasse*. New York: Metropolitan Books.

Adam, André. 1965. "Qu'apporte la psychanalyse à la connaisance des sociétés Nord-Africaines?" Pp. 15–35 in Universita degli studi di Caligari, Facoltà di giurisprudenza e scienze politiche (Eds.), *Atti del I Congresso internazionale di studi Nord-Africani (Cagliari 22–25 Gennaio 1965)*. Cagliari: Stab. tip. edit. G. Fossataro.

———. 1972. *Bibliographie critique de sociologie, d'ethnologie et de géographie humaine du Maroc*. Alger: Centre de recherches anthropologiques, préhistoriques et ethnographiques.

Adams, Julia. 1994. "The Familial State: Elite Family Practices and State-Making in the Early Modern Netherlands." *Theory and Society* 23 (4): 505–539.

———. 1999. "Culture in Rational-Choice Theories of State-Formation." Pp. 98–122 in Steinmetz (1999).

———. 2005a. *The Familial State: Ruling Families and Merchant Capitalism in Early Modern Europe.* Ithaca, N.Y.: Cornell University Press.

———. 2005b. "The Rule of the Father: Patriarchy and Patrimonialism in Early Modern Europe." Pp. 237–266 in Charles Camic, Philip S. Gorski, and David M. Trubek (Eds.), *Max Weber's "Economy and Society": A Critical Companion.* Stanford, Calif.: Stanford University Press.

Adams, Julia, Elisabeth Clemens, and Ann Orloff, eds. 2005. *Remaking Modernity: Politics, History, and Sociology.* Durham, N.C.: Duke University Press.

Adas, Michael. 1989. *Machines as the Measure of Men: Science, Technology, and Ideologies of Western Dominance.* Ithaca, N.Y.: Cornell University Press.

Agamben, Giorgio. 1998. *Homo Sacer: Sovereign Power and Bare Life.* Translated by Daniel Heller-Roazen. Stanford, Calif.: Stanford University Press.

———. 2003. *State of Exception.* Chicago: University of Chicago Press.

Agani, Fehmi. 2002. *Partitë dhe grupet politike në Shqipëri, 1939–1945.* Prishtina: Dukagjini.

Ageron, Charles Robert. 1978. *France coloniale ou parti colonial?* Paris: Presses universitaires de France [hereafter PUF].

———. 1997. "L'exposition coloniale de 1931: mythe républicain ou mythe impérial?" Pp. 493–515 in Pierre Nora (Ed.), *Les lieux de mémoire. La république.* Paris: Gallimard.

Agger, Ben. 2000. *Public Sociology: From Social Facts to Literary Acts.* Lanham, Md.: Rowman and Littlefield.

Ahmad, Aijaz. 2004. "Imperialism of Our Time." In Leo Panitch and Colin Leys (Eds.), *Socialist Register 2004: The New Imperial Challenge.* New York: Monthly Review Press.

Akenson, D. 1992. *God's Peoples: Covenant and Land in South Africa, Israel, and Ulster.* Ithaca, N.Y.: Cornell University Press.

Akimenko, M. A. 2007. *Institut im. V. M. Bekhtereva: ot istokov do sovremennosti, 1907–2007.* St. Petersburg: GU SPb NIPNI im. V. M. Bekhtereva.

Akimoto, Ritsuo. 2004. *Kindai nihon to shakaigaku.* Tokyo: Bakubunsha.

Alavi, Hamza. 1981. "Structure of Colonial Social Formations." *Economic and Political Weekly* 16 (10–12): 475–486.

Albright, Madeleine, and Bill Woodward. 2003. *Madam Secretary.* New York: Miramax.

Aldrich, Robert. 1996. *Greater France: A History of French Overseas Expansion.* London: Macmillan.

Aliaj, Besnik, Keida Lulo, and Genc Myftiu. 2003. *Tirana: sfida e Zhvillimit Urban.* Tirana: Seda and Co-Plan.

Allen, William H. 1903. "Sanitation and Social Progress." *American Journal of Sociology* 8:631–643.

Alongi, Giuseppe. 1890. *La camorra. Studio di sociologia criminale*. Turin: Bocca.

———. 1904. *La mafia: fattori, manifestazioni, rimedi*. Palermo: Sandron.

———. 1914. *In Tripolitania*. Palermo: Sandron.

Alter, Peter. 1994. *Nationalism*. Second edition. London: Edward Arnold.

Amadori-Virgilij, Giovanni. 1903. *L'istituto famigliare nella società primordiale*. Roma-Bari: Laterza.

———. 1905. *Il sentimento imperialista. Studio psico-sociologico*. With a preface by Enrico De Marinis. Palermo: Sandron.

Ambrosini, Gaspare. 1940. *L'Albania nella comunità imperiale di Roma*. Rome: Istituto nazionale di cultura Fascista.

Amin, Samir. 1969. *Accumulation on a World Scale: A Critique of the Theory of Underdevelopment*. New York: Monthly Review Press.

Amselle, Jean-Loup. 2003. *Affirmative Exclusion: Cultural Pluralism and the Rule of Custom in France*. Translated by Jane Marie Todd. Ithaca, N.Y.: Cornell University Press.

An Chaehong. 1935. "Chosŏn kwa munwha undong" [Chosŏn and Cultural Movement]. *Sin Chosŏn* [The New Korea] 8:1–3.

Andall, Jacqueline, and Derek Duncan, eds. 2005. *Italian Colonialism: Legacy and Memory*. Bern: Peter Lang.

Anderson, Benedict. 2006. *Imagined Communities*. Revised edition. London: Verso.

Anderson, Warwick. 1995a. "Excremental Colonialism: Public Health and the Poetics of Pollution." *Critical Inquiry* 21:640–669.

———. 1995b. "'Where Every Prospect Pleases and Only Man is Vile': Laboratory Medicine as Colonial Discourse." Pp. 83–112 in Vicente Rafael (Ed.), *Discrepant Histories: Translocal Essays on Filipino Cultures*. Philadelphia: Temple University Press.

Annasse, Arthur. 1975. *Les comptoirs français de l'Inde (Trois siècles de présence Française) 1664–1954*. Paris: La pensée universelle.

Anonymous. 1907. "Informations." *Revue internationale de sociologie* 15:478.

———. 1921. "Mysore Census in 1921." *Daily Post*, May 10.

Anter, Andreas. 2008. "Die Europäische Union als Großraum. Carl Schmitt und die Aktualität seiner Theorie." Pp. 57–70 in Rüdiger Voigt (Ed.), *Großraum-Denken. Carl Schmitts Kategorie der Großraumordnung*. Stuttgart: Franz Steiner Verlag.

AOD [*Addresses of the Dewans of Mysore to the Mysore Representative Assembly at Mysore*]. [1881–1899] 1914. Vol. 1. Bangalore: Government Press.

———. [1913–1938] 1938. Vol. 3. Bangalore: Government Press.

Appadurai, Arjun. 1991. "Global Ethnoscapes: Notes and Queries for a Transnational Anthropology." Pp. 191–210 in Richard Fox (Ed.), *Recapturing Anthropology*. Santa Fe: SAR Press.

———. 1996. *Modernity at Large*. Minneapolis: University of Minnesota Press.

———, ed. 2001. *Globalization*. Durham, N.C.: Duke University Press.

———. 2006. *Fear of Small Numbers*. Durham, N.C.: Duke University Press.

Appiah, Kwame Anthony. 1996. "Race, Culture, Identity: Misunderstood Connections." Pp. 30–105 in Kwamy Anthony Appiah and Amy Gutmann (Eds.), *Color*

Conscious: The Political Morality of Race. Princeton, N.J.: Princeton University Press.

Aquarone, A. 1977. "Politica estera e organizzazione del consenso nell'età Giolittiana: il Congresso dell'Asmara e la fondazione dell'istituto coloniale Italiano." *Storia contemporanea* 8:57–119, 291–334, 549–570.

Are, G. 1985. *La scoperta dell'imperialismo: il dibattito nella cultura Italiana del primo Novecento.* Rome: Edizioni Lavoro.

Arendt, Hannah. 1945/1946. "Imperialism: Road to Suicide: The Political Origins and Use of Racism." *Commentary* 1:27–35.

———. [1950] 1958. *The Origins of Totalitarianism.* New York: World Publishing.

Aresen'ev, K. K., P. G. Vinogradov, V. A. Wagner, S. K. Gogel, I. A. Ivanovskii, N. I. Kareev, E. P. Kovalevsky, N. D. Kondratiev, A. F. Koni, P. N. Miliukov, eds. 1917. *M. M. Kovalevsky: Uchenyi, gosudarstvennyi i obshchestvennyi deiatel', grazhdanin.* Petrograd: A. F. Marx.

Armitage, David. 2000. *The Ideological Origins of the British Empire.* Cambridge: Cambridge University Press.

Arnold, James. 1981. *Modernism and Negritude.* Cambridge, Mass.: Harvard University Press.

Aron, Raymond. 1945. *L'âge des empires et l'avenir de la France.* Paris: Éditions défense de la France.

Asad, T., ed. 1973. *Anthropology and the Colonial Encounter.* London: Ithaca University Press.

Austen, Ralph. 1967. "The Official Mind of Indirect Rule: British Policy in Tanganyika, 1916–1939. Pp. 577–606 in P. Gifford and W. R. Louis (Eds.), *Britain and Germany in Africa: Imperial Rivalry and Colonial Rule.* New Haven, Conn.: Yale University Press.

Bacevich, Andrew. 2002. *American Empire.* Cambridge, Mass.: Harvard University Press.

Bade, Klaus. 1980. "German Emigration to the United States and Continental Immigration to Germany in the Late Nineteenth and Early Twentieth Centuries." *Central European History* 13:348–377.

Balakrishna, R. 1940. *Industrial Development of Mysore.* Bangalore: Government Press.

Balandier, Georges. 1951. "La situation coloniale: Approche théorique." *Cahiers internationaux de sociologie* 11:44–79.

———. 1955a. *Sociologie actuelle de l'Afrique noire; dynamique des changements sociaux en Afrique centrale.* Paris: PUF.

———. 1955b. *Sociologie des Brazzavilles noires.* Paris: A. Colin.

———. 1966. "The Colonial Situation: A Theoretical Approach." Pp. 34–61 in I. Wallerstein (Ed.), *Social Change: The Colonial Situation.* New York: John Wiley and Sons.

Baldacci, Antonio. 1929. *L'Albania.* Rome: Istituto per l'Europa orientale.

Baldaccini, Anneliese, and Elspeth Guild, eds. 2006. *Terrorism and the Foreigner: A Decade of Tension around the Rule of Law in Europe.* Leiden: Brill.

Bancel, Nicolas, Pascal Blanchard, and Françoise Vergès. 2003. *La république coloniale: essai sur une utopie*. Paris: A. Michel.

Banerji, Sir Albion. [1922] 1926. "Speech at the Sixth Installation of the Cauvery Power Scheme, Sivasamudram, April 25, 1922." Pp. 320–324 in Banerji (1926).

———. [1923] 1926. "Address to the Mysore Representative Assembly, October 22, 1923." Pp. 683–732 in Banerji (1926).

———. [1925] 1926. "Speech at the Mysore Legislative Council, June 25, 1925." Pp. 1157–1159 in Banerji (1926).

———. 1926. *Speeches by Sir Albion Banerji, April 1916 to April 1926*. Bangalore: Government Press.

Barbano, Filippo. 1998. *La sociologia in Italia*. Rome: Carocci.

Barbano, Filippo, and Giorgio Sola. 1985. *Sociologia e scienze sociali in Italia, 1861–1890*. Milan: Angeli.

Barber, John. 1981. *Soviet Historians in Crisis, 1928–1932*. London: Macmillan Press.

Barkey, Karen. 1994. *Bandits and Bureaucrats*. Ithaca, N.Y.: Cornell University Press.

———. 2008. *Empire of Difference*. Cambridge: Cambridge University Press.

Barnes, Harry Elmer. 1919a. "The Struggle of Races and Social Groups as a Factor in the Development of Political and Social Institutions. An Exposition and Critique of the Sociological System of Ludwig Gumplowicz." *Journal of Race Development* 9 (4): 394–419.

———. 1919b. "Two Representative Contributions of Sociology to Political Theory: The Doctrines of William Graham Sumner and Lester Frank Ward. Part II." *American Journal of Sociology* 25:150–170.

———, ed. 1948. *An Introduction to the History of Sociology*. Chicago: University of Chicago Press.

Barnes, Harry Elmer, and Howard Becker. 1938. *Social Thought from Lore to Science*. Vol. 1. Boston: D.C. Heath.

Barrera, Giulia. 2003. "Mussolini's Colonial Race Laws and State-Settler Relations in Africa Orientale Italiana (1935–41)." *Journal of Modern Italian Studies* 8:425–443.

———. 2005. "Patrilinearity, Race, and Identity: The Upbringing of Italo-Eritereans during Italian Colonialism." Pp. 97–108 in Ruth Ben-Ghiat and Mia Fuller (Eds.), *Italian Colonialism*. New York: Palgrave Macmillan.

Bartlett, Robert. 1993. *The Making of Europe*. London: Penguin Books.

Bastide, Roger. 1948. *Initiation aux recherches sur l'interpénétration des civilizations*. Paris: Centre de documentation universitaire.

———. 1958. *Le candomblé de Bahia (rite nagô)*. Paris: Mouton.

———. 1960. *Les religions Afro-Brésiliennes*. Paris: PUF.

———. 1970–1971. "Mémoire collective et bricolage." *L'année sociologique* (3rd series) 21:65–110.

Baud, Michel. 1998. "The Quest for Modernity: Latin American Technocratic Ideas in Historic Perspective." Pp. 13–35 in Miguel Centeno and Patricia Silva (Eds.), *The Politics of Expertise in Latin America*. New York: St. Martin's Press.

Bauman, Zygmunt. 1992. "Legislators and Interpreters: Culture as the Ideology of the Intellectuals." In *Intimations of Postmodernity*. London: Routledge.

Baumgart, Winfried. 1982. *Imperialism: The Idea and Reality of British and French Colonial Expansion, 1880–1914*. Oxford: Oxford University Press.

Bayly, C. A. 2004. *The Birth of the Modern World, 1780–1914*. Oxford: Blackwell.

Bazin, Jean. 1985. "A chacun son bambara." Pp. 87–127 in Jean-Loup Amselle and Elikia M'Bokolo (Eds.), *Au coeur de l'ethnie: ethnies, tribalisme et etat en Afrique*. Paris: La découverte.

Beaud, Stéphane, and Gérard Noiriel. 1990. "Penser 'l'intégration' des immigrés." *Hommes et migrations* 1183:43–53.

Beck, N. 2005. "Enrico Ferri's Scientific Socialism: A Marxist Interpretation of Herbert Spencer's Organic Analogy." *Journal of the History of Biology* 38 (2): 301–325.

Beck, Ulrich. 2006. *The Cosmopolitan Vision*. Cambridge: Polity.

Becker, Howard P. 1932. "Space Apportioned Forty-Eight Topics in the *American Journal of Sociology*, 1895–1930." *American Journal of Sociology* 38 (1): 71–78.

———. 1938. "Sociology in Italy." Pp. 1002–1029 in Howard P. Becker and Harry Elmer Barnes (Eds.), *Social Thought from Lore to Science*. New York: Dover.

Beetham, David. 1977. "From Socialism to Fascism: The Relation between Theory and Practice in the Work of Robert Michels." *Political Studies* 25 (1–2): 3–24, 161–181.

Beinart, W. 2001. *Twentieth Century South Africa*. Oxford: Oxford University Press.

Beinin, Joel. 2006. "The Oslo Process and the Limits of a Pax Americana." Pp. 21–37 in Beinin and Stein (2006).

Beinin, Joel, and Rebecca L. Stein, eds. 2006. *The Struggle for Sovereignty: Palestine and Israel, 1993–2005*. Stanford, Calif.: Stanford University Press.

Belich, James. 2009. *Replenishing the Earth: The Settler Revolution and the Rise of the Anglo-World, 1783–1939*. Oxford: Oxford University Press.

Bell, David Avrom. 2001. *The Cult of the Nation in France: Inventing Nationalism, 1680–1800*. Cambridge, Mass.: Harvard University Press.

Bellamy, Richard. 1987. *Italian Social Theory*. Cambridge: Cambridge University Press.

Ben-Ghiat, Ruth. 2001. *Fascist Modernities: Italy, 1922–1945*. Berkeley: University of California Press.

———. 2008. "Italy and Its Colonies: Introduction." Pp. 262–268 in Prem Poddar, Lars Jensen, and Rajeev Patke (Eds.), *A Historical Companion to Postcolonial Literatures in Continental Europe and its Empires*. Edinburgh: Edinburgh University Press.

Ben-Ghiat, Ruth, and Mia Fuller, eds. 2005. *Italian Colonialism*. New York: Palgrave Macmillan.

Ben Salem, Lilia. 2009. " 'Propos sur la sociologie en Tunisie.' Entretien avec Sylvie Mazzella." *Genèses: sciences sociales et histoire* 75:125–142.

Bensa, Alban. 1988. "Colonialisme, racisme et ethnologie en Nouvelle-Calédonie." *Ethnologie Française* 18:187–197.

Benson, Lee. 1950. "Achille Loria's Influence on American Economic Thought: Including His Contributions to the Frontier Hypothesis." *Agricultural History* 24 (4): 182–199.

Benvenisti, M. 1984. *The West Bank Data Project: A Survey of Israel's Policies*. Washington, D.C.: American Enterprise Institute for Public Policy Research.

Berezin, Mabel. 1997. *Making the Fascist Self*. Ithaca, N.Y.: Cornell University Press.

Berger, Peter L. 1963. *Invitation to Sociology*. Garden City, N.Y.: Doubleday.

Bergesen, Albert, and Ronald Schoenberg. 1980. "Long Waves of Colonial Expansion and Contraction." Pp. 231–277 in Albert Bergesen (Ed.), *Studies of the Modern World-System*. New York: Academic Press.

Berlin, Isaiah. 1965. "The Thought of de Tocqueville." *History* 50 (169): 199–206.

———. 1978. *Russian Thinkers*. London: Hogarth Press.

Berman, Bruce. 1984. "Structures and Process in the Bureaucratic States of Colonial Africa." *Development and Change* 15 (April): 161–202.

Berman, Bruce, and John Lonsdale. 1992. *Unhappy Valley: Conflict in Kenya and Africa*. London: James Currey.

Bernardy, A. A. 1941. "Forme e colori della tradizione Albanese." *Lares* 12.

Berque, Jacques. 1958. "L'inquiétude Arabe des temps moderns." *Revue des études Islamiques* 18 (1): 87–107.

———. 1964. *Dépossession du monde*. Paris: Seuil.

Berr, Henri. 1926. "Foreword." Pp. ix–xxx in Alexandre Moret and Georges Davy, *From Tribe to Empire*. New York: Knopf.

Bertinaria, Francesco. 1865. "Principi di biologia e di sociologia, proposti agli studiosi di filosofia del diritto." *Rivista contemporanea* 40:345–385.

Besnard, P. 1979. "La formation de l'équipe de l'année sociologique." *Revue Française de sociologie* 20 (1): 7–31.

———, ed. 1983. *The Sociological Domain: The Durkheimians and the Founding of French Sociology*. Cambridge: Cambridge University Press.

Betts, Raymond F. 1961. *Assimilation and Association in French Colonial Theory, 1890–1914*. New York: Columbia University Press.

Bhabha, Homi. 1994a. *The Location of Culture*. London: Routledge.

———. 1994b. "Of Mimicry and Man: The Ambivalence of Colonial Discourse." Pp. 85–92 in Bhabha (1994a).

Bhambra, G. K. 2007. *Rethinking Modernity: Postcolonialism and the Sociological Imagination*. London: Palgrave Macmillan.

Bhaskar, Roy. 1986. *Scientific Realism and Human Emancipation*. London: Verso.

Biersteker, T. 1992. "The 'Triumph' of Neoclassical Economics in the Developing World: Policy Convergence and the Bases of Government in the International Economic Order." In James Rosenau and E.-O. Czempiel (Eds.), *Governance without Government: Order and Change in World Politics*. Cambridge: Cambridge University Press.

Biervert, Bernd, and Josef Wieland. 1993. "The Ethical Content of Economic Categories: The Concept of Utility." *Research in the History of Economic Thought and Methodology* 11:93–116.

Biko, S. 1978. *I Write What I Like*. Oxford: Heinemann Educational Publishers.

Billiard, Albert. 1899. *Politique et organisation coloniales*. Paris: V. Giard.

Birnbaum, Pierre. 2003. "French Jews and the 'Regeneration' of Algerian Jewry." Pp. 88–103 in Ezra Mendelsohn (Ed.), *Jews and the State: Dangerous Alliances and the Perils of Privilege*. Oxford: Oxford University Press.

Bishara, M. 2002. *Palestine/Israel: Peace or Apartheid*. London: Zed Books.

Blackmar, Frank Wilson. 1929. "The Socialization of the American Indian." *American Journal of Sociology* 34 (4): 653–669.

Blanchard, Pascal, Nicolas Bancel, and Sandrine Lemaire. 2005. *La fracture coloniale*. Paris: La découverte.

Bleek, Wilhelm. 2001. *Geschichte der Politikwissenschaft in Deutschland*. München: C. H. Beck.

Blévis, Laure. 2003. "La citoyenneté Française au miroir de la colonisation." *Genèses* 53 (4): 25–47.

Blustein, Paul. 2001. *The Chastening*. New York: Public Affairs.

Bobbio, Norberto. 1969. *Saggi sulla scienza politica in Italia*. Roma-Bari: Laterza.

Boccardo, Gerolamo. 1864. *Le colonie e l'Italia: sei lezioni*. Turin: Franco.

———. 1881. *La sociologia nella storia, nella scienza, nella religione e nel cosmo: saggio filosofico*. Turin: Unione tipografico editrice.

Bond, P. 2000. *Elite Transition: From Apartheid to Neo-liberalism in South Africa*. London: Pluto Press.

Boot, Max. 2002. *The Savage Wars of Peace*. New York: Basic Books.

Boralevi, Alberto. 1986. "Le 'città dell'Impero': urbanistica fascista in Etiopia, 1936–1941." Pp. 235–286 in Alberto Mioni (Ed.), *Urbanistica fascista*. Milan: Franco Angeli.

Borkenau, Franz. 1931. *Pareto*. New York: John Wiley and Sons.

Boronoev, A. O., ed. 1996. *M. M. Kovalevsky v istorii rossiiskoi sotsiologii i obshchestvennoi mysli: sbornik statei k 145-letiiu rozhdeniia M. M. Kovalevskogo*. St. Petersburg: Izdatel'stvo St. Petersburgskogo Gosudarstvennogo Universiteta.

Bosc, Olivier. 2000. "Eugénisme et socialisme en Italie autour de 1900: Robert Michels et l' 'education sentimentale des masses.'" *Mil neuf cent* 18:81–108.

Bosco, A., and Cavaglieri, G. 1897. *Rivista Italiana di sociologia* 1 (1): 1n1.

Bose, Sugata. 1998. "Instruments and Idioms of Colonial and National Development: India's Historical Experience in Comparative Perspective." Pp. 45–63 in Cooper and Packard (1997).

Boswell, Terry. 1989. "Colonial Empires and the Capitalist World-Economy: A Time Series Analysis of Colonization, 1640–1960." *American Sociological Review* 54 (2): 180–196.

Boudhiba, A. 1964. "Review of Jacques Berque." *Dépossession du monde. Cahiers internationaux de sociologie* 37:178–179.

Bourdieu, Pierre. 1958. *Sociologie de l'Algérie*. First edition. Paris: PUF.

———. 1959. "La logique interne de la civilisation Algérienne traditionnelle." Pp. 40–51 in Secrétariat social d'Alger (Ed.), *Le sous-développement en Algérie*. Alger: Éditions du secrétariat social d'Alger.

———. 1961a. "Révolution dans la revolution." *Esprit* 1:27–40.

———. 1961b. *Sociologie de l'Algérie*. Second, revised edition. Paris: PUF.

———. 1962. *The Algerians*. Boston: Beacon Press.

———. 1977. *Outline of a Theory of Practice*. Cambridge: Cambridge University Press.

———. 1979. *Algeria 1960*. Cambridge: Cambridge University Press.

—. [1980] 1990. *The Logic of Practice*. Stanford, Calif.: Stanford University Press.

—. 1984. *Distinction*. Cambridge, Mass.: Harvard University Press.

—. 1991a. *Language and Symbolic Power*. Cambridge, Mass.: Harvard University Press.

—. 1991b. "On the Possibility of a Field of World Sociology." Pp. 373–387 in Pierre Bourdieu and James S. Coleman (Eds.), *Social Theory for a Changing Society*. Boulder, Colo.: Westview Press.

—. 1993a. "For a Sociology of Sociologists." Pp. 49–53 in *Sociology in Question*. London: Sage.

—. 1993b. "Some Properties of Fields." Pp. 72–77 in *Sociology in Question*. London: Sage.

—. 1996a. *The Rules of Art*. Stanford, Calif.: Stanford University Press.

—. 1996b. *The State Nobility*. Stanford, Calif.: Stanford University Press.

—. 1999. "Rethinking the State: Genesis and Structure of the Bureaucratic Field." Pp. 53–75 in Steinmetz (1999).

—. 1999/2000. "Die Internationale der Intellektuellen. Wissenschaft als Beruf, Politik als Engagement: Plädoyer für eine neue politische Arbeitsteilung." *Berliner Zeitung*, June 10.

—. 2000. *Pascalian Mediations*. Stanford, Calif.: Stanford University Press.

—. 2001. "For a Scholarship with Commitment." Pp. 17–25 in *Firing Back*. New York: New Press.

—. 2002. "Les conditions sociales de la circulation internationale des idées." *Actes de la recherche en sciences sociales* 145:3–8.

—. 2004. *Science of Science and Reflexivity*. Chicago: University of Chicago Press.

—. 2007. *Sketch for a Self-Analysis*. Chicago: University of Chicago Press.

—. 2012. *Sur l'état*. Paris: Seuil.

Bourdieu, Pierre, and Abdelmalek Sayad. 1964. *Le déracinement*. Paris: Éditions de minuit.

Bourdieu, Pierre, and Loïc Wacquant. 1992. *An Invitation to Reflexive Sociology*. Chicago: University of Chicago Press.

Bourgholtzer, Frank, ed. 1999. *Aleksandr Chayanov and Russian Berlin*. London: Frank Cass.

Braudel, Fernand. 1980. *On History*. Chicago: University of Chicago Press.

Brenner, Neil. 1999. "Globalization as Reterritorialization: The Re-Scaling of Urban Governance in the European Union." *Urban Studies* 36 (3): 431–451.

—. 2004. *New State Spaces: Urban Governance and the Rescaling of Statehood*. Oxford: Oxford University Press.

Brenner, Neil, Bob Jessop, Martin Jones, and Gordon Macleod, eds. 2003. *State/Space: A Reader*. Malden, Mass.: Blackwell.

Brentano, Lujo. 1871. "Abstracte und realistische Volkswirthe." *Zeitschrift des königlich-preußischen statistischen Bureaus* 11:383–385.

Breschi, Danilo, and Gisella Longo. 2003. *Camillo Pellizzi: la ricerca delle élites tra politica e sociologia (1896–1979)*. Soveria Mannelli: Rubbettino.

Breslau, Daniel. 2007. "The American Spencerians: Theorizing a New Science." Pp. 39–62 in Calhoun (2007).

Breuilly, John 2000. "Nationalism and the History of Ideas." *Proceedings of the British Academy* 105:187–223.

Brewer, Anthony. 1990. *Marxist Theories of Imperialism: A Critical Survey*. Second edition. London: Routledge.

Breyfogle, Nicholas B. 2005. *Heretics and Colonizers: Forging Russia's Empire in the South Caucasus*. Ithaca, N.Y.: Cornell University Press.

Breyfogle, Nicholas B., Abby Schrader, and Willard Sunderland, eds. 2007. *Peopling the Russian Periphery: Borderland Colonization in Eurasian History*. London: Routledge.

Brocheux, Pierre. 1972. "Vietnamiens et minorités en Cochinchine pendant la période coloniale." *Modern Asian Studies* 6 (4): 443–457.

———. 1995. *The Mekong Delta: Ecology, Economy, and Revolution, 1860–1960*. Monograph Number 12. Madison: University of Wisconsin, Center for Southeast Asian Studies.

Brocheux, Pierre, and Daniel Hémery. 2001. *Indochine: la colonisation ambiguë 1858–1954*. Paris: La découverte.

Brubaker, Rogers 1992. *Citizenship and Nationhood in France and Germany*. Cambridge, Mass.: Harvard University Press.

Brunialti, A. 1897. *Le colonie degli Italiani con appendice*. Turin: UTET.

B'Tselem. 2002. *Land Grab: Israeli Settlement Policy in the West Bank*. Jerusalem: B'Tselem.

Bucolo, P., ed. 1980. *The Other Pareto*. London: St. Martin's Press.

———. 2004. "Public Sociologies: Contradictions, Dilemmas, and Possibilities." *Social Forces* 82 (4): 1–16.

———. 2006. "Open Letter to C. Wright Mills." *Antipode* 40 (3): 365–375.

Burbank, Jane. 2006. "An Imperial Rights Regime: Law and Citizenship in the Russian Empire." *Kritika: Explorations in Russian and Eurasian History* 7 (3): 397–431.

Burgalassi, Marco M. 1996. *Itinerari di una scienza: la sociologia Italiana tra Otto e Novecento*. Milan: Angeli.

Burgess, John W. 1899. "How May the United States Govern Its Extra-Continental Territory?" *Political Science Quarterly* 14:1–18.

———. 1900. "The Relation of the Constitution of the United States to Newly Acquired Territory." *Political Science Quarterly* 15:381–398.

Burke, Edmund III. 2002. "The Terror and Religion: Brittany and Algeria." Pp. 40–50 in Gregory Blue, Martin Bunton, and Ralph Croizier (Eds), *Colonialism and the Modern World*. Armonk, N.Y.: M. E. Sharpe.

Burnett, Christina Duffy, and Burke Marshall. 2001. *Foreign in a Domestic Sense: Puerto Rico, American Expansion, and the Constitution*. Durham, N.C.: Duke University Press.

Butler, J., Rotberg, R., and J. Adams, eds. 1977. *The Black Homelands of South Africa*. Berkeley: University of California Press.

Buttinger, Joseph. 1967. *Viet-Nam: A Dragon Embattled*. London: Pall Mall.

Calhoun, Craig. 1995. *Critical Social Theory*. Oxford: Blackwell.

———. 2006. "Pierre Bourdieu and Social Transformation: Lessons from Algeria." *Development and Change* 37 (6): 1403–1415.

———, ed. 2007. *Sociology in America: A History*. Chicago: University of Chicago Press.

Calhoun, Craig, Frederick Cooper, and Kevin W. Moore. 2006a. "Introduction." Pp. 1–15 in Calhoun et al. (2006b).

———, eds. 2006b. *Lessons of Empire: Imperial Histories and American Power*. New York: New Press.

Camavitto, Dino. 1935. *La decadenza delle popolazioni Messicane al tempo della conquista*. Rome: Failli.

Camic, Charles. 1995. "Three Departments in Search of a Discipline: Localism and Interdisciplinary Interaction in American Sociology, 1890–1940." *Social Research* 62:1003–1033.

Camic, Charles, and Neil Gross. 2000. "The New Sociology of Ideas." Pp. 236–249 in J. R. Blau (Ed.), *The Blackwell Companion to Sociology*. Malden, Mass.: Blackwell.

Camic, Charles, and Yu Xie. 1994. "The Statistical Turn in American Sociology." *American Sociological Review* 59:773–805.

Cardoso, Fernando Henrique, and Enzo Faletto. 1979. *Dependency and Development in Latin America*. Berkeley: University of California Press.

Carli, Filippo. 1919. *L'equilibrio delle nazioni secondo la demografia applicata*. Bologna: Zanichelli.

———. 1921. *Le esportazioni*. Milano: Treves.

———. 1925a. *Introduzione alla sociologia generale*. Bologna: Zanichelli.

———. 1925b. *Le teorie sociologiche*. Padova: Cedam.

Carpi, L. 1874. *Delle colonie e dell'emigrazione degli Italiani all'estero*. Milan: Lombarda.

Carr, Raymond. 2000. "Introduction." Pp. 1–9 in Raymond Carr (Ed.), *Spain: A History*. Oxford: Oxford University Press.

Carter, Jimmy. 2006. *Palestine: Peace Not Apartheid*. New York: Simon and Schuster.

Cassata, Francesco. 2006a. *Il fascismo razionale: Corrado Gini tra scienza e politica*. Roma: Carocci.

———. 2006b. *Molti sani e forti: l'eugenetica in Italia*. Turin: Bollati boringhieri.

Castells, Manuel. 1977. *The Urban Question: A Marxist Approach*. Cambridge, Mass.: MIT Press.

Castrilli, Vincenzo. 1941. "L'insegnamento della sociologia nelle università Italiane." *Rivista internazionale di filosofia del Diritto* 2:265–279.

Cavaglieri, Guido. 1906. "Augusto Bosco." *Rivista Italiana di sociologia* 10:269–277.

Cawthra, G. 1986. *Brutal Force: The Apartheid War Machine*. London: International Defense and Aid Fund for Southern Africa.

Çelik, Zeynep. 1997. *Urban Forms and Colonial Confrontations: Algiers under French Rule*. Berkeley: University of California Press.

Çelik, Zeynep, Diane Favro, and Richard Ingersoll, eds. 1994. *Streets: Critical Perspectives on Public Space*. Berkeley: University of California Press.

Centeno, Miguel Angel, and Elaine Enriquez. 2010. "Legacies of Empire?" *Theory and Society* 39:343–360.

Chae, Ou-Byung. 2006. "Non-Western Colonial Rule and Its Aftermath: Postcolonial State Formation in South Korea." Ph.D. diss., University of Michigan (Sociology).

———. Forthcoming. "Homology Unleashed: Colonial, Anticolonial, and Postcolonial State Culture in South Korea, 1930–1950." *Positions: Asia Critique.*

Chafer, Tony, and Amanda Sackur, eds. 2002. *Promoting the Colonial Idea: Propaganda and Visions of Empire in France.* New York: Palgrave.

Chaianov, Alexander [Ivan Kremnev]. 1976. "Journey of My Brother Alexey to the Land of Peasant Utopia." *Journal of Peasant Studies* 4 (1): 63–108.

———. 1977. "The Journey of My Brother Alexey to the Land of Peasant Utopia." Pp. 63–116 in R. E. F. Smith (Ed.), *The Russian Peasant, 1920 and 1984.* London: Frank Cass.

Chaianov, V. A. 1998. *A. V. Chaianov—chelovek, uchenyi, grazhdanin.* Moscow: Izdatel'stvo MSKhA.

Chakrabarty, Dipesh. 1992. "Postcoloniality and Artifice of History: Who Speaks for Indian Pasts?" *Representations* 37:1–27.

———. 1997. "The Difference—Deferral of a Colonial Modernity: Public Debates on Domesticity in British Bengal." Pp. 373–405 in Cooper and Stoler (1997).

———. 2000. *Provincializing Europe.* Princeton, N.J.: Princeton University Press.

Chakravarty, Sukhamoy. 1997. "Development Economics in Perspective." In Mihir Rakshit (Ed.), *Writings on Development.* New Delhi: Oxford University Press.

Champagne, Duane. 2006. "Native American Studies." In Clifton D. Bryant and Dennis L. Peck (Eds.), *Handbook of 21st Century Sociology.* Thousand Oaks, Calif.: Sage.

Chandrasekhara, N. S. 1981. *Dewan Seshadri Iyer.* New Delhi: Publications Division, Ministry of Information and Broadcasting.

Chang, Pao-min. 1982. *Beijing, Hanoi, and the Overseas Chinese.* Berkeley: Institute of East Asian Studies, University of California.

Chase-Dunn, Christopher, and Michael P. Smith. 1984. "Urbanization in the World-System: New Directions for Research." Pp. 111–120 in *Cities in Transformation.* Beverly Hills, Calif.: Sage.

Chatterjee, Partha. 1986. *Nationalist Thought and the Colonial World: A Derivative Discourse.* Minneapolis: University of Minnesota Press.

———. 1993. *The Nation and Its Fragments.* Princeton, N.J.: Princeton University Press.

Chen, Edward I-te. 1984. "The Attempt to Integrate the Empire: Legal Perspectives." Pp. 240–274 in Myers and Peattie (1984).

Cheung, Melissa. 2002. "The Legal Position of Ethnic Chinese in Indochina under French Rule." Pp. 32–64 in M. Barry Hooker (Ed.), *Law and the Chinese in Southeast Asia.* Singapore: Institute of Southeast Asian Studies.

Chevalier, Louis. 1973. *Labouring Classes and Dangerous Classes in Paris during the First Half of the Nineteenth Century.* London: Routledge and Kegan Paul.

Chōsen sōtokufu [Government General of Korea]. 1914. *Chōsen sisei no hōsin oyobi zitseki* [The policy and achievement of the administration of Korea]. Seoul: Chōsen sōtokufu.

———. 1936. *Chōsen kensei benran* [Handbook of current conditions in Korea]. Seoul: Chōsen sōtokufu.

Chōsen tōkei kyōkai [Statistical Association of Korea]. 1939. *Chōsen tōkei zibō* [Statistical Bulletin of Korea] 14.

Christ, Karl. 1982. *Römische Geschichte und deutsche Geschichtswissenschaft.* München: C. H. Beck.

Cianferotti, G. 1984. *I giuristi Italiani di fronte all'impresa libica.* Milan: Giuffrè.

Ciano, Galeazzo. 1953. *Ciano's Hidden Diary, 1936–1938.* New York: Dutton.

Clairon, M. 1926. *La renonciation au statut personnel dans l'Inde Française.* Paris: Société annonyme du Recueil Sirey.

Clancy-Smith, Julia Ann, and Frances Gouda. 1998. *Domesticating the Empire: Race, Gender, and Family Life in French and Dutch Colonialism.* Charlottesville: University Press of Virginia.

Clark, Terry N. 1973. *Prophets and Patrons: The French University and the Emergence of the Social Sciences.* Cambridge, Mass.: Harvard University Press.

Clark, Wesley. 2001. *Waging Modern War: Bosnia, Kosovo, and the Future of Combat.* New York: Public Affairs.

Clarke, Richard. 2004. *Against All Enemies.* New York: Simon and Schuster.

Clarno, Andrew. 2008. "A Tale of Two Walled Cities: Neo-Liberalization and Enclosure in Johannesburg and Jerusalem." *Political Power and Social Theory* 19:161–207.

———. 2009. "Empire's New Walls: Sovereignty, Neo-Liberalism, and the Production of Space in Post-Apartheid South Africa and Post-Oslo Palestine/Israel." Ph.D. diss., University of Michigan (Sociology).

Clemente, P., A. R. Leone, S. Puccini, C. Rossetti, and P. Solinas. 1985. *L'antropologia Italiana. Un secolo di storia.* Rome-Bari: Laterza.

Clifford, J., and G. Marcus, eds. 1986. *Writing Culture.* Berkeley: University of California Press.

Closets d'Errey, H. de. 1934. *Précis chronologique de l'histoire de l'Inde Française (1664–1816).* Pondichéry: Imprimerie du gouvernement.

Cohen, Patrick. 2007. "Scholars and the Military Share a Foxhole, Uneasily." *New York Times,* Dec. 22: A23, A27.

Cohn, Bernard S., and Nicholas B. Dirks. 1988. "Beyond the Fringe: The Nation State, Colonialism, and the Technologies of Power." *Journal of Historical Sociology* 1 (2): 224–229.

Colajanni, Napoleone. 1891. *Politica colonial.* Palermo: Clausen.

———. 1909. *Manuale di demografia.* Naples: Pierro.

Cole, Fay-Cooper. 1916. "Relations between the Living and the Dead." *American Journal of Sociology* 21:611–622.

Coletti, F. 1899. "Psicologia ed economia politica: prime linee d'una teoria psicologica dell'emigrazione." *Rivista Italiana di sociologia* 3 (3).

———. 1908. "Alcuni caratteri antropometrici dei Sardi e la questione della degenerazione della razza." *Rivista Italiana di sociologia* 12 (1).

———. 1912. *Dell'emigrazione Italiana*. Milan: Hoepli.

———. 1918. *I nostri irredenti*. Milan: Unione generale degli insegnanti Italiani, Comitato Lombardo.

———. 1926. "La forza demografica dell'Italia e il suo valore per la civiltà del mondo: discorso tenuto il 5 Novembre 1925 per l'inaugurazione degli studi (1925–26) nella R. Universita di Pavia." *Rivista bancaria* 5(1).

Collier, James. 1905. "The Theory of Colonization." *American Journal of Sociology* 11 (2):252–265.

Collins, James B. 1995. *The State in Early Modern France*. Cambridge: Cambridge University Press.

Collins, John. 2008. "Confinement under an Open Sky: Following the Speed Trap from Guernica to Gaza and Beyond." *Globalizations* 5 (4): 555–569.

Collins, Randall. 1978. "Some Principles of Long-Term Social Change: The Territorial Power of States." *Research in Social Movements, Conflicts and Change* 1:1–34.

———. 1997. "A Sociological Guilt Trip: Comment on Connell." *American Journal of Sociology* 102:1511–1557.

Colonna, Fanny. 1975. *Instituteurs Algériens, 1883–1939*. Paris: Presses de la fondation nationale des sciences politiques.

Comaroff, Jean, and John Comaroff. 1992. "Homemade Hegemony." Pp. 265–285 in *Ethnography and the Historical Imagination*. Boulder, Colo.: Westview Press.

Comaroff, John. 1998. "Reflections on the Colonial State, in South Africa and Elsewhere: Factions, Fragments, Facts and Fictions." *Social Identities* 4:321–361.

Commission of the Central Committee of the C.P.S.U. (B.), eds. 1939. *History of the Communist Party of the Soviet Union (Bolsheviks): Short Course*. New York: International Publishers.

Comte, Auguste. [1830–1842] 1975. *Cours de philosophie positive, leçons 1 à 45: philosophie première*. Paris: Hermann.

Congrès international de sociologie coloniale. 1901. 2 vols. Paris: A. Rousseau.

Conklin, Alice L. 1997. *A Mission to Civilize: The Republican Idea of Empire in France and West Africa, 1895–1930*. Stanford, Calif.: Stanford University Press.

———. 2002. "Civil Society, Science, and Empire in Late Republican France: The Foundation of Paris's Museum of Man." *Osiris* 17:255–290.

Connell, Raewyn (R. W.). 1997. "Why Is Classical Theory Classical?" *American Journal of Sociology* 102:1511–1557.

———. 2006. "Northern Theory: The Political Geography of General Social Theory." *Theory and Society* 35:237–264.

———. 2007. *Southern Theory: The Global Dynamics of Knowledge in Social Science*. Cambridge: Polity Press.

———. 2011. *Confronting Equality: Gender, Knowledge and Global Change*. Cambridge: Polity Press.

Conze, Werner, ed. 1957. *Quellen zur Geschichte der deutschen Bauernbefreiung.* Göttingen: Musterschmidt.

Cooley, Charles H. 1897. "The Process of Social Change." *Political Science Quarterly* 12:63–81.

Cooley, Charles H., J. Q. Dealey, C. A. Ellwood, H. P. Fairchild, Franklin H. Giddings, Edward C. Hayes, Edward A. Ross, Albion W. Small, Ulysses G. Weatherly, and Jerome Dowd. 1912. "Report of the Committee of Ten." *American Journal of Sociology* 17:620–636.

Cooper, Frederick. 1994. "Conflict and Connection: Rethinking Colonial African History." *American Historical Review* 99 (5): 1516–1545.

———. 2005a. *Colonialism in Question.* Berkeley: University of California Press.

———. 2005b. "States, Empires, and Political Imagination." Pp. 153–203 in Cooper (2005a).

Cooper, Frederick, and Ann Laura Stoler, eds. 1997. *Tensions of Empire: Colonial Cultures in a Bourgeois World.* Berkeley: University of California Press.

Cooper, Frederick, and Randall Packard. 1997. "Introduction." Pp. 1–41 in Frederick Cooper and Randall Packard (Eds.), *International Development and the Social Sciences: Essays on the History and Politics of Knowledge.* Berkeley: University of California Press.

Coquery-Vidrovitch, Catherine. 1969. "Recherches sur un mode de production Africaine." *La pensée* 144:61–78.

———. 1988. *Africa: Endurance and Change South of the Sahara.* Berkeley: University of California Press.

Cornell, Stephen E. 1988. *The Return of the Native: American Indian Political Resurgence.* New York: Oxford University Press.

Cosentini, Francesco. 1919. *Woodrow Wilson e la sua opera scientifica e politica.* Torino: UTET.

Crawford, W. R. 1948. "Representative Italian Contribution to Sociology: Pareto, Loria, Vaccaro, Gini and Sighele." Pp. 553–585 in Barnes (1948).

Cresti, Carlo. 1996. *Gherardo Bosio: architteto fiorentino, 1903–1941.* Firenze: Pontecorboli editore.

Cumings, Bruce. 1981. *The Origins of the Korean War.* Vol. 1. Princeton, N.J.: Princeton University.

———. 1999a. *Parallax Visions: Making Sense of American-East Asian Relations at the End of the Century.* Durham, N.C.: Duke University Press.

———. 1999b. "Webs with No Spiders, Spiders with No Webs: The Genealogy of the Developmental State." Pp. 61–92 in Meredith Woo-Cumings (Ed.), *The Developmental State.* Ithaca, N.Y.: Cornell University Press.

Cushing, Terence. 2003. "Pakistan's General Pervez Musharraf: Deceitful Dictator or Father of Democracy?" *Pennsylvania State International Law Review* 21:621–647.

Cusset, François. 2003. *French Theory. Foucault, Derrida, Deleuze & Cie et les mutations de la vie intellectuelle aux Etats-Unis.* Paris: La découverte.

Daalder, Ivo, and James Lindsay. 2003. *America Unbound: The Bush Revolution in Foreign Policy*. Washington, D.C.: Brookings Institution.

Dalberg-Acton, John Emerich Edward. [1862] 1996. "Nationality." Pp.141–70 in Gertrude Himmelfarb (Ed.), *Essays on Freedom and Power*. London: Thames and Hudson.

Dareste, Pierre. 1916. "Les nouveaux citoyens Français." *Recueil de législation, de doctrine et de jurisprudence coloniales* 2:1–16.

Datta, Bhabhatosh. 1978. *Indian Economic History*. New Delhi: Tata McGraw Hill.

Davis, Kingsley. 1955. "The Origin and Growth of Urbanization in the World." *American Journal of Sociology* 60:429–437.

Davis, Mike. 2006. *Planet of Slums*. London: Verso.

Davis, U. 1989. *Israel: An Apartheid State*. London: Zed Books.

———. 2003. *Apartheid Israel: Possibilities for the Struggle Within*. London: Zed Books.

De l'Estoile, Benoît. 2007. *Le goût des autres. De l'exposition coloniale aux arts premiers*. Paris: Flammarion.

De Marinis, Errico. 1901. *Sistema di sociologia*. Turin: Unione tipografica Torinese.

De Quieroz, Maria Pereira. 1975. "Les années Brésiliennes de Roger Bastide." *Archives de sciences sociales des religions* 40:79–87.

De Roberti, E. V., Iu. S. Gambarov, M. M. Kovalevsky, eds. 1905. *Russkaia vysshaia shkola obshchcestvennykh nauk v Parizhe*. St. Petersburg: G. O. L'vovich.

De Roberti, Evgenii. 1905. "Kotsenke osnovnykh predposylok sotsiologicheskoi teorii Karla Marksa." Pp. 32–57 in de Roberti, Gambarov, and Kovalevsky (1905).

De Wet, Erika. 2004. *The Chapter VII Powers of the United Nations Security Council*. Portland, Ore.: Hart.

Decoteau, Claire Laurier. 2008. "The Bio-Politics of HIV/AIDS in Post-Apartheid South Africa." Ph.D. diss., University of Michigan (Sociology).

Dedering, Tilman. 1988. "Problems of Pre-Colonial Namibian Historiography." *South African Historical Journal* 20:95–104.

Del Boca, Angelo. 1969. *The Ethiopian War, 1935–1941*. Chicago: University of Chicago Press.

———. 1992. *L'Africa nella coscienza degli Italiani*. Rome: Laterza.

———. 2003. "The Myths, Suppressions, Denials, and Defaults of Italian Colonialism." Pp. 17–36 in Patrizia Palumbo (Ed.), *A Place in the Sun: Africa in Italian Colonial Culture from Post-Unification to the Present*. Berkeley: University of California Press.

Delavignette, Robert. 1950. *Freedom and Authority in French West Africa*. London: Oxford University Press.

———. 1939. *Les vrais chefs de l'empir*. Paris: Gallimard.

Demm, Eberhard. 1990. *Ein Liberaler in Kaiserreich und Republik: Der politische Weg Alfred Webers bis 1920*. Boppard am Rhein: H. Boldt.

———. 1997. "Alfred Weber als Wissenschaftsorganisator." Pp. 97–116 in R. Blomert, H.-U. Eßlinger, and N. Giovannini (Eds.), *Heidelberger Sozial- und Staatswissenschaften: Das Institut für Sozial- und Staatswissenschaften zwischen 1918 und 1958*. Marburg: Metropolis.

————. 2000a. *Geist und Politik im 20. Jahrhundert: Gesammelte Aufsätze zu Alfred Weber*. Frankfurt: Lang.

————. 2000b. "Klaus von Beyme. Interview am 5.5.1993 in Heidelberg." Pp. 219–221 in Eberhard Demm, *Alfred Weber zum Gedächtnis: Selbstzeugnisse und Erinnerungen von Zeitgenossen*. Frankfurt am Main: Peter Lang.

Der Derian, James. 2010. *Human Terrain*. DVD. Oley, PA: Bullfrog Films.

Deringil, Selim. 2003. "'They Live in a State of Nomadism and Savagery': The Late Ottoman Empire and the Post-Colonial Debate." *Comparative Studies in Society and History* 45:281–310.

Derrida, Jacques. 1976. *Of Grammatology*. Baltimore, Md.: Johns Hopkins University Press.

Derrida, Jacques, and Jürgen Habermas. 2006. "February 15, or: What Binds Europeans." Pp. 39–56 in Habermas (2006).

Deschamps, Damien. 2003. "En attendant le vote des indigènes." *Outre-Mers* 90:338–339.

Dimier, Véronique. 2004. *Le gouvernement des colonies, regards croisés Franco-Britanniques*. Brussells: Editions de l'université de Bruxelles.

Diouf, Mamadou. 2000. "Assimilation coloniale et identites religieuses de la civilite des originaires des quatre communes (Senegal)." *Canadian Journal of African Studies* 34 (3): 565–587.

Dirks, Nicholas B. 1987. *The Hollow Crown: Ethnohistory of an Indian Kingdom*. Cambridge: Cambridge University Press.

————. 1992a. "Castes of Mind." *Representations* 37:56–78.

————, ed. 1992b. *Colonialism and Culture*. Ann Arbor: University of Michigan Press.

Doumanis, Nicholas. 1997. *Myth and Memory in the Mediterranean: Remembering Fascism's Empire*. New York: St. Martin's Press.

Doyle, Michael W. 1986. *Empires*. Ithaca, N.Y.: Cornell University Press.

Dragomanov, Mikhail. 1881. "Chto takoe ukrainofil'stvo." *Russkoe Bogatstvo* 11.

Drahos, Peter, and John Braithwaite. 2002. *Information Feudalism*. New York: New Press.

Drake, Richard. 1981. "The Theory and Practice of Italian Nationalism, 1900–1906." *The Journal of Modern History* 53 (2): 213–241.

Drake, St. Clair. 1954. "Value Systems, Social Structure, and Race Relations in the British Isles." Ph.D. diss., University of Chicago (Social Anthropology).

————. 1956. "Prospects for Democracy in the Gold Coast." *Annals of the American Academy of Political and Social Science* 306:78–87.

————. 1960. "Traditional Authority and Social Action in Former British West Africa." *Human Organization* 19 (3): 150–158.

Drake, St. Clair, and Horace R. Cayton. 1945. *Black Metropolis: A Study of Negro Life in a Northern City*. New York: Harcourt, Brace.

Duara, Prasenjit. 1997. *Rescuing History from the Nation*. Chicago: University of Chicago Press.

————. 2003. *Sovereignty and Authenticity*. Chicago: University of Chicago Press.

Dubois, Laurent. 2004. *A Colony of Citizens: Revolution and Slave Emancipation in the French Caribbean, 1787–1804.* Chapel Hill, N.C.: University of North Carolina Press.

Dudden, Alexis. 2005. *Japan's Colonization of Korea.* Honolulu: University of Hawai'i Press.

Duiker, William J. 1995. *Vietnam: Revolution in Transition.* Boulder, Colo.: Westview Press.

Duka, Valentina. 1997. *Qytetet e Shqipërisë në vitet 1912–1924.* Tirana: Toena.

Dumont, Louis. 1966. "The 'Village Community' from Munro to Maine." *Contributions to Indian Sociology* 9:67–89.

Durkheim, Emile. [1912] 1995. *The Elementary Forms of Religious Life.* New York: Free Press

———. 1927. *Les règles de la méthode sociologique.* Eighth edition. Paris: Alcan.

———. 1956. *Education and Sociology.* Glencoe, Ill.: Free Press.

———. 1957. *Professional Ethics and Civic Morals.* London: Routledge and Kegan Paul.

———. 1960. *Montesquieu and Rousseau: Forerunners of Sociology.* Ann Arbor: University of Michigan Press.

———. 1965. "The Determination of Moral Facts." Pp. 35–62 in *Sociology and Philosophy.* New York: Free Press.

———. 1970a. "Cours de science sociale: leçon d'ouverture." Pp. 77–110 in *La science sociale et l'action.* Paris: PUF.

———. 1970b. "L'individualisme et les intellectuels." Pp. 261–278 in *La science sociale et l'action.* Paris: PUF.

———. 1973. *Moral Education: A Study in the Theory and Application of the Sociology of Education.* New York: Free Press.

———. 1975. "L'état actuel des études sociologiques en France." Pp. 73–108 in *Textes.* Vol. 1. Paris: Minuit.

———. 1977. *The Evolution of Educational Thought: Lectures on the Formation and Development of Secondary Education in France.* London: Routledge and Kegan Paul.

———. 1984. *The Division of Labor in Society.* New York: Free Press.

Durkheim, Emile, and Marcel Mauss. 1969a. "De quelques formes primitives de classification: contribution à l'étude des représentations collectives." Pp. 13–89 in *Oeuvres.* Vol. 2. Paris: Minuit.

———. 1969b. "Note sur la notion de civilisation." Pp. 451–455 in *Oeuvres.* Vol. 2. Paris: Minuit.

Durrenberger, E. Paul. 1980. "Chayanov's Economic Analysis in Anthropology." *Journal of Anthropological Research* 36 (2): 133–148.

Dutt, R. C. [1901] 1970. *The Economic History of India.* Vol. 1. New Delhi: Ministry of Information and Broadcasting.

Duus, Peter. 1995. *The Abacus and the Sword: The Japanese Penetration of Korea, 1895–1910.* Berkeley: University of California Press.

Easton, Stewart C. 1964. *The Rise and Fall of Western Colonialism*. New York: Frederick A. Praeger.

Eberhard, Wolfram. 1965. *Conquerors and Rulers: Social Forces in Medieval China*. Second Edition. Leiden: E. J. Brill.

Economy, Elizabeth. 2006. "China, Africa and Oil." Council on Foreign Relations, http://www.cfr.org/publication/9557/china Africa and oil (accessed April 10, 2006).

Economy, Elizabeth, and Karen Monaghan. 2006. "The Perils of Beijing's Africa Strategy." *International Herald Tribune*, Nov. 1: 1.

Eichengreen, Barry. 1996. *Globalizing Capital: A History of the International Monetary System*. Princeton, N.J.: Princeton University Press.

———. 2006. *Global Imbalances and the Lessons of Bretton Woods*. Cambridge, Mass.: MIT Press.

Einaudi, Luigi. 1899. *Un principe mercante: studio sull'espansione coloniale Italiana*. Turin: Bocca.

Eisenstadt, S. N. 1963. *The Political Systems of Empires*. London: Free Press of Glencoe.

———. [1963] 2010. *The Political Systems of Empires*. Revised edition, with new introduction. London: Free Press of Glencoe.

———, ed. 1967. *The Decline of Empires*. Englewood Cliffs, N.J., Prentice-Hall.

———, ed. 2002. *Multiple Modernities*. New Brunswick, N.J.: Transaction Publishers.

Eisenstein, Hester. 2009. *Feminism Seduced: How Global Elites Use Women's Labor and Ideas to Exploit the World*. Boulder, Colo.: Paradigm Publishers.

Elias, Norbert. 1978. *The History of Manners*. Translated by Edmund Jephcott. New York: Pantheon Books.

———. 2000. *The Civilizing Process*. New York: Blackwell.

Eliott, J. H. 1984. *Richelieu and Olivares*. Cambridge: Cambridge University Press.

———. 1992. "A Europe of Composite Monarchies." *Past and Present* 137:48–71.

Elkin, W. B. 1902. "An Inquiry into the Causes of the Decrease of the Hawaiian People." *American Journal of Sociology* 8:398–411.

Elkins, Caroline, and Susan Pedersen, eds. 2005. *Settler Colonialism in the Twentieth Century*. New York: Routledge.

Elliott, J. H. 2006. *Empires of the Atlantic World: Britain and Spain in the Americas, 1492–1830*. New Haven, Conn.: Yale University Press.

Ellman, M., and Laacher, S. 2003. *Migrant Workers in Israel: A Contemporary Form of Slavery*. Paris: Euro-Mediterranean Human Rights Network and International Federation for Human Rights, www.fidh.org/magmoyen/rapport/2003/il1806a.pdf.

Em, Henry. 1999. "*Minjok* as a Modern and Democratic Construct: Sin Ch'aeho's Historiography." Pp. 336–361 in G.-W. Shin and M. Robinson (Eds.), *Colonial Modernity in Korea*. Cambridge, Mass.: Harvard University Press.

Emerson, Rupert. 1960. *From Empire to Nation: The Rise to Self-Assertion of Asian and African Peoples*. Cambridge, Mass.: Harvard University Press.

Ennis, Thomas E. 1936. *French Policy and Developments in Indochina.* Chicago: University of Chicago Press.

Epstein, Steven. 2001. *Speaking of Slavery: Color, Ethnicity, and Human Bondage in Italy.* Ithaca, N.Y.: Cornell University Press.

Escobar, Arturo. 1995. *Encountering Development: The Making and Unmaking of the Third World.* Princeton, N.J.: Princeton University Press.

Esteva, Gustavo. 2010. "Development." Pp. 1–23 in Wolfgang Sachs (Ed.), *The Development Dictionary.* Second edition. London: Zed Books.

Etherington, Norman. 1984. *Theories of Imperialism.* London: Croom Helm.

Eugenics Education Society. 1912. *Problems in Eugenics: Papers Communicated to the First International Eugenics Congress Held at the University of London, July 24th to 30th, 1912.* London: Knight & Co.

Evans, Ivan. 1997. *Bureaucracy and Race: Native Administration in South Africa.* Berkeley: University of California Press.

Evans, Peter. 1995. *Embedded Autonomy: States and Industrial Transformation.* Princeton, N.J.: Princeton University Press.

Evans, Peter, Dietrich Rueschemeyer, andTheda Skocpol, eds. 1985. *Bringing the State Back In.* New York: Cambridge University Press.

Evans-Pritchard, Ambrose. 2004. "Art Show Sees Europe as 'New Roman Empire.'" *Daily Telegraph,* Sept. 14.

Fabian, Johannes. 1983. *Time and the Other: How Anthropology Makes Its Object.* New York: Columbia University Press.

Falasca-Zamponi, Simonetta. 1997. *Fascist Spectacle: The Aesthetics of Power in Mussolini's Italy.* Berkeley: University of California Press.

Fanno, Marco. 1906. *L'espansione commerciale e territoriale degli stati moderni.* Turin: Bocca.

———. 1907. "Il fattore economico dell'espansione colonial." *Rivista Italiana di sociologia* 11 (2).

Fanon, Frantz. 1967. *Black Skin, White Masks.* New York: Grove Press.

Farrell, Michael P. 2003. *Collaborative Circles.* Chicago: University of Chicago Press.

Farsakh, Leila. 2002. "Palestinian Labor Flows to the Israeli Economy: A Finished Story?" *Journal of Palestine Studies* 32 (1): 13–27.

———. 2005. *Palestinian Labour Migration to Israel: Labour, Land, and Occupation.* London: Routledge.

Favre, Pierre. 1983. "The Absence of Political Sociology in the Durkheimian Classifications of the Social Sciences." Pp. 199–216 in Besnard (1983).

Fedele, Francesco G., and Alberto Baldi, eds. 1988. *Alle origini dell'antropologia Italiana.* Naples: Guida.

Federici, Nora. 1938. "Le correnti migratorie e le correnti commerciali tra colonie e madre-patria." *Annali dell'Africa Italiana* 1 (1).

———. 1942a. "Demografia ed espansione dei popoli." *Statistica* 2 (1): 67–81

———. 1942b. "Sul ricambio sociale: teorie sociologiche e contributi statistici." *Statistica* 2 (3): 257–272.

———. 1950. "L'importanza sociologica delle inchieste del comitato Italiano per lo studio dei problemi della popolazione." Pp. 330–43I in *Atti del XIV congresso internazionale di sociologia.* Rome: S.I.S.

Ferguson, James. 2006. *Global Shadows: Africa in the Neoliberal World Order.* Durham, N.C.: Duke University Press.

Ferguson, Niall. 2004. *Empire: How Britain Made the Modern World.* London: Penguin Books.

———. 2005. *Colossus: The Rise and Fall of the American Empire.* New York: Penguin Books.

Ferguson, Priscilla Parkhurst. 1998. "A Cultural Field in the Making: Gastronomy in 19th-Century France." *American Journal of Sociology* 104 (3): 597–641.

Ferrari, Celso. 1896. "Saggio sulla vita e la morte degli organismi sociali." *Rivista di sociologia* 3 (8–9): 476–494.

———. 1898. *La libertà politica e il diritto internazionale: saggio d'interpretazione sociologica della storia.* Turin: Roux frassati e c.

Ferrero, Guglielmo. 1898. *Il militarismo: dieci conferenze.* Milan: Treves.

———. 1902–1907. *Grandezza e decadenza di Roma.* Milan: Treves.

Ferri, Enrico. 1899. *Criminal Sociology.* New York: Appleton.

Fiamingo, Giuseppe. 1895. "Sociology in Italy: The Sociological Tendency of Today." *American Journal of Sociology* 1 (3): 333–352.

Fieldhouse, D. K. 1961. "Imperialism: A Historiographical Revision." *Economic History Review* 14 (2): 187–209.

Fine, Gary Alan, and Janet S. Severance. 1985. "Great Men and Hard Times: Sociology at the University of Minnesota." *Sociological Quarterly* 26:117–134.

Finkel, Stuart. 2005. "Sociology and Revolution: Pitirim Sorokin and Russia's National Degeneration." *Russian History. Histoire Russe* 32 (2): 155–169.

Finkin, Matthew W., and Robert C. Post. 2009. *For the Common Good: Principles of American Academic Freedom.* New Haven, Conn.: Yale University Press.

Firsov, Boris. 2001. *Istoriia sovetskoi sotsiologii 1950–1970 gg. Kurs lektsii.* St. Petersburg: European University at St. Petersburg Press.

Fisch, Jörg, Dieter Groh, and Rudolf Walther. 1982. "Imperialismus." Pp. 171–236 in Otto Brunner, Werner Conze, and Reinhart Koselleck (Eds.), *Geschichtliche Grundbegriffe: Historisches Lexikon zur politisch-sozialen Sprache in Deutschland.* Vol. 3. Stuttgart: Klett-Cotta.

Fischer, Bernd J. 1999. *Albania at War, 1939–1945.* West Lafayette, Ind.: Purdue University Press.

Fisher, Michael. 1991. *Indirect Rule in India: Residents and the Residency System, 1764–1858.* New Delhi: Oxford University Press.

Fishta, Iljaz. 1979. *Ndërhyrja e kapitalit të huaj dhe pasojat e saj skllavëruese për Shqipërinë (1925–1931).* Tirana: Akademia e Shkencave e RPS të Shqiperisë, Instituti i Historisë.

———. 1989. *Ndërhyrja e kapitalit të huaj dhe pasojat e saj skllavëruese për Shqipërinë (1931–1936).* Tirana: Akademia e shkencave e RPS të shqiperisë, instituti i historisë.

————. 1999. *Ndërhyrja e kapitalit të huaj dhe roli i saj për pushtimin e Shqipërisë (1936–1939)*. Tirana: Dituria.

Fleck, Christian. 1990. *Rund um "Marienthal." Von den Anfängen der Soziologie in Österreich bis zu ihrer Vertreibung*. Vienna: Verlag für Gesellschaftskritik.

————. 2007. *Transatlantische Bereicherungen: Zur Erfindung der empirischen Sozialforschung*. Frankfurt am Main: Suhrkamp.

Folz, Robert 1969. *The Concept of Empire in Western Europe, from the Fifth to the Fourteenth Century*. Translated by Sheila Ann Ogilvie. London: Edward Arnold.

Fortunati, Paolo. 1940. "L'importanza delle colonie per la scienza e la politica della popolazione." *Annali dell'Africa Italiana* 3 (3).

Foucault, Michel. [1975] 1995. *Discipline and Punish: The Birth of the Prison*. New York: Vintage Books.

————. 1978. *The History of Sexuality*. Vol. 1. New York: Vintage Books.

————. 1980. "Questions on Geography." Pp. 63–77 in *Power/Knowledge: Selected Interviews and Other Writings, 1972–1977*. New York: Pantheon Books.

————. 1982. "The Subject and Power." Pp. 208–226 in H. Dreyfus and P. Rabinow (Eds.), *Michel Foucault: Beyond Structuralism and Hermeneutics*. Chicago: University of Chicago Press.

————. 1991. "Governmentality." Pp. 87–104 in Graham Burchell, Colin Gordon, and Peter Miller (Eds.), *The Foucault Effect: Studies in Governmentality*. Chicago: University of Chicago Press.

————. 1994. "Polémique, politique et problématisations." Pp. 591–598 in *Dits et écrits*. Vol. IV. Paris: Gallimard.

Fournier, Marcel. 2005. *Marcel Mauss: A Biography*. Princeton, N.J.: Princeton University Press.

Francis, David R. 1913. *The Universal Exposition of 1904*. St. Louis: Louisiana Purchase Company.

Frank, Andre Gunder. 1969. *Capitalism and Underdevelopment in Latin America*. New York: Monthly Review Press.

Fraser, Cary. 1992. "Understanding American Policy towards the Decolonization of European Empires, 1945–64." *Diplomacy and Statecraft* 3:105–125.

Frazer, J. G. 1922. *The Golden Bough*. London: Macmillan.

Frazier, E. Franklin. 1955. "Impact of Colonialism on African Social Forms and Personality." Pp. 70–96 in Calvin W. Stillman (Ed.), *Publication of Norman Harris Memorial Foundation Lectures on Africa in the Modern World*. Chicago: University of Chicago Press.

French, Howard W. 2006. "Commentary: China and Africa." *African Affairs* 106 (422): 127–132.

Frétigné, Jean-Yves. 2002. *Biographie intellectuelle d'un protagoniste de l'Italie liberale: Napoleone Colajanni (1847–1921)*. Rome: Ecole Francaise de Rome.

————. 2007. *Dall'ottimismo al pessimismo: itinerario politico ed intellettuale di colajanni dalla svolta liberale al fascism*. Rome: Archivio Guido Rizzi.

Freyer, Hans. 1948. *Weltgeschichte Europas*. 2 vols. Wiesbaden: Dieterich.

Freyre, Gilberto. [1933] 1946. *The Masters and the Slaves: A Study in the Development of Brazilian Civilization*. New York: A. A. Knopf.

Frisby, David. 1986. *Fragments of Modernity: Theories of Modernity in the Work of Simmel, Kracauer, and Benjamin*. Cambridge, Mass.: MIT Press.

Frum, David, and Perle, Richard. 2003. *An End to Evil: How to Win the War on Terror*. New York: Random House.

Frynas, Jedrzej George, and Manuel Paulo. 2006. "A New Scramble for African Oil? Historical, Political, and Business Perspectives." *African Affairs* 106 (423): 229–251.

Fuller, Mia. 1988. "Building Power: Italy's Colonial Architecture and Urbanism, 1923–1940." *Cultural Anthropology* 3:455–487.

———. 2007. *Moderns Abroad: Architecture, Cities, and Italian Imperialism*. New York: Routledge.

Furber, David B. 2003. "Going East: Colonialism and German Life in Nazi-Occupied Poland." Ph.D. diss., State University of New York at Buffalo (History).

Furber, David, and Wendy Lower. 2008. "Colonialism and Genocide in Nazi-Occupied Poland and Ukraine." Pp. 372–400 in A. Dirk Moses (Ed.), *Empire, Colony, Genocide: Conquest, Occupation, and Subaltern Resistance in World History*. New York: Berghahn.

Furedi, Frank. 1994. *Colonial Wars and the Politics of Third World Nationalism*. London: I. B. Tauris.

Gallagher, John, and Ronald Robinson. 1953. "The Imperialism of Free Trade." *Economic History Review* 6:1–15.

Gandhi, Ramachandra. 1984. *I Am Thou: Meditations on the Truth of India*. Pune: Indian Philosophical Quarterly Publications

———. 2005. *Muniya's Light: A Narrative of Truth and Myth*. New Delhi: IndiaInk.

Ganguli, B. N. 1977. *Indian Economic History: Nineteenth Century Perspectives*. New Delhi: Tata McGraw Hill.

Gaonkar, Dilip Parameshwar, ed. 2001a. *Alternative Modernities*. Durham, N.C.: Duke University Press.

———. 2001b. "On Alternative Modernities." Pp. 1–23 in Gaonkar (2001a).

Garofalo, Raffaele 1906. *Della sociologia come scienza autonoma e delle cattedre di sociologia*. Napoli: Tip. della R. Universita.

———. 1908. *Relazione del procuratore generale barone Garofalo sul codice penale per la colonia eritrea approvato dal consiglio coloniale nelle sedute del 22 Aprile e 21 Maggio 1906 e del 12 Maggio 1907*. Roma: Stamperia reale.

———. 1909a. "Il codice penale della colonia eritrea." *Rivista colonial*, March: 133–139.

———. 1909b. *Relazione sul codice di procedura penale per la colonia eritrea*. Rome: Stamperia reale.

Garroutte, Eva Marie. 2001. "The Racial Formation of American Indians: Negotiating Legitimate Identities within Tribal and Federal Law." *American Indian Quarterly* 25 (2): 224–239.

———. 2003. *Real Indians: Identity and the Survival of Native America*. Berkeley: University of California Press.

―――. 2008. "Native American Identity in Law." Pp. 302–307 in Garrick A. Bailey (Ed.), *Indians in Contemporary Society*. Washington, D.C.: Smithsonian.

Garth, Bryant G., and Yves Dezalay. 2002. *The Internationalization of Palace Wars*. Chicago: University of Chicago Press.

Garzia, Mino. 1992. "For the History of Sociological Analysis. A Scientific Laboratory. The *Rivista Italiana di sociologia* of Guido Cavaglieri." Introduction to *Rivista Italiana di sociologia*. Reprint, Vol. 1. Bad Feilnbach: Schmidt.

―――. 1998. *Political Communities and Calculus: Sociological Analysis in the Italian Scientific Tradition (1924–1943)*. Bern: P. Lang.

Gasster, Michael. 1998. "Anti-Manchuism." Pp. 11–13 in Ke-Wen Wang (Ed.), *Modern China: An Encyclopedia of History, Culture, and Nationalism*. New York: Garland.

Geddes, Patrick. 1917. *Ideas at War*. London: Williams and Norgate.

―――. 1918. *Town Planning towards City Development. A Report to the Durbar of Indore*. 2 vols. Indore: Holkar State Printing Press.

Gellner, Ernest. 1983. *Nations and Nationalism*. Oxford: Blackwell.

―――. 1998. *Nationalism*. London: Phoenix.

Gentile, Emilio. 1996. *The Sacralization of Politics in Fascist Italy*. Cambridge: Harvard University Press.

―――. 1999. *La grande Italia. Ascesa e declino del mito della nazione nel ventesimo secolo*. Milan: Mondadori.

Gerasimov, Ilya. 1997. *Dusha cheloveka perekhodnogo vremeni: Sluchai Aleksandra Chaianova*. Kazan: Anna.

―――. 2009. *Modernism and Public Reform in Late Imperial Russia: Rural Professionals and Self-Organization, 1905–30*. Basingstoke: Palgrave Macmillan.

Germov, John. 2005. *Histories of Australian Sociology*. Carlton, Vic.: Melbourne University Publishing.

Gerth, Hans, and C. Wright Mills. 1953. *Character and Social Structure: The Psychology of Social Institutions*. New York: Harcourt, Brace.

Ghirardo, D. 1989. *Building New Communities: New Deal America and Fascist Italy*. Princeton, N.J.: Princeton University Press.

Gibson, Mary. 1998. "Biology or Environment? Race and Southern 'Deviancy' in the Writings of Italian Criminologists, 1880–1900." Pp. 99–104 in Jane Schneider (Ed.), *Italy's "Southern Question": Orientalism in One Country*. New York: Berg.

―――. 2002. *Born to Crime: Cesare Lombroso and the Origins of Biological Criminology*. Westport: Praeger.

Giddens, Anthony. 1984. *The Constitution of Society: Outline of the Theory of Structuration*. Berkeley: University of California Press.

Giddings, Franklin. 1894. "The Relation of Sociology to Other Scientific Studies." *Journal of Social Science* 32:144–150.

―――. 1898. "Imperialism?" *Political Science Quarterly* 13:585–605.

―――. 1900. *Democracy and Empire, with Studies of Their Psychological, Economic, and Moral Foundations*. New York: Macmillan.

————. 1904. "The Concepts and Methods of Sociology." *American Journal of Sociology* 10:161–176.

————. 1909. *Inductive Sociology.* New York: Macmillan.

————. 1911. "The Relation of Social Theory to Public Policy." *American Journal of Sociology* 16:577–592.

————. 1915. *The Elements of Sociology: A Text-Book for Colleges and Schools.* New York: Macmillan.

Giglio, Carlo. 1973. "L'imperialismo coloniale in Achille Loria." Pp. 273–289 in *Studi in onore di Carlo Emilio Ferri.* Vol. 2, *Diritto e storia.* Milan: Giuffrè.

Gillette, Aaron. 2002. *Racial Theories in Fascist Italy.* London: Routledge.

Gilloch, Graeme. 2006. "Kracauer, Siegfried." Pp. 307–308 in Austin Harrington, Barbara L. Marshall, and Hans-Peter Müller (Eds.), *Encyclopedia of Social Theory.* London: Routledge.

Gilman, Nils. 2003. *Mandarins of the Future: Modernization Theory in Cold War America.* Baltimore, Md.: Johns Hopkins University Press.

Gini, Corrado. 1911. "Sui fattori demografici dell'evoluzione delle Nazioni." *Rivista Italiana di sociologia* 15 (5): 205–221.

————. 1912a. "Contributi statistici ai problemi dell'eugenica." *Rivista Italiana di sociologia* 16 (3–4): 317–326.

————. 1912b. *I fattori demografici dell'evoluzioni delle Nazioni.* Turin: Bocca.

————. 1927a. *Il neo-organicismo: prolusione al corso di sociologia.* Catania: Studio editoriale moderno.

————. 1927b. "The Scientific Basis of Fascism." *Political Science Quarterly* 42 (1): 99–115.

————. 1927c. *Sociologia: lezioni raccolte e compilate ecc.* Roma: Sampaolesi.

————. 1930a. "The Cyclical Rise and Fall of Populations." Pp. 1–140 in *Population.* Chicago: University of Chicago Press.

————. 1930b. *Nascita, evoluzione e morte delle Nazioni.* Rome: Libreria del littorio.

————. 1931. *Le basi scientifiche della politica demografica.* Rome: CISPP.

————. 1935. *Prime linee di patologia economica.* Third edition. Milan: Giuffrè.

————. 1936. "Colonie e materie prime." *La vita economica Italiana,* 2nd series 9 (1–2): 16–31.

————. 1938. "Emigrazione e colonie." *Rivista di politica economica* 28 (4): 341–352.

————. 1939. "Rural Ritual Games in Libya (Berber Baseball and Shinny)." *Rural Sociology* 4 (3): 283–299.

————. 1941a. "Il fattore demografico nella politica colonial." *Gli annali dell'Africa Italiana* 4 (3): 795–821.

————. 1941b. "La lotta attuale tra popoli conservatori e popoli espansionisti e l'evoluzione organica delle Nazioni." *Archivio di studi corporativi* 12 (3).

————. 1954. *Appunti di sociologia generale e coloniale.* Rome: Libreria Eredi V. Veschi.

————. 1957. *Corso di sociologia, con elementi di sociologia coloniale.* Rome: Edizioni ricerche.

Gini, Corrado, and Nora Federici. 1943. *Appunti sulle spedizioni scientifiche del comitato Italiano per lo studio dei problemi della popolazione (Febbraio 1933–Aprile 1940)*. Rome: Tipografia operaia romana.

Girault, Arthur. 1929. *Principes de colonisation et de législation coloniale*. Fifth edition. Vol. 2. Paris: Sirey.

Girollet, Anne. 2000. *Victor Schoelcher, abolitionniste et républicain: approche juridique et politique de l'œuvre d'un fondateur de la république*. Paris: Karthala.

Given, James. 1990. *State and Society in Medieval Europe: Gwynedd and Languedoc under Outside Rule*. Ithaca, N.Y.: Cornell University Press.

Gluck, Carol. 1985. *Japan's Modern Myth: Ideology in the Late Meiji Period*. Princeton, N.J.: Princeton University Press.

Go, Julian. 2000a. "Chains of Empire, Projects of State: Colonial State-Building in Puerto Rico and the Philippines." *Comparative Studies in Society and History* 42 (2): 333–362.

———. 2003a. "The Chains of Empire: State Building and 'Political Education' in Puerto Rico and the Philippines." Pp. 182–216 in Go and Foster (2003).

———. 2003b. "Introduction: Global Perspectives on the U.S. Colonial State in the Philippines." Pp. 1–42 in Go and Foster (2003).

———. 2004. "'Racism' and Colonialism: Meanings of Difference and Ruling Practices in America's Pacific Empire." *Qualitative Sociology* 27:35–58.

———. 2005a. "America's Colonial Empire: The Limit of Power's Reach." Pp. 201–216 in Calhoun et al. (2006b).

———. 2005b. "Modes of Rule in America's Overseas Empire." Pp. 209–229 in Sanford Levinson and Bartholomew H. Sparrow (Eds.), *The Louisiana Purchase and American Expansion*. Lanham, Md.: Rowman and Littlefield.

———. 2007. "The Provinciality of American Empire: 'Liberal Exceptionalism' and U.S. Colonial Rule." *Comparative Studies in Society and History* 49 (1): 74–108.

———. 2008a. *American Empire and the Politics of Meaning: Elite Political Cultures in the Philippines and Puerto Rico during U.S. Colonialism*. Durham, N.C.: Duke University Press.

———. 2008b. "Global Fields and Imperial Forms: Field Theory and the U.S. and British Empires." *Sociological Theory* 26 (3): 201–229.

Go, Julian, and Anne Foster, eds. 2003. *The U.S. Colonial State in the Philippines in Comparative Perspective*. Durham, N.C.: Duke University Press.

Göçek, Fatma Müge. 1987. *East Encounters West: France and the Ottoman Empire in the Eighteenth Century*. New York: Oxford University Press.

———. 2011. *The Transformation of Turkey: Redefining State and Society from the Ottoman Empire to the Modern Era*. London: I. B. Tauris.

Goh, Daniel P. S. 2005. "Ethnographic Empire: Imperial Culture and Colonial State Formation in Malaya and the Philippines, 1880–1940." Ph.D. diss., University of Michigan (Sociology).

———. 2007a. "Imperialism and 'Medieval' Natives: The Malay Image in Anglo-American Travelogues and Colonialism in Malaya and the Philippines." *International Journal of Cultural Studies* 10 (3): 323–341.

————. 2007b. "States of Ethnography: Colonialism, Resistance and Cultural Transcription in Malaya and the Philippines, 1890s–1930s." *Comparative Studies in Society and History* 49 (1): 109–142.

————. 2008. "Genèse de l'état colonial. Politiques colonisatrices et résistance indigène (Malaisie Britannique, Philippines Américaines)." *Actes de la recherche en sciences sociales* 171 (2): 56–73.

Gokhale, G. K. 1962. *Speeches and Writings of Gopala Krishna Gokhale.* Vol. 1. Poona: The Deccan Sabha.

Goldstone, Jack A. 1991. *Revolution and Rebellion in the Early Modern World.* Berkeley: University of California Press.

Goldstone, Jack A., and John E. Haldon. 2010. "Ancient States, Empires and Exploitation." Pp. 3–29 in Ian Morris and Walter Scheidel (Eds.), *The Dynamics of Ancient Empires.* Oxford: Oxford University Press.

Golosenko, I. A. 1991. *Pitirim Sorokin.* Syktyvkar: Komi.

Golosenko, I. A., and V. V. Kozlovskii. 2005. *Istoriia russkoi sotsiologii, 19–20 v.* Moscow: Onega.

Gootenberg, Paul. 1993. *Imagining Development: Economic Ideas in Peru's "Fictitious Prosperity" of Guano, 1840–1880.* Berkeley: University of California Press.

Gordon, Michael, and General Bernard Trainor. 2006. *Cobra II: The Inside Story of the Invasion and Occupation of Iraq.* New York: Random House.

Gorski, Philip. S. 2000. "The Mosaic Moment: An Early Modernist Critique of Modernist Theories of Nationalism." *American Journal of Sociology* 105 (5): 1428–1468.

Goswami, Manu. 2004. *Producing India: From Colonial Economy to National Space.* Chicago: University of Chicago.

Gott, Richard. 1989. "Little Englanders." Pp. 90–102 in Raphael Samuel (Ed.), *Patriotism: The Making and Unmaking of British National Identity.* Vol. 1. London: Routledge.

Goudsblom, J., and J. Heilbron. 2001. "Sociology, History of." Pp. 14574–14580 in Neil J. Smelser and Paul B. Baltes (Eds.), *International Encyclopedia of the Social and Behavioral Sciences.* Vol. 21. Amsterdam: Elsevier.

Gould, Erica. 2003. "Money Talks: Supplementary Financiers and IMF Conditionality." *International Organization* 57:551–586.

Gowan, Peter. 1999. *The Global Gamble: Washington's Faustian Bid for World Domination.* London: Verso.

Gowda, Chandan. 2007. "Development, Elite Agency and the Politics of Recognition in Mysore State, 1881–1947." Ph.D. diss., University of Michigan (Sociology).

Grajdanzev, Andrew. 1978. *Modern Korea.* New York: Octagon Press.

Gransow, Bettina. 1992. *Geschichte der chinesischen Soziologie.* Frankfurt: Campus Verlag.

Gray, Marion W. 1986. "Prussia in Transition: Society and Politics under the Stein Reform Ministry of 1808." *Transactions of the American Philosophical Society* 76:1–175.

Greenberg, S. 1980. *Race and State in Capitalist Development: Comparative Perspectives.* New Haven, Conn.: Yale University Press.

Greenfeld, Liah. 1992. *Nationalism: Five Roads to Modernity.* Cambridge, Mass.: Harvard University Press.

Greenstein, R. 1995. *Genealogies of Conflict: Class, Identity, and State in Palestine/Israel and South Africa.* Hanover, N.H.: Wesleyan University Press/University Press of New England.

Gregory, Derek, and John Urry. 1985. *Social Relations and Spatial Structures.* New York: St. Martin's Press.

Gresleri, Giuliano. 1993. "La via dell'est: da tirana a Lubiana." Pp. 323–331 in Gresleri, Pier Giorgio Massaretti, and Stefano Zagnoni (Eds.), *Architettura Italiana d'Oltremare 1870–1940.* Venice: Marsilio.

Gresleri, Giuliano, Pier Giorgio Massaretti, and Stefano Zagnoni, eds. 1993. *Architettura Italiana d'Oltremare 1870–1940.* Venice: Marsilio.

Grimal, Henri. 1978. *Decolonization: The British, French, Dutch, and Belgian Empires, 1919–1963.* Boulder, Colo.: Lynne Rienner.

Grimmer-Solem, Erik. 2003a. "Imperialist Socialism of the Chair: Gustav Schmoller and German Weltpolitik, 1897–1905." Pp. 106–122 in Geoff Eley and James Retallack (Eds.), *Wilhelminism and Its Legacies: German Modernities, Imperialism, and the Meanings of Reform, 1890–1930.* New York: Berghahn Books.

———. 2003b. *The Rise of Historical Economics and Social Reform in Germany, 1864–1894.* Oxford: Clarendon Press.

———. 2007. "The Professors' Africa: Economists, the Elections of 1907, and the Legitimation of German Imperialism." *German History* 25:313–347.

Grundy, Kenneth W. 1986. *The Militarization of South African Politics.* Bloomington: Indiana University Press.

Guha, Ranajit. 1992. "Dominance without Hegemony and Its Historiography." Pp. 210–309 in *Subaltern Studies VI.* Delhi: Oxford University Press.

Guilhaumou, Jacques. 2006. "Sièyes et le non-dit de la sociologie: du mot à la chose." *Revue d'histoire des sciences humaines* 15:117–134.

Gumplowicz, Ludwig. 1875. *Raçe und Staat: Eine Untersuchung über das Gesetz der Staatenbildung.* Wien: Manz.

———. 1879. *Das Recht der Nationalitäten und Sprachen in Oesterreich-Ungarn.* Innsbruck: Wagner.

———. 1883. *Der Rassenkampf. Sociologische Untersuchungen.* Innsbruck: Wagner'sche Universitäts-Buchhandlung.

———. 1909. *Der Rassenkampf. Sociologische Untersuchungen.* Second edition. Innsbruck: Wagner'sche Universitäts-Buchhandlung.

———. 1910. *Sozialphilosophie im Umriss.* Innbruck: Wagner'sche Universitäts-Buchhandlung.

Gundappa, D. V. [1941] 1998. "Preface to T. T. Sharma's *Mysooru Rajakeeya Sudharanegala Thirulu*" (in Kannada). Pp. 447–458 in H. M. Nayaka (Ed.), DVG *Krtihi Shreni.* Vol. 8. Bangalore: Department of Kannada and Culture.

———. [1971] 1997. "Dewan Rangacharlu" (in Kannada). Pp. 13–21 in H. M. Nayaka (Ed.), DVG *Krtihi Shreni*. Vol. 7. Bangalore: Department of Kannada and Culture.

Gutiérrez Rodríguez, Encarnación, Manuela Boatcǎ, and Sérgio Costa, eds. 2010. *Decolonizing European Sociology: Transdisciplinary Approaches.* Burlington, Vt.: Ashgate.

Gutnov, Dmitrii. 2004. *Russkaia Vysshaia Shkola Obshchestvennykh Nauk v Parizhe (1901–1906).* Moscow: ROSSPEN.

Guttenplan, D. D. 2011. "Attaching a Price to Academic Freedom?" *International Herald Tribune,* April 4: 10.

Habermas, Jürgen. 1984. *The Theory of Communicative Action.* 2 vols. Boston: Beacon Press.

———. 2006. *The Divided West.* Cambridge: Polity Press.

Hacking, Ian. 1995. "The Looping Effects of Human Kinds." Pp. 351–394 in Dan Sperber, David Premack, and Ann James Premack (Eds.), *Causal Cognition: A Multidisciplinary Debate.* New York: Oxford University Press.

Hall, Catherine, and Sonya O. Rose. 2006. "Introduction: Being at Home with the Empire." Pp. 1–31 in Catherine Hall and Sonya O. Rose (Eds.), *At Home with the Empire: Metropolitan Culture and the Imperial World.* Cambridge: Cambridge University Press.

Hall, Peter. 2001. *Cities of Tomorrow: An Intellectual History of Urban Planning and Design in the Twentieth Century.* Oxford: Blackwell.

Hall, Stuart. 1996. "Introduction: Who Needs Identity?" Pp. 1–17 in S. Hall and P. Gay (Eds.), *Questions of Cultural Identity.* London: Sage.

Halliday, R. J. 1968. "The Sociological Movement, the Sociological Society and the Genesis of Academic Sociology in Britain." *Sociological Review* 16:377–398.

Halsey, A. H. 2004. *A History of Sociology in Britain: Science, Literature, and Society.* Oxford: Oxford University Press.

Hammami, Rema, and Salim Tamari, S. 2006. "Anatomy of Another Rebellion: From Intifada to Interregnum." Pp. 263–281 in Beinin and Stein (2006).

Han, Suk-Jung. 1995. "Puppet Sovereignty: The State Effect of Manchukuo, from 1932 to 1936." Ph.D. diss., University of Chicago (Sociology).

Hanafi, Sari, ed. 2006. *Crossing Borders, Shifting Boundaries: Palestinian Dilemmas.* Cairo Papers in Social Science. Vol. 29, no. 1. Cairo: American University in Cairo Press.

Hanieh, Adam. 2006. "The Politics of Curfew in the Occupied Territories." Pp. 324–227 in Beinin and Stein (2006).

Hara, Takashi. [1919] 1990. "Chōsen tōchi shiken" [Private opinion on governing Korea]" Pp. 59–94 in *Saitō Magoto bunsho* [Saitō Magoto documents]. Vol. 13. Seoul: Koryŏ sŏrim.

Harcourt, Wendy. 2009. *Body Politics in Development: Critical Debates in Gender and Development.* London: Zed Books.

Hardin, Bert. 1977. *The Professionalization of Sociology. A Comparative Study: Germany–USA.* Frankfurt/New York: Campus.

Harding, Sandra. 2008. *Sciences from Below: Feminisms, Postcolonialities, and Modernities*. Durham, N.C.: Duke University Press.

Hardt, Michael, and Antonio Negri. 2000. *Empire*. Cambridge, Mass.: Harvard University Press.

———. 2004. *Multitude*. New York: Penguin Press.

Harnisch, Hartmut. 1993. "Georg Friedrich Knapp: Agrargeschichtsforschung und Sozialpolitisches Engagement im Deutschen Kaiserreich." *Jahrbuch fur Wirtschaftsgeschichte* 1:95–132.

Harper, Samuel N. 1945. *The Russia I Believe In: The Memoirs of Samuel N. Harper, 1902–1941*. Chicago: University of Chicago Press.

Harris, John H. [1912] 1968. *Dawn in Darkest Africa*. Reprint. London: Frank Cass.

Harrison, Mark. 1975. "Chayanov and the Economics of the Russian Peasantry." *Journal of Peasant Studies* 2 (4): 389–417.

———. 1977. "The Peasant Mode of Production in the Work of A. V. Chayanov." *Journal of Peasant Studies* 4 (4): 323–336.

———. 1979. "Chayanov and the Marxists." *Journal of Peasant Studies* 7 (1): 86–100.

Harvey, David. 1990. *The Condition of Postmodernity*. Cambridge: Blackwell.

———. 2001. "Cartographic Identities: Geographical Knowledges under Globalization." In *Spaces of Capital: Towards a Critical Geography*. New York: Routledge.

———. 2003. *The New Imperialism*. Oxford: Oxford University Press.

———. 2005. *A Brief History of Neoliberalism*. Oxford: Oxford University Press.

Harvey, Elizabeth R. 2005. "Management and Manipulation: Nazi Settlement Planners and Ethnic German Settlers in Occupied Poland." Pp. 95–112 in Elkins and Pedersen (2005).

Haskell, Thomas L. 1977. *The Emergence of Professional Social Science*. Urbana: University of Chicago Press.

Hatada, Takashi. 1969. *Nihonjin no Chōsenkan* [Japanese view of Korea]. Tokyo: Keiso shobō.

Haudrère, Philippe. 2003. "Le rêve brisé de Dupleix." *L'histoire* 278:56–59.

Hawkins, Mike. 1997. *Social Darwinism in European and American Thought, 1860–1945*. Cambridge: Cambridge University Press.

Heckscher, Eli. 1935. *Mercantilism*. Vol. 1. London: Allen and Unwin.

Heesterman, J. C. 1998. "The Conundrum of the King's Authority." Pp. 1–27 in J. F. Richards (Ed.), *Kingship and Authority in South Asia*. New Delhi: Oxford University Press.

Heilbron, Johan. 1984. "Les métamorphoses du Durkheimisme, 1920–1940." *Revue Française de sociologie* 26 (2): 203–237.

———. 1995. *The Rise of Social Theory*. Minneapolis: University of Minnesota Press.

———. 2004. "A Regime of Disciplines: Toward a Historical Sociology of Disciplinary Knowledge." Pp. 23–42 in Charles Camic and Hans Joas (Eds.), *The Dialogical Turn: New Roles for Sociology in the Postdisciplinary Age*. Lanham, Md.: Rowman and Littlefield.

———. 2008. "Qu'est-ce qu'une tradition nationale en sciences sociales?" *Revue d'histoire des sciences humaines* 18:3–16.

Heinge, David. 1970. *Colonial Governors*. Madison: University of Wisconsin Press.

Heitman, H. 1985. *South African War Machine*. Novato, Calif.: Presidio Press.

Hell, Julia. 2008. "Ruins Travel: Orphic Journeys through 1940s Germany." Pp. 123–160 in John Zilcosky (Ed.), *Writing Travel*. Toronto: University of Toronto Press.

———. 2009. "*Katechon*: Carl Schmitt's Imperial Theology and the Ruins of the Future." *Germanic Review* 86:283–326.

———. 2010. "Imperial Ruin Gazers, or Why Did Scipio Weep?" Pp. 169–192 in Julia Hell and Andreas Schönle (Eds.), *Ruins of Modernity*. Durham, N.C.: Duke University Press.

———. Forthcoming. *Ruin Gazing: The Third Reich and the Fall of Rome*. Chicago: University of Chicago Press.

Henry, Jean-Robert. 1989. "Approches ethnologiques du droit musulman." Pp. 133–171 in M. Flory and J.-R. Henry (Eds.), *L'enseignement du droit Musulman*. Paris: CNRS.

Herder, J. G. [1784] 1966. *Outlines of a Philosophy of the History of Man*. New York: Bergman.

Herder, Johann Gottfried. [1784] 1985. *Ideen zur Philosophie der Geschichte der Menscheit*. Wiesbaden: Fourier Verlag.

Hermassi, Elbaki. 1972. *Leadership and National Development in North Africa*. Berkeley: University of California Press.

Herskovits, Melville. 1937. *Life in a Haitian Valley*. New York: Knopf.

———. 1938. *Acculturation: The Study of Culture Contact*. New York: J. J. Augustin.

———. 1941. *The Myth of the Negro Past*. New York: Harper.

Herskovits, Melville J., and Frances S. Herskovits. [1947] 1964. *Trinidad Village*. New York: Octogon Books.

Herskovits, Melville, and Malcolm Willey. 1923. "The Cultural Approach to Sociology." *American Journal of Sociology* 29 (2): 188–199.

Hettne, Bjorn. 1978. *The Political Economy of Indirect Rule, Mysore 1881–1947*. London: Curzon Press.

Heuman, Susan. 1998. *Kistiakovsky: The Struggle for National and Constitutional Rights in the Last Years of Tsarism*. Cambridge, Mass.: Harvard Ukrainian Research Institute.

Hietala, Thomas R. 1985. *Manifest Design: Anxious Aggrandizement in Late Jacksonian America*. Ithaca, N.Y.: Cornell University Press.

Hill, C. 1964. *Bantustans: The Fragmentation of South Africa*. London: Oxford University Press.

Hill, David Jayne. 1911. *World Organization as Affected by the Nature of the Modern State*. New York: Columbia University Press.

Hindson, D. 1987. *Pass Controls and the Urban African Proletariat*. Johannesburg: Ravan Press.

Hinkle, Gisela, and Roscoe Hinkle. 1969. "Introduction." Pp. vii–lx in Edward Ross, *Social Control: A Survey of the Foundations of Order*. Cleveland, Ohio: Case Western Reserve University.

Hinkle, Roscoe. 1980. *Founding Theory of American Sociology, 1881–1915*. Boston: Routledge and Kegan Paul.

Hintze, Otto. [1907] 1970. "Imperialismus und Weltpolitik." Pp. 457–469 in *Gesammelte Abhandlungen*. Vol. 1. Third edition. Göttingen: Vandenhoeck and Ruprecht.

Hirsch, Francine. 2005. *Empire of Nations: Ethnographic Knowledge and the Making of the Soviet Union*. Ithaca, N.Y.: Cornell University Press.

Hobhouse, L. T. 1899. "The Foreign Policy of Collectivism." *Economic Review* 9:197–220.

———. 1902. "Democracy and Imperialism." *The Speaker* 5 (January 18): 443–445.

———. 1904. *Democracy and Reaction*. London: Unwin.

Hobhouse, L. T., G. C. Wheeler, and M. Ginsberg. 1915. *The Material Culture and Social Institutions of the Simpler Peoples*. London: Chapman and Hall.

Hobsbawm, E. J. 1987. *The Age of Empire, 1875–1914*. London: Weidenfeld and Nicolson.

———. 1992. *Nations and Nationalism since 1780*. Second edition. Cambridge: Cambridge University Press.

———. 1994. *Age of Extremes: The Short Twentieth Century, 1914–1991*. London: Abacus.

Hobsbawm, Eric, and T. Ranger, eds. 1983. *Invention of Tradition*. Cambridge: Cambridge University Press.

Hobson, J. A. 1898. *John Ruskin, Social Reformer*. Boston: D. Estes.

———. 1901. *The Psychology of Jingoism*. London: Grant Richards.

———. [1902] 1965. *Imperialism: A Study*. Ann Arbor: University of Michigan Press.

———. [1902] 1988. *Imperialism: A Study*. Third edition. London: Unwin Hyman.

———. 1926. *Free Thought in the Social Sciences*. New York: The Macmillan Company.

———. 1938. *Confessions of an Economic Heretic*. London: G. Allen & Unwin.

Holland, R. F. 1985. *European Decolonization, 1918–1981*. New York: St. Martin's Press.

Hollier, Dennis, ed. 1988. *The College of Sociology (1937–39)*. Minneapolis: University of Minnesota Press.

Holt, Thomas. 1990. *The Problem of Freedom: Race, Labor, and Politics in Jamaica and Britain, 1832–1938*. Baltimore, Md.: Johns Hopkins University Press.

Holton, Robert John. 2002. "Cosmopolitanism or Cosmopolitanisms? The Universal Races Congress of 1911." *Global Networks* 2 (2): 153–170.

Horkheimer, Max, and Theodor Adorno. 1972. *Dialectic of Enlightenment*. New York: Seabury Press.

Horn, David. 1994. *Social Bodies: Science, Reproduction, and Italian Modernity*. Princeton, N.J.: Princeton University Press.

Horowitz, Donald L. 1985. *Ethnic Groups in Conflicts*. Berkeley: University of California Press.

Horsman, Reginald. 1981. *Race and Manifest Destiny: The Origins of American Racial Anglo-Saxonism*. Cambridge, Mass.: Harvard University Press.

Hoselitz, Bert F. 1951. "Review of Joseph Schumpeter, *Imperialism and Social Classes*." *Journal of Political Economy* 59 (4): 360–363.

Hosking, Geoffrey. 1997. *Russia: People and Empire, 1552–1917*. Cambridge, Mass.: Harvard University Press.

Hountondji, Paulin. 2002. "Knowledge Appropriation in a Post-Colonial Context." Pp. 23–38 in Catherine A. Odora Hoppers (Ed.), *Indigenous Knowledge and the Integration of Knowledge Systems*. Claremont: New Africa Books.

Howe, Anthony. 2002. "Free-Trade Cosmopolitanism in Britain, 1846–1914." Pp. 87–105 in Patrick Karl O'Brien and Arman Cleese (Eds.), *Two Hegemonies: Britain 1846–1914 and the United States 1941–2001*. Aldershot: Ashgate.

Howse, Robert. 2006. "Europe and the New World Order: Lessons from Alexandre Kojève's Engagement with Schmitt's 'Nomos der Erde.'" *Leiden Journal of International Law* 19 (1): 93–103.

Hudson, Michael. 2003. *Super Imperialism: The Origins and Fundamentals of U.S. World Dominance*. London: Pluto.

Hunt, Michael H. 1987. *Ideology and Foreign Policy*. New Haven, Conn.: Yale University Press.

Huntington, Samuel P. 1999. "The Lonely Superpower." *Foreign Affairs*, March–April: 35–49.

Hutchins, Francis G. 1967. *The Illusion of Permanence: British Imperialism in India*. Princeton, N.J.: Princeton University Press.

Hutchinson, M. 2001. "A Cure Worse than the Disease? Currency Crises and Output Costs of Supported Stabilization Programs." Pp. 321–360 in Michael P. Dooley and Jeffrey A. Frankel (Eds.), *Managing Currency Crises in Emerging Markets*. Chicago: University of Chicago Press.

Hyland, William. 1999. *Clinton's World: Remaking American Foreign Policy*. Westport, Conn.: Praeger.

Ibn Khaldun. 1967. *The Muqaddimah: An Introduction to History*. Princeton, N.J.: Princeton University Press.

Ileto, Reynaldo. 1988. "Cholera and the Origins of the American Sanitary Order in the Philippines." Pp. 125–148 in David Arnold (Ed.), *Imperial Medicine and Indigeneous Societies*. Manchester: Manchester University Press.

Inden, Ronald. 1990. *Imagining India*. Oxford: Basil Blackwell.

Inglis, Amirah. 1974. *"Not a White Woman Safe": Sexual Anxiety and Politics in Port Moresby 1920–1934*. Canberra: ANU Press.

Ipsen, Carl. 1992. *Dictating Demography: The Problem of Population in Fascist Italy*. Princeton, N.J.: Princeton University Press.

Isaacman, Allen, and Barbara Isaacman. 1977. "Resistance and Collaboration in Southern and Central Africa, c. 1850–1920." *International Journal of African Historical Studies* 10 (1): 31–62.

Ismail, Mirza. [1931] 1936. "At the Opening of the Session of the All-India Ophthalmological Society at Bangalore, July 20, 1931." Pp. 66–69 in Ismail (1936).

————. [1932] 1936. "Concluding Remarks at the Mysore Representative Assembly, June 13, 1932." Pp. 123–126 in Ismail (1936).

———— [1933] 1936. "Speech at the Distribution of Prizes at the Dasara Exhibition, October 4, 1933." Pp. 240–245 in Ismail (1936).

————1936. *Speeches*. Vol. 2. Bangalore: Government Press.

———— [1936] 1942. "Address to the Mysore Representative Assembly, October 26, 1936." Pp. 15–40 in *Speeches*. Vol. 3. Bangalore: Government Press.

Israeli-Palestinian Interim Agreement on the West Bank and Gaza Strip. 1995. http://www.mfa.gov.il/MFA/Peace+Process/Guide+to+the+Peace+Process/THE+israeli-palestinian+interim+agreement.htm.

Iuzhakov, S. N. 1894. *Dobrovoletz Peterburg: Dvazhdy vokrug Azii: putevye vpechatleniia*. St. Petersburg: B. M. Volf.

Ivanov, A. E. 1998. "Psikhonevrologicheskii institut v Peterburge." Pp. 264–270 in A. A. Fursenko (Ed.), *Rossiia v XIX–XX vv. Sbornik statei k 70–letiiu so dnia rozhdeniia R.Sh. Ganelina*. St. Petersburg: Dmitrii Bulanin.

Iyenaga, Toyokichi. 1912. "Japan's Annexation of Korea." *Journal of Race Development* 3 (2): 201–223.

Iyer, Raghavan. 1960. "Utilitarianism and All That (The Political Theory of British Imperialism in India)." Pp. 9–71 in Iyer Raghavan (Ed.), *South Asian Affairs*, No. 1 (St. Anthony's Papers No. 8). London: Chatto and Windus.

Jabbour, George. 1970. *Settler Colonialism in Southern Africa and the Middle East*. Beirut: Palestine Liberation Organization Research Center.

Jacomoni, Francesco. 1965. *La politica dell'Italia in Albania: Nelle testimonianze del luogotenente del Re*. Bologna: Cappelli.

Jagirdar, Prabhakar Janardan. 1963. *Studies in the Social Thought of M. G. Ranade*. New Delhi: Asia Publishing House.

Jasny, Naum. 1972. *Soviet Economists of the Twenties: Names to Be Remembered*. Cambridge: Cambridge University Press.

Jawara, Fatoumata, and Eileen Kwa. 2003. *Behind the Scenes at the WTO: The Real World of International Trade Negotiations*. London: Zed.

Jenista, Frank, Jr. 1971. "Conflict in the Philippine Legislature: The Commission and the Assembly from 1907 to 1913." Pp. 77–101 in Norman G. Owen (Ed.), *Compadre Colonialism: Studies on the Philippines under American Rule*. Ann Arbor: Center for South and Southeast Asian Studies, University of Michigan.

Jenks, Albert Ernest. 1914. "Assimilation in the Philippines, as Interpreted in Terms of Assimilation in America." *American Journal of Sociology* 19 (6): 773–791.

Jenkyns, Richard. 1992. "The Legacy of Rome." Pp. 1–35 in Richard Jenkyns (Ed.), *The Legacy of Rome: A New Appraisal*. Oxford: Oxford University Press.

Jessop, B. (1990). *State Theory: Putting Capitalist States in their Place*. University Park: Pennsylvania University Press.

Jesudason, James. 2001. "Legitimacy, Participation, and Ethnic Conflict." Pp. 65–98 in Nat J. Colletta, Teck Ghee Lim, and Anita Kelles-Viitanen (Eds.), *Social Cohesion and Conflict Prevention in Asia: Managing Diversity through Development*. Washington, D.C.: World Bank.

Joerges, C. 2003. "Europe a *Großraum*?" Pp. 167–191 in C. Joerges and N. S. Ghaleigh (Eds.), *Darker Legacies of Law in Europe: The Shadow of National Socialism and Fascism over Europe and Its Legal Traditions*. Oxford: Hart.

Johnson, Chalmers A. 2000. *Blowback: The Costs and Consequences of American Empire*. New York: Metropolitan Books.

———. 2005. *The Sorrows of Empire*. New York: Henry Holt.

Johnston, Barry V. 1995. *Pitirim A. Sorokin: An Intellectual Biography*. Lawrence: University Press of Kansas.

Johnston, William M. 1972. *The Austrian Mind*. Berkeley: University of California Press.

Jones, Colin. 1999. *The Cambridge Illustrated History of France*. Cambridge: Cambridge University Press.

Jones, Rhys, and Richard Phillips. 2005. "Unsettling Geographical Horizons: Exploring Premodern and Non-European Imperialism." *Annals of the Association of American Geographers* 95 (1): 141–161.

Jordheim, Helge. 2007. "Conceptual History between Chronos and Kairos. The Case of 'Empire.'" *Redescriptions. Yearbook of Political Thought, Conceptual History and Feminist Theory* 11:115–145.

Josyer, G. R. 1930. *Politics, Philosophy and Phantasy*. Mysore: Coronation Press.

Juhazs, Antonia. 2006. *The Bush Agenda: Invading the World, One Economy at a Time*. London: Duckworth.

Junger, Sebastian. 2007. "Enter the Giant." *Vanity Fair* 563 (July): 126–138.

Kagan, Robert, and William Kristol, eds. 2000. *Present Dangers: Crisis and Opportunity in American Foreign and Defense Policy*. New York: Encounter Publications.

Kaiser, J. H. 1968. "Europäisches Großraumdenken. Die Steigerung geschichtlicher Größen als Rechtsproblem." Pp. 529–548 in H. Barion, E. Böckenförde, E. Forsthoff, and Werner Weber (Eds.), *Epirrhosis. Festgabe für Carl Schmitt*. Berlin: Duncker and Humblot.

Kaloev, B. A. 1979. *M. M. Kovalevsky i ego issledovaniia gorskikh narodov kavkaza*. Moscow: Nauka.

Kanazawa, Shozaburo. [1929] 1978. *Nissen dōsoron* [Theses on the same ancestry of Japan and Korea]. Tokyo: Seiko Shobō.

Kang, Chang-Il. 2003. *Kŭndae Ilbon ŭi Chosŭn chimryak kwa daeasiajŭi* [Modern Japan's Invasion of Korea and Great-Asianism]. Seoul: Yŏksa Pip'yŏngsa.

Kann, Robert A. 1974. *A History of the Habsburg Empire, 1526–1918*. Berkeley: University of California Press.

Kant, Immanuel. 1784. "Idee zu einer allgemeinen geschichte in weltbürgerlicher Absicht." Pp. 15–31 in *Akademieausgabe von Immanuel Kants Gesammelten Werken*, Abt. I, Bd. VIII.

Kaplan, Amy. 2005. *The Anarchy of Empire in the Making of U.S. Culture*. Cambridge, Mass.: Harvard University Press.

Kaplan, Amy, and Donald E. Pease, eds. 1993. *Cultures of United States Imperialism*. Durham, N.C.: Duke University Press.

Kappeler, Andreas. 2001. *The Russian Empire: A Multiethnic History.* Harlow: Longman.

Karady, Victor. 1976. "Durkheim, les sciences sociales et l'université: bilan d'un semi-échec." *Revue Française de sociologie* 17 (2): 267–311.

———. 1979. "Stratégies de réussite et modes de faire-valoir de la sociologie chez les Durkheimiens." *Revue Française de sociologie* 20 (1): 49–82.

———. 1983. "The Durkheimians in Academe: A Reconsideration." Pp. 71–89 in Besnard (1983).

Kareev, Nikolai. 1907. *Vvedenie v sotsiologiiu.* Second edition. St. Petersburg: M. M. Stasiulevich.

———. 1996. *Osnovy russkoi sotsiologii.* St. Petersburg: Izdatel'stvo Ivana Limbakha.

Kaske, Elisabeth. 2002. *Bismarcks Missionäre: Deutsche Militärinstrukteure in China 1884–1890.* Wiesbaden: Harrassowitz.

Käsler, Dirk. 1984. *Die frühe deutsche Soziologie 1900 bis 1934 und ihre Entstehungs-Milieus.* Opladen: Westdeutscher Verlag.

———. 1991. *Sociological Adventures: Earle Edward Eubank's Visits with European Sociologists.* New Brunswick, N.J.: Transaction.

Käsler, Dirk, and Ludgera Vogt, eds. 2000. *Hauptwerke der Soziologie.* Stuttgart: A. Kröner.

Kaufmann, Eric P., ed. 2004. *Rethinking Ethnicity: Majority Groups and Dominant Minorities.* London: Routledge.

Kedourie, Elie 1961. *Nationalism.* London: Hutchinson.

———. 1971. "Introduction." Pp. 1–160 in Elie Kedourie (Ed.), *Nationalism in Asia and Africa.* London: Weidenfeld and Nicolson.

Keet, Dot. 2007. "China as 'Partner' or Neo-Colonial Operator in Africa?" Transnational Institute: A Worldwide Fellowship of Committed Scholar-Activists, http://www.tni.org/detail_page.phtm?andact_id=16959.

Keller, Albert G. 1906. "The Value of the Study of Colonies for Sociology." *American Journal of Sociology* 12:417–420.

Kelly, John D., ed. 2010. *Anthropology and Global Counterinsurgency.* Chicago: University of Chicago Press.

Kempner, Robert M. W. 1941. "The New Constitution of Albania: A Model Constitution for European Vassal States." *Tulane Law Review* 15:430–434.

Kennedy, Charles H. 2004. "The Creation and Development of Pakistan's Anti-Terrorism Regime, 1997–2002." Pp. 387–411 in Satu P. Limaye, Mohan Malik, and Robert Wirsing (Eds.), *Religious Radicalism and Security in South Asia.* Honolulu, Hawaii: Asia-Pacific Center for Security Studies.

Kennedy, Michael D., and Miguel A. Centeno. 2007. "Internationalism and Global Transformations in American Sociology." Pp. 666–712 in Calhoun (2007).

Kennedy, Paul M. 1987. *The Rise and Fall of the Great Powers.* New York: Random House.

Kenyatta, Jomo. 1938. *Facing Mount Kenya: The Tribal Life of the Gikuyu.* London: Secker and Warburg.

Kettler, David. 2005. "The Symbolic Uses of Exile: Erich Kahler at Ohio State." Pp. 269–310 in Alexander Stephan (Ed.), *Exile and Otherness: New Approaches to the Experience of Nazi Refugees*. Oxford: Peter Lang.

Khalid, Adeeb. 2006. "Backwardness and the Quest for Civilization: Early Soviet Central Asia in Comparative Perspective." *Slavic Review* 65 (2): 231–251.

Kharuzin, M.N. 1885. *Svedeniia o kazatskikh obshchinakh na Donu: Materialy dlia obychnogo prava*. Vol. 1. Moscow: M. N. Shchepkin.

Kidd, Benjamin. 1894. *Social Evolution*. New York and London: Macmillan and Co.

———. 1898. *The Control of the Tropics*. New York and London: Macmillan and Co.

Kim, Dong No. 2006. "Ilbon jekukjuŭi ŭi chosŏn jibaeŭi doktŭksŏng" [Special characteristics of Japanese colonial rule in Korea]. *Dongbang Hakji* 133:199–242.

Kim, Jun-Yeop, and Chang-Sun Kim. 1986. *Hankuk konsanjŭui undongsa* [History of communist movements in Korea]. Vol. 2. Seoul: Chŏngkye.

King, Anthony D. 1976. *Colonial Urban Development: Culture, Social Power, and Environment*. London: Routledge and Paul.

———. 1990. *Urbanism, Colonialism, and the World-Economy: Cultural and Spatial Foundations of the World Urban System*. London: Routledge.

———. 1995. "Writing Colonial Space: A Review Article." *Comparative Studies in Society and History* 37:541–554.

———. 2004. *Spaces of Global Cultures: Architecture, Urbanism, Identity*. London: Routledge.

King, Irving. 1903. "Influence of the Form of Change upon the Emotional Life of a People." *American Journal of Sociology* 9:124–135.

Kita, [Sadakichi] Teikichi. 1910. *Kankoku no heigo to kokushi* [Annexation of Korea and national history]. Tokyo: Sanseido Shōten.

Klingemann, Carsten. 1989. "Angewandte Soziologie im Nationalsozialismus." *1999. Zeitschrift für Sozialgeschichte des 20. und 21. Jahrhunderts* 4 (1): 10–34.

———. 2009. *Soziologie und Politik: Sozialwissenschaftliches Expertenwissen im Dritten Reich und in der frühen westdeutschen Nachkriegszeit*. Wiesbaden: VS Verlag für Sozialwissenschaften.

Kloosterhuis, Jürgen. 1994. *Friedliche Imperialisten: Deutsche Auslandsvereine und auswärtige Kulturpolitik, 1906–1918*. Frankfurt am Main: P. Lang.

Knapp, Georg Friedrich. 1891. *Die Landarbeiter in Knechtschaft und Freiheit: Vier Vorträge*. Leipzig: Duncker and Humblot.

———. 1925. "Landarbeiter und innere Kolonisation." Pp. 124–142 in *Einführung in einige Hauptgebiete der Nationalökonomie: Siebenundzwanzig Beiträge zur Sozialwissenschaft*. Munich: Duncker and Humblot.

———. 1927. *Die Bauernbefreiung und der Ursprung der Landarbeiter in den älteren Theilen Preußens*. 2 vols. Munich: Duncker and Humblot.

Koebner, Richard. 1954. "Imperium. The Roman Heritage." *Scripta Hierosolymitana* 1:120–144.

———. 1955. "From Imperium to Empire." *Scripta Hierosolymitana* 2:119–175.

———. 1961. *Empire*. Cambridge: Cambridge University Press.

Koebner, Richard, and Helmut Dan Schmidt. 1964. *Imperialism: The Story and Significance of a Political Word, 1840–1960*. Cambridge: Cambridge University Press.

Koenigsberger, Helmut 1987. "*Dominium Regale* or *Dominium Politicum et Regale*: Monarchies and Parliaments in Early Modern History." Pp. 1–25 in *Politicians and Virtuosi: Essays in Early Modern History*. London: Hambledon Press.

Kohli, Atul. 2004. *State-Directed Development: Political Power and Industrialization in the Global Periphery*. Cambridge: Cambridge University Press.

Kohn, Hans 1932. *Nationalism and Imperialism in the Hither East*. London: Routledge and Sons.

Kojève, Alexandre. 2002. "Outline of a Doctrine of French Policy." *Policy Review* 126:3–40.

Koka, Viron. 1985. *Rrymat e mendimit politiko-shoqëror në Shqipëri në vitet 30 të shekullit XX*. Tirana: Instituti i Historisë.

Kolerov, M. A. 1996. *Ne mir, no mech'. Russkaia religiozno-filosofskaia pechat' ot "Problem idealizma" do "Vekh," 1902–1909*. St. Petersburg: Aleteia.

Kolonialpolitischen Aktionskomité. 1907. *Kolonialpolitischer Führer*. Berlin: Wedekind.

Kopf, David. 1969. *British Orientalism and the Bengal Renaissance*. Berkeley: University of California Press.

Koselleck, Reinhart. 1975. *Preußen zwischen Reform und Revolution: Allgemeines Landrecht, Verwaltung und soziale Bewegung von 1791 bis 1848*. Second edition. Stuttgart: Klett-Cotta.

Kostof, Spiro. 1973. *The Third Rome: Traffic and Glory*. Berkeley, Calif.: University Art Museum.

———. 1994. "His Majesty the Pick: The Aesthetics of Demolition." Pp. 9–22 in Çelik et. al (1994).

Kovalevsky, M. M. 1879. *Obshchinnoe zemlevladenie, prichiny, khod i posledstviia ego razlozheniia*. Part 1. Moscow: F. B. Miller.

———. 1880. *Istoriko-sravnitel'nyi metod v iurisprudentsii i priemy izucheniia istorii prava*. Moscow: F. B. Miller.

———. 1890a. *Tableau des origines et de l'évolution de la famille et de la propriété*. Stochholm: Samson and Wallin.

———. 1890b. *Zakon i obychai na Kavkaze*. Vol. 1. Moscow: A. I. Mamontov.

———. 1891. *Modern Customs and Ancient Laws of Russia, Being the Ilchester Lectures for 1889–90*. London: David Nutt.

———. 1902a. *Russian Political Institutions*. Chicago: University of Chicago Press.

———. 1902b. *Sotsiologiia i sravnitel'naia istoriia prava*. Moscow: I. N. Kushnerev.

———. 1905. "Otnoshenie Rossii k okrainam." *Russkie Vedomosti*, Oct. 9: 2–5.

———. 1997. *Sochineniia*. Vol. 2. St. Petersburg: Aleteia.

———. 2002. "Zadacha progressivnykh partii na budushchikh vyborakh." Pp. 257–58 in *Partii demokraticheskikh reform, mirnogo obnovleniia, progressistov: Dokumenty i materialy, 1906–1916*. Moscow: ROSSPEN.

————. 2005. *Moia zhizn'*. Moscow: ROSSPEN.

Kovel, J. 2007. *Overcoming Zionism: Creating a Single Democratic State in Israel/ Palestine*. Ann Arbor: University of Michigan Press.

Kracauer, Siegfried. 1922. *Soziologie als wissenschaft*. Dresden: Sibyllen-Verlag.

————. 1928. *The Salaried Masses: Duty and Distraction in Weimar Germany*. London: Verso.

Kramer, Paul. 2003. "Empires, Exceptions, and Anglo-Saxons: Race and Rule between the British and U.S. Empires, 1880–1910." Pp. 43–91 in Go and Foster (2003).

————. 2006. *The Blood of Government: Race, Empire, the United States, and the Philippines*. Chapel Hill: University of North Carolina Press.

Kreissler, Françoise. 1989. *L'action culturelle allemande en Chine*. Paris: Maison des sciences de l'homme.

Kruse, Volker. 1990. *Soziologie und "Gegenwartskrise." Die Zeitdiagnose Franz Oppenheimers und Alfred Webers*. Wiesbaden: Deutscher Universitäts-Verlag.

————. 1999. *Analysen zur deutschen historischen Soziologie*. Münster: LIT.

Kumar, Krishan. 2000. "Nation and Empire: English and British National Identity in Comparative Perspective." *Theory and Society* 29 (5): 578–608.

————. 2003. *The Making of English National Identity*. Cambridge: Cambridge University Press.

————. 2005. "When Was the English Nation?" Pp. 137–156 in Atsuko Ichijo and Gordana Uzelac (Eds.), *When Is the Nation?: Towards an Understanding of Theories of Nationalism*. London: Routledge.

Kunz, Diane 1997. *Butter and Guns: America's Cold War Economic Diplomacy*. New York: Free Press.

Kurasawa, F. 2003. "Primitiveness and the Flight from Modernity: Sociology and the Avant-Garde in Interwar Paris." *Economy and Society* 32 (1): 7–28.

————. 2004. *The Ethnological Imagination*. Minneapolis: University of Minnesota Press.

Kuzio, Taras 2002. "The Myth of the Civic State." *Ethnic and Racial Studies* 25 (1): 20–39.

Laaser, Andreas. 1981. *Wissenschaftliche Lehrfreiheit in der Schule: Geschichte und Bedeutungswandel eines Grundrechts*. Königstein/Ts.: Athenäum.

Labanca, Nicola. 2002. *Oltremare*. Bologna: Il mulino.

————. 2003. "Studies and Research on Fascist Colonialism, 1922–1935: Reflections on the State of the Art." Pp. 37–61 in Patrizia Palumbo (Ed.), *A Place in the Sun: Africa in Italian Colonial Culture from Post-Unification to the Present*. Berkeley: University of California Press.

Lacan, Jacques. [1975] 1991. *The Seminar of Jacques Lacan*. Book I. *Freud's Papers on Technique 1953–1954*. New York: Norton.

Laclau, Ernesto, and Chantal Mouffe. 1985. *Hegemony and Socialist Strategy*. London: Verso.

Lagerquist, P. 2003. "Privatizing the Occupation: The Political Economy of an Oslo Development Project." *Journal of Palestine Studies* 32 (2): 5–20.

Lamprakos, Michele. 1992. "Le Corbusier and Algiers: The Plan Obus as Colonial Urbanism." Pp. 183–210 in Nezar AlSayyad (Ed.), *Forms of Dominance: On the Architecture and Urbanism of the Colonial Enterprise*. Aldershot: Avebury.

Lanaro, Silvio. 1979. *Nazione e lavoro: saggio sulla cultura borghese in Italia, 1870–1925*. Venice: Marsilio.

Landmann, Robert von. 1907. *Kommentar zur Gewerbeordnung für das Deutsche Reich*. 2 vols. Munich: C. H. Beck.

Landshut, Siegfried. 1929. *Kritik der Soziologie*. München: Duncker and Humblot.

Lane, Jeremy F. 2000. *Pierre Bourdieu: A Critical Introduction*. London: Pluto Press.

Lange, Matthew. 2004. "British Colonial Legacies and Political Development." *World Development* 32 (6): 905–922.

———. 2006. "Colonialism and Development: A Comparative Analysis of Spanish and British Colonies." *American Journal of Sociology* 111 (5): 1412–1462.

Lardinois, R. 2007. *L'invention de l'Inde: entre ésotérisme et science*. Paris: CNRS Editions.

Larebo, Haile M. 1994. *The Building of an Empire: Italian Land Policy and Practice in Ethiopia, 1935–1941*. Oxford: Clarendon Press.

———. 2005. "Empire Building and Its Limitations: Ethiopia (1935–1941)." Pp. 83–94 in Ben-Ghiat and Fuller (2005).

LAW—The Palestinian Society for the Protection of Human Rights and the Environment. n.d. *Apartheid, Bantustans, Cantons: The ABC of the Oslo Accords*. Jerusalem: LAW.

Lazzarato, Maurizio. 2002. *Puissances de l'invention: la psychologie économique de Gabriel Tarde contre l'économie politique*. Paris: Empêcheurs de penser en rond.

Le Cour Grandmaison, Olivier. 2005. *Coloniser, exterminer: sur la guerre et l'état colonial*. Paris: Fayard.

———. 2010. *De l'indigénat. Anatomie d'un "monstre" juridique: le droit colonial en Algérie et dans l'empire Français*. Paris: Zones/La découverte.

Le Sueur, James D. 2001. *Uncivil War: Intellectuals and Identity Politics during the Decolonization of Algeria*. Philadelphia: University of Pennsylvania Press.

Le Teguilly, Philippe, and Monique Moraze. 1995. *L'Inde et la France: deux siècles d'histoire communes*. Paris: CNRS éditions.

Lebovics, Herman. 2004. *Bringing the Empire Back Home: France in the Global Age*. Durham, N.C.: Duke University Press.

Lee, J. M., and M. Petter. 1982. *The Colonial Office, War, and Development Policy*. London: Institute of Commonwealth Studies.

Leenhardt, Maurice. [1902] 1976. *Le mouvement Éthiopien au sud de l'Afrique de 1896 à 1899*. Paris: Académie des sciences d'outre-mer.

———. 1953. *Gens de la grande terre*. Second edition. Paris: Gallimard.

Lefebvre, Henri. [1974] 1991. *The Production of Space*. Malden, Mass.: Blackwell.

———. 2003. "Space and the State." Pp. 84–100 in Brenner et al. (2003).

Lefèvre, Kim. 1992. "Eves jaunes et colons blancs." Pp. 111–119 in Philippe Franchini (Ed.), *Saigon 1925–1945*. Paris: Autrement.

Leiris, Michel. 1934. *L'Afrique fantôme*. Paris: Gallimard.

———. 1966. "L'ethnographe devant le colonialisme." Pp. 125–145 in *Brisées*. Paris: Gallimard.

———. 1989. "The Ethnographer Faced with Colonialism." In *Brisées = Broken Branches*. San Francisco: North Point Press.

Lentini, Osvaldo. 1974. *L'analisi sociale durante il fascism*. Naples: Guida.

———. 1983. "Tendenze della teoria sociale durante il fascism." Pp. 62–66 in Alberto Izzo and Carlo Mongardini (Eds.), *Contributi di storia della sociologia*. Milan: Angeli.

Lepsius, M. Rainer. 1983. "The Development of Sociology in Germany after World War II (1945–1968)." *International Journal of Sociology* 13 (3): 3–88.

Lerner, M. 2004. *The Geneva Accord and Other Strategies for Healing the Israeli-Palestinian Conflict*. Berkeley, Calif.: North Atlantic Books.

Leroy-Beaulieu, Paul. 1874. *De la colonisation chez les peuples modernes*. Paris: Guillaumin.

Lescourret, Marie-Anne, ed. 2009. *Pierre Bourdieu: un philosophe en sociologie*. Paris: PUF.

Lester, Alan. 1998. *From Colonization to Democracy: A New Historical Geography of South Africa*. London: I. B. Tauris.

Leveau, Arnaud. 2003. *Le destin des fils du dragon: l'influence de la communauté Chinoise au Viêt Nam et en Thaïlande*. Paris: L'harmattan.

Levi della Vida, Giuseppina. 1935. "La teoria della circolazione delle aristocrazie del Pareto e la teoria del ricambio sociale del Gini." *Genus* 2 (1–2): 83–136.

Levine, Donald. 1995. *Visions of the Sociological Tradition*. Chicago: University of Chicago Press.

———. 2005. "The Continuing Challenge of Weber's Theory of Rational Action." Pp. 101–226 in Charles Camic, Philip S. Gorski, and David M. Trubek (Eds.), *Max Weber's "Economy and Society": A Critical Companion*. Stanford, Calif.: Stanford University Press.

Lévi-Strauss, Claude. 1971. "French Sociology." Pp. 503–537 in G. Gurvitch and W. E. Moore (Eds.), *Twentieth Century Sociology*. Freeport, N.Y.: Books for Libraries Press.

———. 1997. *Tristes tropiques*. New York: Modern Library.

Levy, Jack. 1983. *War in the Modern Great Power System, 1495–1975*. Lexington: University of Kentucky Press.

Lévy-Bruhl, Lucien. [1910] 1966. *How Natives Think*. New York: Washington Square Press.

———. 1923. *Primitive Mentality*. London: Allen and Unwin.

Lewis, Martin Deming. 1962. "One Hundred Million Frenchmen: The 'Assimilation' Theory in French Colonial Policy." *Comparative Studies in Society and History* 4:129–153.

Lichtheim, George. 1974. *Imperialism*. Harmondsworth: Penguin Books.

Lieven, Dominic. 2000. *Empire: The Russian Empire and Its Rivals from the Sixteenth Century to the Present*. London: John Murray.

Light, Ivan. 1983. *Cities in World Perspective*. New York: Macmillan.

Lindenfeld, David F. 1997. *The Practical Imagination: The German Sciences of State in the Nineteenth Century.* Chicago: University of Chicago Press.

List, Friedrich. [1841] 1904. *The National System of Political Economy.* Translated by Sampson S. Lloyd. London: Longmans, Green and Company.

Lloyd, T. O. 2002. *Empire, Welfare State, Europe: History of the United Kingdom, 1906–2001.* Oxford: Oxford University Press.

Lochak, Danièle. 1991. "La citoyenneté: un concept juridique flou." Pp. 179–207 in Dominique Colas, Claude Emeri, and Jacques Zylberberg (Eds.), *Citoyenneté et nationalité: perspectives en France et au Québec.* Paris: PUF.

Lombroso, Cesare. 1871. *L'uomo bianco e l'uomo di colore: letture sull'origine e la varietà delle razze umane.* Padua: Sacchetto.

———. 1911a. *Crime: Its Causes and Remedies.* New York: Little, Brown.

———. 1911b. *The Criminal Man.* New York: Putnam.

Lombroso, Cesare, and G. Ferrero. 1893. *La donna delinquente, la prostituta e la donna normale.* Turin: Roux.

Lorcin, Patricia M. E. 1995. *Imperial Identities: Stereotyping, Prejudice and Race in Colonial Algeria.* London: I. B. Tauris.

Loria, Achille. 1882. *La legge di popolazione ed il sistema sociale.* Siena: Lazzari.

———. 1898. "L'importance sociologique des etudes economiques sur les colonies." *Annales de l'institut international de sociologie* 4:137–166.

———. 1899. *Economic Foundations of Society.* New York: Sambiner.

———. 1905. *La morphologie sociale.* Brussels: Veuve F. Larcier.

———. 1927. *Ricordi di uno studente settuagenario.* Bologna: Zanichelli.

Losito, Marta, and Segre Sandro. 1991. "Ambiguous Influences. Italian Sociology and the Fascist Regime." Pp. 42–87 in S. P. Turner and Dirk Käsler (Eds.), *Sociology Responds to Fascism.* London: Routledge.

Louis, William Roger. 1967. "Great Britain and German Expansion in Africa, 1884–1919." Pp. 3–46 in Prosser Gifford and William Roger Louis (Eds.), *Britain and Germany in Africa: Imperial Rivalry and Colonial Rule.* New Haven, Conn.: Yale University Press.

Louis, William Roger, and Ronald Robinson. 1993. "The Imperialism of Decolonization." *Journal of Imperial and Commonwealth History* 22 (3): 462–511.

Löwith, Karl. 1949. *Meaning in History.* Chicago: University of Chicago Press.

Lowry, John S. 2006. "African Resistance and Center Party Recalcitrance in the Reichstag Colonial Debates of 1905/06." *Central European History* 39:244–269.

Ludden, David. 1992. "India's Development Regime." In Nicholas Dirks (Ed.), *Colonialism and Culture.* Ann Arbor: University of Michigan Press.

———. 2005. "Development Regimes in South Asia." *Economic and Political Weekly* 40 (37): 4042–4051.

Lugard, Frederick John Dealtry. 1928. *Representative Forms of Government and "Indirect Rule" in British Africa.* Edinburgh: W. Blackwood and Sons.

Luhmann, Niklas. 1995. *Social Systems.* Stanford, Calif.: Stanford University Press.

Lukács, György. 1981. *The Destruction of Reason*. Atlantic Highlands, N.J.: Humanities Press.

Lukes, S. 1985. *Emile Durkheim*. Stanford, Calif.: Stanford University Press.

Lustick, Ian. 1993. *Unsettled States, Disputed Lands: Britain and Ireland, France and Algeria, Israel and the West Bank-Gaza*. Ithaca, N.Y.: Cornell University Press.

Lyman, Stanford M. 1992. *Militarism, Imperialism, and Racial Accomodation*. Fayetteville: University of Arkansas Press.

MacClintock, Samuel. 1903. "Around the Island of Cebu on Horseback." *American Journal of Sociology* 8 (4): 433–441.

Macintyre, Stuart. 2010. *The Poor Relation. A History of Social Sciences in Australia*. Carlton, Vic.: Melbourne University Press.

Mack Smith, Denis. 1976. *Mussolini's Roman Empire*. New York: Viking Press.

MacKenzie, John M., ed. 1986. *Imperialism and Popular Culture*. Manchester: Manchester University Press.

MacLachlan, A. 1996. "'A Patriotic Scripture': The Making and Unmaking of English National Identity." *Parergon* 14 (1): 1–30.

Madoui, Mohamed. 2007. "Les sciences sociales en Algérie: regards sur les usages de la sociologie." *Sociologies pratiques* 2 (15): 149–160.

Magubane, Zine. 2005. "Overlapping Territories and Intertwined Histories: Historical Sociology's Global Imagination." Pp. 92–108 in Adams et al. (2005b).

Mamdani, Mahmood. 1996. *Citizen and Subject. Contemporary Africa and the Legacy of Colonialism*. Princeton, N.J.: Princeton University Press.

Mam-Lam-Fouck, Serge. 2006. *Histoire de l'assimilation: des "vieilles colonies" Françaises aux départements d'outre-mer*. Matoury Guyane: Ibis rouge.

Manasse, Ernst Moritz. 1947. "Max Weber on Race." *Social Research* 14:191–221.

Mann, James. 2004. *The Rise of the Vulcans: The History of Bush's War Cabinet*. New York: Viking Press.

Mann, Michael. 1984. "The Autonomous Power of the State: Its Origins, Mechanisms, and Results." *European Journal of Sociology* 25:185–213.

———. 1986. *The Sources of Social Power*. Vol. 1. *A History of Power from the Beginning to AD 1760*. Cambridge: Cambridge University Press.

———. 1988. "The Roots and Contradictions of Contemporary Militarism." In *States, War and Capitalism*. Oxford: Basil Blackwell.

———. 1993. *The Sources of Social Power*. Vol. 2. *The Rise of Classes and Nation-States, 1760–1914*. Cambridge: Cambridge University Press.

———. 2003. *Incoherent Empire*. London: Verso

———. 2004. *Fascists*. Cambridge: Cambridge University Press.

———. 2005. *The Dark Side of Democracy: Explaining Ethnic Cleansing*. Cambridge: Cambridge University Press.

———. 2008. "Impérialisme économique et impérialisme militaire Américains: un renforcement mutuel?" *Actes de la recherche en sciences sociales* 171 (2): 21–39.

Manor, James. 1978. *Political Change in an Indian State: Mysore, 1917–1955*. New Delhi: Manohar Publications.

Mantena, Karuna. 2010. *Alibis of Empire: Henry Maine and the Ends of Liberal Imperialism*. Princeton, N.J.: Princeton University Press.

Mantovani, Claudia. 2004. *Rigenerare la società: l'eugenetica in Italia dalle origini*. Soveria Mannelli: Rubbettino.

Marais, Hein. 2001. *South Africa: Limits to Change: The Political Economy of Transition*. Cape Town: University of Cape Town Press.

Marcus, George E., and Michael M. J. Fischer. 1986. *Anthropology as Cultural Critique: An Experimental Moment in the Human Sciences*. Chicago: University of Chicago Press.

Marcuse, Herbert. 1969. *An Essay on Liberation*. Boston: Beacon Press.

Marks, Shula, and Richard Rathbone, eds. (1982). *Industrialisation and Social Change in South Africa*. New York: Longman.

Marotta, Gary. 1983. "The Academic Mind and the Rise of U.S. Imperialism: Historians and Economists as Publicists for Ideas of Colonial Expansion." *American Journal of Economics and Sociology* 42 (2): 217–34.

Marsh, Peter, and Andrew Bounds. 2007. "Chinese Steel Dumping." *Financial Times*, Sept. 28: 2.

Martin, Terry. 2001. *The Affirmative Action Empire: Nations and Nationalism in the Soviet Union, 1923–1939*. Ithaca, N.Y.: Cornell University Press.

Martins, Herminio. 1974. "Time and Theory in Sociology." Pp. 246–294 in John Rex (Ed.), *Approaches to Sociology*. London: Routledge and Kegan Paul.

Marucco, Dora. 2001. "Filippo Virgilii: problemi teorici e tematiche." Pp. 485–509 in M. Guidi and L. Michelini (Eds.), *Marginalismo e socialismo nell'Italia liberale 1870–1925*. Milan: Feltrinelli.

Marx, Anthony. 2003. *Faith in Nation: Exclusionary Origins of Nationalism*. New York: Oxford University Press.

Marx, Karl. [1853a] 1969. "The Future Results of British Rule in India." Pp. 132–139 in Marx (1969).

———. [1853b] 1969. "Revolution in China and in Europe." Pp. 67–75 in Marx (1969).

———. 1967. *Capital*. Vol. 3. New York: International Publishers.

———. 1969. *Karl Marx on Colonialism and Modernization*. Edited by Schlomo Avineri. Garden City, N.Y.: Anchor Books.

———. 1976. *Capital*. Vol. 1. New York: Random House.

Masala, C. 2004. "Europa sollte ein Reich werden." *Frankfurter Allgemeine Zeitung*, Oct. 10: 15.

Maskovsky, Jeff, and Ida Susser, eds. 2009. *Rethinking America: The Imperial Homeland in the 21st Century*. Boulder, Colo.: Paradigm.

Massad, Joseph. 2006. "Blaming the Lobby." *Al-Ahram Weekly*, n. 787 (March 23–29), http://weekly.ahram.org.eg/2006/787/op35.htm (accessed January 5, 2013).

Massey, Douglas S. 2002. "Residential Segregation." Pp. 348–354 in David Theo Goldberg and John Solomos (Eds.), *A Companion to Racial and Ethnic Studies*. Malden, Mass.: Blackwell.

Matsuo, Takayoshi. 1974. *Taishō temokurashi* [Taishō democracy]. Tokyo: Iwanami shōten.

Matteucci, Ugo. 1913. *Le colonie nella sociologia, nella storia e nel diritto.* Pisa: Mariotti.

Maunier, René. 1932. *Sociologie coloniale.* Paris: Domat-Montchrestien.

———. 1943. *L'empire Français: propos et projets.* Paris: Recueil sirey.

———. 1949. *The Sociology of Colonies.* Vol. 1. London: Routledge and Kegan Paul.

Maurenbrecher, Max. 1900. "The Moral and Social Tasks of World Politics ('Imperialism')." *American Journal of Sociology* 6 (3): 307–315.

Mauss, Marcel. 1969a. "Les civilisations: éléments et formes." Pp. 456–523 in *Oeuvres.* Vol. 2.

———. 1969b. "L'ethnographie en France et à l'étranger." Pp. 303–358 in *Oeuvres.* Vol. 3.

———. 1969c. "Lucien Lévy-Bruhl (1857–1939)." Pp. 560–565 in *Oeuvres.* Vol. 3.

———. 1969d. "Mentalité primitive et participation." Pp. 125–131 in *Oeuvres.* Vol. 2.

———. 1969e. "La sociologie en France depuis 1914." Pp. 436–459 in *Oeuvres.* Vol. 3.

———. 1988. *The Gift.* London: Routledge.

———. 1997. *Écrits politiques.* Paris: Fayard.

May, Ernest R. 1968. *American Imperialism: A Speculative Essay.* New York: Atheneum.

Mazrui, Ali A. 1968. "From Social Darwinism to Current Theories of Modernization: A Tradition of Analysis." *World Politics* 21 (1): 69–83.

McKenzie, Fayette Avery. 1911. "The Assimilation of the American Indian." *American Journal of Sociology* 19 (6): 761–772.

Medushesvkii, Andrei. 1993. *Istoriia russkoi sotsiologii.* Moscow: Vysshaia shkola.

Mehta, Uday. 1997. "Liberal Strategies of Exclusion." Pp. 59–86 in Cooper and Stoler (1997).

———. 1999. *Liberalism and Empire.* Chicago: University of Chicago Press

Meller, Helen Elizabeth. 1990. *Patrick Geddes: Social Evolutionist and City Planner.* London: Routledge.

Memmi, Albert. 1957. "Sociologie des rapports entre colonisateurs et colonisés." *Cahiers internationaux de sociologie* 23:85–96.

———. 1967. *The Colonizer and the Colonized.* Boston: Beacon Press.

Mennasemay, M. 1997. "Adwa: A Dialogue between the Past and the Present." *Northeast African Studies* 4 (2): 43–89.

Mercier, Paul. 1954. "Aspects des problèmes de stratification sociale dans l'Ouest Africain." *Cahiers internationaux de sociologie* 17:47–65.

———. 1965a. "Les classes sociales et les changements politiques récents en Afrique noire." *Cahiers internationaux de sociologie* 38 (n.s. 12): 143–154.

———. 1965b. "On the Meaning of 'Tribalism' in Black Africa." Pp. 483–501 in Pierre L. Van den Berghe (Ed.), *Africa: Social Problems of Change and Conflict.* San Francisco: Chandler.

———. 1966. *Histoire de l'anthropologie.* Paris: PUF.

Mérimée, J. 1931. *De l'accession des Indochinois à la qualité de citoyen Français.* Toulouse: Imprimerie andrau et laporte.

Merle, Isabelle. 1995. *Expériences coloniales: la nouvelle-calédonie, 1853–1920.* Paris: Belin.

————. 2002. "Retour sur le régime de l'indigénat: genèses et contradictions des principes répressifs dans l'empire Français." *French Politics, Culture and Society* 20 (2): 77–97.

Metcalf, Thomas. 1989. *An Imperial Vision: Indian Architecture and Britain's Raj.* Berkeley: University of California Press.

————. 1994. *Ideologies of the Raj.* Cambridge: Cambridge University Press.

Meyer, John W., John Boli, George M. Thomas, and Francisco O. Ramirez. 1997. "World Society and the Nation State." *American Journal of Sociology* 103 (1): 144–181.

Michalon, Paul. 1990. *Des Indes Françaises aux Indiens Français ou comment peut-on être Franco-Pondichérien?* Mémoire de D.E.A. de sociologie, Université Aix-Marseille.

Michel, Ute. 2005. "Neue ethnologisches Forschungsansätze im Nationalsozialismus? Aus der Biographie Wilhelm Emil Mühlmann (1904–1988)." Pp. 141–167 in Thomas Hauschild (Ed.), *Lebenslust und Fremdenfurcht.* Frankfurt am Main: Suhrkamp.

Michels, Robert. 1906. "Divagazioni sullo imperialismo Germanico e la questione del Marocco." *La riforma sociale* 13 (16), 2nd series.

————. 1910. "Das Proletariat in der Wissenschaft und die Okonomisch-anthropologische Synthese." Pp. 3–28 in A. Niceforo (Ed.), *Anthropologie der nichtbesitzenden Klassen: studien und untersuchungen.* Leipzig and Amsterdam: Maas & Van Suchtelen.

————. 1911. *Zur Soziologie des Parteiwesens in der modernen Demokratie; Untersuchungen über die oligarchischen Tendenzen des Gruppenlebens.* Leipzig: W. Klinkhardt.

————. 1912. "Elemente zur Entstehungsgeschichte des imperialismus in Italien." *Archiv für Sozialwissenschaft und Sozialpolitik* 34 (1–2): 55–120.

————. 1914. *L'imperialismo Italiano: studi politico-demografici.* Milan: Società editrice libraria.

————. 1917. "La sphère historique de Rome." *Scientia* 22 (11): 55–66.

————. 1924. *Fattori e problemi dell'espansione commerciale.* Torino: Bocca.

————. 1927. *Corso di sociologia politica.* Milan: Istituto editoriale scientifico.

————. 1929. *Il problema della popolazione: conferenza fatta sulla forza del numero nell'aula Benito Mussolini della R. Universita di Perugia il di 21 Gennaio 1929.* Perugia: Tipografia G. Guerra.

————. 1930. "The Status of Sociology in Italy." *Social Forces* 9 (1): 20–39.

————. 1932a. "Il concetto coloniale nelle teorie degli economisti classici Italiani." *Rivista di politica economica* 22, fasc. 5.

————. 1932b. "Die Theorien des Kolonialismus." *Archiv für Sozialwissenschaft und Sozialpolitik* 67 (6): 693–710.

————. 1934. *Il boicottaggio.* Turin: Einaudi.

————. 1935. "Sul ricambio sociale in genere e su quello del dopoguerra in ispecie." In comitato Italiano per lo studio dei problemi della popolazione, institut international de sociologie (Ed.), *La sezione Italiana dell'istituto internazionale di sociologia al congresso di Bruxelles, 25–29 agosto 1935-XIII* [S.l.: s.n.].

Mierendorff, M. 1959. "Kracauer, Siegfried." Pp. 280–281 in Wilhelm Bernsdorf (Ed.), *Internationales Soziologenlexikon*. Stuttgart: F. Enke.

Miho, Dhimitër. 1976. "Veprimtaria kolonizuese e shoqërisë EIAA në Shqipëri dhe lufta kundër saj." *Studime historike* 30:103–128.

Miles, William F. S. 1995. *Imperial Burdens: Countercolonialism in Former French India*. Boulder, Colo.: L. Rienner.

Miller, Alexei. 2000. *Ukrainskii vopros v politike vlastei i russkom obshchestvennom mnenii (vtoraia polovina 19 veka)*. St. Petersburg: Aleteia.

Mills, C. Wright. 1944. "The Powerless People." *Politics* 1 (3): 68–72.

———. 1948. "International Relations and Sociology: Discussion." *American Sociological Review* 13 (3): 271–273.

———. 1958. *The Causes of World War III*. New York: Ballatine Books.

———. 1959a. "Crackpot Realism." *Fellowship. The Journal of the Fellowship of Reconciliation* 25 (1): 3–8.

———. 1959b. *The Sociological Imagination*. Oxford: Oxford University Press.

Miner, Horace. 1953. *The Primitive City of Timbuctoo*. Princeton, N.J.: Princeton University Press.

———. 1960. *Oasis and Casbah: Algerian Culture and Personality in Change*. Ann Arbor: University of Michigan Press.

———. 1965. "Urban Influences on the Rural Hausa." Pp. 110–130 in Hilda Kuper (Ed.), *Urbanization and Migration in West Africa*. Berkeley: University of California Press.

Mioni, Alberto. 1986. "Storia urbana dell'Italia fascista." In Alberto Mioni (Ed.), *Urbanistica fascista: ricerche e saggi sulle città e il territorio e sulle politiche urbane in Italia tra le due guerre*. Milan: Franco Angeli.

Mirowski, Philip. 1989. *More Heat Than Light: Economics as Social Physics, Physics as Nature's Economics*. Cambridge: Cambridge University Press.

Misha, Kristaq. 1970. *Lëvizja punëtore në Shqipëri*. Tirana: Naim frashëri.

Mitchell, Timothy. 1988. *Colonizing Egypt*. Berkeley: University of California Press.

Moe, Nelson. 2001. " 'This Is Africa': Ruling and Representing Southern Italy." Pp. 119–153 in Albert Russell Ascoli and Krystyna Von Henneberg (Eds.), *Making and Remaking Italy*. New York: Berg Publishing.

———. 2002. *The View from Vesuvius*. Berkeley: University of California Press.

Mogilner, Marina. 2009. *Homo imperii: Istoriia fizicheskoi antropologii v Rossii*. Moscow: Novoe Literaturnoe Obozrenie.

Mohan, Raj P., and Arthur S. Wilke, eds. 1994. *International Handbook of Contemporary Developments in Sociology*. Westport, Conn.: Greenwood Press.

Mommsen, Wolfgang J. 1978. "Power Politics, Imperialism and National Emancipation." Pp. 121–140 in T. W. Moody (Ed.), *Nationality and the Pursuit of National Independence*. Belfast: Appletree Press.

———. 1981. "Max Weber and Roberto Michels: An Asymmetrical Partnership." *European Journal of Sociology* 22:100–111.

———. 1982. *Theories of Imperialism*. Chicago: University of Chicago Press.

————. 1984. *Max Weber and German Politics, 1890–1920*. Chicago: University of Chicago Press.

————. 1990. "The Varieties of the Nation State in Modern History: Liberal, Imperialist, Fascist and Contemporary Notions of Nation and Nationality." Pp. 210–26 in Michael Mann (Ed.), *The Rise and Decline of the Nation State*. Oxford: Basil Blackwell.

Mondaini, Gennaro. 1906. "Le colonie e le popolazioni indigene." *Rivista Italiana di sociologia* 10:43–83.

Monina, Giancarlo. 2002. *Il consenso coloniale: le società geografiche e l'istituto coloniale Italiano, 1896–1914*. Roma: Carocci.

Monroe, Paul. 1913. "Influence of the Growing Perception of Human Interrelationship on Education." *American Journal of Sociology* 18:622–640.

Morandi, Mario. 1942. *La comunità imperiale e l'Albania: prime esperienze*. Rome: Istituto nazionale di cultura fascista.

Morasso, Mario. 1903. *L'imperialismo artistico*. Turin: Bocca.

Moret, Alexandre, and Georges Davy. 1926. *From Tribe to Empire*. New York: Knopf.

Morgan, J. Graham. 1970. "Contextual Factors in the Rise of Academic Sociology in the United States." *Canadian Review of Sociology and Anthropology* 7 (3): 159–171.

————. 1982. "Preparation for the Advent: The Establishment of Sociology as a Discipline in American Universities in the Late Nineteenth Century." *Minerva* 20:25–58.

Morrell, Robert. 2001. *Changing Men in South Africa*. Natal: University of Natal Press.

Morris, Aldon. 2007. "Sociology of Race and W. E. B. DuBois: The Path Not Taken." Pp. 503–534 in Calhoun (2007).

Morselli, Enrico. 1879. *Il suicidio: saggio di statistica morale comparata*. Milan: Dumolard.

Mosca, Gaetano. 1882. "I fattori della nazionalità." *Rivista Europea* 13 (27): 703–720.

————. 1912. *Italia e Libia: considerazioni politiche*. Milan: Treves.

————. 1933. "Cenni storici e critici sulle dottrine razziste: nota." *Rendiconti della R. accademia dei lincei, classe di scienze morali, storiche e filologiche* Series VI, 9:456–470.

————. 1939. *The Ruling Class*. New York: McGraw-Hill.

————. 2003. *Discorsi parlamentari*. Bologna: Il mulino.

Motyl, Alexander J. 2001. *Imperial Ends: The Decay, Collapse, and Revival of Empires*. New York: Columbia University Press.

Mozetič, Gerald. 1985. "Ludwig Gumplowicz: Das Programm einer naturalistischen Soziologie." Pp. 189–210 in Kurt Freisitzer (Ed.), *Tradition und Herausforderung: 400 Jahre Universität Graz*. Graz: Akademische Druck- u. Verlagsanstalt.

Mucchielli, Laurent. 1998. *La découverte du social: Naissance de la sociologie en France (1870–1914)*. Paris: La découverte.

Mühlmann, W. E. 1942. "Umvolkung und volkwerdung." *Deutsche Arbeit* 42 (1): 287–297.

————, ed. [1961] 1968. *Messianismes révolutionnaires du ties monde.* Trans. Jean Baudrillard. Paris: Gallimard.

————. 1962. "Bewegung, Kulturwandel, Geschichte." *Zeitschrift für Ethnologie* 87 (2):163–190.

Mukherjee, Ramkrishna. 1936. *Migrant Asia. With an Introduction by Corrado Gini.* Rome: Failli (Comitato Italiano per lo studio dei problemi della popolazione).

————. 1979. *Sociology of Indian Sociology.* Bombay: Allied.

Muldoon, James. 1999. *Empire and Order: The Concept of Empire, 800–1800.* Houndmills: Macmillan.

Müller, Rainer A., and Rainer Christoph Schwinges, eds. 2008. *Wissenschaftsfreiheit in Vergangenheit und Gegenwart.* Basel: Schwabe.

Mulrine, Anna. 2007. "The Culture Warriors." *U.S. News and World Report,* Dec. 10: 34–37.

Münkler, Herfried. 2005. *Imperien: Die Logik der Weltherrschaft—Vom Alten Rom bis zu den Vereinigten Staaten.* Berlin: Rowohlt.

Mussgnug, Dorothee. 1988. *Die vertriebenen Heidelberger Dozenten: Zur Geschichte der Ruprecht-Karls-Universität nach 1933.* Heidelberg: C. Winter.

Mustilli, Domenico. 1940. *Roma e L'Albania.* Rome: Edizioni Universitarie.

Muthu, Sankar. 2003. *Enlightenment against Empire.* Princeton, N.J.: Princeton University Press.

Myers, R. H., and M. R. Peattie, eds. 1984. *Japanese Colonial Empire, 1895–1945.* Princeton, N.J.: Princeton University Press.

Nagel, Joane. 2006. *American Indian Ethnic Renewal: Red Power and the Resurgence of Identity and Culture.* New York: Oxford University Press.

Naipaul, V. S. [1967] 1985. *The Mimic Men.* New York: Vintage.

Nandy, Ashis. 1983. *The Intimate Enemy.* New Delhi: Oxford University Press.

————. 1995. "History's Forgotten Doubles." *History and Theory* 3:44–66.

Naroll, Raoul. 1966. *Imperial Cycles and World Order.* N.p.

Naumann, Friedrich. [1915] 1964. "Mitteleuropa." Pp. 485–767 in Theodor Schieder (Ed.), *Werke.* Vol. 4. Köln: Westdeutscher Verlag.

Nesanelis, D., and V. A. Semyonov. 1991. "Traditsionnaia etnografiia naroda Komi v rabotakh P.A. Sorokina." *Rubezh: Al'manakh Sotsiologicheskikh Issledovanii* 1:47–56.

Nesbitt, Nick. 2003. *Voicing Memory.* Charlottesville: University of Virginia Press.

Nese, Marco. 1993. *Soziologie und Positivismus im präfaschistischen Italien 1870–1992.* Basel: Social Strategies Publishers.

Neumann, Franz L. [1942] 2009. *Behemoth: The Structure and Practice of National Socialism.* Oxford: Oxford University Press.

Ng, Franklin. 1994. "Knowledge for Empire: Academics and Universities in the Service of Imperialism." Pp. 123–146 in Robert David Johnson (Ed.), *On Cultural Ground.* Chicago: Imprint Publications.

Niceforo, Alfredo. 1897. *La delinquenza in Sardegna.* Turin: Bocca.

————. 1898. *L'Italia barbara contemporanea: studi e appunti.* Palermo: Sandron.

————. 1901. *Italiani del nord e Italiani del sud.* Turin: Bocca.

———. 1906. *Forza e ricchezza: studi sulla vita fisica e economica delle classi sociali.* Turin: Bocca.

———. 1907. *Antropologia delle classi povere.* Milan: Vallardi.

———. 1919. *La misura della vita.* Torino: n.p.

———. 1925. *La demografia, le sue scienze ausiliarie e la sociologia.* Rome: Centenari. *PubblicazioneRoma : Tip. F. Cente*

Nicolaysen, Rainer. 1997. *Siegfried Landshut: Die Wiederentdeckung der Politik.* Frankfurt am Main: Jüdischer Verlag.

Nicotri, Gaspare. 1910. *Rivoluzioni e rivolte in Sicilia: studio di sociologia storica, con prefazione di Enrico Ferri.* Turin: Unione tipografico-editrice Torinese.

———. 1912. *Primavera libica: studi e impressioni di viaggio.* Turin: Unione tipografico-editrice Torinese.

Nitobe, Inazo. 1911. "Japan as a Colonizer." *Journal of Race Development* 2:347–336.

No Sizwe. 1979. *One Azania, One Nation: The National Question in South Africa.* London: Zed Press.

"Non-Aggression Pact between South Africa and Venda." 1982. In *"Homeland" Tragedy: Function and Farce.* Information Publication, no. 6. Johannesburg: University of Witwatersrand Development Studies Group/Southern Africa Research Service.

Nye, Joseph. 2004. *Soft Power: The Means to Success in World Politics.* New York: Public Affairs.

Nye, Robert A. 1986. "The Influence of Evolutionary Theory on Pareto's Sociologo." *Journal for the History of the Behavioral Sciences* 22 (2): 99–106.

Oatley, Thomas, and Jason Yackee. 2004. "American Interests and IMF Lending." *International Politics* 41:415–429.

Odum, Howard. 1951. *American Sociology: The Story of Sociology in the United States through 1950.* New York: Longmans, Green and Company.

O'Leary, Brendan 2002. "In Praise of Empires Past: Myths and Method of Kedourie's *Nationalism.*" *New Left Review* 18:106–130.

Ong, A. 2006. *Neoliberalism as Exception: Mutations in Citizenship and Sovereignty.* Durham, N.C.: Duke University Press.

Oppenheim, Heinrich Bernhard. 1872. *Der Katheder-sozialismus.* Berlin: R. Oppenheim.

Oppenheimer, Franz. 1919. *Der staat.* Frankfurt am Main: Rütten and Loening.

———. 1922–1933. *System der Soziologie.* 4 vols. Jena: Gustav Fischer.

———. 1926. *Der Staat.* Vol. 2 of Oppenheimer (1922–1933).

———. 1929. *Rom und die Germanen.* Vol. 4, part 1 of Oppenheimer (1922–1933).

———. 1933. *Adel und Bauernschaft.* Vol. 4, part 2 of Oppenheimer (1922–1933).

———. 1935. *Stadt und Bürgerschaft.* Vol. 4, part 3 of Oppenheimer (1922–1933).

———. 1944. "Japan and Western Europe: A Comparative Presentation of Their Social Histories (I)." *American Journal of Economics and Sociology* 3 (4): 539–551.

———. 1958. "A First Program for Zionist Colonization (1903)." Pp. 71–82 in I. H. Bilski (Ed.), *Means and Ways towards a Realm of Justice: A Collection of Articles*

Dedicated to the Memory of Professor Franz Oppenheimer (1864–1943). Tel Aviv: Mesharim.

Ortner, Sherry B. 1995. "Resistance and the Problem of Ethnographic Refusal." *Comparative Studies in Society and History* 37 (1): 173–193.

Orum, Anthony M., and Xiangming Chen. 2002. *The World of Cities: Places in Comparative Historical Perspective*. Malden, Mass.: Blackwell.

Osterhammel, Jürgen. 1986. "Semi-Colonialism and Informal Empire in Twentieth-Century China: Towards a Framework of Analysis." Pp. 290–314 in Wolfgang J. Mommsen and Jürgen Osterhammel (Eds.), *Imperialism and After: Continuities and Discontinuities*. London: Allen and Unwin.

———. 2005. *Colonialism: A Theoretical Overview*. Second edition. Princeton, N.J.: Markus Wiener.

———. 2009. *Die Verwandlung der Welt: Eine Geschichte des 19. Jahrhunderts*. München: Beck.

Packer, George. 2005. *The Assassin's Gate: America in Iraq*. New York: Farrar, Straus and Giroux.

Padovan, Dario. 1999. *Saperi strategici. le scienze sociali e la formazione dello spazio pubblico Italiano tra le due guerre mondiali*. Milan. Angeli.

Pagden, Anthony. 1994. *European Encounters with the New World*. New Haven, Conn.: Yale University Press.

———. 1995. *Lords of All the World*. New Haven, Conn.: Yale University Press.

———. 2003. *Peoples and Empires*. New York: Modern Library.

Paige, Jeffery M. 1975. *Agrarian Revolution*. New York: Free Press.

Palumbo, Patrizia. 2003a. "Introduction: Italian Colonial Cultures." In Palumbo (2003b).

———, ed. 2003b. *A Place in the Sun: Africa in Italian Colonial Culture from Post-Unification to the Present*. Berkeley: University of California Press.

Pan, Esther. 2006. *Hamas and the Shrinking PA Budget*. Washington, D.C.: Council on Foreign Relations, http://www.cfr.org/publication/10499/.

———. 2007. *China, Africa, and Oil*. Washington, D.C.: Council on Foreign Relations, http://www.cfr.org/publication/9557.

Pankhurst, Richard. 2001. *The Ethiopians: A History*. Oxford: Blackwell.

———. 2005. "Racism in the Service of Fascism, Empire-Building and War: The History of the Italian Fascist Magazine 'La Difesa della Razza.'" In Stefan Brüne and Heinrich Scholler (Eds.), *Auf dem Weg zum Moderned Äthiopien: Festschrift für Bairu Tafla*. Münster: Lit Verlag.

Paredes, Ruby R. 1988. "The Origins of National Politics: Taft and the Partido Federal." Pp. 41–69 in Ruby R. Paredes (Ed.), *Philippine Colonial Democracy*. New Haven, Conn.: Yale University Southeast Asia Studies.

Pareto, Vilfredo. 1893. "The Parliamentary Regime in Italy." *Political Science Quarterly* 8 (4): 677–721.

———. 1896. *Cours d'economie politique*. Lausanne: F. Rouge.

———. [1902] 1951. *I sistemi socialisti*. Turin: UTET.

———. 1916. *Trattato di sociologia generale*. Florence: Barbera.

——. 1935. *Mind and Society*. 4 vols. New York: Harcourt, Brace.

Park, Robert E., and Ernest W. Burgess. 1924. Second edition. *Introduction to the Science of Sociology*. Second edition. Chicago: University of Chicago Press.

Pastorelli, Pietro. 1967. *Italia e Albania, 1924–1927: Origini diplomatiche del trattato di tirana del 22 Novembre 1927*. Florence: n.p.

——. 1970. *L'Albania nella politica estera Italiana, 1914–1920*. Naples: Jovene.

Patriarca, Silvana. 1995. *Numbers and Nationhood*. Cambridge: Cambridge University Press.

Paulsen, Jörg. 1988. *Zur Geschichte der Soziologie im Nationalsozialismus*. Oldenburg: BIS.

Peattie, Mark R. 1984. "Japanese Attitude towards Colonialism, 1895–1945." Pp. 80–127 in Myers and Peattie (1984).

Peled, Yoav. 2006. "From Zionism to Capitalism: The Political Economy of the Neoliberal Welfare State in Israel." Pp. 38–53 in Beinin and Stein (2006).

"Performance-based Roadmap to a Permanent Two-State Solution to the Israeli-Palestinian Conflict." 2003. Washington, D.C.: U.S. Department of State, http://www.mfa.gov.il/MFA/Peace+Process/Guide+to+the+Peace+Process/A+Performance-Based+Roadmap+to+a+Permanent+Two-Sta.htm (accessed January 5, 2013).

Petit, Carlos. 2007. "Lombroso en Chicago: presencias Europeas en la 'Modern Criminal Science' Americana." *Quaderni Fiorentini per la storia del pensiero giuridico moderno* 36:801–890.

Petitjean, Patrick, Catherine Jami, and Anne Marie Moulin, eds. 1992. *Science and Empires: Historical Studies about Scientific Development and European Expansion*. Dordrecht: Kluwer Academic Publishers.

Pick, Daniel. 1989. *Faces of Degeneration: A European Disorder, c.1848–1918*. Cambridge: Cambridge University Press.

Pickering-Iazzi, Robin. 2003. "Mass-Mediated Fantasies of Feminine Conquest, 1930–1940." Pp. 197–224 in Patrizia Palumbo (Ed.), *A Place in the Sun: Africa in Italian Colonial Culture from Post-Unification to the Present*. Berkeley: University of California Press.

Pinson de Ménerville, Charles-Louis. 1884. *Dictionnaire de la législation Algérienne*. Vol. 1. Algiers: Jourdan and Challamel.

Pirumova N. M. 1970. *Bakunin*. Moscow: Molodaia Gvardiia.

Pitts, Jennifer. 2005. *A Turn to Empire: The Rise of Imperial Liberalism in Britain and France*. Princeton, N.J.: Princeton University Press.

Plaatje, Sol. T. [1916] 1982. *Native Life in South Africa: Before and since the European War and the Boer Rebellion*. Braamfontein: Ravan Press.

Platt, Jennifer. 2002. "The History of the British Sociological Association." *International Sociology* 17 (2): 179–198.

——. 2010. "Transatlantic Voyages and National Sociologies." Pp. 53–67 in Schrecker (2010).

Platzky, L., and C. Walker. 1985. *The Surplus People: Forced Removals in South Africa*. Johannesburg: Ravan Press.

Ploetz, Alfred et al. 1911. "Die Begriffe Rasse und Gesellschaft und einige damit zusammenhängende Probleme" and discussion. Pp. 111–165 in *Verhandlungen des Ersten Deutschen Soziologentages vom 19.–22. Oktober 1910 in Frankfurt a.m.* Tübingen: J. C. B. Mohr.

Pocock, John 2005. "Empire, State and Confederation: The War of American Independence as a Crisis in Multiple Monarchy." Pp. 134–63 in *The Discovery of Islands: Essays in British History.* Cambridge: Cambridge University Press.

Pogodin, S. N. 2005. *Maksim Maksimovich Kovalevsky.* St. Petersburg: Nestor.

Pokrovsky, M. N. 1966. *History of Russia from the Earliest Times to the Rise of Commercial Capitalism.* Second edition. Bloomington, Ind.: University Prints and Reprints.

Pollock, Floyd Allen. 1984. *A Navajo Confrontation and Crisis.* Tsaile, Ariz.: Navajo Community College Press.

Polybius. 1979. *The Rise of the Roman Empire.* London: Penguin.

Porter, Bernard. 1968. *Critics of Empire: British Radical Attitudes to Colonialism in Africa, 1895–1914.* London: Macmillan.

———. 2004. *The Absent- Minded Imperialists: Empire, Society, and Culture in Britain.* Oxford: Oxford University Press.

Poulain, C. 1894. *Notes sur l'Inde Française: le régime politique.* Chalon-sur-Saône: Imprimerie de L. Marceau.

Prévost, Jean-Guy. 2002. "Genèse particulière d'une science des nombres. L'autonomisation de la statistique en Italie entre 1900 et 1914." *Actes de la recherche en sciences sociales* 141–142:98–109.

Price, David H. 2011. *Weaponizing Anthropology: Social Science in Service of the Militarized State.* Oakland, Calif.: AK Press Distribution.

Psycho-Neurological Institute. 1907. "Psikho-nevrologicheskii institute." *Vestnik psikhologii, kriminal'noi antropologii i gipnotizma* 4:306–320.

Pula, Besnik. 2008. "Becoming Citizens of Empire: Albanian Nationalism and Fascist Empire, 1939–1943." *Theory and Society* 37:567–596.

Pusceddu, Augusto. 1989. *La sociologia positivistica in Italia (1880–1920).* Rome: Bulzoni.

Rabbani, Mouin. 2006. "Palestinian Authority, Israeli Rule." Pp. 75–83 in Beinin and Stein (2006).

Rabbeno, Ugo. 1892. "Loria's Landed System of Social Economy." *Political Science Quarterly* 7 (2): 258–293.

———. 1898. *La questione fondiaria nelle grandi colonie dell'Australasia.* Turin: Bocca.

Rabinovitch, Eyal. 2004. "The Making of the Global Public." Ph.D. diss., UCLA (Sociology).

Rabinow, Paul. 1989. *French Modern: Norms and Forms of the Social Environment.* Cambridge, Mass.: MIT Press.

Ram, Uri. 2000. "'The Promised Land of Business Opportunities': Liberal Post-Zionism in the Global Age." Pp. 217–240 in Gershon Shafir and Yoav Peled (Eds.), *The New Israel: Peacemaking and Liberalization.* Boulder, Colo.: Westview Press.

Ranade, Mahadev Govind. [1890] 1990. "Netherlands, India and the Culture System." In Bipan Chandra (Ed.), *Ranade's Economic Writings*. New Delhi: Gian Publishing House.

———. 1900. *Essays on Indian Economics*. Bombay: D. B. Tarporewalla and Sons.

Randolph, John. 2007. *The House in the Garden: The Bakunin Family and the Romance of Russian Idealism*. Ithaca, N.Y.: Cornell University Press.

Rangacharlu, C. [1874] 1988. "The British Administration of Mysore." *Quarterly Journal of the Mythic Society* 79 (1–2).

Ranger, Terence. 1983. "The Invention of Tradition in Colonial Africa." Pp. 211–262 in Hobsbawm and Ranger (1983).

Rao, N. Rama. 1915. "Village Improvement." *Mysore Economic Journal* 1(2).

Rao, Shama M. 1891. *Ten Years of Native Rule in Mysore*. Madras: National Press.

Ratzel, Friedrich. 1882. *Anthropo-Geographie, oder Grundzüge der Anwendung der Erdkunde auf die Geschichte*. Stuttgart: J. Engelhorn.

———. 1897. "Der Staat und sein Boden." *Abhandlungen der Philologisch-Historischen Classe der Königlich Sächsischen Gesellschaft der Wissenschaften* 17 (4): 1–127.

———. 1901. "Der Lebensraum: Eine biogeographische Skizze." Pp. 103–189 in Karl Bücher (Ed.), *Festgaben für Albert Schäffle zur siebenzigsten Wiederkehr seines Geburtstages am 24. Februar 1901*. Tübingen: Verlag der H.Laupp'sche Buchhandlung.

———. 1923. *Politische Geographie*. Third edition. München: R. Oldenbourg.

Reece, Ernest J. 1914. "Race Mingling in Hawaii." *American Journal of Sociology* 20:104–116.

Reinsch, Paul S. 1904. "Colonial Autonomy, with Special Reference to the Government of the Philippine Islands." *Proceedings of the American Political Science Association* 1:116–139.

———. 1905. *Colonial Administration*. New York: Macmillan.

———. 1907. "Colonial Affairs." *American Political Science Review* 1:505–507.

Remnick, D. 2007. "The Apostate: A Zionist Politician Loses Faith in the Future." *New Yorker* 83 (July 30): 32.

Renan, Ernest. [1882] 2001. "What Is a Nation?" Pp. 162–76 in Vincent P. Pecora (Ed.), *Nations and Identities: Classic Readings*. Malden, Mass.: Blackwell.

Resis, Albert. 1970. "*Das Kapital* Comes to Russia." *Slavic Review* 29 (2): 219–237.

Rex, John. 1986. *Race and Ethnicity*. Philadelphia: Open University Press.

Rey, Pierre-Philippe. 1973. *Les alliances de classes*. Paris: Maspero.

Reynolds, Henry. 1982. *The Other Side of the Frontier: Aboriginal Resistance to the European Invasion of Australia*. Ringwood, Australia: Penguin.

Rich, Paul. 1984. "The Baptism of a New Order: The 1911 Universal Races Congress and the Liberal Ideology of Race." *Ethnic and Racial Studies* 7 (4): 534–550.

Richards, J. F. 1998. "Introduction." Pp. 1–12 in J. F. Richards (Ed.), *Kingship and Authority in South Asia*. New Delhi: Oxford University Press.

Richardson, J. S. 1991. "*Imperium Romanum*: Empire and the Language of Power." *Journal of Roman Studies* 8 (1): 1–9.

Richman, M. H. 2002. *Sacred Revolutions: Durkheim and the Collège de Sociologie.* Minneapolis: University of Minnesota Press.

Ritzer, George, ed. 2007. *The Blackwell Encyclopedia of Sociology.* Malden, Mass.: Blackwell.

Roach, Kent. 2003. *September 11: Consequences for Canada.* Montreal: McGill-Queens University Press.

Robinson, Robert. 1984. "Imperial Theory and the Question of Imperialism after Empire." Pp. 42– 54 in Robert F. Holland and Gowher Rizvi (Eds.), *Perspectives on Imperialism and Decolonization.* London: Frank Cass.

Robinson, Ronald. 1972. "Non-European Foundations of European Imperialism: Sketch for a Theory of Collaboration." Pp. 117–140 in Roger Owen and Bob Sutcliffe (Eds.), *Studies in the Theory of Imperialism.* London: Longman.

———. 1986. "The Excentric Idea of Imperialism, with or without Empire." Pp. 267–289 in Wolfgang J. Mommsen and Jürgen Osterhammel (Eds.), *Imperialism and After: Continuities and Discontinuities.* London: Allen and Unwin.

Robinson, William. 1996. *Promoting Polyarchy: Globalization, U.S. Intervention, and Hegemony.* New York: Cambridge University Press.

Rodgers, Daniel T. 1998. *Atlantic Crossings: Social Politics in a Progressive Age.* Cambridge, Mass.: Harvard University Press.

Roff, William R. 1994. *The Origins of Malay Nationalism.* Kuala Lumpur: Oxford University Press.

Rogers, Howard J., ed. 1905. *Congress of Arts and Science: Universal Exposition, St. Louis, 1904.* Boston: Houghton Mifflin.

Roggero, E. 1990. "Il contributo della 'rivista Italiana di sociologia' alla nascita e allo sviluppo della sociologia in Italia." *Sociologia* 4:89–122.

Rosanvallon, Pierre. 1992. *Le sacre du citoyen: histoire du suffrage universel en France.* Paris: Gallimard.

Ross, Dorothy. 1991. *The Origins of American Social Science.* Cambridge: Cambridge University Press.

Ross, Edward Alsworth. 1897. "Social Control. IX. Personality." *American Journal of Sociology* 3:236–247.

———. 1901. "The Causes of Race Superiority." *Annals of the American Academy of Political and Social Science* 18:67–89.

———. [1901] 1969. *Social Control: A Survey of the Foundations of Order.* Cleveland, Ohio: Press of Case Western Reserve University.

———. 1904. "Moot Points in Sociology. VIII. The Factors of Social Change." *American Journal of Sociology* 10:189–207.

———. 1918. "Adult Recreation as Social Problem." *American Journal of Sociology* 23:516–528.

———. 1936. *Seventy Years of It: An Autobiography.* New York: D. Appleton-Century.

Ross, Robert J., and Gerard J. Telkamp. 1985. *Colonial Cities: Essays on Urbanism in a Colonial Context.* Hingham, Mass.: Kluwer Academic.

Rossi, Lino. 1988. *Dalla filosofia alle scienze dell'uomo: riviste scientifiche e origine delle scienze sociali in Italia (1871–1891).* Milan: Angeli.

Roussillon, Alain. 2003. "Sociology in Egypt and Morocco." Pp. 432–449 in Theodore M. Porter and Dorothy Ross (Eds.), *The Cambridge History of Science*. Vol. 7. Cambridge: Cambridge University Press.

Rowe, L. S. 1904. *The United States and Puerto Rico*. New York: Longmans, Green and Company.

RPA [*Report on the Progress of Agriculture in Mysore (First Edition), Department of Agriculture, Mysore State*]. 1926. Bangalore: Government Press.

Russell, Conrad. 1995. "Composite Monarchies in Early Modern Europe: The British and Irish Example." Pp. 133–46 in Alexander Grant and Keith J. Stringer (Eds.), *Uniting the Kingdom? The Making of British History*. London: Routledge.

Russian Society for Normal and Pathological Psychology. 1904. "Zasedanie Russkogo obshchestva obychnoi i patologicheskoi psikhologii, 13 aprelia 1904 g." *Vestnik psikhologii, kriminal'noi anthropologii i gipnotizma* 4:359.

Rüstow, Alexander. [1950–1957] 1980. *Freedom and Domination: A Historical Critique of Civilization*. Princeton, N.J.: Princeton University Press.

Rydell, Robert W. 1984. *All the World's a Fair: Visions of Empire at American International expositions, 1876–1916*. Chicago: University of Chicago Press.

Saada, Emmanuelle. 2002. "The Empire of Law: Dignity, Prestige, and Domination in the "Colonial Situation.'" *French Politics, Culture and Society* 20 (2): 98–120.

———. 2003. "The History of the Lessons: Power and Rule in Imperial Formations." *Items and Issues*, Social Sciences Reseach Council, 4 (4): 16.

———. 2005. "Entre 'assimilation' et 'décivilisation': l'imitation et le projet colonial républicain." *Terrain* 44, http://terrain.revues.org/document2618.html.

———. 2006. "Un racisme de l'expansion: les discriminations raciales au regard des situations coloniales." Pp. 55–71 in Didier Fassin and Eric Fassin (Eds.), *De la question sociale à la question raciale?* Paris: La découverte.

———. 2012a. "The Absent Empire. The Colonies in French Constitutions." Pp. 205–15 in Alfred McCoy, Josep M. Fradera, and Stephen Jacobson (Eds.), *Endless Empire: Spain's Retreat, Europe's Eclipse, America's Decline*. Madison: The University of Wisconsin Press.

———. 2012b. *Empire's Children: Race, Filiation, and Citizenship in the French Colonies*. Chicago: University of Chicago Press.

Sabagh, Georges, and Iman Ghazalla. 1986. "Arab Sociology Today: A View from Within." *Annual Review of Sociology* 12:373–399.

Saeki, Ariyoshi. 1910. *Kankoku heigo no Shishu* [Purport of the annexation of Korea]. Tokyo: Shokaitsusha.

Safronov, B. G. 1960. *M. M. Kovalevsky kak sotsiolog*. Moscow: Izdatel'stvo MGU.

Said, Edward W. 1978. *Orientalism*. New York: Vintage.

———. 1989. "Representing the Colonized: Anthropology's Interlocutors." *Critical Inquiry* 15:205–225.

———. 1993. *Culture and Imperialism*. New York: Knopf.

———. 1996. *Peace and Its Discontents: Essays on Palestine in the Middle East Peace Process*. New York: Vintage.

———. 2001. *The End of the Peace Process: Oslo and After*. New York: Vintage.

———. 2004. *From Oslo to Iraq and the Road Map*. New York: Pantheon.

Sakai, Naoki. 1997. *Translation and Subjectivity: On "Japan" and Cultural Nationalism.* Minneapolis: University of Minnesota Press.

Salaün, Marie. 2005. *L'école indigène: nouvelle-calédonie, 1885–1945.* Rennes: Presses Universitaires de Rennes.

Salz, Arthur. 1923. "Der Imperialismus der Vereinigten Staaten." *Archiv für Sozialwissenschaft und Sozialpolitik* 50:565–616.

———. 1931. *Das wesen des imperialismus.* Leipzig: B. G. Teubner.

Samara, A. 2000. "Globalization, the Palestinian Economy, and the 'Peace Process.'" *Journal of Palestine Studies* 29 (2): 20–34.

Sandomirskii, G. 1919. "Voprosy kooperativnogo izdatel'stva." *Kooperativnaia zhizn'* (7–9).

Santoro, Marco. 1992. "Per una storia sociale della giuspubblicistica Italiana. L'insegnamento del diritto amministrativo e della scienza dell'amministrazione nell'Italia liberale." *Cheiron* 3 (16): 115–152.

———. Forthcoming. "An Episode in the History of Sociology: Corrado Gini and Robert K. Merton at Harvard, 1935." *Sociologica.*

Sartre, Jean-Paul. [1961] 1963. "Preface." Pp. 7–31 in Frantz Fanon, *The Wretched of the Earth.* New York: Grove Press.

———. 2001. *Colonialism and Neocolonialism.* New York London: Routledge.

Sassen, Saskia. 2006. *Territory, Authority, Rights: From Medieval to Global Assemblages.* Princeton, N.J.: Princeton University Press.

Sastri, Venkatasubba K. N. 1932. *The Administration of Mysore under Sir Mark Cubbon.* London: George Allen and Unwin.

———. 1937. *An Introduction to the History of the Administration of Mysore.* Mysore: Wesley Press and Publishing House.

Saul, John S., and Stephen Gelb. 1986. *The Crisis in South Africa.* New York: Monthly Review Press.

Sautman, Barry, and Yan Hairong. Forthcoming. "The Forest for the Trees: Trade, Investment and the China-in-Africa Discourse," *Pacific Affairs* 81.1 (spring).

Savorgnan, Franco. 1918. *La guerra e la popolazione: studi di demografia.* Bologna: Zanichelli.

———. 1921. *Demografia di guerra e altri saggi.* Bologna: Zanichelli.

Sayad, Abdelmalek. 2004. *The Suffering of the Immigrant.* Cambridge: Polity Press.

Sayyid, Afaf al-. 1968. *Egypt and Cromer.* New York: Praeger.

Scaff, Lawrence A. 1998a. "The 'Cool Objectivity of Sociation': Max Weber and Marianne Weber in America." *History of the Human Sciences* 11:61–82.

———. 1998b. "Max Weber's *Amerikabild* and the African American Experience." Pp. 82–94 in David McBride, Leroy Hopkins, and C. Aisha Blackshire-Belay (Eds.), *Crosscurrents: African Americans, Africa, and Germany in the Modern World.* Columbia, S.C.: Camden House.

———. 2011. *Max Weber in America.* Princeton, N.J.: Princeton University Press.

Scalapino, Robert, and Chong-Sik Lee. 1972. *Communism in Korea.* Vol. 1. Berkeley: University of California Press.

Schäffle, Albert. 1886–1888. "Kolonialpolitische Studien." *Zeitschrift für die gesamte Staatswissenschaft* 42 (1886): 625–665; 43 (1887): 123–217, 343–416; 44 (1888): 59–96, 263–306.

Scheltema, J. F. 1907. "The Opium Trade in the Dutch East Indies. I." *American Journal of Sociology* 13 (1): 79–112.

Scheppele, Kim Lane. 2004. "A *Realpolitik* Defense of Social Rights." *University of Texas Law Review* 82 (7): 1921–1961.

————. 2005. " 'We Forgot about the Ditches': Russian Constitutional Impatience and the Challenge of Terrorism." *Drake Law Review* 53:963–1027.

Schissler, Hanna. 1978. *Preußische Agrargesellschaft im Wandel: Wirtschaftliche, Gesellschaftliche und politische von 1763 bis 1847*. Göttingen: Vandenhoeck und Ruprecht.

Schivelbusch, Wolfgang 2004. *The Culture of Defeat: On National Trauma, Mourning, and Recovery*. London: Granta Books.

Schmitt, Carl. 1922. *Politische Theologie*. Munich: Duncker and Humblot.

————. [1932] 1940. "Völkerrechtliche Formen des modernen Imperialismus." Pp. 184–203 in *Positionen und Begriffe im Kampf mit Weimar-Genf-Versailles, 1923–1939*. Berlin: Duncker and Humblot.

————. 1950. *Der Nomos der Erde im Völkerrecht des Jus Publicum Europaeum*. Cologne: Greven.

————. [1950] 2003. *The Nomos of the Earth in the International Law of the Jus Publicum Europaeum*. New York: Telos Press.

————. [1955] 1995. "Der Neue Nomos der Erde." Pp. 518–522 in *Staat, Großraum, nomos. Arbeiten aus den Jahren 1916–1969*. Berlin: Duncker and Humblot.

————. 1988. "Die Rheinlande als Objekt internationaler Politik." Pp. 29–37 in *Positionen und Begriffe im Kampf mit Weimar-Genf-Versailles, 1923–1939*. Third edition. Berlin: Duncker and Humblot.

————. 1996. *The Concept of the Political*. Chicago: University of Chicago Press.

————. 2005. *Political Theology*. Chicago: University of Chicago Press.

Schmoller, Gustav. 1886. "Die preußische Kolonisation des 17. und 18. Jahrhundert." Pp. 1–43 in Verein für Socialpolitik, *Zur Inneren Kolonisation in Deutschland: Erfahrungen und Vorschläge*. Leipzig: Duncker and Humblot.

————. 1888. "Der Kampf des preußischen Königthums um die Erhaltung des Bauernstandes." *Jahrbuch für Gesetzgebung, Verwaltung und Volkswirthschaft im Deutschen Reich* 12:245–255.

————. 1900. *Grundriß der allgemeinen Volkswirtschaftslehre*. Vol. 1. Leipzig: Duncker and Humblot.

————. 1902. Comments on Freiherr von Herman, "Plantagen und Eingeborenen-Kulturen in den Kolonien." Pp. 507–517 in *Verhandlungen des Deutschen Kolonialkongresses 1902 zu Berlin*. Berlin: Dietrich Reimer.

Schmoller, Gustav, Bernhard Dernburg, Walter Delbrück et al. 1907. *Reichstagsauflösung und Kolonialpolitik*. Berlin: Wedekind.

Schnapper, Dominique. 1998a. *Community of Citizens: On the Modern Idea of Nationality*. New Brunswick, N.J.: Transaction.

————. 1998b. *La relation à l'autre: au coeur de la pensée sociologique*. Paris: Gallimard.

Schneider, Jane, ed. 1998. *Italy's Southern Question: Orientalism in One Country.* New York: Berg.

Schrecker, Cherry, ed. 2010. *Transatlantic Voyages and Sociology: The Migration and Development of Ideas.* Surrey: Ashgate.

Schroer, Markus. 2007. "Auf der Suche nach der verlorenen Wirklichkeit: Aufmerksamkeit und Dingwahrnehmung bei Siegfried Kracauer." *Osterreichische Zeitschrift fur Soziologie* 32 (1): 3–24.

Schueller, Malini Johar. 1998. *U.S. Orientalisms: Race, Nation, and Gender in Literature, 1790–1890.* Ann Arbor: University of Michigan Press.

Schumpeter, Joseph Alois. [1919] 1951. *Imperialism and Social Classes.* Cleveland: The World Publishing Company.

Schwendinger, Herman, and Julia R. Schwendinger. 1974. *The Sociologists of the Chair.* New York: Basic Books.

Scott, James C. 1985. *Weapons of the Weak.* New Haven, Conn.: Yale University Press.

Seeley, J. R. [1883] 1971. *The Expansion of England.* Chicago: University of Chicago Press.

Sell, Susan. 2002. "Intellectual Property Rights." Pp. 171–188 in David Held and Anthony McGrew (Eds.), *Governing Globalization.* Cambridge: Polity.

Semyonov, Alexander. 2009. " 'The Real and Live Ethnographic Map of Russia': The Russian Empire in the Mirror of the State Duma." Pp. 191–228 in Ilya Gerasimov, Jan Kusber, and Alexander Semyonov (Eds.), *Empire Speaks Out: Languages of Rationalization and Self-Description in the Russian Empire.* Boston: Brill.

Sergi, Giuseppe. 1881. "La sociologia e l'organismo della società umana." Pp. v–lx in Spencer (1881).

———. 1895. *Origine e diffusione della stirpe Mediterranea.* Rome: D. Alighieri, Rome; English translation: *The Mediterranean Race: A Study of the Origins of European Peoples.* London: W. Scott, 1901.

———. 1911. "Differences in Customs and Morals, and their Resistance to Rapid Change." Pp. 67–73 in *Papers on Inter-Racial Problems. A Record of the Proceedings of the First Universal Races Congress.* London: P. S. King & Son.

———. 1916. "Sociologia e nazionalita." *Rivista Italiana di sociologia* 20:1–7.

———. 1919. "I possedimenti coloniali e la giustizia internazionale." *Rivista Italiana di sociologia* 23:385–415.

Sering, Max. 1893. "Die innere Kolonisation in östlichen Deutschland." *Schriften des Vereins für Socialpolitik.* Vol. 56. Leipzig: Duncker and Humblot.

Serra Zanetti, P. 1976. "Il recupero critico di un antropologo culturale: Mario Morasso." Pp. 89–119 in Renato Barilli (Ed.), *Estetica e società tecnologica.* Bologna: Il mulino.

Seton-Watson, Hugh. 1964. "Nationalism and Multi-National Empires." Pp. 3–35 in *Nationalism and Communism: Essays 1946–1963.* New York: Praeger.

Sewell, William, Jr. 1992. "A Theory of Structure: Duality, Agency, and Transformation." *American Journal of Sociology* 98 (1): 1–29.

———. 1996. "Historical Events as Transformations of Structures: Inventing Revolution at the Bastille." *Theory and Society* 25:841–881.

Shafaeddin, Mehdi. 2005. "Friedrich List and the Infant Industry Argument." Pp. 42–61 in Jomo K.S. (Ed.), *The Pioneers of Development Economics: Great Economists on Development*. New Delhi: Tulika Books.

Shafir, G., and Peled, Y. 2000a. "Introduction: The Socioeconomic Liberalization of Israel." Pp. 1–13 in Shafir and Peled (2000b).

———, eds. 2000b. *The New Israel: Peacemaking and Liberalization*. Boulder, Colo.: Westview Press.

Shah, Aqil. 2003. "Pakistan's 'Armored' Democracy." *Journal of Democracy* 14 (4): 26–40.

Shanin, Teodor. 1972. *The Awkward Class*. Oxford: Oxford University Press.

Shils, Edward. 1970. "Tradition, Ecology, and Institution in the History of Sociology." *Daedalus* 99:760–825.

Shin, Gi-Wook, and Michael Robinson, eds. 1999. *Colonial Modernity in Korea*. Cambridge: Cambridge University Press.

Sibeud, Emmanuelle. 2002. *Une science impériale pour l'Afrique?* Paris: Ecole des hautes études en sciences sociales.

Siddique, Osama. 2006. "The Jurisprudence of Dissolutions: Presidential Power to Dissolve Assemblies under the Pakistani Constitution and Its Discontents." *Arizona Journal of International and Comparative Law* 23:615–715.

Sigrist, Christian and Reinhart Kössler. 1985. "Soziologie in Heidelberg." Pp. 79–99 in Karin Buselmeier, Dietrich Harth, and Christian Jansen (Eds.), *Auch eine Geschichte der Universität Heidelberg*. Mannheim: Edition Quadrat.

Simmel, Georg. 1950. *The Sociology of Georg Simmel*. Glencoe, Ill.: Free Press.

Simons, Sarah E. 1901a. "Social Assimilation. I." *American Journal of Sociology* 6:790–822.

———. 1901b. "Social Assimilation. VII. Assimilation in the Modern World." *American Journal of Sociology* 7:234–248.

Skocpol, Theda. 1979. *States and Social Revolutions: A Comparative Analysis of France, Russia, and China*. Cambridge: Cambridge University Press.

———. 1985. "Bringing the State Back In: Strategies of Analysis in Current Research." Pp. 3–37 in Evans et al. (1985).

Slocum, John W. 1998. "Who, and When, Were the Inorodtsy? The Evolution of the Category of 'Aliens' in Imperial Russia." *Russian Review* 57 (2): 173–190.

Slotkin, Richard. 1992. *Gunfighter Nation: The Myth of the Frontier in Twentieth-Century America*. New York: Atheneum.

Small, Albion W. 1895. "The Era of Sociology." *American Journal of Sociology* 1:1–15.

———. 1900a. "The Scope of Sociology. I. The Development of Sociological Method." *American Journal of Sociology* 5:506–526.

———. 1900b. "The Scope of Sociology. VI. Some Incidents of Association." *American Journal of Sociology* 6:324–380.

———. 1923–1924. "Some Contributions to the History of Sociology." Parts 1–15. *American Journal of Sociology* 28 (4): 385–418; through 30 (3): 310–336.

Smith, Anthony D. 1986. *The Ethnic Origins of Nations*. Oxford: Blackwell.

———. 1991. *National Identity*. London: Penguin Books.

————. 2003. *Chosen Peoples: Sacred Sources of National Identity*. Oxford: Oxford University Press.

Smith, David A. 1991. "Review Article." *Social Forces* 70:553–555.

————. 1996. *Third World Cities in Global Perspective: The Political Economy of Uneven Urbanization*. Boulder, Colo.: Westview Press.

Smith, Neil. 2005. *The Endgame of Globalization*. New York: Routledge.

Smith, Peter. 2000. *Talons of the Eagle: Dynamics of U.S.-Latin American Relations*. New York: Oxford University Press.

Smith, R. B. 1969. "Bui Quang Chieu and the Constitutionalist Party." *Modern Asian Studies* 3 (2): 132–136.

Smith, Tony. 1981. *The Pattern of Imperialism*. Cambridge: Cambridge University Press.

Snipp, C. Matthew. 1985. "Essentially, American Indians Are Captive Nations." In Remmelt and Kathleen Hummelen (Eds.), *Stories of Survival: Conversations with Native North Americans*. New York: Friendship Press.

————. 1986. "The Changing Political and Economic Status of the American Indians: From Captive Nations to Internal Colonies." *American Journal of Economics and Sociology* 45 (2): 145–157.

————. 1992. "Sociological Perspectives on American Indians." *Annual Review of Sociology* 18:351–371.

Snyder, Jack. 1991. *Myths of Empire*. Ithaca, N.Y.: Cornell University Press.

Soederberg, Susanne. 2004. *The Politics of the New International Financial Architecture*. London: Zed.

Soffer, Reba N. 1982. "Why Do Disciplines Fail? The Strange Case of British Sociology." *English Historical Review* 97 (385): 767–802.

Solomon, Susan Gross. 1977. *The Soviet Agrarian Debate: A Controversy in Social Science, 1923–1929*. Boulder, Colo.: Westview Press.

————. 1978. "Rural Scholars and the Cultural Revolution." Pp. 129–153 in Sheila Fitzpatrick (Ed.), *Cultural Revolution in Russia, 1928–1931*. Bloomington: Indiana University Press.

Solus, Henry. 1927. *Traité de la condition des indigènes en droit privé, colonies et pays de protectorat et pays sous mandat*. Paris: Recueil sirey.

Sombart-Ermsleben. 1887. "Ueber innere Kolonisation mit Rücksicht auf die Erhaltung und Vermehrung des mittleren und kleineren ländlichen Grundbesitzes." Pp. 77–138 in *Verhandlungen der zweiten Generalversammlung des Vereins für Socialpolitik am 24. und 25. September 1886, Schriften des Vereins für Socialpolitik*. Vol. 33. Leipzig: Duncker and Humblot.

Somerville, Margaret, and Tony Perkins. 2010. *Singing the Coast*. Canberra: Aboriginal Studies Press.

Sonnabend, E. H. 1935. *Il fattore demografico nell'organizzazione sociale dei Bantù*. Rome: Arti grafiche Zamperini e Lorenzini.

Sorgoni, Barbara. 2003. "'Defending the Race': The Italian Reinvention of the Hottentot Venus during Fascism." *Journal of Modern Italian Studies* 8 (3): 411–424.

Sorokin, Pitirim. 1914. *Prestuplenie i kara, podvig i nagrada. Sotsiologicheskii etiud ob osnovnykh formakh obshchestvennogo povedeniia i morali.* St. Petersburg: Ia. g. dolbyshev.

———. 1918. *Programma po izucheniiu zyrianskogo kraia.* Iarensk: Komi Kotyr.

———. 1920. *Obshchedostupnyi uchebnik sotsiologii.* Part 1. Iaroslavl': n.p.

———. [1920a] 1993. *Sistema sotsiologii.* Vol. 1. Moscow: Nauka.

———. [1920b] 1993. *Sistema sotsiologii.* Vol. 2. Moscow: Nauka.

———. 1922. *Sovremennoe sostoianie Rossii.* Prague: Lingva.

———. 1923. *Populiarnye ocherki sotsial'noi pegagogiki i politiki.* Uzhgorod: Komitet delovodchikov narodo-prosvetitel'nykh rad v Podkarpatskoi Rusi.

———. 1925. *The Sociology of Revolution.* Philadelphia: J. B. Lippincott.

———. 1928. *Contemporary Sociological Theories.* New York: Harper and Row.

———. 1944. *Russia and the United States.* New York: E. P. Dutton.

———. 1950. *Leaves from a Russian Diary, and Thirty Years After.* Boston: Beacon Press.

———. 1956. "Review of Leon Petrazycki, Law and Morality." *Harvard Law Review* 69 (6): 1150–1157.

———. 1963. *A Long Journey: The Autobiography of Pitirim A. Sorokin.* New Haven, Conn.: College and University Press.

———. 1967. "The Essential Characteristics of the Russian Nation in the Twentieth Century." *Annals of the American Academy of Political and Social Science* 370:99–115.

———. 1990. "Kolonizatsionnyi vozhdeleniia." *Sotsiologicheskie Issledovaniia* 2:134–138.

———. 1991. "Sorokin P. A.: Dokumental'nye shtrikhi k sud'be i tvorcheskoi deiatel'nosti." *Sotsiologicheskie Issledovaniia* 10:125–130.

Soustelle, Jacques. 1937. *La famille otomi-pame du Mexique central.* Paris: Institut d'ethnologie.

———. 1971. *The Four Suns: Recollections and Reflections of an Ethnologist in Mexico.* New York: Grossman.

Spann, Othmar. 1923. "Imperialismus." Pp. 383–385 in Ludwig Elster, Adolf Weber, and Friedrich Wieser (Eds.), *Handwörterbuch der Staatswissenschaften.* Vol. 5. Jena: G. Fischer.

Sparrow, Bartholomew H. 2006. *The Insular Cases and the Emergence of the American Empire.* Lawrence: University Press of Kansas.

Spencer, Herbert. 1881. *Introduzione allo studio della sociologia.* Milan: Dumolard.

———. 1887. *Principi di sociologia.* Torino: UTET.

———. 1902a. *Facts and Comments.* New York: D. Appleton.

———. 1902b. "Imperialism and Slavery." Pp. 157–171 in Spencer (1902a).

———. 1902c. "Re-Barbarization." Pp. 172–188 in Spencer (1902a).

Spengler, Oswald. 1920–1922. *Der Untergang des Abendlandes.* 2 vols. München: C. H. Beck.

Spiller, G., ed. 1911. *Papers on Inter-Racial Problems Communicated to the First Universal Races Congress Held at the University of London, July 26–29, 1911.* London: P. S. King and Son.

Squillace, Fausto. 1902. *Critica della sociologia. I. Le dottrine sociologiche.* Palermo: Sandron.

———. 1911. *Dizionario di sociologia.* Second edition. Palermo: Sandron.

Srikantaiya, S. 1941. "Sri Krishnaraja Wadiyar IV." *Quarterly Journal of Mythic Society* 33 (4).

Srinivas, M. N. 1996. *Caste in Modern India and Other Essays.* Bombay: Media Promoters and Publishers PVT.

Stacey, Judith. 2011. *Unhitched: Love, Marriage, and Family Values from West Hollywood to Western China.* New York: New York University Press.

Stanley, Peter W. 1974. *A Nation in the Making: The Philippines and the United States, 1899–1921.* Cambridge, Mass.: Harvard University Press.

"Statement from PM's Bureau." 2003. Israeli Government Press Office (May 25), http://www.imra.org.il/story.php3?id=16972 (accessed January 5, 2013).

Staubmann, Helmut. 1999. "Das Ornament als 'Erzahlung' der Moderne: Zu Siegfried Kracauers soziologischer Dekodierung einer asthetischen Metapher." *Österreichische Zeitschrift für Soziologie* 24 (1): 31–46.

Steinfeld, Robert J. 2001. *Coercion, Contract, and Free Labor in the Nineteenth Century.* Cambridge: Cambridge University Press.

Steinmetz, George. 1993. *Regulating the Social: The Welfare State and Local Politics in Imperial Germany.* Princeton, N. J.: Princeton University Press.

———, ed. 1999. *State/Culture: State-Formation after the Cultural Turn.* Ithaca, N.Y.: Cornell University Press.

———. 2002. "Precoloniality and Colonial Subjectivity: Ethnographic Discourse and Native Policy in German Overseas Imperialism, 1780s–1914." *Political Power and Social Theory* 15:135–228.

———. 2003a. "'The Devil's Handwriting': Precolonial Discourse, Ethnographic Acuity and Cross-Identification in German Colonialism." *Comparative Studies in Society and History* 45 (1): 41–95.

———. 2003b. "The State of Emergency and the New American Imperialism: Toward an Authoritarian Post-Fordism." *Public Culture* 15 (2): 323–346.

———. 2004. "Odious Comparisons: Incommensurability, the Case Study, and 'Small N's in Sociology." *Sociological Theory* 22 (3): 371–400.

———. 2005a. "American Sociology's Epistemological Unconscious and the Transition to Post-Fordism: The Case of Historical Sociology." Pp. 109–157 in Adams et al. (2005).

———, ed. 2005b. *The Politics of Method in the Human Sciences: Positivism and Its Epistemological Others.* Durham, N.C.: Duke University Press.

———. 2005c. "Positivism and Its Others in the Social Sciences." Pp. 1–56 in Steinmetz (2005b).

———. 2005d. "Return to Empire: The New U.S. Imperialism in Theoretical and Historical Perspective." *Sociological Theory* 23 (4): 339–367.

———. 2005e. "Scientific Authority and the Transition to Post-Fordism: The Plausibility of Positivism in American Sociology since 1945." Pp. 275–323 in Steinmetz (2005b).

————. 2006a. "Decolonizing German Theory: An Introduction." *Postcolonial Studies* 9 (1): 3–13.

————. 2006b. "Imperialism or Colonialism? From Windhoek to Washington, by Way of Basra." Pp. 135–156 in Calhoun et al. (2006b).

————. 2007a. "American Sociology before and after World War Two: The (Temporary) Settling of a Disciplinary Field." Pp. 314–366 in Calhoun (2007).

————. 2007b. *The Devil's Handwriting: Precolonial Ethnography and the German Colonial State in Qingdao, Samoa, and Southwest Africa.* Chicago: University of Chicago Press.

————. 2007c. "Transdisciplinarity as a Nonimperial Encounter." *Thesis Eleven* 91 (1): 48–65.

————. 2008a. "The Colonial State as a Social Field." *American Sociological Review* 73 (4): 589–612.

————. 2008b. "Empire et domination mondiale." *Actes de la recherche en sciences sociales* 171–172:4–19.

————. 2008c. "La sociologie historique en Allemagne et aux Etats-Unis: un transfert manqué (1930–1970)." *Genèses* 71:123–147.

————. 2009a. "The Imperial Entanglements of Sociology in the United States, Britain, and France since the 19th Century." *Ab Imperio* 4:1–56.

————. 2009b. "Neo-Bourdieusian Theory and the Question of Scientific Autonomy: German Sociologists and Empire, 1890s–1940s." *Political Power and Social Theory* 20:71–131.

————. 2010a. "Charles Tilly, Historicism, and the Critical Realist Philosophy of Science." *American Sociologist* 41 (4): 312–336.

————. 2010b. "Entretien avec Georges Balandier." *Actes de la recherche en sciences sociales* 185 (December): 44–61.

————. 2010c. "Ideas in Exile: Refugees from Nazi Germany and the Failure to Transplant Historical Sociology into the United States." *International Journal of Politics, Culture, and Society* 23 (1): 1–27.

————. 2011a. "The Anti-Comparative Imperative: German Historicism in the Human Sciences." Paper delivered to workhop on "The Comparative Imperative: Capitalism, Comparison and Social Transformation," New York University, February 1819.

————. 2011b. "Historicizing and Spatializing Field Theory: A Study of Disciplinary Separation and Interaction between Sociology and History." Paper prepared for conference on "The Sociology of the Social Sciences 1945–2010," Copenhagen, June 9–11.

————. 2012a. "British and French Sociology after 1945: The Colonial Connection." *Timelines* (Newsletter of the Section on the History of Sociology, American Sociological Association), 20 (August): 2, 4–6.

————. 2012b. "Geopolitics." Pp. 800–822 in George Ritzer (Ed.), *The Wiley-Blackwell Encyclopedia of Globalization.* Vol. 2. Malden, Mass.: Wiley-Blackwell.

————. 2012c. "Toward a Bourdieusian Analysis of Empires: Rescaling Field Theory." Paper presented at the Social Science History Association meetings, Vancouver, November 2.

————. 2013. "Toward Socioanalysis: On Psychoanalysis and Neo-Bourdieusian Theory." Pp. 108–130 in Phil Gorski (Ed.), *Bourdieusian Theory and Historical Analysis*. Durham, N.C.: Duke University Press.

————. Forthcoming-a. "Comparative History and its Critics: A Genealogy of the Debates and a Possible Resolution." In Prasenjit Duara, Viren Murthy, and Andrew Sartori (Eds.), *A Companion to Global Historical Thought*. London: Blackwell.

————. Forthcoming-b. *Imperial Intellectuals: Sociologists as Theorists, Advisers, and Critics of Empire in Germany, France, Britain and the United States, 1880s–1960s.*

Steinmetz, Selbald R. 1903. *Rechtsverhältnisse von eingeborenen völkern in Afrika und Ozeanien.* Berlin: Springer.

Steinwedel, Charles. 2002. "Tribe, Estate, or Nationality? Changing Conceptions of Bashkir Particularity within the Tsar's Empire." *Ab Imperio* 2:249–278.

Stewart, W. K. 1928. "The Mentors of Mussolini." *American Political Science Review* 22 (4): 843–869.

Stocking, George W., Jr. 1968. *Race, Culture, and Evolution.* Chicago: University of Chicago Press.

Stokes, Eric. [1959] 1992. *The English Utilitarians and India.* New Delhi: Oxford University Press.

Stokes, Kenneth Michael. 1995. *Paradigm Lost: A Cultural and Systems Theoretical Critique of Political Economy.* London: M. E. Sharpe.

Stoler, Ann Laura. 1989. "Rethinking Colonial Categories: European Communities and the Boundaries of Rule." *Comparative Studies in Society and History* 31:134–161.

————. 2002. *Carnal Knowledge and Imperial Power: Race and the Intimate in Colonial Rule.* Berkeley: University of California Press.

————. 2006. "On Degrees of Imperial Sovereignty." *Public Culture* 18 (1): 125–146.

————. 2009. *Along the Archival Grain: Epistemic Anxieties and Colonial Common Sense.* Princeton, N.J.: Princeton University Press.

Stoler, Ann Laura, and Frederick Cooper, 1997. "Between Metropole and Colony: Rethinking a Research Agenda." Pp. 1–56 in Cooper and Stoler (1997).

Stone, Alfred Holt. 1908. "Is Race Friction between Blacks and Whites in the United States Growing and Inevitable?" *American Journal of Sociology* 13:676–697.

Stone, Randall 2004. "The Political Economy of IMF Lending in Africa." *American Political Science Review* 98:577–591.

Stora, Benjamin. 1999. *Le transfert d'une mémoire: de l'Algérie Française au racisme anti-Arabe.* Paris: Le découverte.

Strang, David. 1990. "From Dependency to Sovereignty: An Event History Analysis of Decolonization, 1870–1987." *American Sociological Review* 55:846–860.

Strassoldo, R. 1988. "The Austrian Influence on Italian Sociology." Pp. 101–117 in Josef Langer (Ed.), *Geschichte der österreichischen Soziologie.* Vienna: Verlag für Gesellschaftskritik.

Struve, Petr. 1908. "Velikaia Rossiia: iz razmyshlenii o probleme russkogo mogushchestva." *Russkaia Mysl'* (1): 143–157.

Sulstarova, Enis. 2006. *Arratisje nga lindja: orientalizmi shqiptar nga Naimi te Kadareja.* Tirana: Dudaj.

Sulzbach, Walter. 1926. "Der wirtschaftliche Wert der Kolonien." *Der deutsche Volkswirt. Zeitschrift für Politik und Wirtschaft* 1:300–304.

———. 1929. *Nationales Gemeinschaftsgefühl und wirtschaftliches Interesse*. Leipzig: Hirschfeld.

———. 1942. *"Capitalistic Warmongers," a Modern Superstition*. Chicago: University of Chicago Press.

———. 1959. *Imperialismus und Nationalbewusstsein*. Frankfurt am Main: Europaische Verlagsanstalt.

———. 1963. "Die Vereinigten Staaten und die Auflösung des Kolonialsystems." *Schweizer Monatshefte* 43 (3): 233–245.

Sumner, William Graham. 1911. *War and Other Essays*. New Haven, Conn.: Yale University Press.

Sunderland, Willard. 2004. *Taming the Wild Field: Colonization and Empire on the Russian Steppe*. Ithaca, N.Y.: Cornell University Press.

Suny, Ronald. 2006. "Learning from Empire: Russia and the Soviet Union." Pp. 73–93 in Calhoun et al. (2006b).

Suny, Ronald, and Terry Martin, eds. 2001. *A State of Nations: Empire and Nation-Making in the Age of Lenin and Stalin*. New York: Oxford University Press.

Sylvest, Casper. 2007. *Liberal International Thought in Britain, 1880–1918*. Ph.D. diss., University of Cambridge (History).

Tadiar, N. 2004. "Challenges for Cultural Studies under the Rule of Global War." *Kritika Kultura* 4:34–47.

Tanaka, Stefan. 1993. *Japan's Orient: Rendering Past into History*. Berkeley: University of California Press.

Tannenbaum, Nicola. 1984. "The Misuse of Chayanov: 'Chayanov's Rule' and Empiricist Bias in Anthropology." *American Anthropologist* 86 (4): 927–942.

Tarde, Gabriel. 1895. *Les lois de l'imitation: étude sociologique*. Paris: F. Alcan.

———. 1899. *Les transformations du pouvoir*. Paris: Félix Alcan.

———. 1902. *Psychologie économique*. 2 vols. Paris: Félix Alcan.

Tarrow, Sidney. 1998. *Power in Movement: Social Movement and Contentious Politics*. Cambridge: Cambridge University Press.

Taylor, Charles. 2001. "Two Theories of Modernity." Pp. 172–191 in Gaonkar (2001a).

Taylor, P. J. 1994. "The State as Container: Territoriality in the Modern World-System." *Progress in Human Geography* 18 (3): 151–162.

———. 1996. "Embedded Statism and the Social Sciences: Opening Up to New Spaces." *Environment and Planning A* 28:1917–1995.

Tenet, George. 2007. *At the Center of the Storm: My Years at the C.I.A.* New York: Harper-Collins.

Teschke, Benno. 2006. "Imperial Doxa from the Berlin Republic." *New Left Review* 40:128–140.

Thomas, William I. 1896. "The Scope and Method of Folk-Psychology." *American Journal of Sociology* 1:434–445.

———. 1905a. "The Province of Social Psychology." *American Journal of Sociology* 10:445–455.

————. 1905b. "Review of *The Bontoc Igorot*, by Albert Ernest Jenks and *The Negritos of Zambales*, by William Allen Reed." *American Journal of Sociology* 11:273.

————. 1908. "The Significance of the Orient for the Occident." *American Journal of Sociology* 13:729–755.

————. 1909a. *Source Book for Social Origins*. Chicago: University of Chicago Press.

————. 1909b. "Standpoint for the Interpretation of Savage Society." *American Journal of Sociology* 15:145–163.

————. 1912a. "Letter from William I. Thomas to Samuel N. Harper, July 18, 1912." "Letter from William I. Thomas to Samuel N. Harper, July 19, 1912" in University of Chicago Library, Special Collections and Research Center, Samuel N. Harper collection, box 1, folder 16.

————. 1912b. "Race Psychology: Standpoint and Questionnaire, with Particular Reference to the Immigrant and the Negro." *American Journal of Sociology* 17 (6): 741–742.

Thomas, William I., and Florian Znaniecki. 1918–1920. *The Polish Peasant in Europe and America: Monograph of an Immigrant Group*. 3 vols. Chicago: University of Chicago Press.

Thompson, Elizabeth. 2000. *Colonial Citizens: Republican Rights, Paternal Privileges, and Gender in French Syria and Lebanon*. New York: Columbia University Press.

Thompson, Lanny. 2002. "The Imperial Republic: A Comparison of the Insular Territories under U.S. Dominion after 1898." *Pacific Historical Review* 71:535–574.

Thorner, D., B. Kerblay, and R. E. F. Smith, eds. 1968. *A. V. Chayanov on the Theory of the Peasant Economy*. Homewood, Ill.: Irwin.

Thornton, A. P. 1968. *The Imperial Idea and Its Enemies: A Study in British Power*. New York: Anchor Books.

Thurnwald, Richard. 1931–1935. *Die Menschliche Gesellschaft in ihren ethnosoziologischen Grundlagen*. 5 vols. Berlin: W. de Gruyter.

————. 1935. *Black and White in East Africa. The Fabric of a New Civilization*. London: Routledge.

————. 1936. "The Crisis of Imperialism in East Africa and Elsewhere." *Social Forces* 15 (1): 84–91.

————. 1938. "Zur persönlichen Abwehr." *Archiv für Anthropologie*, N.F. 24(3/4): 300–302.

————. 1939a. *Koloniale Gestaltung. Methoden und Probleme überseeischer Ausdehnung*. Hamburg: Hoffmann und Campe Verlag.

————. 1939b. "Methoden in der völkerkunde." Pp. 420–428 in Otto Reche, *Kultur und Rasse*. München: J. F. Lehmanns Verlag.

Tilly, Charles. 1975. "Reflections on the History of European Statemaking." Pp. 3–82 in Charles Tilly (Ed.), *The Formation of National States in Western Europe*. Princeton, N.J.: Princeton University Press.

————. 1985. "War Making and State Making as Organized Crime." Pp. 169–191 in Evans et al. (1985).

————. 1990. *Coercion, Capital, and European States, AD 990–1990*. Cambridge: Blackwell.

———. 1995. "To Explain Political Processes." *American Journal of Sociology* 100:1594–1610.

———. 1997a. "How Empires End." Pp. 1–11 in Karen Barkey and Mark von Hagen (Eds.), *After Empire: Multiethnic Societies and Nation-Building.* Boulder, Colo.: Westview Press.

———. 1997b. *Roads from Past to Future.* Lanham, Md.: Rowman and Littlefield.

———. 2001. "Historical Sociology." Pp. 6753–6757 in *International Encyclopedia of the Behavioral and Social Sciences.* Vol. 10. Amsterdam: Elsevier. .

———. 2003. "Contention over Space and Place." *Mobilization* 8 (2): 221–226.

———. 2004. "Social Boundary Mechanisms." *Philosophy of the Social Sciences* 34:211–236.

Tilly, Charles, and Bruce Stave. 1998. "A Conversation with Charles Tilly: Urban History and Urban Sociology." *Journal of Urban History* 24:184–225.

Tilly, Virginia. 2005. *The One-State Solution.* Ann Arbor: University of Michigan Press.

Timasheff, N. S. 1948. "The Sociological Theories of Maksim M. Kovalevsky." Pp. 441–457 in Barnes (1948).

Timm, Klaus. 1977. "Richard Thurnwald: 'Koloniale Gestaltung'—Ein 'Apartheids-Projekt' für die koloniale Expansion des deutschen Faschismus in Afrika." *Ethnographisch-Archäologische Zeitschrift* 18:617–649.

Tipps, Dean C. 1973. "Modernization Theory and the Comparative Study of Societies: A Critical Perspective." *Comparative Studies in Society and History* 15 (2): 199–226.

Tipton, Frank B., Jr. 1974. "Farm Labor and Power Politics: Germany, 1850–1914." *Journal of Economic History* 34:951–979.

Tocqueville, Alexis de. [1837] 2001. "Second Letter on Algeria (22 August 1837)." Pp. 14–26 in Tocqueville (2001).

———. [1842] 2001. "Essay on Algeria (October 1842)." Pp. 59–116 in Tocqueville (2001).

———. [1843] 1962. "Ébauches d'un ouvrage sur l'Inde." Pp. 443–475 in J. P. Mayer (Ed.), *Alexis de Tocqueville, Œuvres completes).* Vol. 3. Paris: Gallimard.

———. 2001. *Writings on Empire and Slavery.* Edited by Jennifer Pitts. Baltimore, Md.: Johns Hopkins University Press.

Todorova, Maria. 1997. *Imagining the Balkans.* Oxford: Oxford University Press.

Toniolo, G. 1905. *L'odierno problema sociologico: studi storico-critico.* Florence: Libreria editrice Fiorentina.

Toscano, Alberto. 2007. "Powers of Pacification: State and Empire in Gabriel Tarde." *Economy and Society* 36 (4): 597–613.

Treves, Renato. 1959. "Gli studi e le ricerche sociologiche in Italia." Pp. 172–211 in *Atti del 4: congresso mondiale di sociologia biblioteca di cultura moderna: la sociologia nel suo contesto sociale.* Roma-Bari: Laterza.

———. 1987. "Continuità o rottura nella storia della sociologia italiana." *Quaderni di sociologia* 7:97–102.

Triulzi, Alessandro. 1982. "Italian Colonialism and Ethiopia." *Journal of African History* 23 (2): 237–243.

————. 2003. "Adwa: From Monument to Document." *Modern Italy* 8 (1): 95–108.

Trocki, Carl A. 1999. "Political Structures in the Nineteenth and Early Twentieth Centuries." Pp. 75–126 in Nicholas Tarling (Ed.), *The Cambridge History of Southeast Asia*. Cambridge: Cambridge University Press.

Trouillot, Michel-Rolph. 1991. "Anthropology and the Savage Slot. The Poetics and Politics of Otherness." Pp. 18–44 in Richard Fox (Ed.), *Recapturing Anthropology*. Santa Fe, N.M.: SAR Press.

Turner, Stephen Park, and Jonathan H. Turner. 1990. *The Impossible Science: An Institutional Analysis of American Sociology*. Newbury Park, N.J.: Sage.

Tylor, E. B. 1974. *Primitive Culture: Researches into the Development of Mythology, Philosophy, Religion, Art, and Custom*. Vol. 1. New York: Gordon Press.

Ullmann, Walter. 1979. " 'This Realm of England Is an Empire.' " *Journal of Ecclesiastical History* 30:175–203.

Urs, Kantaraj. [1917] 1953. "Reply to Mysore Municipal Address after Sir M. Kantharaj Urs' Return from Japan, 1917 (the exact date not mentioned)." Pp. 189–190 in Urs (1953).

————. [1920] 1953. "Address Presented by the Adikarnatakas and Adidravidas (Harijans) of Mysore, October 25, 1920." Pp. 276–277 in Urs (1953).

————. 1953. *Speeches of Sirdar Sir M. Kantharaj Urs*. Edited by Sirdar K. Basavaraj Urs. Bangalore: Government Press.

Uspenskii, Gleb. 1908. "Poezdki k pereselentsam." Pp. 3–165 in *Polnoe sobranie sochinenii*. Sixth edition. Vol. 6. St. Petersburg: A. F. Marx.

Vaccaro, Michele Angelo. 1917. *Il problema della pace e del futuro assetto del mondo*. Turin: Bocca.

————. 1927. *Crispi: dal martirio all'apoteosi*. Rome: Industrie grafiche editoriali.

Vann, Michael G. 1999. "White City on the Red River: Race, Power, and Culture in French Colonial Hanoi, 1872–1954." Ph.D. diss., University of California, Santa Cruz (History).

Vanni, Icilio. 1886. *Saggi critici sulla teoria sociologica della popolazione*. Città di Castello: Lapi.

Verein für Socialpolitik. 1883. *Bäuerliche Zustände in Deutschland*, Vol. 1. *Schriften des vereins für Socialpolitik*, Vol. 22. Leipzig: Duncker and Humblot.

————. 1884. "Massregeln der Gesetzgebung und Verwaltung zur Erhaltung des Bäuerlichen Grundbesitzes." Pp. 1–76 in *Verhandlungen 6. und 7. October 1884 abgehaltenen Generalversammlung des Vereins für Socialpolitik. Schriften des Vereins für Socialpolitik*. Vol. 28. Leipzig: Duncker and Humblot.

Vidich, Arthur J., and Stanford M. Lyman. 1985. *American Sociology: Worldly Rejections of Religion and Their Directions*. New Haven, Conn.: Yale University Press.

Vierkandt, Alfred. 1896. *Naturvölker und Kulturvölker: Ein Beitrag zur Socialpsychologie*. Leipzig: Duncker and Humblot.

Virgilii, Filippo. 1892. "Il problema della popolazione: critica dei sistemi." *Giornale degli economisti* (March): 566–599.

————. 1898. *La sociologia e le trasformazioni del diritto: prolusione ad un corso libero di sociologia tenuto all'università di Siena.* Turin: Bocca.

————. 1916. *Il costo della guerra Europea.* Milan: Treves.

————. 1917. *Per un trattato di sociologia.* Turin: Bocca.

————. 1919. "L'emigrazione tedesca prima della guerra e le conseguenze per la Germania dell'intervento dell'America nel conflitto mondiale." *Scientia* 25 (13): 132–141.

————. 1924. *Il problema della popolazione.* Milan: Vallardi.

————. 1927. *Le colonie Italiane nella storia, nella vita presente e nel loro avvenire.* Milan: Hoepli.

————. 1937. "Espansione coloniale e demografica dell'Italia." In *Terra e nazioni: Italia.* Milan: Vallardi.

Visser, Romke. 1992. "Fascist Doctrine and the Cult of Romanità." *Journal of Contemporary History* 27 (1): 5–22.

Visvesvaraya, Sir M. [1913a] 1917. "Opening of Harihar Pump Installation, August 11, 1913." Pp. 86–91 in Visvesvaraya (1917).

————. [1913b] 1917. "Reply to an Address by the Citizens of Mysore, January 7, 1913." Pp. 60–65 in Visvesvaraya (1917).

————. [1914a] 1917. "Address to Dasara Representative Assembly, September 30, 1914." Pp. 165–205 in Visvesvaraya (1917).

————. [1914b] 1917. "Address to the Fifth Session of Mysore Economic Conference, June 3, 1914." Pp. 142–152 in Visvesvaraya (1917).

————. [1915a] 1917. "Address to Dasara Representative Assembly, October 19, 1915." Pp. 257–299 in Visvesvaraya (1917).

————. [1915b] 1917. "Address to the Sixth Session of Mysore Economic Conference, June 21, 1915." Pp. 231–240 in Visvesvaraya (1917).

————. 1917. *Speeches, 1910–17.* Bangalore: Government Press.

————. 1920. *Reconstructing India.* London: P. S. King and Son Limited.

Volney, Constantin-François. 1796. *The Ruins: Or, a Survey of the Revolutions of Empires.* London: J. Johnson.

Von Hagen, Mark. 2007. "Federalisms and Pan-movements: Re-Imagining Empire." Pp. 503–505 in Jane Burbank, Mark von Hagen, and Anatolyi Remnev (Eds.), *Russian Empire: Space, People, Power, 1700–1930.* Bloomington: Indiana University Press.

Von Henneberg, Krystyna Clara. 1994. "Tripoli: Piazza Castello and the Making of a Fascist Colonial Capital." Pp. 135–150 in Çelik et. al. (1994).

Vreeland, James. 2003. *The IMF and Economic Development.* Cambridge: Cambridge University Press.

Vucinich, Alexander. 1976. *Social Thought in Tsarist Russia: The Quest for a General Science of Society, 1861–1917.* Chicago: University of Chicago Press.

Wacquant, Loïc. 2002. "From Slavery to Mass Incarceration." *New Left Review* 13:41–60.

Wadiyar, Sri Krishnaraja [1907] 1934. "Speech on the Occasion of the Opening of the Dasara Exhibition on 5th October, 1907." Pp. 61–64 in Wadiyar (1934).

————. [1913] 1942. "Joint Reply to the Welcome Addresses Presented by the Bangalore City Municipal Council and the Vokkaligara Sangha, Bangalore, October

6, 1913." Pp. 30–36 in *Speeches by His Highness Yuvaraja Sri Kantirava Narasimharaja Wadiyar Bahadur, 1910–1939*. Bangalore: Government Press.

———. [1919] 1934. "Speech as First Chancellor of the Benares Hindu University at the Convocation held on 17th January, 1919." Pp. 167–177 in Wadiyar (1934).

———. [1921] 1934. "Speech as Chancellor of the Benares Hindu University on the Occasion of the Degree of Doctor of Laws upon His Royal Highness The Prince of Wales on 13th December, 1921." Pp. 190–193 in Wadiyar (1934).

———. [1924] 1934. "Address to the Reconstituted Mysore Legislature, March 12, 1924." Pp. 228–233 in Wadiyar (1934).

———. [1926] 1934. "Speech on the Occasion of the Jubilee of the Maharaja's Sanskrit College, Mysore, October 20, 1926." Pp. 252–257 in Wadiyar (1934).

———. 1934. *Speeches by His Highness Maharaja Sri Krishnaraja Wadiyar Bahadur, Maharaja of Mysore, 1902–1933*. Mysore: Government Branch Press.

Wagner, Peter, Carol Hirschon Weiss, Björn Wittrock, and Helmutt Wollman, eds. 1999. *Social Sciences and Modern States: National Experiences and Theoretical Crossroads*. Cambridge: Cambridge Univesity Press.

Walicki, Andrzej. 1975. *The Slavophile Controversy: History of a Conservative Utopia in Nineteenth-Century Russian Thought*. Oxford: Clarendon Press.

———. 1979. *A History of Russian Thought: From the Enlightenment to Marxism*. Stanford, Calif.: Stanford University Press.

———. 1987. *Legal Philosophies of Russian Liberalism*. Oxford: Clarendon Press.

Wallace, Alfred Russel. [1869] 1986. *The Malay Archipelago: The Land of the Orang-Utan, and the Bird of Paradise*. Oxford: Oxford University Press.

Wallerstein, Immanuel. [1970] 1986. "The Colonial Era in Africa: Changes in the Social Structure." Pp. 13–35 in Wallerstein (1986).

———. 1971. "The Range of Choice: Constraints on the Policies of Governments of Contemporary African Independent States." Pp. 19–33 in Michael F. Lofochie (Ed.), *The State of Nations*. Berkeley: University of California Press.

———. [1974–2011] 2011. *The Modern World-System*. 4 vols. Berkeley: University of California Press.

———. 1979. "The Rise and Future Demise of the World Capitalist System." Pp. 1–36 in *The Capitalist World-Economy*. Cambridge: Cambridge University Press.

———. 1986. *Africa and the Modern World*. Trenton: Africa World Press.

———. 1991. *Unthinking Social Science: The Limits of Nineteenth-Century Paradigms*. Cambridge: Polity.

———. 2003. *The Decline of American Power: The U.S. in a Chaotic World*. New York: New Press.

———. 2004. *World Systems Analysis: An Introduction*. Durham, N.C.: Duke University Press.

Wallis, William, and Rececca Bream. 2007. "Chinese Deal with Congo Prompts Concern." *Financial Times*, Sept. 20: 10.

Walt, Stephen, and John Mearsheimer. 2007. *The Israel Lobby and U.S. Foreign Policy*. New York: Farrar, Straus, and Giroux.

Walther, Andreas. 1927. *Soziologie und Sozialwissenschaften in Amerika*. Karlsruhe: Verlag G. Braun.

Ward, Lester F. 1896. "Contributions to Social Philosophy. VI. The Data of Sociology." *American Journal of Sociology* 1:738–752.

———. 1901. *Sociology at the Paris Exposition of 1900*. Washington, D.C.: Government Printing Office.

———. 1902a. "Contemporary Sociology. II." *American Journal of Sociology* 7:629–658.

———. 1902b. "Contemporary Sociology. III." *American Journal of Sociology* 7:749–762.

———. 1903. *Pure Sociology: A Treatise on the Origin and Spontaneous Development of Society*. New York: Macmillan.

———. 1906. *Applied Sociology: A Treatise on the Conscious Improvement of Society by Society*. Boston: Ginn.

———. 1907. "Social and Biological Struggles." *American Journal of Sociology* 13:289–299.

———. 1908. "Social Classes in the Light of Modern Sociological Theory." *American Journal of Sociology* 13:617–627.

Warren, Bill. 1980. *Imperialism, Pioneer of Capitalism*. London: NLB.

Wax, Murray L. 1971. *Indian Americans: Unity and Diversity*. Englewood Cliffs, N.J.: Prentice-Hall.

———. 1979. "The Reluctant Merlins of Camelot: Ethics and Politics of Overseas Research." Pp. 83–102 in Murray L. Wax (Ed.), *Federal Regulations: Ethical Issues and Social Research*. Boulder, Colo.: Westview Press.

Wax, Murray Lionel, and Robert W. Buchanan, eds. 1975. *Solving "the Indian Problem": The White Man's Burdensome Business*. New York: New Viewpoints.

Weatherly, Ulysses G. 1910. "Race and Marriage." *American Journal of Sociology* 15:433–453.

Weaver, Frederick. 2000. *Latin America in the World Economy: Mercantile Colonialism to Global Capitalism*. Boulder, Colo.: Westview.

Weber, Alfred. 1904. "Deutschland und der wirtschaftlicher Imperialismus." *Preussische Jahrbücher* 116:298–324.

———. 1920–1921. "Prinzipielles zur Kultursoziologie. (Gesellschaftprozeß, Zivilisationsprozeß und Kulturbewegung)." *Archiv für Sozialwissenschaft und Sozialpolitik* 47:1–49.

———. 1935. *Kulturgeschichte als Kultursoziologie*. Leiden: A. W. Sijthoff's uitgeversmaatschappij, n.v.

Weber, Eugen. 1976. *Peasants into Frenchmen*. Stanford, Calif.: Stanford University Press.

Weber, Jacques. 1988. *Les etablissements Français en Inde au XIXe siècle (1816–1914)*. Vol. 5. Paris: Librairie de l'Inde.

———. 1991. "Chanemougam, the King of India: Social and Political Foundations of an Absolute Power under the Third Republic." *Economic and Political Weekly* (Bombay), Sept. 2: 291–302.

———. 1996. *Pondichéry et les comptoirs de l'Inde après dupleix: la démocratie au pays des castes*. Paris: Editions denoël.

Weber, Marianne. 1975. *Max Weber: A Biography*. New York: Wiley.

Weber, Max. 1891. *Die römische Agrargeschichte in ihrer Bedeutung für das Staats-und Privatrecht*. Stuttgart: F. Enke.

———. [1891] 2010. *Roman Agrarian History in Its Relation to Roman Public and Civil Law*. Claremont, Calif.: Regina Books.

———. 1892. *Die Verhältnisse der Landarbeiter im ostelbischen Deutschland: Schriften des Vereins für Socialpolitik*. Vol. 55. Leipzig: Duncker and Humblot.

———. [1896] 1924. "Die sozialen Gründe des Untergangs der antiken Kultur." Pp. 289–311 in Max Weber (1924a).

———. [1896] 1998. "The Social Causes of the Decline of Ancient Civilization." Pp. 387–411 in *The Agrarian Sociology of Ancient Civilizations*. London: Verso.

———. 1906. "The Relations of the Rural Community to Other Branches of Social Science." Pp. 725–746 in Howard J. Roger (Ed.), *Congress of Arts and Science: Universal Exposition, St. Louis, 1904*. Vol. 7. Boston: Houghton Mifflin.

———. [1909] 1998. "The Agrarian Sociology of Ancient Civilizations." Pp. 35–386 in *The Agrarian Sociology of Ancient Civilizations*. London: Verso.

———. 1922. *Gesammelte Aufsätze zur Religionssoziologie*. 3 vols. Tübingen: J. C. B. Mohr.

———. 1924a. *Gesammelte Aufsätze zur Sozial- und Wirtschaftsgeschichte*. Tübingen: J. C. B. Mohr.

———. 1924b. "Zur Psychophysik der instriellen Arbeit (1908–09)." Pp. 62–255 in Max Weber (1924a).

———. 1971. *Gesammelte Politische Schriften*. Third edition. Edited by Johannes Winckelmann. Tübingen: J. C. B. Mohr.

———. 1978. *Economy and Society*. Fourth edition. 2 vols. Berkeley: University of California Press.

Wehler, Hans-Ulrich. 1972. "Industrial Growth and Early German Imperialism." Pp. 71–92 in Edward Owen and Bob Sutcliffe (Eds.), *Studies in the Theory of Imperialism*. London: Longman.

Weiler, Bernd. 2003. "Ludwig Gumplowicz (1838–1909) e il suo allievo triestino Franco Savorgnan (1879–1963): analisi del rapporto fra la sociologia Austriaca e quella Italiana." *Sociologia* 37 (1): 9–34.

———. 2007. "Gumplowicz, Ludwig (1838–1909)." Pp. 2038–2040 in George Ritzer (Ed.), *The Blackwell Encyclopedia of Sociology*. Malden, Mass.: Blackwell.

Weinstein, David. 2005. "Imagining Darwinism." Pp. 189–210 in Bart Schultz and Georgios Varouxakis (Eds.), *Utilitarianism and Empire*. Oxford: Lexington Books.

Weisman, Alan. 2007. *Prince of Darkness: Richard Perle, the Kingdom, the Power, and the End of Empire in America*. New York: Union Square Press.

Weizman, Eyal. 2002. "The Politics of Verticality." April 24, 2002, www.opendem ocracy.org.

———. 2007. *Hollow Land: Israel's Architecture of Occupation*. London: Verso.

West, Max. 1900. "The Fourteenth Amendment and the Race Question." *American Journal of Sociology* 6:248–254.

Wickham, Gary, and Harry Freemantle. 2008. "Some Additional Knowledge Conditions for Sociology." *Current Sociology* 56:922–939.

Wiese, Leopold von. 1914a. "Die gegenwärtige Stellung Ceylons in der Weltwirtschaft im Vergleich mit Vorder- und Hinterasien." *Weltwirtschaftliches Archiv* 3 (1): 139–162.

———. 1914b. "Die Rodias auf Ceylon." *Archiv für Rassen-und Gesellschaftsbiologie* 11 (1): 33–45.

———. 1915. "Englands Herrschaft in Indien." *Die neue Rundschau* 26 (1): 465–479.

Wilder, Gary. 2005. *The French Imperial Nation-State: Negritude and Colonial Humanism between the Two World Wars*. Chicago: University of Chicago Press.

Williams, Raymond. 1983. "Utilitarian." Pp. 327–329 in *Keywords: A Vocabulary of Culture and Society*. New York: Oxford University Press.

Williams, William Appleman. 1959. "Imperial Anticolonialism." Pp 23–44 in *The Tragedy of American Diplomacy*. Cleveland, Ohio: World Publishing.

———. 1980. *Empire as a Way of Life*. New York: Oxford University Press.

Willoughby, William F. 1905. *Territories and Dependencies of the United States*. New York: Century Co.

———. 1909. "The Reorganization of Municipal Government in Porto Rico: Political." *Political Science Quarterly* 24:409–443.

Wilson, Woodrow. 1901. "Democracy and Efficiency." *Atlantic Monthly* 87 (521): 289–299.

Wimmer, Andreas 2002. *Nationalist Exclusion and Ethnic Conflict: Shadows of Modernity*. Cambridge: Cambridge University Press.

Wolf, Eric R. 1982. *Europe and the People without History*. Berkeley: University of California Press.

Wolff, Larry. 1994. *Inventing Eastern Europe*. Stanford, Calif.: Stanford University Press.

Wolin, Sheldon. 1973. "The Politics of the Study of Revolution." *Comparative Politics* 5 (3): 343–358.

———. 2004. *Politics and Vision: Continuity and Innovation in Western Political Thought*. Princeton, N.J.: Princeton University Press.

Wolpe, Harold. 1972. "Capitalism and Cheap Labour-Power in South Africa: From Segregation to Apartheid." *Economy and Society* 1 (4): 425–456.

———, ed. 1980. *The Articulation of Modes of Production*. London: Routledge and Kegan Paul.

Wood, Ellen Meiksins. 2005. *Empire of Capital*. London: Verso.

Woodward, Bob. 2004. *Plan of Attack*. New York: Simon and Schuster.

Woolf, Greg. 2001. "Inventing Empire in Ancient Rome." Pp. 311–322 in Susan E. Alcock et al. (Eds.), *Empires: Perspectives from Archaeology and History*. Cambridge: Cambridge University Press.

Worms, René. 1908. *Études de sociologie coloniale. Les populations indigènes du Cambodge et du Laos*. Paris: V. Giard & E. Brière.

Wortman, Richard. 1967. *The Crisis of Russian Populism*. Cambridge: Cambridge University Press.

Wright, Gwendolyn. 1991. *The Politics of Design in French Colonial Urbanism*. Chicago: University of Chicago Press.

Wright, Quincy. 1942. *A Study of War*. Chicago: University of Chicago Press.

Yadov, Vladimir. 2008. "Dlia chego nuzhna segodnia russkaia sotsiologiia?" *Sotsiologicheskie Issledovaniia* 4:16–20.

Young, Crawford. 1994. *The African Colonial State in Comparative Perspective*. New Haven, Conn.: Yale University Press.

Young, Louise. 1998. *Japan's Total Empire*. Berkeley: University of California Press.

Young, Nick. 2007. "China in Africa: A Relationship Still in the Making." *China Development Brief*, June 5, http://www.chinadevelopmentbrief.com/node/1126.

Young, Robert. 1990. *White Mythologies: Writing History and the West*. London: Routledge.

Younis, Mona. 2000. *Liberation and Democratization: The South African and Palestinian National Movements*. Minneapolis: University of Minnesota Press.

Yu, Henry. 2001. *Thinking Orientals: Migration, Contact, and Exoticism in Modern America*. New York: Oxford Universtiy Press.

Zeghidi, M'Hamed. 1976. "Décolonisation et développement dans la sociologie Tunisienne." Pp. 251–264 in Yvonne Roux (Ed.), *Questions à la sociologie Française*. Paris: PUF.

Zimmer, Oliver 2003. *Nationalism in Europe, 1890–1940*. Houndmills: Palgrave Macmillan.

Zimmerman, Andrew. 2001. *Anthropology and Antihumanism in Imperial Germany*. Chicago: University of Chicago Press.

———. 2005. "A German Alabama in Africa: The Tuskegee Expedition to German Togo and the Transnational Origins of West African Cotton Growers." *American Historical Review* 110:1362–1398.

———. 2006a. "Decolonizing Weber." *Postcolonial Studies* 9:53–79.

———. 2006b. " 'What Do You Really Want in German East Africa, *Herr Professor*?' Counterinsurgency and the Science Effect in Colonial Tanzania." *Comparative Studies in Society and History* 48:419–461.

———. 2010. *Alabama in Africa: Booker T. Washington, the German Empire, and the Globalization of the New South*. Princeton, N.J.: Princeton University Press.

Žižek, Slavoj. 1989. *The Sublime Object of Ideology*. London: Verso.

Zweig, David, and Bi Jianhai. 2005. "China's Hunt for Energy." *Foreign Affairs* 84/85:25–38.

Contributors

ALBERT J. BERGESEN is professor and director of the School of Sociology, University of Arizona. Recent publications include "Frankian Triangles," in Manning and Gills (eds.), *Andre Gunder Frank and Global Development* (Routledge, 2011); and "Geography and War," in Chase-Dunn and Babones (eds.), *The Handbook of World-System Analysis* (Routledge, in press). He is presently writing a book on the basic principles of geopolitics.

OU-BYUNG CHAE is assistant professor of sociology at Kookmin University, Seoul, Korea. As a historical sociologist, he is interested in modern colonialism, East Asian state formation, globalization, and cultural diffusion. His articles available in English include "Sociology in an Era of Fragmentation" (*Sociological Quarterly* 2002, with George Steinmetz) and "The 'Moment of the Boomerang' Never Came: Resistance and Collaboration in Colonial Korea, 1919–1945" (*Journal of Historical Sociology*, 2010), and "Homology Unleashed: Colonial, Anticolonial, and Postcolonial State Culture in South Korea, 1930–1950" (*positions: east asia cultures critique*, forthcoming).

ANDY CLARNO is assistant professor of sociology and African American studies at the University of Illinois at Chicago. He is working on a book manuscript, *The Empire's New Walls*, analyzing the walled enclosures that mark the urban landscapes of contemporary South Africa and Palestine/Israel. He has published two related articles based on this research: "A Tale of Two Walled Cities: Neoliberalization and Enclosure in Johannesburg and Jerusalem," *Political Power and Social Theory* 19 (2008) and "Or Does It Explode? Collecting Shells in Gaza," *Social Psychology Quarterly* 72:2 (2009).

RAEWYN CONNELL is university professor at the University of Sydney, a fellow of the Academy of Social Sciences in Australia, and one of Australia's leading social scientists. Her most recent books are *Confronting Equality* (2011), about social science and politics; *Gender: In World Perspective* (2009); and *Southern Theory* (2007), about social thought beyond the global metropole. Her other books include *Masculinities, Schools & Social Justice, Ruling Class Ruling Culture, Gender & Power,* and *Making the Difference.* Her work has been translated into fifteen languages. She has taught at universities in Australia, Canada, and the United States, in departments of sociology, political science, and education. A long-term participant in the labor movement and peace movement, Raewyn has tried to make social science relevant to social justice. Details at www.raewynconnell.net.

ILYA GERASIMOV (Ph.D. in History, Rutgers University, 2000; Candidate of Sciences in History, Kazan University, Russia, 1998) is the executive editor of *Ab Imperio,* which is dedicated to studies of new imperial history and nationalism in the post-Soviet space; and director at the Center for the Studies of Nationalism and Empire (Kazan, Russia). His most recent books include *Ethnic Crime, Imperial City: Practices of Self-Organization and Paradoxes of Illegality in Late Imperial Russia, 1905–1917* (under review); *Modernism and Public Reform in Late Imperial Russia: Rural Professionals and Self-Organization, 1905–30* (Palgrave Macmillan, 2009); *Writing. Degree. The Naughties* [in Russian] (Moscow: Novoe izdatelstvo, 2009).

JULIAN GO is associate professor of sociology at Boston University. He is also editor of the journal *Political Power and Social Theory* and Chair of the Comparative-Historical Sociology Section of the American Sociological Association. His books include *Patterns of Empire: The British and American Empires, 1688–Present* (Cambridge University Press, 2011) and *American Empire and the Politics of Meaning: Elite Political Cultures in the Philippines and Puerto Rico during U.S. Colonialism* (Duke University Press, 2008). He is currently writing about postcolonial and global sociology.

DANIEL P. S. GOH is assistant professor of sociology at the National University of Singapore. He is the coeditor of *Race and Multiculturalism* in Malaysia and Singapore (2009), and his articles on culture and colonialism have been published in *Comparative Studies in Society and History,* the *International Journal of Cultural Studies, Postcolonial Studies,* the *British Journal of Sociology,* and *positions: east asia cultures critique.* His current research focuses on urban aspirations, heritage cultural politics, and the remaking of Hong Kong, Malacca, Penang, and Singapore in the age of Asian global city competition.

CHANDAN GOWDA is professor of sociology at Azim Premji University, Bengaluru. His interests include social theory, sociology of knowledge, contemporary South Asia, Indian normative traditions, and Kannada literature and cinema. In addition to his academic publications, he has written for newspapers and published translations of Kannada fiction and nonfiction in English. He is presently completing a book on the cultural politics of development in the old Mysore state.

KRISHAN KUMAR is university professor, William R. Kenan Jr. professor and chair, at the Department of Sociology, University of Virginia. He was previously professor of social and political thought at the University of Kent at Canterbury, England. Among his publications are *Utopia and Anti-Utopia in Modern Times* (Blackwell, 1987), *1989: Revolutionary Ideas and Ideals* (University of Minnesota Press, 2001),

The Making of English National Identity (Cambridge University Press, 2003), and *From Post-Industrial to Post-Modern Society* (2nd ed., Blackwell, 2005). He is currently working on a comparative study of European empires.

FUYUKI KURASAWA is associate professor of sociology, political science, and social and political thought at York University in Toronto, Canada. He is the author of *The Ethnological Imagination: A Cross-Cultural Critique of Modernity* (University of Minnesota Press, 2004) and *The Work of Global Justice: Human Rights as Practices* (Cambridge University Press, 2007). He is currently researching the history of Western visual representation of humanitarian crises.

MICHAEL MANN is distinguished professor of sociology at UCLA. He has honorary doctorates from McGill University and the University of the Aegean and is an honorary professor at Cambridge University. Mann is the author of the four-volume *The Sources of Social Power: A History of Power from the Beginning to 1760* (1986); *The Rise of Classes and Nation-States, 1760–1914* (1993); *Global Empires and Revolution, 1890–1945* (2012); and *Globalizations, 1945–2011* (2013). He has also published *Incoherent Empire; Fascists; The Dark Side of Democracy;* and *Power in the 21st Century: Conversations with John Hall.* He is the subject of John Hall and Ralph Schroeder (eds.), *The Anatomy of Power: The Social Theory of Michael Mann.*

MARINA MOGILNER is research fellow at the Center for the Studies of Nationalism and Empire (Kazan, Russia) and a founder and editor of the international quarterly *Ab Imperio.* She got her Russian Candidate of Sciences degree in 1998 and a Ph.D. from Rutgers University in 2000. Her book, *Mythology of the "Underground Man": Russian Radical Microcosm in the Early Twentieth Century as an Object of Semiotic Analysis,* came out in 1999 (in Russian), followed by *Homo Imperii: A History of Physical Anthropology in Russia* (2008). The revised English-language version of this book is due in March 2013 from Nebraska University Press.

BESNIK PULA is a postdoctoral researcher at the Center for the Study of Social Organization at Princeton University under the ASA/NSF fellowship program. He received his Ph.D. in sociology from the University of Michigan and holds an M.A. in Russian and East European Studies from Georgetown University. His work on colonialism, nationalism and empire has appeared in *Theory and Society* and *Nationalities Papers.* His current research examines the relationship between socialist and postsocialist transformations and major shifts in the world economy since 1970.

ANNE RAFFIN is associate professor of sociology at the National University of Singapore. She is the author of *Youth Mobilization in Vichy Indochina and Its Legacies, 1940–1970* (Lexington Books, 2005). She has written not only on colonial but also on contemporary Vietnam, and her recent publications include "Assessing State and Societal Functions of the Military and the War Experience in *Doi Moi* Vietnam" (*Armed Forces and Society,* 2011). Expanding her research to French colonialism in Asia, she is currently working on a manuscript entitled "Who Belongs to My Community? Cultural Particularism vs. the Universal Nation in French Colonial Pondicherry, 1870s–1914."

EMMANUELLE SAADA is associate professor of French, history, and sociology at Columbia University. Her first book was translated into English by the University of Chicago Press in 2012 under the title of *Empire's Children: Race, Filiation and Citizenship in the French Colonies*. She is currently writing a book on the historiography of European colonialisms. She is also working on a project on law and violence in nineteenth-century Algeria.

MARCO SANTORO is associate professor of sociology at the University of Bologna. A research director at the Istituto Carlo Cattaneo (Bologna) and an associate member of the Centre européen de sociologie et de science politique (Paris), he has published widely in both Italian and English on professions, intellectuals, arts (especially music), the Mafia, social theory, and the history of sociology. He is a founding editor of the journal *Sociologica: Italian Journal of Sociology online* and a member of the editorial boards of *Poetics, Cultural Sociology*, and the *American Journal of Cultural Sociology*. He is currently writing a book on the political dimension of Mafias, and working on suicide and artistic consecration, on the Chicago School of sociology, and on the sociology of Italian sociology. He is also coediting, with George Steinmetz, a book on the global circulation of Bourdieu.

KIM LANE SCHEPPELE is the Laurance S. Rockefeller professor of sociology and international affairs in the Woodrow Wilson School and the University Center for Human Values as well as director of the Program in Law and Public Affairs, Princeton University. After 1989, Scheppele studied the emergence of constitutional law in Hungary and Russia, living in both places for extended periods. After 9/11, Scheppele has researched the effects of the international "war on terror" on constitutional protections around the world. In short, when the Berlin Wall fell, she studied the transition of countries from police states to constitutional rule-of-law states, and after the Twin Towers fell, she studied the process in reverse. Her forthcoming book is called *The International State of Emergency: The Rise of Global Security Law*.

ALEXANDER SEMYONOV is professor of history at the Faculty of History, National Research University-Higher School of Economics in St. Petersburg and a founder and editor of the international scholarly journal *Ab Imperio: Studies of New Imperial History and Nationalism in the Post-Soviet Space*. He also teaches history at the Faculty of Liberal Arts and Sciences, St. Petersburg State University. He edited and authored: *Empire Speaks Out: Languages of Rationalization and Self-Description in the Russian Empire* (Leiden: Brill, 2009), in English; *New Imperial History of the Post-Soviet Space* (2004); *Myths and Misconceptions in Studies of Nationalism and Empire* (2010), in Russian.

GEORGE STEINMETZ is the Charles Tilly Professor of Sociology at the University of Michigan. He wrote *Regulating the Social: The Welfare State and Local Politics in Imperial Germany* (Princeton University Press) and *The Devil's Handwriting: Precoloniality and the German Colonial State in Qingdao, Samoa, and Southwest Africa* (University of Chicago Press). He edited *State/Culture* (Cornell University Press), *The Politics of Method in the Human Sciences* (Duke University Press), and *Sociology* and *Empire* (Duke University Press). He codirected the film "Detroit: Ruin of a City" (2005). Currently he is writing a history of the emergence of sociology in imperial settings.

ANDREW ZIMMERMAN is professor of history at George Washington University. He is the author of *Anthropology and Antihumanism in Imperial Germany* (University of Chicago Press, 2001) and *Alabama in Africa: Booker T. Washington, the German Empire, and the Globalization of the New South* (Princeton University Press, 2010). He is currently working on a global history of the American Civil War.

Index

Armitage, David, 283–84
Armitage, Dick (Richard), 234
Aron, Raymond, 33–34
ASR. See American Sociological Review
Assab (Eritrea): Italian colony, 107
Asian Financial Crisis (1997), 223
Asianism, discourse: in Japan, 403–5; in
    Korea, 410–12
assimilation, 405; in American Philippines,
    98–99, 471–74, 476, 479; "benevolent
    assimilation" (McKinley), 472; in French
    Empire, 50n37, 196–201, 206, 290–91,
    323–24, 334–37, 14n10, 419–20, 426–27,
    433; in Germany, 35, 184; in Italian
    Empire, 373–5, 382, 390, 392; in Japanese
    Korea, 404–6, 409–12, 413n7, 414n9; in
    United States, 68, 91, 103, 104n5
Austen, Ralph, xiii
Australia: indigenous peoples in, 20, 192,
    194, 494, 496; sociology in, 9
Austria: sociology in, 47n10
Austro-Hungarian Empire, 12, 16–18, 26, 39,
    42, 50n39, 281, 288, 377. See also Habsburg
    Empire
"autonomy" (Clarno): in Palestine/Israel
    and South Africa, 437–39, 448, 461
autonomy of science, xvin12
L'Avanti (newspaper, Italy), 164n24
"axis of evil" (Frum), 233
d'Azeglio, Massimo, 286

Bagehot, Walter, 147
Bakongo people (French Congo), 36–37
Bakunin, Mikhail, 56
Balandier, Georges, ix, xivn2, 4, 45;
    Sociologie actuelle de l'Afrique noire,
    36–37; Sociologie des Brazzavilles noires,
    37
Baldacci, Antonio: L'Albania, 395n31
Balkans, 377; crisis in (pre-WWI), 121
Bandits and Bureaucrats (Barkey), 38
Bantu Mining Corporation, 457
Bantu peoples (Africa), 154
bantustans. See South Africa: Bantustan
    system
"Bantustization" (West Bank) 436, 439
Barkey, Karen, 45; Bandits and Bureaucrats,
    38; Empire of Difference, 38

Barnes, Harry, 6
Bartlett, Robert, 284
Basques (Spain), 283, 285
Bastide, Roger, ix, xivn2, 1, 4, 32, 45
Bataille, Georges, 192
Baudrillard, Jean, 50n36
BBC (British Broadcasting Corporation),
    240
Bearing Point (U.S. company), 239
Beccaria, Cesare, 112
Bechtel (U.S. corporation), 241
Bechuanaland (Botswana): as British
    protectorate, 85
Becker, Howard, 6, 104n6, 105n17
Bedouin, 90
Behemoth (Neumann), 34
"Beijing Consensus" (Bergesen), 301–2,
    306–12
Bekhterev, Vladimir, 70–71
Belgian Empire, 167, 182, 184–85, 307
Belgium: as Austrian colony, 39
Benelux countries, 184
"benevolent assimilation" (McKinley), 472
Bengal, 349
Benini, Rodolfo, 135
Bentham, Jeremy, 346, 363n20
Berbers. See Kabyle
Bergesen, Albert, 496–97; "Long Waves of
    Colonial Expansion and Contraction"
    (with Schoenberg), 302–3, 306
Berkeley, University of California at, 96
Berlin, Congress of, 377
Berlin, Isaiah, 167
Berlin University, xivn2, 19, 50n35, 174
Berlin Wall, 436
Berlin West Africa Conference, 49n20, 167,
    183–84. See also Africa: partition of
Berque, Jacques, ix, 4, 32, 44
Beuchat, Henri, 207n2
Bhabha, Homi, 45
Bhutto, Benazir, 271
Biko, Steve, 448–49, 457
Bin Laden, Osama, 231, 271
"biopower" (Foucault), 446, 455
Bishara, Marwan, 439
Bismarck, Otto von, 169–70, 172
Blackman, W. F., 97
Blackmar, Frank Wilson xvn8

Comaroff, Jean and John, xiiin1
Comitato Italiano per lo studio delle
    popolazioni, 154
Commissione per le colonie (Italy), 107,
    160n1
communes (administrative divisions,
    France), 420
"communicative action" (Habermas),
    183–84
Communist Academy (Soviet Union), 79
Communist International, 410
Compania Mexicana de Petroleo Aguila,
    149
comparative methodology, 20, 86–87, 90
"composite monarchies" (Kumar), 283,
    296n6
comprador class, 215, 223
Comte, Auguste, 8, 13, 44, 63, 191; 208n4,
    350; *Cours de philosophie positive*, 13
Concept of the Political (Schmitt), 182–83
Concert of Europe, 377
Condorcet, Marquis de, 191; *Sketch for a
    Historical Picture of the Progress of the
    Human Mind*, 208n4
Conference of Ambassadors, 377
Confucianism, 180
Cong Luan (newspaper, French Vietnam),
    422, 429–30
Congo, 175: Bakongo people in, 36–37; as
    Belgian colony, 182, 184–85; China,
    relations with, 301, 307; as French colony,
    36–37; United States' recognition as
    independent, 378
Congo Free State, 183
Congo Reform Association, 182
Congress of Arts and Sciences (United
    States), 84, 97, 105n14
Congress of Berlin, 377
Congress of Colonial Studies (Italy),
    163n16, 164n22
Connell, Raewyn (R. W.), xi, 85–88, 104n3,
    161n5, 208n3; "metropole apparatus," 497
Conoco (U.S. corporation), 239
consciencism, 401
conseils municipaux (administrative
    divisions, France), 420
Conseil supérieur des colonies (France),
    419

Cooley, Charles, 88, 92, 97
Cooper, Frederick, 291, 294–95, 326, 415
Cornell, Stephen E., xvn8
Cornell University (United States), 85,
    96–97
Corradini, Enrico, 148, 164n4
Corsica: independence movements in, 322
Cosentini, Francesco, 111, 113
cosmopolitanism, 41
Costa, Sérgio, 491
cour de cassation (France), 419
Cours de philosophie positive (Comte), 13
C.P.S.U. (Communist Party of the Soviet
    Union), Central Committee: *History of
    the Communist Party of the Soviet Union
    (Bolsheviks): Short Course*, 80
"crackpot realism" (Mills), xii–xiii
*Crime and Punishment, Achievement and
    Reward* (Sorokin), 72
Criminal Sociology (Ferri), 144
Crispi, Francesco, 130–31, 163n17
Croce, Benedetto, 111, 161n6
Cromer, Lord (Evelyn Baring), 214
Crusades: state formation and, 284. *See also*
    Christianity; religion
Cuba: as Spanish colony, 85; U.S. occupa-
    tion of, 85, 95, 98–99, 481
Cumings, Bruce: "defensive colonialism,"
    396

Dalberg-Acton, Lord (John Emmerich
    Edward), 293
Damaras (Namibia), 90
Darwin, Charles, 141, 147
datsu-A (discourse, Japan), 403
Davis, Mike, 460
Davis, Uri, 439
Davy, George: *From Tribe to Empire* (with
    Moret), 29
"decentralized despotism" (Mamdani), 38,
    470
Decline of the West (Spengler), 26
decolonization, 36, 38, 109, 379, 483–84, 496
"defensive colonialism," 396
degeneration, discourse of, 26, 158
Dell'Acqua, Enrico, 163n17
De Marinis, Enrico, 122, 133, 136
De Martiis, Salvatore Cognetti, 122

Elkin, W. B., 98

Ellis Island (United States), 81n6

empire: definition of, 9, 213, 280; direct
  empire, 214; "empire of bases," 48;
  empires of domination" (Mann) 41–43,
  48n17; forms, 43–44; hegemony as form
  of empire, 216–17; indirect empire, 214
  (*see also* "indirect rule"); "informal
  empire," xivn4, 33, 43, 214, 228–43;
  military relation to, xvn9, 214–15,
  227–44; nation-states relation to, 3–4, 17,
  21, 48n19, 251–52, 279–99; periodizations
  of (waves, cycles, etc.), 4, 13–44, 281–82,
  302–3, 306; "territorial empires" (Mann),
  41–43; "world state" (Tarde), 21. *See also*
  colonialism; colonies; colonization;
  imperialism; *individual countries'*
  empires (e.g., British Empire, German
  Empire)

Empire (Hardt and Negri), x, 250, 436,
  449–51, 491

"empire of bases," 48

Empire of Difference (Barkey), 38

"empires of domination" (Mann), 41–43,
  48n17

"enclosures" (Palestine/Israel), 443–46,
  453–60

Energy Task Force (United States), 238

Engels, Friedrich, 169

England: Act in Restraint of Appeals (1533),
  283; Angevin monarchy, 296n6; Norman
  Conquest, 284

"Englishness," 287

Enlightenment thought, 55, 58, 190–92,
  199–200, 202, 281, 293, 364n27, 365n31,
  394n23

Ente Italiana agricolo Albania (EIAA,
  Italy), 374

environmentalists, opposition to "new
  imperialism" (Mann), 226

epistemology, xi, xiv, 62, 91, 192, 400,
  490

Equatorial Guinea: China, relations with,
  301

Eritrea: as Italian colony, 107, 139, 368,
  371–72

Erzberger, Matthias, 176

Espinas, Alfred, 68

Estland (Estonia), 80

Etherington, Norman, 105n16

Ethiopia: "ethnic zoning" in, 368–69, 381,
  383; as Italian colony, 154, 156, 366–95;
  Italian defeat in (Adwa), 107, 130

ethnographic discourse, 13, 31, 39, 45, 128,
  131, 206, 469, 471, 484–5; in Britain, 341,
  380, 466, 468, 470, 473, 476, 481, 483; in
  France, 18, 190–96, 206, 208n6, 327–28,
  470; in Germany, ix, 175, 177, 183–84,
  186n8, 468; Italy, 13, 112, 127, 132–35, 139,
  142, 151, 154, 380, 382, 387, 389, 390; in
  Russia, 57, 63–65, 68, 70, 73, 80n4;
  written by "the colonized," 493–95

Ethnological Survey of the Philippines
  (United States), 98

ethnology, xivn2, 26, 46n2, 83–84, 97–98,
  188, 195–96, 199, 204–5

ethno-sociologists, 26, 29–32

eugenics movement: in Italy, 115–16, 124–25,
  134; Eugenics Education Society, 162n9;
  International Congress of Eugenics, 116,
  145

European Commission, 50n34

European Union (EU), 297, 452; as bloc
  with Russia, 316–18; as form of empire,
  50n34; in "Mideast Quartet," 445, 454; in
  "the Quad," 225–26

Evans-Pritchard, E. E., 183

L'evolution de la morale et sociologie après
  l'ethnographie (Letourneau), 142

evolutionism, social. See social
  evolutionism

Evolution of Educational Thought (Durkheim), 209n14

"excentric" theories of colonialism, 2, 38,
  400, 467–68

Exposition universelle (Paris), 145

Facing Mount Kenya: The Tribal Life of the
  Gikuyu (Kenyatta), 493–95

"faith-based analysis" (United States),
  232

Falkland Islands: as British colony, 236–37

Fang people (Gabon), 36–37

Fanno, Marco, 123

Fanon, Frantz, 32, 399, 401

Farsakh, Leila, 439–40

Germany (*continued*)
nation-state concept (Brubaker), 337–38,
339n6; Poles, treatment of, 167–68,
171–74, 178–81, 185; social democracy in,
8, 169–70, 173, 178, 408; social evolutionism in, 183; socialism in, 169; sociology
in, x, xivn4, 2, 4, 6–8, 18, 23–26, 28, 86,
166–87; on race, 171–82, 185; state
formation, 42, 284, 286. *See also* German
Empire; Nazi Germany; *Verein für
Sozialpolitik* (Social Policy Association);
Weimar Republic
Germany, Prussia, 42, 178, 286; political
figures: Frederick the Great, King, 168;
vom Steim, Karl, Baron, 168; Wilhelm,
Friedrich, III, 168; Prussian reform
movement, 168; Prussian Settlement
Commission, 170–72, 179, 183
Geronimo (United States), 84
Gerth, Hans: *Character and Social Structure*
(with Mills), xii, 33
Giddens, Anthony, 490
Giddings, Franklin, 18, 84–86, 90, 92,
96–101, 103, 105n8; *Democracy and
Empire*, 100–101; "democratic empire,"
101, 103; *Elements of Sociology*, 11; *Scientific
Study of Human Society*, 103
Gikuyu Central Association (British
Kenya), 493
Gikuyu people (British Kenya), 493–95
Gilani, Yousuf Raza, 271
Gillen, Francis James, 194
Gini, Corrado, 27, 44, 107–8, 111, 113–15, 117,
135, 150–57, 159, 162nn9–10, 164nn21–22,
164n26, 165nn30–32; *Prime linee di
patologia economica*, 165n32; "social
metabolism," 153
Ginsberg, M., 13
globalization, 294, 450, 453–4, 497;
economic, 245, 239, 249, 251–52; theories
of, 250–52, 491
Gluckman, Max, 29
Go, Julian, 39–40, 45, 449
Goh, Daniel, 45, 492
Gokhale, G. K., 342, 345, 362n12
The Golden Bough (Frazer), 209n15
Goudsblom, J., 8
"governmentality" (Foucault), 363n17

governors, colonial, 466–67, 481, 485
Gowda, Chandan, 492
Gramsci, Antonio, 113, 161n6, 163n14, 216
"Greater East Asia Co-Prosperity Sphere,"
213, 411. *See also* Japanese Empire
"Great Japanese Empire," 413n4
"Great Power" wars, 316–17
Great War. *See* World War I
Grimmer-Solem, Erik, 177
Großraum/Großräume (Schmitt), 33–34,
185, 379. See also *nomos/nomoi*
Groppali, Alessandro, 113
Guadeloupe: as French colony, 322, 333, 418
Guam: as U.S. colony, 95
Guantanamo Bay (detention camp), 452
Guillemard, Laurence, 479, 482
Guinea: as French colony, 85
Gulf War, 436, 448
Gumplowicz, Ludwig, 4, 9, 12, 15–17, 44–45,
63, 94, 113, 134, 155
"gunboat diplomacy," 402
Guru, Narayana, 358
Gutiérrez Rodríguez, Encarnación, 491
Guyana: as French colony, 322, 333, 418

Habermas, Jürgen, 167, 185–86; on
"communicative action," 183–84; on
"lifeworld," 184
Habsburg Empire, 42, 63, 288, 291, 293–94.
See also Austro-Hungarian Empire
Haeckel, Ernst, 141
Haiphong (French Vietnam), 415, 420, 430
Halbwachs, Maurice, 207n2
Halliburton (U.S. corporation), 240
Hamas, 454
Hamburg (Germany), 177
Han, Suk-Jun, xiiin1
Hanoi (French Vietnam), 415, 420, 427–28,
430
Harding, Sandra, 491
Harding, Warren, 480–81
Hardt, Michael: "deterritorialization"
(with Negri), 449–51; *Empire* (with
Negri), x, 250, 436, 491
Harper, Samuel, 81
Harris, John H., 182
Harris Foundation (United States), 151
Harrison, Francis, 479

Harvard University, 28, 48n16, 117

Harvey, David, 491; "time-space compression" 457

Hastings, Warren, 364n22

Haushofer, Karl, 34

Hawaii: U.S. annexation of, 85, 95–99, 214

Heavily Indebted Poor Countries (HIPC) Initiative, 225

Hebrew society, ancient, 87

Hebrew University, 8

Hegel, G. W. F. (Georg), 17

Hegelianism: in Italy, 161n6; in Russia, 56

hegemony: as form of empire: 216–17; stages of, 315–18

Heidelberg, University of, 50n36

Heilbron, J., 8

Henry VIII (King, England), 283

Herder, J. G. (Johann Gottfried), 39, 44, 200

Hermassi, Elbaki, 38

Herskovits, Melville, 31, 38, 45

Hertz, Robert, 207n2

Hezbollah, 229

Hilferding, Rudolf, 10

Hinduism, 180, 348–49, 355–56, 364n24, 365n33, 416–19, 422–27, 432, 435n7

Hintze, Otto, 10, 23–24, 43

Hirobumi, Itō, 403, 468

Histoire de la civilization en Angleterre (Buckle), 147

historical sociology, x, xi, 2–3, 12, 24, 36, 42, 44, 48n19,104n4, 465, 468, 491

History and Theory (journal, United States), 47

History of the Communist Party of the Soviet Union (Bolsheviks): Short Course (C.P.S.U.), 80

Hitler, Adolf, 231, 235

Hobbes, Thomas, 55, 81n6

Hobhouse, Leonard, 13, 23, 45

Hobsbawm, Eric, 47n11, 298n19

Hobson, J. A., 4, 10, 13, 18, 41, 44, 100, 105n16, 125, 136, 220, 290–93; *Imperialism*, 22, 24

Hollander, Jacob, 96

Holy Roman Empire, 283, 288, 292, 296nn4–5

Homer: *Odyssey*, 183

Hong Kong, 481

Horkheimer, Max, 183

Horowitz, Donald, 428

Horsman, Reginald, 287

Hrushevsky, Mykhailo, 70

Hubert, Henri, 207n2

Huerta, Victoriano, 149–50

Hull, Cordell, 215

human geography, 46n2

"humanitarian interventionism" (Mann), 228, 231, 234

L'humanité (newspaper, France) 208n7

human rights, 231, 265, 269. *See also* United Nations

human sciences. *See* social sciences

Human Terrain Project (United States/ Afghanistan), xiii

Husband, W. W., 81n6

Hussein, Sadam, 215, 228, 230, 236–38, 242

hybridity, 29–31, 197, 493. *See also* métissage; mimicry; syncretism; transculturation

"Idea for a Universal History with a Cosmopolitan Intent" (Kant), 167, 185

"ideal types" (Weber), 166

Igorots (Philippines), 84, 100

Imagined Communities (Anderson), 280–81

Imperialismo artistico (Morasso), 120

Imperialismo Italiano (Michels), 120

"imperial formation" (Stoler), 449

imperialism, 22–23, 28–29, 184–85; definition of, 9–10; economic imperialism, 215–27, 230, 243–44, 249, 251–52; "free trade imperialism," 224, 314, 316; "informal imperialism," 43; "social imperialism," 45

"imperial nationalism," 282, 286–90

"Imperialism of Free Trade" (Gallagher and Robinson), 214, 313, 315–16, 400

"imperialism of the weak" (Kim): Japanese Empire as, 396

"imperial overreach,"44, 313–14

Import Substitution Industrialization (ISI), 217, 222

Incan Empire, 147

Incoherent Empire (Mann), 42–43, 229

incommensurability," cultural, 39

Lefèvre, Kim, 434n4

Leiris, Michel, 44, 192; *Afrique fantôme*, 31

"leisure class" theory (Veblen), 113

Lenin, Vladimir (V. I.), 10, 58, 69, 100, 105n16, 220, 297n14, 309

Lesotho, 457

Letourneau, Charles: *L'evolution de la morale et sociologie après l'ethnographie*, 142

Levasseur, E. (Emile), 135

Levine, Donald, 161n5

Lévi-Strauss, Claude, 30; *bricolage*, 32; *Race and History*, 191, 205; *Triste tropiques*, 30

Lévy-Bruhl, Lucien, 208n9

liberalism, 56, 401; in British Empire, 281, 400; in Europe (general), 102; in France, 321, 332; in Germany, 8, 182; in Italy, 122; in Japan, 403–4; in Japanese Korea, 408–10; in Russia, 56; in United States, 229

Liberation of the Serfs (Schmoller), 170

Liberia, 184

Libya: as Italian colony, 107, 121, 127, 131–32, 139, 154

"lifeworld" (Habermas), 184

Liliuokalani, Queen (Hawaii), 85

List, Friedrich: India, reception in, 343–36, 363n15; *National System of Political Economy*, 169, 344;

"Little Englanders" (Britain), 291–92, 297n15

Locke, John, 363n20

logocentrism, 183

Lombroso, Cesare, 107, 113–4, 120–21, 130, 139–46, 149, 161n8; *L'uomo delinquente*, 140, 158

London, City of, 219–20

London, University of, 137

London School of Economics (LSE), 6

Lorenzoni, Giovanni, 111, 113

Loria, Achille, 10, 111, 113, 122–25, 132–37, 161n6, 162n9, 162n11, 163n15; *Economia politica*, 123

La lotta per l'esistenza (Vaccaro), 131

Louisiana Purchase (United States), 84, 472

Louvre, 207

Lubbock, John: *Prehistoric Times and the Origins of Civilization*, 147

Luchitskii, Ivan, 70

Ludden, David, 341

Lugard, Frederick (Lord), 468

Luogoteneza (Albania), 385–87

Luxemburg, Rosa, 10

Luzzatto, Gino, 136

Macaulay, Lord (Thomas Babington), 281

MacClintock, Samuel, 98

Machiavelli, Niccolò, 112–13, 129, 161n5

Madagascar: as French colony, 85, 107

Madaro, Francisco, 149

Mafia (Italy), 132

Mahan, Admiral (Alfred Thayer), 313

Maharishi, Ramana, 358, 364n23

Mahdism: in Sudan, 401

Maine, Henry Sumner, 20, 64–65; *Ancient Law and Village Communities in the East and West*, 352, 365n29

Malaya (British): 465–88, 473 map 1; Chinese resistance in, 475, 478–84; conservative-technocrat conflict in, 474–80; protectionism in, 471–74

Malaysia: as British colony, 92

Maldives: as British colony, 236–37

Malinowski, Bronislaw, 154, 493

Mamdani, Mahmood, 38, 43, 470

Manchester School (political economy), 169, 175

Mandate system, 18

Mandela, Nelson, 456

Mann, Michael, xvn9, 5, 15–16, 35, 40–45, 50nn39–40, 298n17, 496–97; "empires of domination," 41–43, 48n17; *Incoherent Empire*, 42–43, 229; *Sources of Social Power*, 40–44; "territorial empires," 41–43

Mannheim, Karl, 7

Mannoni, Octave, 32

Manor, James, 341

Mantegazza, Paolo, 160n1

maquiladoras, 495

Marcuse, Herbert, 15

Marro, Antonio, 162n9

Marshall, Alfred, 7

Martello, Tullio, 164n26

Martinique: as French colony, 322, 333, 418

Marx, Anthony, 282

Marx, Karl, 14–15, 22, 41, 44, 49n24, 309, 350, 365n29; *Capital*, 14; critiques of, 22, 28, 166, 493; status as sociologist, 49n21; *Theses on Feuerbach*, 56–57

Marxist approaches, 10, 15, 24, 27, 33, 35–38, 76, 298n14; critiques of, 28, 37–38; in Italy, 125, 161n6, 164n24; in Japanese Korea, 410; in Russia, 57–58, 69, 72; in Soviet Union, 79–80. *See also* Lenin, Vladimir

Marzolo, Paolo, 141

masculinity: empire and, 496

Massad, Joseph, 454

Matabeleland (Zimbabwe), 85

Matteucci, Ugo, 162n11

Mau Mau uprising (British Kenya), 50n36

Maunier, René, ix, xivn2, 4, 32–33, 44–45; *colonistics*, 31; *Sociology of Colonies*, 32

Maurenbrecher, Max, 92

Mauss, Marcel, 29, 31, 38, 68, 188–209

Maxwell, William, 476

Mazzarella, Giuseppe, 136–37

Mazzini, Giuseppe, 289

McKenzie, Fayette Avery, xvn8

McKinley, William: "benevolent assimilation," 472

Mearsheimer, John, 454

"mechanical solidarity" (Durkheim), 194

Mechnikov, Ilya, 68

medievalism, discourse of, 474

Medvedev, Dmitri, 264–65

Meiji Constitution, 402

Meiji Restoration, 403

Melanesia, 30

Memmi, Albert, ix, 5, 32–33

mercantilism, 23, 362n10. *See also* neo-mercantilism

merchant capitalism, 39

A Merchant Prince: A Study of Italian Colonial Expansion (Einaudi), 163n17

Mercier, Paul, 5, 37

Merton, Robert K., 155, 165n32

methodological nationalism, x, xivn3, 160, 189, 195

métissage, 31. *See also* hybridity; mimicry; syncretism; transculturation

metropole: impact of colonialism on, 13–14, 22–23, 44, 100, 198

"metropole apparatus" (Connell), 497

Mexican Empire, 147

Mexico: anti-terrorism laws in, 257; as Spanish colony, 154, 302, 307; U.S. relations with, 149–50

Miceli, Vincenzo, 135, 137

Michels, Robert, ix, 23, 114, 122, 124, 133, 146, 150, 159, 162n9, 163nn16–17, 164n22; *Le colonie Italiane in Isvizzera durante la guerra*, 125; "demographic imperialism," 125–26; *Imperialismo Italiano*, 120; *Political Parties*, 125

Michigan, University of, x, 46n6, 47n11, 88, 96

"Mideast Quartet" (United States, European Union, Russia, United Nations), 445, 454

Milan, as city-state, 283

military (general): empire and, xvn9, 214–15, 217, 228–44, 497; sociology and, xiii, xvin13

Mill, John Stuart, 13, 281, 342, 346; *On Liberty*, 363n16

Mills, C. Wright: on American imperialism, xi, 33; *Character and Social Structure* (with Gerth), xii, 33; on "crackpot realism," xii–xiii; on intellectuals' and their role, xii; on positivism, xii; on "power elite," xii; *Sociological Imagination*, xii

Mikhailovsky, N. K. (Nikolai), 58–59

The Mimic Men (Naipaul), 295

mimicry, 29, 32. *See also* hybridity; *métissage*; syncretism; transculturation

Mind and Society (Pareto), 148

Mindanao (Philippines), 481

Miner, Horace, xvn7, 46n6

Minerva Project, xiii, xvin13

Minnesota, University of, 85, 96–97, 117

missionaries, 176, 193, 495–96

"missionary nationalism," 287. *See also* "imperial nationalism"

mission civilisatrice (France, French Empire), 199–201, 285, 288, 338, 416

Mitchell, Charles, 477

Mitchell, Clyde, ix, xivn2

Mitchell, Timothy: *Colonizing Egypt*, 39

modernities: theories of alternate or multiple, 2, 39, 401, 410, 413n3
modernity: European discourse of, 17, 21, 24, 44, 55–60, 71, 135, 183–84, 193–194, 202, 204, 249, 350–51, 357, 364n27, 370, 389–90, 400–401, 441, 485
modernization theories, 20–21, 35–36, 102, 104, 340, 361n8, 369
Mogilner, Marina, 490
Mommsen, Wolfgang, 289–90
Mondaini, Gennaro, 136–37
Moneta, Ernesto Teodoro, 124
Monroe Doctrine, 34, 183
Monroe, Paul, 99
Montaigne, Michel de, 191
Montesquieu, Baron de, 55, 209n14; *Persian Letters*, 191; *Spirit of Laws*, 204
monumentalism (architecture), 382–83
The Moon (Klein), 82n17
Moral Education (Durkheim), 198
Morasso, Mario: *Imperialismo artistico*, 120
Morel, B. A. (Bénédict Augstin), 141–42
Morel, E. D. (Edmund Dene), 182, 184
Morène, Jean, 429
Moret, Alexandre: *From Tribe to Empire* (with Davy), 29
Morocco: as French colony, 197–98, 208n11, 324, 338n2, 339n3; sociology in, 46n2, 47
Moro people (Philippines), 481
Morrell, Robert, 496
Morselli, Enrico, 111, 113, 135, 160n1, 162n9, 162n11
Mosca, Gaetano, 107, 112–4, 126–31, 133, 136, 146, 159–60; critique of ethnography, 128–29; *Elementi di scienza politica*, 112, 129, 163n17; *Italia e Libia. Considerazioni politiche*, 127
Moscow Agricultural Institute, 76
Moses, Bernard, 96
Mühlmann, Wilhelm: *Umvolkung*, 35
"multiple kingdoms" (Kumar), 283, 296n6
Munro, Thomas, 351
Mus, Paul, 4
Musée d'ethnographie du Trocadéro, 206
Musée de l'homme, 206–7, 208n9
Musée d'Orsay, 207
Musée du quai Branly, 207
Muslim League: in Pakistan, 269

Mussolini, Benito, 117, 121, 132, 148, 150, 153, 155, 157, 372, 381, 387–88, 394n25, 395n31
Mysore (India), 340–65 (chap. 12)
Mysore Economic Conference (MEC), 342, 346, 364n26
Mysore Legislative Council (MLC), 342, 355–56
Mysore Representative Assembly (MRA), 342, 345, 350, 352, 355–56

Nagel, Joanne, xvn8
Naipaul, V. S.: *The Mimic Men*, 295
Namibia: as German colony, 186n8, 186n10, 468
Namier, Lewis (Sir), 282
Nandy, Ashis: *Intimate Enemy*, 496
Naoroji, Dadabhai, 342
Naples, University of, 118, 120, 122, 160n1, 161n6, 164n19
Napoleon (Bonaparte), 9, 23, 168–69, 317, 321, 323
Napoleon III, 10
Natal: as British colony, 496
nation-states: empire and, 17, 251–52, 279–99, 321–22
National System of Political Economy (List), 169
Native Life in South Africa (Plaatje), 494–95
Native Princes of India (Aitchison), 365n32
National Congress of Urbanism (Italy), 383
nationalism: empire and, 29, 279–99; "imperial nationalism," 282, 286–90; "organic nationalism," 289
Nationalism (Kedourie), 298n18
Nations and Nationalism (Gellner), 280–81
Native Americans, 40; ethnological representations of, 84; internal colonialism and, 48n19; sociological study of, xvnn7–8, 98. *See also* Bureau of Indian Affairs (United States)
native policy, 18, 30, 39, 398, 400; in American Philippines, 465–88; in British Malaya, 465–88; in French Empire, 414n10; in French India (Pondicherry), 415–35
Native States (India), 340–41, 361n2, 365n32
nativism, 401; Gandhi and, 413n2; in Japanese Korea, 410–12

natural sciences relation to social sciences and sociology. *See* social sciences: relation to natural sciences; sociology: relation to natural sciences

Naumann, Friedrich, 12, 172

Nazi Germany, 8, 33–35, 46nn6–7, 50n35, 317

Nazism, 8, 49n31, 381; as form of empire, 26, 33–35, 43, 47n13, 185; nationalism and, 289

Neapolitan società Africana d'Italia, 122

Nebraska, University of, 97, 105n8

Negri, Antonio, 491; "deterritorialization" (with Hardt), 449–51; *Empire* (with Hardt), x, 250, 436, 491

negritude, 401, 412

"Negro question," writings on: in United States, 31, 67, 99; in Germany, 171–72, 175, 177–82

Nehru, Jawaharlal, 413n2

neoconservatism (United States), 231–32, 242

neo-institutionalist theory, 38

neoliberalism, 219, 221–23, 227, 229, 233, 239, 242–43, 300, 306–9, 311, 306, 436, 440, 443, 448–49

neomercantilism: in British India, 343–36

Netanyahu, Benjamin, 455

Netherlands: sociology in, 20

Neumann, Franz, 33; *Behemoth*, 34

New Caledonia: as French colony, 30, 322, 325–27, 330. *See also* Kanak

New Delhi, 495

New Guinea: as German colony, 19, 19 fig. 1.1

"New World," 31

"New World Order" (Bush, G. H. W.), 436, 449

New York Post (newspaper, United States), 15

Nguyen Phu Kai, 422, 429

Nice (France), 321

Niceforo, Alfredo, 111, 113–14, 133, 135, 137, 139, 145–46, 162n9, 164n22; *Italia barbara contemporanea*, 145; *Italiani del nord e Italiani del sud*, 145; *Forza e ricchezza: studi sulla vita fisica ed economica delle classi sociali*, 145

Nicolucci, Giustiniano, 160n1

Nicotri, Gaspare, 132

Nigeria: as British colony, 85, 467–70; China, relations with, 301

Nissen dōsoron (discourse, Japan), 404, 413n8

Nitobe, Inazo, 413n9

Nixon, Richard, 218

Nkrumah, Kwame, 401

"noble savage," discourse of, 30. *See also* primitivism

nomos (Bourdieu), 6

nomos/nomoi (Schmitt), 33–34, 43, 45, 378, 389, 394n25, 398n20. See also *Großräum/ Großräume*

Nomos of the Earth (Schmitt), x, 183

Norman Conquest (England), 284

Normandy (France), 285

North American Free Trade Agreement (NAFTA), 448

North Atlantic Treaty Organization (NATO), 183–84, 228

Norway, 291

"Not a White Woman Safe" (Inglis), 496

Novicow, J. (Jacques), 134

Nye, Joseph: "soft power," 216

Odum, Howard, 105n17

Odyssey (Homer), 183

Ohio State University, xvn8

oil: imperialism and, 218–20, 228, 230, 235–43, 300–318

Olivares, Count-Duke (Gaspar de Guzmán), 280

"one-drop rule" (United States), 182

Ong, Aihwa, 452

On Liberty (Mill), 363n16

"Open Door" policy (U.S./China), 40, 471

Operation Desert Storm, 436, 448

L'opinion (newspaper, France), 429

Oppenheimer, Franz, 27–28, 45; *Der Staat*, 27–28

"organic nationalism," 289

"organic solidarity" (Durkheim), 194

Organization for Economic Co-Operation and Development (OECD), 226

Organization of Petroleum Exploring Countries (OPEC), 219, 239–40

Orientalism (discourse), 39, 45, 348–50, 399; indigenous responses to, 364n23

Race and History (Lévi-Strauss), 191, 205
"racial colonialism" (Pula): in Italian
    Empire, 375, 381–90
Ranade, M. G., 342, 344–45, 352
Rangacharlu, C. (Dewan), 342, 345, 347,
    350, 352, 264n25
Rassegna di science sociali e politiche, 161
Rathgen, Karl, 177
Ratzel, Friedrich, 4, 17–18, 34, 43, 45, 92;
Ratzenhofer, Gustav, 84, 94
Razze inferiori e razze superiori: Latini e
    Anglosassoni (Colajanni), 121
Reagan, Ronald, 219, 228, 234
Reconstructing India (Visvesvaraya), 352–53
Reece, Ernest J., 98
Reed, William Allen, 98
reflexivity, social sciences and, xi, xvn10
refugees, hostility towards, 497
Reinsch, Paul. S., 96
religion, 180–82, 185, 192–93, 197, 282. See
    also Christianity; Catholicism;
    Confucianism; Hinduism; Islam;
    Jainism; Protestantism; Shintoism
Renan, Ernest, 295, 297n9
renonçants (French Empire), 419, 423, 427,
    435n7
republicanism, French, 190, 195, 199–200,
    206, 288, 238, 416, 420–23, 427
Republican Revolution (China), 9
resistance, of colonized, 45, 466, 469–70; in
    Philippines and Malaya, 483–85
Réunion: as French colony, 322, 418
Reuter, Edward, 98
Revue international de sociologie (journal,
    France), 107
Rhee, Syngman 409
Rhodes-Livingston Institute, xiv n2
Ribot, Theodule, 76
Ricardo, David, 342
Ricci, Marcello, 395
Richtofen, Ferdinand von, 18
Rivet, Paul, 196, 208n9
Rivista di filosofia scientifica, 161
Rivista di sociologia, 107, 133–34, 161n8
Rivista internazionale de sience sociali e
    discipline ausiliarie, 161
Rivista Italiana di sociologia (RIS),107, 111,
    133–39, 150, 161n8

"Roadmap for peace" (Israeli-Palestinian
    conflict), 445, 459
Roberti, Evgenii de, 20, 68–70, 82n12
Robinson, Ronald, 45; "The Imperialism of
    Free Trade" (with Gallagher), 214, 313,
    315, 400
Rockefeller Foundation, 363n18
"rogue states" (U.S. definition), 228, 230, 242
Rohfls, Gerhard, 137
Romagnosi, Gian Domenico, 112–3
Roman Empire, 9–11, 15, 17, 21–28, 41–42,
    44, 109, 120, 134, 137–38, 141, 147, 152,
    162–63, 214, 280, 283, 287–89, 292; as
    model, 48n16, 50, 108–11, 155, 159, 163n16,
    371–72, 383–84, 390, 391n5, 394n24
Romanticism, 21, 58, 190–92, 200, 202, 364
Rome (city, Italy), 134; as showcase of
    fascist urbanism, 371
Rome, University of, 145, 160n1. See also
    Sapienza (La)
Roosevelt, Franklin Delano, 231
Roosevelt, Theodore, 139, 476
Ross, E. A. (Edward Alsworth), ix, 84, 86,
    88, 97, 99–100, 105n8; Social Control, 89
Rossi, Pasquale, 113–4, 163n13
Rousseau, Jean-Jacques, 55; Discourse on the
    Origins of Inequality, 191
"rule of colonial difference" (Chatterjee),
    21, 32, 43, 48n14, 368, 370, 397–98
Rules of Sociological Method (Durkheim),
    201
Rumsfeld, Donald, 229–30, 232
Rural Sociology (journal), 154
rural sociology, 132, 154, 494
Russell, Conrad, 296
Russia: anarchism in, 56; anthropology in,
    70, 80n4; anti-terrorism laws in, 258–65;
    as "backward," 20, 55–57; as bloc with
    European Union, 316–18; Bolshevik
    censorship in, 72, 82n13; Chechnya, wars
    with, 259; Hegelianism in, 56; Marxism
    in, 56–58, 71–72; in "Mideast Quartet,"
    445, 454; terrorist attacks in, 264; United
    States, relations with, 228. See also
    Caucasus; Russian Empire; Russian
    Revolution (1905); Russian Revolution
    (1917); Russo-Japanese War; Soviet
    Empire; Soviet Union

Sicily (Italy): as "barbarous," 158

La sienza sociale (journal, Italy), 161

Sièyes, Abbé, 8

Sighele, Scipio, 111, 113–14, 137, 149

Simmel, George, 7, 120, 167, 402

Simons, Sarah: "Social Assimilation" series, 91

Sino-Japanese War, 85

Skënderbeg Square (Albania), 366, 385

Sketch for a Historical Picture of the Progress of the Human Mind (Condorcet), 208n4

Skocpol, Theda, 48, 484

slavery, 13–14, 21, 24, 31–32, 36, 124, 135, 171–72, 175, 196, 302, 323, 329–36

Slavophilism, 56

Small, Albion, 6, 84, 86, 88, 91–92, 98, 101, 105n10, 105nn14–15

smallholding (Germany), 170–71, 175–76, 185

Smith, Adam, 169, 342, 363n20; *Wealth of Nations*, 362n10

Smith, Anthony: on core "ethnies," 286–87

Smith, Cecil, 476, 481

Smith, James, 478

Snipp, C. Matthew, xvn8

Social Control (Ross), 89

Social Darwinism. *See* evolutionism, social

social democracy: in Europe, 221; in Germany, 8, 169–70, 173, 178, 408; in Russia, 81n8

social evolutionism, 14, 16, 20–21, 30, 41–42, 59, 86–88, 92, 400, 414n10; in Britain, 473; in British India, 350–53; in France, 142, 190–91, 203–6, 209n14, 326, 331, 334; in Germany, 181; in Italy, 113, 127, 131, 133, 135, 140–44, 151, 161n6, 165n29; in Russia, 20, 57, 62–70, 74–85, 79; in United States, 88–90, 93–94, 96, 101, 104, 112, 120

socialism: colonialism and, 310–12, 401; in France, 197–98, 208n7, 208n11, 219; in Germany, 169; in Italy, 111, 114, 116, 121–26, 130, 146, 159, 161n6, 164n19, 164n24, 366; in Japanese Korea, 408–12; in Russia, 59–60, 62, 79, 80n2, 81n8; in United States, 88

Il socialismo (Colajanni), 121

"social metabolism" (Gini), 153

social sciences, as field, xi, xvn10

Società degli agricoltori Italiani, 132

Società internazionale della pace, 124

Società Italiana di sociologia, 107, 117, 139

Société de sociologie de Paris, 145

Society of American Indians, xvn8

Society of the Lovers of Natural Sciences, Anthropology, and Ethnography (Russia), 80

Sociologia criminale (Colajanni), 121

Sociological Imagination (Mills), xii

Sociological Papers (journal, Britain), 22

Sociological Review (journal, Britain), 20

Sociologie actuelle de l'Afrique noir (Balandier), 36–37

Sociologie de l'Algérie (Bourdieu), 37

Sociologie des Brazzavilles noires (Balandier), 37

Sociologus (journal, German), xivn2

sociology: anthropology and, xivn2, xvnn7–8, 1, 3, 29–32, 46n6, 49n29, 188–89, 190, 192, 206, 208n6; "colonial sociology," 18, 30, 46n5, 136, 140, 156, 159, 336; disciplinary boundaries of, 3–9, 13, 18; empire and, ix–xvi, 1–50, 189–90, 489–92; European (general), 86–88; historical sociology, x, xi, 2–3, 12, 24, 36, 42, 44, 48n19, 104n4, 465, 468, 491; military involvement and, xiii, xvin13; natural sciences and, x, xi, 20, 45 (*see also* under social sciences); predisciplinary history of, 8, 47n9; populist sociology (Russia), 58–62; postcolonial theory and, 3, 189; on race, 13–14, 16, 50n36, 57, 89, 91–99, 105n18, 121, 124, 127, 139, 146, 148, 171–82, 185, 343; rural sociology, 132, 154, 494; on the state, 3, 11–12, 24, 17, 27–28, 42–44, 48n19, 465; urban sociology, xivn2, 370, 291n4. *See also individual universities for specific departments of sociology; social sciences; individual national sociologies* (e.g., Germany: sociology in)

Sociology of Colonies (Maunier), 32

Sociology of Imperialism (journal, Abdel-Malek, ed.), ix

Sociology of Religion (Weber), 180, 184

Somalia: as Italian colony, 122, 157, 372; United States intervention in, 228

Sombart, Werner, 181–82

Somerville, Margaret: *Singing the Coast* (with Perkins), 494

Sorokin, Pitirim, 48n16, 68, 72–74; 79, 114, 155, 161n7; *Crime and Punishment, Achievement and Reward*, 72; sociology of revolution, 75; *System of Sociology*, 74–75

Source Book for Social Origins (Thomas), 89

Sources of Social Power (Mann), 40–43

Soustelle, Jacques, 32, 49n32

South Africa, 38, 43, 93, 462–63; Afrikaner-British conflicts in, 83, 85, 92, 438; apartheid in, 38, 43, 436, 439–43, 454, 456, 497; "autonomy" in (Clarno), 437–39, 448, 457–58, 461; Bantustan system, 439–43, 453–60 (*see also* Bantustization); Bophuthatswana, 457; citizenship in, 441; Department of Native Affairs, 442; Labor Bureau, 442, 453, 458; Non-Aggression Pacts, 457; Suppression of Communism Act, 456; *swart gevaar* (black peril), 456; Transkei, 457; Transvaal Republic, 85

sovereignty, 2, 9, 11, 27, 36, 43, 109, 182–85, 214–16, 221, 247, 250, 253, 270–74, 283, 296n4, 306, 308, 377–79, 393n21, 397, 465; in French Empire, 321–24, 331; in Italian Empire, 373, 376, 380, 389; in Palestine/Israel and South Africa, 436–64

Soviet Empire, 280, 289: "informal colonies" of, 282. *See also* Russian Empire

Soviet Union, 33–35, 78, 234, 237, 242, 293, 310; censorship in, 82n17; collapse of, 228, 282, 295, 436, 448; forced emigration in, 79–80; "internal colonies" of, 282; sociology in, 57, 75–76, 79. *See also* Russia

"spaces of exception" (Clarno), 437, 440, 461

Spain: anti-terrorism laws in, 257; as "composite monarchy," 283; state formation in, 284. *See also* Spanish-American War, Spanish Empire

Spanish-American War, 92, 95, 97, 103, 105n16, 130, 471

Spanish Empire, 65, 85, 171, 287–88, 291, 297n13, 302, 306–7, 316, 495

"spectator-sport militarism" (Mann), 237

Spencer, Herbert, 13, 16, 22, 59, 88, 97, 147, 203, 342; *Principles of Sociology*, 127; *Study of Sociology*, 107

Spencer, Walter Baldwin, 194

Spengler, Oswald, 44; *Decline of the West*, 26

Spirit of Laws (Montesquieu), 204

Srinivas, M. N., 424

Staatswissenschaft, 11, 17, 48n19, 402

Stacey, Judith, 491

"stagflation," 217

Stalinism: sociology and, 80

Standard Oil Company, 149

Stanford University, 96, 105n8

state: spatial strategies of, 436–64; sociology of, 3 11–12, 24, 17, 27–28, 42–44, 48n19, 465. *See also* colonial state; nation-state; *Staatswissenschaft*; state formation

State Bankruptcy (Zak), 82n17

state formation, 40: in American Philippines, 465–88; in Britain, 284–87; in British Malaya, 465–88; in Europe, 284; in France, 284–86, 297n9, 297n11; in Italy, 286; in Germany, 286; in Spain, 285–86

"state of exception" (Schmitt/Agamben), 184–85, 446–47, 497

statistics, as field, 103, 113–14, 117

Steinmetz, George, 39, 44–45, 186n8, 251, 451, 468–69, 471, 485, 489

Steinmetz, S. R. (Sebald), 20

Stoler, Ann Laura, 291, 415; "imperial formation," 449

Stone, Alfred, 99

St. Petersburg Psycho-Neurological Institute, 70–71, 73, 82n12

St. Petersburg University (Russia), 20, 63

Strang, David, 38

Strasbourg, University of, 170

structural adjustment policies, 216, 219–23, 230, 239, 242

structural functionalism, 102, 104

Structure of Social Action (Parsons), 7

Struve, Petr, 72

Study of Sociology (Spencer, H.), 107

Sturzo, don Luigi, 165n34

Suárez, Francisco, 21

Sudan: China, relations with, 301, 316; Mahdism in, 401

Sulzbach, Walter, 10, 29

Sumner, William Graham, 18, 86, 100

Sun Yat-sen: *Three Principles of the People*, 492

"surgical colonialism" (Bergesen), 300–18 (chap. 10), 496–97

surrealism, 192

Sverdlov Communist University (Soviet Union), 79

swadeshi movement (India), 362

swart gevaar (black peril, South Africa), 456

Swettenham, Frank, 477, 479

syncretism, 1, 26, 29–32. *See also* hybridity; *métissage*; mimicry; transculturation

Syria: as French colony, 324, 415; United States relation with, 229

System of Sociology (Sorokin), 74–75

Taft, William, 476, 481

Taiping Rebellion, 15, 48n16

Taiwan: as Japanese colony, 85

Taliban: in Afghanistan; in Pakistan, 259, 268

Tamamshev, Mikhail, 70

Tanganyika: as British colony, 30

Tanzania, 225; as Germany colony, 175, 186n10

Tarde, Gabriel, 4, 18, 2, 43, 65, 68; *Psychologie economique*, 21; *Les transformations du pouvoir*, 21; "world state," 21

Taylor, Charles, 184

Tenet, George, 232, 236–37

"territorial empires" (Mann), 41–43

Thatcher, Margaret, 236

Thoi Bao (newspaper, French Vietnam), 422, 429

Thomas, William I., 67, 84, 88–89, 97–99, 101; *Polish Peasant in Europe and America* (with Znaniecki), 89, 104; *Source Book for Social Origins*, 89

Thompson, Elizabeth, 415

Three Principles of the People (Sun), 492

Thurnwald, Richard, ix, xivn2, 1, 4, 19, 19 fig 1.1, 31, 44–45, 49n31

Tilly, Charles, xi, 16, 47n11

Tilly, Virginia, 439

Tirana (Albania): as Italian colonial city, 366, 368, 381–88

Tittoni, Tommaso, 122

Tocqueville, Alexis de, 13, 14; *Democracy in America*, 14

Togo: French colonialism in, 324; as German colony, 175–77, 186n10

Tolstoi, Aleksei: *Prince Serebriannyi*, 82n17

Tonga: as British colony, 85

Toniolo, Guiseppe, 165n34

Tonkin: as French colony, 324

Tonkin, Gulf of, 236

Tönnies, Ferdinand, 84, 134, 137, 167

totalitarianism, 44, 101–2; fascist, 150, 156, 392n15; Nazi, 34

"trade overreach" (Bergesen), 313–15

transculturation, 1, 29–30, 45. *See also* hybridity; *métissage*; mimicry; syncretism

transdisciplinarity, 3

Les transformations du pouvoir (Tarde), 21

Transvaal Republic (South Africa): Boer War and, 85

Trattato di sociologia generale (Pareto), 107

travel narratives, 193

Treaty of Paris (1815), 418

"triadic" colonialism (Chae): Japanese Empire as, 396–414

Tribune indigène (newspaper, French Vietnam), 422, 429

Tripoli (Libya), 132, 371, 385

Tripolitania (Libya), 132, 154

La Tripolitiana settentrionale e la sua vita sociale studiate dal vero (Coletti), 132

Triste tropiques (Lévi-Strauss), 30

Trouillot, Michel-Rolph, xv n8

Truman, Harry S., 340

Tsingtao (German colony), 186n8. *See also* Qindao

Tunisia: as French colony, 324, 338n2, 339n3; sociology in, 47n10

Turin, University of, 106, 118, 140

Turkey, 222

Turner, Frederick, 163n15

Tuskegee Institute (United States), 177, 179

Twain, Mark: *The Prince and the Pauper*, 82n17

Tylor, E. B., 209n15

Uganda: as British protectorate, 85, 107
Ukraine, 60, 70, 74–5
Umvolkung (Mühlmann), 35
underdevelopment, theories of, 35, 44
UNESCO. *See* under United Nations
United Kingdom. *See* Britain; England;
Ireland; Scotland; Wales
United Nations (UN), 223, 228, 231, 379; in
"Mideast Quartet," 445, 454; Universal
Declaration of Human Rights, 282
United Nations, Security Council, 184,
245–47, 250, 254, 264, 267, 272–3;
Chapter VII authority, 254–55;
Counter-Terrorism Committee (CTC),
256–57, 263, 268; Resolution 1373, 255–58,
260–62, 269; Resolution 1624, 263
United Nations, UNESCO (United Nations
Educational, Scientific, and Cultural
Organization), 156; Division of Applied
Social Sciences, xivn3, 156
United States: anti-terrorism laws in, 257,
272–73; assimilation in, 68, 91, 103, 104n5;
China, relations with, 40, 215, 228, 231,
242, 471–72; ethnology, 97–98;
immigration in, 81n6, 88–89, 91–92, 101,
103, 105n9, 169; imperial culture of,
95–96; Israel, relations with: 215, 229,
234, 241; Jews in, 235; in "Mideast
Quartet," 445, 454; Pearl Harbor,
bombing of, 235; religion in, 232; Russia,
relations with, 228; social evolutionism
in, 88–90, 93–94, 96, 101, 104, 112, 120;
socialism in, 88. *See also* 9/11; Gulf War;
Korean War; United States (American)
Empire; Vietnam War
United States, government bodies:
CENTCOM (Central Command), 238;
Central Intelligence Agency (CIA), 215,
232–34, 242; Commerce Department,
234; Defense Department, xiii; Defense
Policy Board, 236; Joint Chiefs of Staff,
231; Labor Department, 81n6; Office of
Special Plans, 234; Pentagon, 229,
233–34; Secret Service, 239; State
Department, 233–34, 240, 242; Treasury,
220, 234, 239; USAID (United States
Agency for International Development),
239

United States, political parties: Democratic
Party, 102, 228, 231, 243, 475, 478–82, 485;
Progressive Party, 475–80; Republican
Party, 102, 228, 231–32, 234, 239, 242–43,
475–76, 478–80, 482, 485
United States, sociology in, 2, 6, 9, 18,
83–86, 118; American imperialism and,
95–101; on assimilation and immigration,
68, 91, 103, 104n5; on empire, 101–4,
105n8; European sociology, influence of,
86–88, 94–95; military funding, xiii, xvi
n13; on race, 31, 67, 88–94, 98–99, 104n5,
105n18. *See also* United States: social
evolutionism in
United States (American) Empire, xii, 12,
15–16, 18, 21, 33, 39–40, 42–43, 48n15,
84–85, 88, 95–104, 184, 213–44, 282, 295,
296n2, 436, 452, 461
United States Empire, features: assimilation in, 98–99, 471–74, 476, 479;
comprador class in, 215, 223; decline of,
312–18; indigenous elites, role of, 39,
465–88; military, role of, 214–15, 227–44,
497; native policy in, 465–88
United States Empire, places: Afghanistan,
230, 237, 250; Caribbean, 95; Caucasus,
230; Central America, 95; Cuba, 95,
98–99; Guam, 95, 315; Hawaii, 95–98,
214; Iran, 229, 238; Iraq, 47n13, 183–84,
185, 229–31, 233, 236–43, 250, 451–52, 436,
448; Korea (North), 229, 231, 242; Korea
(South), 223; Latin America (region), 40,
217, 227; Lebanon, 242; Mexico, 149–50;
Middle East (region), 217, 228, 230, 238,
243, 315; Native Americans, 214; Panama,
228, 315; Philippines, 39–40, 84–85,
95–100, 103, 214, 315, 465–88, 492; Puerto
Rico, 39–40, 84, 95–99, 103, 214, 315;
Samoa, 95; Santa Domingo, 98; Saudi
Arabia, 238–39, 242, 315; Somalia, 228;
Syria, 229; Yugoslavia (former), 228–31
Universal Expositions. *See* World Fairs
Universal Races Congress, 137, 164n23
Università popolare (Palermo), 132
Université nouvelle de Bruxelles, 132, 145
universities, role of, xii–xiii, 18. *See also*
individual universities by name
L'uomo delinquente (Lombroso), 140, 158

608 · Index